# Toward Justice

Designed as a text for Criminal Justice and Criminology capstone courses, *Toward Justice* encourages students to engage critically with conceptions of justice that go beyond the criminal justice system, in order to cultivate a more thorough understanding of the system as it operates on the ground in an imperfect world—where people aren't always rational actors, where individual cases are linked to larger social problems, and where justice can sometimes slip through the cracks. Through a combined focus on content and professional development, *Toward Justice* helps students translate what they have learned in the classroom into active strategies for justice in their professional lives—preparing them for careers that will not simply maintain the status quo and stability that exists within our justice system, but rather challenge the system to achieve justice.

**Dr. Kristi Holsinger** is Professor and Chair of the Department of Criminal Justice and Criminology at the University of Missouri-Kansas City, where she has been on the faculty since 1999. She received her Masters and Doctoral degrees in Criminal Justice from the University of Cincinnati. Her primary research interests include policies and practices related to girls and women in correctional systems as well as innovations in teaching. Each fall, she teaches a mentoring course in collaboration with the Jackson County Family Court, in which students mentor and develop programming for incarcerated girls. Dr. Holsinger's book, *Teaching Justice: Solving Social Justice Problems through University Education* was published in 2012. She has more than 30 academic articles, and has delivered more than 50 conference presentations. She is an active member of the American Society of Criminology and its Division on Women and Crime, and the Academy of Criminal Justice Sciences.

**Dr. Lori Sexton** is Assistant Professor of Criminal Justice and Criminology at the University of Missouri-Kansas City. She earned her Ph.D. in Criminology, Law and Society from the University of California, Irvine, and an M.A. in Criminology from the University of Pennsylvania. Her research focuses primarily on prisons and punishment, with a secondary focus on marginalized populations and intersectionality. She has worked on numerous studies of incarcerated populations, including two studies focusing specifically on transgender prisoners. Her work has been funded by the National Science Foundation, the National Institute of Justice, and the Fletcher Jones Foundation. Findings from her research have informed criminal justice policy and practice through publication in peer-reviewed journals and books, inclusion in testimony to legislative bodies and for civil legal proceedings, and incorporation into trainings for criminal justice practitioners.

There are so many aspects to admire and respect about *Toward Justice*, including the authors' clear and engaging coverage of expansive topics, the untangling of seemingly simple concepts such as "justice," the timeliness of such a book, and the remarkable included activities and exercises. But more than anything, I appreciate how *Toward Justice* provides students with hope, concrete strategies and potential solutions, and with some of the leadership, creativity, and responsibility necessary to advocate for social and legal justice.

**Joanne Belknap,** *Professor of Ethnic Studies, University of Colorado-Boulder*

# TOWARD JUSTICE

## BROADENING THE STUDY OF CRIMINAL JUSTICE

**Kristi Holsinger**

**Lori Sexton**

NEW YORK AND LONDON

First published 2017
by Routledge
711 Third Avenue, New York, NY 10017

and by Routledge
2 Park Square, Milton Park, Abingdon, Oxon, OX14 4RN

*Routledge is an imprint of the Taylor & Francis Group, an informa business*



*Library of Congress Cataloging in Publication Data*
Names: Holsinger, Kristi, author. | Sexton, Lori, author.
Title: Toward Justice / Kristi Holsinger, Lori Sexton.
Description: 1 Edition. | New York: Routledge, 2017.
Identifiers: LCCN 2016037530 | ISBN 9781138184732 (hardback) | ISBN 113818473X (hardback) | ISBN 9781138184749 (pbk.) | ISBN 1138184748 (pbk.) | ISBN 9781315644950 (ebook) | ISBN 1315644959 (ebook) | ISBN 9781317290568 (web pdf) | ISBN 1317290569 (web pdf)
Subjects: LCSH: Criminal justice, Administration of. | Social justice.
Classification: LCC HV7231 .H65 2017 | DDC 364—dc23
LC record available at https://lccn.loc.gov/2016037530

ISBN: 978-1-138-18473-2 (hbk)
ISBN: 978-1-138-18474-9 (pbk)
ISBN: 978-1-315-64495-0 (ebk)

Typeset in Warnock Pro
by codeMantra

This book is dedicated to all of the Capstone students who have changed the way we think—and teach—about justice. Without you, this book wouldn't exist.

# Contents

# Journals Cooperation Sheet

The editors of this book would like to express their gratitude to the Taylor and Francis Journals division for providing the following articles for publication:

*Criminal Justice Studies:*

"A feminist analysis of the American criminal justice system's response to human trafficking"

"Build to sustain: collaborative partnerships between university researchers and criminal justice practitioners"

"Pretrial detention and guilty pleas: if they cannot afford bail they must be guilty"

"Race, neighbourhood context, and risk prediction"

"Women in policing: changing the organizational culture by adopting a feminist perspective on leadership"

"Worlds apart: The views on crime and punishment among white and minority college students"

*Journal of Human Behavior in the Social Environment:*

"The Ecology of Homelessness"

*Justice Quarterly:*

"Broken Windows or Window Breakers: The Influence of Physical and Social Disorder on Quality of Life"

"Perceived Criminal Threat from Undocumented Immigrants: Antecedents and Consequences for Policy Preferences"

"Serious Youth Violence and Innovative Prevention: On the Emerging Link Between Public Health and Criminology"

"Where the Margins Meet: A Demographic Assessment of Transgender Inmates in Men's Prisons"

*The Justice Professional:*

"A writing-intensive approach to criminal justice education: the California Lutheran university model"

*Women and Criminal Justice:*

"Women and Drug Use: The Case for a Justice Analysis"

Without their generous cooperation, *Toward Justice: Broadening the Study of Criminal Justice* would not have been possible.

# Part I

# Understanding Justice

The purpose of this book is to encourage Criminal Justice and Criminology (CJC) students to consider justice in the broadest possible sense. You might be asking yourself, why this broad focus on justice? The answer is simple: criminal justice is not the only kind of justice that matters. Criminal justice systems (CJSs) don't operate in a vacuum. They work alongside other governmental and nongovernmental agencies, operate in different cultural contexts, and affect diverse groups of people. Ignoring the context around the CJS—acting as though the CJS is a closed system—prevents us from seeing the many factors that affect the CJS in diverse ways. In order to understand criminal justice in context, we need to first *see* the context. Once we understand the context, we can identify the relationships between the criminal justice system—its components, processes, and people—and outside forces and institutions.

One way in which we limit our view of the CJS is by failing to see the people who are caught up in the system and the contexts in which their lives unfold. The CJS is not a machine that blindly processes identical individuals; it consists of people enforcing written strictures against other people, individuals making decisions and exercising discretion, consciously and unconsciously, that impact the lives of others. When we ignore the people on both sides of the equation, we are unable to see how their identities, experiences, and cultures shape their perspectives on the world and the ways they behave; how their material circumstances affect their life chances via blocked opportunity or inequality; and how the CJS protects or fails them.

What does all of this mean? Consider a woman who is arrested for drug possession and doesn't have enough money to make bail. This sounds like a criminal justice issue, right? Now consider that this woman has a child. When the woman is arrested and detained, her child is left with no one to care for her and is swept into the foster care system. When we zoom out on this picture to see the CJS in its surrounding context, suddenly a wealth of new information becomes available to us. Even with the addition of a single detail (the woman has a daughter), we've already involved another governmental agency, impacted another human being—a juvenile at that—and invoked the economy, social stratification, and inequality. We haven't even begun to consider elements like race, ethnicity, sexual orientation, religion, ability status, geographic region, or the many other elements that impact our lives.

This book will help you to make sense of the myriad factors that affect the CJS, but are all too often regarded as falling outside its purview. Consider this book a roadmap to justice—but not the type you get when you plan your route via Google maps, perfectly zoomed in to contain only the path that you will take from point A to point B, planned out for you in the most efficient and logical way. This book is more like an old-school, paper map that needs to be unfolded and examined bit by bit, one that provides more information than you think you need. We have some ideas of how you, as a CJC student, can achieve justice once you finish your degree. But that is not for us to decide. Instead of prescribing a route for you to take from here to justice (as if it were that simple!), we wrote a book that maps the terrain of justice so you can plot your own course. We begin, in Chapter 1, with a critical examination of justice—what it is, the forms it can take, and the complicated relationship that it has to the law in general and the CJS in particular. In Chapter 2, we turn our attention not to justice, but to injustice. We discuss the many forms that injustice can take and the complex interrelationships between the various social problems that we face in our society today. We place a particular emphasis on social and economic inequality, two factors that undergird much of the injustice that we see (and sometimes fail to see) around us. In Chapter 3, we tackle the knotty issues of social status, privilege, and oppression. As in Chapter 2, this chapter has an in-depth focus on a particular type of injustice that abounds in criminal justice: racism. We briefly consider the nature, causes, and manifestations of racism, as well as its implications for criminal justice.

# Chapter 1

# Defining Justice

## INTRODUCTION

Before you read any further in this text, stop and ask yourself what justice means to you. How would you define the word itself? When was the last time you stopped to think about the meaning of the word "justice"—or have you ever? Although college classes across multiple disciplines—criminology, sociology, and urban studies, for example—touch upon various justice-related issues in the context of criminal justice (CJ), they often do not spend much time exploring the complex, abstract, and sometimes contradictory notions of justice as a concept in and of itself. Similarly, when criminal justice is examined, it is not often situated within the larger framework of justice studies. This chapter will provide a starting point for you to explore the concept of justice (and the related concept of *social justice*). We will consider how both concepts have emerged and evolved over time, and provide contemporary and historical examples of how they have been realized in our society and how we have sometimes fallen short. It is impossible to provide comprehensive coverage to such broad, frequently addressed, but seldom explicitly defined concepts. Beginning to think about criminal justice as first and foremost a *justice* issue (rather than the reverse) will allow for a deeper, broader, and more critical consideration of how these concepts make sense within the field of criminal justice.

In the 1960s and 1970s, when the academic discipline of criminology was young, it was critiqued for focusing predominantly on the individual offender and ignoring larger social, political, economic, and historical contexts (Capeheart & Milovanovic, 2007; Southerland, Merlo, Robinson, Benekos, & Albanese, 2007). Criminal justice as a discipline is best known for its focus on describing and understanding how systems and subsystems operate, and less on articulating the overarching goals of the systems or evaluating whether justice has been achieved by these systems (Arrigo, 2008; Klofas, 2010). In this book, we consider criminal justice and criminology as two parts of the same field, which we will abbreviate as CJC studies. (This is not to be confused with the abbreviation "CJS," which we use to refer to the criminal justice system.)

There have been calls within CJC studies for developing a more philosophical approach to better understand the concept of justice, one that educates on the inequality and failures of current systems of justice and provides a closer examination of the relationships between offenders, victims, agents of social control, and the community (Arrigo, 2008; Hunter, 2011). Criminal justice policies can actually perpetuate injustice, so a critical focus must be given to how justice is administered and thoughtful attention given to the underlying principles and goals of criminal justice systems.

Given the critical justice issues that are faced by criminal justice practitioners, policymakers, and academics, developing a deeper understanding of justice as a CJC student will be useful. If you have not completed the activity noted in the introduction to this chapter, take a minute to write down how you would define the word "justice." As we explore this concept, you will be able to categorize how you defined justice, and see how that definition could be expanded. You may find that justice has multiple, overlapping, and at times even seemingly contradictory dimensions.

## CATEGORIZING TYPES OF JUSTICE

There are many ways to understand the different aspects of justice; one useful approach is to categorize justice into discrete types. For instance, an important distinction that can be drawn is between *formal or procedural justice* and *distributive or substantive justice*. *Formal justice* is also referred to as corrective or rectificatory justice, a nod to the main goal of making unjust situations right, meaning to "rectify" them. Formal justice is frequently the purview of criminal justice courses because it is the basis of our legal system, which outlines procedures to be followed to ensure that justice is served (hence the name *procedural* justice). The rights afforded to all people who are involved in the CJS—from their first interaction with the police, through their court proceedings, all the way to what we refer to as the "back end" of the system where sentences are carried out, often in prison or community corrections—are born of this type of justice. It is important to remember, however, that "law" and "justice" are not one and the same. Laws were created to mediate relations between people, and they are not immutable representations of justice. Many laws have been protested and broken when they were deemed unjust (Hurlbert, 2011). It is important to remember that such seemingly outdated (and clearly unjust) elements of our nation's history as slavery, Jim Crow, and Japanese internment were, at one time, enshrined in law.

*Distributive or substantive justice*, on the other hand, deals not with the process by which justice is achieved, but rather with the outcome: the distribution of goods, rewards, burdens, and opportunities in society. This type of justice recognizes that sometimes it is necessary to treat different people differently to achieve justice. Looking at the world with a distributive lens requires an examination of whether everyone's needs are met according to a baseline, agreed-upon standard of what individuals should receive. Access to nutritious food, health care, housing, or education could, for example, be deemed basic rights that should, on some level, be provided to all people. Because our CJS focuses on process rather than outcome (e.g., the right to a fair and speedy trial), the substantive rights that distributive justice emphasizes are often considered secondary to criminal justice issues.

Weisheit and Morn (2015) propose a different way of breaking down the multifaceted concept of justice. They delineate four components of justice: equality, merit (also referred to as desert), need, and fairness. Equality is defined as all people having equal rights and equal access to resources. Any efforts that take the most disadvantaged into account would be based on this notion of equality and equal opportunity. Merit refers to getting what one deserves, whether it is recognition and rewards or punishments and consequences (deserts). For example, military and political actions in response to the terrorist attacks of September 11, 2001, were rooted in this type of justice. The concept of need is about providing access to basic resources for those who find themselves most in need. Providing shelter and food to the homeless is an example of attending to justice needs. Fairness involves treating equals equally and, when necessary, treating unequals unequally. For example, hiring preferences that are given to a group that has historically experienced disadvantage can help to achieve fairness.

In her taxonomy of justice, Hurlbert (2011) also includes ethical practice, which is defined by the concepts of moral righteousness, virtue, and altruism. Any attempts to make society a better place, from helping others or behaving altruistically on a personal level, to civic engagement (e.g., political or religious efforts in pursuit of justice) and public action (e.g., social justice activism), would fall into this category. This perspective on justice prioritizes ensuring that the most marginalized people in a society are valued and protected. Consequently, many examples of ethical practice take the form of advocacy for or engagement with marginalized groups. Take, for instance, the acts of volunteering at a soup kitchen, participating in a protest against human trafficking, or attending an event to raise awareness about racial disproportionality in incarceration rates. All of these efforts use individual action to achieve justice for oppressed or marginalized people.

A very closely related concept—one that is central to our discussion of justice in this text and essential to any comprehensive conceptualization of justice—is *social justice*. The use of the term social justice in the United States came into prominence at the end of the 19th century. Using the categories discussed previously, social justice is most closely related to distributive justice. Social justice is governed by the basic structure of society or the major institutions that allocate (or bring about an allocation of) rights, opportunities, and resources (Rawls, 1971). Social justice deals with fairness and equality of opportunity for groups or classes of people. Implicit in this definition is an expectation that those with power will consider and attend to the needs of those who are not in power. A just society attempts to diminish significant disparities between groups even if it requires a redistribution of resources to ensure fairness in meeting basic needs (Weisheit & Morn, 2015). Social justice is the broadest form of justice and relates to "whether people have access to the things they need to live a secure and dignified life" (Hurlbert, 2011, p. 19). Social justice focuses on discrimination against groups based on characteristics such as class, race and ethnicity, gender, sexual identity, as well as the provision of basic human rights, and justice related to the environment. Hulbert (2011, p. 19) sets forth this ideal definition of social justice:

> Social justice is a set of ideas, values and social practices to ensure that all persons and groups enjoy economic security, can participate effectively in democratic decision-making, exercise mutual respect and caring for one another and live their lives in ways that protect and sustain the natural environment for future generations.

## HISTORY OF IDEAS ABOUT JUSTICE

One commonality between these many different types and forms of justice is that they all concern the relationship between individuals and the complex structures and institutions of society. This was not always the case, however. Less than 200 years ago, justice was thought of primarily as a characteristic of individuals, rather than societies, with a focus on individual property rights. The application of justice to institutions began largely through the concerns for individual rights in criminal courts in terms of providing fair trials and appropriate punishments (Barry, 2005). The evolution of the concept of justice only broadened from there.

The roots of justice can be seen in philosophical, religious, and moral thought. Ancient philosophers set the stage for the discussion of issues related to justice. In Greece, philosophers such as Socrates, and his students, Plato and Aristotle, developed "ethical theory" that focused on what it meant to be a just person, and how "human excellence" required possessing moral virtues, such as acting courageously, justly, and in moderation (Parry, 2014). These ideas were linked to achieving personal happiness, and became the basis for moral psychology (Parry, 2014). These early ideas about justice did not include the concept of equality, as people were not viewed as inherently equal or deserving of equal shares (Reisch, 2002).

Concepts of justice are present in the teachings and literature associated with Buddhism, Christianity, Hinduism, Islam, and Judaism. In Medieval times, theologians and philosophers often drew on religious texts with Saint Augustine and Thomas Aquinas being a few of the many influential writers. Philosophical thought on this topic greatly expanded by focusing on justice in politics, economics, and public life through the work of Thomas Hobbes (1588–1679) in the United Kingdom, David Hume (1711–1776) in Scotland, Immanuel Kant (1724–1804) in Germany, and John Stuart Mill (1806–1873) in England, again, just to name a few. This work helped solidify what came to be known as "natural rights" and ideas about "the pursuit of happiness" and is reflected in such documents as the U.S. Declaration of Independence. Throughout the 17th and 18th centuries in the West, ideas about justice were also linked with the scientific revolution, which sought to establish universal truths that stood separate from religious beliefs (Reisch, 2002).

One contemporary American philosopher, John Rawls (1921–2002), became a leading figure in the development of moral and political philosophy. In explaining his theory of justice, Rawls poses the following question: Assuming that some sort of a social contract is necessary if we are to live together in a civilized society, what sort of contract would ensure the most just distribution of income and opportunity? To complicate that decision, he suggests that this decision be made with a "veil of ignorance" preventing us from seeing whether we might be born into disadvantage (e.g., in poverty, as an oppressed minority, with a physical or mental handicap), or into advantage (e.g., in a wealthy, educated family, part of the privileged majority). Rawls believed that if we did not know whom we would be born as, we, being rational and self-interested individuals, would only allow a society in which the distribution of income and opportunity would benefit those least well off.

Despite contemporary understandings of social justice that recognize the crucial nature of including marginalized or oppressed groups, early philosophical teaching on justice came from (and advanced) the perspective of a very elite few. It did not escape our notice—and it probably will not escape yours—that our discussion of the philosophy of justice presented a list of European men. In this sense, our understandings of justice have come a long way toward advancing justice for, and from the perspective of, marginalized populations since the time of the early philosophical scholars.

## THE EMERGENCE OF SOCIAL JUSTICE

The modern concept of social justice emerged in France and Britain in the 1840s during the time of early industrialization, and became the central message of social democratic parties across Europe (Barry, 2005). This message challenged the justice of institutions, primarily by questioning the power of the owners of capital, the dominance of the market system (i.e., capitalism), unequal relations between employers and employees, and the distribution of income and wealth. By the end of World War II in 1945, social democratic parties had these key ideas: (1) Worker representation should exist to insure that people's rights and welfare are more important than an institution's profits; (2) The unequal distribution of income and wealth created by capitalism should be corrected through taxation and/or a transfer of funds to provide for those without adequate incomes; and (3) High-quality education and health care (and housing, although strategies varied) should be provided for all (Barry, 2005).

In the United States, some of the same ideals were put forth under presidential social and economic programs and initiatives with the goal of addressing existing inequality and injustice. Franklin Roosevelt's economic programs of the 1930s, known as The New Deal, promoted recovery of the economy in response to the Great Depression, providing relief to unemployed farmers and reforming business and financial practices. A "Second New Deal" included The Social Security Act, The Wagner Act to promote labor unions, and the Works Progress Administration, a relief program that used millions of unskilled workers to carry out public works projects, such as the construction of buildings, parks, roads, and bridges. In 1938, the Fair Labor Standards Act was passed; it set minimum wages and maximum hours for different groups of workers.

Although some of these programs were later ruled unconstitutional by the Supreme Court or shut down by the Congressional opponents of the New Deal known as the Conservative Coalition, many of these programs still exist. For example, the Social Security System, the Securities and Exchange Commission, Fannie Mae, the Federal National Mortgage Association, the Federal Deposit Insurance Corporation, and the Federal Housing Administration are all lasting innovations of the New Deal.

President Harry Truman created The Fair Deal, a program designed to address social welfare and economic development. In his State of the Union Address in 1949, Truman declared that "Every segment of our population, and every individual, has a right to expect from his government a fair deal." Although some Fair Deal programs were successfully implemented, others received opposition from conservatives who envisioned a smaller role played by the federal government. The Fair Deal was notable for establishing the call for universal health care, a topic that remains controversial today. Another major legislative accomplishment of The Fair Deal was the Housing Act of 1949, which led to the allocation of federal funds for new housing projects, urban renewal, and increased public housing. The Social Security Act of 1950 extended the coverage of social security to elderly Americans and raised the minimum wage, benefiting middle-class and working-class Americans.

Some of Truman's largest and most lasting social justice achievements were integrating the armed forces, denying government contracts to firms with racially discriminatory practices, and naming African Americans to federal posts. In a 1947 speech to the National Association for the Advancement of Colored People (NAACP), Truman (the first President to address this organization) said, "Every man should have the right to a decent home, the right to an education, the right to adequate medical care, the right to a worthwhile job, the right to an equal share in the making of public decisions through the ballot, and the right to a fair trial in a fair court." Notably, this statement designed to promote social justice included sexist language that was standard for this time period. This demonstrates the elasticity of the concept of social justice, which has expanded and deepened over time as people have become more aware of different forms of societal disadvantage.

President Lyndon Johnson also implemented a set of programs to address injustice, referred to as The Great Society. Two main goals of these social reforms were the elimination of poverty and racial injustice. New programs that addressed education, medical care, urban problems, and transportation were launched during this period. Some of these proposals were the continuation of initiatives of President John F. Kennedy's New Frontier. Although some of the programs have been eliminated or had their funding reduced, many of them, including Medicare, Medicaid, and federal education funding, continue. The Great Society's programs expanded under the administrations of Richard Nixon (who enacted the National Wilderness Act) and Gerald Ford.

More recent presidents, such as Jimmy Carter, Bill Clinton, and Barack Obama, can also be credited with promoting legislation and creating federally funded programs in line with the ideals of social justice. In each of these presidencies, however, we could also detail actions that resulted in injustice, such as the internment of Japanese Americans in concentration camps during World War II, welfare-to-work policies, and policies related to the treatment of ex-felons and undocumented immigrants. Just as there have been social programs designed to promote social justice, laws have also been enacted that diminish social justice, such as the Poor Laws, lowering the capital gains tax (which primarily benefits the wealthy), and the Defense of Marriage Act. Debates over what basic needs the government is—or ought to be—obligated to provide are perennial. This debate hinges on striking a balance between two components of justice: providing individual liberty and ensuring social equality.

The government is structured in such a way that social justice simply cannot be a primary focus; because presidents (and other elected officials) have to be concerned with elections, they are typically not in a position to champion causes that question the status quo. This situation is exacerbated by the politicization of many justice issues, fostered by divergent perspectives about justice across the political spectrum. Consider, for instance, the unexpected role that public bathrooms have played in our history of both justice and politics, from the racial segregation of Jim Crow to the more recent spate of "bathroom laws" that dictate where transgender people can relieve themselves. In both examples, a justice issue with a mundane subject matter (access to public bathrooms) becomes fodder for heated political debate.

Despite the politicization of justice issues, justice and social justice are not inherently ideological. Individuals can reach different conclusions about what justice and social justice are, or what is best for the common good, and individuals can also reach different conclusions about how to achieve justice and social justice. Theories of justice and of social justice tend to question the prevailing status quo, however—providing a frame that fits well with contemporary understandings of left-leaning politics. Because conservatives generally opt for approaches to justice that include viewing problems as being caused by individuals (rather than social conditions), advocating for solutions outside of government, a focus on the fiscal costs associated with reforms, and a concern that justice unfairly runs the risk of depriving certain people who deserve greater rewards, there is not a contemporary theory of justice that can be classified as conservative. Clearly, it is not possible to avoid political ideology in discussions of justice; Chapter 4 addresses ideology and politics with regard to issues of justice head-on and in greater detail.

## JUSTICE AND THE LAW

As demonstrated previously, government can sometimes be ill-equipped to produce social justice, and, at times, laws can even codify injustice. Even though we often think of the laws that comprise the CJS as being synonymous with justice, the reality is far more complex. The law can enshrine, implement, ensure, or promote justice—but law and justice are not synonymous. Hurlbert (2011, p. 29) addresses this complexity by noting that the law provides "a skeleton or framework for justice. It sets out certain attributes of the justice system but it is only one social institution in the study of justice." By invoking "social institutions," Hurlbert is referring to the many different realms of our social lives that interact with issues of justice.

*Social institution* may seem like a confusing term (in fact, the concept has proven itself almost as slippery as "justice" (Martin, 2004)), but at its core it refers to well-established, enduring "patterns of social activity that give shape to collective and individual experience" (Bellah, Marsden, Sullivan, Swidler, & Tipton, 1991, p. 40). Examples of social institutions include the government, economy, family, education, religion—all abstract concepts that structure and constrain the way individuals and groups act. In explaining that "the law is but one social institution that mediates relations between people and has influence on the actions and choices of people," (Hurlbert, 2011, p. 29) provides a helpful reminder that as scholars and students of justice, we must expand our understanding of the issue well beyond the boundaries of criminal justice. Considering the many social institutions that relate to justice—rather than myopically focusing on the CJS to the exclusion of other pertinent factors—allows us to view justice in the appropriate social context.

Doing this in turn allows us to orient to injustice as a *social problem*, rather than individual circumstance. Because individual cases do not occur in a social vacuum, it is important to understand how their unique circumstances represent a wider social issue. Take, for instance, the hypothetical sexual assault of a teenage girl at a party. Considering this horrific event as an individual case would entail understanding the circumstances of the sexual assault (perhaps it occurred at a party, perhaps she was drinking, perhaps she knew the perpetrator) and might have implications for assessments of desert that inform our idea of how to remedy the situation (perhaps the perpetrator should be charged with sexual assault). Although this view is natural and clearly has merit, it eclipses many other important considerations.

If we consider the larger context of gender inequality, cultural expectations for how women and men behave in social and dating situations, and the pervasiveness of "rape culture" (Williams, 2007), it is easy to see how this young woman's experience is related to misogyny—linking her sexual assault not only to other women's similar experiences, but also to issues as far-flung as the gender-wage gap and the social phenomenon known as "mansplaining." Had the individuals' genders been different in this scenario, our understanding of this sexual assault would also change. If a young man were sexually assaulted at the same party, or if the young woman were known to be transgender, or even if the perpetrator were female as well, our discussion of the injustice would be altered. In all of these variations of the scenario, gender is as important a social institution as the law. Consequently, our understanding of how to address the injustice *as a social problem* will be broader than simply charging the perpetrator with sexual assault and providing services to the victim. Although these are clearly remedies to the individual case, they will do nothing to diminish sexual assault more broadly, or to address the larger social forces of misogyny that facilitate sexual assault.

Because our CJS is structured to deal with individual cases rather than tackle larger social problems, it is often challenging for CJC students (and consumers of criminal justice, as we all are) to make this connection between injustice as a personal problem and injustice as a social problem. Using what Mills (1959) refers to as our "sociological imagination" can help us grasp this relationship between personal biography and social history. By examining how institutions, culture, and social structure provide the opportunity for personal injustice, we can link our own experiences to the broader systems of the social world. And by viewing ourselves and others in the broader context of the social institutions that influence us, we can more fully understand *in*justice in order to begin to achieve justice.

# STUDYING JUSTICE

Pursuing justice in this way requires that the perspective of marginalized people be considered and that they be given a voice. Without this approach, injustice will not be fully seen or challenged. Marginalized and oppressed people have far poorer life chances than those whose lives are privileged and stable. For example, marginalized populations are more likely to be incarcerated, hospitalized, and/or die younger than people who are not marginalized or oppressed. Part of the work of understanding justice requires exploring how and why this occurs. One problem quickly encountered is the realization that existing structures are based on and perpetuate inequality, begging the question of whether justice can be fully achieved in these contexts (Reisch, 2002)

Studying justice also requires acknowledging our own *ethnocentrism* (Hurlbert, 2011). *Ethnocentrism* refers to our often automatic and subconscious preferences for practices and values reflective of our own culture. Ethnocentrism entails thinking *normatively*, or thinking within the confines of our own values, experiences, and perspectives without taking into consideration the perspectives of others. As individuals, we are the product of our own cultural, religious, and class backgrounds, so it makes perfect sense that normative thinking comes naturally to us. One challenge that must be overcome to study justice is to acknowledge and reflect on our own *positionality* in the world—how we are situated with regard to the larger social world. Positionality reflects the idea that gender, race, class, and other aspects of our identities are markers of relational positions rather than essential qualities.

We will discuss all of this more in Chapter 3 when we address issues of identity, privilege, and oppression. For now, it's important to keep in mind that each of us sees the world through our own individual lenses that have been shaped and colored by our cultures and experiences. *Reflexivity* is the process of paying attention to your own position within this larger social or cultural context, with regard to what you are describing; it means examining your assumptions critically and reflecting on how your positionality affects your interpretation of the world. By examining our own positionality in the world in reflexive ways, we can combat (but not eliminate) the ethnocentrism that comes naturally to all of us.

## References

Arrigo, B.A. (2008). Crime, justice, and the under-laborer: On the criminology of the shadow and the search for disciplinary identity and legitimacy. *Justice Quarterly, 25*(3), 439–468.

Barry, B. (2005). *Why social justice matters*. Cambridge, UK: Polity Press.

Bellah, R. N., Marsden, R., Sullivan, W. M., Swidler, A., & Tipton, S. M. (1991). *The good society.* New York: Vintage Books.

Capeheart, L., & Milovanovic, D. (2007). *Social justice: Theories, issues, and movements.* New Brunswick, NJ: Rutgers University Press.

Hunter, R.D. (2011). Presidential address: The future of justice studies. *Justice Quarterly, 28*(1), 1–14.

Hurlbert, M.A. (Ed.). (2011). *Pursuing justice: An introduction to justice studies.* Nova Scotia, Canada: Fernwood Publishing.

Klofas, J.M. (2010). Postscript: Teaching the new criminal justice. In J.M. Klofas, N. Kroovand Hipple, & E. McGarrell (Eds.), *The new criminal justice: American communities and the changing world of crime control* (pp. 147–155). New York: Routledge.

Martin, P. Y. (2004). Gender as social institution. *Social Forces, 82*(4), 1249–1273.

Mills, C. W. (1959). *The sociological imagination.* New York: Oxford.

Parry, R. (2014). Ancient ethical theory. In E.N. Zalta (Ed.), *The Stanford encyclopedia of philosophy.* Retrieved from http://plato.stanford.edu/archives/fall2014/entries/ethics-ancient/.

Rawls, J. (1971). *A theory of justice.* Cambridge, MA: Harvard University Press.

Reisch, M. (2002). Defining social justice in a socially unjust world. *Families in Society: The Journal of Contemporary Social Services, 14*(2), 343–354.

Southerland, M.D., Merlo, A.V., Robinson, L., Benekos, P.J., & Albanese, J.S. (2007). Ensuring quality in criminal justice education: Academic standards and the reemergence of accreditation. *Journal of Criminal Justice Education, 18*(1), 87–105.

Weisheit, R., & Morn, F. (2015). *Pursuing justice: Traditional and contemporary issues in our communities and the world.* New York: Routledge.

Williams, J. E. (2007). Blackwell Encyclopedia of Sociology - Rape Culture. In G. Ritzer (Ed.), *Blackwell Encyclopedia of Sociology.* Oxford, UK: Blackwell Publishing Inc.

## Selected Readings

Smith & Sullivan, Student conceptions of Justice, original article for book.
The Universal Declaration of Human Rights.

## Discussion Questions/Writing Assignments

1. Where do your ideas about justice come from? Which meaning of justice resonates most with you: deserts, fairness, equality, or moral righteousness? Provide an example of justice that is rooted in each of these four aspects of justice. How might these distinct conceptions of justice compete with or contradict one another?
2. Every day we make decisions that reflect our own beliefs about justice, so justice can be thought of, in part, as an individualized practice. What are "rules"

you personally live by? Think of all of the day-to-day decisions and long-term decisions you make. Are they influenced by your ideas about justice?

3. What does this image tell us about justice? Which one gives us justice? Provide a real-world example that could be applied to this image.

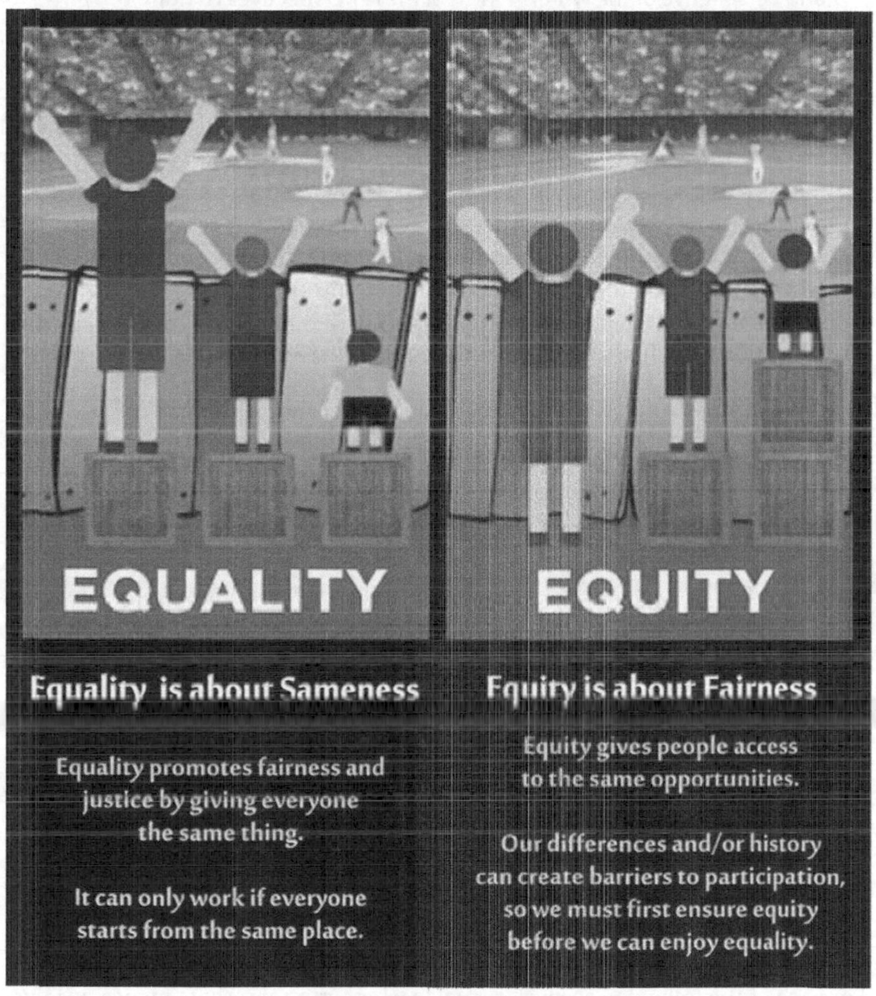


4. In this chapter, federal funding for education was given as an example of a justice-related government priority under President John F. Kennedy. Have you received federal (or other) funding for your college education? Do your experiences paying for your college education reflect justice, or injustice? How so?
5. Provide examples of several U.S. laws that over time came to be seen as unjust. Do you think they were considered just at the time? According to which definition(s) of justice? How did they come to be seen as unjust over time?
6. Read the satirical piece here: http://www.theonion.com/article/brave-mountain-lion-fends-off-group-of-hikers-2526. How does this (comically) demonstrate

ethnocentrism? What might the headline have been if presented from the hikers' perspective? Now let's examine the context of humans only (sorry, no mountain lions). Consider the 2012 shooting of Trayvon Martin by George Zimmerman; how could this encounter be reported differently depending on the positionality and perspective of the writer? Which of these perspectives is "right"?
7. Why might people disagree on how to correct injustice?
8. How can the law be used to combat injustice? How has the law been used to perpetuate or create injustice? Is the law ever neutral in the face of injustice?
9. We know that our criminal justice system is designed to deal with individual injustices; does this mean that the criminal justice system is ill-equipped to treat injustice as a social problem? What about Criminal Justice and Criminology as a field—do we approach injustice as a social problem?
10. After reading the 30 articles in The Universal Declaration of Human Rights, where and how is the U.S. falling short in terms of providing these universal human rights?
11. How do the students' views on justice presented in Smith and Sullivan's reading compare to your views?

## ACTIVITIES/ASSIGNMENTS

### Visualizing Justice

Now that you've pondered the meaning of justice, let's try something creative to apply your ideas. Take a few minutes to jot down what justice means to you; you can use the new terminology you learned from this chapter or any other words that resonate with how you conceptualize justice. Next, challenge yourself to create a visual depiction of justice. Using nothing more than a pencil and a clean sheet of paper, draw what justice means to you. Your drawing can be as literal or symbolic as you'd like; just make sure that it represents all of the facets of justice that you jotted down. As if this wasn't already tricky enough, there is one restriction: you can't draw the scales of justice! (That would be too easy.)

### What Is Justice?

For each of the following scenarios, decide whether it represents justice or injustice. Explain why you think that situation is just or unjust, using terminology from the chapter (e.g., fairness, equality). Using your sociological imagination, explain how this individual case is connected to social institutions and can be viewed in the context of a larger social problem.

1. A woman is required by her employer to wear makeup (powder, blush, lipstick, and mascara) as part of the appearance guidelines of the company. She is fired for refusing to comply with the policy.
2. Many Native Americans were removed from their homeland by white immigrants and put on reservations.

3. During a time of war, men can be drafted into the armed forces and compelled to fight in a war, but women cannot.
4. Men's football programs at most major universities are given 10 times the amount of money given to women's basketball, volleyball, and lacrosse programs combined.
5. Convicted sex offenders must register with state and local criminal justice authorities. Their names (and sometimes pictures) are available on the Internet.
6. All students are required to say the pledge of allegiance, including the phrase, "one nation, under God."
7. A principal of a school hits on a teacher wearing a low cut blouse and a miniskirt. He invites her to dinner and says she will be "sure to get a good rating this year." She files a sexual harassment complaint and the principal is fired.
8. A husband repeatedly beats his wife and she kills him. She is convicted of first-degree murder and sent to prison for life.
9. A student with dyslexia (a learning disorder marked by impairment of the ability to recognize and comprehend written words) is given double the time of other students to take the SAT.
10. A university renames two buildings named after former school presidents who sold university-owned slaves to pay off campus debts in the 1800s.
11. Gay couples can get married in the United States.
12. People at your university aren't allowed to smoke on campus.
13. Women are allowed to get abortions in the first trimester of their pregnancy.
14. Convicted murderers in your state are put to death.
15. One athletic team was required to eliminate the use of Native American words and images to represent their team, whereas another team in a different state kept a similar name and image.

## Miscarriage of Justice in CJ

Watch: http://www.cbsnews.com/news/30-years-on-death-row-exoneration-60-minutes/ and answer the following questions:

1. Do the prosecutor and the acting district attorney both define what happened as an injustice?
2. What are the important differences in how these two individuals define justice?

## Justice Documentaries

Many documentaries have been made to bring injustices to light. Pick a documentary to view that addresses a social problem. Briefly summarize the movie. What are the justice issues portrayed in the film? What makes them justice issues? Are they social justice issues? Why? What solutions are presented to the injustice portrayed?

## Contemporary Activists for Justice

Read the following document: http://www.thenation.com/article/fifty-most-influential-progressives-twentieth-century/. Choose one person interesting to you. Google their name and learn more about how they named and responded to a justice issue. How did this person define justice/injustice?

## The Danger of a Single Story

Watch Chimamanda Ngozi Adichie's TED talk on "The Danger of a Single Story": http://www.ted.com/talks/chimamanda_adichie_the_danger_of_a_single_story?language=en. How does Adichie touch upon justice, positionality, and ethnocentrism in her talk?

# SEMESTER-LONG JUSTICE PROJECT

Step One: Choose one of the following assignments:

1. Write a three-page paper that describes and examines an incident of injustice in your life (it can be an experience in which you witnessed, experienced, or participated in injustice). Make sure to use your sociological imagination to link your personal experiences to broader issues of injustice.
   Be reflexive in your paper—discuss how your experiences (including your understanding of these experiences and reactions to them) have been shaped by your positionality in the world.
2. What areas of injustice are you most interested in learning more about? Based on your own experiences with injustice, are there particular justice issues you feel personally connected to or passionate about? Why is this a justice issue?

## Selected Reading

# UNIVERSAL DECLARATION OF HUMAN RIGHTS

## WHAT ARE HUMAN RIGHTS?

Human rights are rights inherent to all human beings, whatever our nationality, place of residence, sex, national or ethnic origin, color, religion, language, or any other status. We are all equally entitled to our human rights without discrimination. These rights are all interrelated, interdependent and indivisible.

Universal human rights are often expressed and guaranteed by law, in the forms of treaties, customary international law, general principles and other sources of international law. International human rights law lays down obligations of Governments to act in certain ways or to refrain from certain acts, in order to promote and protect human rights and fundamental freedoms of individuals or groups.

## UNIVERSAL AND INALIENABLE

The principle of universality of human rights is the cornerstone of international human rights law. This principle, as first emphasized in the Universal Declaration on Human Rights in 1948, has been reiterated in numerous international human rights conventions, declarations, and resolutions. The 1993 Vienna World Conference on Human Rights, for example, noted that it is the duty of States to promote and protect all human rights and fundamental freedoms, regardless of their political, economic and cultural systems.

All States have ratified at least one, and 80% of States have ratified four or more, of the core human rights treaties, reflecting consent of States which creates legal obligations for them and giving concrete expression to universality. Some fundamental human rights norms enjoy universal protection by customary international law across all boundaries and civilizations.

Human rights are inalienable. They should not be taken away, except in specific situations and according to due process. For example, the right to liberty may be restricted if a person is found guilty of a crime by a court of law.

## INTERDEPENDENT AND INDIVISIBLE

All human rights are indivisible, whether they are civil and political rights, such as the right to life, equality before the law and freedom of expression; economic, social and cultural rights, such as the rights to work, social security and education, or collective rights, such as the rights to development and self-determination, are indivisible, interrelated and interdependent. The improvement of one right facilitates advancement of the others. Likewise, the deprivation of one right adversely affects the others.

## EQUAL AND NONDISCRIMINATORY

Nondiscrimination is a cross-cutting principle in international human rights law. The principle is present in all the major human rights treaties and provides the central theme of some of international human rights conventions such as the International Convention on the Elimination of All Forms of Racial Discrimination and the Convention on the Elimination of All Forms of Discrimination against Women.

The principle applies to everyone in relation to all human rights and freedoms and it prohibits discrimination on the basis of a list of nonexhaustive categories such as sex, race, color, and so on. The principle of nondiscrimination is complemented by the principle of equality, as stated in Article 1 of the Universal Declaration of Human Rights: "All human beings are born free and equal in dignity and rights."

## BOTH RIGHTS AND OBLIGATIONS

Human rights entail both rights and obligations. States assume obligations and duties under international law to respect, to protect, and to fulfill human rights. The obligation to respect means that States must refrain from interfering with or curtailing the enjoyment of human rights. The obligation to protect requires States to protect individuals and groups against human rights abuses. The obligation to fulfill means that States must take positive action to facilitate the enjoyment of basic human rights. At the individual level, although we are entitled our human rights, we should also respect the human rights of others.

Citation: http://www.ohchr.org/EN/Issues/Pages/WhatareHumanRights.aspx

## HISTORY OF THE DOCUMENT

The Universal Declaration of Human Rights, which was adopted by the United Nations (UN) General Assembly on December 10, 1948, was the result of the experience of the Second World War. With the end of that war, and the creation of the UN, the international community vowed never again to allow atrocities like those of that conflict happen again. World leaders decided to complement the UN

Charter with a road map to guarantee the rights of every individual everywhere. The document they considered, and which would later become the Universal Declaration of Human Rights, was taken up at the first session of the General Assembly in 1946. The Assembly reviewed this draft Declaration on Fundamental Human Rights and Freedoms and transmitted it to the Economic and Social Council "for reference to the Commission on Human Rights for consideration ... in its preparation of an international bill of rights." The Commission, at its first session early in 1947, authorized its members to formulate what it termed "a preliminary draft International Bill of Human Rights." Later, the work was taken over by a formal drafting committee, consisting of members of the Commission from eight States, selected with due regard for geographical distribution.

In 1950, on the second anniversary of the adoption of the Universal Declaration of Human Rights, students at the UN International Nursery School in New York viewed a poster of the historic document. After adopting it on December 10, 1948, the UN General Assembly had called upon all Member States to publicize the text of the Declaration and "to cause it to be disseminated, displayed, read and expounded principally in schools and other educational institutions, without distinction based on the political status of countries or territories."

The Commission on Human Rights was made up of 18 members from various political, cultural and religious backgrounds. Eleanor Roosevelt, widow of American President Franklin D. Roosevelt, chaired the UDHR drafting committee. With her were René Cassin of France, who composed the first draft of the Declaration, the Committee Rapporteur Charles Malik of Lebanon, Vice-Chairman Peng Chung Chang of China, and John Humphrey of Canada, Director of the UN's Human Rights Division, who prepared the Declaration's blueprint. But Mrs. Roosevelt was recognized as the driving force for the Declaration's adoption.

The Commission met for the first time in 1947. In her memoirs, Eleanor Roosevelt recalled:

> Dr. Chang was a pluralist and held forth in charming fashion on the proposition that there is more than one kind of ultimate reality. The Declaration, he said, should reflect more than simply Western ideas and Dr. Humphrey would have to be eclectic in his approach. His remark, though addressed to Dr. Humphrey, was really directed at Dr. Malik, from whom it drew a prompt retort as he expounded at some length the philosophy of Thomas Aquinas. Dr. Humphrey joined enthusiastically in the discussion, and I remember that at one point Dr. Chang suggested that the Secretariat might well spend a few months studying the fundamentals of Confucianism!

The final draft by Cassin was handed to the Commission on Human Rights, which was being held in Geneva. The draft declaration sent out to all UN member States for comments became known as the Geneva draft.

The first draft of the Declaration was proposed in September 1948 with more than 50 Member States participating in the final drafting. By its resolution 217 A (III) of December 10, 1948, the General Assembly, meeting in Paris, adopted the Universal Declaration of Human Rights with eight nations abstaining from the vote but none dissenting. Hernán Santa Cruz of Chile, member of the drafting sub-Committee, wrote:

> I perceived clearly that I was participating in a truly significant historic event in which a consensus had been reached as to the supreme value of the human person, a value that did not originate in the decision of a worldly power, but rather in the fact of existing—which gave rise to the inalienable right to live free from want and oppression and to fully develop one's personality. In the Great Hall...there was an atmosphere of genuine solidarity and brotherhood among men and women from all latitudes, the like of which I have not seen again in any international setting.

The entire text of the UDHR was composed in less than two years. At a time when the world was divided into Eastern and Western blocks, finding a common ground on what should make the essence of the document proved to be a colossal task.

Citation: http://www.un.org/en/sections/universal-declaration/history-document/

# THE UNIVERSAL DECLARATION OF HUMAN RIGHTS

## Preamble

Whereas recognition of the inherent dignity and of the equal and inalienable rights of all members of the human family is the foundation of freedom, justice and peace in the world,

Whereas disregard and contempt for human rights have resulted in barbarous acts which have outraged the conscience of mankind, and the advent of a world in which human beings shall enjoy freedom of speech and belief and freedom from fear and want has been proclaimed as the highest aspiration of the common people,

Whereas it is essential, if man is not to be compelled to have recourse, as a last resort, to rebellion against tyranny and oppression, that human rights should be protected by the rule of law,

Whereas it is essential to promote the development of friendly relations between nations,

Whereas the peoples of the United Nations have in the Charter reaffirmed their faith in fundamental human rights, in the dignity and worth of the human person and in the equal rights of men and women and have determined to promote social progress and better standards of life in larger freedom,

Whereas Member States have pledged themselves to achieve, in co-operation with the United Nations, the promotion of universal respect for and observance of human rights and fundamental freedoms,

Whereas a common understanding of these rights and freedoms is of the greatest importance for the full realization of this pledge,

Now, Therefore THE GENERAL ASSEMBLY proclaims THIS UNIVERSAL DECLARATION OF HUMAN RIGHTS as a common standard of achievement for all peoples and all nations, to the end that every individual and every organ of society, keeping this Declaration constantly in mind, shall strive by teaching and education to promote respect for these rights and freedoms and by progressive measures, national and international, to secure their universal and effective recognition and observance, both among the peoples of Member States themselves and among the peoples of territories under their jurisdiction.

## Article 1

All human beings are born free and equal in dignity and rights. They are endowed with reason and conscience and should act towards one another in a spirit of brotherhood.

## Article 2

Everyone is entitled to all the rights and freedoms set forth in this Declaration, without distinction of any kind, such as race, colour, sex, language, religion, political or other opinion, national or social origin, property, birth or other status. Furthermore, no distinction shall be made on the basis of the political, jurisdictional or international status of the country or territory to which a person belongs, whether it be independent, trust, non-self-governing or under any other limitation of sovereignty.

## Article 3

Everyone has the right to life, liberty and security of person.

## Article 4

No one shall be held in slavery or servitude; slavery and the slave trade shall be prohibited in all their forms.

## Article 5

No one shall be subjected to torture or to cruel, inhuman or degrading treatment or punishment.

## Article 6

Everyone has the right to recognition everywhere as a person before the law.

## Article 7

All are equal before the law and are entitled without any discrimination to equal protection of the law. All are entitled to equal protection against any discrimination in violation of this Declaration and against any incitement to such discrimination.

## Article 8

Everyone has the right to an effective remedy by the competent national tribunals for acts violating the fundamental rights granted him by the constitution or by law.

## Article 9

No one shall be subjected to arbitrary arrest, detention or exile.

## Article 10

Everyone is entitled in full equality to a fair and public hearing by an independent and impartial tribunal, in the determination of his rights and obligations and of any criminal charge against him.

## Article 11

1. Everyone charged with a penal offence has the right to be presumed innocent until proved guilty according to law in a public trial at which he has had all the guarantees necessary for his defense.
2. No one shall be held guilty of any penal offence on account of any act or omission which did not constitute a penal offence, under national or international law, at the time when it was committed. Nor shall a heavier penalty be imposed than the one that was applicable at the time the penal offence was committed.

## Article 12

No one shall be subjected to arbitrary interference with his privacy, family, home or correspondence, nor to attacks upon his honour and reputation. Everyone has the right to the protection of the law against such interference or attacks.

## Article 13

1. Everyone has the right to freedom of movement and residence within the borders of each state.
2. Everyone has the right to leave any country, including his own, and to return to his country.

## Article 14

1. Everyone has the right to seek and to enjoy in other countries asylum from persecution.
2. This right may not be invoked in the case of prosecutions genuinely arising from non-political crimes or from acts contrary to the purposes and principles of the United Nations.

## Article 15

1. Everyone has the right to a nationality.
2. No one shall be arbitrarily deprived of his nationality nor denied the right to change his nationality.

## Article 16

1. Men and women of full age, without any limitation due to race, nationality or religion, have the right to marry and to found a family. They are entitled to equal rights as to marriage, during marriage and at its dissolution.
2. Marriage shall be entered into only with the free and full consent of the intending spouses.
3. The family is the natural and fundamental group unit of society and is entitled to protection by society and the State.

## Article 17

1. Everyone has the right to own property alone as well as in association with others.
2. No one shall be arbitrarily deprived of his property.

## Article 18

Everyone has the right to freedom of thought, conscience and religion; this right includes freedom to change his religion or belief, and freedom, either alone or in community with others and in public or private, to manifest his religion or belief in teaching, practice, worship and observance.

## Article 19

Everyone has the right to freedom of opinion and expression; this right includes freedom to hold opinions without interference and to seek, receive and impart information and ideas through any media and regardless of frontiers.

## Article 20

1. Everyone has the right to freedom of peaceful assembly and association.
2. No one may be compelled to belong to an association.

## Article 21

1. Everyone has the right to take part in the government of his country, directly or through freely chosen representatives.
2. Everyone has the right of equal access to public service in his country.
3. The will of the people shall be the basis of the authority of government; this will shall be expressed in periodic and genuine elections which shall be by universal and equal suffrage and shall be held by secret vote or by equivalent free voting procedures.

## Article 22

Everyone, as a member of society, has the right to social security and is entitled to realization, through national effort and international co-operation and in accordance with the organization and resources of each State, of the economic, social and cultural rights indispensable for his dignity and the free development of his personality.

## Article 23

1. Everyone has the right to work, to free choice of employment, to just and favorable conditions of work and to protection against unemployment.
2. Everyone, without any discrimination, has the right to equal pay for equal work.
3. Everyone who works has the right to just and favorable remuneration ensuring for himself and his family an existence worthy of human dignity, and supplemented, if necessary, by other means of social protection.
4. Everyone has the right to form and to join trade unions for the protection of his interests.

## Article 24

Everyone has the right to rest and leisure, including reasonable limitation of working hours and periodic holidays with pay.

## Article 25

1. Everyone has the right to a standard of living adequate for the health and well-being of himself and of his family, including food, clothing, housing and medical care and necessary social services, and the right to security in the event of unemployment, sickness, disability, widowhood, old age or other lack of livelihood in circumstances beyond his control.
2. Motherhood and childhood are entitled to special care and assistance. All children, whether born in or out of wedlock, shall enjoy the same social protection.

## Article 26

1. Everyone has the right to education. Education shall be free, at least in the elementary and fundamental stages. Elementary education shall be compulsory. Technical and professional education shall be made generally available and higher education shall be equally accessible to all on the basis of merit.
2. Education shall be directed to the full development of the human personality and to the strengthening of respect for human rights and fundamental freedoms. It shall promote understanding, tolerance and friendship among all nations, racial or religious groups, and shall further the activities of the United Nations for the maintenance of peace.
3. Parents have a prior right to choose the kind of education that shall be given to their children.

## Article 27

1. Everyone has the right freely to participate in the cultural life of the community, to enjoy the arts and to share in scientific advancement and its benefits.
2. Everyone has the right to the protection of the moral and material interests resulting from any scientific, literary or artistic production of which he is the author.

## Article 28

Everyone is entitled to a social and international order in which the rights and freedoms set forth in this Declaration can be fully realized.

## Article 29

1. Everyone has duties to the community in which alone the free and full development of his personality is possible.
2. In the exercise of his rights and freedoms, everyone shall be subject only to such limitations as are determined by law solely for the purpose of securing due

recognition and respect for the rights and freedoms of others and of meeting the just requirements of morality, public order and the general welfare in a democratic society.

3. These rights and freedoms may in no case be exercised contrary to the purposes and principles of the United Nations.

## Article 30

Nothing in this Declaration may be interpreted as implying for any State, group or person any right to engage in any activity or to perform any act aimed at the destruction of any of the rights and freedoms set forth herein.

http://www.un.org/en/documents/udhr/index.shtml

## Selected Reading

# Student Conceptions of Justice

*Sarah M. Smith and Kaley Sullivan*

What is justice? How would you define justice? Just as the authors asked you to consider these questions at the beginning of the book, we asked our students to tell us. Many of us use the term "justice" in everyday speech, likely without thinking very deeply about what it actually means. But conceptions and perceptions of justice are complex and subjective, depending on any number of individual characteristics, including upbringing, education, and personal experiences. In what follows, we will share how our students defined justice and our thoughts and reflections about these conceptions. We imagine that many of these ideas will resonate with you, whether you are a student of criminal justice, or simply someone interested in justice. We hope that some perspectives are different from yours and inspire you to think in new ways or more deeply about justice. As you read this piece, we entreat you to think about how the different conceptions and perspectives presented here speak to the social justice concerns discussed in the Introduction of this book.

At the beginning of the semester, over 100 students at public universities in California and Missouri were tasked with a short writing assignment that asked them to define justice. They were asked to write a two-page paper describing their personal definition of justice and how their understanding of justice has been shaped by their positions in the world. They were instructed not to use any course materials for the assignment. The vast majority were advanced students in criminal justice programs, as the assignment was used in only capstone courses. Despite years of education about criminal justice that most of these students had undergone, students often offered unclear, vague, or conflicting statements about the meaning of the term "justice." We do not believe that this is due to the lack of sophistication of our students, but rather the difficulty in articulating a clear, concise definition of a multifaceted term. We believe this difficulty is partly a product of American exceptionalism and partly created by the complexity of human experience and perceptions. As we discuss next, students frequently offered what we call "negative" retributive conceptions of the term, which we also think is a product of these issues.

# JUSTICE AS A NEGATIVE CONCEPTION AND THE ROLE OF THE POLITICAL SYSTEM

Students frequently offered negative conceptions of justice, as one-third of them defined it using the term "injustice," and nearly two-thirds defined it in the broader context of injustice. Scholars (Finkel, Watanabe, & Crystal, 2001) explain this tendency, arguing that it is easier to determine what is *not* acceptable or moral rather than what is because different circumstances call for different judgments. Examples of injustices were plentiful—students seemed to have no problem identifying situations lacking justice, while examples affirming it were less often cited. Many students, in fact, identified justice as retributive in nature, referring to it as the act of correcting an injustice, or righting a wrong, rather than affirming how justice is being achieved.

The reactive character of these definitions seems reflective of American criminal justice and how it operates as part of the political system.

Rather than investing in proactive, long-term strategies that experts argue are more effective at curbing crime and violence such as early childhood prevention and community policing (Sherman et al., 1998), U.S. crime control measures in the past several decades have been overwhelmingly punitive, reactive policies (Percival, 2015). The United States' uniquely punitive nature is caused by several different factors, but pivotal among them is the politicized nature of crime (Gottschalk, 2009; Tonry, 2007). Beginning with Richard Nixon, most political candidates have used "tough on crime" platforms to win political elections. The American public is generally uninformed about how the criminal justice system works, but politicians have often been able to garner support by appealing to voters' fear of crime through emotive advertisements about increasing crime or opponents' "soft on crime" records. The use of crime as a populist tool of politicians is particularly common in the United States because criminal justice actors in the United States are elected, and they do so within an adversarial political system in which two parties compete for dominance and power (Gottschalk, 2009; Tonry, 2007). In such systems, the politicization of crime through sensational media stories is encouraged in an effort to gain support for candidates' rhetoric (Chevigny, 2003; Gottschalk, 2009; Tonry, 2007). Given social media exposure of injustices in society and a general increase in familiarity with criminal justice processes, politicians are now using the term "smart on crime" in order to garner the same support received in previous elections (Cusac, 2015; Fairfax, 2010; Percival, 2015).

The United States is also faced with crime problems that are slightly different and seemingly intractable when compared with other western democracies (Lynch & Pridemore, 2011). Compared with other western democracies, the United States maintains relatively high violent victimization rates, particularly lethal violence, in the face of years of punitive criminal justice policies (Lynch & Pridemore, 2011; Percival, 2016). More Americans have come to understand that many punitive policies are not effective and are very expensive, such as long prison sentences for federal drug offenders. Given fiscal exigencies in many states, both the political left and right have agreed to reconsider some extreme sentencing policies including mandatory minimums and recidivism statutes such as three strikes laws. Many states are now relying on community corrections programs given that they are almost always cheaper and just as effective as prison (Henrichson & Delaney, 2012; Vera Institute of Justice, 2013). Yet, many of these programs fail to focus on prevention, which would require addressing inequalities that lead to crime, and instead serve as short-term solutions to larger correctional problems. The financial crisis of 2008 and the resulting recession may have necessitated innovative criminal justice policies, but retribution may still be the leading sentiment informing correctional policy in the United States, and changing financial situations may reverse this trend. Students' understanding of the criminal justice system may reflect our longstanding cultural emphasis on individual accountability and retribution.

Students' negative or reactive conceptions of justice may be influenced by the impact of these cultural emphases in their education. Many students discussed justice in terms of reparation or retribution for wrongs, often in the form of punishment. Those who cited dictionary definitions included criminal justice concepts, describing justice as "the process or result of using laws to fairly judge and punish crimes and criminals"; "the administration of law; the act of determining rights and assigning rewards or punishments"; or "the process or result of using law to fairly judge and punish crimes, and a judge in the court of law." Similarly, those who offered their own definitions often cited criminal justice-oriented views: "paying for and learning from wrongdoing"; "holding individuals accountable for their actions"; "the execution of a punishment for a wrongdoing or crime"; or the "ability to be treated fairly for the actions committed."

Many students' conceptions of justice reflected traditional notions of retribution, or "eye for an eye" sentiments, and viewed desert as proper punishment. For example, one student wrote, "in my opinion, justice means getting what you deserve." Another wrote, "justice means to me, that a person who has been fairly tried and convicted of a crime [is] properly sentenced or punished." However, that same student viewed retributive desert in a more positive sense, as meeting a need created by the injustice, stating, "I also feel justice means the victim's family feels vindicated by the result of a trial." Some students' conceptions reflected retributive justice notions that specifically referred to the equality of a response to a wrongdoing or crime: "justice means that if a person has done something wrong then there will be equal consequences for their actions"; "justice to me is the ability to be treated equally for the actions committed"; or "making an unjust situation equal." In this way, "equality" and "fairness" were qualities used to characterize how retributive notions of desert should be distributed in the face of wrongdoing. Although students rarely explicitly acknowledged inherent inequalities, some were able to conceptualize justice as the act of redressing a previously unfair or unequal situation.

Even students who did not use criminal justice terms often offered negative conceptions such as "righting a wrong" as ways to achieve justice; in fact, this was one of the most common ways justice was explained. One student stated that justice is "a response to injustice anywhere and in any form." Another defined it as "what is fair to both the victim and the perpetrator," and yet another described it as "when a conflict between two or more entities is resolved morally so that the entities can carry out their existence without further conflict." Most students conceived of justice as a *result* of a process, a distributive *outcome*, rather than the process itself. In students' papers, this orientation seems to favor negative conceptions, involving a response to an injustice or to an unjust system.

Students' framing of justice in negative terms seems to reflect their perspective on the current state of affairs. Many students juxtaposed what justice *is* with what justice *should* be in an ideal sense, acknowledging the difficulty of meeting such standards in our contemporary society and in the world in general. Although most students' perspectives of justice reflected traditional, vengeful retributive conceptions, some referred to justice as reparation or restoration for victims and offenders. For example, one student stated, "I believe that justice should be distributed equally to all people and all situations and should be a tool used to restore peace." Another stated, "I believe justice comes in the form of explanation and punishment of the offender so that the victim and their family can rest easy" but added, "justice should be granted to the offender because of the actions and experiences which led them down a criminal life course." In this way, some students communicated the idea that justice can be an outcome, a "tool" in a process, or the process itself.

The emphasis on the restoration of both the victim and the offender in some of these definitions is a central tenet of restorative justice, a type of justice response that many feel is a more proactive and balanced strategy than traditional criminal justice approaches. These reintegrative approaches have gained much attention recently for providing positive outcomes in terms of reduced recidivism and higher victim and offender satisfaction when compared with traditional criminal justice processes (Dolling & Hartmann, 2003; Latimer, Dowden, & Muise, 2001; Hayes & Daly, 2003; Maxwell & Morris, 2001; McCold & Wachtel, 2002; Umbreit, 2001). Though restorative justice approaches are not ideal for all criminal offenses (Johnstone, 2011), in many cases, they may be viable alternatives that often avoid the negative effects of traditional responses (Morris, 2002). Though very few students cited restorative justice in their original essays, some became interested in the perspectives advocated in restorative justice programs and cited such programs or their founding philosophies in subsequent paper assignments addressing justice issues and conceptions.

## POSITIVE CONCEPTIONS; FAIRNESS, EQUALITY, AND MORALITY

Outside of criminal justice perspectives, many students referred to justice using positive conceptions, referring to it simply as "equality" or "fairness." For example, one student stated that justice means "to be unbiased or equal" and another characterized justice as "equal rights and opportunities for all." Another described it as "equality, right and fair treatment," and another wrote "I believe justice is the fair, objective treatment of people." Notions of justice that cited the qualities "equality" or "fairness" were more often discussed in relation to procedures or *processes* rather than an outcome or result. For example, one student stated, "my personal definition of justice is that each person is treated fairly. There is no person that is above the law or subject to any additional punishment for who they are."

Also, although most students described fairness and equality as synonymous and relied on the notion of impartiality to define them, a few stated that fairness does not always mean equal treatment. For example, one student wrote, "individuals should not treat others differently because of their race, class, or gender, but that sometimes in order to achieve fairness in society certain groups of people should be treated unequally." Statements like these that discussed inequalities signal the prominence of social justice in students' conceptions of justice (even when the emphasis on outcome inherent in social justice stood at odds with students' emphasis on process), and may reflect the overlap of criminal justice and sociological theory in these capstone classes.

Sociolegal scholars, particularly critical legal scholars, focus on the inability of the law to achieve social justice because of the difficulty of using the law to meet substantive (or outcome-focused) justice demands (Milovanovic, 2003). American law, as a "formally rational" system, is based on notions of equality where all legal actors (all citizens) are assumed to be equals (Milovanovic, 2003). The reality is that individuals have different capabilities, attributes, and resources—differences that the legal system does not always recognize. An important component in capstone classes involves discussing the idea that equality before the law does not always acknowledge individuals' or groups' substantive differences, including differences in access to resources. The difficulty in meeting these demands through the use of law parallels the problem with identifying "justice" as either "fairness" or "equality" and with conflating fairness and equality when conceptualizing justice. A few students argued that "equality" or "fairness," on their own do not encompass the entirety of the value judgments that are made when determining whether something is "just." Therefore, it may not be surprising that some students preferred to identify justice as morality, or incorporated morality in their definitions.

Several students included notions of morality in their definitions of justice, and these conceptions reflected justice in the most positive light. Both dictionary definitions and those offered by students included the concepts "morality," "righteousness," "distinguishing right from wrong," and "moral rightness." Some students defined justice as, "to make sure everyone is getting the treatment that he or she deserves morally." Moral definitions depicted justice as a proactive process. For example, one student wrote, "justice means doing something for the greater good." Another student wrote that justice "brings hope to the less fortunate, empowers the powerless, and strives to attain a perfect world."

The difficulty of defining justice given competing demands for equality and fairness is evidenced in some students' definitions of justice as a combination of multiple elements. For example, a student stated, "justice is simply this: a mixture of equality, moral rightness, and law." In addition, another student defined justice as, "the fair, moral, ethical treatment of all people, all of the time." Incorporating several concepts may be the least precise, but perhaps the most accurate, of definitions of justice because these conceptualizations acknowledge the complexity of the term and embody the role of balance. For example, emphasizing "equality" in one situation or circumstance and emphasizing "fairness," or "morality" in another may more sufficiently meet justice demands. Each element identified may be an important part of justice, but is not sufficient in itself to constitute justice as a whole (see Bell, 1965). A few students demonstrated this idea through the concept of balance. For example, one wrote, "justice is a continual balance in relationships which adapts through time and social or worldly conditions," and another student stated, "to maintain balance… is the epitome of justice." One student's personal definition of justice as embodying the concept of compromise illustrates the idea of prioritizing one or more elements of justice over others to achieve balance. Balance in this sense may not evoke the concept of "equality," but nevertheless is important in achieving justice.

## THE ROLE OF THE MEDIA

Social media's role in the exposure of injustices was a common element students discussed in their papers. Many students discussed media portrayals of incidents in which police officers dealt with citizens unjustly, and some identified these unjust interactions as indicative of widespread distrust of the criminal justice system. The media, but most specifically social media, played an important role in raising awareness of justice issues and served as a mechanism for provoking students' contemplations and discussions of justice. Social media, including Facebook, Twitter, and YouTube, often comprise the majority of sources of news information for undergraduate students (Kushin & Yamamoto, 2010). Social media influence is differentiated from the general media in that the personal intimacy level and amount of user-generated information, particularly from friends and family, can have an increased impact on the individual as compared to information received from general media sources such as television broadcast networks (Kushin & Yamamoto, 2010). Though there were few students who made direct in-text references to social media applications such as Facebook, studies agree that the majority of the young adult population is now more reliant on social media as an immediate source of their political information including justice-related issues (Twenge, Campbell, & Freeman, 2012).

The media's impact in increasing student interest in social justice issues is important given the declining role of civic participation in young people's lives (Twenge, Campbell, & Freeman, 2012) and the attenuation of social ties (McPherson, Smith-Lovin, & Brashears, 2006). Compared with past generations, many students, particularly those attending state schools, spend more of their time working, either completing assignments for school or working low-wage jobs to pay for their educations, rather than participating in community and extracurricular activities (Twenge, Campbell, & Freeman, 2012). Some have found that millennials are less involved in formal politics due to cynicism and ambivalence about politics as a vehicle for genuine change (Kiesa et al., 2007). From failed wars abroad to political corruption and continuing economic pressures in the wake of the financial crisis of 2008, millennials may have become even more cynical than these studies originally cited. They also may be even less likely to have time to participate in civic action due to the economic pressures the financial collapse created. Studies indicate that people have responded to the financial crises by taking on more debt and working more hours (Roubini, 2008).

Media exposure to political issues and social movements may play an important role in students' development by generating an investment in social justice issues that can lead to more meaningful engagement with justice-related coursework. For example, some students incorporated social movement groups such as Black Lives Matter and All Lives Matter into their discussion of justice. Social awareness of these movements helped students connect personal experiences of injustice to larger social inequalities. For these reasons, we believe incorporating media portrayals of justice issues in coursework is generally beneficial; however, these depictions can shape students' initial, and often lasting, views of current events. Indeed, it may be because of millennials' cynicism and the role of some media outlets in spreading misinformation that certain types of social media, particularly videos uploaded to Twitter and Facebook, are perceived as reliable sources of information insofar as the viewer holds the power of interpretation. The idiom "seeing is believing" may seem like a hackneyed phrase, but it may be representative of students who seem to lack faith in public officials and put more trust in their own judgments.

Nevertheless, some students seemed to base their discussion of justice almost entirely on information received from media videos, images, and articles. The tone of these papers reflects the emotional impact of their initial exposure to the media portrayals rather than an analysis of the meaning of justice itself in relation to these issues. The emotional quality of written responses to video clips may signal a lack of critical assessment of the issue and instead indicate that students' previously held beliefs are merely reinforced. In fact, studies of news outlets find that stories about crime are often focused on violent aspects and certain demographic groups in an effort to serve the perceived viewer preferences (Beale, 2006).

## RECOMMENDATIONS FOR JUSTICE STUDIES

One of the issues we have addressed is students' use of social media in their discussions of justice. We believe that it is important to critically examine the sources of the information we all consume, acknowledging the possible biases, motivations, and perspectives of these sources. It may be most important for those engaged in justice studies to make this a regular habit, particularly regarding material provided by social media outlets. Although many such outlets are openly biased, politically motivated, and intended to influence viewers, others may merely operate as a forum for information. This information, particularly video recordings of events, however, is typically limited in perspective, as they are often citizens' phone recordings that provide little context. Many students, in fact, acknowledged as important missing information in social media coverage of interactions between law enforcement and community members as well as bias in commentators' and the public's depictions of them, specifically that they portrayed police officers as racist or violent.

These assessments bring up common academic debates about political corruption, police misconduct and the best ways to bring about change. These are areas that we encourage you, as students of justice studies, to explore, particularly those interested in pursuing careers in law enforcement and corrections. In general, the media tends to focus on negative aspects of the criminal justice system rather than positive interactions between citizens and criminal justice actors. This, too, may be reflective of the reactive nature of our political and criminal justice system processes and of the relative ease of identifying injustices compared to identifying examples of justice. While we entreat you to contextualize and critique one-sided portrayals, as we did with our students, it may be in the interest of "justice" that our exercise evidenced that students' perceptions were more often critical of criminal justice actors. There is no indication that racialized violence by police officers is any more common today than in the past, and in fact the opposite is probably true, but media coverage seems to have increased with the availability of video recordings (McLaughlin, 2015; Rizzo, 2015). Today, the pervasiveness of handheld recording devices and other advancements in technology have increased exposure to human rights violations and abuse at the hands of law enforcement. This exposure, which our students often cited in their discussions of justice, can contribute to reform through class action lawsuits addressing misconduct and negligence, particularly regarding use of excessive force.

Though students' conceptions of justice more often reflected retributive notions of desert that are common in U.S. political rhetoric, their descriptions of the term "justice" included a diverse set of principles and virtues, such as "equality," "fairness," "balance," "morality," and indicated an interest in "the greater good." Although we call attention to the fact that most students defined justice "negatively" in that they identified justice as a response to injustice, a reaction rather than an affirmative state of being, we are encouraged by their sincere interest in addressing injustices. Generational shifts in trust of formal politics and government notwithstanding, many students made passionate arguments about unethical and unfair practices, particularly regarding the treatment of citizens by law enforcement officers. We entreat you to approach your studies with the same passion and commitment to social justice.

In conclusion, social media and political depictions of incidents may not tell the whole story, but their utility in increasing awareness of and interest in social justice problems may be immeasurable. Given increasing demands on students' time and their limited civic engagement, exposure to these issues through media outlets may serve as an important tool in engendering commitment to social justice issues. This may become more significant as economic pressures maintain and public school students pursue local government and law enforcement positions for the benefits and stability they offer. Critical thought and analysis of justice issues can serve us all as the next generation takes on these important public service roles.

## References

Beale, S. (2006). The news media's influence on criminal justice policy: How market-driven news promotes punitiveness. *William and Mary Law Review, 48*(2), 397–481.

Bell, D.R. (1965). Impartiality and intellectual virtue. *The Philosophical Quarterly, 15*(60), 229–239.

Chevigny, P. (2003). The populism of fear: Politics of crime in the Americas. *Punishment & Society, 5*(1), 77–96.

Cusac, A. (2015, October). Getting smart on crime: conservatives discover prison reform [Electronic version]. *The Progressive, 79*(10), 27–31.

Dolling, D. & Hartmann, A. (2003). Re-offending after victim-offender mediation in juvenile court proceedings. In Weitekamp & Kerner (Eds.), *Restorative justice in context: International practice and directions*. (pp. 208–228). Portland, OR: Willan Publishing.

Fairfax, R.A. (2010). From overgeneralization to smart on crime: American criminal justice reforms legacy and prospects. *Journal of Economics, Law and Policy, 7*(4), 597–616.

Finkel, N.J., Crystal, D.S. & Watanabe, H. (2001). Commonsense notions of unfairness in Japan and the United States. *Psychology, Public Policy, and Law, 7*(2), 345–380.

Gottschalk, M. (2009). Review: The long reach of the carceral state: the politics of crime, mass imprisonment and penal reform in the United States and abroad. *Law & Social Inquiry, 34*(2), 439–472.

Hayes, H. & Daly, K. (2003) Youth justice conferencing and reoffending. *Justice Quarterly, 20*(4), 725–764.

Henrichson, C. & Delaney, R. (2012). *The price of prisons: What incarceration costs taxpayers*. New York: Vera Institute of Justice.

Johnstone, G. (2011). *Restorative justice: Ideas, values, debates*. New York: Routledge.

Lynch, J.P. & Pridemore, W.A. (2011). Crime in international perspective. In J.Q. Wilson & J. Petersilia (Eds.), *Crime and Public Policy* (pp. 5–52). Oxford: Oxford University Press.

Kiesa, A., Orlowski, A.P., Levine, P., Both, D., Kirby, E.H., Lopez, M.H., & Marcelo, K.B. (2007). Millennials talk politics: A study of college student political engagement. College Park, MD: Center for Information and Research on Civic Learning and Engagement.

Kushin, M.J. & Yamamoto, M. (2010). Did social media really matter? College students' use of online media and political decision making in the 2008 Election. *Mass Communication & Society, 10*(3), 608–630.

Latimer, J., Dowden, C. & Muise, D. (2001). The effectiveness of restorative justice practices: A meta-analysis. Ottawa, Canada: Research and Statistics Division, Department of Justice.

Maxwell, G. & Morris, A. (2001). Family group conferences and reoffending. In A. Morris & G. Maxwell (Eds.), *Restorative justice for juveniles: Conferencing, mediation and circles*. (pp. 243–263). Oxford: Hart.

McCold, P. & Wachtel, T. (2003). Restorative justice theory validation. In E.G.M. Weitekamp and H.-J. Kerner (Eds.), *Restorative justice: Theoretical foundations*. (pp. 110–142). Portland, OR: Willan Publishing.

McLaughlin, E.C. (2015, April 21). We're not seeing more police shootings, just more news coverage. CNN. Retrieved May 20, 2016, from http://www.cnn.com/2015/04/20/us/police-brutality-video-social-media-attitudes/.

McPherson, M., Smith-Lovin, L., & Brashears, M. E. (2006). Social isolation in America: Changes in core discussion networks over two decades. *American Sociological Review, 71*(3), 353–375.

Milovanovic, D. (2003). *An introduction to the sociology of law*. Monsey, NY: Criminal Justice Press.

Morris, A. (2002). Critiquing the critics: A brief response to critics of restorative justice. *The British Journal of Criminology, 42*(3), 596–615.

Percival, G.L. (2015). *Smart on crime: The struggle to build a better American penal system*. Boca Raton, FL: CRC Press.

Rizzo, K. (2015, April 30). Are police shootings on the rise, and why isn't the government counting? *Law Street Media*. Retrieved May 20, 2016, from http://lawstreetmedia.com/blogs/crime/police-shootings-rise-government/.

Roubini, N. (2008). Written Testimony for the House of Representatives Financial Services Committee Hearing. http://www.archives.financialservices.house.gov/hearing110/roubini022608.pdf.

Sherman, L.W., Gottfredson, D., MacKenzie, D., Eck, J., Reuter, P., & Bushway, S. (1998). *Preventing crime: What works, what doesn't, what's promising*. College Park, MD: University of Maryland.

Tonry, M., ed. (2007). Determinants of penal policy. In Tonry, M. (Ed.), *Crime, punishment and politics in comparative perspective—Crime and justice: A review of research, 36*, 1–48. Chicago: University of Chicago Press.

Twenge, J., Campbell, W.K., & Freeman, E.C. (2012). Generational differences in young adults' life goals, concern for others, and civic orientation, 1966–2009. *Journal of Personality and Social Psychology, 102*(5), 1045–1062.

Umbreit, M.S. (2001). *The handbook of victim offender mediation*. San Francisco: Jossey-Bass, Inc.

Vera Institute of Justice. (2013). *The potential of community corrections to improve communities and reduce incarceration*. New York: Vera Institute of Justice.

# Chapter 2

# GAPS IN JUSTICE

## INTRODUCTION

Despite a common desire for justice and equality, examples of injustice are all around us. Drawing upon the multiple definitions of justice discussed in Chapter 1, we know that acts of injustice can occur on many levels and can be perpetrated by individuals, groups, corporations, or governments. Injustice occurs when the assumptions of formal justice, social justice, or human rights are violated, or when their guarantees are not upheld. Rather than focusing on justice, as we did in Chapter 1, here we examine its breach. We begin by describing the various types of injustice relevant to criminal justice, followed by discussion of three key theoretical perspectives on the causes of injustice. Without adequately and accurately assessing the causes of injustice, we will be ill-equipped to begin the work of achieving justice. In the second half of the chapter, two topics with important implications for criminal justice will be examined in further detail: economic inequality and unequal access to social opportunity. Within these sections, we will focus on the ways in which income inequality and poverty produce lopsided *economic opportunity*, with implications for individuals involved in the CJS and for the functioning of the system itself. We will also begin to examine the ways in which *statuses* such as race, ethnicity, gender, and sexual identity interact with economic opportunity to affect *social opportunity*, further disadvantaging marginalized groups and producing additional gaps in justice.

## INJUSTICE AND CRIMINAL JUSTICE

One of the most common types of injustice covered in criminal justice classes is crime itself. From a criminal justice perspective, injustice can be found in all crimes, for example, domestic violence, human trafficking, or any crime that deprives others of their most basic rights, such as safety, security and the ability to determine one's own destiny. In the CJC literature, injustices that occur as a result of the CJS's *response* to crime are also examined. For example, disproportionate minority contact and confinement, various types of bias that enter into decision-making, inadequate legal representation for poor defendants, and violence within correctional facilities are all injustices that result from the functioning of the CJS. Last, injustices in the *context* surrounding the CJS can play a large role in whether and how justice is achieved. This type of injustice can take many forms: a lack of material resources, blocked opportunities, social disorganization and low cultural capital, racism, sexism, homophobia, and other kinds of bigotry or bias, to name just a few. We examine these examples, and others, in the remainder of this chapter.

## TYPES OF INJUSTICE

One major type of injustice occurs when people lack access to the basic resources they need to survive and/or thrive. Injustice related to material resources often comes down to issues of imbalances in access and quality. Examples include poverty, food instability, lack of affordable health care and housing, subpar education, and inability to make a living wage. The content of this list is likely to prompt discussion and debate, as individuals hold differing ideas about what exactly constitutes "basic needs." Definitions of social justice suggest that attempts should be made to ensure a dignified and fulfilled life for all people (Hurlbert, 2011). If access to basic needs is synonymous with a dignified and full life, then perhaps this list should be expanded considerably. For instance, to lead a dignified and fulfilled life in the digital age, is access to the Internet a necessity? What about access to transportation, enabling people to get to work, the grocery store, the doctor, or the voting booth?

When considering any form of injustice related to resources, we must examine the issue in terms of both *access* and *quality*. All access is not created equal. Take, for instance, the example of education. In the United States, all children are legally entitled to free public education. In this sense, there is equality of access. But we know that the quality of schools can vary substantially from one district to another, based largely on resources. One of the most influential factors creating inequality in school resources is the income level of the surrounding area. Public schools are funded in part by local income and property taxes, which vary dramatically based on wealth. This creates well-funded schools in wealthy areas, whereas schools in poor areas are left woefully underfunded. In addition to the direct impact on school funding, income inequality also has many indirect effects on students. For instance, students in low-income districts may be experiencing strain in other areas of their life, in the form of food instability, precarious housing situations, poor health, and financial strain on their families from low wages or underemployment; this is compounded by overworked and underpaid teachers who are likely in similar positions. The advantages of being in a wealthy school district compound just as quickly. Students in these districts have access to a wider variety of classes with well-equipped classrooms and highly paid teachers, they have resources at home to support their academic success and are often shielded from the type of strain that low-income students experience. Students in both types of schools have the *same access* to education—but they do not have access to the *same education*. It is easy to slip into thinking that access to opportunity is all that matters when thinking about justice, but hopefully this example demonstrates how substantive inequality can lurk under the surface of formal equality.

Another important element to consider is the role of bias in injustice or inequality. Bias can exist in the everyday actions of individuals, in the policies and procedures that individuals implement, and in the historical roots of the systems that structure them. When access to material resources is limited, bias often plays a role in both the cause and the result. Many individuals and groups who lack material or social resources have found themselves in this position as a result of long and complex American histories of racism, sexism, and classism. African Americans are consistently overrepresented among Americans who live in poverty. It is difficult to imagine that descending from slaves who were themselves considered material resources would not have an impact on racial inequalities in the current distribution of material resources. This is just one example of the intergenerational transmission of wealth and poverty—a topic we will discuss in greater detail toward the end of this chapter.

Bias can also exacerbate existing injustices, as is the case when a context already characterized by injustice has policies and procedures that are carried out in a biased manner based on race, ethnicity, gender, sex, sexual orientation, religion, age, ability status, or any other number of characteristics. For instance, when a transgender woman is turned away from a homeless shelter because she is not biologically female, her individual injustice is exacerbated. Although we may think of this type of injustice as being perpetuated by individuals, our sociological imaginations prompt us to consider that the individual case might be part of a larger pattern related to injustice. As this woman is discriminated against due to her transgender status, outmoded notions about gender and sex are reinforced, facilitating similarly biased treatment against others; thus, the gap in social justice is deepened. Patterns like these become institutionalized, rendering marginalized groups of people further disadvantaged and incorporating bias into the very fabric of the system.

## DOMAINS OF INJUSTICE

Injustices occur across a variety of domains. For example, in the workplace injustice can occur through exploitation, unfair procedures related to employment or wages, and violations of workers' rights. Another type of injustice, classified as "political injustice," involves the denial of voting rights, violations of the rights of freedom of speech, religion, and protection from cruel and unusual punishment. Because injustices are so often intertwined or cooccurring, these types of injustice affect certain groups of people more than others. In this section, we examine various sites of injustice and how they relate to the CJS.

One very broad area of injustice exists with issues surrounding the environment. Clean air, water, and access to healthy living environments are not equally distributed in the world. Current practices, often driven by large corporations, are leading to extensive pollution, a reduction in biodiversity, and a loss of nonrenewable resources. Many of these practices, from the production of food sources to the use of energy, are not being carried out in a sustainable way and are causing irreversible damage to both people and the Earth. Competition over these declining natural resources is also, and will continue to be, a significant contributor to global conflicts and wars. Environmental justice relates to criminal justice in many ways. Take the recent example of the 2014 water crisis in Flint, MI, which exposed thousands of residents (mostly low-income) to lead-poisoned water. The injustices involved in this crisis are many, but foremost among them is the role that the government played in allowing the lead-contaminated water to be piped into Flint families' houses, covering up the information once it became known, and failing to remedy the problem once it had come to light. In 2016, the Michigan Attorney General filed criminal charges against three individuals related to the scandal, and numerous government agencies are still conducting concurrent investigations. The injustices perpetrated against the people of Flint don't end there; lead exposure has been linked to a variety of poor health outcomes at both the individual and community levels, and has even been shown to be a predictor of city-level homicide rates (Feigenbaum & Muller, 2016).

If the economy has the power to constrain and shape government's response to (or role in) injustice, imagine the possibilities for injustice in the private sector. Many times, injustice can be seen by looking at the practices of businesses and corporations, which tend to make decisions based solely on the economic bottom line without regard for the justice implications of their practices. Social justice ideals would position people's rights and welfare above profits, but this simply is not how the incentive structure of capitalism operates. Misuse of power and basic human greed have created great amounts of injustice that are difficult to address. Similarly, the policies and practices of wealthy countries, and the international institutions that they control, often perpetuate injustice in less powerful countries.

At times, the link between corporate injustice and crime is clear: take, for instance, white collar crimes like embezzlement or wage theft. At other times, however, the connection is a bit more abstract. Elliot Currie, a prominent critical criminologist, has proposed that some forms of capitalism can actually cause crime. He posits that countries with strong capitalist economies and strong social safety nets (e.g., Japan, Great Britain) have *market economies*, but do not constitute *market societies*. In a market society (like the United States), capitalist principles dictate not only the economy, but also become the "dominant organizing principle of social life" (Currie, 1997, p. 147). This can be seen in the frequent use of the language of cost-benefit analysis in everyday conversation (e.g., "get more bang for your buck"). Consequently, the inequalities produced by our economic system are reinforced and reinscribed in other domains of life. The inequalities and insecurities engendered by market societies result in higher violent crime rates as compared to countries with market economies that practice what Currie calls "compassionate capitalism."

As we've discussed before, injustice is not uniformly distributed across the population. Some groups are marginalized, oppressed, or treated unjustly more frequently than others. One such group that often gets overlooked is native populations. In many countries, including our own, examples of the mistreatment and violation of indigenous people are plentiful. As victims of conquest and colonization, indigenous people have been massacred, displaced, robbed of their lands, and denied many of their basic rights. In the United States, historical injustices—from the Trail of Tears to the systematic removal of babies from Native homes—have led to ongoing injustices, resulting in higher rates of poverty and many other disadvantages. Even today, for example, higher rates of sexual violence against indigenous women in the United States are well-documented—a fact that traces its roots to systematic atrocities committed by White settlers. The complex relationship between sovereign tribal governments and federal/state governments further exacerbates this injustice, creating what has been referred to as a "maze of injustice" for Native Americans (Amnesty International, 2006).

Extreme poverty can also leave individuals—indigenous and otherwise—vulnerable to bonded labor, forced migrant/immigrant labor, and sexual slavery. Often, individuals in the most desperate circumstances are the most exploited. Bonded labor occurs when individuals or families take loans intending to work off their debt. Typically, these debts are impossible to pay off, and because of the stark power differential, this form of slavery is difficult to escape and can continue over generations. Although the largest numbers of slaves exist in India, China, and Pakistan, trafficking and forced labor exist in the United States as well, with an estimate of about 60,000 individuals involved in slavery (http://www.globalslaveryindex.org/). Unfortunately, slavery and slave labor remain a worldwide problem with an ever-changing face. In recent years, we have witnessed heightened international commitment to combatting modern-day slavery in the form of intergovernmental task forces, international treaties, and collaborations among nongovernmental organizations like Amnesty International, Walk Free, and an impressive number of faith-based organizations. Despite these efforts, factors including income inequality, racism, patriarchal social norms, and globalization have all contributed to the enduring injustice of modern-day slavery. A major factor in the perpetuation of slavery is war. Slavery is but one of the injustices associated with war and war crimes, however. Rape, torture, civilian casualties, genocide, and circumstances creating the potential for exploitation that arise from these scenarios are disturbing and clear examples of injustice. Wars themselves are frequently initiated in response to vastly different access to resources and different grades of citizenship that create inequality, both material and social. Just as these factors are impactful on a small scale, they can easily have a global impact as well.

## CAUSES OF INJUSTICE

Because injustices stem from complex and interrelated political, social, and economic problems, it is often difficult to pinpoint the exact cause of injustice. Various theoretical explanations contribute unique ideas about the causes of social problems that exist in the world. In our examination of justice in this book, we draw upon three main theoretical perspectives: ***structural functionalism***, ***conflict theory***, and *symbolic interactionism*. So far in this book, we have addressed the multifaceted nature of justice, detailing its many dimensions and manifestations. It follows, then, that the study of justice must be equipped to handle the nuance and complexity of justice. By drawing upon diverse theoretical perspectives, we are able to examine justice issues from all possible angles. Although some theories are better suited to understanding individual injustices (symbolic interactionism), others focus on the structural context (structural functionalism) or larger political and cultural backdrop (conflict theory) in which injustices are situated. In the section below, we very briefly summarize these three perspectives and demonstrate their utility for the study of justice issues. You may recognize elements of these perspectives that have been implicitly embedded in the book thus far, and you will certainly see them play out in the chapters that follow.

*Symbolic interactionism* views society as a socially constructed network in which individuals interact to create shared meaning to make sense of the world around them (Mead, 1934). According to symbolic interactionism, objects have no inherent meaning or value; rather, their meaning is created and refined by people through continual social interaction. This perspective informs the underlying premise of our discussion of justice in this book. We present justice as a slippery concept with many different definitions; despite this, common understandings of justice (e.g., fairness, equality, desert) represent shared meanings. This blend of individual subjectivity and shared meaning can trace its roots to symbolic interactionism; it casts justice as a manifold, socially constructed phenomenon.

Similarly, terms like "crime" and "offender" have no objective, innate meaning. Crimes are acts that have been deemed harmful by society and consequently prohibited by law; offenders are individuals who have committed these acts and have been labeled as such. Symbolic interactionism is one framework that helps us make sense of why some actions are criminal in one context, but lawful in another. Let's consider the example of marital rape. Although rape within the context of marriage is now criminal in all 50 states, shockingly, this was not the case until 1993. If we expand our view beyond the United States, there are many countries that do not have marital rape as we know it. According to the symbolic interactionist perspective, the crime of rape can only occur in the presence of a law prohibiting rape—a law that was created by humans through social interaction and a shared process of meaning-making. If no law exists identifying, defining, and labeling sexual assault between spouses, then no crime has been committed when nonconsensual sex occurs within a marriage. In cultures without marital rape (whether other countries or the United States of the recent past), a marriage contract is often legally interpreted as blanket sexual consent for the remainder of the marriage. Although it might be tempting to view this issue through our own ethnocentric lenses and claim that marital rape is an act that should always be considered a crime, the fact remains that this is not true. Symbolic interactionism helps us understand that the acts that we call crime are not inherently bad or evil, but are reflective of the shared meaning that we, in a given society at a specific point in time, have assigned to them.

One critique of symbolic interactionism is that its emphasis on micro-level interpersonal interactions can eclipse larger macro-level, societal concerns. The two remaining perspectives that we draw upon in this book operate at this macro-level. The first, *structural functionalism*, views society as a complex system of interrelated parts that work together to produce social stability (Merton, 1957; Parsons, 1951).

This perspective views a stable society as a functional and balanced one with the ability to properly socialize individuals through customs, norms, and institutions. This process breaks down when rapid social change occurs, leading to a weakening of the institutions that in the past were used to achieve order and exert social control.

By way of illustration, let's briefly examine the Black Lives Matter (BLM) movement through the lens of structural functionalism. BLM emerged in 2012 in response to police killings of unarmed Black people. From a structural functionalist perspective, BLM can be seen as a grassroots response to the failure of the CJS to maintain social stability. The name "Black Lives Matter" sends a clear message challenging the stability of a system that allows people in uniform to kill unarmed Black citizens. (Note that the use of the word "allow" does not imply that police killings of unarmed citizens are sanctioned by the CJS; from a structural functionalist perspective, such killings are allowed in as much as they happen, and when they do, they go largely under-addressed.) In this time of instability, BLM can be viewed as a new social institution that has arisen to address the failure of existing institutions (e.g., our CJS) to ensure justice for the Black community.

A different perspective on justice at the macro-level can be seen in conflict theories. *Conflict theories* trace their roots back to Karl Marx, who conceptualized society as a system of competing parts (rather than interdependent parts, as structural functionalism posits) in continual conflict for scarce resources. Because resources are scarce, injustice results from lopsided power struggles that occur between a small group of powerful elites and the larger, disempowered citizenry. This competition between groups, and the power of one group over others, engenders oppression and exploitation. In Marx's original formulation, members of the dominant group were determined by ownership of the means of production in a society; more recent conflict perspectives have broadened this power position to include other factors that systematically give advantages to members of their group, such as ethnicity, race, or religion. At times, these advantages are embedded in the legal system, but they also occur as a result of decisions being made in a biased manner (Hurlbert, 2011).

Consider the many roles that money plays in our government: well-paid lobbyists that exert an undue influence on elected officials, the increasing necessity of massive political fundraising to secure a seat in the government, and the recent U.S. Supreme Court Decision *Citizens United*, which extended First Amendment protections to corporations by interpreting their campaign donations as constitutionally protected speech, effectively eliminating many checks and balances on campaign spending. All of these examples lend support to the conflict perspective by demonstrating the ways in which powerful elites can work within the system to retain their power, even in the absence of outright bias.

## POVERTY AND WEALTH INEQUALITY

There are many different ways to measure the economic justice of a country: income inequality, broader measures of wealth inequality, poverty rates, and economic mobility, to name a few. In this section, we choose two—poverty and wealth inequality—to discuss in detail. *Poverty* as a measure of economic injustice focuses our attention on the lowest rungs of the socioeconomic ladder, examining the extent and nature of insufficient material resources. *Wealth inequality* broadens the focus beyond just the poor, shifting attention to disparities in income and other assets between the poor and the rich.

The U.S. Census Bureau collects the most up-to-date data on poverty in this country, relying on a survey of approximately 100,000 households nationwide (www.census.gov). It has determined the poverty rate since the mid-1960s, using poverty thresholds that set the minimum annual amount of cash income required to support individuals and families of various sizes. For example, to be categorized as living in poverty, one person under 65 years of age must earn less than $12,316 annually. For two parents and one child, the amount is $16,317. These figures do not include noncash benefits such as public housing, food stamps, Medicaid, or employer-provided health insurance.

In 2012, the poverty rate was 15%. In its first decline since 2006, this figure dropped to 14.5% in 2013. A poverty rate of 14.5% translates to 45.3 million people living in poverty in the United States. The poverty rate varies by age and is the highest for children under the age of 18 (19.9%), lower for individuals between 18 and 64 (13.6%), and lowest for those 65 and older (9.5%). It also varies substantially by race. Twenty-seven percent of Black citizens and 24% of Hispanic citizens live in poverty compared with 10% of non-Hispanic White citizens. A similarly large gap is evident when comparing the poverty rates of those with disabilities (29%) and those without disabilities (12%) (DeNavas-Walt & Proctor, 2014).

One way in which the United States attempts to cushion the blow of poverty is through federal and state assistance. Levels of public assistance rise and fall over time; in recent years, the totals have been climbing. For instance, from 2000 to 2011, the use of federal assistance has increased 171% (Ziliak, 2013). Recent estimates show that 14% of the U.S. population (or one in seven people) receives assistance through the Supplemental National Assistance Program (SNAP) (Ziliak, 2013). Despite the common assumption that people living in poverty are unemployed, in reality 36% of SNAP recipients come from working families who make so little money that they qualify for state assistance. In fact, almost three-quarters of those receiving assistance designed to help the poor are in families headed by someone who works (Jacobs, Perry, & MacGillvary, 2015).

Rising levels of reliance on public assistance are often blamed on the weak U.S. economy. Food stamp use mirrors the unemployment rate in this country, but stagnant or falling incomes, and increased wealth and income inequality are also blamed. For most workers in the United States, wages are flat or declining (taking inflation into account). Workers who are experiencing increasing wages are predominantly located in the upper income brackets (DeSilver, 2014). Families report feeling the effect of this reality with a growing number (56%, as compared with 44% in 2007) reporting that their income is not keeping up with the cost of living and that they are falling behind financially (Pew Research Center, 2014).

In terms of income inequality, large shifts have taken place in the United States over the past few decades. In 1965, chief executive officers (CEOs) in major companies made 24 times more than the average worker, while today, top CEOs make more than 300 times the average workers (Mishel & Davis, 2015). Another way in which wealth inequality is exacerbated is through our labyrinthine tax code. Although our federal income tax is graduated (meaning that individuals in lower income brackets pay a smaller percentage of their income than those in higher brackets), varying state tax codes and a constellation of tax breaks often invert this relationship; in fact, the government generally ends up collecting *more* in state and local taxes from the poor in terms of a percentage of their overall income. Figures from 2015 reveal that the bottom 20% of earners paid state and local taxes at a rate twice that of the top 1% of earners.

You may be asking yourself why wealth disparity matters. Why not just look at the absolute amount of money that an individual or family has in order to determine whether it is sufficient to ensure that their basic needs are met? Looking at the relative distribution of wealth in a society prompts us to look beyond the individual injustice of not having enough money to ensure a dignified and sustainable life, in order to see the ways in which society as a whole is impacted by the imbalance of resources. Wealth inequality actually perpetuates and aggravates poverty, with increasing gaps between the rich and the poor resulting in a rise in the poverty rate (Danziger & Gottschalk, 1995). Bernstein and Spielberg (2015, p. 1) note that the "the lack of opportunity for those in poverty is not some separate problem from the unequal distribution of wealth and income across society" because "disadvantages faced by children in low- and middle-income families and advantages held by their wealthy peers are two sides of the same coin." In fact, a growing body of research demonstrates a strong link between poverty, inequality, and opportunity—the topic we turn to next.

## EQUAL OPPORTUNITY

Equal opportunity is the premise of "The American Dream"—a well-known phrase which suggests that anyone, through hard work, can be successful. Unequal access to opportunity offends deeply held American values. In truth, however, the opportunity to succeed in our country is very unequally distributed, and only becoming more lopsided over time. Research on social mobility (the ability to advance in terms of social status) has demonstrated that it is a long and steep climb up the socioeconomic ladder.

One explanation for the intransigence of low socioeconomic status (SES) is the path-dependency of success. In the United States, individuals' lives are determined by their parents' income and educational level to a greater degree than in other comparable countries (Stiglitz, 2013). This means that poor children in the United States have less of an opportunity to be successful than middle and upper class children. Stiglitz (2013) suggests that this is largely the result of gender and racial/ethnic discrimination and vast differences in the quantity and quality of education received by youth in the United States. Although success is frequently thought about in monetary terms, there are other ways to define wealth (or poverty), including opportunities for positive social interactions and relationships, inclusion in political decision-making, positive regard of a person's culture and social identity, connection to supportive communities, and fulfillment of basic human rights (Hurlbert, 2011). As journalists Bernstein and Spielberg (2015, p. 1) eloquently put it: "Poverty is not only a matter of near-term material deprivation—too often, it also robs low-income children of the chance to realize their intellectual and economic potential."

The mechanisms of social immobility are varied and overlapping. (Put more plainly, there are a lot of ways that poor people are kept poor.) A large body of research has demonstrated the downstream consequences of low SES in childhood in the areas of health, education, and employment. Some of the inequalities that characterize low SES begin even before conception, affecting children's life chances before they are born. This is most evident with regard to the health of the mother. Women living in poverty are less likely to have access to nutritious food and pre-/postnatal care, more likely to be exposed to environmental pollutants, and are besieged by an array of stressors particular to low SES. These are realities that can affect the baby both before and after it is born.

As discussed earlier in this chapter, the vastly unequal education system in this country does little to correct for these early inequalities. Once children reach school, middle class advantage is well-established and difficult to overcome, producing a widening gap in educational performance (Barry, 2005). One study found that the gap in test scores between rich and poor kids has grown significantly (by about 40%) since the 1960s, and exceeds the racial gap in parental involvement in a child's cognitive development (Reardon, 2011). Further exacerbating the situation for poor kids, Barry notes that, "...social disadvantage tends to be compounded by poor schooling, rather than compensated for by superior schooling" (2005, p. 56). The quality of a school can be assessed on a number of factors, including class size; teacher experience and education; enrichment opportunities provided by schools, such as music, arts, and sports programs; and school resources, such as a school nurse, counselor, and librarian. When more affluent schools experience budget cuts, they solicit parent contributions to avoid losing resources like these, and the inequality between schools grows. Another example of how wealthier parents interact differently with schools is their reluctance to accept that their child is simply bad at reading or disruptive; instead, they are more likely to get a diagnosis (e.g., dyslexia, attention deficit hyperactivity disorder [ADHD]) through a health care provider that necessitates special treatment and additional resources. A poor child without the same advocacy may be put on a track that leads him or her to juvenile justice system involvement. The example of compounded cumulative disadvantage could be elaborated on as these disadvantages can produce negative peer relationships and further cut off opportunities.

Another way that the intergenerational transmission of disadvantage persists is in terms of health care. The United States outspends other developed countries on health care, but has far from the best health outcomes and only an average life expectancy. Further, health outcomes and life expectancy are stratified by group, with factors such as class, ethnicity, and race impacting the quality of health. This unjust distribution of health has large cumulative effects: Citizens in the top 5% of the income distribution can expect to live about nine years longer than those in the bottom 10% (Carpenter, 2013). There are behavioral differences related to health as well, as wealthy people are quicker to decide to see a doctor when they suspect something is wrong, and are more easily able to make it to an appointment due to job/childcare flexibility and access to transportation. Interpersonally, they are generally more comfortable demanding attention, likely due to a greater sense of entitlement and self-confidence navigating an unfamiliar professional context. The wealthy also have more discretionary time to exercise and more disposable income for gym memberships, equipment, and healthy food.

An important, yet often easily dismissed, way in which SES impacts health is through stress. We know that anxiety and stress increase as we move down the socioeconomic ladder. The less job security, job flexibility, and control over working conditions an individual has, the more stress she experiences; the more stress, the worse her short- and long-term health consequences (Thoits, 2010). Stress can even compound financial disadvantage on a daily basis, leading to further poverty-related stress in a vicious cycle. Not only do low-income individuals' daily financial decisions carry greater stakes (due to the instability of living at or near the poverty line), stress can also negatively affect decision-making capabilities, leading to poor financial decisions that further entrench poverty. In fact, researchers recently found that conditions of scarcity can impose a mental burden on decision-making that is the equivalent of losing 13 IQ points (Mani, Mullainathan, Shafir, & Zhao, 2013). One author of this particular study emphasizes that this finding "isn't about poor people, it's about people who happen to be in poverty. All the data suggest it is not the person, it's the context they're inhabiting" (Shafir, as quoted in Badger, 2013). And unfortunately, the context of low SES is difficult to escape, even across generations. As Thoits (2010, p. S41) notes, "stressors proliferate over the life course and across generations, widening health gaps between advantaged and disadvantaged group members."

A just society would allow for second chances to compensate for early disadvantage and should promote chances for success later on (Barry, 2005); unfortunately, there is ample evidence that our society does exactly the opposite. The discussion of poverty, income inequality, and lopsided access and opportunity doesn't even scratch the surface of the injustice that can be experienced when bias and oppression are added to the mix. It is to these topics that we turn in Chapter 3.

## References

Amnesty International (2006). *Maze of injustice: The failure to protect Indigenous women from sexual violence in the USA*. New York: Amnesty International USA.

Badger, E. (2013). How poverty taxes the brain. *CityLab*, August 29, 2013. Retrieved from http://www.citylab.com/work/2013/08/how-poverty-taxes-brain/6716/.

Barry, B. (2005). *Why social justice matters*. Cambridge, UK: Polity Press.

Bernstein, J., & Spielberg, B. (2015). Inequality matters. *The Atlantic Monthly*, June 5, 2015. Retrieved from http://www.theatlantic.com/business/archive/2015/06/what-matters-inequality-or-opportuniy/393272/.

Carpenter, Z. (2013). Inequality is (literally) killing America. *The Nation*. Retrieved from http://www.thenation.com/article/inequality-literally-killing-america/.

Currie, E. (1997). Market, crime and community. *Theoretical Criminology, 1*(2), 147–172.

Danziger, S., & Gottschalk, P. (1995). *American unequal.* Cambridge, MA: Harvard University Press.

DeNavas-Walt, C., & Proctor, B.D. (2014) U.S. Census Bureau, Current Population Reports, P60-249, Income and Poverty in the United States: 2013, U.S. Government Printing Office, Washington, DC.

DeSilver, D. (2014). For most workers, real wages have barely budged for decades. Washington D.C.: Pew Research Center. (October 9).

Feigenbaum, J. J., & Muller, C. (2016). *Lead exposure and violent crime in the early 1900s*. Unpublished research paper.

Hurlbert, M.A. (Ed.). (2011). *Pursuing justice: An introduction to justice studies.* Nova Scotia, Canada: Fernwood Publishing.

Jacobs, K., Perry, I., & MacGillvary, J. (2015, April). The High Public Cost of Low Wages: Poverty-Level Wages Cost U.S. Taxpayers $152.8 Billion Each Year in Public Support for Working Families. Berkeley, CA: UC Berkeley Labor Center.

Mani, A., Mullainathan, S., Shafir, E., & Zhao, J. (2013). Poverty impedes cognitive function. *Science, 341*(6149), 976–980.

Mead, G. H. (1934). *Mind, self, and society: From the standpoint of a social behaviorist.* Chicago: University of Chicago Press.

Merton, R. (1957). *Social theory and social structure.* London: The Free Press of Glencoe.

Mishel, L., & Davis, A. (2015). Top CEOs make 300 times more than typical workers. *Economic Policy Institute.* July 21. Retrieved from: http://www.epi.org/publication/top-ceos-make-300-times-more-than-workers-pay-growth-surpasses-market-gains-and-the-rest-of-the-0-1-percent/.

Parsons, T. (1951). *The social system.* London: Routledge.

Pew Research Center (2014). Views of Job Market Tick Up, No Rise in Economic Optimism. Washington, D.C. (September 4).

Reardon, S.F. (2011). The widening academic achievement gap between the rich and the poor: New evidence and possible explanations. In R. Murnane & G. Duncan (Eds.), *Whither opportunity? Rising inequality and the uncertain life chances of low-income children.* New York: Russell Sage Foundation Press.

Stiglitz, J.E. (2013). Equal opportunity, our national myth. The New York Times. February 16. Retrieved from http://opinionator.blogs.nytimes.com/2013/02/16/equal-opportunity-our-national-myth/?_r=0.

Thoits, P. A. (2010). Stress and health: Major findings and policy implications. *Journal of Health and Social Behavior, 51*(1), S41-S53.

Ziliak, J. (2013) "Why Are So Many Americans on Food Stamps," University of Kentucky Center for Poverty Research, *Discussion Paper* DP2013-01 (September 2013). Retrieved from https://pdfs.semanticscholar.org/f282/e086786281ed60b70fe147d809a2979094ed.pdf on March 5, 2014.

## Selected Readings

Comfort, M. (2012). "It was basically college to us": Poverty, prison, and emerging adulthood. *Journal of Poverty, 16*(3): 308–322.

Sacks, M., & Ackerman, A.R. (2012). Pretrial detention and guilty pleas: If they cannot afford bail they must be guilty. *Criminal Justice Studies, 25*(3), 265–278.

## Discussion Questions/Writing Assignments

1. Does "equality" demand some sharing of the collective economic resources of society?
2. What needs to be done to ensure that everyone has a decent material standard of living? What does that include? What are the basic necessities of life?
3. Use CNN's middle class calculator (http://money.cnn.com/interactive/economy/middle-class-calculator/) to determine where you fall relative to your U.S. peers in terms of income. Now use the Pew Research Center's global middle class calculator (http://www.pewresearch.org/fact-tank/2015/07/16/are-you-in-the-global-middle-class-find-out-with-our-income-calculator/) to determine your standing worldwide. How different are the two numbers? What are your thoughts on your class categorizations, national and global?
4. How should college students who did not come from the best school systems, and therefore did not learn how to write well in high school, be responded to? What is fair in terms of the grades they receive relative to other students?
5. Read the short article "Rich Kids Stay Rich, Poor Kids Stay Poor" (http://fivethirtyeight.com/features/rich-kids-stay-rich-poor-kids-stay-poor/?ex_cid=538fb). How do gender and parental structure impact social immobility? Are these effects likely the result of bias, or something else? Explain.
6. Choose one gap in justice that was discussed as an example in this chapter (e.g., educational inequality, marital rape, indigenous rights). Identify elements of the three primary theoretical frameworks in these examples; where can you see the influence of symbolic interactionism? Structural functionalism? Conflict theory?
7. In *It Was Basically College to Us*, Comfort notes that, "A discussion of building social and educational infrastructure in poor neighborhoods and embarking upon serious efforts to pursue alternatives to incarceration for juveniles and facilitate that from universities is beyond the scope of this article." What efforts can you imagine being useful in poor neighborhoods?
8. What are the effects of the growing gap between rich and poor from a justice perspective?
9. What might prisons and universities have in common in terms of an experience for 18 to 25 year olds? How might they differ?
10. In *Pretrial Detention and Guilty Pleas*, Sacks and Ackerman find that pretrial incarceration provides a powerful incentive for defendants to plead guilty. What implications does this powerful finding have for formal or procedural justice?

# ACTIVITIES/ASSIGNMENTS

## The High Cost of Poverty: Why the Poor Pay More

http://www.washingtonpost.com/wp-dyn/content/article/2009/05/17/AR2009051702053_3.html?sid=ST2009051801162

How do the poor end up paying more on a daily basis? Give some specific examples from the article and discuss them in terms of justice. Now think of some structural changes or policy solutions that might ease these burdens on the poor.

## Wealth Inequality in the United States

https://www.youtube.com/watch?v=LfgSEwjAeno&list=PLmKbqjSZR8TZa7wyVoVq2XMHxxWREyiFc

Watch the video about income inequality. What did you learn from the video about the extent of income inequality in our country? What was most surprising to you?

## Race and Income Distribution

http://www.justicemap.org/

Play around with the justice map, zooming in and selecting different cities and states, and displaying the intersection of income and race in any way that interests you. What patterns jumped out at you? How might you explain them?

## The Social Justice of Countries

http://www.nytimes.com/imagepages/2011/10/29/opinion/29blow-ch.html?ref=opinion

Examine the table in the link. What factors are used to determine social justice; are there any other factors that you think should be included? What are some of the findings that are most striking to you about the United States? How can you explain them?

## Simulation Game on Poverty

http://playspent.org/

Play "spent" at the link above. How much money did you end up with at the end of the day? What did you need to do to accomplish that—what difficult choices did you make, and what obstacles did you have to overcome? What does this game tell us about the instability that poverty induces?

## Myths and Realities

http://www.upworthy.com/if-you-think-only-poor-people-need-welfare-wait-till-you-see-what-really-rich-folks-do-with-it?c=upw1
http://www.dailydot.com/opinion/minimum-wage-myths-poverty-seattle/
http://benirwin.me/2013/12/03/20-things-the-poor-do-every-day/

Watch the three videos above that seek to challenge some of the myths of poverty. How do they challenge commonly held notions about government assistance, minimum wage, poverty, and even wealth?

## International Perspective on Parenting

http://www.theatlantic.com/health/archive/2016/02/hospital-bags-around-the-world/460434/?utm_source=SFFB
http://womansvibe.com/every-newborn-in-finland-sleeps-in-a-cardboard-box-for-the-most-brilliant-reason/

How do so-called birth necessities vary across countries? What patterns do you see in what items are considered necessary (or not)? Did most countries' governments provide the necessities for newborns, or were parents expected to supply them? How does the United States compare internationally?

# SEMESTER-LONG JUSTICE PROJECT

Step Two: Choose an area of injustice that you would like to learn more about. Locate one recent, peer-reviewed academic article on this topic. Read the article and write a summary of it. Format your summary as follows: Put the full APA-style citation at the top, with subheadings that correspond to the article and summaries under each subheading. Note: the topic you choose will become the one you work on addressing and creating justice in in upcoming weeks. Topics chosen by students of ours in the past have included specific types of crime (e.g., domestic violence, trafficking, health care fraud, drug and alcohol use/policies on campus, cyber crime), issues specific to police (e.g., racial profiling, police misconduct), courts (death penalty, wrongful conviction, unfair sentencing), corrections (reentry, abuse in institutions, felony employment exclusions), crime prevention (programs for at-risk youth, community prevention organizations), a variety of other local (public school closings, poverty, hunger, homelessness, dress codes in local entertainment district) and broad national or global issues (environment, suicide rates among Native American populations, financial regulations, death with dignity).

## Selected Reading

# "It Was Basically College to Us"

## Poverty, Prison, and Emerging Adulthood

***Megan Comfort***

The period from 18 to 25 years of age has been theorized as a distinct life stage of "emerging adulthood" (Arnett 2000) during which people explore social roles, occupational directions, and behavioral choices that set the foundation for their adult lives. In the United States, certain key events often characterize this liminal phase, such as moving out of one's childhood home, entering full-time employment, or pursuing higher education. Yet for sizeable numbers of young men of color from impoverished backgrounds, this time of exploration and experimentation is dominated by a less ebullient event: incarceration. Within the last four decades, historically high numbers of people have been swept into U.S. jails and prisons, an "incarceration binge" that has had particularly severe consequences for residents of destitute, predominantly black neighborhoods. (Bobo and Thompson 2010; see also: Sampson and Loeffler 2010; Wacquant 2010). Indeed, Western (2006) has demonstrated that going to prison has become more common in the lives of African-American men than enrolling in college or enlisting in the military, and the likelihood of being sent behind bars is highest before age 30 (Steffensmeier, Kramer et al. 1995; Bonczar and Beck 1997; Bushway, Tsao et al. 2011).

Emerging adulthood is conceived of as a time when "many different directions remain possible, when little about the future has been decided for certain, when the scope of independent exploration of life's possibilities is greater for most people than it will be at any other period of the life course" (Arnett 2000). Imprisonment is starkly antithetical to this conception, and certainly for the majority of young men, the aftereffects of an early stay in the penitentiary serve to restrict life's possibilities and determine much about the future in ways that are harmful to their health, employment prospects, family life, and civic participation (Western, Lopoo et al. 2004; Uggen and Manza 2005; Pager 2007; Massoglia 2008; Western and Pettit 2010).

Within this context, it is striking to encounter young men who retrospectively describe a prison sentence as having played a positive role in their emergence into adulthood. Such narratives give pause, and invite dismissal as shaky attempts to rationalize a stigmatizing experience or as applying to too rare a minority to justify scholarly attention. However, as we broaden our investigations to examine the full scope of incarceration's impact on historically high numbers of people born into poverty, a close analysis of these stories is instructive and necessary for three intertwined reasons. First, it raises our awareness of the range of youth being drawn into the penal net under the nation's continued aggressive punishment policies, such that men who might have formerly aged out of crime in their late twenties having nothing more to show than a few misdemeanor charges now have several years of "hard time" under their belts. Second, it pushes us to consider more deeply what is "gained" through imprisonment, and in particular whether what is delivered to the poor in the tainted guise of "rehabilitation" is provided to their more privileged peers through valorized and supportive social institutions. And third, it expands our understanding of the "rhetoric of redemption" (Maruna 2001) by focusing on those who offer narratives of desistance from criminalized behavior relatively early in the life cycle, before they have become seasoned in imprisonment and recidivism.

This article provides a starting point for such an analysis and argues for the need for further research by drawing on qualitative data from a multi-method study of men who had been recently released from a California state prison and their female partners. Study recruitment focused primarily on Oakland, a city of 400,000 residents which lies east of San Francisco and has 19% of its population living below the federal poverty line, is 28% African American and 25% Latino, and during the time of the fieldwork received 3,000 parolees from California state prisons annually (City of Oakland 2008; Urban Strategies Council 2006; U.S. Census Bureau 2010). Potential participants were recruited using street outreach, venue-based presentations, and flyers advertising the study, with a total of 172 couples (344 individuals) completing a cross-sectional survey interview. Qualitative interviews were conducted with a subsample of participants: ten couples were interviewed prior to the start of quantitative data collection as a pilot study for the feasibility of interview procedures (2005–2006), and eleven couples, one woman whose partner had been reincarcerated, and one man whose partner had left the country were interviewed after participating in the quantitative survey (2009–2012). Couples came together to a scheduled appointment at community-based organizations in the recruitment neighborhoods, where they were interviewed separately and simultaneously in private rooms. For the qualitative interviews, I interviewed the women and a male colleague interviewed the men.

In order to be eligible for study participation, both parties had to be 18 years of age or older and consider that they were in a relationship with each other during the male partner's most recent incarceration as well as at the time of eligibility screening. Men in the qualitative sample ranged from 1–15 months since they were released from prison. Four couples had been in a relationship for eleven to fifteen years, twelve had been together for between three and eight years and seven for one to two years. Two men had most recently served sentences of seven years, three had been behind bars for between four and six years, seven had served one to three years, and ten had been confined for between two and seven months.[1] Thirty-three participants self-identified as African American, seven as Latino and four as other ethnicities, with ages ranging from nineteen to fifty-eight years (the average participant age was thirty-five years).

The primary focus of the multi-method study was sexual health and HIV risk among recently released men and their female partners, and the qualitative interview guide concentrated on exploring couples' interactions and relationship dynamics during the post-incarceration period. Within this broader framework, the meaning of imprisonment in one's personal trajectory emerged as a theme warranting analytical attention. While men of diverse ages claimed to some degree that "prison saved my life" – not an unusual utterance in the redemption narratives of those trying to move forward and "make good" (Maruna 2001; see also McCall 1994; Veysey, Christian et al. 2009) – young men constructed this experience differently, placing less emphasis on a need for a punitive "wake-up call" to disrupt a long history of crime and deviance (which, as youthful convicts, they did not have), and more on the benefits of having time to reflect on "various life possibilities and gradually moving toward making enduring decisions" (Arnett 2000) compatible with non-incarcerated people of a similar age. Indeed, the girlfriends and wives of these young men tended to offer hopeful narratives that resonated with those of their partners, in contrast to those of more weathered and hence more skeptical women. Scholars have argued that impoverished youth of color are denied many of the graces customarily granted to children and adolescents to experiment, rebel, and misbehave, and instead have their behaviors construed as foreshadowing more serious criminality and thus requiring repression (for example, see Ferguson 2001; Jones 2009; Rios 2011). By reinterpreting the years spent in the grip of the penitentiary in a manner that rejects the need for punishment and asserts desires for the protective period of emerging adulthood, young men and women signal the importance of this developmental stage and highlight the necessity of understanding the dominant role of the prison as a shaping institution at this critical juncture in the lives of those born into poverty.

## "I GOT TO REALLY UNDERSTAND MYSELF": MEANINGS OF IMPRISONMENT FOR EMERGING ADULTS

A first prison sentence often marks a point of "upping the game" from misdemeanor charges, juvenile detention, and jail stays, and frequently places people on the slippery slope of parole violations, recidivism, and in-facility infractions that can result in decades of correctional involvement. Yet on the heels of having gone to prison for the first time, young men do not necessarily see themselves as being on this bleak path, particularly if they have not already had extensive contact with the criminal justice system. At the time of his interview, 23-year-old Calvin[2] had been in correctional custody twice in his lifetime: once for one day in jail in his mid-teens, and once for two and a half years in prison. Prior to his imprisonment at age 19, Calvin had surrounded himself with various trappings that typically signify an adult status: two children (one of whose mother he married while behind bars) and "my money, my cars, my wardrobe, you know, everything materialistic" acquired through an early career in the illegal economy. Nevertheless, during his interview he repeatedly describes having contemplated the next phase of his life from within the prison walls with a sense of youthful openness to unknown possibilities:

> I just knew I wanted stuff to go good when I got out, everything to fall into place. But I didn't know exactly what it was gonna be. I had goals: I had wanted to get in school [community college], wanted to get a job. Wanted to be with my kids, wanted to have a good girlfriend. But I never got in-depth of what exactly what I was gonna be doing. It was like, 'Dang!' Whatever came. So I was like really undecided.

Previous studies have found that milestones such as parenthood, marriage, or embarking on a career rank low among people in their teens and early twenties as important criteria for the attainment of adulthood, whereas high notes are given to more subjective transitions such as learning to accept responsibility for oneself and undertaking independent decision making (Greene, Wheatley et al. 1992; Scheer, Unger et al. 1994; Arnett 1998; Arnett 2000). Calvin's musings are in harmony with these findings: despite his early paternal and occupational obligations, he articulates the crystallization while he was in prison of a strong desire for emotional growth and maturation:

> [Before I went to prison] I didn't know myself as a person, as a human being, like what I wanted in life. Because I didn't have no father figure, no mother figure. They was drug addicts. And I really, you know, never had a idea of what a man was. So when I was incarcerated I was doing a lot of reading and just reflecting on past relationships, like, "Dang. That was wrong. You was wrong for doing that girl like that." So I just went back, all the way, just like reevaluating myself ... I was thinking about how could I be a better person.

Calvin shares many similarities with 31-year-old Rasheed, who had been out of prison for fifteen months at the time that he and his 30-year-old wife, Fatima, were interviewed. The couple had met thirteen years prior, when Fatima was still in high school: she was standing on the street one day when Rasheed approached her and asked for her phone number. Just eighteen years old, the young man had left school several years earlier, around the time he was first locked up in a juvenile detention facility. The son of a substance-addicted mother and an absent father, he knew how to fend for himself and made a solid living selling illegal drugs. Shortly after they met, Fatima recalls, Rasheed "ended up going to jail... and that's how our relationship kinda built." While her new beau spent sixty days in detention, Fatima wrote him letters and accepted his collect phone calls, opening up a conversation between them about their troubled family lives. As soon as Rasheed was released, she says, "we talked and everything and from there we just started being real close. And then I had some problems at home, and he was having problems at home, which caused us to move in together and we've been together ever since."

Despite the romance and courtship, these two vulnerable young people struggled to make a life together. Fatima already had a daughter to whom she had given birth at age fifteen, which added parenting responsibilities and additional economic demands into the mix. Fatima describes early in her interview how she and Rasheed would argue frequently about his other girlfriends, and how being a young mother with no family support exacerbated her feelings of depression and isolation. When she shifts to talk about the maturation of their relationship and how the young couple struggled to learn how to communicate with each other and establish a monogamous partnership, I ask whether this transformation was simply a matter of the two of them getting older. "No," she replies, "Actually it took for him to be incarcerated for six years."

As both partners tell it, Rasheed had spent time in juvenile facilities as a teenager and had gone to jail a handful of times as an adult, but had never been to state prison. Five years after he met Fatima, however, there was a warrant out for his arrest for a felony charge and he decided to turn himself in to the authorities. Several days before he went to the police, he and Fatima drove to Reno, Nevada and got married. This series of events was a turning point for Fatima:

> He coulda played it two ways. He coulda been a man that said, "You know what, I'm not gonna go ahead and deal with this. I'm just gonna run. I don't want to deal with you no more," and leave and do what he want to do. But... he committed himself to go and turn himself in and do his six years and get it over with. So when he made that decision I said, "Okay if you're strong enough to say I'm going to go ahead and turn myself in and do the six years and separate myself from my family, then I'm going to be there with you every step of the way."

Rasheed was first housed in California's High Desert State Prison, nearly 200 miles and a three-hour drive away from Oakland, which made it difficult for Fatima to visit regularly. But the newlyweds immediately took to constructing a fresh way of life together, one in which communication and "presence creation," or the sharing and synchronizing of activities to simulate feelings of togetherness (Comfort 2008), featured prominently. Rasheed remembers:

> I got actually so deep that anything that I found out or learned I would turn my wife and daughter onto it instantly. ... I'd pull them in on studying with me and we'd go into it together. ... I would tell [Fatima] about my day and what I was learning. What books she should pick up and start reading and try to catch up. "I'm on chapter this. Hurry up and catch up with me." And what books I would like her to get for me and get an extra copy for herself so we could read together.

After two years at High Desert, Rasheed was moved to San Quentin State Prison, just 18 miles from Oakland. Fatima and her daughter began to visit him for eight hours each Saturday and Sunday and participate in a three-day "family visit"[3] once a month for which Fatima would take time off from her job as the office manager at a construction company. While behind bars, Rasheed took classes to earn his General Educational Development (GED) credential and worked for the California state Joint Ventures program, which offers minimum-wage employment to a small group of prisoners. About a year before he was released from custody he converted to Islam, and Fatima decided to do so as well.

Like Calvin, when Rasheed looks back on his time behind bars, he evokes a period of self- reflection driven by a yearning for metamorphosis and maturation:

> I did so much studying and so much analyzing myself and self-evaluation that it was a trip to actually come to the understanding that I was really in prison. ... Because that was a time to where I got to really understand myself. When I was on the streets I was moving so fast you know. The street life and whatnot it just got you moving so much to where from the time you wake up in the morning you're moving until the time you go to sleep. So it's like I've never had no solitude time for me to know who I am, to understand myself, to analyze things that took place within that day or whatever. And most importantly to reflect on my family. Before I went to prison I neglected them a lot. ... It's safe to say that I really didn't know my wife like I should have. I didn't know my daughter neither, like I should have known her. And also myself. ... So I dove real deep into that. I started seeing things about myself that I didn't see out there [on the streets]. So immediately when I started seeing the negative parts of things about myself that I didn't see when I was out, immediately I started making changes to better myself. But I started seeing things about my wife and daughter that I never really paid attention to that was so beautiful and I couldn't understand how I didn't see it the first time. So it really drew us real close.

Fatima's perspective on the processes that occurred during these six years closely echoes that of her husband:

> Most importantly it [incarceration] was some time for him just to sit down and focus on him. Because before that he was like he was ripping and running into this, into that, into this, into that while he was out on the streets. ... Just not slowing down to really do some self evaluation. And that [prison] did it. That gave him the time. Because he couldn't go nowhere. He couldn't escape from himself. He had to sit down and face himself head on of who he was and who he wanted to be and where he wanted to go, and what he came from. And once he started sitting down and figuring out those pieces it's easy. The hardest part is sitting down doing it. ... We both felt like, okay this is like our time to be away from each other. We can grow. I can grow as a woman. I can grow as a mother. He can grow as a man. And when you come out we'll know exactly where we want to go. And it was basically college to us. We were separated but wasn't separated. ... it's a bad thing to be

> separated from your family and everything but I looked at this as a beautiful experience. ... It's like so many blessings have come to us through him being incarcerated. It's just – I feel like God just said, "Look, let me take you over here and let me work with you personally for a few minutes and [help] get you together and then [you'll] come out and maybe you can have changed some people and showed them that this is not the way to go."

These rich passages speak to multiple nuanced and complex aspects of the experiences of young people whose lives are dominated by the penitentiary. First, it is notable that incarceration is seen as an opportunity to think deeply about one's life due to the break it provides from the fast-paced existence young men lead in the outside world. This observation highlights the peculiar trajectory of entrepreneurs like Calvin and Rasheed, whose impoverished backgrounds and family histories of substance use catapult them into a precocious adulthood replete with business duties and action, but void of occasions to ripen into the "grown-ups" they want to be (Sanchez-Jankowski 1992; Bourgois 1995; Venkatesh 2009). The clearly expressed appreciation for having time to develop self-understanding, tune into personal relationships, and contemplate future goals and possibilities strongly relates to the conceptualization of emerging adulthood, and corresponds to the recognition of higher education and military institutions as providing this kind of protected time for self-exploration during this critical life stage (Arnett 2000).

Fatima's declaration that a six-year prison sentence "was basically college to us" pushes us to examine this parallel further. On the one hand, her pronouncement movingly encapsulates the tremendous change, advancement, and maturity that she and her husband accomplished during the long stretch of their twenties. Yet with these words, Fatima also brings into piercing focus the fact that she and Rasheed were not able to access the form of socially valorized passage to adulthood offered by costly centers of higher learning, but rather were consigned to salvage what they could from a degraded institution primarily concerned with confining bodies instead of elevating minds. In doing so, she articulates the subjective counterpart to Western's (2006) statistical analyses of model life experiences, namely that prison has become the college of the poor and the dark-skinned.

It is obvious that the criteria for entering college and entering prison differ. A discussion of building social and educational infrastructure in poor neighborhoods and embarking upon serious efforts to pursue alternatives to incarceration for juveniles in order to avoid their "graduation" to the adult penitentiary and facilitate that from universities is beyond the scope of this article (but see Miller 1996; Ferguson 2001; Perry 2006; Justice Policy Institute 2009; Nurse 2010; Comfort, Nurse et al. 2011). My intent here is to engage the ways that young people who have traversed incarceration retroactively narrate that experience in order to catalyze social scientists' thinking about the implications of spending one's emerging adulthood years inside of or intimately connected to a punitive social institution, and to remind us that the current breadth of this phenomenon is a product of the neoliberal age. To do so thoroughly, it is vital to extend the analysis to encompass the full spectrum of these narratives, including the indications of "sociological ambivalence" (Merton and Barber 1976) folded within. For example, 25-year-old John had left San Quentin just a month prior to coming to his interview appointment, and many of his comments mirror those of Calvin and Rasheed. When asked if his time in prison was a positive, negative, or neutral experience, he responds:

> It sounds funny for me to say it because of where I was at, but it was more positive. Because when I first got there, for twenty-three hours in the day I'm locked up in the cell with one guy you know. And so a lot of times I just went into my little inner circle, and thought about the things I was doing and thought about the things I was going through, what led me to get in there. And it just really tripped me out. I thought about things in my past that I never really put into perspective about when I was a little kid and stuff like that. And it just like really woke me up. So I had to come to the conclusion, like I sat down and was thinking, "Why am I here? What did I do?" You know what I'm saying? Not exactly the crime that I did but what led me along this path you know. So I started thinking about what I was doing in my life when I was happy, when I wasn't struggling too much and when I was doing something positive.

Also like Calvin and Rasheed, the fourteen months John spent behind bars constituted the first prison sentence he had served. Talking in a separate moment of the interview about his first weeks in lock up, he expresses a sense of vulnerability and unease:

> John: [It was] my first time to the penitentiary. And I was scared too... .
> Interviewer: And why were you scared?
> John: Cause I watch movies you know. They be talking about you get stabbed up in there and this, that and the other. When I first got to the penitentiary it got a real big sign at San Quentin in West Block says, "No warning shots will be fired."[4] You know, they walk around with Mini-14s[5], talking about no warning shots will be fired. Yeah! ... And I'm a little guy, you got these big buff dudes up in here....
> Interviewer: Different world?
> John: Yeah, yeah, it shocked me.

Rasheed and Fatima, too, intertwine stories of worry and hardship in their accounts. Fatima provides an evocative detail indicating the weight of "doing time" in tandem with her husband: "I would buy calendars and mark off months and months and I'd be like, 'Okay I got thirty-two months left' and [sighs heavily] it was crazy." For his part, in addition to the strain of navigating his way through the correctional environment, Rasheed was deeply concerned about Fatima's health: "For the whole time I was in prison, my wife, she went through a real stress mode. She even lost a little hair at the time, like a patch of hair fell out behind her stressing. She was thinner than she is [now], so it was like hurting for me to see that."

Here, then, are indicators of the many ways in which prison is emphatically *not* "like college." Prison is scary, shocking, and organized around intimidation and threats of violence. Prison holds one captive, whether while waiting to exit or waiting for a loved one to come home. It provokes profound stress and distress, causing weight loss, hair loss, and other health complications. And even for those who manage to use their time within its grasp to reflect, to learn, and to grow, it bestows upon them not the positive credential of a degree acclaiming their transition to a higher status, but instead the "negative credential" of a criminal record proclaiming them unworthy to participate in the social body (Wacquant 2005; see also: Maruna 2011). In sum, as Carlen and Tomb (2006) bluntly state, "a prison is a prison" and the punitive mission at its core fundamentally interferes with any other purpose young adults may attempt to extract from it.

## CONCLUSION

In her critique of the psychological approach to "thriving," Blankenship (1998) notes that "it sometimes appears in the thriving literature as if adversity or challenge are the most important factors promoting thriving." This can lead to a mindset that those at the bottom of the social ladder have the most "opportunity" to thrive because they face the most hardship, which in turn promotes the belief that those who do not overcome adversity either lack the will to do so or need to sink further toward "rock bottom" in order to "stimulate a response on the part of individual [actors] to transform their lives" (Blankenship 1998). As an alternative approach, Blankenship offers a sociological conceptualization of thriving that emphasizes the centrality of position in the social hierarchy as determining both the odds that certain groups of people will encounter adversity *and* the (un)likelihood that those people will have access to the resources they need to overcome adverse experiences. She also advocates replacing the standard consideration of individuals as the unit of analysis in thriving research with an approach that examines social groups as a whole.

Without question, African Americans in impoverished neighborhoods face dramatically high odds of their own or their loved one's incarceration (Bonczar and Beck 1997; Green, Ensminger et al. 2006; Wildeman 2009). And young adults' narratives of transforming a prison sentence into a meaningful experience may lead us to think of the carceral environment as fecund ground for thriving, lending credence to arguments for rehabilitation delivered through punishment (see Miller, this issue). But relocating these narratives into Blankenship's framework and focusing not only on the positive elements people managed to wring out of imprisonment but also the fear, loneliness, despair, and burden that characterized this time in their lives weakens this case. Rather than narratives of thriving, then, we can hear these young people as articulating Bourdieu's (1984) notion of "*amor fati*, the choice of destiny, but a forced choice, produced by conditions of existence which rule out all alternatives as mere daydreams and leave no choice but the taste for the necessary." In the neoliberal era of collapsing or defunct social services, meager labor markets that look askance at would-be workers without high school diplomas or professional skills, and a correctional ethos that chides those at "rock bottom" to pull themselves up by their bootstraps, redemption through imprisonment resonates as a tale of lemonade squeezed out under duress from the bitter, subpar fruit a deregulated society thrusts upon its most needy denizens. Indeed, in another passage in which he reflects on the meaning of imprisonment in his life, Calvin conveys a longing to substitute the "mere daydream" for the destiny produced by his social circumstances:

> I think it [being in prison] was a positive experience all the way around. Because I look at it as a blessing. Because the stuff I was into, it was like I was hanging around the wrong crowd. All my friends now that I was hanging around with are either dead or in prison for a long time, for like murders and stuff. So I think it was like a blessing from God, or whoever, that I was taken away to learn that lesson. Because I don't think I'd be the person I am right now if it wasn't for that. One, because it gave me time to focus, and just really you know you at the bottom then. All this material stuff took away from you now – you're not just a big popular guy for all this stuff. You just you now. It's like – a perfect chance to really find *you*. I don't know, it was refreshing. *Not the sense of being in jail, like if I could go away and not be in jail, like go somewhere on an island or a mountaintop or something and just think, and really be able to just think and not [have] all these... distractions*. It's good [to have time to reflect]. I think people should do that.

Being in a place with uninterrupted time to think about one's life and one's future is a standard practice afforded to youth during their emerging adulthood, some of whom enjoy the liberty of doing this on an island or mountaintop, and many of whom do so in the halls and on the campuses of academe. Were large batches of these high-resourced young people suddenly rerouted to the penitentiary, it is unlikely their ensuing stories would decree the correctional environment well-suited to fostering personal development and growth. That emerging adulthood is construed for the better-off as a time to indulge in privilege and promise while impoverished young adults are expected to learn from and even thrive through suffering can alert us to further layers of inequality and disadvantage that merit exploration. By probing more deeply into the ambivalence and daydreams of those who manage to convert their carceral experiences into positive life lessons, we may come closer to a comprehensive understanding of the conditions needed for all of society to flourish.

## ACKNOWLEDGMENTS

I am very grateful to the people who participated in this study and shared their experiences with us. My thanks as well to Reuben Miller, Javier Auyero, Jessica Fields, Lynne Haney, Shadd Maruna, and Loïc Wacquant for their helpful comments on this manuscript, and to Olga Reznick, Diane Binson, Nicolas Alvarado, and John Weeks for their assistance with carrying out the study. This research was funded by grants P30MH62246 and R01MH078743 from the National Institutes of Health. All procedures were approved by the UCSF Committee on Human Subjects Research and the RTI International Institutional Review Board.

## Notes

1 Data missing for 1 participant.

2 All names are pseudonyms.

3 California permits 43-hour overnight visits to the parents, children, and legal spouses of prisoners who have not been convicted of domestic violence or sexual crimes and who have a release date (meaning that they are not on Death Row or serving a life sentence). The eligibility criteria for family visits combined with the necessity of having family members who are willing to participate and can afford to take time off of work, travel to the prison, and pay for 3 days worth of food limits the number of prisoners who receive such visits.

4 West Block is a housing unit at San Quentin where newly arrived prisoners are held. The "No warning shots will be fired" sign refers to California Department of Corrections and Rehabilitation policy that correctional officers will not give warning if they determine there is a need to intervene with weapons in a violent situation.

5 A Mini-14 is a type of automatic rifle.

## References

Arnett JJ. Learning to stand alone: The contemporary American transition to adulthood in cultural and historical context. Human Development. 1998; 41:295–315.

Arnett JJ. Emerging Adulthood: A Theory of Development From the Late Teens Through the Twenties. American Psychologist. 2000; 55(5):469–480. [PubMed: 10842426].

Blankenship KM. A Race, Class, and Gender Analysis of Thriving. Journal of Social Issues. 1998; 54(2):393–404.

Bobo, LD.; Thompson, V. Racialized Mass Incarceration: Poverty, Prejudice, and Punishment. In: Markus, HR.; Moya, P., editors. Doing Race: 21 Essays for the 21st Century. New York: Norton; 2010. pp. 322–355.

Bonczar, TP.; Beck, AJ. Lifetime Likelihood of Going to State or Federal Prison. Washington DC: Bureau of Justice Statistics; 1997.

Bourdieu, P. Distinction: A Social Critique of the Judgement of Taste. Cambridge, MA: Harvard University Press; 1984.

Bourgois, P. In Search of Respect: Selling Crack in El Barrio. Cambridge: Cambridge University Press; 1995.

Bushway, SD.; Tsao, H-S., et al. Has the U.S. Prison Boom Changed the Age Distribution of the Prison Population?. Working paper. 2011. http://www.irp.wisc.edu/newsevents/workshops/2011/participants/papers/2016-BushwayTsaoSmith.pdf.

Carlen P., Tombs J. Reconfigurations of Penality: The Ongoing Case of the Women's Imprisonment and Reintegration Industries. Theoretical Criminology. 2006; 10(3):337–360.

City of Oakland. Oakland: 2003. Press Release: Oakland Mayor Jerry Brown Comments on Visit to San Quentin Prison. http://www.oaklandnet.com/government/mayor/press-releases/SanQuentin.html.

Comfort, M. Doing Time Together: Love and Family in the Shadow of the Prison. University of Chicago Press; 2008.

Comfort M., Nurse A., et al. Taking children into account: Addressing intergenerational effects of parental incarceration. Criminology & Public Policy. 2011; 10(3):839–850.

Ferguson, AA. Bad Boys: Public Schools in the Making of Black Masculinity. Ann Arbor: University of Michigan Press; 2001.

Green KM, Ensminger ME, et al. Impact of Adult Sons' Incarceration on African American Mothers' Psychological Distress. Journal of Marriage and Family. 2006; 68(2):430–441.

Greene AL, Wheatley SM, et al. Stages on life's way: Adolescents' implicit theories of the life course. Journal of Adolescent Research. 1992; 7:364–381.

Jones, N. Between Good and Ghetto: African American Girls and Inner-City Violence. New Brunswick, NJ: Rutgers University Press; 2009.

Justice Policy Institute. The Costs of Confinement: Why Good Juvenile Justice Policies Make Good Fiscal Sense. Washington, DC: 2009.

Maruna, S. Making Good: How Ex-Convicts Reform and Rebuild Their Lives. Washington, DC: American Psychological Association; 2001.

Maruna S. Reentry as a Rite of Passage. Punishment & Society. 2011; 13(1):3–28.

Massoglia M. Incarceration as Exposure: The Prison, Infectious Disease, and Other Stress Related Illnesses. Journal of Health and Social Behavior. 2008 Mar.49:56–71. [PubMed: 18418985].

McCall, N. Makes Me Wanna Holler: A Young Black Man in America. New York: Vintage Books; 1994.

Merton, RK.; Barber, E. Sociological Ambivalence and Other Essays. New York: Free Press; 1976. Sociological Ambivalence.

Miller, JG. Search and Destroy: African-American Males in the Criminal Justice System. New York: Cambridge University Press; 1996.

Nurse, A. Locked Up, Locked Out: Young Men in the Juvenile Justice System. Nashville, TN: Vanderbilt University Press; 2010.

Pager, D. Marked: Race, Crime, and Finding Work in an Era of Mass Incarceration. Chicago: University of Chicago Press; 2007.

Perry BL. Understanding social network disruption: The case of youth in foster care. Social Problems. 2006; 53(3):371–391.

Rios, VM. Punished: Policing the Lives of Black and Latino Boys. New York, NY: NYU Press; 2011.

Sampson RJ, Loeffler C. Punishment's Place: The Local Concentration of Mass Incarceration. Daedalus: the Journal of the American Academy of Arts & Sciences. 2010; 139(3):20–31.

Sanchez-Jankowski, M. Islands in the Street: Gangs and American Urban Society. Berkeley, CA: University of California Press; 1992.

Scheer, SD.; Unger, DG., et al. Society for Research on Adolescence. San Diego, CA: 1994. Adolescents becoming adults: Attributes for adulthood.

Steffensmeier D, Kramer J, et al. Age Differences in Sentencing. Justice Quarterly. 1995; 12(3):583– 602.

U.S. Census Bureau. Washington, DC: 2010. State & County Quick Facts. http://quickfacts.census.gov/qfd/states/06/0653000.html.

Uggen, C.; Manza, J. Disenfranchisement and the Civic Reintegration of Convicted Felons. In: Mele, C.; Miller, TA., editors. Civil Penalties, Social Consequences. New York: Routledge; 2005. pp. 67–84.

Urban Strategies Council. Community report on parole & probation in Alameda County. Oakland, CA: Urban Strategies Council; 2005.

Venkatesh, S. Off the Books: The Underground Economy of the Urban Poor. Cambridge, MA: Harvard University Press; 2009.

Veysey, MB.; Christian, J., editors. How Offenders Transform Their Lives. Cullompton, UK: Willan; 2009.

Wacquant L. Race as Civic Felony. International Social Science Journal. 2005 Spring;181:127–142.

Wacquant L. Class, Race & Hyperincarceration in Revanchist America. Daedalus: the Journal of the American Academy of Arts & Sciences. 2010; 139(3):74–90.

Western, B. Punishment and Inequality in America. New York: Russell Sage Foundation; 2006.

Western, B.; Lopoo, LM., et al. Incarceration and the Bonds between Parents in Fragile Families. In: Pattillo, M.; Weiman, D.; Western, B., editors. Imprisoning America: The Social Effects of Mass Incarceration. New York: Russell Sage Foundation; 2004. pp. 21–45.

Western B, Pettit B. Incarceration and Social Inequality. Daedalus: the Journal of the American Academy of Arts & Sciences. 2010; 139(3):8–19.

Wildeman C. Paternal Imprisonment, the Prison Boom, and the Concentration of Childhood Disadvantage. Demography. 2009; 46:265–280. [PubMed: 21305393].

Selected Reading

# Pretrial Detention and Guilty Pleas

## If They Can't Afford Bail They Must Be Guilty

*Meghan Sacks and Alissa R. Ackerman*

## INTRODUCTION

Criminal case processing has received a great deal of attention among legal scholars concerned with the fair administration of justice. Specifically, many researchers have focused on inequities in sentencing practices (Demuth & Steffensmeier, 2004; Spohn & Holleran, 2000; Western, 2006). Increasing attention has also been devoted to potential disparities in pretrial processing (Katz & Spohn, 1995; Demuth, 2003; Schlesinger, 2005). However, as Frenzel and Ball (2007) point out, research on other decision points in case processing is limited.

The trial is often thought of as the hallmark of justice in the USA; however, almost all criminal cases are disposed through plea bargaining and while there is extensive research on the practice (Alshuler, 1979; McCoy, 1993, 2005; Schulhofer, 1984; Smith, 1984), current research on factors that affect the process is limited. Additionally, these studies seldom include bail decisions and outcomes as potential influences on guilty pleas. The current study, while employing primarily a quantitative analysis and supplemental qualitative data, is intended to fill this gap by analyzing the effect of pretrial detention on guilty pleas. Further, the current research goes one step further in that it examines the timing of such guilty pleas to gauge the potential impact of pretrial detention on a defendant's decision to plead guilty.

## FACTORS AFFECTING GUILTY PLEAS

Plea bargaining is the 'middle point' of case processing, falling between the pretrial process and determination of guilt and (in 97% of cases) sentencing (Kycelhahn &

Cohen, 2008). While definitions of plea bargaining vary, McCoy (2005) notes that certain critical features remain: mainly that there is a confession and a defendant's waiver of the right to trial. Opponents point to the coercive nature of the process, positing that defendants are either promised some form of leniency or threatened with a harsher punishment should they opt for trial, lending credence to the coercion objection. This problem is further compounded by the problem of the escalating 'trial penalty' suffered by defendants who choose to go to trial. While this is not a new phenomenon, the trial penalty has escalated due to stricter crime control policies and mandatory laws and has resulted in an increase in the 'going rate', or expected punishment for a certain crime.

Previous research that has analyzed the coercive nature of the plea found that defendants who took their cases to trial received harsher sentences than those who pleaded guilty (Brereton & Casper, 1981–1982; Kurlychek & Johnson, 2004; Uhlman & Walker, 1980). Albonetti (1990) contends that the finality of the conviction emphasizes the importance of studying factors that contribute to a defendant's decision to plead guilty. In her analysis, Albonetti (1990) found that a confession, the presence of physical evidence and the number of charges increase the probability of a guilty plea whereas the severity of the penalty, use of a weapon and the number of witnesses decrease the odds that a defendant will plead guilty. In their study of guilty pleas and sentencing, Meyer and Gray (1997) also found that offense severity was the strongest predictor of guilty pleas and other notable studies have demonstrated the impact of both offense severity and prior criminal record on plea decisions (Frenzel & Ball, 2007; Ulmer & Bradley, 2006).

However, legal determinants are not the only factors that influence plea bargaining. Meyer and Gray (1997) also found that race plays a strong role, in that white defendants were more likely to plead not guilty. However, most of the empirical data have found that black defendants are less likely than white defendants to plead guilty (Albonetti, 1990; Frenzel & Ball, 2007; Kellough & Wortley, 2002). Kellough and Wortley (2002) found that younger defendants are more likely than their older counterparts to plead guilty. While the research shows that both legal and extralegal characteristics influence the decision to engage in plea negotiations, Feeley (1979) suggested that pretrial detention would increase the probability of a defendant pleading guilty. Logically, individuals who cannot afford bail will have to wait in jail until their cases are concluded and according to the Bureau of Justice Statistics (BJS, 2008), approximately 43% of defendants are detained until case disposition. Being held in jail provides defendants with a strong incentive to plead guilty. The length of pretrial detention plays a role as well. After all, it is plausible to expect that the longer a defendant is held in custody, the stronger the incentive he or she has to plead guilty in order simply to be released – particularly in cases involving misdemeanors, where the actual sentence may not exceed time spent in pretrial detention and the judge may set the sentence upon conviction as 'time served'.

Few studies to date have examined this hypothesis, but two of these studies found that being held in jail prior to trial did not significantly impact a defendant's decision to plead guilty (Albonetti, 1990; Meyer & Gray, 1997). However, in their

Canadian study of bail and plea bargaining, Kellough and Wortley (2002) found that individuals held in pretrial detention are more likely to enter into guilty pleas. Kellough and Wortley (2002) suggest several reasons why individuals held pretrial may plead guilty, including the following: the plea agreement may not involve any prison time; a plea may result in a sentence of time served and therefore a release from jail; and pleading guilty might mean moving to a better correctional facility. For various reasons, pleading guilty while in pretrial detention might be a more appealing option than trial. McCoy (2007) also posits that low-level offenders facing short jail terms or non-incarcerative sentences will plead guilty simply to get out of jail.

## TIMING OF CASE DISPOSITION

The research on factors affecting guilty pleas is not nearly as extensive as the research on factors affecting bail and sentencing decisions. The studies that have examined this decision point have commonly measured case disposition as a binary variable, whereby a defendant enters a guilty plea or opts for trial (Brereton & Casper, 1981–1982; Engen & Steen, 2000; Meyer & Gray, 1997; Walsh, 1990).[1] However, the majority of criminal cases are resolved through guilty pleas so for most criminal defendants the issue is not if they will enter a guilty plea but when. According to the BJS (2006), the average case processing time for felony crimes is approximately 10.1 months, while cases involving misdemeanors take approximately 4.6 months to settle. At the same time, the Sixth Amendment to the US Constitution provides criminal defendants with the right to a 'speedy and public trial', mandating the courts to provide justice in an expeditious manner and bringing the issue of case processing timing to the forefront.

In *Barker v. Wingo*, the court announced a four-prong test to determine whether a defendant has been afforded his/her right to a speedy trial. The court laid out the following criteria in determining whether a delay was unduly excessive: '[l]ength of delay, the reason for the delay, the defendant's assertion of his right, and prejudice to the defendant' (p. 530). New Jersey subsequently adopted this four-part test in *State v. Szima*, and although no specific rule addresses pretrial detention, the court considers length of detention in cases where excessive delay is the issue (*State v. Farrell*).[2]

Prompted by an interest in how the courts balance these objectives, some researchers have examined factors that contribute to case processing time (Church, 1982; Flemming, Nardulli, & Eisenstein, 1987; Ostrom & Hanson, 1999), often speculating that court-level characteristics have a strong influence on timing of case dispositions. In a notable study of case processing time, Luskin and Luskin (1986) examined the impact of both case-related and court-level factors on the pace of case processing time. In doing so, the authors considered the impact of pretrial detention on disposition timing, positing that both defendants and the courts have an interest in expeditious processing. Specifically, defendants do not want to be held in jail and the courts are concerned about jail overcrowding and incarcerating individuals who are presumed innocent. Luskin and Luskin (1986) found that detained defendants have faster case dispositions, as well as defendants with lengthy prior records and those facing long incarcerative sentences. The authors also found that court-related characteristics, such as docket type, impact disposition timing, but ultimately confirmed the findings of Church, Carlson, Lee, and Tan (1978), that case processing time is best attributed to the 'local legal culture'. Church (1986) further developed this concept, which refers to the notion that case processing timing is usually determined by the shared beliefs and norms of the local courtroom work group.

In their study of nine state criminal trial courts, Ostrom and Hanson (1999) investigated the impact of case characteristics, management strategies and resources on the speed of felony litigation. According to Ostrom and Hanson (1999), prosecutors and public defenders in courts with a faster pace of litigation hold similar views on management strategies and resources, i.e. they share expectations about the timing of case disposition and they feel satisfied with their resources. Ostrom and Hanson (1999) also found that case characteristics impact disposition timing. Specifically, cases involving the most serious offenses take the longest to resolve. Similarly, trial cases take longer to settle than those disposed of via guilty pleas and even more pertinent to the current study, cases involving defendants detained prior to trial are settled faster than cases in which defendants are released. According to Ostrom and Hanson, this finding can be attributed to court considerations, in that the courts are concerned with costs of incarceration and protection of defendant liberties.

Ostrom and Hanson's (1999) interpretation of their conclusions is that quicker case dispositions for defendants who are detained prior to trial is a function of court efficiency. While the researchers operationalize bond status as a defendant-level characteristic, they attribute its impact to *intra-* court considerations of management. Additionally, the potential influence of bail operations on case dispositions was not the focus of Ostrom and Hanson's (1999) study. In light of these considerations, the current research posits that defendants held before trial will plead guilty earlier to get out of jail quickly, a reason that may coincide with court efficiency explanations.

## THE CURRENT STUDY

The literature on factors that affect bail and sentencing practices is vast, yet the research on determinants of guilty pleas is limited in comparison. Many of the studies that have been conducted on this topic have measured case disposition as a binary variable – guilty plea or trial. However, it is well-established that most criminal cases are resolved through plea bargaining and ultimately, a guilty plea. Some researchers have examined the issue of criminal case processing time; however, there is little empirical research that includes the effect of bail operations on plea bargaining in the USA. The current study analyzes the legal and extralegal factors that influence a defendant's decision to plead guilty, with a central focus on the coercive element of plea bargaining that influences detained defendants to plead guilty to get out of jail. We hypothesize that cases in which defendants are held prior to trial will result in faster case dispositions. This study is intended to add to current research on the administration of justice, particularly since a guilty plea is the most common form of case disposition.

## METHODOLOGY AND DATA

The current study utilizes individual-level secondary data collected from the State of New Jersey's Criminal Disposition Commission (CDC). Data were obtained on all summons and complaints issued in New Jersey from 18 October 2004, to 24 October 2004. The movement of these cases from arrest through sentencing was followed and recorded, which culminated in the creation of a database containing 2093 initial cases. Of these, nearly half of the sample ($n$ = 1118) cases were 'screened out'. The screening process in New Jersey refers to the County Prosecutor's review of the charges and subsequent decision to file these as indictable offenses in Superior Court. Cases that are charged as indictable offenses in Superior Court are considered cases that are 'screened in'.

Cases that are screened out are those that are not charged as indictable offenses in Superior Court. Prosecutors screen cases early in the criminal case process, usually just following the defendant's first court appearance or as early as after the complaint is filed. There are several circumstances under which cases are screened out. In some instances the judge dismisses the cases at arraignment or defendants plead guilty immediately, pay fines and are released. Often cases are downgraded and remanded to municipal court for prosecution as 'disorderly persons' offenses (misdemeanors). These are cases in which the prosecutor has determined that the evidence does not support charging a defendant with an indictable offense. Cases that are screened out can also be transferred to Family Court. These are cases that involve juveniles under the age of eighteen.[7] In this sample, ($n$ = 975) cases were screened in. The screening process is common and illustrates what is referred to as 'the funnel of justice', which describes the high attrition rate of cases as they progress through the process from arrest to sentencing. As illustrated very well by a study published by the Vera Institute of Justice (1977), the number of felony arrests diminishes as cases are dismissed, downgraded and adjudicated.

The 975 cases that remained in the sample were further diminished as this analysis focused on cases of those defendants who had bail decisions and subsequently proceeded all the way through the system to conviction and sentencing. This resulted in a final sample of ($n$ = 634) cases for this analysis. Even though the sample is reduced as the study progresses, the numbers are still sufficiently adequate for robust statistical analyses. The cases in this sample were collected from all twenty-one counties in New Jersey, which include rural, suburban and urban jurisdictions. Data include demographic factors, such as gender, age and race; a comprehensive list of legal variables, including criminal history and information about offense seriousness; and information about the various decision points in each case. The sample of cases recorded in one week is representative of the typical decisions made in New Jersey's courts as well as those made in trial courts in other states, so the findings in this study have general relevance to state trial courts. In addition to the quantitative data, we interviewed members of the judiciary and observed bail proceedings to help place the statistical findings in the appropriate context.

## VARIABLES

Two dependent variables are utilized in this analysis to examine the hypothesis about the timing for defendants' plea bargains. The first, a binary variable, assesses whether the case disposition occurs before or after indictment. A second continuous variable measures the number of days that elapsed between the time when bail was set and the date of the final disposition. This measurement is used to discern if defendants held before trials have earlier case dispositions, i.e. plead guilty earlier. A third binary variable measuring whether a defendant has pled guilty to any charges was originally intended to be included as a dependent variable in this analysis. However, and consistent with the literature, very few cases went to trial in this sample: 16 to be precise. As this number is too small for statistical analysis, this variable was not included.

The database compiled by the CDC includes both demographic and legal information that was used to construct independent variables in the current study. The demographic variables utilized in the study include the following: gender (male/female), race (white/black/Hispanic), age (in years), jurisdiction type (urban/non-urban), and defense attorney type (public defender/private counsel/none). Defendants deemed indigent are eligible for a public defender while those with financial means retain private counsel. Jurisdictions were assessed as urban/non-urban based on the population per square mile of each county and as New Jersey is the most densely populated state in the nation, no counties could be categorized as 'rural' compared to less populous states.

This study uses several independent legal variables relevant to guilty pleas. Offense type is measured as a four-category variable consisting of 'person and weapons offenses' (otherwise known as violent offenses), property offenses, drug offenses, and other offenses. 'Other' offenses include a range of non-violent, public-order offenses such as solicitation for prostitution, disorderly conduct, as well as 'crimes of dishonesty' such as forgery and perjury. Previous research suggests that offense severity is a predictor of guilty pleas (Albonetti, 1990; Meyer & Gray, 1997). Based on this information, we created dummy variables for the latter three offense types, making violent offenses the reference category.

The number of charges pending, a continuous measure of offense severity, is also included in the analyses. As previously discussed, the number of charges has been shown to impact guilty pleas and may play a critical role in plea bargaining. Along with the seriousness of the offense, the defendant's criminal history has been found to be the strongest predictor of judicial decisions at all stages of criminal procedure (Gottfredson & Gottfredson, 1990). Therefore, this study includes the number of prior convictions as a continuous variable to measure a defendant's criminal history.

While certain legal factors such as prior record and offense severity, and demographic variables, such as race, have been examined for their effect on guilty pleas, this research adds to the standard list of variables by testing whether 'pretrial status' affects subsequent procedure. This research focuses on the coercive element of plea bargaining that influences defendants who are detained before trial to plead guilty to get out of jail. As this focus is central to the current study, bail outcomes were used in the analyses of the factors that affect guilty pleas.

A few approaches are used in this study to determine the potential impact of bail practices on plea bargaining. Logistic regression was selected for one of the analyses involving disposition timing where the dependent variable was dichotomized to reflect cases in which defendants pleaded guilty prior to indictment and those in which defendants pleaded guilty after being indicted. As this dependent variable is dichotomous and categorical in nature and the independent variables used in the analysis are both categorical and continuous, logistic regression is the preferred statistical procedure (Mertler & Vannatta, 2005). Multiple regression is also employed to analyze the predictors of a continuous dependent variable measuring disposition timing in days. Finally, we supplement the quantitative analysis with qualitative data collected from observations of bail hearings and interviews with members of the courtroom work group in New Jersey.

## RESULTS

Table 2.1 provides the descriptive data for the variables used in this study. A majority 87% ($n$ = 553) of the defendants in this sample were males, and about 66% ($n$ = 419) of defendants were ethnic minorities. Defendants in this sample had an average of 3.8 of charges pending and about 3.1 prior convictions. The offense types were distributed as follows: 30% ($n$ = 187) of the charges involved violent offenses (these offenses include the use or sale of firearms), 41% ($n$ = 262) involved drug offenses, 22% ($n$ = 141) involved property offenses, and 7% ($n$ = 44) involved other types of offenses. Approximately 24% ($n$ = 151) of the arrestees were released on their own recognizance, while 76% ($n$ = 483) were subjected to a financial bail requirement. The average bail amount in this sample was $48,725 but the most common bail amount set by the court was $10,000. Approximately 64% ($n$ = 308) of the defendants in the sample were able to post bail, whereas about 36% ($n$ = 175) could not meet financial requirements and were therefore held in jail while awaiting trial. Regarding legal counsel, about 84% ($n$ = 510) of defendants were assigned a public defender while only about 16% ($n$ = 98) retained private counsel. Less than one-fifth of the case dispositions, 14% ($n$ = 91), occurred before an indictment, with an average of 210 days from the day when bail was set to the disposition of the case.

Table 2.2 shows the results of a logistic regression predicting disposition timing (pre- or post-indictment). Interestingly, only one factor in this model appears to impact the timing of case disposition ($\chi^2 = 12, n = 593 = 29.96, p < .005$). Specifically, the odds of a case disposition occurring post-indictment are significantly higher for defendants who have been released from jail on bail (Wald = 6.12, odds = 2.06, $p$ = .013). This finding lends support to the hypothesis that cases in which defendants are held in pretrial detention are more likely to reach faster case

**Table 2.1** Sample description ($N = 634$)

| Name | Coding | n | % | M | SD |
|---|---|---|---|---|---|
| Age | In years | | | 30 | 9.9 |
| Gender | 1 = female | 80 | 12.6 | | |
| | 0 = male | 553 | 87.4 | | |
| Race | 1 = white | 213 | 33.7 | | |
| | 2 = Hispanic | 104 | 16.5 | | |
| | 3 = black | 315 | 49.8 | | |
| County type | 1 = urban | 451 | 71.1 | | |
| | 2-non-urban | 183 | 28.9 | | |
| Offense type | 1 = person and weapons | 187 | 29.5 | | |
| | 2 = property | 141 | 22.2 | | |
| | 3 = CDS (controlled dangerous substance) | 262 | 41.3 | | |
| | 4 = other | 44 | 6.9 | | |
| Prior convictions | Number of prior convictions | | | 3.1 | 4.1 |
| Number of counts | Number of current charges | | | 3.8 | 3.4 |
| Release | 1 = Release | 459 | 72.4 | | |
| | 0 = In jail | 175 | 27.6 | | |
| Defense attorney type | 1 = private counsel | 98 | 16.1 | | |
| | 0 = assigned counsel | 510 | 83.9 | | |
| Disposition time | 1 = pre-indictment | 91 | 14.4 | | |
| | 2 = post-indictment | 543 | 85.6 | | |
| Days to disposition | | | | 210 | 168 |

dispositions. One prosecutor discussed this issue as well, stating that most guilty pleas occur pre-indictment. According to the prosecutor, defendants plead guilty to get out of jail, 'to get time served or to get it over with' (Interview, 10 March 2010).

Table 2.3 presents the results of a multiple regression predicting time to disposition. Both legal and demographic factors are significant ($F(12, n = 499) = 8.218$, $p < .001$) in this model. Race emerged as a significant predictor of disposition timing when this variable was measured in units of days rather than as a binary variable (pre- or post-indictment). The results show that case dispositions for black ($t = 3.13$, $b = .29$, $p = .002$) and Hispanic ($t = 2.30$, $b = .27$, $p < .05$) defendants took longer than those for white defendants. Secondly, attorney type was a significant predictor in this analysis ($t = -2.82$, $b = -.31$, $p = .005$) in that defendants represented by public defenders had a significantly shorter number of days

**Table 2.2** Logistic regression analysis: dependent variable = disposition timing (0 = Pre-Indictment; 1 = Post-Indictment) ($n$ = 593)

| | B | SE | Wald | Exp(B) |
|---|---|---|---|---|
| Gender (female) | −0.19 | 0.40 | 0.22 | 0.83 |
| Age | 0.01 | 0.01 | 0.78 | 1.01 |
| Race (White) | | | | |
| Hispanic | 0.85 | 0.44 | 3.71 | 2.34 |
| Black | 0.38 | 0.31 | 1.49 | 1.47 |
| Attorney type (private) | −0.76 | 0.45 | 2.84 | 0.47 |
| County type (non-urban) | −0.48 | 0.32 | 2.35 | 0.62 |
| Prior convictions | 0.06 | 0.04 | 1.85 | 1.06 |
| Number of charges | 0.09 | 0.05 | 3.40 | 1.10 |
| Offense type (violent) | | | | |
| Property | 0.15 | 0.38 | 0.15 | 1.16 |
| Drugs | 0.10 | 0.33 | 0.09 | 1.10 |
| Other | −0.86 | 0.46 | 3.44 | 0.42 |
| Release (in jail) | 0.72 | 0.29 | 6.12 | 2.06* |
| Model $\chi^2$ | 23.10* | | | |
| −2LL | 406.53 | | | |
| Nagelkerke $R^2$ | 0.08 | | | |

Note: Reference categories are in parentheses. *$p < .05$. **$p < .01$. ***$p < .001$.

to disposition than defendants represented by private attorneys. This result is not surprising since lack of resources and high caseloads give public defenders a stronger incentive to settle cases faster than private attorneys.

Turning to legal predictors, the number of charges pending was a significant predictor of disposition timing ($t$ = 4.24, $b$ = .05, $p$ < .001). As the number of charges pending increased, so did the days from bail hearing to the disposition of a case. Regarding the offense type, property ($t$ = −2.31, $b$ = −.25, $p$ < .022) and drug felony offenses ($t$ = −2.71, $b$ = −.24, $p$ = .007) had significantly faster disposition times when compared to violent offenses. Finally, and central to the current study, a defendant's pretrial release status was a significant predictor of disposition timing ($t$ = 7.22, $b$ = .61, $p$ < .001) in that defendants who were held in jail prior to trial had shorter case dispositions than defendants who were on release. This finding supports the hypothesis that defendants who are held in jail before trial will have earlier case dispositions because they plead quicker to get out of jail. The results in this analysis are consistent with the previous logistic regression predicting case disposition as before or after the indictment. However, examination of disposition timing as a continuous variable revealed other significant legal and demographic predictors. The qualitative data also indicate that most defendants plead guilty

**Table 2.3** OLS regression: dependent variable = days to disposition (logged) ($n$ = 499)

| | b | SE | β | t |
|---|---|---|---|---|
| Gender (female) | 0.01 | 0.11 | 0.00 | 0.09 |
| Age | 0.00 | 0.00 | 0.03 | 0.74 |
| Race (White) | | | | |
| Hispanic | 0.27 | 0.12 | 0.12 | 2.30* |
| Black | 0.29 | 0.09 | 0.16 | 3.13** |
| Attorney Type (private) | −0.31 | 0.11 | −0.13 | -2.82** |
| County type (non-urban) | −0.12 | 0.09 | −0.62 | -1.42 |
| Prior convictions | 0.01 | 0.01 | 0.06 | 1.30 |
| Number of charges | 0.05 | 0.01 | 0.18 | 4.24*** |
| Offense type (violent) | | | | |
| Property | −0.25 | 0.11 | −0.11 | -2.31* |
| Drugs | −0.24 | 0.09 | −0.14 | -2.71* |
| Other | −0.26 | 0.16 | −0.07 | -1.61 |
| Release (in jail) | 0.61 | 0.08 | 0.32 | 7.22*** |
| $R^2$ | 0.41 | | | |

Note: Reference categories are in parentheses. *$p < .05$, **$p < .01$, ***$p < .001$.

and many of them do so to get out of jail. The following quotes, taken from interviews, support this conclusion:

> Most cases are disposed of through guilty pleas. They plead earlier to get out earlier if they are detained. Yes, yes, they definitely plead guilty to get out of jail. You would want to get out too. They plead guilty to get out, get time served or to get it over with. (Interview with prosecutor, 11 March 2010)
>
> They plead guilty to get out; that happens a lot. The thought of collateral consequences is the furthest thing from their minds - they just want to get out. (Interview with public defender, 16 March 2010)
>
> Ten percent of people in jail are innocent but people plead guilty because they save themselves time in jail. (Interview with judge, 16 March 2010)[4]

Information from the qualitative analyses also provides support for the shared dynamics of the courtroom work group. While not included as a variable in this study, the norms of this work group have been offered as an explanation for manner and frequency of plea bargains. The dynamic of the courtroom work group appears to play a role in the bail process as well as subsequent procedures in the criminal case process. Observations indicate that public defenders and prosecutors are friendly with each other as well as with the judge presiding over bail hearings. They joke, laugh and share in casual conversations. One public defender explained that the players are usually the same (Interview, 11 March 2010). Even if not particular to guilty pleas themselves, the following quote, taken from an interview with a public defender, helps illustrate the operating dynamic of the courtroom work group:

> Bail decisions made in advance happens a lot. Usually there is the same judge, prosecutor and sometimes public defenders. We get to know each other and what the judge wants and expects. There is definitely a dynamic among the players. (Interview, 16 March 2010)

# DISCUSSION

As previously established, plea bargaining has become the most common form of case disposition in the USA. Approximately 97% of felony cases are disposed through plea bargaining (Kycelhahn & Cohen, 2008). Of the 722 cases in the entire sample that resulted in a finding of guilt, only 11 were the result of a trial while the remainder stemmed from a plea bargain. Ideally, one analysis would have focused on predictors of disposition type (guilty plea or trial). However, this analysis was not possible due to the small number of cases in the sample that were resolved through trial. Although plea bargaining has become the norm, certain factors, such as number of charges pending, have been found to increase the odds of a defendant engaging in the plea bargaining process.

Even more important for the current research, this study looks at factors that affect the timing of a plea bargain. Most cases will result in a plea bargain but the court is still charged with providing speedy justice, making the issue of timing an important one. The number of charges, while increasing a defendant's likelihood of pleading guilty, also increased the number of days until disposition. Defendants with more charges pending took longer to plea bargain; a finding that is consistent with previous research and sensible considering that cases involving more charges are usually more complex and therefore require more due diligence. Similarly, cases involving property and drug offenses were settled quicker than those involving violent offenses; another indicator that more serious and more complex cases take longer to dispose.

Cases involving public defenders have a shorter disposition timing than those with private attorneys. This finding may highlight the lack of resources and the burden of the caseload pressures faced by public defenders that undoubtedly need to dispose of cases in an expeditious manner. However, it may also be another indicator of the efficiency of the courtroom work group. This study joins several other notable studies in efforts to understand these courtroom relationships (Clynch & Neubauer, 1981; McCoy, 1993; Schulhofer, 1984; Spohn, 1991). Another finding, consistent with previous research (Albonetti, 1990; Frenzel & Ball, 2007; Kellough & Wortley, 2002) is the role of race. The results indicate that cases involving black and Hispanic defendants will take longer to resolve than those involving their Caucasian counterparts. One explanation for this finding, offered by Albonetti (1990), is that black defendants may be less likely to plea bargain as they are more distrustful of the legal system. This argument can be applied to the finding that minority defendants may also express their distrust of the legal system by a comparatively long resistance to plea bargaining.

The hypothesis that defendants, held in jail before trial, will be more likely to plea bargain early to get out of jail quickly is essential to the present research. The results of this study appear to support this hypothesis. Specifically, pretrial detention had the strongest impact on when defendants plead guilty. Defendants who were held pretrial in this sample had their cases disposed of quicker than defendants who were released. According to the BJS (2008), approximately 43% of defendants are held until case disposition, thus providing defendants with an incentive to plead guilty quicker than those released in the community on bail.

The results in this analysis are also consistent with the findings from Kellough and Wortley's (2002) study of bail decisions and plea bargaining. They found that individuals held in jail prior to trial were more likely to engage in plea negotiations. Kellough and Wortley (2002) offered several reasons why pretrial detention affects plea bargaining. They reasoned that defendants may plead guilty to a crime when prison time might not result or when a guilty plea would result in a release from jail. McCoy (2007) echoes this sentiment as well, suggesting that low-level offenders plead guilty to get out of jail. It is possible that defendants also plead early for other reasons, perhaps for better correctional accommodations and/or facilities and privileges.[5] Ostrom and Hanson (1999) explain that guilty pleas occur faster because of court concerns. Specifically, the courts are concerned with the costs of incarceration and the defendant's potential loss of freedom, which suggests that court-level factors are responsible for timing of guilty pleas. While this is a possible explanation, the combined quantitative and qualitative results in this study suggest that defendants will plead guilty earlier to get out of jail faster.

The results of this study implicate inherent flaws in both plea bargaining practices and bail operations. Pretrial detention of defendants who cannot afford to purchase their freedom is a strong incentive for defendants to enter guilty pleas quickly. Although non-financial release is an option for the courts, cash bail is used much more frequently, likely due to the renewed focus on 'crime control' and the more punitive trend in sentencing of the last 30 years. However, an increase in the use of non-financial bail options is a realistic goal. Another option that would reduce the number of defendants held in pretrial detention, although not as aggressive, is to reduce the amount of cash bail set by the court, particularly for cases involving low-level offenders. The findings of this study demonstrate that the decision points in the criminal justice system are connected and that defendants held in pretrial detention plead guilty quickly. Therefore, any correction of flaws at the pretrial stage could greatly improve criminal case processing as a whole.

## CONCLUSION AND FUTURE RESEARCH

The main finding of the current study is that pretrial detention has a strong impact on guilty pleas and more specifically, the timing of such pleas. There are some limitations to the current study that should be considered when evaluating the results. This study utilized a sample of felony cases. The New Jersey CDC collected bail data for misdemeanor cases but did not track the cases through the entire criminal process and in many instances, there was no information beyond the bail decision. Therefore, it was not possible to analyze these cases. Future research should include an examination of misdemeanor cases.

The data did not contain information regarding the type of evidence involved in each case. For example, Albonetti (1990) found that the presence of confession, eye-witness and other physical evidence significantly impacted plea decisions. More recently, with advances in technology, forensic evidence has become more common in criminal investigations. However, as Strom and Hickman (2010) explain, the high demand for forensic evidence analysis has led to a substantial backlog in crime laboratory capabilities, which may result in what they refer to as 'justice delayed' in the criminal courts. Unfortunately, our data did not contain indicators of evidence type but future research would do well to consider the impact of evidence in plea negotiations.

This study consisted primarily of quantitative analyses supplemented with observations of bail hearings and by interviews with members of the courtroom work group. Future research on this topic would also benefit from more qualitative research. Kellough and Wortley (2002) also combined research methods and in doing so interviewed pretrial detainees. Observations and interviews certainly help to highlight the findings of these studies and also provide invaluable information that cannot be expressed solely by examining the numbers. To this end, Ostrom and Hanson (1999) included a comprehensive analysis of factors internal to the court. Future research should also incorporate measures of the courtroom culture and organization as these factors play a role in timing of case dispositions as well.

Finally, this study sought to examine the impact of pretrial detention on guilty pleas. Future research should also seek to do the same and when possible, studies should examine the effect of pretrial outcomes on all subsequent decision points in a case. A substantial body of literature has amassed on sentencing and several important studies have examined bail decisions and outcomes; however, very little research has addressed the factors that affect the plea bargaining process. This study was conducted to fill the gap in knowledge on this topic and to highlight the impact of bail on subsequent stages of the process. The findings here suggest that early decisions may just be the most important ones.

## Notes

1 Johnson (2003) uses a four-category measure of conviction type which includes negotiated plea, non-negotiated plea, bench trial and jury trial in his analysis of disparities in sentencing departures.

2 While we do not have data containing the precise time from case inception to indictment, we note that the average time to case disposition in this sample is 210 days or approximately seven months, which is considerably shorter than the ten-month nationwide average.

3 There are very few of these cases in our sample.

4 We note that this statement was expressed as an opinion by a judge who has since retired. It was later suggested that this judge might have been referring to cases involving an *Alford* plea (as enunciated in *North Carolina v. Alford*), where the defendant enters a guilty plea without actually admitting guilt and thereby preserving his/her claims of innocence; however, we did not make this inference given the context of the interview and the judge did not mention *Alford* pleas at any time during the course of the interview. Although there is no way to know the actual percentage of innocent defendants who plead guilty, some scholars in the field believe that false guilty pleas are very rare (Hoffman, 2007; McConville & Baldwin, 1981).

5 Another possible explanation relates to guilt. As pointed out by Bibas (2004), guilty defendants usually know that they are guilty. Therefore, they are aware of the potential evidence that can be used against them at a trial, thus placing them in a better position to predict trial outcomes when compared with similarly situated innocent defendants. The defendant who is able to make this calculation might have a stronger incentive to accept a guilty plea.

## NOTES ON CONTRIBUTORS

Meghan Sacks, PhD, is an Assistant Professor and Director of Criminology in the Department of Social Sciences and History at Fairleigh Dickinson University. Her research interests include bail reform, plea bargaining, sentencing policy, and correctional program evaluations.

Alissa R. Ackerman, PhD, is an Assistant Professor of Criminal Justice in the Department of Social Work at the University of Washington, Tacoma. Her research and publications focus on US sex offender policy and management and the impact of registration, community notification, and residency restrictions on offender reintegration. She is currently involved in a national study of US state sex offender registries.

## References

Albonetti, C.A. (1990). Race and the probability of pleading guilty. *Journal of Quantitative Criminology, 6*, 315–334.

Alshuler, A.W. (1979). Plea bargaining and its history. *Law and Society Review, 13*, 211–245.

Bibas, S. (2004). Plea bargaining outside the shadow of trial. *Harvard Law Review, 117*, 2463–2547.

Brereton, D., & Casper, J.D. (1981–1982). Does it pay to plead guilty: Differential sentencing and the functioning of the criminal courts. *Law and Society Review, 16*, 45–70.

Bureau of Justice Statistics (BJS). (2006). *Compendium of Federal Justice Statistics, 2004*. Washington, DC: US Department of Justice. Retrieved from http://bjs.ojp.usdoj.gov/ index.cfm?ty=pbdetail&iid=564.

Bureau of Justice Statistics (BJS). (2008). *Jail statistics*. Washington, DC: US Department of Justice. Retrieved from http://www.ojp.usdoj.gov/bjs/jails.htm.

Church, T.W.Jr. (1982). The 'Old and the New' conventional wisdom of court delay. *Justice System Journal, 7,* 395–412.

Church, T.W.Jr. (1986). Examining local legal culture. *American Bar Foundation Research Journal, 3,* 449–518.

Church, T.W. Jr., Carlson, A., Lee, J., & Tan, T. (1978). *Justice delayed: The pace of litigation in urban trial courts.* Williamsburg, VA: National Center for State Courts.

Clynch, E.J., & Neubauer, D.W. (1981). Trial courts as organizations: A critique and synthesis. *Law and Policy Quarterly, 3,* 69–94.

Demuth, S. (2003). Racial and ethnic differences in pretrial release decisions and outcomes: A comparison of Hispanic, black and white felony arrestees. *Criminology, 41,* 873–907.

Demuth, S., & Steffensmeier, D. (2004). The impact of gender and race-ethnicity in the pre-trial release process. *Social Problems, 51,* 222–242.

Engen, R.L., & Steen, S. (2000). The power to punish: Discretion and sentencing reform in the war on drugs. *American Journal of Sociology, 105,* 1357–1395.

Feeley, M.M. (1979). *The process is the punishment.* New York: Russell Sage Foundation.

Flemming, R., Nardulli, P., & Eisenstein, J. (1987). The timing of justice in felony trial courts. *Law and Policy, 9,* 179–206.

Frenzel, E.D., & Ball, J.D. (2007). Effects of individual characteristics on plea negotiations under sentencing guidelines. *Journal of Ethnicity in Criminal Justice, 5,* 59–82.

Gottfredson, M.R., & Gottfredson, D.M. (1990). *Decision making in criminal justice: Toward the rational exercise of discretion* (2nd ed.). New York: Plenum.

Hoffman, M.B. (2007). The myth of factual innocence. *Chicago-Lent Law Review, 82,* 663–690.

Johnson, B. (2003). Racial and ethnic disparities in sentencing departures across modes of conviction. *Criminology, 41,* 449–490.

Katz, C.M., & Spohn, C.C. (1995). The effect of race and gender on bail outcomes: A test of an interactive model. *American Journal of Criminal Justice, 19,* 161–184.

Kellough, G., & Wortley, S. (2002). Remand for plea: Bail decisions and plea bargaining as commensurate conditions. *British Journal of Criminology, 42,* 186–210.

Kurlychek, M., & Johnson, B. (2004). The juvenile penalty: A comparison of juvenile and young adult sentencing outcomes in criminal court. *Criminology, 42,* 485–515.

Kycelhahn, T., & Cohen, T.P. (2008). *State court processing statistics: Felony defendants in large urban counties, 2004.* Bureau of Justice Statistics. Washington, DC: US Department of Justice.

Luskin, M.L., & Luskin, R. C. (1986). Why so fast, why so slow?: Explaining case processing time. *The Journal of Criminal Law and Criminology, 77,* 190–214.

Mcconville, M., & Baldwin, J. (1981). *Courts, prosecution and conviction.* Oxford: Oxford Clarendon Press; Oxford University Press.

McCoy, C. (1993). *Politics and plea bargaining: Victim's rights in California.* Philadelphia, PA: University of Pennsylvania Press.

McCoy, C. (2005). Plea bargaining as coercion: The trial penalty and plea bargaining reform. *Criminal Law Quarterly, 50,* 1–41.

McCoy, C. (2007). Caleb was right: Pretrial decisions determine mostly everything. *Berkeley Journal of Criminal Law, 12*, 135–149.

Mertler, C.A., & Vannatta, R.A. (2005). *Advanced and multivariate statistical methods: Practical application and interpretation* (2nd ed.). Glendale: Pyrczak.

Meyer, J.A., & Gray, T. (1997). Drunk drivers in the courts: Legal and extra-legal factors affecting pleas and sentences. *Journal of Criminal Justice, 25*, 155–163.

Ostrom, B.J., & Hanson, R.A. (1999). *Efficiency, timeliness, and quality: A new perspective from nine state criminal trial courts.* Washington, DC: National Institute of Justice and the State Justice Institute.

Schlesinger, T. (2005). Racial and ethnic disparity in pretrial criminal processing. *Justice Quarterly, 22*, 170–192.

Schulhofer, S.S. (1984). Is plea bargaining inevitable? *Harvard Law Review, 97*, 1037–1107.

Smith, D.A. (1984). The plea bargaining controversy. *Journal of Criminal Law and Criminology, 77*, 949–968.

Spohn, C. (1991). Decision making in sexual assault cases: Do Black and female judges make a difference? *Women and Criminal Justice, 2*, 83–105.

Spohn, C., & Holleran, D. (2000). The imprisonment penalty paid by young, unemployed black and Hispanic male offenders. *Criminology, 38*, 281–306.

Strom, K.J., & Hickman, M.J. (2010). Unanalyzed evidence in law enforcement agencies: A national examination of forensic processing in police departments. *Criminology and Pub-lic Policy, 9*, 381–404.

Uhlman, T.M., & Walker, N.D. (1980). He takes some of my time: I take some of his: An analysis of judicial sentencing patterns in jury cases. *Law and Society Review, 14*, 323–341.

Vera Institute of Justice. (1977). *Felony arrests: Their prosecution and disposition in New York city courts*. New York: Longman.

Ulmer, J., & Bradley, M. (2006). Variation in trial penalties among serious violent offenses. *Criminology, 44*, 631–670.

Walsh, A. (1990). Standing trial versus copping a plea: Is there a penalty? *Journal of Con-temporary Criminal Justice, 6*, 226–236.

Western, B. (2006). *Punishment and inequality in America*. New York: Russell Sage Foundation.

## Cases cited

*Barker v. Wingo*, 407 US 514 (1972).
*North Carolina v. Alford*, 400 US 25 (1970).
*State v. Farrell*, 320 NJ Super. 425 (App. Div. 1999).
*State v. Szima*, 70 NJ 196 (1976).

# Chapter 3

# JUSTICE, PRIVILEGE, AND IDENTITY

## INTRODUCTION

Chapter 1 introduced us to the critical examination of justice, emphasizing subjectivity, positionality, and reflexivity. Chapter 2 put these concepts into practice, using them to expose gaps in justice, many of which related to access to resources. In Chapter 3, we examine these gaps in close detail, widening our discussion of inequality through a focus on the concepts of *social stratification, privilege,* and *oppression. Social stratification* categorizes and ranks individuals based on assessments of their value to society, resulting in a hierarchy of status. In justice terms, social stratification is an unequal distribution of the rewards and burdens of society. In the social stratification game, there are advantages to being at the top (or to being at least positioned above others), and disadvantages to being toward the bottom. The impact of this difference in status can be understood in terms of privilege and oppression. *Privilege* is simply the advantages that people benefit from in society as a result of their social status (Hurlbert, 2011). The flip side of this is *social exclusion,* defined as the disadvantages that are experienced as a result of social status. When social exclusion is experienced continually by a group of people, the end result is *oppression.*

## SOCIAL STRATIFICATION

Social stratification is the root of all privilege, social exclusion, and oppression. Although people clearly don't walk around with value labels affixed to their foreheads like price tags, it goes without saying that in our society, certain individuals and groups are valued more than others. The process that forms this hierarchy of social value is social stratification, defined by Hurlbert (2011, p. 68) as "the systematic process by which individuals, groups and places are categorized and ranked on a scale of social worth." Despite the simplicity of this definition, social stratification is actually quite complex. We, as a society, do not think and act as an undifferentiated mass. Our diverse society reflects myriad culturally and individually determined sets of values and ideas about the social world, borne of different perspectives and life experiences. Consequently, there is no exact consensus on who is valued or devalued in society, or how much an individual or group is valued. This value is context-dependent, subject to change over time and space, and is often predicated on any number of intersecting *statuses* (more on that later).

So, if we can't determine who is valued or how much, what is the point of talking about social stratification? Because social stratification is about relative, rather than absolute, value, it is a useful tool for understanding how some individuals or groups are positioned in society in relation to others. Let's start with a clear-cut example: wealth. In our society, the wealthy are valued more than the poor. This is evident in the way that we talk about and treat the poor, whether through the dehumanizing language of "bum" or "hobo" or the dearth of both formal and informal social support for people at or near the poverty line. It is just as evident in reverse, in the way that we valorize the rich. Take Donald Trump's unpredictable success in the 2016 presidential primary season. Despite being a political newcomer who had never run for, let alone served in, public office, Trump had already beaten out his competitors for the Republican nomination well before the last primary election took place. Despite his complete lack of political experience and his limited adherence to traditional Republican values, Trump had social status on his side: he was incredibly wealthy and not timid about equating his financial success to the type of power and authority necessary to lead a country.

In this example, Trump's economic status garnered significant social status for him. It is important to remember, however, that social stratification is not the same as economic stratification—even though the two are closely related. Being at the bottom of the SES ladder means you not only have relatively little money, but also that you have less power, authority, responsibility, and self-determination. There are many other factors that can affect someone's location on the social hierarchy—things that have little to do with money (e.g., race, gender, sexual orientation, religion), but have major implications for SES. For instance, gender inequality results in a number of economic inequalities for women, from the "pink tax" experienced by women as they purchase unnecessarily expensive (and unnecessarily pink) "female" versions of everyday products, such as pens and razors, to the gender wage gap that pays women 79 cents on the dollar compared with men (Institute for Women's Policy Research, 2016). It also contributes to other forms of social disadvantage or oppression that cannot be easily monetized, such as domestic violence, sexual objectification, decreased credibility as witnesses in court, and limits on reproductive rights.

The concept that captures these varied forms of injustice is *social status*: the rank or position that someone occupies within the social hierarchy. Status is not something innate or inherent to a person; it is a quality that can be understood only in relation to others in a society. There are two types of status: ascribed and achieved. *Ascribed status* is based on innate factors over which individuals have no control, for instance their race, sexual orientation, or age. *Achieved status* is based on behavior or characteristics over which people do have some measure of control—factors such as income, education, and even religion. Statuses are more than just attributes or characteristics, however. In order for an attribute to also be a status, it must have some bearing on position within the social hierarchy.

For instance, attributes such as "funny" or "athletic" are not considered statuses, because they have no direct implication for the relative value attached to those traits and the position this affords someone in the social stratification order. Although humor and athleticism can produce statuses through career choice and attractiveness to others, for example, they themselves are not statuses.

Because status value is relative, there is no absolute numerical value attached to different status labels (remember—no price tags on our foreheads). But it isn't difficult to sort people roughly into hierarchical groups along these dimensions. For instance, we know that people of Christian faith occupy a higher status than people of Muslim faith in our society. Muslim Americans face a great deal of suspicion and prejudice in the United States, particularly in the years since the terrorist attacks of September 11, 2001. Of course, we know that this does not mean that Christians are inherently better or more valuable to society than are Muslims; in fact, social stratification has absolutely no bearing on inherent worth. It simply reflects that certain statuses are valued more in society, relative to others. *Status value*, then, can be understood as the socially assigned value that some characteristics impart to those who embody them. The result is a society in which some people are regarded and treated as more valuable (Hurlbert, 2011).

Because status value is socially assigned, the ranking system of statuses (social stratification) rests on the perceived value of a status, rather than an actual measure of social value. Social status is highly context-dependent; not all social statuses are valued equally everywhere. Although being a woman is not valued in our society, it could confer higher social standing in matriarchal societies, and even in the context of certain professions, such as nursing or modeling, in our society. Context can also change over time; the status value assigned to being identified as homosexual in the 1950s was quite different from the status value that members of the LGBTQIA (lesbian, gay, bisexual, transgender, queer, intersex, and asexual) community experience today. Although LGBTQIA people still do not enjoy high status in our society (as evident by the many rights that have still not been extended to this group and the lingering stigma attached to LGBTQIA identity), this is a far cry from the days of criminalization of same-sex affection in public and police raids of gay bars.

Now that you have a handle on what status is, let's make things a bit more complicated by introducing the concept of identity. *Identity* is simply a person's conception and expression of his or her individuality or group affiliations. Identity labels reflect a person's sense of who they are in ways that matter to them. Some common identity labels are adopted by individuals to claim membership in a group along the lines of race, ethnicity, nationality, gender, sex, sexual orientation, religion, and ability. Here's where it gets tricky: identity labels and status labels can often use the same words (e.g., bisexual, atheist, White, deaf, elderly). Further, both can be ascribed or achieved, and both can be used to link an individual to a larger social group. The difference between identity and status is easy to discern with a little context, however. Identities are chosen and adopted by individuals to define themselves and connect them to larger communities and groups within society. Status is assigned by others based on assumptions or perceptions of individuals' characteristics and their presumed societal worth.

To illustrate, let's extend our earlier example of the gender gap to the discussion of status and identity. "Woman" is both an identity label and a status. It is an important part of many people's sense of who they are as individuals, and can provide a powerful feeling of community. The authors of this book, for instance, both identify as women. Identifying as a woman unites us as part of a larger group that shares similarity of experience and perspective (to a degree). "Woman" is also a status, however—one with implications that go far beyond the "pink tax" discussed earlier. Being a woman in our society means being situated below men in the social stratification order.

This is particularly impactful in terms of economic standing, where gender inequality becomes apparent at a shockingly early age. One study revealed a two-hour difference in the amount of time girls and boys spend doing chores in the home on a weekly basis (Stafford, 2007). Further, the types of chores boys are assigned (e.g., mowing the lawn) tend to be valued more than those girls are assigned (e.g., laundry), garnering more "wages" in terms of allowance as well as greater actual wages when children age and take on part-time jobs. This not only provides evidence of the early application of status value along gender lines, but also helps us understand the gendered division of labor in the current workforce. Domestic jobs tend to be female-dominated, whereas jobs outside the home remain male-dominated in terms of gender representation, career advancement, and pay disparities. Although these disparities can trace their roots back to childhood, they have significant cumulative effects over time. Over the course of the average American woman's career, she loses $434,000 due to the gender wage gap (Arons, 2008).

## PRIVILEGE, OPPRESSION, AND SOCIAL EXCLUSION

In a socially stratified society, some groups benefit at the expense of others. Because social stratification advantages some and disadvantages others, it results in an imbalance of rewards and burdens. This unequal distribution of rewards and burdens engenders vastly different individual and collective experiences based on status. Those who receive an excess of rewards due to their status experience *privilege*. Those who experience an excess of burdens experience *oppression*. Privilege means something slightly different in the context of social justice than in everyday life. Because privilege confers special advantages that are unearned, many people consider these advantages to therefore be undeserved. Consequently, notions of responsibility and blame easily become implicated discussions of privilege. Given this, it is understandable that people may become upset when others point out their privilege. Bovy (2014, p. 2) contends that "to call someone 'privileged' is to say that his or her successes are undeserved. It's a personal insult posing as social critique." In terms of social justice, however, the benefits and rewards of privilege are not the problem—so eliminating them (or making people feel guilty about them) does not help to achieve justice. In a just society, the goal should not be to reduce everyone's status to the lowest common denominator, leveling the playing field so that all people have an equally low number of both rewards and burdens. Instead, the trappings of privilege—the economic security, social approval, and positive regard that come along with high status—are things that everyone should be able to expect, rather than something that only high status individuals can enjoy. The problem with privilege isn't that some people are treated that way... it's that some people are not.

The people who are not treated well in society by virtue of their low social status experience the flip side of privilege: oppression. Oppression can take many forms: lack of access to material wealth and income, poor health outcomes, increased risk of victimization, entanglement with the CJS, and civic disenfranchisement or denied opportunities to participate in society. Some of the most powerful impacts of oppression fall into this last category, which can be captured under the larger umbrella of *social exclusion*, or "the inability of certain groups or individuals to participate fully... due to structural inequalities in access to social, economic, political, and cultural resources arising out of the often intersecting experiences of oppression relating to race, gender, class, disability, sexual orientation, and immigrant status" (Galabuzi, 2006, p. 173). We could add to Galabuzi's list any number of additional statuses associated with social exclusion: gender identity, religion, employment, felony status, etc. If this sounds familiar, it should. Social exclusion is the inverse of *social opportunity*, which we discussed in Chapter 2.

Because social stratification is such a normalized and expected part of our society, it can be difficult to see the privilege, oppression, and social exclusion that it creates. Although privilege has become something of a buzzword lately, it is very easy for privilege to go unnoticed in daily life. For instance, imagine yourself heading to your next class. What did you picture? Did you stroll into the building, climb a flight of stairs, open the door, and take your regular seat? If so, you just imagined a mundane, everyday scenario of relatively hidden privilege. The privilege of being able to easily and conveniently access buildings of all varieties—whether for school or just to buy groceries—is something that many able-bodied individuals take for granted. For those who don't experience this type of privilege (e.g., people with limited mobility from disability or injury), its counterpart, social exclusion, is far more evident. Although legislation such as the 1990 Americans with Disabilities Act has brought us a long way in terms of lessening societal burdens on people with disabilities, there are still many ways in which daily life is more onerous for people of different ability levels.

## INTERSECTIONALITY

As we have discussed, privilege is distributed along a range of axes (e.g., gender, race, sexual orientation) and attached to a number of different social statuses (e.g., female, Asian, straight). *Intersectionality* is the idea that where these statuses overlap has interesting implications for either the compounding of privilege and oppression, or their attenuation. You may have noticed the phrase "intersecting experiences of oppression" in the definition of social exclusion provided previously.

Individuals are multifaceted and can claim many identities at once; similarly, they may embody many statuses at once. Some of these statuses may confer privilege, whereas others connote disadvantage and oppression. In some cases, privilege can be attenuated (or complicated) by marginalization or oppression along other axes.

Take, for instance, the statuses mentioned at the beginning of this section; when these are all shared by an individual (in this case, a straight Asian woman), *intersectionality* helps us understand how these axes come together to form a unique position in the social world, and thus in the stratification order. Variation along any of these axes would result in a slightly different positionality with different associated status. For instance, if we change the individual's gender, we may now be talking about a straight Asian man, who has higher social status than a straight Asian woman. If we alter the individual's sexual orientation, we could be talking about an Asian lesbian, who would have lower social status than a straight Asian woman and a far lower social status than a straight Asian man. These intersectional statuses can be impactful in all arenas of life, from daily interactions on the bus, to employment opportunities, to dating prospects.

Coston and Kimmel (2012) illustrate the complexity of intersectional status through an examination of what it means to be a disabled man, a gay man, and a poor man in our society. In the United States, there is an idealized, normative standard for men that is referred to as "hegemonic masculinity." According to hegemonic masculinity, men are expected to be providers who are brave, dependable, strong, powerful, stable, and logical. Coston and Kimmel explore the ways in which men who hold marginalized statuses in terms of ability, sexual orientation, and class manage the tension between their gender and hegemonic masculinity's expectations for its embodiment. According to the authors, men have a choice to conform to the dominant view of masculinity and make attempts to minimize their difference from other men, or to resist hegemonic masculinity by developing a masculinity of resistance. Resistance can take a number of forms: exaggerating and embracing the difference from ideal masculinity, or embracing a militant male chauvinism that focuses on both the difference and superiority of their identity (Coston & Kimmel, 2012).

Key to understanding Coston and Kimmel's analysis is the idea of gender as something that is accomplished, rather than something that is natural and constant. This idea, referred to as the "doing gender" framework (West & Zimmerman, 1987), separates maleness from masculinity. In Coston and Kimmel's examples, gay, disabled, and poor men are no less male from a biological perspective, but are less masculine by virtue of their marginalized statuses with regard to sexual orientation, ability, and class. Because gay men are viewed as effeminate, disabled men viewed as less physically powerful, and poor men viewed as less capable providers, their accomplishment of masculinity is markedly different from the heterosexual, able-bodied, financially stable ideal. Similar dynamics can be seen when low status men are unable to achieve the culturally idealized "provider" role prescribed by hegemonic masculinity. When legitimate opportunities to earn a living are absent or difficult to come by, as is often the case in areas of concentrated disadvantage, for men of color, or when the economy is weak, for instance, some men opt for alternative paths such as criminal behavior to achieve the same result (Messerschmidt, 1993). The accomplishment of hegemonic masculinity through crime and violence is well documented among various age groups, across races and ethnicities, and even in various countries.

# RACE, RACISM, AND INJUSTICE

To better understand and address social stratification in the context of criminal justice, we must have a working understanding of race and racism. Racism plays a major role in producing, maintaining, and compounding injustice within the criminal justice system, and in society as a whole. Racism is a complex phenomenon to understand, and can be better understood by breaking it down into two main types: *individual* and *systemic racism.* The type of racism that typically comes to mind first is individual racism. *Individual racism* is when a person holds prejudicial views and/or acts in a discriminatory manner based on those beliefs. It's important to emphasize that no action is required for individual racism to occur; racist thoughts are racism, too.

Individual racism can take different forms. One form is overtly biased or prejudicial thoughts, statements, or actions. This type of overt bias can be seen in ways small and large—in playground taunts and purses clenched tight, in the burning of crosses and the bombing of churches. It is clear that, over time, our country has become less overtly, individually racist. This does not mean that racism is dying out, however. It may simply be changing form. Covert racism can be seen in everyday interactions, and is the result of either intentional (albeit veiled) racism, or implicit bias that individuals may not even realize they harbor. Even though these acts of individual racism may seem like the personal injustices that we discussed in Chapter 1, they are often linked to larger social injustices in the form of systemic racism.

*Systemic racism* is defined by Hurlbert (2011, p. 105) as "a form of oppression that excludes some groups of people from opportunities in society on the basis of their race or ethnicity." In the language of social stratification, systemic racism is the oppression that results from the low status assigned to people of certain races. In our society, it is clear that White Americans are at the very top of the social stratification order, with people of color located beneath them. White Americans have more prestige, hold more positions of power, and have greater access to opportunity than any other racial group in the United States. This has been the case historically since the arrival of Europeans on the shores of North America (then called "Turtle Island" by many indigenous people), and is perpetuated still. For instance, the long-standing, historical nature of racism has led to the creation of the dominant White middle class through access to resources such as home ownership, college education, health care, and safe neighborhoods.

One crucial form of systemic racism to consider in the context of criminal justice is *institutional racism.* Institutional racism occurs when racist ideas are reinforced by our social and political institutions. In its most extreme form, institutional racism becomes codified in policy—literally written into our laws.

Without a doubt, many of our country's most overtly racist policies have been eliminated. Take, for instance, the denial of voting rights. By the mid-1870s, all U.S. citizens—including newly emancipated African American citizens—were guaranteed the right to vote by the 14th and 15th amendments to the U.S. Constitution. The 1965 Voting Rights Act strengthened these constitutional guarantees by prohibiting all discrimination in voting procedures and detailing specific provisions for monitoring and compliance.

Less visible, however, are the policies still in place that make voting difficult or impossible for certain groups, thereby marginalizing if not eliminating their civic voice. In recent years, the Supreme Court has steadily weakened the Voting Rights Act through piecemeal rulings striking down many of its provisions. The result has been the disenfranchisement of many voters, particularly voters of color. As polling locations in low-income neighborhoods and communities of color have closed, and voter registration requirements have been made more onerous, African American citizens are once again finding themselves in the same position they were in 50 years ago—a position that bears a disheartening resemblance to one century prior, when voting rights had yet to be granted. Thus, the modern forms of systemic, covert discrimination are inextricably linked to the overtly racist laws of our nation's past.

The claim is sometimes made that we live in a "post-racial society," indicating that racism is a social problem of a bygone era, and that race is simply not a relevant issue any longer. This idea is best exemplified by statements such as "I don't see race" (also known as "color blindness") or the reminder "... but we had a Black president." If race no longer matters, how do we explain persistent disparities among racial groups? Race still affects people's experiences and outcomes (i.e., access to opportunity) to a great degree, and therefore remains an important factor in addressing oppression and injustice. If we act as though race does not affect opportunities when all evidence points to the contrary, we are failing to acknowledge the existence of injustice, and thus perpetuating injustice ourselves.

## WORKING TOWARD SOCIAL INCLUSION

Hopefully, the chapters in the first section of this book have opened your eyes to some of the injustices around you that you may not have noticed before. And it's all right that you haven't seen them. Privilege, oppression, and social exclusion are often invisible to those who do not experience them; this is a function of ethnocentrism. Recall that our perspectives are shaped by our positionality in society (which encompasses our identities, statuses, and location in the social stratification order). But now you know about them, and there's no going back. So it's time to start to think concretely about how to work toward social inclusion.

What does it mean to start working toward social inclusion? Social inclusion assumes equality among people, addresses the manifestations of social inequalities that threaten social cohesion (the bonds that link members of groups), and attempts to include the excluded (Galabuzi, 2006). These directives for social inclusion are somewhat vague, but we can at least try to make the starting point more concrete. To get to the point where we "assume equality," individuals will have to examine racist thoughts or feelings and confront them. Only through critical, reflexive self-examination can we recognize and address any thoughts that reinforce oppression. This is obviously just a starting point—but it is an important one. Without reflexively analyzing our own personal assumptions, biases and prejudices, we will have no way of knowing how we are reproducing or reinforcing oppression.

Another path toward social inclusion is to engage in what Anzaldúa (1987) calls "open-hearted listening": listening to people who have been excluded in ways that acknowledge their experience even though we may not fully understand it and value their perspective even though it is different from our own. This approach requires people in privileged positions to give up some power and be willing to follow the leadership of others, particularly those most affected by oppression and social exclusion. Being respectful of marginalized people's right to direct the conversation around issues that face them is paramount to helping create more justice.

These two strategies will certainly not achieve justice on their own. At this point in the book, we could present a handful of hypothetical examples of justice issues and how to begin to address them. Instead, we leave you with the first section of the book under your belt, armed with the two suggestions given previously, and direct you to the semester-long justice project assignment at the end of this chapter.

## References

Anzaldúa, G. (1987). *Borderlands/La Frontera: The new Mestizo.* San Francisco, CA: Aunt Lute Books.

Arons, J. (2008). *Lifetime losses: The career wage gap.* Washington, D.C.: Center for American Progress Action Fund.

Bovy, P. M. (2014). Checking privilege checking. *The Atlantic Monthly,* May 7, 2014. Retrieved from http://www.theatlantic.com/politics/archive/2014/05/check-your-check-your-privilege/361898/.

Coston, B.M., & Kimmel, M. (2012). Seeing privilege where it isn't: Marginalized masculinities and the intersectionality of privilege. *Journal of Social Issues, 68*(1), 97–111.

Galabuzi, G.E. (2006). *Canada's economic apartheid: The social exclusion of racialized groups in the new century.* Toronto, ON: Canadian Scholar's Press.

Hurlbert, M.A. (Ed.). (2011). *Pursuing justice: An introduction to justice studies.* Nova Scotia, Canada: Fernwood Publishing.

Institute for Women's Policy Research. (2016). *The gender wage gap and public policy.* Washington, D.C.: Institute for Women's Policy Research.

Messerschmidt, J. (1993). *Masculinities and crime: Critique and reconceptualization of theory.* Lanham, MD: Rowman & Littlefield Publishers.

Stafford, F. P. (2007). *Time, money and who does the laundry.* Ann Arbor, MI: Institute for Social Research.

West, C., & Zimmerman, D. H. (1987). Doing gender. *Gender & Society, 1*(2), 125–151.

## Selected Readings

Jones, T.R., & Kingshott, B.F. (2016). A feminist analysis of the American criminal justice system's response to human trafficking, *Criminal Justice Studies, 29*(3), 272–287.

Sexton, L., Jenness, V., & Sumner, J.M. (2009). Where the margins meet: A demographic assessment of transgender men's prisons. *Justice Quarterly, 27*(6), 835–866.

## Discussion Questions/Writing Assignments

1. Write down five identity labels that apply to you. What kind of statuses do those identities afford you? What are some of the ways that your social status has affected your access to opportunities?
2. Revisit your "Who Am I?" assignment from the beginning of the semester. Which of the characteristics that you wrote down are statuses? Which are merely attributes? Do you rely more on attributes or statuses to conceptualize your identity? Why do you think this is?
3. How have you experienced privilege and/or oppression in your life? Relate your experiences to our definitions of justice and injustice.
4. Which is easier to address: individual racism or systemic racism? Which is more important to address? Discuss.
5. Provide an example of institutional racism that has literally been written into law or policy. It doesn't have to be explicit—for instance, it can be a policy that had a decidedly racist intent and/or impact, even without the explicit mention of race.
6. What are some possible sources of unintentional or accidental racism? What can we do to combat these forms of racism?
7. Sometimes, when two identities intersect, they can have an unexpected effect on status. For instance, even though being a woman and being gay are both generally associated with lower status, being a lesbian might temper some of the low status of being gay, paradoxically putting lesbians above gay men in the social hierarchy. Why is this? Is this a good thing?
8. What are the various ways that social stratification affects the issue of human trafficking? Be sure to consider the social status of trafficking victims and offenders, the impact of this status on criminal justice interventions into human trafficking, and the larger, gendered structure of our society.
9. In *Where the Margins Meet*, Sexton et al. present the many intersecting statuses of transgender women in men's prisons. Discuss some of the implications of their findings for justice, using the vocabulary of Part I of this book.

# ACTIVITIES/ASSIGNMENTS

## Comedy Sketches

The following clips use comedy to highlight how White people, as the majority racial group, may be unaware or insensitive about race. Watch the clips and consider whether comedy is a good approach to understanding more about privilege and oppression in society. Why or why not?

https://www.youtube.com/watch?v=lJKIQXO0YqM
http://www.youtube.com/watch?v=A1zLzWtULig
http://www.youtube.com/watch?v=XnFUDx3wC-Y
http://www.youtube.com/watch?v=PMJI1Dw83Hc
http://www.youtube.com/watch?v=xdyin6uipy4

## Other Types of Privilege

Watch http://www.cnn.com/2013/02/17/opinion/russell-model-genetic-lottery/index.html?hpt=hp_c1
How does this talk by Model Cameron Russell add to the discussion on privilege?

## Harvard Implicit Association Test

Complete any one Harvard Implicit Association Test found at https://implicit.harvard.edu/implicit/selectatest.html. These tests offer a unique way to look at status. The goal of the test is to measure unconscious or automatic biases, which may be one of the roots of stereotypes and prejudice in our society. What did you learn from this experience?

## Confronting Our Biases

https://www.ted.com/talks/verna_myers_how_to_overcome_our_biases_walk_boldly_toward_them?language=en#
https://www.youtube.com/watch?v=9VGbwNI6Ssk&feature=youtu.be (watch after doing the implicit bias tests).

## Racist Little Shapes

Run through the "Parable of the Polygons" simulation. What did you learn from it? What implications does this have for justice?
http://ncase.me/polygons/

## The Whiteness Project

Choose three people from the website below and listen to their stories. What did you learn about their experience of whiteness? How was intersectionality evident in their stories? What implications did the stories have for social stratification, privilege, and oppression?

http://www.whitenessproject.org/checkbox

## SEMESTER-LONG JUSTICE PROJECT

Step Three: You chose an area of injustice after reading Chapter 2. How do the concepts of social stratification, status, identity, privilege, and oppression relate to the topic you have chosen? And how does your experience of these concepts (e.g., your social status) inform your understanding of this topic? Write a two-page paper addressing both of these questions.

## ACTIVITIES FOR INSTRUCTOR

http://www.buzzfeed.com/nathanwpyle/this-teacher-taught-his-class-a-powerful-lesson-about-privil#.ih8Bw5vAE

## Garden of Privilege Exercise

Read the following statements to your students. Have them keep track of statements that characterize them. If they agree with four or more of these statements in each category, give them the corresponding color of crayon.

**Red (Race)**

I can choose Band-Aids in "flesh" color and have them more or less match my skin.

I can turn on the TV or open a magazine and see people of my race widely represented.

When I am told about this country's national heritage, I am shown that people of my color made it what it is.

I can be sure that the majority of my professors will be of my race.

I can take a job at a company with an affirmative action policy without having my coworkers assume I got the job because of my race.

**Orange (Religion)**

My place of work or school is closed on my major religious holidays.

I can talk openly about my religious practices without concern for how it will be received by others.

When swearing an oath, I am probably making this oath by placing my hand on the scripture of my religion.

I can travel without others assuming that I put them at risk because of my religion.
My citizenship and immigration status will likely not be questioned, and my background will likely not be investigated, because of my religion.

**Yellow (Sexual Orientation)**
I can be pretty sure my classmates and coworkers will be comfortable with my sexual orientation.
People don't ask why I "chose" my sexual orientation.
No one will ever question whether it is appropriate for me to have children or get married because of my sexual orientation.
I can walk in public with my significant other and not have people stare.
I will be able to sit at my partner's deathbed in a hospital.

**Green (Sex/Gender)**
I do not worry about walking alone at night in a rough neighborhood.
If I choose not to have children, my gender will not be invoked to question my decision.
I can have multiple sexual experiences and be patted on the back and not be called derogatory names.
When people look at me, they don't wonder what my biological sex is.
When I ask to see "the person in charge," odds are I will face a person of my own sex.

**Blue (Class)**
Each student in my high school classroom had his or her own textbook.
My family owned the home that I grew up in.
Where I went to college was not dependent on tuition costs or financial aid.
At least one of my parents has a college degree.
I have travelled internationally.

**Purple (Ability)**
I don't have to worry about being able to enter a building with a staircase.
I can easily complete a test without asking for special accommodation from a teacher.
If I need to move, I can easily be assured of finding a place that I can access easily.
My dietary needs are met at most public locations.
My first language is spoken most places that I go.

Give the students 10-15 minutes to draw as realistic and colorful a garden as they can.
Tell them you will be judging the pictures according to how beautiful and realistic they are. Make your choice or choices (you could choose the top three).
Have a discussion about the winning picture, or top three winners.
What made this picture the "best" or most realistic? Was it more colorful?
Does artistic talent play a role in this drawing being the winner?
How do privilege and talent interact to produce a winning picture?
What happens to those who didn't win? Why didn't they win? What does privilege have to do with it? What about ability/talent?

## Reflection Questions

What were your initial feelings/thoughts about the activity?

Was there anything that was confusing or surprising?

How did you feel when your drawings were being judged? Did you feel this was fair? Was it just?

What types of privilege were reflected in the statements? Are there types of privilege that weren't touched upon in the activity, but should have been?

Did any one type of privilege trump the others in this activity? Is that the case in real life?

How often do you think about privilege in your life? Did seeing it physically help you to understand your privilege differently?

## Selected Reading

# WHERE THE MARGINS MEET

## A Demographic Assessment of Transgender Inmates in Men's Prisons

***Lori Sexton, Valerie Jenness, and Jennifer Macy Sumner***

## INTRODUCTION

A recently released report by The Pew Center on the States (2008) revealed a startling figure: "For the first time, more than one in every 100 adults is now confined in an American jail or prison" (p. 3). This number has received considerable attention from the media, policymakers, academics, activists, and corrections officials alike, at least in part because it dramatically emphasizes mass incarceration in the USA. Growing mass incarceration, in turn, raises a plethora of social, legal, and fiscal issues related to how US prisons have become "warehouses" for a sizeable, and growing, portion of the American population (Tonry, 2004). In the words of Mauer and Chesney-Lind, "[U]ltimately, a society in which mass imprisonment becomes the norm is one in which questions of justice, fairness and access to resources are being altered in ways hitherto unknown" (2002, p. 2).

Mass imprisonment has been accompanied by newfound challenges confronting criminal justice officials charged with managing diverse and changing inmate populations while attending to human rights issues as well as legislative and judicial mandates. In a historical context in which prisons have become "warehouses" for criminals rather than institutions designed to rehabilitate offenders (e.g., Irwin, 2005; Simon & Feeley, 1992; Tonry, 2004), departments of corrections have increasingly had to confront the realities of incarcerating transgender women—biologically male inmates who identify and/or present themselves as female—in men's prisons. From a managerial point of view, these realities include reconsidering intake, screening, and classification processes and other custodial challenges related to medical care, housing, physical presentation, disproportionately high rates of victimization, and litigation resulting in high institutional costs (Blight, 2000; Jenness, Maxson, Matsuda, & Sumner, 2007; Mann, 2006; Petersen, Stephens, Dickey, & Lewis, 1996; Tarzwell, 2006; Tewksbury & Potter, 2005).

Among the millions of people currently incarcerated, transgender inmates have become increasingly visible. Over a decade ago, the U.S. Supreme Court heard a case in which a transgender inmate, Dee Farmer, alleged "deliberate indifference" to her safety. In this case the Court affirmed that prison officials have a duty to protect inmates' rights under the "Cruel and Unusual Punishment" clause of the Eighth Amendment of the U.S. Constitution by protecting them from violence at the hands of other prisoners (*Farmer v. Brennan* [114 S.Ct. 1970 (1994)]).[1] More recently, the issue of conditions of confinement for transgender inmates was made even more visible to the American public in *Cruel and Unusual* (Baus, Hunt, & Williams, 2006). This award-winning documentary follows the lives and stories of a handful of transgender women in men's prisons to reveal the complex nature of their identities as well as the unique challenges they face as prisoners. Bringing mainstream media attention to transgender inmates, more than one corrections agency in the USA has made the news when announcing new policies providing for the treatment of transgender inmates. In 2008, for example, New York corrections made national news when Governor Paterson's office announced a new anti-discrimination policy that allows transgender youth in New York detention centers to wear whatever uniform they choose, be called by whatever name they want, and request (and be considered for) specialized housing (Kates, 2008). More recently, the Washington D.C. Department of Corrections issued a new policy on "Gender Classification and Housing" that will allow for housing placement according to gender identity (Najafi, 2009). Furthermore, in California, State Assemblyman Tom Ammiano (D-13th District) recently introduced a Bill (The LGBT Prisoner Safety Act, AB 382 [2009]) that, if adopted, would require the California Department of Corrections and Rehabilitation (CDCR) to add "self-reported safety concerns related to the sexual orientation and gender identity of the inmate or ward" to the list of "risk factors to be considered" when classifying inmates and wards "in order to prevent inmate and ward sexual violence and to promote inmate and ward safety" (p. 1). At the heart of this legislative proposal, which recently passed the State Senate, is a concern about how best to keep lesbian, gay, bisexual, and transgender inmates and wards safe while incarcerated in California.

In a context in which the judicial decision-makers, the media, elected officials from the executive and legislative branches, and corrections officials are increasingly focused on transgender inmates, there is little empirical social science research devoted to this particular population of inmates. As Tewksbury and Potter (2005) recently concluded, "Despite the fact that transgender individuals are fairly likely to end up in prison… there is very little scholarly information available about transgender inmates" (p. 15-2). While select works examine correctional policies that do and do not address transgender inmates (see Petersen et al., 1996; Tarzwell, 2006; Tewksbury & Potter, 2005), systematic social science work that examines the demographic patterns and lived experiences of this population is, at best, in a nascent state. In 2007, the Sylvia Rivera Law Project, a non-profit group dedicated to providing legal services to transgender, gender non-conforming, and intersexed low-income communities, released a report based on a systematic analysis of first-hand accounts obtained through in-person interviews with legal clients (Sylvia Rivera Law Project, 2007). Also in 2007, research on violence in California correctional facilities by Jenness et al. (2007) revealed that transgender inmates are disproportionately victims of sexual assault. Specifically, comparing the results from in-person interviews with a convenience sample of 39 transgender inmates and a random sample of 322 inmates in California prisons for adult men, Jenness and her colleagues reported that 59% of transgender inmates reported having been sexually assaulted in a California correctional facility in contrast to 4.4% of the random sample of inmates (Jenness et al., 2007). Moreover, incident-level data from this study revealed that when transgender inmates are sexually assaulted in prison by another inmate, the incident is more likely to involve the use of a weapon, yet less likely to evoke medical attention if needed. Through these and other empirical findings, this report makes clear that the prevalence rate of sexual assault for transgender inmates is significantly higher than for their non-transgender counterparts in prison; moreover, transgender inmates experience different institutional interactions and responses than their non-transgender counterparts in prison.

These recently conducted studies are the exception, rather than the rule, when it comes to relying on systematically analyzed empirical data to delineate the demographic parameters of transgender inmates as a uniquely situated prison population. This is surprising given the wealth of information provided through decades of ethnographic research on inmate culture and lives. Although the term "transgender" is absent in most research on prison culture and inmate violence, a well-established literature on inmate culture nonetheless details the characteristics, behaviors, and status of the "punk" and the "queen"—each of whom *could*, presumably, be included in current umbrella understandings of the term "transgender."[2] A queen is an inmate who displays visible feminine characteristics and plays a submissive role to the "men." The queen is often referred to by female pronouns and is generally understood to have presented as feminine/female when outside of prison (Donaldson, 1993, 2003; Fleisher & Krienert, 2009; Sykes, 1958). While not occupying the lowest position within the prison hierarchy, *she* is located not far above the truly despised punk (but see also Coggeshall, 1988; Fleisher & Krienert, 2009; Hensley, Wright, Tewksbury, & Castle, 2003).[3] The punk is distinct from the queen and, from the point of view of inmate culture, occupies a lower status within the prison hierarchy because *he* has been forcibly "turned out" or forced to play the submissive sexual role through force or threat of force.

In their recent work, Fleisher and Krienert (2009) report that "the prison sexual hierarchy does not exist on a simple continuum from homosexual to straight" (p. 66). In light of this finding, they provide rich empirical evidence of crucial distinctions between punks, "true" homosexuals, and queens.[4] True homosexuals, who may or may not present as effeminate, occupy a higher status position in the inmate hierarchy than punks because they were, presumably, homosexual before coming to prison and are thus, presumably, being "true to themselves" in prison. In contrast, punks are despised because they did not have the strength to resist the force or pressures of other inmates and were "turned out" (i.e., became homosexual). Queens, who look, dress, and act as women, have an elevated status compared to punks for several reasons. Most notably, queens are seen as being who they were prior to incarceration and not willing to hide who they are in prison, whereas punks are viewed as lacking respect for themselves as indicated by their "choice" to engage in sexual submission, something they probably would not do outside of prison (Fleisher & Krienert, 2009). This important recent work is careful to delineate the social roles of differentially vulnerable inmate groups within prison culture as well as the roles each type of inmate plays in prison culture (e.g., Fleisher & Krienert, 2009; c.f., Hensley et al., 2003); however, it does not provide a systematic empirical examination of the demographic contours of these groups of inmates (but see Table 5.1. in Fleisher & Krienert, 2009, p. 73).

Similarly, while empirical research that examines the causes and correlates of inmate violence or other inmate issues often includes inmates with non-normative sexual identities, it does not allow for the separate and distinct consideration of transgender inmates.[5] In prison settings, references to sexual and gender identities are frequently conflated and inconsistently used by both inmates and staff. According to Donaldson (1993), "[t]he prisoner subculture fuses sexual and social roles and assigns all prisoners accordingly" (p. 7). Thus, not surprisingly, even as the more established literature on "homosexuality" in inmate culture details the characteristics, behaviors, and status of those who may presumably be considered transgender, we have yet to fully understand this population within a rubric of non-normative gender and sexual identities. Transgender inmates are a unique and empirically underexamined population whose labels and images are subject to interpretation both inside and outside of prison by inmates, researchers, lawmakers, and lay persons alike.

Drawing on official data and original interview data with transgender inmates in prisons for men, the following research provides the first systematic empirical portrayal of a population that is exceptionally vulnerable by virtue of being both transgender and incarcerated. The focus is on demographic and well-being factors that characterize this population in ways that render it distinct from other inmate populations as well as non-incarcerated populations. We begin by detailing the research methodology employed and the data collected. Next, we provide an examination of the demographic characteristics of transgender inmates in California prisons for adult men. We then compare transgender inmates in California prisons for men to the non-incarcerated transgender population, the incarcerated populations of both the USA and California specifically, and the non-incarcerated populations of the USA and California in order to determine whether these populations are comparable or distinct when it comes to a host of demographic and social factors that correlate with victimization and life chances more generally. We do so to address the following overarching, interrelated questions: Are transgender inmates more marginalized than other groups in terms of their basic demographic and social profile? And, if so, how?

## RESEARCH METHODOLOGY AND DATA

This article draws on data collected from a larger study focused exclusively on transgender inmates in California prisons (Jenness, Sexton, & Sumner, 2009; see also, Jenness, in press).[6] As described below, it makes use of both official and original data collected for the purposes of this larger study as well as secondary data on the US population, the California population, the US men's prison population, the California men's prison population, and the transgender population in the community for comparative purposes. We begin this section by defining the target population. Thereafter, we describe the research sites, how we collected original interview data and official data from the CDCR, and how we amassed the best available secondary data to be used for comparative purposes.

## Defining the Target Population

Our focus on transgender inmates immediately raised a dilemma best phrased as a question: Who is transgender in prison and how can we identify transgender inmates in prisons? Varying definitions in the activist and research communities, and a lack of consensus with regard to what transgender means in a prison setting and by what criteria an inmate should be classified as transgender, made this task quite challenging. To further complicate matters, the CDCR, the research site for this work, does not employ an agreed-upon definition of transgender to identify or classify inmates. Also, the most recent and most comprehensive research on prison sexual culture does not provide clear direction along these lines (Fleisher & Krienert, 2009, pp. 63–84).

In light of this morass of real-life ambiguity and lack of clear direction from the literature, in order to collect reliable and valid data in prisons for men, we operationalized transgender by utilizing four specific criteria. For the purposes of this study, a transgender inmate is an inmate in a men's prison who: (1) self-identifies as transgender (or something analogous); (2) presents as female, transgender, or feminine in prison or outside of prison; (3) receives any kind of medical treatment (physical or mental) for something related to how she presents herself or thinks about herself in terms of gender, including taking hormones to initiate and sustain the development of secondary sex characteristics to enhance femininity; or (4) participates in groups for transgender inmates. Meeting any one of these criteria would qualify an inmate for inclusion in this study.[7]

## Selecting Research Sites

The State of California currently has the largest correctional population in the country (Petersilia, 2008; The Pew Center on the States, 2008). When field data collection began, approximately 160,000 adult prisoners were incarcerated in California's 33 prisons.[8] Despite the rising rate at which females are being incarcerated in California (Petersilia, 2006), well over 90% of these inmates are housed in 30 prisons for adult men. Rather than sample transgender inmates from these institutions, we worked collaboratively with CDCR officials to identify and make face-to-face contact with all transgender inmates in California prisons for men in order to obtain data on the population. We asked for all inmates on our lists to be educated[9] for confidential interviews and, once face-to-face with inmates on the list, we asked them if they are transgender.[10] Inmates who met our criteria as described above were invited to participate in the study.

## Collecting Original Interview Data

The field data collection process began in late April 2008 and ended in late June 2008; in eight weeks, the interview team traveled to 27 prisons for adult men in California, met face-to-face with over 500 inmates, and completed interviews with over 300 transgender inmates.[11] The interview instrument included questions about transgender inmates' daily prison life, fear of victimization in prison, perceptions of sexual and non-sexual victimization in prison, personal victimization from sexual and non-sexual assaults in California correctional facilities and in the community, opinions on safety and reporting, and demographics.[12] The shortest interview was less than a half an hour (19 minutes), while the longest extended to just under three hours (2 hours and 55 minutes). The mean duration for interviews was slightly less than one hour (56 minutes). The total amount of live interview time approached 300 hours (294 hours and 6 minutes).

Predictably, there was some sifting and attendant loss of cases from the interview data as we moved from the total number of names provided on all of the lists from 27 prisons for adult men ($n$ = 705) to the number of inmates we actually saw face-to-face at a prison ($n$ = 505) to the number of inmates who met our eligibility requirements for participation ($n$ = 332) to the number of inmates who consented to an interview ($n$ = 316) and the number of inmates who completed a usable interview ($n$ = 315).[13]

There are two potential sources of bias introduced in our data collection strategy. First, there were possibly transgender inmates who were not identified by CDCR officials for inclusion in the study and thus did not appear on our original interview lists. Second, it was the case that many of the inmates who were listed were not transgender (according to our study definition). Our method corrects for error resulting from inmates being on our lists who do not qualify for participation. However, it does not address the opposite source of error: the omission of inmates who qualify for participation in the study from our lists. Fortunately, we have no reason to believe this introduced systematic bias and, in fact, our experience in the field suggests that CDCR officials were—just as we had requested—over-inclusive. This process resulted in a 95% participation rate.[14] This exceptionally high participation rate does not leave much room for consequential bias in the data born of transgender inmates declining to be interviewed. Using age, sex, race/ethnicity, occupational status, and language used in the interview as key interviewer indicators, we found no evidence to suggest that the characteristics of the interviewer had an impact on transgender inmates' willingness to participate in the study.

## Collecting Official Data

We concatenated existing official data retrieved from the CDCR's database on inmates—the Offender Based Information System—to the self-report data described above.[15] To protect the identity of each inmate participating in the research, we assigned each a unique study identification number for the purposes of this project only. This study ID was used to link the interview and official data for each inmate in the study. Official data variables include age, race/ethnicity, mental health status, verified gang membership, custody level, commitment offense, lifer status, and sex offender registration.

## Secondary Data Collection

Finally, for comparative purposes, we retrieved the most comparable data possible on all relevant indicators of social status and welfare across other populations. To do so, we first chose several key demographic and social dimensions on which to compare transgender inmates to other populations, including education and employment, marital status, health, sex work, homelessness, and victimization. We also identified empirical research that examined these variables for each of the following populations: the non-incarcerated transgender population, the incarcerated populations of both California and the USA (in adult men's prisons only), and the non-incarcerated California and USA populations. A total of 27 data sources were ultimately selected for inclusion in the study. These range from decennial Census reports to small-scale studies of transgender health and economic needs conducted by small non-profit organizations, with the methodological rigor and sampling quality of each study informing the ultimate decision for inclusion.

This approach has its limitations, which are largely born of those that are characteristic of secondary data collection more generally. First, the large number of distinct data sources—each with its own particular operationalization of key constructs—results in imperfect comparisons across several dimensions. This is most problematic when differences are evident in the unit of analysis or time frame, or when constructs themselves were differentially operationalized. This limitation was minimized through the selection of sources with data that best approximate measures used for the transgender inmate population in order to maximize validity of comparisons across data. Second, because the study of transgender populations is in a nascent state, several data sources and analyses did not meet the high standards of methodological rigor evident in data for the other populations. In an effort to remedy this, wherever possible multiple measures were used from multiple studies, in order to triangulate the estimates and achieve convergence—or, at the very least, display the breadth in estimates evident in the larger literature. Limitations aside, the official and unofficial data utilized in the next section constitute the best available data given the limited information on this population.

# FINDINGS

To make systematic comparisons between the transgender inmate population and the entire men's prison population in California, we analyzed official data on eight demographic variables: age, race/ethnicity, offense category, custody level, type of life sentence (or not), registered sex offender (or not), verified gang affiliation (or not), and mental health status.[16] Table 3.1 reveals that transgender inmates are distinguishable from the larger population of inmates in prisons for adult men in terms of age, with transgender inmates more represented in the middle ages (36–45);[17] race/ethnicity, with transgender inmates disproportionately White and Black; commitment offense, with transgender inmates disproportionately admitted to prison for property crimes; custody level, with transgender inmates disproportionately classified as Level 3 and Level 4 inmates;[18] sex offender status, with transgender inmates more frequently classified as sex offenders; gang status, with transgender inmates less frequently identified as gang members; and mental health status, with transgender inmates more often classified as CCCMS[19] and EOP.[20] The magnitude of the difference (i.e., the effect size) for all of these dimensions is not large. Transgender inmates and the larger population of inmates in prisons for men are roughly equivalent on only one dimension reported in Table 3.1. Namely, 15.7% of transgender inmates are serving life sentences and 16.9% of inmates in prisons for adult men are serving life sentences. Combined, these findings suggest that the demographic composition of the transgender population is considerably different from the demographic composition of the total population of inmates in prisons for adult men.

Tables 3.2 through 3.6 present a bricolage that expands the domain of comparisons between transgender inmates in California and other populations. It does so in two ways: (1) by making comparisons across more populations, including the US population, the US prison population (men's prisons only), the California prison population (men's prisons only), the transgender community (non-incarcerated), and the transgender population in California prisons for men; and (2) by moving beyond age, race/ethnicity, criminal history, and offender status—standard demographic variables—to consider other variables related to health and welfare, including education and employment, marital status, health status (mental health, substance abuse, and HIV status), participation in sex work, homelessness, and experiences with victimization (sexual and non-sexual).[21] These features of social life serve as a lens through which specific dimensions of the economic and social status of transgender people (in general) and transgender inmates (in particular) are rendered evident.

## EDUCATION AND EMPLOYMENT

A comparison of transgender populations in the community and in prison to their non-transgender counterparts reveals notable differences in terms of education and employment, two important measures of class status. The highest level of educational attainment for 32.4% of the transgender inmates in California prisons is a high school degree or GED, while only 8% have a college degree. This compares favorably to the population of inmates in men's prisons in California and the population of inmates in men's prisons in the USA; however, it does not compare favorably to the transgender community outside of prison, the California population, or the US population (see Table 3.2).

Just over 10% of Americans were unemployed or marginally employed as of August 2008 (U.S. Department of Labor, 2008). This stands in stark contrast to the figures for the US and California men's prison populations one month prior

**Table 3.1** A comparison of select characteristics of the transgender inmate population in CDCR prisons for men and the total population in CDCR prisons for men

| | Total transgender population in CDCR prisons for men | | Total adult population in CDCR prisons for men[1] | |
|---|---|---|---|---|
| | *N* | % | *N* | % |
| *Total* | 332 | 146,360 | | |
| *Age* | | | | |
| Mean | | 38.05 | | 37.69 |
| Median | | 38.50 | | 37.00 |
| SD | | 9.61 | | 11.18 |
| Range | | 19, 63 | | 18, 92 |
| 18–25 | 33 | 9.9 | 21,383 | 14.6 |
| 26–35 | 90 | 27.1 | 46,933 | 32.1 |
| 36–45 | 135 | 40.7 | 40,971 | 28.0 |
| 46+ | 74 | 22.3 | 37,073 | 25.3 |
| *Race/Ethnicity* | | | | |
| Hispanic | 94 | 28.3 | 56,880 | 38.9 |
| White | 93 | 28.0 | 37,954 | 25.9 |
| Black | 115 | 34.6 | 43,451 | 29.7 |
| Asian/Pacific Islander | 3 | .9 | 1,337 | .9 |
| Other | 27 | 8.1 | 6,738 | 4.6 |
| *Offense* | | | | |
| Crimes against persons | 162 | 49.8 | 80,202 | 54.8 |
| Property | 98 | 30.2 | 26,892 | 18.4 |
| Drug | 53 | 16.3 | 26,418 | 18.1 |
| Other | 12 | 3.7 | 12,841 | 8.8 |
| *Custody level* | | | | |
| 1 | 39 | 13.3 | 25,226 | 19.6 |
| 2 | 75 | 25.6 | 43,288 | 33.6 |
| 3 | 85 | 29.0 | 31,037 | 24.1 |
| 4 | 94 | 32.1 | 29,405 | 22.8 |
| *Life sentence* | | | | |
| Life | 44 | 13.3 | 21,271 | 14.5 |
| Life without parole | 8 | 2.4 | 3,524 | 2.4 |
| Death row | - | - | 64 | 0 |
| *Sex offender registration* | | | | |
| Yes | 68 | 20.5 | 21,381 | 14.6 |
| *Gang (verified)* | | | | |
| Yes | 17 | 5.1 | 22,070 | 15.1 |
| *Mental health (official)* | | | | |
| CCCMS | 180 | 54.2 | 25,148 | 17.2 |
| EOP | 33 | 9.9 | 4,458 | 3.0 |

[1] The total adult male prison population figures include the study population and exclude those residing in camps.

*Note*: CCCMS, Correctional Clinical Case Management System; EOP, Enhanced Outpatient.

**Table 3.2** A comparison of educational status and employment of the transgender inmate population in California prisons for men and various other populations

| | US population | CA population | US prison population (men's prisons only) | CA prison population (men's prisons only) | Transgender community | Transgender inmate population in CA men's prisons[1] |
|---|---|---|---|---|---|---|
| *Education* | | | | | | |
| Some grade school | 18.2%[2] | 23.2%[2] | 60.8%[3] | 50.1%[3] | 34.5%[4] | 38.1% |
| High school graduate or GED | 28.6%[2] | 20.1%[2] | 24.6%[3] | 31.9%[3] | 28.2%[4] | 32.4% |
| Some college | 21.1%[2] | 22.9%[2] | 10.3%[3] | 13.3%[3] | 17.9%[4] | 21.3% |
| College graduate | 21.8%[2] | 24.2%[2] | 1.1%[3] | 2.7%[3] | 6.3%[4] | 7.0% |
| Any post-graduate | 8.9%[2] | 9.5%[2] | | | 7.6%[4] | 1.0% |
| *Employment* | | | | | | |
| Unemployed | 10.7%[5] (unemployed or marginally employed as of August 2008) | 7.3%[6] (percent of civilian labor force unemployed) | 26.6%[3] (unemployed one month prior to arrest) | 31.6%[3] (unemployed one month prior to arrest) | 23.0%[7]<br>35.0%[8]<br>42.0%[4]<br>51.0%[9] | 28.7% (unemployed before most recent incarceration) |

[1] Population $N = 332$ (includes 16 refusals and one unusable interview).
[2] U.S. Census Bureau (2000).
[3] U.S. Department of Justice, Bureau of Justice Statistics (2004).
[4] Xavier (2000).
[5] U.S. Department of Labor (2008).
[6] California Employment Development Department (2008).
[7] Herbst et al. (2008).
[8] San Francisco Bay Guardian and Transgender Law Center (2006).
[9] Clements-Nolle et al. (2006).

to their arrest, which hover around 30% (U.S. Department of Justice, Bureau of Justice Statistics, 2004). For the transgender population in the community, unemployment estimates range from 23% to over 50% (Herbst et al., 2008 and Clements-Nolle, Marx, & Katz, 2006, respectively). By some accounts, the prevalence of unemployment for transgender people is even higher than the US and California prison populations, and by all accounts it exceeds the percentage of the general population that is unemployed (Table 3.2). In accordance with estimates for both transgender and incarcerated populations, joblessness for transgender inmates in California prior to their incarceration is just below 30%.

Throughout the interviews with transgender inmates in California prisons for men, transgender inmates expressed awareness of their marginalized status along these lines. For example, a Level 1 African-American transgender inmate who worked as a prostitute on the streets of Los Angeles for over 20 years explained it this way: "Look at me. That's the only line of business some of us can get. They aren't going to hire us at Target. Only real girls get hired at Target." Related, some of the transgender inmates expressed that the value of securing conventional employment outside of prison is as much about securing respect as it is about the pursuit of financial self-sufficiency. As a White transgender inmate who reported considerable problems with drug addiction and mental illness surmised when asked how transgender people get respect outside of prison: "You have to show you can be productive as a transgender. You'll get a lot of respect if you can get a real job." Those who reported having a "real" job—which means conventional, legal employment—outside of prison often emphasized their atypical status. As a biracial transgender inmate distinguished herself from other transgender inmates when she wrote in a follow-up letter:

> I am a caring, respectful, productive, self-supported member of society that developed an addiction to meth. I was clean for four years, relapsed, and ended up here. I always have a job, I graduated high school, and have parents that support me being transsexual 100%.

This constellation of factors, especially employment and the presence of social support from family members, is rare among the transgender inmates in California prisons for men.

## Marital Status

As shown in Table 3.3, differences emerge when comparing marital status—as just one measure of social integration[22]—across various populations. More than half of all US adults are married and approximately one in five prison inmates in the USA and California is married (U.S. Census Bureau, 2000; U.S. Department of Justice, Bureau of Justice Statistics, 2004, respectively). In contrast, only 8.7% of transgender community members reported being married in a survey of over 250 transgender community members in Washington, D.C. (Xavier, 2000). Over 20% of these respondents were reportedly partnered, but unmarried, perhaps due to

**Table 3.3** A comparison of marital status of the transgender inmate population in California prisons for men and various other populations

| | US population | CA population | US prison population (men's prisons only) | CA prison population (men's prisons only) | Transgender community | Transgender inmate population in CA men's prisons[1] |
|---|---|---|---|---|---|---|
| Married | 54.3%[2] | 52.4%[2] | 19.5%[3] | 21.4%[3] | 8.7%[4] | 13.3% |
| Partnered (not married) | 1.9%[2] (unmarried partner household members) | 2.0%[2] | | | 21.4%[4] | 28.7% |
| Separated | 2.2%[2] | 2.5%[2] | 6.6%[3] | 7.9%[3] | | 4.7% |
| Single | 27.1%[2] | 30.1%[2] | 53.6%[3] | 51.0%[3] | 68.7%[4] | 40.7% |
| Divorced | 9.7%[2] | 9.5%[2] | 18.0%[3] | 17.7%[3] | | 8.3% |
| Widowed | 6.6%[2] | 5.6%[2] | 2.0%[3] | 2.1%[3] | | 2.0% |

[1] Population $N = 332$ (includes 16 refusals and one unusable interview).
[2] U.S. Census Bureau (2000).
[3] U.S. Department of Justice, Bureau of Justice Statistics (2004).
[4] Xavier (2000).

legal limitations on same-sex marriage and the complications of legal sex change documentation. Approximately 40% of transgender inmates in California prisons reported being currently married or partnered, which is considerably more than transgender people in the community outside of prison (30.1%). Of course, these numbers should be interpreted through the lens of what it means to be partnered for transgender inmates and the degree to which the term signifies something distinct for transgender inmates.[23]

## Health

Far more revealing than demographic comparisons, however, are the differences shown in Table 3.4 between the transgender population and the larger population with regard to health, most notably mental health, substance abuse, and HIV/AIDS status. Over 60% of respondents in a San Francisco survey of 362 male-to-female transgender people reported that they were currently suffering from clinical depression (Clements-Nolle et al., 2006)—a figure more than twice the rate of mental illness as a whole for the US population in a given year and over twice the lifetime prevalence of a mental illness diagnosis for male prisoners. Furthermore, estimates of transgender individuals in the community who have had suicidal ideation or who have attempted suicide range from 30% to over 50% (Kenagy, 2005 and Herbst et al., 2008, respectively). Among the incarcerated transgender population in California, over 70% reported having had a mental health problem at some point in their lives, most of whom (66.3%) reported experiencing mental health problems since being incarcerated (Table 3.4).

Alcohol and drug abuse are similarly overrepresented among transgender populations. Over one-third of transgender people in the community suffer from drug and alcohol abuse problems (Xavier, 2000). The level of alcohol abuse among the non-incarcerated transgender population is slightly higher than among prisoners in general, but the estimate of drug abuse among transgender inmates falls short of the levels for prisoners in general. For the incarcerated transgender population, however, these numbers rise precipitously, with estimates that exceed those of the larger California men's prison population (see Table 3.4).

The prevalence rates for HIV are even more disparate. While an estimated .5% of the US population is HIV-positive (McQuillan & Kruszon-Moran, 2008), an estimated 1.6% of inmates in men's prisons in the US are HIV positive (Marus-chak, 2006). The figure for California's transgender inmates in prisons for men far exceeds that number. According to Dr. Lori Kohler, the founder of California's only health clinic for transgender inmates (located at the California Medical Facility (CMF) in Vacaville): "Anywhere from 60–80 percent [of transfeminine prisoners] at any given time are HIV-infected. And many are also Hep-C infected. The next greatest problem is addiction" (Alpert, 2005). To worsen the situation, most health care professionals have had little to no exposure to transgender people. Dr. Kohler explained: "Care of transpeople is not something that most medical people understand. As far as I know of, CMF and now CMC [California Men's Colony] are the only two prisons in the country that actually have a physician who's dedicated to providing good care [for

**Table 3.4** A comparison of health status of the transgender inmate population in California prisons for men and various other populations

| | US population | CA population | US prison population (men's prisons only) | CA prison population (men's prisons only) | Transgender community | Transgender inmate population in CA men's prisons[1] |
|---|---|---|---|---|---|---|
| *Mental health* | | | | | | |
| Mental health problem | 26.2%[2] (suffer from a diagnosable mental disorder in a given year) | 16.3%[3] (self-reported current need for mental health treatment) | 25.3%[4] (ever diagnosed) | 26.0%[4] (ever diagnosed) | 60.2%[5] (currently meet criteria for depression) | 66.3% (mental health problem since incarcerated) |
| Serious mental illness | 5.9%[2] (serious mental illness in a given year) | 6.5%[6] (serious mental illness in a given year) | | | 30.1%[7] (lifetime attempted suicide) 34.9%[8] (lifetime suicidal ideation) 53.8%[9] (lifetime suicidal ideation) | 70.7% (ever had mental health problem) |
| *Substance abuse* | | | | | | |
| Alcohol abuse | 7.6%[10] (dependence or abuse of alcohol in past year) | 8.23%[10] (dependence or abuse of alcohol in past year) | 33.4%[11] (current alcohol abuse "high need") | 33.0%[11] (current alcohol abuse "high need") | 34.1%[9] (self-reported current alcohol problem) | 37.0% (ever had alcohol problem) |
| Drug abuse | 2.9%[10] (depend ence or abuse of illicit drugs in past year) | 2.9%[10] (dependence or abuse of illicit drugs in past year) | 40.6%[11] (current substance abuse "high need") 53.0%[12] (drug dependence/abuse) | 48.3%[11] (current substance abuse "high need") | 36.1%[8] (self-reported current drug problem) | 59.3% (ever had drug problem) |

| | | | | | | |
|---|---|---|---|---|---|---|
| *HIV status* | | | | | | |
| HIV positive | 0.5%[13] | 0.4%[14,15] | 1.6%[15] | | 10.0%[7]<br>27.7%[9] (weighted mean of prevalence across 4 studies)<br>32.0%[8]<br>35.0%[5]<br>35.0%[18] | 60–80%[17] |

[1] Population $N = 332$ (includes 16 refusals and one unusable interview).
[2] National Institute of Mental Health (2005).
[3] Lund (2005).
[4] U.S. Department of Justice, Bureau of Justice Statistics (2004).
[5] Clements-Nolle et al. (2006).
[6] California Department of Mental Health (2000).
[7] Kenagy (2005).
[8] Xavier (2000).
[9] Herbst et al. (2008).
[10] U.S. Department of Health and Human Services (2006).
[11] Petersilia (2006). "High need" is defined as reporting at least eight alcohol-related issues across several areas (out of 25 possible areas) or at least 10 drug-related issues (out of 34 possible areas). In short, responding positively to at least 30% of substance-need criteria qualified an individual as "high need." These criteria were adapted from *Prisoner Reentry and Crime in America* (Petersilia, 2005).
[12] Mumola and Karberg (2004).
[13] McQuillan and Kruszon-Moran (2008).
[14] California Department of Health (2007).
[15] U.S. Census Bureau (2007).
[16] Maruschak (2006).
[17] Alpert (2005).
[18] Clements and Clynes (1999).

transgender inmates], including cross-hormone therapies."[24] This observation was confirmed by a middle-aged, White, HIV-positive transgender inmate with a history of drug abuse who said the following when asked "if there was one thing you'd want people to understand about being transgender in prison, what would it be?":

> I would like to see a lot more of certain staff in here that aren't too familiar with transgenders to be more familiar and not be prejudiced towards us. I'd like to see some sensitivity training. I wish they knew that being transgender is hard. Going from prison to the community is hard. We need drug treatment that is HIV-and transgender-friendly.

## Sex Work

By their own account, over 40% of transgender inmates in California prisons for men have participated in sex work (see Table 3.5). It is difficult to put this number into context by making comparisons to the US population, the California population, or other prison populations because comparable data for these populations do not exist, but qualitative data suggest this feature of transgender inmates' lives is relevant to understanding their marginalization insofar as it often forms a nexus with drug use, health and well-being, engagement with law enforcement, and victimization. It is telling that this self-reported rate approximates the rate estimated by Herbst et al. (2008) in their analysis of 29 studies of HIV prevalence and risk behaviors of transgender persons in the USA; to be exact, our study estimates 42.7% and Herbst et al.'s (2008) study estimated 41.5%. It is difficult to imagine a higher prevalence of sex work in the US population, the California population, or the population in men's prisons.

Compatible with these numbers, it is not surprising that transgender inmates in this study who reported engaging in sex work often did so in a matter-of-fact way, such that the taken-for-grantedness of selling sex was emphasized and the problematic nature of prostitution understood to be an unfortunate part of sex work. When asked about the frequency of engaging in "sexual things against one's will" or "sexual things one would rather not do," some transgender inmates could not recall exact numbers, but frequently told accounts of prostitution in response to these inquiries. When they were prompted to estimate a number, the response was often some version of "too many times to count" or "more times than I can remember." On occasion and without prompting, some transgender inmates compared working on the streets to serving time in prison. For example, an African-American transgender inmate who reported engaging in prostitution for decades while coming in and out of prison explained: "I was prostituting for 20 years, more than 20 years. It's [the violence is] much worse on the streets than in prison." Similarly, a recently incarcerated young White transgender inmate who recently tested positive for HIV described being stabbed in the chest while engaging in street prostitution: "I did prostitution for drugs to support myself, my habit. It was easy and fast money, but then there's the risk. I'm going to die. That's the risk." Also revealing a theme of life-threatening risk, another transgender inmate explained the circumstances in

**Table 3.5** A comparison of sex work and homelessness among the transgender inmate population in California prisons for men and various other populations

| | US population | CA population | US prison population (men's prisons only) | CA prison population (men's prisons only) | Transgender community | Transgender inmate population in CA men's prisons[1] |
|---|---|---|---|---|---|---|
| *Sex work* | | | | | | |
| Participated in sex work | | | | | 36.0%[2] (past 30 days)<br>41.5%[3] (average across 29 studies)<br>48.0%[4] (past 6 months)<br>80.0%[4] (lifetime prevalence) | 42.7% (lifetime prevalence) |
| *Homelessness* | | | | | | |
| Homeless | .5%[5] (sheltered homeless in a given year)<br>.82–1.2%[9] (homeless in a given year) | .4%[5] (sheltered homeless in a given year) | 9.0%[5] (ever homeless) | 12.4%[6] (ever homeless) | 6.4%[7] (current)<br>10.0%[8] (current)<br>12.9%[3] (weighted mean of prevalence across 29 studies)<br>25.5%[2] (current) | 21.7% (homeless right before most recent incarceration)<br>47.7% (ever homeless) |

1 Population $N = 332$ (includes 16 refusals and one unusable interview).
2 Reback and Lombardi (1999).
3 Herbst et al. (2008).
4 Clements and Clynes (1999).
5 U.S. Department of Housing and Urban Development (2008).
6 U.S. Department of Justice, Bureau of Justice Statistics (2004).
7 Xavier (2000).
8 San Francisco Bay Guardian and Transgender Law Center (200[illegible]).
9 National Law Center on Homelessness and Poverty (2007).

which engaging in prostitution led to being raped on the streets by a local law enforcement officer:

TRANSGENDER INMATE: He [a municipal police officer] penetrated me with a foreign object. It was a routine stop in a prostitution area. He arrested me and took me to a secluded area.
INTERVIEWER: What foreign object?
TRANSGENDER INMATE: His billy club.
INTERVIEWER: Did you report it?
TRANSGENDER INMATE (MILDLY LAUGHING): No, god no. Why?

The frequency and severity of violence associated with prostitution notwithstanding, a handful of transgender inmates described engaging in prostitution as a rite of passage of transgender people. As a transgender inmate serving a life sentence who reported engaging in prostitution "for about four months... just to fit in" explained:

> It just wasn't me. I'd rather go get a credit card—someone else's credit card—and go shopping. I didn't have to prostitute to survive like some of the girls in here. I got money from credit cards and then told some of the other girls I made it as a prostitute. I'd tell them I had a date for $200. They would be impressed.

In a similar vein, a Mexican-American transgender inmate who reported coming from a wealthy family explained the importance of engaging in prostitution this way:

> No matter how much money I had, I wanted to know how much I was worth. How much would a guy pay for me. I went to prostitution to see how much I could get—I got $1,000 once. I'm not joking. A $1,000—and I could have got more.

This is not to say that transgender inmates *routinely* took pride in engaging in prostitution, nor did they deny the physical harm associated with prostitution. Rather, most frequently, transgender inmates who reported engaging in prostitution described sex work as a way to survive in light of their limited prospects for employment. As one of the oldest transgender inmates interviewed for this study, a biracial transgender inmate who reported engaging in prostitution both inside and outside of prison, explained: "Prostitution. It's something I have to do to survive. Of course I'd prefer to not do it. I'd prefer to not be in here. But, I am. You just make the best of it. That's all you can do, really." Elaborating along these lines, another older African-American transgender inmate who reported engaging in prostitution off-and-on since becoming a teenage runaway said:

> I was a sex worker beginning when I was 18. But, I stopped when I was 40 once I got SSI. When I was a prostitute, there would be dates I really didn't

want, but I did it for the money. I didn't want to do it, but it wasn't against my will. I did it willingly, but I didn't want to.

These and other comments by transgender inmates point to the multiple ways in which engaging in sex work and being transgender outside prison intersect in the lives of transgender inmates. At the aggregate level, these are lives defined by considerable economic and social marginalization, including exceptionally high rates of homelessness.

## Homelessness

Estimates of homelessness for transgender people who are not incarcerated range from 6.4% to 25.5% of the population reporting being currently homeless (Xavier, 2000 and Reback & Lombardi, 1999, respectively). The prevalence of homelessness among transgender people, according to a meta-analysis of 29 studies, averaged almost 13%—a figure over 10 times as high as the largest estimate for the US population (Herbst et al., 2008). This number increases further still when considering the incarcerated transgender population. Nearly half (47.7%) of California's transgender inmates experienced homelessness at some point in their adult lives, and over 20% reported being homeless right before their most recent incarceration (Table 3.5).

Transgender inmates in California prisons described homelessness as an outgrowth of not being able to work, lacking social support in the form of dependable family and friends, and being confronted with no viable alternatives upon parole. An African-American transgender inmate described daily life prior to coming to prison this way: "I was a girl on the street. I can't read well enough to get a job. I lived homeless and panhandled to eat every day. I go to the mission to shower and change my clothes." This transgender inmate went further to express a desire to learn to read past the sixth-grade level, a concern about having no place to live upon release, a defeatist attitude about any prospects for improvement in her life, and an acceptance of the inevitable: that upon release from prison, life outside prison would be "all the same" as it was before being incarcerated due to a lack of programming in prison and a lack of alternatives outside of prison. In this case, "all the same" includes prostitution and considerable victimization in the form of verbal harassment and sexual assault on the street.

Others are beginning to document the ways in which the consequences of being homeless are exacerbated for transgender people, including acting as a catalyst for criminal behavior and attendant incarceration (see, e.g., the Sylvia Rivera Law Project, 2007). As Raschka (2008) recently explained to a national audience after examining the lives of homeless transgender youth: "Transgender people face—often bravely—hostility and other obstacles that complicate their homelessness" (p. C08). Homelessness, like many of the other dimensions of marginalization associated with being transgender, correlates with victimization.

## Victimization

In terms of physical victimization, transgender individuals do not fare well—and transgender inmates worse still. Compared to the 2.3% of the US population who were victims of a violent crime in a given year (Rand & Catalano, 2006), an estimated 37% of transgender people reported having experienced physical abuse *because of their gender identity or presentation* (Clements & Clynes, 1999) and 43%, 51.3%, and 59.5%, respectively, report lifetime violent victimization (Xavier, 2000), lifetime physical abuse (Kenagy, 2005), and lifetime harassment or violence (Wilchins, Lombardi, Priesing, & Malouf, 1997). While reports from a single year cannot be directly compared to lifetime prevalence rates, the sheer magnitude of the difference suggests that transgender people are differentially vulnerable to victimization. As compared to inmates in US and California men's prisons—by all reports, populations that have also suffered high rates of physical abuse—transgender people experienced more than five times as many incidents of non-sexual physical victimization. Even when compared to other relatively vulnerable populations, transgender people are perilously situated. When examining a population that is doubly vulnerable—transgender inmates—lifetime prevalence of physical assault while presenting as female outside of prison is 67.3%, a number that rises to 88% when considering assault both in and out of a carceral setting (Table 3.6). Statistics are just as revealing for sexual victimization. While approximately one in 10 Americans—and one in six American women—has experienced rape or attempted rape (Tjaden & Thoennes, 1998), numerous estimates for the transgender population range from 13.5% to nearly 60% (Clements & Clynes, 1999; Kenagy, 2005; Wilchins et al., 1997; Xavier, 2000). The corresponding figure for transgender inmates in California prisons is higher still, with over 75% of the population reporting a lifetime prevalence of sexual victimization (Table 3.6).

# DISCUSSION AND CONCLUSION

The demographic profile of transgender inmates presented in this article reveals multiple dimensions of social and economic marginality. Although transgender inmates constitute a diverse group in terms of continuity of gender presentation, gender identity, sexual orientation, and sexual attractions,[25] it is nonetheless useful to consider "transgender" an umbrella term that encompasses multiple non-normative identities, sexual orientations, and presentations of self. With regard to the social, economic, and experiential status of transgender inmates, the larger picture is clear: with the possible exceptions of having a partner (in the interpersonal sense of the word) and educational attainment, transgender inmates are marginalized in ways that are not comparable to other prison populations.

As the focus shifts from the transgender population outside of prison to the incarcerated transgender population, these multiple sources of marginalization continue—and along some dimensions are exacerbated. Most significantly, transgender inmates fare far worse in terms of their health, participation in sex work,

**Table 3.6** A comparison of victimization among the transgender inmate population in California prisons for men and various other populations

| | US population | CA population | US prison population (men's prisons only) | CA prison population (men's prisons only) | Transgender community | Transgender inmate population in CA men's prisons[1] |
|---|---|---|---|---|---|---|
| Physical victimization | 2.3%[2] (victims of violent crime [including sexual victimization] in a given year) | | 11.9%[3] (lifetime physical abuse)<br>13.4%[5] (lifetime physical abuse) | 12.4%[3] (lifetime physical abuse) | 37.0%[4] (lifetime physical abuse because of gender)<br>43.0%[6] (lifetime violent victimization)<br>51.3%[7] (lifetime physical abuse)<br>59.5%[8] (lifetime harassment or violence) | 67.3% (ever been physically assaulted outside of prison)<br>88.0% (ever been physically assaulted) |
| Sexual victimization | 10.5%[9] (lifetime rape/attempted rape)<br>17.6%[9] (females only)<br>3.0%[9] (males only) | | 5.7%[3] (lifetime forced sexual contact)<br>5.8%[5] (lifetime sexual abuse) | 5.6%[3] (lifetime forced sexual contact) | 13.5%[6] (lifetime sexual assault)<br>14.0%[8] (lifetime rape or attempted rape)<br>53.8%[7] (lifetime forced sex)<br>59.0%[6,4] (lifetime forced sex or rape) | 42.7% (ever had to do sexual things against will outside of prison)<br>59.3 (ever had to do sexual things would rather not have done outside prison)<br>75.3% (ever had to do sexual things against will) |

[1] Population $N = 332$ (includes 16 refusals and one unusable interview).
[2] Rand and Catalano (2006).
[3] U.S. Department of Justice, Bureau of Justice Statistics (2004).
[4] Clements and Clynes (1999).
[5] Harlow (1999).
[6] Xavier (2000).
[7] Kenagy (2005).
[8] Wilchins et al. (1997).
[9] Tjaden and Thoennes (1998).

homelessness, and history of sexual victimization. It is not surprising that these factors cluster together. Homelessness has dire consequences for both physical and mental health (a relationship which is often reciprocal) and can be intimately linked to sex work as a means of survival—a means that carries with it a high risk of victimization. Stories of violence recounted by transgender inmates were common both as they related to living on the streets and, more generally, simply living as transgender—prompting the vast majority of transgender inmates to report sexual assault in the community and/or while incarcerated. These accounts not only reveal drastically disproportionate marginalization at multiple turns, but also highlight the interconnectedness of these marginalities inside and outside of prison.

Taken together, the findings presented in this article illustrate the familiar point attributed to the philosopher de Tocqueville: "It is well known that most individuals on whom the criminal law inflicts punishment have been unfortunate before they become guilty" (Beaumont & de Tocqueville, 1964, p. 172). This quote is perhaps nowhere more true, as an empirical matter, than with regard to transgender inmates in California prisons. Related, it is shocking that volumes of research on prisons and prison populations have heretofore not put forth a basic understanding of the demographic, health, and welfare related characteristics of transgender inmates and systematically discerned the degree to which they are similar to or dissimilar from other populations of inmates and the larger communities from which they derive. Having done so, this article is a first.

The final issue to be addressed in this article is criminal justice policy. First and foremost, the findings presented in this work suggest that it would behoove law enforcement officials, especially corrections officials charged with providing custody and care to transgender inmates, to understand that this population is a uniquely marginal one, both inside and outside prison. As an empirically discernable population above and beyond just being transgender, transgender inmates are uniquely stigmatized, are less advantaged in terms of "life chances," and have comparatively few resources to draw upon to navigate prison life such that their experiences in prison are conducive to safety, rehabilitation, and successful reentry into their—and our—communities.

The incarceration of transgender women in prisons for adult males poses a range of managerial challenges to correctional officials charged with ensuring the safety and security of all inmates, including transgender inmates. As others are beginning to document, managerial challenges emerge in light of considerable ambiguity surrounding what it means to be transgender; unique medical concerns for transgender inmates, especially those related to initiating and sustaining hormone therapy; complicated questions about where best to house transgender inmates—in the general population or in segregated housing assignments—in light of their amplified vulnerability to assault (both sexual and non-sexual); and an array of dilemmas related to the physical appearance and grooming standards for transgender inmates, including the wearing of female clothing, especially bras and other underwear, the use of cosmetics that accentuate femininity, and the ability to wear long hair and be respectfully referenced by female names and pronouns in men's prisons (Mann, 2006; Petersen et al., 1996; Rosenblum, 2000; Sumner, 2009; Tewksbury & Potter,

2005). With these and other concerns in mind, the development of correctional policies for transgender inmates is, at best, in the incipient stages.[26]

It would be premature to use this one study and the central finding it advances—that being transgender and being incarcerated is "where the margins meet" in discernable ways—as the basis for recommending specific managerial policy directives to corrections officials. However, it is entirely reasonable to encourage those charged with providing custody and care to the transgender population to be sensitive to what others have called "the dilemma of difference." As Minow (1990) succinctly explained in *Making All the Difference: Inclusion, Exclusion, and American Law*:

> The stigma of difference may be recreated both by ignoring and by focusing on it. Decisions about education, employment, benefits, and other opportunities in society should not turn on an individual's ethnicity, disability, race, gender, religion, or membership in any other group about which some have deprecating or hostile attitudes. Yet refusing to acknowledge these differences may make them continue to matter in a world constructed with some groups, but not others, in mind. These problems of inequality can be exacerbated both by treating members of minority groups the same as members of the majority and by treating the two groups differently (p. 20).

With regard to transgender inmates, a population that certainly exists on an important axis of differentiation and related inequality in modern life, this comes down to developing correctional policy that finds a balance between treating them the same as other inmates and recognizing their minority differences and the implications of those differences. The dilemma of difference evokes a tension between recognizing the unique characteristics and vulnerabilities associated with the transgender population, and, at the same time, remaining true to the value of fairness, which often is most recognizable as avoiding the temptation to single out various types of inmates for treatment that might inadvertently increase vulnerability and amplify disadvantage in prison and beyond.

## ACKNOWLEDGMENTS

This project was funded by the California Department of Corrections and Rehabilitation and the School of Social Ecology at the University of California, Irvine. We would like to thank the following contributors for consultation on and assistance with data collection and interpretation: the CDCR's Offender Information Services Branch and the CDCR's Office of Research as well as key CDCR personnel, including Nola Grannis, Karen Henderson, Tim Lockwood, Betty Viscuso, and especially Suzan Hubbard and Wendy Still; the wardens who made their prisons available to us and their staff who ensured we could conduct face-to-face interviews with hundreds of transgender inmates in a confidential setting; academic colleagues, including Francesca Barocio, Victoria Basolo, Kitty Calavita, Sarah Fenstermaker, Ryken Grattet, Cheryl Maxson, Richard McCleary, Merry Morash,

Jodi O'Brien, and Joan Petersilia; many people outside the CDCR and academic settings who offered their expertise including, Patrick Callahan, Dr. Lori Kohler, Alexander L. Lee, Julie Marin, Linda McFarlane, Andie Moss, Lovisa Stannow, Dr. Denise Taylor, Jeanne Woodford, and anonymous reviewers for *Justice Quarterly*; a team of hardworking and talented research assistants, including Akhila Ananth, Lyndsay Boggess, Tim Goddard, Philip Goodman, Kristy Matsuda, Randy Myers, Gabriela Noriega, Lynn Pazzani, and Sylvia Valenzuela; and most importantly, hundreds of transgender inmates in California prisons who agreed to be interviewed, thus making it possible to understand their lives in prison.

## Notes

1 The Court's ruling in this case was a landmark decision insofar as it affirmed that being violently assaulted and raped in prison is not part of the penalty and serves no penological objective.

2 Although there is a growing academic literature on transgender people and lives, there is not a concomitant consensus on how best to define transgender. At one end of a range of definitions, transgender is used as an umbrella term to refer to gender variant individuals, with gender variance referring to individuals whose gender expression and behavior do not match the expectations associated with a binary understanding of sex/gender (Girshick, 2008; see also Gagné & Tewksbury, 1998, 1999; Tewksbury & Potter, 2005). This understanding includes all non-normative sexual and gender identities and lifestyles. At the other end of a range of definitions, transgender is used as a proxy for transsexuals (i.e., those who have undergone, or will undergo, sex reassignment surgery), or transvestites in the narrowest sense of the term (i.e., those who wear "opposite" gendered clothing).

3 Hensley et al. (2003) argue that sexual and gendered hierarchies are being reconfigured such that female-presenting inmates may occupy a higher status within the larger inmate culture.

4 For Fleisher and Krienert (2009), "the term hierarchy does not imply the operation of a formal system of ranked social statuses defined by rights and duties as we find in the military, corporations, or university professors. [Rather] it means that prison culture creates mutually exclusive sexual roles by ascribing to each role a set of differentiating criteria" (p. 82).

5 For example, Alarid (2000) surveyed (presumably) gay and bisexual men about their sexual identities, behavioral preferences, and perceptions of treatment by others. The author reports that 7% of the sample "would rather be female than male," 14% "frequently dress in drag" when on the street, and 30% report that they are more feminine than masculine, all characteristics that fit easily within recent "umbrella" definitions of transgender outside carceral settings and that correspond with inmate cultural understandings of "the queen." However, none of the groups are afforded separate examination within the author's analyses.

6 For a more detailed description of the research methodology employed in the larger project, see Jenness et al. (2009).

7 By deploying these criteria, we bypassed larger debates about who is and is not transgender and, instead, relied on a comprehensive understanding that would maximize inclusion without diluting the target population beyond recognition. In particular, the third criterion—participation in groups for transgender inmates—was utilized to be as inclusive as possible. While there was the potential for slippage in terms of transgender identification of all inmates who participate in such groups, the actual number of research subjects who were recruited through this means was small.

8 This represents the total population of CDCR prisons in April 2008, just a few weeks prior to the commencement of data collection in the field (see http://www.cdcr.ca.gov/Reports_Research/Offender_Information_Services_Branch/Monthly/TPOP1A/TPOP1Ad0804.pdf, last retrieved May 21, 2009).

9 In prison, a ducat is written permission to move throughout the institution for a particular appointment or responsibility, such as a medical appointment or a work assignment.

10 In compliance with the protocol approved by the University of California, Irvine's Institutional Review Board (IRB), all interviews were conducted in confidential settings after obtaining informed consent. No potential respondents were questioned about inclusion criteria until a confidential setting was secured.

11 For more details on the experience of collecting data on transgender inmates in California prisons, see Jenness et al. (2009).

12 The complete interview schedule is available upon request.

13 The loss of *potential* cases—going from the name on the master list to actually seeing the person at the prison—is due to a variety of factors, including inmates paroling, dying, or being transferred to another prison after we received our list and before we arrived at the prison; inmates being unwilling to come out of their cell; inmates being unavailable as a result of an urgent medical or psychiatric appointment; and inmates—believe it or not—being "lost" in the prison and thus unavailable for an interview. We emphasize that these are *potential* losses of cases because we have no way of knowing how many would have met our eligibility requirements and, therefore, have been given the opportunity to participate in the study. If, upon arrival at a prison, we learned that an inmate on our list had been transferred to a prison at which we had not yet collected data, we made every effort to ducat the inmate at that prison; however, if an inmate on our list transferred to a prison from which we had already collected data, we did not return to that prison to ducat the inmate.

14 We also identified four transgender inmates in a prison for women. Three of these inmates completed an interview. These interviews were exceptionally illuminating, both in and of themselves and in light of interviews conducted in men's prisons; however, because there are so few cases it is difficult to extrapolate statistical trends from these interviews. Therefore, this research focuses exclusively on transgender inmates in prisons and reception centers for men.

15 Because the University of California, Irvine's Institutional Review Board, the research design, and our own professional ethics required that the identities

of research participants be kept confidential, we received central file information on *all* individuals currently housed in California adult correctional facilities from the CDCR, from which the research team extracted information for study participants. This enabled us to collect official data without revealing to the CDCR which inmates are included in this study (for more along these lines, see Jenness et al. (2009)).

16 These variables were chosen for two reasons: (1) they are typically used to profile inmate populations; and (2) they represent factors identified by extant research as potential correlates of sexual and/or non-sexual violence—the main focus of the larger study from which this article derives.

17 This finding is no doubt related to the age at which transgender people "come out" (i.e., a process whereby gay men, lesbians, bisexuals, and transgender people inform others of their non-normative identity). A recent study based on a survey of 3,474 transgender people from across the USA revealed the following: although the vast majority of transwomen "felt different" and reported feeling "uncertain about their gender identity" very early in life (age 12 and under), only 1% disclosed their gender identity to others when they were age "12 and under." According to this study, 6% of transwomen disclosed their gender identity to others between the ages of 13 and 19, 16% disclosed their gender identity in their 20s, 17% disclosed their gender identity in the 30s, and 38% disclosed their gender identity when they were 40 or older. In other words, transwomen most often come out as such later in life (Beemyn & Rankin, in press; but, see a related Power Point presentation at: http://www.umass.edu/stonewall/translives/, last retrieved May 21, 2009). For a more complicated view of coming out as transgender, see Gagné, Tewksbury, and McGaughey (1997).

18 Classification level is based upon the Inmate Classification Score System (ICSS) and represents the recommended custody level at which an offender is to be housed. Inmates with a Level 1 placement score (0–18) are normally housed in Level 1 facilities and camps consisting primarily of open dormitories with a low security perimeter. Inmates with a Level 2 placement score (19–27) are normally housed in Level 2 facilities consisting primarily of open dormitories with a security perimeter, which may include armed coverage. Inmates with a Level 3 placement score (28–51) are normally housed in Level 3 facilities primarily having a secure perimeter with armed coverage and housing units with cells adjacent to exterior walls. Inmates with a Level 4 placement score (52 and above) are normally housed in Level 4 facilities primarily having a secure perimeter with internal and external armed coverage and housing units with cells adjacent to exterior walls or cell block housing with cells non-adjacent to exterior walls. Inmates with Close Custody must be housed in a celled environment, whereas inmates with Minimum or Medium Custody can be housed in a celled or dormitory environment.

19 CCCMS stands for Correctional Clinical Case Management System.

20 EOP stands for Enhanced Outpatient. According to the *Mental Health Services Delivery System Program Guide* (MHSDS, 2009), EOP inmates experience "Acute

Onset or Significant Decompensation of a serious mental disorder" and "an inability to function in a general population" (p. 12-1-8).

21 Unfortunately, there is very little research on the health and welfare of transgender people in the community that reports systematic data along these lines and what does exist consists of convenience samples from a few select regions of the country. As a result, basic demographic characteristics of the transgender community are difficult to document.

22 The presence or absence of children, another conventional measure of social integration, is also an important consideration. Unfortunately, data along these lines are typically collected with "household" as the unit of analysis, thus comparisons to the transgender inmates in California prisons are problematic.

23 Related work in progress suggests that for some transgender inmates, a partner is simply someone with whom a transgender inmate is currently having sexual relations, while for others it can be operationalized as equivalent to legally recognized marriage. In other words, there is considerable variability in how transgender inmates make sense of the word "partner." This kind of difference in understandings associated with the word partner in prison and among members of the transgender community may very well account for this large discrepancy.

24 See Alpert (2005).

25 Work in progress reveals that transgender inmates are a diverse prison population in terms of four important dimensions of self and identity—continuity in terms of female presentation, gender identity, sexual orientation, and sexual attraction(s)—as well as the considerable variation among transgender inmates in California prisons for men in terms of collective identity and collective efficacy.

26 For example, in the USA there is no clear and definitive legal standard for determining the placement of transgender prisoners in particular types of prisons or housing units within prisons. Most states routinely assign convicted felons to male or female prisons on the basis of their genitalia even as it is both rare and increasingly common for jails and prisons to segregate inmates by sexual orientation and, to some degree, gender (Tarzwell, 2006). Although still rare, an increasing number of states are developing policies related to hormonal treatment for transgender inmates; the modal method is one of treatment "maintenance" that continues treatment existing prior to incarceration but does not further it (Tarzwell, 2006). A few recent progressive policies and practices for transgender inmates in correctional systems throughout the USA have begun to provide a multi-dimensional approach to the management of transgender inmates that not only addresses housing placement and medical treatment but also gender expression and identification in the form of attention to and respect for chosen name and pronoun use as well as clothing, makeup, and hygiene items (Kates, 2008; Najafi, 2009). In other words, although the issues related to transgender issues are increasingly clear, there is little agreement on how to resolve them and even less social science research to be utilized in the resolve. This, then, presents a challenge to correctional officials who embrace an "evidence-based corrections" approach to developing and implementing correctional policy.

## References

Alarid, L. F. (2000). Sexual orientation perspectives of incarcerated bisexual and gay men: The county jail protective custody experience. *Prison Journal, 80*(1), 80–95.

Alpert, E. (2005, November 21). Gender outlaws. *In the Fray Magazine*. Retrieved May 21, 2009, from http://www.inthefray.com/html/print.php?sid=1381

Baus, J., Hunt, D., & Williams, R. (Directors/Producers). (2006). *Cruel and unusual* [Motion Picture]. United States: Reid Productions LLC.

Beaumont, G., & de Tocqueville, A. (1964). *On the penitentiary system in the United States and its application in France*. Carbondale, IL: Southern Illinois University Press.

Beemyn, B. G., & Rankin, S. (in press). *Understanding transgender lives*. New York: Columbia University Press.

Blight, J. (2000). Transgender inmates (*Trends and Issues in Crime and Criminal Justice No. 168*). Griffith: Australian Institute of Criminology.

California Department of Health. (2007). California AIDS surveillance report: Cumulative cases of AIDS as of June 30, 2007 (Office of AIDS, HIV/AIDS Case Registry Section). Retrieved May 21, 2009, from http://www.cdph.ca.gov/data/statistics/Documents/OA-2007-06AIDSMerged.pdf

California Department of Mental Health. (2000). Estimates of need for mental health services for California for year 2000 for serious mental illnesses by age, sex, race/ ethnicity for household population. Retrieved May 21, 2009, from http://www.dmh. ca.gov/Statistics_and_Data_Analysis/CNE2/Calif_CD/q5asr_htm/California/q5asr2k_ wsmi01_ca_excel_Index_demographics.htm

California Employment Development Department. (2008). News release: California's unemployment rate increases to 7.3 percent. Retrieved May 21, 2009, from http:// www.edd.ca.gov/About_EDD/pdf/urate200808.pdf

Clements, K., & Clynes, C. (1999). *Transgender community health project: Descriptive results*. San Francisco, CA: The San Francisco Transgender Health Project, San Francisco Department of Public Health. Retrieved May 21, 2009, from http://hivinsite.ucsf.edu/InSite?page=cftg-02-02

Clements-Nolle, K., Marx, R., & Katz, M. (2006). Attempted suicide among TG persons: The influence of gender-based discrimination and victimization. *Journal of Homosexuality, 51*(3), 53–69.

Coggeshall, J. M. (1988). Ladies behind bars: A liminal gender as cultural mirror. *Anthropology Today, 4* (4), 6–8.

Donaldson, S. (1993). Survivor testimony (A million jockers, punks, and queens. Stop prisoner rape: Sex among American male prisoners and its implications for concepts of sexual orientation). Retrieved May 21, 2009, from http://www.justdetention.org/en/docs/doc_01_lecture.aspx

Donaldson, S. (2003). Hooking up: Protective pairing for punks. In N. Scheper-Hughes & P. Bourgois (Eds.), *Violence in war and peace: An anthology* (pp. 348–353). Malden, MA: Blackwell.

Farmer *v.* Brennan, 511 U.S. 825; 114 S.Ct. 1970; 128 L.Ed. 2d 811; LEXIS 4274 (USA, 1994).

Fleisher, M. S., & Krienert, J. L. (2009). *The myth of prison rape: Sexual culture in American prisons*. Lanham, MD: Rowman & Littlefield.

Gagné, P., & Tewksbury, R. (1998). Conformity pressures and gender resistance among transgendered individuals. *Social Problems, 45*(1), 81–101.

Gagné, P., & Tewksbury, R. (1999). Knowledge and power, body and self: An analysis of knowledge systems and the transgendered self. *Sociological Quarterly, 40*(1), 59–83.

Gagné, P., Tewksbury, R., & McGaughey, D. (1997). Coming out and crossing over: Identity formation and proclamation in a transgender community. *Gender & Society, 11*(4), 478–508.

Girshick, L. (2008). *Transgender voices: Beyond women and men.* Lebanon, NH: University Press of New England.

Harlow, C. W. (1999). *Prior abuse reported by inmates and probationers* (NCJ 172879). Washington, DC: U.S. Department of Justice, Office of Justice Programs, Bureau of Justice Statistics.

Hensley, C., Wright J., Tewksbury, R., & Castle, T. (2003). The evolving nature of prison argot and sexual hierarchies. *Prison Journal, 83*(3), 289–300.

Herbst, J. H., Jacobs, E. D., Finlayson, T. J., McKleroy, V. S., Neumann, M. S., & Crepaz, N. (2008). Estimating HIV prevalence and risk behaviors of TG persons in the United States: A systematic review. *AIDS and Behavior, 12*(1), 1–17.

Irwin, J. (2005). *The warehouse prison: Disposal of the new dangerous class.* Los Angeles, CA: Roxbury.

Jenness, V. (in press). Getting to know "the girls" in an "alpha-male community": Notes on fieldwork on transgender inmates in California prisons. In S. Fenstermaker & N. Jones (Eds.), *Sociologists backstage: Answers to 10 questions about what they do.* New York: Routledge Press.

Jenness, V., Maxson, C. L., Matsuda K. N., & Sumner, J. (2007). *Violence in California correctional facilities: An empirical examination of sexual assault* (Report). Sacramento, CA: California Department of Corrections and Rehabilitation.

Jenness, V., Sexton, L., & Sumner, J. (2009). *The victimization of transgender inmates: An empirical examination of a vulnerable population in prison* (Report). Sacramento, CA: California Department of Corrections and Rehabilitation.

Kates, W. (2008, June 20). Advocates hail new policy for transgender youth at New York's juvenile detention centers. *International Herald Tribune*, n.p.

Kenagy, G. P. (2005). Transgender health: Findings from two needs assessment studies in Philadelphia. *Health and Social Work, 30*(1), 19–26.

Lund, L. E. (2005). Mental health care in California counties: Perceived need and barriers to access, 2001. California Department of Health Services, Center for Health Statistics. Retrieved May 21, 2009, from http://www.cdph.ca.gov/pubsforms/Pubs/OHIRmentalhealthCareCA2001.pdf

Mann, R. (2006). The treatment of transgender prisoners, not just an American problem: A comparative analysis of American, Australian, and Canadian prison policies concerning the treatment of transgender prisoners and a "universal" recommendation to improve treatment. *Law and Sexuality: Review of Lesbian, Gay, Bisexual, and Transgender Legal Issues, 15*, 91–133.

Maruschak, L. M. (2006). *HIV in prisons* (NCJ 222179). Washington, DC: U.S. Department of Justice, Bureau of Justice Statistics. Retrieved May 21, 2009, from http://www.ojp.usdoj.gov/bjs/pub/pdf/hivp06.pdf

Mauer, M., & Chesney-Lind, M. (Eds.). (2002). *Invisible punishment: The collateral consequences of mass imprisonment.* New York: The New Press.

McQuillan, G., & Kruszon-Moran, D. (2008). HIV infection in the United States household population aged 18–49 years: Results from 1999–2006. Centers for Disease Control and Prevention and National Center for Health Statistics. Retrieved May 21, 2009, from http://www.natap.org/2008/newsUpdates/013008_03.htm

MHSDS (Mental Health Services Delivery System). (2009). *Chapter 1: Program guide overview* (Revision). Sacramento, CA: California Department of Corrections and Rehabilitation.

Minow, M. (1990). *Making all the difference: Inclusion, exclusion, and American law.* Ithaca, NY: Cornell University Press.

Mumola, C. J., & Karberg, J. C. (2004). *Drug use and dependence, state and federal prisoners* (NCJ 213530). Washington, DC: U.S. Department of Justice, Bureau of Justice Statistics. Retrieved May 21, 2009, from http://www.ojp.usdoj.gov/bjs/pub/pdf/dudsfp04.pdf

Najafi, Y. (2009, March 5). Prison progress: Activists offer measured praise for transgender plans. *Metroweekly.* Retrieved May 21, 2009, from http://www.metroweekly. com/gauge/?ak=4090

National Institute of Mental Health. (2005). *The numbers count: Mental disorders in America.* Retrieved February 27, 2009, from http://www.nimh.nih.gov/health/publications/the-numbers-count-mental-disorders-in-america.shtml

National Law Center on Homelessness and Poverty. (2007). *2007 annual report.* Retrieved May 21, 2009, from http://www.nlchp.org/content/pubs/2007_Annual_Report2.pdf

Petersen, M., Stephens, J., Dickey, R., & Lewis, W. (1996). Transsexuals within the prison system: An international survey of correctional services policies. *Behavioral Sciences & the Law,* 14, 219–229.

Petersilia, J. (2005). From cell to society: Who is returning home? In J. Travis & C. Visher (Eds.), *Prisoner reentry and crime in America* (pp. 15–49). New York: Cambridge University Press.

Petersilia, J. (2006). *Understanding California corrections.* Berkeley, CA: California Policy Research Center, University of California.

Petersilia, J. (2008). Influencing public policy: An embedded criminologist reflects on California prison reform. *Journal of Experimental Criminology, 4* (4), 335–356.

Rand, M., & Catalano, S. (2006). *Criminal victimization, 2006* (NCJ 219413). Washington, DC: U.S. Department of Justice, Office of Justice Programs, Bureau of Justice Statistics. Retrieved May 21, 2009, from http://www.ojp.usdoj.gov/bjs/pub/pdf/cv06.pdf

Raschka, L. (2008, July 28). Trans formed: To be homeless and transgender. *The Washington Post,* p. C08.

Reback, C., & Lombardi, E. (1999). HIV risk behaviors of male-to-female transgenders in a community-based harm reduction program. *International Journal of Transgenderism, 3* (1+2). Retrieved May 21, 2009, from http://www.symposion.com/ijt/hiv_risk/reback.htm

Rosenblum, D. (2000). "Trapped" in Sing Sing: Transgendered prisoners caught in the gender binarism. *Michigan Journal of Gender and Law, 6*, 499–571.

San Francisco Bay Guardian and Transgender Law Center. (2006). Good jobs NOW! A snapshot of the economic health of San Francisco's TG communities. Retrieved May 21, 2009, from http://www.transgenderlawcenter.org/pdf/Good%20Jobs%20NOW%20report.pdf

Simon, J., & Feeley, M. (1992). The new penology: Notes on the emerging strategy of corrections and its implications. *Criminology, 30*(4), 449–474.

Sumner, J. M. (2009). *Keeping house: Understanding the transgender inmate code of conduct through prison policies, environments, and culture.* Unpublished doctoral dissertation, University of California, Irvine.

Sykes, G. (1958). *Society of captives.* Princeton, NJ: Princeton University Press.

Sylvia Rivera Law Project. (2007). "It's war in here:" A report on the treatment of transgender and intersex people in New York State men's prisons. Retrieved May 21, 2009, http://www.srlp.org/files/warinhere.pdf

Tarzwell, S. (2006). The gender lines are marked with razor wire: Addressing state prison policies and practices for the management of transgender prisoners. *Columbia Human Rights Law Review, 38*, 167–220.

Tewksbury, R., & Potter, R. H. (2005). Transgender prisoners: A forgotten group. In S. Stojkovic (Ed.), *Managing special populations in jails and prisons* (pp. 15-1–15-14). New York: Civic Research Institute.

The Pew Center on the States. (2008). One in 100: Behind bars in America 2008. Retrieved May 21, 2009, from http://www.pewcenteronthestates.org/uploadedFiles/8015PCTS_Prison08_FINAL_2-1-1_FORWEB.pdf

Tjaden, P., & Thoennes, N. (1998). *Prevalence, incidence and consequences of violence against women: Findings from the National Violence Against Women Survey* (NCJ 172837). Washington, DC: U.S. Department of Justice, National Institute of Justice and Centers for Disease Control and Prevention. Retrieved May 21, 2009, from http://www.ncjrs.gov/pdffiles/172837.pdf

Tonry, M. (Ed.). (2004). *The future of imprisonment.* New York: Oxford University Press.

U.S. Census Bureau. (2000). *Census 2000.* Retrieved May 21, 2009, from http:// www.census.gov/Press-Release/www/2002/demoprofiles.html

U.S. Census Bureau. (2007). *Population estimates as of July 1, 2007.* Retrieved May 21, 2009, from http://www.census.gov/popest/national/

U.S. Department of Health and Human Services. (2006). *Results from the 2006 National Survey on Drug Use and Health.* Washington, DC: Substance Abuse and Mental Health Services Administration. Retrieved May 21, 2009, from http://www.oas.samhsa.gov/NSDUH/2K6NSDUH/2K6results.cfm

U.S. Department of Housing and Urban Development. (2008). *Third annual homeless assessment report to congress.* Washington, DC: Office of Community Planning and Development. Retrieved May 21, 2009, from http://www.hudhre.info/documents/3rdHomelessAssessmentReport.pdf

U.S. Department of Justice, Bureau of Justice Statistics. (2004). *Survey of inmates in State and Federal correctional facilities, 2004* [Data file]. Retrieved August 1, 2007, from the National Archive of Criminal Justice Data website, http://www.icpsr.umich.edu/NACJD/archive.html

U.S. Department of Labor. (2008). *News release: The employment situation August 2008*. Washington, DC: Bureau of Labor Statistics.

Wilchins, R. A., Lombardi, E., Priesing, D., & Malouf, D. (1997). First national survey of transgender violence. GenderPAC. Retrieved May 21, 2009, from http://transreference.transadvocacy.org/reference/TransViolenceSurveyResults.pdf

Xavier, J. M. (2000). Washington transgender needs assessment survey: Final report for phase two. Report to Us Helping Us, People Into Living, Inc. Retrieved May 21, 2009, http://www.glaa.org/archive/2000/tgneedsassessment1112.shtml

Selected Reading

# A Feminist Analysis of the American Criminal Justice System's Response to Human Trafficking

*Tonisha Renee Jones and Brian Frederick Kingshott*

## INTRODUCTION

Recently, the topic of human trafficking has received significant attention in the form of media coverage (Denton, 2010), the formation of anti-human trafficking advocacy groups and task forces (Stolz, 2005, 2010), the adoption of international human trafficking legislation, and the increase of human trafficking governmental reports, theoretical literature, and empirical research on the issue (see Gozdziak & Bump, 2008; Gozdziak & Collett, 2005; Gozdziak, Graveline, Skippings, & Song, 2015). Criminological and criminal justice scholarship on the topic of human trafficking has consisted of a critical examination of human trafficking legislation, as well as how law enforcement, the legal community, and victim service providers respond to the crime (for some examples see Farrell & Pfeffer, 2014; Farrell, Owens, & McDevitt, 2014; Farrell, Pfeffer, & Bright, 2015; Kerodal, Freilich, & Galietta, 2015; Nichols & Heil, 2015).

While criminological and criminal justice scholarship has made important contributions to enhance human trafficking awareness and inform anti-human trafficking policy and practice, to date, it has been devoid of a feminist analysis of the topic. While human trafficking is considered a gender-based phenomenon, disproportionately impacting women and girls (International Labour Office, 2012; U.N. Office of Drugs & Crime, 2012), and while gender-based factors that contribute to the activity have been identified (Ebbe & Das, 2008; Territo & Kirkham, 2010), criminological and criminal justice scholars have spent little time reflecting on how patriarchy impacts the criminal justice system's response to the crime. Examining the topic of human trafficking through a feminist lens is necessary to understand how the issue of patriarchy impacts criminal justice system approaches to the crime as well as the outcomes of such anti-human trafficking efforts.

Therein, the purpose of this analysis is to examine the patriarchy/criminal justice system nexus to build understanding within criminological and criminal justice literature concerning how patriarchy impacts the criminal justice system's response to human trafficking. In effect, this analysis discusses the influence of patriarchy on criminal justice system policy development and practices and postulates that such influence ultimately undermines the system's anti-human trafficking efforts. The following analysis first provides a general overview of the issue of human trafficking. Then, human trafficking as a gender-based phenomenon is explored. This is followed by an analysis of the interface between a patriarchal criminal justice system and the system's response to human trafficking. Finally, implications for future human trafficking public policy and research are discussed.

## THE ISSUE OF HUMAN TRAFFICKING

The term human trafficking refers to, 'the act of recruiting, harboring, transporting, providing, or obtaining a person for compelled labor or commercial sex acts through the use of force, fraud, or coercion' (U.S. Department of State, 2014, p. 29). Human trafficking has been considered a problem for some time, evidenced by international human trafficking legislation in existence since the early 1900s. For example, in 1905, the League of Nations adopted the International agreement for the Suppression of the 'White Slave Traffic'. In 1910, the United States (U.S.) passed the White Slave Traffic act, also known as the Mann act, federal legislation designed to stop the interstate transportation of women and girls for the purposes of prostitution. Additional human trafficking legislation followed in 1934, when the League of Nations entered into force the International Convention for the Suppression of the Traffic in Women of Full Age, followed in 1951, by the United Nations (U.N.) Convention for the Suppression of the Traffic in Persons and the Exploitation of the Prostitution of Others. More recent human trafficking legislation was enacted in 2000, including the U.N. Protocol to Prevent, Suppress and Punish Trafficking in Persons, Especially Women and Children (the Palermo Protocol), and the U.S. Victims of Trafficking and Violence Protection act (TVPa), the first comprehensive federal legislation to address human trafficking. In addition, by 2015, every state in the U.S. had enacted human trafficking legislation or legal provisions (Polaris Project, 2014).

While human trafficking legislation has been enacted to address and combat the crime, due to definitional and methodological challenges (International Organization for Migration, 2010; Nawyn, Birdal, & Glogower, 2013), establishing the prevalence of the activity has proved difficult. As a result, available human trafficking statistics are largely derived from estimates (see International Labour Office, 2012; U.N. Office of Drugs & Crime, 2012; U.S. Department of State, 2014). These estimates, however, vary widely from official human trafficking statistics, including confirmed human trafficking investigations, arrests, prosecutions, convictions, and victim certifications (see Banks & Kyckelhahn, 2011; Federal Bureau of Investigation, 2014; Kyckelhahn, Beck, & Cohen, 2009; Motivans & Kyckelhahn, 2006; Office of Refugee Resettlement, 2012). Despite the lack of empirical information on the prevalence of human trafficking, human trafficking scholarship has contributed to a growing knowledgebase on the topic, especially concerning gender-based factors that contribute to the crime.

## GENDER AND HUMAN TRAFFICKING

Human trafficking is considered a gender-based phenomenon (Russell, 2014; Zimmerman, 2005), disproportionately impacting the lives of women and girls. The U.N. states that women account for 55–60% of all human trafficking victims detected globally, while two-thirds of trafficked children are girls (U.N. Office of Drugs & Crime, 2012). Human trafficking scholars have identified a complex set of 'push and pull' factors that make women and girls particularly vulnerable to becoming trafficking victims (Ebbe & Das, 2008; Territo & Kirkham, 2010) such as violence against women (U.N. Office of Drugs & Crime, 2013; World Health Organization, 2012, 2014), the feminization of poverty and migration (Barner, Okech, & Camp, 2014; Baykotan, 2014; Bertone, 2000; Russell, 2014; Samarasinghe, 2015; Sassen, 2000), globalization and the capitalist market system (Aronowitz, 2001; Bales, 2000; Bertone, 2000; Sassen, 2000), and the practice of consumerism and commodification (Bales, 2000; Bertone, 2000; Chase & Statham, 2005; Clift & Carter, 2000; Dong-Hoon, 2004; Ekberg, 2004). However, the one factor suggested to condition the factors mentioned above, and contribute to women's vulnerable social, political, and economic positioning, is the system of patriarchy.

### Patriarchy

Patriarchy, defined as 'a sex/gender system in which men dominate women and what is considered masculine is more highly valued than what is considered feminine' (Chesney-Lind, 2006, p. 9), is suggested to influence the context in which women and girls are trafficked (Busch, Fong, & Williamson, 2004; Samarasinghe, 2015; U.N. Office of Drugs & Crime, 2013). In highly patriarchal societies, women are often viewed as inferior beings and are expected to be subordinate to men (Ebbe & Das, 2008; Jungudo, 2014). Ascribed second-class citizen status in social institutions, women are not afforded the same rights and liberties as men and experience limited or restricted access to social, political, or economic spheres (Baykotan, 2014; Watson & Silkstone, 2006). Women's less privileged status produces gender-based inequality and discrimination, resulting in women's low educational attainment and gender-based division of labor and wages, ultimately producing deep social, political, and economic disadvantage for women (Busch et al., 2004; Jungudo, 2014; Russell, 2014; Samarasinghe, 2015; Watson & Silkstone, 2006). It is stated, within this context, human traffickers capitalize on women's desire to elevate their weak status, as well as broad cultural acceptance of gender-based violence, including viewing the trafficking of women as socially acceptable (Barner et al., 2014; Baykotan, 2014; Russell, 2014; Samarasinghe, 2015; U.N. Office of Drugs & Crime, 2012, 2013; World Health Organization, 2012, 2014).

It is also stated that in highly patriarchal societies human trafficking for the specific purpose of commercial sexual exploitation is likely to flourish. In such societies, patriarchal perspectives ascribe to the ideology that women's sole purpose is to please men, especially sexually (Leidholdt, 2003). Male privilege entitles men to sexual access to women, with women obliged to provide such access (Monto, 2004). With male sex-seeking behavior considered a demonstration of masculinity and a normative male experience, a demand is created for unrestricted and affordable sexual access to women, which human trafficking for the purpose of commercial sexual exploitation provides (Monto, 2004).

The system of patriarchy has impacted women on a global scale. However, patriarchy has also impacted the American criminal justice system. Patriarchy's influence on the criminal justice system has shaped the system's approach to human trafficking as well as the outcomes of such anti-human trafficking efforts.

## PATRIARCHY, THE AMERICAN CRIMINAL JUSTICE SYSTEM, AND HUMAN TRAFFICKING

As stated above, in patriarchal societies, men wield considerable power and authority over women. Women are often ascribed second-class citizen status in social institutions resulting in their unequal and disadvantaged social, political, and economic standing (Baykotan, 2014; Watson & Silkstone, 2006). In patriarchal societies, the 'inherent power embedded in masculinity'(Lutze & Symons, 2003, p. 320), affords men, 'the ability to formulate law, institutions, and policy from this position of power' (p. 320). As a result, gendered institutions often develop, including justice systems (Franklin, 2008).

### Patriarchy and the American Criminal Justice System

The American criminal justice system is considered highly gendered and heavily male-dominated with maleness constructed into the system and infused throughout the organizational process (Burgess-Proctor, 2006; Chesney-Lind, 2006; Schram & Koons-Witt, 2004). Specifically, males come to overwhelmingly serve as legislators that make the laws, judges that interpret the laws, police officers that enforce the laws, correctional officers that supervise offenders in male-centric correctional facilities, and practitioners who work to rehabilitate offenders with male-centric curricula (Rafter & Natalizia, 1981). Such a heavily male-dominated institutional framework produces a male-informed ideology in which the criminal justice system tends to 'favor male perspectives and approaches' (Lutze & Symons, 2003, p. 321) often to the detriment of women interfacing with the system as criminal offenders or crime victims, including trafficking victims.

## Patriarchy and the American Criminal Justice System's Response to Human Trafficking

U.S. responses to crime issues often involve 'law and order' approaches that are stated to reflect a 'masculine-defined institutional bias toward problem solving' (Lutze & Symons, 2003, p. 321). The U.S. response to human trafficking is no exception with criminal justice approaches employed to address the crime, including the adoption of the TVPa and the use of the criminal justice system to enforce the federal legislation. However, the TVPa and accompanying criminal justice anti-human trafficking activities have been heavily criticized for their inability to effectively prevent trafficking, prosecute offenders, or protect victims (Sheldon-Sherman, 2012).

The severe limitations of the TVPa and associated criminal justice anti-human trafficking activities are the result of the impact of patriarchy on criminal justice system human trafficking policy development and practice. Specifically, the TVPa was formulated in the highly male-gendered U.S. Congressional system and is implemented through the masculine criminal justice institution. As a result, criminal justice system responses to human trafficking have favored male perspectives, interests, and approaches. Such male-informed and defined responses to human trafficking have resulted in the criminal justice system's preoccupation with sex trafficking, the narrow construction of human trafficking victim, the prioritization of the criminal justice system's goals over human trafficking victims' needs, and the lack of concern for human trafficking victims' lived reality, all of which have subverted the TVPa's intent and undermined the effectiveness of the criminal justice system's anti-human trafficking efforts, with negative consequences for trafficking victims.

## The Preoccupation with Sex Trafficking

Although the TVPa is designed to address all forms of human trafficking, the criminal justice system has been criticized for its singular focus on sex trafficking (Lobasz, 2009; Marcus, Horning, Curtis, Sanson, & Thompson, 2014; Sheldon-Sherman, 2012; Wilson & O'Brien, 2016; Wolken, 2006; Zimmerman, 2005). For example, 'between 2001 and 2005, the Department of Justice filed twice as many sex trafficking cases as labor cases and prosecuted three times as many sex trafficking defendants' (Sheldon-Sherman, 2012, p. 459). It is argued that the criminal justice system's singular focus on sex trafficking can be attributed to criminal justice professionals' adherence to dominant constructions of human trafficking that rely upon sensationalized accounts of passive and sexually exploited women and girls. It is stated these sensationalized accounts were developed by relevant stakeholders to craft a 'sympathetic' victim in order to garner public and political interest and support for anti-human trafficking efforts (Lobasz, 2009; Sheldon-Sherman, 2012; Wilson & O'Brien, 2016; Wolken, 2006; Zimmerman, 2005). However, the criminal justice system's singular focus on the issue of sex when addressing human trafficking mirrors past system responses to crime issues involving women and girls.

The criminal justice system has historically been preoccupied with the morality and sexuality of women and girls as criminal offenders and as crime victims (Franklin, 2008). For example, early criminal justice punishment and treatment strategies were employed to ensure women's conformity to White, middle-class ideals about morality, sexual propriety, and appropriate gender roles. Women whose behavior fell outside these ideals faced harsh criminal punishment. Leniency in criminal punishment only extended to women who adhered to feminine norms and standards of behavior, or who were deemed worthy of protection, largely excluding poor women and women of color. Women who engaged in 'unladylike' or masculine crimes did not encounter a chivalrous criminal justice system, but instead were labeled 'deviant' or 'evil' and faced harsh sanctions (Franklin, 2008; Rafter, 1990; Rafter & Natalizia, 1981).

Such preoccupation with the issue of morality, sexual propriety, and appropriate gender roles was also present in early U.S. criminal justice responses to human trafficking, evidenced by the White Slave Traffic act of 1910. It is argued, this early legislation was enacted as part of the international campaign against 'white slavery' and out of concern to protect white women's virtue, uphold their morality, and sanction their sexual activity committed for 'immoral purposes' (Jahic & Finckenauer, 2005; Lobasz, 2009). It is argued the criminal justice system's preoccupation with the morality and sexuality of women and girls was again present in the 1990s, when the topic of human trafficking received renewed attention by the criminal justice system due only to the 'white slave panic' caused by reports of white Eastern European women trafficked to the U.S. for the purpose of sexual exploitation as part of the 'Natasha Trade' (Doezema, 1999; Jahic & Finckenauer, 2005; Lobasz, 2009; Wilson & O'Brien, 2016).

Preoccupation with white women's virtue, morality, and sexuality, as well as ideological positions about sex work (Marcus et al., 2014; Wilson & O'Brien, 2016) by the highly-gendered and male-dominated political and criminal justice systems likely led to the adoption of the TVPa in 2000 by the U.S. Congress and has likely contributed to the criminal justice system's singular focus on sex trafficking while implementing the federal legislation. Such preoccupation has unjustly prioritized, 'the sexual traffic of white women over the traffic of women and men of all races who are trafficked for purposes including, but not limited to, the sex trade' (Lobasz, 2009, p. 322). In addition, such preoccupation has also influenced the construction of the TVPa's legal definition of human trafficking victim that, 'exploits gender stereotypes, specifically notions of women's passivity'(Zimmerman, 2005, p. 39) and 'selects for only one specific type of trafficking victim-a type that represents only a very small minority of trafficked individuals' (p. 39).

## The Narrow Construction of Human Trafficking Victim

Throughout its history, the criminal justice system has reserved victim status for women considered to be 'true victims'. For example, prior to the 1970s Victim's Rights Movement, during court trials for rape and domestic violence cases, rape myths and victim blaming permeated court proceedings with widely held views by judges, attorneys, and jurists that the victim's own behavior or lifestyle contributed to her victimization (Belknap, 2001; Belknap & Potter, 2006; Caringella, 2006; Muraskin, 2012; Van Wormer & Bartollas, 2000). It is stated the criminal justice system continues to not extend victim status to women whose behavior or lifestyle is believed to have contributed to her victimization (Belknap, 2001; Belknap & Potter, 2006; Caringella, 2006; Muraskin, 2012; Van Wormer & Bartollas, 2000). In addition, it is suggested the criminal justice system only offers protection and rehabilitation to women, whether victims or offenders, who conform to sex-role stereotypes and standards of behavior, and who are willing to accept the criminal justice system's paternal protection (Lutze & Symons, 2003).

The criminal justice system's narrow construction of victim is present in the TVPa's legal definition of human trafficking victim. The TVPa's legal definition is patterned on dominant human trafficking narratives that are based on widely held, but largely inaccurate stereotypes about human trafficking (Cunningham & Cromer, 2016; Hickle & Roe-Sepowitz, 2016; Menaker & Franklin, 2013; Menaker & Miller, 2013). Current human trafficking narratives rely on idealized conceptions of human trafficking victims, offenders, and situations, conceptions that are often steeped in sex-based stereotypes. For example, anti-human trafficking advocates presenting anecdotal accounts of human trafficking situations often depict victims as young, innocent females, who because of their naiveté and helplessness, are tricked or forced into the violent world of sex-trafficking (Wilson & O'Brien, 2016). While human trafficking victims are largely portrayed as devoid of any agency, and therefore blameless, human trafficking offenders are depicted as deviant criminals unknown to the victim, who dominate and control unconsenting victims in oppressive and exploitive slave-like conditions (Wilson & O'Brien, 2016). It is stated, however, that these dominant narratives often do not reflect the lived experiences of trafficked victims (Hickle & Roe-Sepowitz, 2016) bearing 'little if any relationship to the various women caught in the human trafficking trade' (Zimmerman, 2005, p. 50).

Recent empirical research challenges conventional narratives about human trafficking (see Hickle & Roe-Sepowitz, 2016; Marcus et al., 2014). This research suggests that contrary to popular human trafficking depictions, many human trafficking victims possess autonomy and enter human trafficking situations without being tricked or forced. This research states human trafficking offenders play a smaller role in the recruitment and initiation of trafficking victims, and operation of trafficking networks, than what is widely assumed. This research also states that not all relationships between human trafficking victims and offenders are violent, oppressive or exploitive, with such relationships often highly complex and multifaceted, and characterized as encompassing 'a wide spectrum of behaviors, power balances, and mutual compromises (Marcus et al., 2014, p. 242). While it is acknowledged that human trafficking situations of oppression and captivity do exist, this research suggests these situations are rare enough to question dominant human trafficking narratives that perpetuate this idealized victim/offender construction (Hickle & Roe-Sepowitz, 2016; Marcus et al., 2014).

Because the TVPa's legal definition is patterned on dominant human trafficking narratives, it reinforces dominant constructions of human trafficking victims held by criminal justice professionals, potentially impacting their ability to identify human trafficking situations, and when interfacing with potential human trafficking victims, their willingness to extend victim status (Zimmerman, 2005).

For example, to qualify as a trafficking victim and receive social services and immigration relief, a victim must prove they suffered 'severe forms of trafficking' defined in the TVPa as:

a. sex trafficking in which a commercial sex act is induced by force, fraud, or coercion, or in which the person induced to perform such an act has not attained 18 years of age; or
b. the recruitment, harboring, transportation, provision, or obtaining of a person for labor or services, through the use of force, fraud, or coercion for the purpose of subjection to involuntary servitude, peonage, debt bondage, or slavery (U.S. Department of State, 2015, p. 9).

While the elements of force, fraud, and coercion are considered integral to the TVPa's legal definition, it is stated such a narrow construction of human trafficking victims excludes potential victims that cannot prove their situation was entirely involuntary (Hickle & Roe-Sepowitz, 2016; Sheldon-Sherman, 2012; Zimmerman, 2005).

It is stated, many human trafficking victims cannot meet the TVPa's strict legal standard due to the circumstances of their initial entry into the trafficking situation (Lobasz, 2009). As recent empirical research suggests, seeking employment, new opportunities, or new experiences, many trafficking victims know of the work they will be doing, or willingly leave their homes with their traffickers, but do not consent to the slave-like conditions they find themselves in (Hickle & Roe-Sepowitz, 2016; Lobasz, 2009; Marcus et al., 2014; Rieger, 2007; Sheldon-Sherman, 2012; Wolken, 2006; Zimmerman, 2005). Because these victims do not fit the TVPa's strict legal standard or the ideal victim prototype of a trafficking victim held by many criminal justice professionals of a kidnapped, sold, and sexually exploited female, waiting and wanting to be rescued, many trafficking victims are not identified as victims (Lobasz, 2009). In addition, if a trafficking victim cannot prove their situation is the result of force, fraud, or coercion, they are often seen by criminal justice professionals as complicit in and guilty of their victimization, and quickly relabeled a prostitute, labor law violator, or illegal immigrant (Lobasz, 2009; Rieger, 2007; Sheldon-Sherman, 2012; Wolken, 2006). The victim is not seen as a victim, but as a criminal whose situation is unworthy of investigation or prosecution (Rieger, 2007; Sheldon-Sherman, 2012; Wolken, 2006).

The TVPa's narrow construction of human trafficking victim and the dominant construction of a trafficking victim held by many criminal justice professionals enforcing the federal legislation create a 'rhetorical' victim and a 'legal' victim (Zimmerman, 2005). A victim hierarchy is created whereby a distinction is made between 'true' trafficking victims and those underserving of legal rights, criminal justice protection, and social service support (Lobasz, 2009; Rieger, 2007). It is stated this narrow construction of human trafficking victim selects for a kidnapped, sold, and sexually exploited female victim, which is the least likely trafficking scenario (Lobasz, 2009). It is also stated this narrow construction of human trafficking victim is the real cause of low victim identification, case prosecution, and victim certification rates, not because the activity is well-hidden or criminal justice efforts have been minimal, as is commonly suggested (Rieger, 2007; Zimmerman, 2005). For those trafficking victims that are identified and extended victim status, they learn that the goals of the criminal justice system will be prioritized over their needs as victims and that the criminal justice system's response to human trafficking is not as victim-centered as it purports to be.

## The Prioritization of Criminal Justice System Goals over Human Trafficking Victim Needs

Historically, men have dominated the U.S. legal system (Rafter & Natalizia, 1981). Consequently, law has been produced favoring male perspectives and interests (Lutze & Symons, 2003). Women have frequently been denied equal access to the law, or have been granted only limited legal rights (Lutze & Symons, 2003; Rafter & Natalizia, 1981; Van Wormer & Bartollas, 2000). In addition, gender-based laws have helped men retain their status and authority over women, and the law has regularly failed to address issues of critical importance to women, such as rape, incest, domestic violence, and sexual harassment (Belknap, 2001; Lutze & Symons, 2003; Rafter & Natalizia, 1981). It is stated, early criminal law, with differential treatment of women codified into the law and corresponding criminal sentences, was used as the legal apparatus to uphold the status quo as well as women's proper place in society (Belknap, 2001; Lutze & Symons, 2003; Rafter & Natalizia, 1981; Van Wormer & Bartollas, 2000).

When female crime victims have received legal protections they have often encountered a criminal justice system insensitive to their needs as victims and only willing to provide protection to those women who are deemed by criminal justice professionals to be cooperative and worthy of such protection (Lutze & Symons, 2003). When interfacing with the heavily male-dominated and highly gendered criminal justice system, human trafficking victims have had experiences similar to female crime victims.

Like early domestic violence legislation (Lutze & Symons, 2003), the TVPa locates power in the hands of the male-centered criminal justice institution. Consequently, the criminal justice system has had the ability to define its perspective, pursue its interests, and determine its approach when enforcing the federal legislation. As a result, the criminal justice system has prioritized its goals over trafficking victims' needs.

Human trafficking is considered to be a complex human rights issue caused by diverse social, political, and economic factors (U.N. Office of Drugs & Crime, 2012, 2013; World Health Organization, 2012, 2014). To ensure a victim-centered response to human trafficking, it is suggested a human rights paradigm should be used to critically assess human trafficking victims' vulnerabilities, identify their most pressing needs, and make certain their voices are incorporated into anti-human trafficking solutions (Pourmokhtari, 2015; U.N. Office of Drugs & Crime, 2012, 2013; World Health Organization, 2012, 2014). In the U.S., however, human trafficking has largely been framed as a crime issue requiring a law enforcement response. The adoption of this framework has resulted in human trafficking legislation that'stems from a law enforcement perspective rather than a victim-centered perspective' (Jordan, Patel, & Rapp, 2013, p. 364). The criminal justice system's approach to addressing human trafficking has been highly criticized. It is suggested the criminal justice system only extends its protection and support to human trafficking victims willing to accept the system's paternal protection, and only if it is in the system's best interest to do so (Lobasz, 2009; Rieger, 2007; Sheldon-Sherman, 2012; Zimmerman, 2005).

For example, to receive legal rights, social services, and immigration relief, human trafficking victims must submit to the investigation and prosecution goals of the criminal justice system (Rieger, 2007; Sheldon-Sherman, 2012). Specifically, human trafficking victims are not afforded legal rights as victims unless granted by the prosecutor after a decision is made to pursue a human trafficking case. Criminal justice system protection then becomes protection only 'for the sake of prosecution' (Rieger, 2007, p. 252). In addition, while a trafficking victim can request the unreasonable exception to avoid participating in the adversarial court process, the prosecutor makes the final determination whether the victim qualifies for the exception. Furthermore, even if a human trafficking victim participates in the investigation and prosecution of a human trafficking case, they still must prove they would face 'extreme hardship' if deported to their country of origin (Rieger, 2007; Sheldon-Sherman, 2012).

It is stated tying legal protections and social services to cooperation with case investigation and prosecution further victimizes trafficked individuals and ensures their 'needs, concerns, wishes, and goals' (Rieger, 2007, p. 252) come second to the goals of the criminal justice system. It is further asserted that the criminal justice system's approach to human trafficking reveals its true interest, which is not protecting victims, as is often claimed, but advancing its own interests by expanding police powers both domestically and internationally, securing the nation's borders, and shutting down criminal networks thought to be associated with human trafficking activity such as organized crime, illegal immigration, and prostitution (Lobasz, 2009; Wilson & O'Brien, 2016). Furthermore, the distribution of significantly more federal funding for investigation and prosecution efforts over victim service delivery is cited as additional evidence of the prioritization of the goals of the criminal justice system over the needs of human trafficking victims (Sheldon-Sherman, 2012).

## The Lack of Concern for Human Trafficking Victims' Lived Reality

As stated above, the early criminal justice system failed to address issues of critical importance to women as crime victims and often responded to women's victimization in ways that left them feeling twice victimized (Belknap, 2001; Belknap & Potter, 2006; Caringella, 2006; Lutze & Symons, 2003; Muraskin, 2012; Rafter & Natalizia, 1981; Van Wormer & Bartollas, 2000). In addition, early criminological theories on female offending were fraught with sexist stereotypes that trivialized, sexualized, or demonized female offenders (Belknap, 2001). Such theoretical and empirical research marginalized and misrepresented female offending (Chesney-Lind, 2006), rarely accounting for, or even considering, the complexity of women's lives and how their lived experiences potentially contributed to their involvement in criminal activity (Belknap, 2001; Burgess-Proctor, 2006; Franklin, 2008; Schram & Koons-Witt, 2004). Similarly, the criminal justice system's response to human trafficking has been criticized for its lack of understanding of the lived reality of human trafficking victims as well as its failure to consider the complex set of factors that push and pull victims into human trafficking.

It is stated that human trafficking does not occur in social, political, or economic isolation (Wolken, 2006). Human trafficking victims, most of whom are poor women and children, are considered to be vulnerable to trafficking because they come from populations that are 'systematically oppressed and marginalized'(Rieger, 2007, p. 235) and face significant structural inequalities (Hickle & Roe-Sepowitz, 2016; Pourmokhtari, 2015). In addition, it is stated human trafficking victims often have extensive victimization histories including childhood physical, sexual, and psychological abuse and neglect, and as children have been exposed to domestic violence in the home, have witnessed parental alcohol and substance abuse, and because of the multi-problem family dysfunction have become involved in the social services system (Hickle & Roe-Sepowitz, 2016; Jordan et al., 2013; Marcus et al., 2014; Menaker & Franklin, 2013; Menaker & Miller, 2013). It is suggested human trafficking victims also often possess salient risk factors for trafficking such as being a runaway or 'throwaway' youth, homelessness, academic and social challenges, alcohol or drug dependency, mental illness, child welfare or juvenile justice system involvement, and significant economic need (Cunningham & Cromer, 2016; Hickle & Roe-Sepowitz, 2016; Jordan et al., 2013; Marcus et al., 2014; Menaker & Franklin, 2013; Menaker & Miller, 2013).

It is asserted that human trafficking victims' social, political, and economically disadvantaged status, aversive life experiences, and the presence of salient risk factors for trafficking leave them especially vulnerable to being trafficked (Rieger, 2007; Wolken, 2006). It is stated that human trafficking occurs within this larger context where the most disadvantaged individuals, seeking to survive or improve their lives or that of their family, exercise agency by pursuing employment opportunities among the very limited options that are available to them. It is suggested, within this context, trying to secure employment through the assistance of a trafficker becomes a reasonable pursuit (Zimmerman, 2005).

The criminal justice system's approach to human trafficking has been characterized as disaggregated from the social, political, and economic dynamics that structure it, rendering the approach largely disconnected from human trafficking victims' lived experiences (Zimmerman, 2005). For example, to qualify as a victim of 'severe forms of trafficking' an individual must prove the elements of force, fraud, or coercion, and that they did not consent to being trafficked. It is stated this criteria is problematic because it fails to consider that 'social factors always work to condition consent'(Zimmerman, 2005, p. 46), and that 'consent is a social artifact that is inherently contextually embedded' (p. 46). It is argued using the criteria of consent to determine whether an individual is a true victim of human trafficking ignores how larger social, political, and economic conditions 'shape both consent and choice' (p. 49) and fails to acknowledge how these factors can be just as coercive as individual coercive acts and can profoundly impact the choices that individuals make (Zimmerman, 2005). It is argued, the TVPa fails to allow for the very complex social, political, and economic contingencies that compel people into human trafficking where it is possible that an individual can at the same time be a trafficking victim and a choosing agent (Hickle & Roe-Sepowitz, 2016; Marcus et al., 2014). It is stated the TVPa oversimplifies the complex lives of victims (Marcus et al., 2014) where victims often enter trafficking not through force, but act autonomously, but where their decision to enter 'remains one among few very constrained and difficult choices' (Hickle & Roe-Sepowitz, 2016, p. 2), and where this choice is the 'the least worst option or last option to support themselves and their children' (Hickle & Roe-Sepowitz, 2016, p. 14). This 'choice' is often considered by the public and criminal justice officials as consent, and therefore outside the purview of the TVPa's policy apparatus.

## DISCUSSION

Due to the highly gendered and heavily male-dominated criminal justice institution, the system's response to human trafficking has favored male interests, perspectives, and approaches. The criminal justice system's 'masculine-defined institutional bias toward problem solving' (Lutze & Symons, 2003, p. 321) has led to the adoption of a 'law and order' approach to human trafficking that has been deficient in achieving the TVPa's three main goals of preventing human trafficking, protecting victims, and prosecuting offenders. The influence of patriarchy on criminal justice system policy and practice has produced male informed and defined responses to human trafficking that has resulted in the system's preoccupation with sex trafficking, the narrow construction of a trafficking victim, the prioritization of the criminal justice system's goals over the trafficking victim's needs, and the lack of concern for trafficking victims' lived reality, all of which has ultimately undermined the system's anti-human trafficking efforts and negatively impacted trafficking victims. To more effectively address human trafficking, and successfully redress the harms caused by the crime, the criminal justice system must acknowledge the limitations of its current law enforcement approach and adopt a new framework to respond to the crime.

## Public Policy Implications

It is stated, 'human trafficking is first and foremost a violation of human rights' (Lobasz, 2009, p. 321) and that 'traffickers routinely violate the human rights enumerated in the Universal Declaration of Human Rights (UDHR)' (p. 330). Under the UDHR state governments are 'legally obligated to protect individuals within their own territory against human rights abuses even if those individuals are not citizens of the state and even if the government itself is not the group abusing human rights' (p. 331). It is argued the UDHR provides moral and legal ground to reframe the problem of human trafficking from a law enforcement to human rights issue. It is suggested reframing the problem of human trafficking could produce more victim-centered responses to the crime (Lobasz, 2009; Pourmokhtari, 2015; Wolken, 2006).

Adopting a human rights framework to respond to the issue of human trafficking would establish trafficking victims as the category of analysis to allow for the consideration of the complex social, political, and economic factors that make trafficking victims vulnerable, not criminal people (Lobasz, 2009). Within this context, a human rights framework would challenge the TVPa's narrow legal definition of human trafficking and encourage the expansion of the TVPa's legal definition, as well as its enforcement, to reflect the reality of human trafficking situations.

A human rights framework would also challenge the TVPa's rigid requirements that mandate trafficking victims participate in the investigation and prosecution of their traffickers to receive legal rights, social services, and immigration relief (Jordan et al., 2013) on the grounds that, from a human rights perspective, such requirements are fundamentally flawed because they prioritize the goals of the criminal justice system over the needs of the trafficking victim. It can be argued the TVPa's rigid participation requirements deny trafficking victims agency and utilize its own form of forceful and coercive tactics to achieve criminal justice system goals.

Finally, a human rights framework would challenge the current unequal distribution of funding for trafficking investigation and prosecution over victim services and demand that 'funding for education, outreach, and service provisions be distributed effectively and logically – filtered through local immigrants' rights and workers' rights organizations as well as domestic violence and other social justice organizations' (Wolken, 2006, p. 437).

## Future Research Directions

In addition, while criminological and criminal justice scholars have made meaningful contributions to human trafficking literature, future research should continue to critically examine how patriarchy impacts the criminal justice system's response to human trafficking. Specifically, criminological and criminal justice scholars should explore how the construction of human trafficking and human trafficking victim impacts the language and enforcement of the TVPa (Wilson & O'Brien, 2016). Criminological and criminal justice scholars should also assess how the TVPa, 'a legislative tool that patterns its legal definitions of victimization on the stereotype of a passive, sexually violated woman' (Zimmerman, 2005, p. 51) impacts how criminal justice practitioners define human trafficking, identify trafficking victims, and extend trafficking victim status (Cunningham & Cromer, 2016; Menaker & Miller, 2013).

Furthermore, criminological and criminal justice scholars should relocate the crime of human trafficking back in time and space (Zimmerman, 2005), to provide the academic and practitioner community a more sophisticated and nuanced understanding of the complex social, political, and economic factors that condition trafficking victims' consent and choice and make them vulnerable to the crime (Hickle & Roe-Sepowitz, 2016; Marcus et al., 2014).

Finally, criminological and criminal justice scholars should propose innovative anti-human trafficking policy that does not rely so heavily on law enforcement approaches, but that instead has a human rights framework and utilizes harm reduction strategies. Harm reduction strategies that employ empowerment approaches that treat human trafficking victims with respect while at the same time recognizing their autonomy can produce broader and more holistic social justice solutions that actually meet the real needs of human trafficking victims (Marcus et al., 2014; Menaker & Franklin, 2013).

## CONCLUSION

Human trafficking is a complex crime that requires an equally sophisticated response. Such response must be informed by a more nuanced understanding concerning the dynamic factors that condition human trafficking. Human trafficking public policy must be reflective of this understanding if such policy is to be effective and truly victim-centered.

## DISCLOSURE STATEMENT

No potential conflict of interest was reported by the authors.

## NOTES ON CONTRIBUTORS

Tonisha Renee Jones, Ph.D., is an assistant professor at the School of Criminal Justice at Grand Valley State University. Her current research interests include criminal justice interagency collaboration, juvenile justice, and human trafficking.

Brian Frederick Kingshott, Ph.D., is a professor at the School of Criminal Justice at Grand Valley State University. His current research interests include international policing and terrorism.

## References

Aronowitz, A. A. (2001). Smuggling and trafficking in human beings: The phenomenon, the markets that drive it and the organisations that promote it. *European Journal on Criminal Policy and Research, 9,* 163–195.

Bales, K. (2000). Expendable people: Slavery in the age of globalization. *Journal of International Affairs, 53,* 461–485.

Banks, D., & Kyckelhahn, T. (2011). *Characteristics of suspected human trafficking incidents, 2008–2010 (NCJ 233732).* Washington, DC: United States Department of Justice.

Barner, J. R., Okech, D., & Camp, M. a. (2014). Socio-economic inequality, human trafficking, and the global slave trade. *Societies, 4,* 148–160. doi: http://dx.doi.org/10.3390/soc4020148

Baykotan, C. (2014). Human trafficking in Turkey: A feminist analysis. *Fe Dergi, 6,* 14–24.

Belknap, J. (2001). *The invisible woman: Gender, crime, and justice* (2nd ed.). Belmont, Ca: Wadsworth Thomson Learning.

Belknap, J., & Potter, H. (2006). Intimate partner abuse. In C. Renzetti, L. Goodstein, & S. Miller (Eds.), *Rethinking gender, crime, and justice: Feminist readings* (pp. 168–184). New York: Oxford University Press.

Bertone, A. M. (2000). Sexual trafficking in women: International political economy and the politics of sex. *Gender Issues, 18,* 4–22.

Burgess-Proctor, A. (2006). Intersections of race, class, gender, and crime. *Feminist Criminology, 1,* 27–47.

Busch, N. B., Fong, R., & Williamson, J. (2004). Human trafficking and domestic violence: Comparisons in research methodology needs and strategies. *Journal of Social Work Research and Evaluation, 5,* 137–147.

Caringella, S. (2006). Sexual assault reforms: Thirty years and counting. In C. M. Renzetti, L. Goodstein, & S. L. Miller (Eds.), *Rethinking gender, crime, and justice: Feminist readings* (pp. 155–167). New York: Oxford University Press.

Chase, E., & Statham, J. (2005). Commercial and sexual exploitation of children and young people in the UK: a review. *Child Abuse Review, 14,* 4–25.

Chesney-Lind, M. (2006). Patriarchy, crime, and Justice: Feminist criminology in an era of backlash. *Feminist Criminology, 1,* 6–26. doi: http://dx.doi.org/10.1177/1557085105282893.

Clift, S., & Carter, S. (2000). *Tourism and sex: Culture, commerce and coercion.* London: Wellington House. *Convention for the Suppression of the Traffic in Persons and of the Exploitation of the Prostitution of Others,* New York, March 21, 1950, United Nations, Treaty Series, 96, 271. Retrieved from https://treaties.un.org/pages/ViewDetails.aspx?src=TREaTY&mtdsg_no=VII-11-a&chapter=7&lang=en

Cunningham, K. C., & Cromer, L. D. (2016). attitudes about human trafficking: Individual differences related to belief and victim blame. *Journal of Interpersonal Violence, 31*, 228–244. doi: http://dx.doi. org/10.1177/0886250514555369

Denton, E. (2010). International news coverage of human trafficking arrests and prosecutions: a content analysis. *Women & Criminal Justice, 20*, 10–26. doi: http://dx.doi.org/10.1080/08974451003641321

Doezema, J. (1999). Loose women or lost women? The re-emergence of the myth of white slavery in contemporary discourses of trafficking in women. *Gender Issues, 18*, 23–50.

Dong-Hoon, S. (2004). International sex trafficking in women in Korea: Its causes, consequences and countermeasures. *Asian Journal of Women's Studies, 10*, 7–47.

Ebbe, O. N. I., & Das, D. K. (Eds.). (2008). *Global trafficking in women and children*. Boca Raton, FL: CRC Press.

Ekberg, G. (2004). The Swedish law that prohibits the purchase of sexual services: Best practices for prevention of prostitution and trafficking in human beings. *Violence Against Women, 10*, 1187–1218.

Farrell, A., Owens, C., & McDevitt, J. (2014). New laws but few cases: Understanding the challenges to the investigation and prosecution of human trafficking cases. *Crime, Law & Social Change, 61*, 139–168. doi: http://dx.doi.org/10.1007/s10611-013-9442-1

Farrell, A., & Pfeffer, R. (2014). Policing human trafficking: Cultural blinders and organizational barriers. *Annals of the American Academy of Political & Social Science, 653*, 46–64. doi: http://dx.doi. org/10.1177/0002716213515835

Farrell, A., Pfeffer, R., & Bright, K. (2015). Police perceptions of human trafficking. *Journal of Criminal Justice, 38*, 315–333. doi: http://dx.doi.org/10.1080/0735648x.2014.995412

Federal Bureau of Investigation. (2014). *Human trafficking, 2014*. Retrieved from https://www.fbi.gov/about-us/cjis/ucr/crime-in-the-u.s/2014/crime-in-the-u.s.-2014/additional-reports/human-trafficking-report/human-trafficking.pdf

Franklin, C. A. (2008). Women offenders, disparate treatment, and criminal justice: a theoretical, historical, and contemporary overview. *Criminal Justice Studies, 21*, 343–362.

Gozdziak, E. M., & Bump, M. N. (2008). *Data and research on human trafficking: Bibliography of research based literature*. Washington, DC: Georgetown University, Walsh School of Foreign Services, Institute for the Study of International Migration.

Gozdziak, E. M., & Collett, E. A. (2005). Research on human trafficking in North america: a review of literature. *International Migration, 43*, 99–128.

Gozdziak, E. M., Graveline, S., Skippings, W., & Song, M. (2015). *Bibliography of research-based literature on human trafficking: 2008–2014*. Washington, DC: Georgetown University, Institute for the Study of International Immigration.

Hickle, K., & Roe-Sepowitz, D. (2016). "Curiosity and a pimp": Exploring sex trafficking victimization in experiences of entering sex trade industry work among participants in a prostitution diversion program. *Women & Criminal Justice.* doi: http://dx.doi.org/10.1080/08974454.2015.1128376

*International Agreement for the Suppression of the "White Slave Traffic"*, Paris, May 18, 1904, League of Nations, Treaty Series, 1, 83. Retrieved from https://treaties.un.org/Pages/ViewDetails.aspx?src=TREaTY&mtdsg_no=VII-8&chapter=7&lang=en

*International Convention for the Suppression of the Traffic in Women of Full Age*, Geneva, October 11, 1933, League of Nations, Treaty Series, 150, 431. Retrieved from https://treaties.un.org/Pages/ViewDetails.aspx?src=TREaTY&mtdsg_no=VII-5&chapter=7&lang=en

International Labour Office (2012). *ILO global estimate of forced labor.* Geneva: International Labour Office.

International Organization for Migration (2010). *Beneath the surface: Methodological issues in research and data collection with assisted trafficking victims.* Geneva: International Organization for Migration.

Jahic, G., & Finckenauer, J. O. (2005). Representations and misrepresentations of human trafficking. *Trends in Organized Crime, 8,* 24–40.

Jordan, J., Patel, B., & Rapp, L. (2013). Domestic minor sex trafficking: a social work perspective on misidentification, victims, buyers, traffickers, treatment, and reform of current practice. *Journal of Human Behavior in the Social Environment, 23,* 356–369. doi: http://dx.doi.org/10.1080/10911359.2013.764198

Jungudo, M. M. (2014). Gender and human rights implications of women trafficking in Northern Nigeria. *Mediterranean Journal of Social Sciences, 5,* 15–21. doi: http://dx.doi.org/10.5901/mjss.2014.v5n26p15

Kerodal, A. G., Freilich, J. D., & Galietta, M. (2015). The efficacy of sex crime and human trafficking legislations: Introducing the special issue. *International Journal of Comparative and Applied Criminal Justice, 39,* 93–97. doi: http://dx.doi.org/10.1080/01924036.2015.1012704

Kyckelhahn, T., Beck, A. J., & Cohen, T. H. (2009). *Characteristics of suspected human trafficking incidents, 2007–08 (NCJ 224526).* Washington, DC: United States Department of Justice.

Leidholdt, D. a. (2003). Prostitution and trafficking in women: an intimate relationship. *Journal of Trauma Practice, 2,* 167–183.

Lobasz, J. K. (2009). Beyond border security: Feminist approaches to human trafficking. *Security Studies, 18,* 319–344. doi: http://dx.doi.org/10.1080/09636410902900020

Lutze, F. E., & Symons, M. L. (2003). The evolution of domestic violence policy through masculine institutions: From discipline to protection to collaborative empowerment. *Criminology & Public Policy, 2,* 319–329.

Mann Act, 18 U.S.C. §§ 2421-2424 *et seq.* (1910).

Marcus, A., Horning, A., Curtis, R., Sanson, J., & Thompson, E. (2014). Conflct and agency among sex workers and pimps: a closer look at domestic minor sex trafficking. *American Academy of Political and Social Science, 653*, 225–246. doi: http://dx.doi.org/10.1177/0002716214521993

Menaker, T. A., & Franklin, C. A. (2013). Commercially sexually exploited girls and participant perceptions of blameworthiness: Examining the effects of victimization history and race disclosure. *Journal of Interpersonal Violence, 28*, 2024–2051. doi: http://dx.doi.org/10.1177/0886260512471078

Menaker, T. A., & Miller, A. K. (2013). Culpability attributions toward juvenile female prostitutes. *Child Abuse Review, 22*, 169–181. doi: http://dx.doi.org/10.1002/car.2204

Monto, M. A. (2004). Female prostitution, customers, and violence. *Violence Against Women, 10*, 160–188. doi: http://dx.doi.org/10.1177/1077801203260948

Motivans, M., & Kyckelhahn, T. (2006). *Federal prosecution of human trafficking, 2001–2005 (NCJ 215248)*. Washington, DC: United States Department of Justice.

Muraskin, R. (Ed.). (2012). *Women and justice: It's a crime* (5th ed.). Upper Saddle River, NJ: Prentice Hall.

Nawyn, S. J., Birdal, N. B. K., & Glogower, N. (2013). Estimating the extent of sex trafficking: Problems in definition and methodology. *International Journal of Sociology, 43*, 55–71.

Nichols, A. J., & Heil, E. C. (2015). Challenges to identifying and prosecuting sex trafficking cases in the Midwest United States. *Feminist Criminology, 10*, 7–35. doi: http://dx.doi. org/10.1177/1557085113519490

Office of Refugee Resettlement (2012). *Report to Congress, FY 2012*. Washington, DC: United States Department of Health and Human Services.

Polaris Project. (2014, September). *2014 state ratings on human trafficking laws*. Retrieved from http://www.polarisproject.org/resources/2014-state-ratings-human-trafficking-laws

Pourmokhtari, N. (2015). Global human trafficking unmasked: A feminist rights-based approach. *Journal of Human Trafficking, 1*, 156–166. doi: http://dx.doi.org/10.1080/23322705.2014.1000078

*Protocol to Prevent, Suppress and Punish Trafficking in Persons, Especially Women and Children*, New York, November 15, 2000, United Nations, Treaty Series, 2237, 319. Retrieved from: https://treaties.un.org/pages/viewdetails.aspx?src=ind&mtdsg_no=xviii-12-a&chapter=18&lang=en

Rafter, N. H. (1990). *Partial justice: Women, prisons, and social control* (2nd ed.). New Brunswick, NJ: Transaction Publishers.

Rafter, N. H., & Natalizia, E. M. (1981). Marxist feminism: Implications for criminal justice. *Crime & Delinquency, 27*, 81–98. doi: http://dx.doi.org/10.1177/0011/001112878102700106

Rieger, A. (2007). Missing the mark: Why the Trafficking Victims Protection Act fails to protect sex trafficking victims in the United States. *Harvard Journal of Law & Gender, 30*, 231–256.

Russell, A. M. (2014)."Victims of trafficking": The feminization of poverty and migration in the gendered narratives of human trafficking. *Societies, 4*, 532–548. doi: http://dx.doi.org/10.3390/soc4040532

Samarasinghe, V. (2015). Female sex trafficking: Gendered vulnerability. In A. Coles, L. Gray, & J. Momsen (Eds.), *The Routledge handbook of gender and development* (pp. 330–340). New York: Routledge.

Sassen, S. (2000). Women's burden: Counter-geographies of globalization and the feminization of survival. *Journal of International Affairs, 53*, 503–524.

Schram, P. J., & Koons-Witt, B. (2004). *Gendered (in)justice: Theory and practice in feminist criminology*. Long Grove, IL: Waveland Press.

Sheldon-Sherman, J. A. L. (2012). The missing "p": Prosecution, prevention, protection, and partnership in the Trafficking Victims Protection act. *Penn State Law Review, 117*, 443–501.

Stolz, B. (2005). Educating policymakers and setting the criminal justice policymaking agenda: Interest groups and the 'Victims of Trafficking and Violence act of 2000'. *Criminal Justice, 5*, 407–430. doi: http://dx.doi.org/10.1177/1466801250505771 8

Stolz, B. (2010). Human trafficking: Policy. *Criminology & Public Policy, 9*, 267–274. doi: http://dx.doi. org/10.111/j.1745-9122.2010.00625.x

Territo, L., & Kirkham, G. (Eds.). (2010). *International sex trafficking of women and Children: Understanding the global epidemic*. Flushing, NY: Looseleaf Law Publications Inc.

U.N. Office of Drugs and Crime (2012). *Global report on trafficking in persons*. Vienna: United Nations Publication.

U.N. Office of Drugs and Crime (2013). *Abuse of a position of vulnerability and other "means" within the definition of trafficking in persons*. Vienna: United Nations Publication.

U.S. Department of State (2014). *Trafficking in Persons Report June 2014*. Washington, DC: United States Department of State.

U.S. Department of State (2015). *Trafficking in Persons Report July 2015*. Washington, DC: United States Department of State.

Van Wormer, K. S., & Bartollas, C. (2000). *Women and the criminal justice system*. Needham Heights, MA: Allyn & Bacon.

Victims of Trafficking and Violence Protection Act of 2000, P.L. 106-386 (2000). Retrieved from: http:// www.state.gov/j/tip/laws/61124.htm.

Watson, J., & Silkstone, C. (2006). Human trafficking as a form of gender-based violence: Protecting the victim. *Agenda: Empowering Women for Gender-Equity, 1*, 110–118.

White Slave Traffic Act of 1910 (18 U.S.C. § 2421).

Wilson, M., & O'Brien, E. (2016). Constructing the ideal victim in the United States of america's annual trafficking in persons report. *Crime, Law and Social Change, 65*, 29–45. doi: http://dx.doi.org/10.1007/ s10611-015-9600-8

Wolken, C. L. (2006). Feminist legal theory and human trafficking in the United States: Towards a new framework. *U. MD. L.J. Race, Religion, Gender & Class, 6*, 407–438.

World Health Organization. (2012). *Human trafficking*. Retrieved from http://apps.who.int/iris/ bitstream/10665/77394/1/WHO_RHR_12.42_eng.pdf

World Health Organization. (2014, November). *Violence against women*. Retrieved from http://www. who.int/mediacentre/factsheets/fs239/en/

Zimmerman, Y. C. (2005). Situating the ninety-nine: a critique of the trafficking victims protection act. *Journal of Religion & Abuse, 7*, 37–56.

# Part II

# Locating Justice in Criminal Justice

The ultimate goal of this book is to help create critical-thinking, justice-conscious CJS practitioners and CJC scholars. At this point in the book, we've emphasized the importance of understanding the world around the CJS without really getting into the particulars of justice and injustice *within* the CJS. We've examined the larger social context of justice that surrounds the CJS and the individuals implicated therein. In Part II, we turn our attention to the CJS directly, considering how it is situated within this broader social context. Without an understanding of justice and injustice within the CJS itself, knowledge about the larger social world isn't particularly helpful for graduating CJC students. In Part II of this book, we trace the connections between the CJS and its surrounding context by relating individual-level issues to larger social problems, and illustrating the constraints that the CJS faces in trying to achieve justice.

We begin, in Chapter 4, by examining the role of ideology in criminal justice, shedding light on the often implicit—but nonetheless powerful—ideologies that structure our society, infuse our CJS, and influence CJC scholarship. Armed with this understanding, in Chapter 5, we turn to an examination of the different ways in which injustice can relate to the CJS. We discuss crime itself as injustice, the CJS response to injustice, and the reciprocal relationship between broader social injustices and the CJS. Chapter 6 considers the role that theory, research, and policy can play in helping us to understand injustice in the CJS, and moving us further along the path to justice.

Chapter 4

# Ideology in Criminal Justice

## INTRODUCTION

Criminal justice education in the United States tends to focus on describing systems and how they are designed to function, with minimal emphasis on critical analysis of how those systems actually function in our society. This leads to a concern that graduates will be equipped to maintain the status quo and stability that exists in the CJS, rather than challenging the system to achieve justice. To address issues of justice, we must open our eyes to the realities of the CJS that we have, examining its origin and intent while also rigorously and critically assessing how it works and what its varied outcomes are. One of the goals of a liberal arts education is to foster critical thinking by honing students' analytic skills. This goal is particularly relevant to CJC studies. Because criminal justice addresses pressing social issues, the ability to critique the system in order to improve it should be demanded of each and every CJC degree holder and criminal justice practitioner. In a way, we wrote this book for both of these audiences; many CJC students are current or future practitioners. Providing an environment where students can engage in rigorous, critical analysis can increase the likelihood that CJC programs will produce graduates who act ethically and proactively to identify social problems and respond in ways that advance justice.

CJC education's focus on the design and functioning of the CJS can eclipse important issues of power, politics, and ideology (Williams & Robison, 2004). All of these factors have profoundly shaped the formation, trajectory, and current functioning of the CJS. By acknowledging the role that competing ideologies play in the existence and functioning of the system, we can better understand the system and assess whether and how it makes good on its promise of justice. In Part I of this book, we laid the groundwork for a critical examination of justice; in Part II, we bring this critical lens to bear on the CJS, beginning with an examination of the ideologies that impact the system.

## BELIEFS, VALUES, AND IDEOLOGIES

An *ideology* is a set of ideas or beliefs held by a particular group. Ideologies often operate in the background of our society, impacting us in unseen ways by structuring how we see and engage with the world. Just as our positionalities inform our viewpoints by altering our perspective, so too do ideologies. As we go about our lives, we can't help but encounter ideology at every turn. Imagine ideologies, if you will, as invisible currents that run through social life, directing our attention this way and that, shaping our perceptions of what we see and influencing how we behave. Because ideologies are often invisible, they can easily go unacknowledged. But don't let this fool you into underestimating ideology. Despite its invisibility—or perhaps because of it—ideology can be quite powerful. Take the example of hegemonic masculinity introduced in Chapter 3. Hegemonic masculinity can exert such a powerful impact on society's expectations for men and prescriptions for their appearance and behavior because the ideas that it encompasses are so accepted, so taken for granted, that they simply seem normal. No one hands little boys a manual with instructions for how to become the "right" kind of man, because none is needed. Instead, gendered expectations are subtly but strongly communicated through the way we talk to young boys, what we demand of them, and how we treat them relative to young girls. Phrases such as "boys don't cry" and "man up" communicate hegemonic masculinity to children before they can even pronounce the words to describe it.

With regard to justice, ideologies can influence how problems are defined and understood as well as the solutions that are considered and later implemented through policy and practice. For example, at the core of the ideology of feminism is the identification of gender inequality in our current society and a demand for gender equality. Differences within this broad ideology exist with regard to the exact nature and effects of gender inequality, and appropriate solutions to the problem. For instance, mainstream feminism has received well-deserved criticism for its predominantly White, middle-class perspective that further marginalizes the perspectives, experiences, and voices of women of color and poor women. In this way, feminism illustrates that even those who subscribe to a justice-focused ideology can exhibit ethnocentrism as a result of privilege.

A prime example of the diversity of ideology can be found in our political structure. Across political parties, and even within a given party, members may hold different ideas about what is problematic, why, and how to best solve the issue. At the time we wrote this book, the 2016 presidential primary was in full swing, and replete with examples of ideological diversity within parties. Billionaire Donald Trump made waves in the Republican field with broad and unexpected support for his departure from the conservative social values that had characterized the Republican Party for decades. In the Democratic Party, Senator Bernie Sanders reenergized the party by mobilizing young citizens for a "political revolution" that emphasized progressive values over the Party line. Trump and Sanders may have little else in common, but they both reflect the considerable room for variation that exists within even well-established and institutionalized ideological camps.

# IDEOLOGY AND CRIMINAL JUSTICE

Ideologies can affect the CJS in many ways. There are ideologies that structure and power the CJS, ideologies that shape CJC studies (frequently referred to as "schools of thought"), and ideologies in the larger social context that surrounds the CJS. By examining the ideologies that affect the CJS, we can better understand the values upon which the system is premised, the assumptions that are built into the fabric of the system, and the social impact of our policies and practices. The policies and practices that our system implements to solve problems spring from diverse ideological perspectives, and should be evaluated in terms of the justice that they create in a broad sense—including, but not limited to, their effectiveness at reducing crime (Williams & Robison, 2004). An understanding of how ideology informs the CJS, CJC studies, and even our understandings of justice can lead to a more pragmatic and successful plan to achieve justice through criminal justice.

There are two competing schools of thought at the very core of most CJSs. The classical school of thought suggests that crimes are committed by rational individuals acting on their own free will after weighing the costs and benefits of deviant behavior. To produce a law-abiding outcome, proponents argue that punishments should be used to provide a deterrent effect. In short, this perspective posits that all individuals in society have the potential to commit crime, so to reduce crime we need to ensure that the costs of crime outweigh the gains. Positivism, on the other hand, suggests that the causes of criminal behavior can be identified and treated (rather than universally constrained and contained through deterrence). As a result, proponents of this perspective consider rehabilitation and other efforts designed to "fix" the dysfunctional aspects of "the criminal person" to be the best solutions to reducing crime. Many of the policies and practices in CJSs can be traced back to one of these two competing perspectives.

There are also ideologies that undergird the *study* of the CJS—and they aren't necessarily the same as the ideologies that characterize the CJS itself. As noted in the introduction to this chapter, CJC studies provide a working knowledge of the form and function of the CJS. The ideologies that buttress these particular studies are often the same as those that undergird the CJS itself. But because CJC is the study *of* the CJS, rather than simply a discipline in which training is provided to work within the CJS, we think a more critical lens is necessary. Consequently, the perspective that we advance in this book is one in which CJC examines how our society defines, measures and responds to crime, and to what end. The schools of thought that are most represented in this text include the structural-functionalist, symbolic interactionist, and conflict perspectives discussed in Chapter 2. These three perspectives have in common a critical, constructivist lens—meaning that social facts are not taken to be static and absolute, but instead are examined in terms of the meaning that people attach to them (i.e., their *social construction*) and the impact that they have in the real world.

At first glance, it may seem as though the ideologies that guide CJC studies are on a collision course with the ideologies that structure our CJS. But acknowledging and examining this array of ideologies from the beginning enables a deeper, more thorough understanding of the CJS as it actually operates on the ground in our imperfect world—where people aren't always rational actors, where individual cases are part of larger social problems, and where justice can sometimes slip through the cracks. We can use a critical, constructivist lens to critique the assumptions on which our CJS is based (we're looking at you, "rational actor"), revealing irreconcilable differences of perspective between the CJS and CJC. But we can use the same lens to examine how well our CJS embodies its values and fulfills its goals, assessing the CJS on its own merits and using its own internal criteria (assuming, of course, that we find them worthy of justice).

At times, the ideologies represented by the internal goals of the CJS may even conflict with one another. Packer (1968) identifies a tension between two different value systems embodied by the CJS: efficiency and fairness. Although both are important, prioritizing one or the other can result in two very different approaches for policy and practice. Efficiency emphasizes public order, community safety, and crime control. Fairness prioritizes due process, individual rights, including those of the accused, and equal treatment under the law, and demonstrates a concern for governmental abuses of power.

## POLITICAL IDEOLOGY

Most voters in the United States identify as Republicans, Democrats, or Independents (those with no Party affiliation who vote for the candidates on a case-by-case basis). Other smaller parties exist as well, but they are often overshadowed by the two larger parties; in fact, they're frequently referred to as "third parties" in the acknowledgment that we essentially have a two-Party system consisting of Democrats and Republicans. These parties include Libertarians, who prioritize civil liberties over all else and emphasize freedom from government intrusion into private lives; the Constitution Party, which adheres strictly to the original intent of the framers as evident in the Constitution, Bill of Rights, and Declaration of Independence; and the Green Party, which is organized around social democracy, diversity, nonviolence, and environmental justice, placing a high value on equality and fairness. There are also groups with shared political ideologies that are not formal political parties. For instance, the Tea Party emerged in 2009 as a populist blend of conservative and libertarian arguments about fiscal and government issues. Although not a recognized political party, the Tea Party established a large presence within the government on the right side of the aisle, and subsequently drove many Republican Party priorities.

As with any ideological perspective, differences exist between individual members of a particular political party. There are, however, generalizations that can be made about the basic platforms of the two major, contemporary political parties in the U.S. system. Democrats tend to be more liberal on social issues such as reproductive rights, same-sex marriage, stem cell research, gun control, health care, and education. The common theme among these issues is an emphasis on equal rights. With regard to economic issues, Democrats tend to be supportive of higher income taxes for the wealthy, government assistance for those living in poverty, and broader government-sponsored social welfare programs (e.g., Social Security) for all. Democrats do not shy away from stances that require additional government regulations. For instance, they favor laws that protect people from corporations, such as restrictions that limit a company's environmental impact on the earth or legislation that provides teeth to existing antidiscrimination measures. These stances, both social and economic, have one important thing in common: a social justice-oriented ideology. The positions that the Democratic Party promotes attempt to identify and address the root causes of social problems—even if the policies they implicate will increase government involvement in everyday life, curtail the profitability of U.S. businesses, or cost a large sum of money over a long period.

Republicans are generally more socially and fiscally conservative. Key issues for the Republican Party include a strong economic and military presence worldwide, a desire to secure our borders to curb illegal immigration, and conservative views on social issues that range from a pro-life stance to strong support for the death penalty. Overall, Republicans are proponents of small government and minimal regulation, particularly with regard to the federal government. They support states' rights, lower taxes, and personal choice in education and health care. Republicans adhere more to neo-liberalism (despite the misleading name), which emphasizes individual responsibility and orients to problems as individual in nature. Thus, the positions that the Republican Party promotes emphasize an ethic of personal responsibility at the individual level (through a desire for minimal government intrusion into private lives) and the state level (via states' rights and a limited federal government), rather than government-sponsored social change at the macro level. Republicans also tend to address major problems—particularly economic issues—with an eye toward immediate results, rather than through incremental progress toward long-term goals.

Given their platforms, it is not surprising then that these political parties have vastly divergent views on justice issues. Democrats' emphasis on long-term remedies for social problems with historical roots makes their platform compatible with prevailing views of social justice. The party's emphasis on legal, civil, and human rights coincides with a procedural justice perspective. Republicans, too, have platforms with implications for justice. Their emphasis on personal responsibility and tendency to address problems at the individual level lend themselves to notions of justice as desert. The Republican Party's social platform emphasizes conservative, often religious values compatible with conceptions of justice as moral righteousness.

One major area of ideological disagreement between Democrats and Republicans is income inequality. The growing gap between the rich and poor in this country is an empirical reality that we discussed in Chapter 2. This issue came to national attention in 2011 when Occupy Wall Street protests were staged in New York City. Declaring "we are the 99%," protestors occupied Wall Street's Zuccotti Park to draw attention to the widening wealth gap between the top 1% of earners in the country and the remainder of the population. Political attention has been paid to income inequality as well, revealed most notably by President Obama's frequent mentions of the shrinking middle class.

Representatives of both parties acknowledge the gap between the rich and the poor. Where the party platforms differ is with regard to whether they believe that income inequality is an issue to be addressed, and what they think should be done about it. From a Republican standpoint, income inequality is the result of a capitalist system that is working properly for many. Through hard work, those who are disadvantaged in the economy can rise to a level of success by availing themselves of the same opportunities that others have in the past. Thus, the Republican Party tends to view income inequality as a nonissue. According to Democrats, income inequality is evidence of social injustice, and thus very much an issue. They consider it the responsibility of the government to promote social justice. More specifically, Democrats favor the achievement of social justice through social welfare programs that level the playing field for low-income individuals and marginalized groups, and government intervention into the economy through corporate regulation and graduated tax reform.

Data from a Gallup survey of U.S. citizens reveals that 46% believe it is extremely or very important that the federal government in Washington reduces the income and wealth gap between the rich and poor. Seventy percent say the solution lies in the government increasing equality of opportunity (a traditionally Democratic viewpoint), and 82% say it is important for the government to grow and expand the economy (a traditionally Republican viewpoint). Interestingly a slight majority (up from 45% in 1998) agrees that "the fact that some people in the United States are rich and others are poor" is an acceptable part of our economic system (another traditionally Republican viewpoint).

When the same survey data are broken down by political perspective, not surprisingly, substantial differences are revealed. Seventy-two percent of Democrats say it is extremely or very important to reduce the income and wealth gap between rich and poor, whereas only 21% of Republicans agree. In looking at solutions to this issue, more Democrats (87%) think it is important for the government to be involved in increasing equality of opportunity than Republicans (53%). Democrats and Republicans rate the government's role in growing and expanding the economy as important with Republicans placing slightly less emphasis on it than Democrats do (71% and 91%, respectively). Another stark difference is evident between these two groups in whether they see the gap between rich and poor as an acceptable part of the system, with 72% of Republicans and 36% of Democrats identifying such a gap (http://www.gallup.com/poll/151568/americans-prioritize-growing-economy-reducing-wealth-gap.aspx). The Democratic Party's preference for the government playing a role in solving social problems is clear in these findings. Similarly clear is the Republican Party's aversion to government intrusion into personal matters. It is interesting to note, however, that the survey results were not split neatly along party lines—providing further evidence for diversity and nuance of viewpoints.

## THE POLITICAL CRIMINAL JUSTICE SYSTEM

Because political systems create the CJS, these ideological differences are important to examine. Politics is the method through which people create, maintain, and change the rules that govern society, including the processes that determine how resources are distributed. Criminal justice in particular is political in a variety of ways. Many key decision-makers in criminal justice (e.g., judges, prosecutors, chiefs of police, directors of corrections) are either elected by the voting public or appointed by someone already in office; both of these selection methods are based on shared ideology. Voters cast ballots for people who share their ideologies, and elected officials choose political appointees who reflect their own ideological bent. Criminal justice legislation (e.g., sentencing laws) is enacted by state legislators and U.S. Congressional representatives, and is often reflective of their ideologies and those of their electorate. The larger political climate of a community can impact the CJS in less direct, but no less powerful, ways. For instance, political ideology affects police practices, dictating the style and focus of law enforcement. The same culture also impacts corrections, for example through parole board releases and funding priorities for rehabilitative programming.

Given the impact of political ideology on the CJS, where has politics gotten us? We'll address many of the injustices in our CJS in the next chapter, so for now, we'll discuss the current state of the CJS broadly. As it stands, the United States has the highest incarceration rate in the world, with a full 1% of our citizens behind bars. We face widespread criticism for police killings of citizens, and have a court system so overburdened that only a tiny fraction of cases ever make it to a courtroom. Criminal justice costs have increased steadily—primarily because of a swollen prison system—siphoning funds from other social and human services, such as education.

We didn't get here by accident. Politics has played a substantial role in the evolution of the CJS since the "get tough" era of the 1970s. Before this time, criminal justice was not a highly politicized topic. In the ensuing decades, however, politicians have frequently campaigned on punitive law and order platforms, whereas those who don't favor get-tough policies are accused of being soft on crime. And so began the onslaught of politically charged rhetoric about crime that brought our CJS to Draconian new highs (or lows, as the case may be). Although you might think that the increasingly large body of research conducted by CJC scholars would inform criminal justice legislation policies and practices and thereby combat the insidious influence of politics, unfortunately this is rarely the case. This does appear to be changing, however—as indicated by the steadily rising acceptance of evidence-based practices and policies, which we'll discuss in detail in Chapter 6. We like to think it also has a little something to do with the army of critical-thinking social justice warriors that rigorous CJC programs are sending to staff the CJS.

## References

Packer, H. (1968). *The limits of criminal sanction.* Stanford, CA: Stanford University Press.

Williams, E.J. & Robison, M. (2004). Ideology and criminal justice: Suggestions for a pedagogical model. *Journal of Criminal Justice Education, 15*(2), 373–392.

## Selected Readings

Lambert, E.G. (2005). Worlds apart: The views on crime and punishment among white and minority college students. *Criminal Justice Studies, 18*(1), 99–121.

Stupi, E.K., Chiricos, T., & Gertz, M. (2016). Perceived criminal threat from undocumented immigrants: Antecedents and consequences for policy preferences. *Justice Quarterly, 33*(2), 239–266.

## Discussion Questions/Writing Assignments

1. Has your CJC education emphasized critical analysis of the current state of the CJS? In what ways?
2. Is it the government's responsibility to address issues of social justice—such as poverty, racism, and sexism? Does the CJS in particular have a responsibility to work toward social justice?
3. Many of the differences between the two primary political parties are controversial. How comfortable do you feel discussing and debating controversial subjects? What kinds of things could make doing so more comfortable?
4. How does our current CJS balance the internal goals of efficiency and fairness?
5. Does your personal political ideology lend itself to a critical study of the CJS? How so/how not?
6. There is consensus among CJC scholars that the politicization of criminal justice issues has negative effects. What steps could we take to lessen the influence of politics in our CJS? What improvements might these steps result in?
7. What role does the media play in the production and proliferation of ideology? What effects has this had on criminal justice? What effects has it had on justice in general?
8. In the concluding paragraph of *Worlds Apart*, Lambert issues a strong call for CJC education to make numerous changes to incorporate the divergent views of White and minority people on crime and punishment. Which of these has your CJC education provided? Give some examples.
9. According to Chiricos et al., what role does ideology play in views on immigration?

## ACTIVITIES/ASSIGNMENTS

## Political Tests

http://www.politicalcompass.org/test
http://www.isidewith.com/political-quiz
http://www.people-press.org/quiz/political-typology/

After completing these online tests, please write an essay that includes the following components: (1) What you learned about yourself, and your political beliefs; (2) How those beliefs intersect with your ideas about justice and social justice; (3) How those beliefs intersect with stratification, privilege, and oppression.

## Ideological Preferences in News Source

http://www.journalism.org/2014/10/21/section-1-media-sources-distinct-favorites-emerge-on-the-left-and-right/

It is increasingly easy to curate our news consumption to only those with compatible ideologies to our own. What implications does this have for our understanding of justice issues? Now consider your news consumption habits. How do you get your news? Is it from a TV news network, a site such as Facebook, or through another means? How do you think your favorite news sources measure up in terms of their political leanings?

## Understanding Differences

http://www.ted.com/talks/jonathan_haidt_on_the_moral_mind.html

Psychologist Jonathan Haidt studies the five moral values that form the basis of our political choices, showing how the values of liberals and conservatives differ. He argues that there are strengths in these differences and by understanding these moral roots we will be more civil and open-minded about political differences. Do you agree? Do some of the moral values lead people to behave in unethical, discriminatory ways?

## Relating Traits to Political Parties

Please indicate whether you consider each trait to be more characteristic of liberals, more characteristic of conservatives, or whether the trait reflects both groups equally. For each choose "mostly liberal," "equally shared," and "mostly conservative."

Intelligent, Educated, Charitable, Authoritarian, Compassionate, Moral, Religious, Just, Protective, Objective, Wealthy, Strong, Weak, Community-Oriented, Loyal, Callous, Sexist, Racist, Respectful, Scientific, Trustworthy

## Relating Policy Issues to Political Parties

For each of the criminal justice policy initiatives below, indicate your level of support or opposition (do you strongly agree, agree, disagree, or strongly disagree). Next, choose whether you believe that policy would garner more support among liberals or conservatives, or if both parties would support this policy equally.

1. Suspend the use of the death penalty because there are innocent people on death row.
2. Equalize penalties for "crack" cocaine with those for "powder" cocaine.
3. Use drug courts to divert drug offenders from prison and into community-based treatment programs.
4. Support laws that allow law-abiding citizens to carry concealed firearms.
5. Keep three-strikes-and-you're-out laws because of their role in preventing recidivism.
6. Expand the use of faith-based (religious-based) correctional programs.
7. Keep "super-max" prisons as a method of managing dangerous inmates.
8. Abolish the juvenile court and give them the same legal rights and penalties as adults.
9. Put an end to police use of racial profiling.
10. Expand the use of early intervention programs.
11. Retain or expand the use of incapacitation effects in the reduction of crime.
12. Repeal mandatory minimum sentencing, especially for drug offenders.
13. Expand the use of rehabilitation programs with juvenile offenders.
14. Expand the use of restorative justice programs.
15. Support the prosecution of those responsible for the 2007 financial collapse.
16. Expand the use of rehabilitation programs with adult offenders.
17. Pass stricter, national laws on the selling and ownership of firearms.
18. Keep mandatory arrest policies in incidents where people are suspected of domestic violence.
19. Legalize marijuana for recreational use.

Pick the most interesting policy and examine the criminal justice and criminology research literature on this topic. You will use this information again in Chapter 6.

## SEMESTER-LONG JUSTICE PROJECT

Step Four: What roles does ideology play in your topic? Would people with differing political perspectives see this issue differently in terms of whether it is a problem, or in terms of what the cause and solution are? How do your ideologies shape your understanding of the issue?

Selected Reading

# WORLDS APART
## The Views on Crime and Punishment among White and Minority College Students

*Eric G. Lambert*

## INTRODUCTION

The USA, as a society, tends to have a strong resolve to punish criminals in a punitive fashion (McCorkle, 1993). Over the past several decades, the desire for long periods of incarceration and a willingness to impose the sentence of death is found among the majority of the US public. While US society can be described overall as punitive, there is great debate and disagreement among members of the US public in their views of crime and punishment. Indeed, the topic can invoke passionate debate among those with opposing views. There is not agreement among all segments of society on crime and punishment views.

Views toward punishment arise from a multitude of factors, including social values of justice, socialization, and what an offender did to warrant punishment (Chung & Bagozzi, 1997). The difference between men and women in their views toward crime and punishment is one area frequently studied. The literature strongly suggests that there is a gender gap in terms of punishment views. Women tend to be more supportive of rehabilitation and less punitive than men (Applegate, Cullen, & Fisher, 2002; Blumstein & Cohen, 1980; Cullen, Clark, Cullen, & Mathers, 1985; Haghighi, & Lopez, 1998; Hurwitz & Smithey, 1998; Sprott, 1999), especially in terms of the death penalty (Grasmick, Cochran, Bursik, & Kimpel, 1993; Keil & Vito, 1991; Sandys & McGarrell, 1995). One of the reasons for the gender gap in crime and punishment views is different socialization and life experiences (Gilligan, 1982).

Gender is not the only area in which there are different socialization and life experiences. Race is another area. Race and ethnicity are salient forces in the USA and have been for a long time. This is particularly true when dealing with crime and the criminal justice system. Walker, Spohn, and DeLone (2000, p. 1) argued that 'nearly every problem related to criminal justice issues involves matters of race and ethnicity'. Therefore, rather than having a consensus between whites and minorities, there should be significant differences in their views toward crime and punishment issues. There, however, has been little research to determine whether whites and minorities are similar or different in their crime and punishment views. This is a critical oversight. The views of crime and punishment among different groups in society are important. In a democracy, public views, at least in theory, are supposed to shape and guide the criminal justice system (i.e., while the will of the majority rules, government must respect the rights and views of the minority). Moreover, the racial and ethnic make-up of the USA has been changing over time. Minorities in the population are expected to increase dramatically over the next several decades (US Bureau of Census, 2000), and, in the next 30 to 40 years, Whites will no longer be the numerical majority in the country. Therefore, it is important that the crime and punishment views of whites and minorities be better understood. For that reason, a survey of attitudes toward crime and punishment was conducted using undergraduate students at two Midwestern universities. This study examined the views of white and minority students to see whether there were differences between the two groups in their views of crime and punishment.

## LITERATURE REVIEW

There is a division between whites and minorities on many issues. Studies have shown that there are racial differences in voter registration, political party identification, and voting (Lien, 1998). In the 2000 presidential election, only one in 10 blacks voted for George W. Bush (Hutchinson, 2000). Empirical findings suggest that blacks are more supportive of policies intended to deal with racial inequality, such as fair housing laws, busing efforts, and affirmative action college admission policies (Kinder & Sanders, 1996; Schuman, Steeh, Bobo, & Krysan, 1997). Minorities and whites also differ in their views of gays and lesbians. Among social work students, it was found that black and Hispanic males were more homophobic than were white males (Black, Oles, & Moore, 1996). It has also been observed that black women had higher levels of negative views toward gay and lesbian individuals than white women (Ernst, Francis, Nevels, & Lemeh, 1991). Finally, among 190 Southwestern university students, it was observed that white students were less homophobic than black students (Waldner, Sikka, & Baig, 1999); however, there was no difference in homophobic scores between black and Hispanic students.

Less research has explored the similarities and differences in views on crime and punishment among different racial and ethnic groups in the USA. The little research produced to date suggests that whites and minorities do differ in their views of crime and the criminal justice system. Views of the O. J. Simpson trial differed by race (Brigham & Wasserman, 1999). In a study of domestic violence among undergraduate students, black respondents tended to feel more sympathy for black females who were victims of domestic violence than they did for white victims (Locke & Richman, 1999). Ortega and Myles (1987) found that minorities had higher rates of perceived victimization risks, although they also found that whites were more fearful of crime. On the other hand, other research found that minorities tended to have higher levels of fear of crime, along with the elderly and women (Braungart, Braungart, & Hoyer, 1980; Weinrath & Gartell, 1996).

Minorities tend to have a more contentious view of the criminal justice system, particularly the police (Bass, 2001; Escobar, 1999; Russell, 1998; Weitzer & Tuch, 1999). Minorities generally have a less favorable view of the police and how they treat people than do whites (Erez, 1984; Halim & Stiles, 2001; Lasley, 1994; Tuch & Weitzer, 1997; Webb & Marshall, 1995; Weitzer, 2000), but not always (Frank, Brandl, Cullen, & Stichman, 1996). Frank *et al.* (1996) observed that minorities in Detroit had more positive views of the police than did whites. They attributed their findings to the fact that the Detroit Police Department was more racially integrated than most other police agencies. Minorities are more likely to perceive racial discrimination and disparities and report discriminatory treatment by the police than are whites (Weitzer & Tuch, 1999). There may be some foundation for the views of minorities toward the police. Minorities are more likely to be the victims of wrongful shootings by the police, police abuse, police corruption (Shank, 2000), and racial profiling by the police (Harris, 1997). For example, in a survey of Chicago students, more than two-thirds of the African American and Hispanic high school students indicated that they had been stopped by the police, and the majority felt that they had been mistreated by the police (Friedman & Hott, 1995).

There appear to be differences between whites and minorities in their views on punishing criminals. A growing body of research has examined support for punishment of offenders and the degree of punitiveness toward offenders (e.g., Applegate, Wright, Dunaway, Cullen, & Wooldredge, 1993; Mackey & Courtright, 2000; McCorkle, 1993; Miller, Rossi, & Simpson, 1986; Singh & Jayewardene, 1978; Tyler & Boeckmann, 1997). It has been observed that whites and blacks differ somewhat in what they feel is an appropriate sentence for an array of crimes, with black respondents, particularly black females, being slightly harsher on some crimes than white respondents (Miller *et al.*, 1986). On the other hand, Blumstein and Cohen (1980) found that blacks, on average, assigned lower prison sentences than did whites when asked about several violent crimes. Conversely, it was found that race had no significant effect on the punitiveness in a study of drunk driver vignettes among Cincinnati residents (Applegate, Cullen, Link, Richards, & Lanza-Kaduce, 1996). Similarly, in a survey of 200 students at a Midwestern university, race had no significant impact on the harshness of punishment measurement nor on a criminal rights index measurement in multivariate analysis (Tsoudis, 2000).

While the research data has not been conclusive on whether whites and minorities differ in their views on punishment, there is some indication that whites are more punitive in their punishment views. The way in which minorities have been treated by the criminal justice system may explain why minorities are more lenient in their punishment views. Minorities are more likely to feel there is racial discrimination in the criminal justice system (Flanagan & Longmire, 1996; Gabbidon, Penn, & Richards, 2003). Besides negative contact with the police, minorities generally are more likely to be arrested, convicted, and face harsher sentences than whites. There is empirical support that minority offenders are more likely to be sentenced to prison and for longer periods of time (Albonetti, 1997; Britt, 2000; Kramer & Steffensmeier, 1993). Moreover, Bass (2001) reported that while blacks make up 13 percent of drug users, they comprise 38 percent of those arrested, and almost 60 percent of those convicted for drug offenses. Moreover, these drug convictions cause many minorities to have a more difficult time finding employment and to lose the right to vote (Bass, 2001). On a typical day, one in three black males between 20 and 29 are under some governmental custodial care, such as probation, parole, jail or prison (Mauer & Huling, 1995; Taylor, 2000). This is a staggering statistic. Finally, research has shown that race may be an important factor in imposing the death penalty (Applegate et al., 1993; Keil & Vito, 1989; Radelet & Pierce, 1985; Walker et al., 2000), particularly when the victim is white and the offender is a minority (Baldus, Pulaski, & Woodworth, 1983; Gross & Mauro, 1984). Finally, research strongly suggests that whites are more in favor of the death penalty than are blacks and Hispanics (Applegate *et al.*, 1993; Britt, 1998; Durham, Elrod, & Kinkead, 1996; Halim & Stiles, 2001; Walker *et al.*, 2000).

It is argued in the literature that potential victims are more likely to advocate harsher sentences, while potential offenders are more likely to support more lenient punishments (Miller *et al.*, 1986). McCorkle (1993, p. 247) found that non-whites were 'generally more optimistic and supportive of programs designed to correct personal or economic disadvantages of offenders'. In other words, minorities had a greater support for rehabilitation than did whites. This is interesting considering that minorities are more likely to be victims of crimes (Walker *et al.*, 2000) and are also more likely to be arrested (Smith, Visher, & Davidson, 1984), convicted and sentenced to prison (Walker *et al.*, 2000). Therefore, it seems that minorities, even though they are at greater risk of being victimized, are less likely to advocate a punitive approach when sanctioning criminal offenders.

There have been several studies which have examined the views of criminal justice majors toward crime and punishment issues, and race was often a salient variable in the results of these studies. There has been a significant increase in the number of minority students attracted to the major of criminal justice (Gabbidon & Penn, 1999). Yet this increase does not mean that white and minority criminal justice students view the criminal justice system in the same manner. In a survey of 400 students across 12 colleges and universities, it was observed that minority students were less interested in law enforcement careers than were white students, suggesting that there may be an aversion by minorities to seek employment as police officers (Krimmel & Tartaro, 1999). In addition, minority criminal justice majors were less interested in working in the field of criminal justice because of the power to arrest people, nor did they wish to wear a uniform (Krimmel & Tartaro, 1999). In a later analysis of the same survey data, it was found that white criminal justice majors were more likely to have been influenced in seeking a criminal justice career by a family member than were minority students (Tartaro & Krimmel, 2003), and white criminal justice students were more likely to report seeking a criminal justice job because of a law and order mentality (Tartaro & Krimmel, 2003). In another study of college students, it was observed that white students were more interested in a policing career than were minority students (Beckman, 1980). Kaminski (1993) found in a survey of high school students that whites were more than four times more likely to accept a hypothetical offer of a job as a police officer than were blacks, and black students reported feeling more pressure by family members not to seek a career in law enforcement.

In a survey conducted at five historically Black colleges and universities (HBCU), it was also found that criminal justice majors at these institutions were less interested in a career in law enforcement as compared to students at predominately white institutions (PWI) (Gabbidon, Penn, & Richards, 2003). In addition, it was found that students at the HBCU were more interested in legal careers than were students at the PWI (Gabbidon *et al.*, 2003). Gabbidon *et al.* (2003, p. 242) concluded that criminal justice students at HBCU were more likely to have selected criminal justice as a major to 'solve problems, fight oppression, and protect the Constitution'. In a study looking at the attitudes of criminal justice majors toward inmate privileges, minority students were more supportive of providing college education to inmates than were white students (Hensley, Miller, Tewksbury, & Koscheski, 2003). On the other hand, Tsoudis (2000), in a study comparing the attitudes of criminal justice students to students in other majors, found that race had no significant impact on views toward harsh punishments, due process for accused criminals, equal punishment of offenders, regardless of the race of the offender, or treating juvenile offenders differently than adult offenders.

In general, the majority of studies involving criminal justice majors suggest that white and minority students have different views of the criminal justice system. On the other hand, it is important to point out that these studies were mainly limited to criminal justice students, who have been found to be more punitive in their views of criminals than students majoring in other areas (Mackey & Courtright, 2000). It is unclear whether a similar finding would be found among students across a wide array of majors.

## RESEARCH QUESTION

While there has been research on the views of whites and minorities toward crime and punishment, there clearly is a need for more research. First, many of the aforementioned studies were published a decade or more ago. Much has changed in society since then. Second, most of the previous studies asked about appropriate sentences or support for capital punishment. There has been less research that has looked at differences in views on the importance of crime as a social problem, rights for individuals accused of a crime, and reasons for punishing criminals. Third, there has been little research concerning the views of white and minority college students. These are important groups to study since they represent the next generation of citizens who will hopefully become productive, voting members in society during the time period when the racial and ethnic makeup of the USA is predicted to change significantly. Understanding how white and black students differ in their views toward crime and punishment should not only help scholars comprehend those differences, but also discover what the future might hold. Therefore, a survey of college students at two Midwestern universities was undertaken to see whether whites and minorities differed in their views on the importance of crime, their degree of support for rights for non-US criminal defendants, and their level of support for punitive punishments. Finally, in this study, not only were bivariate tests conducted, but multi-variate analysis was performed to see what, if any, differences existed between white and minority students after controlling for the effects of gender, age, academic level, and degree of conservatism/liberalism.

# METHODS

## Sample

The data for this study was derived from a survey of undergraduate students at two Midwestern public universities.[1] One university was a regional four-year Midwestern school, with an enrollment of about 5000 students. The other university was a comprehensive, nationally-ranked Midwestern university, with an enrollment of approximately 20,000 students. It is recognized that the two universities differ from one another in many ways. Nevertheless, since the survey results were similar for students at both universities, the responses from both universities were combined into a single data set. Furthermore, by using more than one university, a broader range of students was surveyed.

A convenience sampling design involving about two dozen academic courses in the 2002 Winter semester was utilized. A convenience sample is where the researcher selects individuals who are available and willing to be part of the study. There is no random sampling in a convenience sample. Classes were selected from a list of courses offered during the Winter 2002 semester. The classes were selected because they are generally taken by students of different majors (e.g., general education courses), and, as such, the respondents represented a wide array of majors, ensuring that students with different experiences, views, beliefs, expectations and so forth would be surveyed. The nature of the survey was explained to the instructors of the selected classes and, while there were requests to reschedule the date of the administration of the survey, no instructor denied access to his or her class. The size of the classes typically ranged between 20 and 40 students. Students were asked to participate in the study by voluntarily completing the questionnaire during class time. While no student was required to participate and all were told that they could decline without penalty, it was estimated that about 95 percent or more of the students who were present completed the survey.

For this study, a total of 302 questionnaires were selected.[2] Missing responses for the attitudinal questions were estimated using statistical estimation procedures (see Shafer, 1997). If a respondent was missing data on demographic measures used in this study (e.g., race, age, academic level, etc.), that survey was dropped from the analysis using listwise deletion. A total of nineteen surveys were dropped for this reason. Approximately 67 percent ($n = 203$) of the surveys were from the comprehensive, national university and 33 percent ($n = 99$) were from the regional university.

The demographics of the respondents are presented in Table 4.1 for the entire group of students, white students, and minority students. About 56 percent of the respondents were female and 44 percent were male. The median age was 20, and ranged from 18 to 68. The mean age was 21.46, with a standard deviation of 5.18. Approximately 28 percent were freshmen, 26 percent were sophomores, 21 percent were juniors, and 25 percent were seniors. Almost 76 percent of the respondents indicated that they were white, 13 percent indicated that they were black, 7 percent indicated that they were Hispanic, and 4 percent indicated that they were another race. Overall, both groups of students were similar on the demographic measures.

**Table 4.1** Profile of Respondents

| Characteristics | All Students | | White Students | | Minority Students | |
|---|---|---|---|---|---|---|
| | n | % | n | % | n | % |
| **Gender** | | | | | | |
| Female | 169 | 56% | 128 | 56% | 41 | 56% |
| Male | 133 | 44% | 101 | 44% | 32 | 44% |
| **Age** | | | | | | |
| Median | 20.00 | | 20.00 | | 20.00 | |
| Mean | 21.46 | | 21.29 | | 22.01 | |
| Standard Deviation | 5.18 | | 5.00 | | 5.70 | |
| **Academic Level** | | | | | | |
| Freshman | 84 | 28% | 67 | 29% | 17 | 23% |
| Sophomore | 79 | 26% | 53 | 23% | 26 | 36% |
| Junior | 63 | 21% | 43 | 19% | 20 | 27% |
| Senior | 76 | 25% | 66 | 29% | 10 | 14% |
| **Race** | | | | | | |
| Black | 40 | 13% | N/A | | N/A | |
| Hispanic | 21 | 7% | N/A | | N/A | |
| Other | 12 | 4% | N/A | | N/A | |
| White | 229 | 76% | N/A | | N/A | |
| **School** | | | | | | |
| National | 203 | 67% | 145 | 63% | 58 | 79% |
| Regional | 99 | 33% | 84 | 37% | 15 | 20% |

Note: School represents the university at which the survey was administered. The survey was given at two universities: a national ranked school with about 20,000 enrollment and a regional ranked school with an enrollment of about 5000. Percentages may not total 100% due to rounding.

# Measures

## Views about Crime and Punishment

The survey had 65 questions. Ten questions measured personal and demographic characteristics, such as age, gender, and race. Fifty-five questions were attitudinal questions about the war on terrorism, punishment of terrorists, crime, and punishment of criminals. Fifteen questions dealing with crime, punishment, and the death penalty were selected from the survey and included in the present study. The questions were selected because they represented a wide array of crime and punishment issues. The questions were measured using a five-point Likert-type of response scale ranging from strongly disagree (coded 1), disagree (2), uncertain (3), agree (4), and strongly agree (5).[3] The 15 questions are presented in Table 4.2.

The single question of 'Crime is one of the most serious social problems facing society today' was used as a single measure of view towards crime as a social problem. The measure had a median value of 4.00 and ranged from 2 to 5. It had a mean of 3.86, with a standard deviation of 0.81. The single question of 'I am afraid of becoming a victim of a violent crime' was used to measure degree of fear of being victimized. The measure had a median value of 3.00 and ranged from 1 to 5. It had a mean of 2.76, with a standard deviation of .89.

The remaining 13 attitudinal questions were entered into factor analysis using the extraction method of Principal Axis Factoring (i.e., Common Factors Method) with a Varimax (i.e., orthogonal) rotation, which is commonly used (Gorsuch, 1983; Kline, 1994). Based upon the Eigen values and the Scree plot, two factors were extracted. The first factor had two questions which represented willingness to extend criminal rights to non-US citizens (see Table 4.2 for the specific questions). The two questions were summed together to form an index. The index had a Cronbach's alpha of .65. The index had a median value of 6.00, ranged from 2 to 10, and had a mean of 6.33, with a standard deviation of 1.982. The other 11 questions loaded on a single factor that represented the degree of support for punitive punishment of criminal offenders (see Table 4.2 for the specific questions). The four items that represented more lenient views of punishment and loaded negatively on the factor were reverse coded. The 11 questions were summed together to form an index of support for punitive punishment which had a Cronbach's alpha of .93. The index had a median value of 34.00, ranged from 13 to 55 and had a mean of 33.74, with a standard deviation of 9.86.

# Race variable

Because the focus of this study was whether there were similar views on crime and punishment between whites and minorities, the measure of race was collapsed into a dichotomous variable with whites in one category (coded 1) and minorities (blacks, Hispanics, and other races) in the other category (coded 0). Different minority groups were collapsed into a single category because of the history of

**Table 4.2** Percentages of the Frequency Responses of Views on Crime, Punishment, and the Death Penalty for the Entire Group, Whites, and Minorities

| Statement | Entire Group ($N$ = 302) | | | | | Whites ($N$ = 229) | | | | | Minorities ($N$ = 73) | | | | |
|---|---|---|---|---|---|---|---|---|---|---|---|---|---|---|---|
| | SD % | D % | U % | A % | SA % | SD % | D % | U % | A % | SA % | SD % | D % | U % | A % | SA % |
| **View of Crime as a Social Problem** | | | | | | | | | | | | | | | |
| Crime is one of the most serious social problems facing society today. | 0 | 7 | 20 | 54 | 20 | 0 | 5 | 18 | 57 | 20 | 0 | 15 | 22 | 45 | 18 |
| **Fear of Being Victimized** | | | | | | | | | | | | | | | |
| I am afraid of becoming a victim of a violent crime. | 13 | 32 | 22 | 26 | 7 | 2 | 40 | 35 | 19 | 4 | 6 | 49 | 30 | 12 | 3 |
| **Rights for Non-US Citizens** | | | | | | | | | | | | | | | |
| If non-US citizens legally living in the US are arrested for a crime, they deserve the same legal rights as US citizens. | 6 | 16 | 17 | 44 | 18 | 6 | 18 | 19 | 42 | 14 | 6 | 10 | 10 | 48 | 27 |
| Illegal immigrants arrested for a crime in the US deserve the same legal rights as a US citizen. | 13 | 32 | 22 | 26 | 7 | 16 | 34 | 22 | 23 | 6 | 4 | 26 | 23 | 34 | 12 |
| **Support for Punitive Punishment** | | | | | | | | | | | | | | | |
| Courts generally are not harsh enough with criminals. | 3 | 22 | 26 | 36 | 12 | 2 | 18 | 26 | 41 | 14 | 6 | 38 | 27 | 23 | 6 |
| The main goals for dealing with criminals should be to treat and rehabilitate them (reverse coded). | 6 | 18 | 24 | 38 | 14 | 7 | 19 | 24 | 41 | 9 | 1 | 14 | 22 | 32 | 32 |
| Society has a right to seek revenge on violent criminals. | 6 | 20 | 21 | 39 | 14 | 5 | 17 | 20 | 42 | 16 | 8 | 27 | 25 | 33 | 7 |
| Showing mercy is more important than seeking revenge (reverse coded). | 9 | 26 | 33 | 28 | 4 | 10 | 26 | 38 | 23 | 4 | 7 | 25 | 19 | 44 | 6 |
| I support the death penalty. | 13 | 13 | 22 | 30 | 23 | 9 | 11 | 20 | 32 | 28 | 26 | 18 | 27 | 22 | 7 |
| Race affects who gets the death penalty (reverse coded). | 12 | 30 | 28 | 24 | 6 | 14 | 34 | 28 | 21 | 3 | 6 | 14 | 29 | 36 | 16 |
| The death penalty is necessary to maintain law and order. | 12 | 20 | 31 | 29 | 8 | 10 | 19 | 31 | 31 | 9 | 18 | 26 | 30 | 22 | 4 |
| It saddens me when a person is executed, regardless of the crime they committed (reverse coded). | 23 | 29 | 15 | 24 | 9 | 28 | 29 | 15 | 20 | 8 | 8 | 29 | 15 | 34 | 14 |
| 16-year olds convicted of first degree murder deserve the death penalty. | 26 | 27 | 24 | 15 | 8 | 22 | 24 | 27 | 18 | 10 | 36 | 37 | 15 | 10 | 3 |
| Murderers deserve the death penalty since they took a life. | 10 | 20 | 27 | 24 | 19 | 8 | 15 | 29 | 26 | 22 | 17 | 34 | 22 | 16 | 10 |
| I become angry when a convicted murderer does not receive the death penalty. | 18 | 35 | 17 | 13 | 13 | 15 | 30 | 19 | 20 | 16 | 26 | 51 | 8 | 10 | 6 |

Note. SD = Strongly Disagree, D = Disagree, U = Uncertain, A = Agree, SA = Strongly Agree. The ordering of the statements in the table does not necessarily reflect the ordering in the survey. Percentage totals may not equal 100% due to rounding.

discrimination and abuse by dominant members of society through various social institutions, including the criminal justice system. Taylor (2000, p. 205) wrote, 'Despite the differences between African Americans, other Blacks, and Latinos, these groups share one commonality: a history of anger, bitterness, violence, and alienation from social institutions such as the criminal justice system.'

## Other Demographic Variables

While race was the focus of the study, it is possible that other demographic factors might account for the difference between the two groups of students. As previously mentioned, men and women often differ on their views of crime and punishment. Men tend to be more punitive, while women tend to be more supportive of treatment efforts. In addition, as people age, they often change their views concerning crime and punishment issues. The type of relationship is unclear. One study found that the young were more punitive (Tyler & Boeckmann, 1997), while another study observed that younger individuals were more supportive of rehabilitation (McCorkle, 1993). While the direction is unclear, there is evidence to support the idea that age affects views on crime and punishment. Similar to age, there are mixed findings on liberal/ conservative ideology and support for harsh punishment, such as the death penalty (Britt, 1998). Those with a conservative ideology tend to be more punitive in their views of punishment than those with a liberal ideology (Mackey & Courtright, 2000). Likewise, some studies have found self-identified conservatives more supportive of the death penalty (Sandys & McGarrell, 1995; Young, 1991), while other studies have found no relationship (Durham *et al.*, 1996; Tyler & Weber, 1982). Education has been found to have a liberalizing effect on views toward crime and punishment (Blumstein & Cohen, 1980; McCorkle, 1993; Tyler & Boeckmann, 1997). Finally, Tartaro and Krimmel (2003) reported that the bivariate relationships between race and career goals in criminal justice among criminal justice college students disappeared in multi-variate analysis when other demographic variables, such as age and gender, were introduced.

In this study, the demographic characteristics of gender, age, academic level, and conservative/liberal ideology were selected as control variables for multi-variate analyses of the impact of race on views toward crime and punishment. Gender was measured as a dichotomous variable with men coded as 1 and women coded as 0. Age was measured in years. Academic level was measured with freshman = 1, sophomore = 2, junior = 3, and senior = 4. Students were asked to check a box which best represented their level of conservatism/liberalism. About 4 percent of the respondents marked that they were very conservative, 13 percent indicated that they were conservative, 30 percent marked that they were somewhat conservative, 25 percent marked that they were somewhat liberal, 22 percent indicated that they were liberal, and 5 percent marked that they were very liberal. The conservatism/liberalism measure was coded as 1 = very conservative, 2 = conservative, 3 = somewhat conservative, 4 = somewhat liberal, 5 = liberal, and 6 = very liberal.

## RESULTS

As shown in Table 4.2, it appears that whites were more likely to view crime as one of the most serious social problems in society. Whites were slightly more likely to fear becoming a victim of violent crime than minority students, even though official victimization statistics indicate that minorities are more likely to be victimized. Minority respondents appeared more willing to extend rights to non-U.S. citizens accused of a crime, even if the accused was an illegal alien. There were differences between the white and minority students in their views on the reasons for sanctioning criminal offenders. White students were more punitive in their views. For example, only half of the white students felt that treatment should be one of the main goals of dealing with criminals, while almost two-thirds of the minority students felt it should be one of the main goals. Fifty percent of whites indicated that they supported the death penalty, while only 29 percent of minorities did.

Based upon results presented in Table 4.2, there appear to be differences between the two groups of students in terms of their views toward crime, rights, and punishment. The independent *t*-test was used to determine whether there was a statistically significant difference between whites and minorities in their views on crime, rights, and punishment. The independent *t*-test examines the difference between the means on the dependent variable of two groups to determine whether the difference is statistically significant (Green, Salkind, & Akey, 1997), and it is frequently used for analyses such as those in this study. The results of the independent *t*-test are presented in Table 4.3.[4] On all four measures, there was a statistically significant difference between white and minority students. White respondents were more likely to see crime as a pressing social problem than were minority respondents, and white students were more likely to be fearful of being victims of violent crime as compared to minority students. Conversely, minority

**Table 4.3** Differences Between Whites and Minorities on Their Crime, Punishment, and Death Penalty Views

| | Whites (*N* = 229) | | Minorities (*N* = 73) | | |
|---|---|---|---|---|---|
| Statement | Mean | SD | Mean | SD | *t*-value |
| View of Crime as a Social Problem | 3.92 | 0.75 | 3.66 | 0.95 | –2.48* |
| Fear of Being Victimized | 2.82 | 0.89 | 2.58 | 0.88 | -2.06* |
| Rights for Non-U.S. Citizens | 6.09 | 1.98 | 7.07 | 1.82 | 3.74** |
| Support for Punitive Punishment | 35.39 | 9.52 | 28.58 | 9.14 | -5.38** |

Note: SD stands for standard deviation. The independent *t*-test was used. The degrees of freedom was 300. The Levene's test for equality of variances was not statistically significant, which means the variances for the two groups of students on the measures are similar to one another.
$^{*}p \leq .05$ $^{**}p \leq .01$

students were more supportive than whites of providing rights to non-US criminal defendants. Finally, white students were much higher on the punitive punishment scale compared to minority students.

While the independent *t*-test tends to be robust even when its assumptions are violated (Boneau, 1960; Gardner, 1975), there was a large difference in the number of white students ($n = 229$) as compared to minority students ($n = 73$) and the surveyed students were not randomly sampled. Therefore, non-parametric tests were also utilized. Specifically, the Kruskal–Wallis H test, and the Mann–Whitney U test were used. For all four questions in Table 4.3, a statistically significant difference at $p \leq .05$ was found between white and minority students using the two non-parametric tests (results not reported).

To see whether the two groups of students were significantly different in their crime views, independent of the effects of gender, age, academic standing, and degree of conservatism/liberalism, ordinary least squares (OLS) regression was utilized. A major advantage of using OLS regression is that it allows for the effects of an independent variable on the dependent variable to be estimated while statistically controlling for the shared effects of other independent variables.

The four measures of views toward crime and punishment were entered into OLS regression models as the dependent variables and gender, age, academic standing, conservative/liberal ideology, and race as the independent variables.[4] The results are reported in Table 4.4.[5] After controlling for gender, age, academic

**Table 4.4** OLS Regression Results for Views Toward Crime, Fear of Victimization, Rights for Non-U.S. Citizens, and Support for Punitive Punishment

| | View of Crime as a Pressing Social Problem | | Fear of Being Victimized | | Rights for Non-U.S. Citizens | | Support for Punitive Punishment | |
|---|---|---|---|---|---|---|---|---|
| Variable | b | β | b | β | b | β | b | β |
| Gender | –.13 | –.08 | –.22 | –.12* | –.49 | –.12* | .68 | .03 |
| Age | .02 | .15* | .01 | .05 | .01 | .01 | –.02 | –.01 |
| Academic Level | –.04 | –.06 | –.05 | –.07 | –.15 | –.09 | .23 | .03 |
| Conser/ Liberal | –.11 | –.16** | –.01 | –.02 | .16 | .10 | –3.14 | –.39** |
| Race | .25 | .13* | .25 | .12* | –.88 | –.16** | 7.70 | .28** |
| R-Squared | .07** | | .03 | | .07** | | .27** | |

Note: b represents the unstandardized regression coefficient, and β the standardized regression coefficient. Gender was measured as males = 1 and females = 0. Age was measured in years. Academic level was measured with 1 = freshman, 2 = sophomore, 3 = junior, and 4 = senior. Conser/Liberal represents the conservatism/liberalism scale, where 1 = very conservative, 2 = conservative, 3 = somewhat conservative, 4 = somewhat liberal, 5 = liberal, and 6 = very liberal. Race was measured with Whites = 1 and Minorities = 0.
$^{*}p \leq .05$. $^{**}p \leq .01$.

level, and conservative/liberal ideology, there was a statistically significant difference between white and minority students on all four dependent measures.[6] White students were more likely to view crime as one of the most serious problems facing society and were more fearful of becoming a victim of violent crime. Minority students were more willing to extend rights to non-US citizens accused of a crime and were less punitive in their punishment views.

## DISCUSSION AND CONCLUSION

There are two general theories of law and punishment in a society: consensus and conflict. The consensus theory holds that there is general agreement among the different groups that comprise a society on appropriate laws and punishments (Bernard, 1983; Barnett, 1993). Under this view, segments of society are in agreement in their views of crime and punishment. Alternatively, the conflict theory postulates that laws and actions of the justice system result from the actions of the dominant group in an attempt to maintain their power (Liska, 1992; Quinney, 1970, 1977; Turk, 1976). According to the conflict theory, the dominant groups' views of crime issues and punishment will significantly differ from the views held by non-dominant group members. Originally, the conflict theory focused on social class (Weitzer, 1996). In the 1980s, the conflict theory grew to incorporate race and ethnicity as reasons for disparate and discriminatory treatment in society, particularly by social institutions (Hawkins, 1987). The results of this study indicate that views of crime and punishment of whites and minorities are more in line with the conflict theory than they are with the consensus theory.

Taylor (2000, p. 199) writes, 'At the beginning of this new century, the fact remains that race still matters in America.' The results of this study suggest that race does matter when looking at crime and punishment views. Whites in this study were more likely to view crime as one of the most important social problems, were more fearful of crime, were less willing to extend constitutional safeguards to both legal and illegal aliens charged with a crime, and were more punitive in their punishment of criminals. The question becomes why was there a difference? It is more than just conservative/ liberal ideology between the two groups which accounts the differences. In multivariate OLS regression analyses, the measure of conservatism/liberalism had a significant impact on two of the four measures, while the measure of race had a significant impact on all four measures. In other words, even after controlling for conservative/ liberal ideology, gender, age, and academic level, there were significant differences between white and minority students. Therefore, there must be other factors that account for the difference between white and minority students in their views of crime and punishment.

Differences in racial attitudinal measures are often hard to explain (Krysan, 2000). The reasons for the differences in views between whites and minorities are complex and sometimes paradoxical (Krysan, 2000). There is no single reason for the differences between whites and minorities in their views on social issues, including crime and punishment. The differences are probably due to a wide array of different forces and experiences. It is postulated that the reasons for these differences are due in part to different social experiences and socialization.

In the USA, minorities generally face two social barriers: classism and racism (Shank, 2000). Minorities have experienced a long legacy of segregation, discrimination, disenfranchisement, and violence in the USA (Johnson & Leighton, 1995; Massey & Denton, 1993). The history of this country is mired in deep racial and ethnic economic disparities, which explains why minorities are disproportionately found among the poor and poverty stricken (Walker *et al.*, 2000). The history of mistreatment was once openly supported by governmental policy. One aspect of the government that was used in the subjugation of the minority community was the criminal justice system (Walker *et al.*, 2000). Walker *et al.* (2000, p. 290) further contended, 'Although reforms have made systematic racial discrimination (i.e., discrimination in all stages, in all places, and at all times) unlikely, the American criminal justice system has never been and is not now color-blind.' As indicated in the literature review, minorities are more likely to feel that the police target and harass them, probably leading to a contentious view of law enforcement. Minorities are more likely to be arrested, convicted, and face harsher sentences than whites, probably leading to a view that the criminal justice system is stacked against those not in power. This unequal treatment, which has lasted generations, has led to distrust towards the criminal justice system by members of the minority community. This is not to imply that all criminal justice employees are racist, but rather, there is a climate of distrust and frustration felt by many in the minority community towards the criminal justice system.

Bass (2001, p. 171) argues that 'even as the number of young men of color are detained, harassed, profiled, labeled, or arrested continues to escalate, few in policymaking positions question whether the fundamental premises of policy choices portend racially skewed outcomes.' Donziger (1996) echoes similar sentiments when he argues that the legislative efforts against crime result in large numbers of minority men being imprisoned. Moreover, some argue that the reason that whites are more punitive than minorities is not due to a fear of crime but rather a fear of minorities (Ortega & Myles, 1987; Stinchcombe, Adams, Heimer, Scheppele, Smith, & Taylor, 1980). Both the negative history and social incidents of disparity and discrimination within the criminal justice system have led minorities to develop different views of crime and punishment than those held by whites. As Davis (1997, p. 442) contends, 'When people of color experience injustices that are tolerated and even sanctioned by the courts and other criminal justice officials, they develop mistrust and disrespect for the justice system.' It is this disparate and discriminatory behavior by the criminal justice system that may have caused minority students in this study to be more supportive of civil rights of offenders, more supportive of treatment efforts, and less supportive of punitive punishments as compared to white students.

Additionally, white students have generally had little contact with agents of the criminal justice system, other than in brief positive episodes, such as a police rendering assistance after car breaking down or motor vehicle accident. This has probably led them to form more positive views of the criminal justice system. In addition, whites are far less likely to be victimized than minorities

(Ortega & Myles, 1987), which means they have less personal experience with offenders and the crimes they have committed, which tend to be either property or drug related. For many whites, their primary source of information on crime and criminals is the mass media. The mass media does not provide an accurate picture of crime or criminals (Marsh, 1991; Vandiver & Giacopassi, 1997). Instead, the mass media tends to present a distorted picture where violence abounds and criminals receive lenient, ineffective sentences (Graber, 1980). The position of 'if it bleeds, it leads' bias that white students are constantly subjected to by the mass media, without personal experiences to contradict the false information, probably leads to myths and misconceptions being formed by whites, which in turn influences their views toward crime and punishment (Kappler, Blumberg, & Potter, 1996).

There are many myths and misconceptions about crime, the criminal justice system, and punishment. Among many whites, there is a view that the police and the courts are equal in their treatment of citizens (Kappler *et al.*, 1996). There is also the view that criminals are let off easy by the criminal justice system. These and many other myths and misconceptions about crime and punishment tend to lead to a heightened fear of crime by whites and this translates into an increased desire to punish offenders (Kappler *et al.*, 1996). This may explain why in this study it was observed that white students were more fearful of being a victim of violence, even though minority students generally are more likely to be victimized. Moreover, minorities, especially blacks and Hispanics, who made up the vast number of minority students in this study, are more likely to live in neighborhoods with higher crime rates than whites, which leads to increased contact with the criminal justice system (Ortega & Myles, 1987; Skogan & Maxfield, 1981). This increased contact probably means that minority students have more knowledge about the reality of crime and punishment in this country, and this knowledge helps shape their views of crime and punishment in a way that is different from whites. In other words, minority students had fewer misconceptions about crime and punishment because they were exposed more to crime and aspects of the criminal justice system than were white students.

There is a history of mistrust between whites and minorities, probably based on the past discriminatory practices and harm done by the majority society (Taylor, 2000). This mistrust is not just limited to the legal system, but also the workplace, schools, and social relationships (Taylor, 2000). In addition, white and minority students in all likelihood have had different experiences involving the criminal justice system that helped shape their views toward crime and punishment. While it is postulated that a history of unfair treatment in society in general, and in the criminal justice system specifically, are the main reasons for the differences observed, it is important to point out that neither postulation was empirically tested in this study. There could be other reasons for the differences in views of crime and punishment between white and minority students. More research is needed; this was only one study. The minority students in this study were mainly black, and to a lesser extent, Hispanic. There is a need to study the views of crime, justice, and punishment among Asians, blacks, Hispanics, and Native Americans. Their views matter, especially in a society that is moving toward cultural pluralism.

Moreover, only students at two universities were surveyed in this exploratory study. Students at other universities/colleges and general citizens in society should be studied. While it is logical to argue that the differences observed between white and minority college students would probably be found among non-college citizens, this is an untested postulation. It is possible that minority college students are different in their crime and punishment views from non-college educated minority citizens. This is something that requires empirical testing. Additionally, the reasons for the differences between whites and minorities must be explored in future research. Only then will a better understanding of how different members of society feel about crime and punishment be gained.

Furthermore, more and different types of questions should be asked. The type of question asked may influence a respondent's response (Mackey & Courtright, 2000). Turner, Cullen, Sundt, and Applegate (1997) contend that views of punishment may change if a respondent is provided more information on crime, sentencing options, and implications toward resource allocation in society. McCorkle (1993) argues that surveys of punishment views should focus on specific offense types and use scenarios (i.e., scenario-based) rather than asking about general views of punishment of criminals (i.e., global measures). There is some indication that global measures of punishment invoke a more punitive view than do scenario-based questions. For example, Applegate, Cullen, Turner, and Sundt (1996) found much higher support for three strikes in a general question than they did in scenario-based questions. While it may be that respondents are more punitive on global rather than scenario-based punishment questions, it is unclear whether the use of scenario-based questions would have led to different results in the differences between white and minority students in their views of crime and punishment.

In closing, the results of this study suggest that there is not a consensus between whites and minorities concerning views on crime and punishment. Instead, there are conflicting views. This pressing social division will continue until the majority recognizes and incorporates many of the crime and punishment views of minority members into the criminal justice system. This is easier said than done. A diverse workforce is necessary in order to have diversity in attitudes and views. The field of criminal justice, unfortunately, is not a very diverse field. Most employees are still disproportionately white and male. One way to include the crime and punishment view of minorities in the criminal justice system is to increase the number of minority criminal justice employees. This requires a dedicated, unremitting recruitment effort of minorities, which, while being undertaken by many criminal justice agencies, needs to be undertaken by even more agencies using more effective methods. Having a diverse criminal justice workforce would hopefully lead to a system with a wide array of views toward crime and how to respond to it more effectively. There also needs to be more opportunities for input by minority citizens in the policy-making decisions of criminal justice agencies. This would require criminal justice agencies to reach out actively to minorities in the community for their views on how to respond to crime-related problems and sanctions for criminal offenders (e.g., citizen advisory boards or having town hall meetings). Seeking the input of minority community members should help create a more diverse view of crime and punishment. There is also the option of trying to educate lawmakers on the diverse and differing views that exist in society. Of the suggested methods for incorporating the views of minority citizens into the criminal justice system, this would be the most difficult. Nevertheless, it is still an option that deserves consideration and debate. Last, a salient way to help incorporate the crime and punishment views of minorities is to have a greater focus in college criminal justice programs on the issue. Criminal justice programs need to increase the diversity among their students. There needs to be more and better outreach to minority students so that they will major in the field of criminal justice.

The results of this study should have an impact on the criminal justice academic community. Criminal justice textbooks and curricula need to incorporate the differing views between white and minority persons on crime and punishment and why these differences exist. Injustices done to minorities by criminal justice agencies and society must be acknowledged, along with pointing out that there are conflicting views of crime and punishment in our pluralistic democracy, even if such views contradict those of the instructor and many of the students. Criminal justice professors should provide students with a socio-historical context of criminal justice from the perspectives of minorities (Gabbidon *et al.*, 2003). The views of minority students need to have a fair presentation and discussion within criminal justice programs. They have merit. Ignoring the differing crime and punishment views exacerbates the feeling of disenfranchisement and alienation felt by many minority students. If minority students feel divorced from the focus of criminal justice programs, it will be unlikely that they will accept it as their major. If they do not major in criminal justice, it is less likely that they will seek and obtain a criminal justice system job and work from the inside to change the system. The views of today's criminal justice students will probably be reflected in the actions of tomorrow's criminal justice professionals. Finally, the pressure to represent the crime and punishment views of minorities will only increase as the number and percentage of minorities increases dramatically in the next 30 years. Now is the time for action.

## ACKNOWLEDGEMENT

The author thanks the editors and anonymous reviewers for their comments and suggestions. Finally, the author is grateful to the help of Daniel Hall, Miami University Hamilton, Alan Clarke, Utah Valley State College, and O. Oko Elechi, University of Wisconsin-Parkside, for helping with the collection of the survey data.

## Notes

1 The survey asked a series of questions concerning views toward crime, punishment, the death penalty, and terrorism. Data from this survey has been used in other studies that have explored the views of college students on the war on terrorism and the importance of having allies in the war against terrorism,

gender differences in views on crime and terrorism, and difference between criminal justice and other majors on the war on terrorism (copies of the papers are available upon request).

2 In addition, 263 criminal justice students were surveyed in a second wave of the administration of the survey. Criminal justice majors were not included in the surveys used in this study unless they were in the selected general education courses. The additional surveys of criminal justice students were not included in this study because they were not the focus in this study. As indicated in the previous endnote, the survey data from criminal justice was used in another study.

3 The inclusion of the uncertain category in a measurement scale is sometimes viewed with concern. Therefore, separate analyses were performed on all the measures with the uncertain category being removed from the measurement scale (results not reported). In terms of statistical significance, the same results were observed. The race measure (i.e., white/minority) had a significant impact on all the measures of views toward crime and punishment in both the bivariate and multi-variate analyses.

4 Besides comparing white and minority students, a separate analysis was done comparing white to black students on the measures (results not reported). There were no differences in statistical significance for any of the measures as compared to what was found when using the dichotomous measure of white and minority students.

5 The view towards crime and fear of victimization measures are ordinal level variables, and OLS regression analysis makes the assumption that the dependent variable is a continuous variable. While OLS results tend to be robust for ordinal data, some argue that it is more appropriate to use ordered regression (Long, 1997; Menard, 1995). Therefore, ordered (ordinal) regression was also performed (results not reported). In terms of statistical significance, there was no difference between the OLS regression and ordered regression results. The measure of race (i.e., white/minority) had the same significant effects on all four measures of views of crime, fear, rights, and punishment.

6 Besides the control variables of gender, age, academic standing, conservative/liberal ideology, and race, a measure representing the survey university (regional university coded as 0 and national university coded as 1) was also used in the multi-variate analyses (results not reported). Race still had significant effects on the crime and punishment measures and the variable representing the survey university did not have a significant impact on any of the crime and punishment measures.

## References

Albonetti, C. A. (1997). Sentencing under the federal sentencing guidelines: Effects of defendants characteristics, guilty pleas, and departures on sentencing outcomes for drug offenses, 1991–1992. *Law and Society Review, 31,* 789–822.

Applegate, B. K., Cullen, F. T., & Fisher, B. S. (2002). Public views toward crime and correctional policies: Is there a gender gap? *Journal of Criminal Justice, 30,* 89–100.

Applegate, B. K., Cullen, F. T., Link, B. G., Richards, P. J., & Lanza-Kaduce, L. (1996). Determinants of public punitiveness toward drunk driving: A factorial approach. *Justice Quarterly, 13,* 57–79.

Applegate, B. K., Cullen, F. T., Turner, M. G., & Sundt, J. L. (1996). Assessing public support for three strikes and you're out laws: Global versus specific attitudes. *Crime and Delinquency, 42,* 517–534.

Applegate, B. K., Wright, J. P., Dunaway, R. G., Cullen, F. T., & Wooldredge, J. D. (1993). Victim-offender race and support for capital punishment: A factorial design approach. *American Journal of Criminal Justice, 18,* 95–115.

Baldus, D., Pulaski, C., & Woodworth, G. (1983). Comparative review of death sentences. *Journal of Criminal Law and Criminology, 74,* 661–753.

Barnett, L. D. (1993). *Legal construct, social concept: A marcosociological perspective on law.* Hawthorne, NY: Aldine.

Bass, S. (2001). Policing space, policing race: Social control imperatives and police discretionary decisions. *Social Justice, 28,* 156–176.

Beckman, E. (1980). Police career planning among university students: The role of agencies' perceived reputation. *Police Studies, 3,* 34–41.

Bernard, T. J. (1983). *The consensus-conflict debate: Form and content in social theories.* New York: Columbia University Press.

Black, B., Oles, T., & Moore, L. (1996). Homophobia among students in social work programs. *Journal of Baccalaureate Social Work, 2,* 23–41.

Blumstein, A., & Cohen, J. (1980). Sentencing of convicted offenders: An analysis of the public's view. *Law and Society Review, 14,* 223–261.

Boneau, C. A. (1960). The effects of violations of assumptions underlying the t test. *Psychological Bulletin, 57,* 49–64.

Braungart, M. M., Braungart, R. G., & Hoyer, W. J. (1980). Age, sex, and social factors in fear of crime. *Sociological Focus, 13,* 55–66.

Brigham, J. C., & Wasserman, A. W. (1999). The impact of race, racial attitude, and gender on reactions to the criminal trial of O. J. Simpson. *Journal of Applied Social Psychology, 29,* 1333–1370.

Britt, C. L. (1998). Race, religion, and support for the death penalty: A research note. *Justice Quarterly, 15,* 175–191.

Britt, C. L. (2000). Social context and racial disparities in punishment decisions. *Justice Quarterly, 17,* 707–732.

Chung, W. S., & Bagozzi, R. P. (1997). The construct validity of measures of the tripartite conceptualization of punishment attitudes. *Journal of Social Service Research, 22,* 1–25.

Cullen, F. T., Clark, G. A., Cullen, J. B., & Mathers, R. A. (1985). Attribution, salience, and attitudes toward criminal sanctioning. *Criminal Justice and Behavior, 12,* 305–331.

Davis, A. (1997). Race, cops, and traffic stops. *University of Miami Law Review, 51,* 425–443.

Donziger, S. (1996). *The real war on crime.* New York: Harper Collins.

Durham, A., Elrod, H. P., & Kinkead, P. T. (1996). Public support for the death penalty: Beyond Gallup. *Justice Quarterly, 13,* 705–736.

Erez, E. (1984). Self-defined desert and citizen's assessment of the police. *Journal of Criminal Law and Criminology, 75,* 1276–1299.

Ernst, F., Francis, R., Nevels, H., & Lemeh, C. (1991). Condemnation of homosexuality in the Blackcommunity: A gender-specific phenomenon? *Archives of Sexual Behavior, 20,* 579–585.

Escobar, E. (1999). *Race, police, and the making of a political identity: Mexican-Americans and the Los Angeles Police Department, 1900–1945.* Berkeley, CA: University of California Press.

Flanagan, T., & Longmire, D. (1996). *Americans view crime and justice: A national public opinion survey.* Thousand Oaks, CA: SAGE.

Frank, J., Brandl, S. G., Cullen, F. T., & Stichman, A. (1996). Reassessing the impact of race on citizens' attitudes toward the police: A research note. *Justice Quarterly, 13,* 321–334.

Friedman, W., & Hott, M. (1995). *Young people and the police: Respect, fear, and the future of community policing in Chicago.* Chicago: Chicago Alliance for Neighborhood Safety.

Gabbidon, S. L., & Penn, E. B. (1999). Criminal justice education at historically Black colleges and universities: Past, present, and future. *The Justice Professional, 11,* 439–449.

Gabbidon, S. L., Penn, E. B., & Richards, W. A. (2003). Career choices and characteristics of African-American undergraduates majoring in criminal justice at historically Black colleges and universities. *Journal of Criminal Justice Education, 14,* 229–244.

Gardner, P. L. (1975). Scales and statistics. *Review of Educational Research, 45,* 43–57.

Gilligan, C. (1982). *In a different voice: Psychological theory and women's development.* Cambridge, MA: Harvard University Press.

Gorsuch, R. (1983). *Factor Analysis* (2nd ed.). Hillsdale, NJ: Lawrence Erlbaum Associates, Publishers.

Graber, D. (1980). *Crime news and the public.* New York: Praeger.

Grasmick, H. G., Cochran, J. K., Bursik, R. J., & Kimpel, M. (1993). Religion, punitive justice, and support for the death penalty. *Justice Quarterly, 10,* 289–314.

Green, S., Salkind, N., & Akey, T. (1997). *Using SPSS for Windows: Analyzing and understanding data.* Upper Saddle River, NJ: Prentice Hall.

Gross, S., & Mauro, R. (1984). Patterns of death: An analysis of racial disparities in capital sentencing and homicide victimization. *Stanford Law Review, 37,* 127–153.

Haghighi, B., & Lopez, A. (1998). Gender and perception of prisons and prisoners. *Journal of Criminal Justice, 26,* 453–464.

Halim, S., & Stiles, B. L. (2001). Differential support for police use of force, the death penalty, and perceived harshness of the courts: Effects of race, gender, and region. *Criminal Justice and Behavior, 28,* 3–23.

Harris, D. (1997). Driving while Black and all other traffic offenses: The Supreme Court and pretextual traffic stops. *Journal of Criminal Law and Criminology, 87,* 544–582.

Hawkins, D. (1987). Beyond anomalies: Rethinking the conflict perspective on race and criminal justice. *Sociological Forces, 65,* 719–745.

Hensley, C., Miller, A., Tewksbury, R., & Koscheski, M. (2003). Students' attitudes toward inmate privileges. *American Journal of Criminal Justice, 27,* 249–262.

Hurwitz, J., & Smithey, S. (1998). Gender differences on crime and punishment. *Political Research Quarterly, 51,* 89–115.

Hutchinson, E. O. (2000, December 15). How bad is Bush for Blacks? *MoJournal.* Retrieved February 10, 2003 from http://www.motherjones.com/reality_check/bushblacks.html.

Johnson, R., & Leighton, P. (1995). Blackgenocide? Preliminary thoughts on the plight of America's poor Blackmen. *Journal of African Men, 1*(2). Retrieved February 20, 2003 from http:// www.paulsjusticepage.com/reality-of-justice/blackgenocide.htm.

Kaminski, R. J. (1993). Police minority recruitment: Predicting who will say yes to an offer for a job as a cop. *Journal of Criminal, 21,* 395–409.

Kappler, V. E., Blumberg, M., & Porter, G. W. (1996). *The mythology of crime and criminal justice* (2nd ed.). Prospect Heights, IL: Waveland Press.

Keil, T. J., & Vito, G. F. (1989). Race, homicide severity, and application of the death penalty: A consideration of the Barnett scale. *Criminology, 27,* 511–531.

Keil, T. J., & Vito, G. F. (1991). Fear of crime and attitudes toward capital punishment: A structural equations model. *Justice Quarterly, 8,* 447–464.

Kinder, D. R., & Sanders, L. (1996). *Divided by color: Racial politics and democratic ideals.* Chicago: University of Chicago Press.

Kline, P. (1994). *An easy guide to factor analysis.* New York: Routledge.

Kramer, J., & Steffensmeier, D. (1993). Race and imprisonment decisions. *Sociological Quarterly, 34,* 357–376.

Krimmel, J. T., & Tartaro, C. (1999). Career choices and characteristics of criminal justice undergraduates. *Journal of Criminal Justice Education, 10,* 277–289.

Krysan, M. (2000). Prejudice, politics, and public opinion: Understanding sources of racial policy attitudes. *Annual Review of Sociology, 26,* 135–168.

Lasley, J. R. (1994). The impact of the Rodney King incident on citizen attitudes toward police. *Policing and Society, 3,* 245–255.

Lien, P. (1998). Does the gender gap in political attitudes and behavior vary across racial groups? *Political Research Quarterly, 51,* 869–894.

Liska, A. E. (1992). *Social threat and social control.* Albany, NY: State University of New York Press.

Locke, L. M., & Richman, C. L. (1999). Attitudes toward domestic violence: Race and gender issues. *Sex Roles: A Journal of Research, 40,* 227–247.

Long, J. (1997). *Regression models for categorical and limited dependent variables: Advanced quantitative techniques in the social sciences.* Thousand Oaks, CA: SAGE.

Mackey, D. A., & Courtright, K. E. (2000). Assessing punitiveness among college students: A comparison of criminal justice majors with other majors. *The Justice Professional, 12,* 423–441.

Marsh, H. (1991). A comparative analysis of crime coverage in newspapers in other countries from 1960 to 1989: Review of literature. *Journal of Criminal Justice, 19,* 67–79.

Massey, D. S., & Denton, N. A. (1993). *American apartheid: Segregation and the making of the underclass.* Cambridge, MA: Harvard University Press.

Mauer, M., & Huling, T. (1995). *Young black Americans and the criminal justice system: five years later.* Washington, DC: The Sentencing Project.

McCorkle, R. C. (1993). Research note: Punish or Rehabilitate? Public attitudes toward six common crimes. *Crime and Delinquency, 39,* 240–252.

Menard, S. (1995). *Applied logistic regression analysis.* Newbury Park, CA: SAGE.

Miller, J. L., Rossi, P. H., & Simpson, J. E. (1986). Perceptions of justice: Race and gender differences in judgments of appropriate prison sentences. *Law and Society Review, 20,* 313–334.

Ortega, S. T., & Myles, J. L. (1987). Race and gender effects on fear of crime: An interactive model with age. *Criminology, 25,* 133–152.

Quinney, R. (1970). *The social reality of crime.* Boston: Little, Brown.

Quinney, R. (1977). *Class, state, and crime: On the theory and practice of criminal justice.* New York: McKay Company.

Radelet, M. L., & Pierce, G. L. (1985). Race and prosecutorial discretion in homicide cases. *Law and Society Review, 19,* 587–621.

Russell, K. K. (1998). *The color of crime: Racial hoaxes, white fear, Black protectionism, police harassment, and other macro-aggressions.* New York: New York University Press.

Sandys, M., & McGarrell, E. F. (1995). Attitudes toward capital punishment: Preference for the penalty or mere acceptance? *Journal of Research in Crime and Delinquency, 32,* 191–213.

Schafer, J. L. (1997). *Analysis of incomplete multivariate data.* New York: Chapman and Hall.

Schuman, H., Steeh, C., Bobo, L., & Krysan, M. (1997). *Racial attitudes in America: Trends and interpretations* (rev. ed.). Cambridge, MA: Harvard University Press.

Shank, G. (2000). Overview of 'race, class, and state crime.' *Social Justice, 27,* 1–8.

Singh, A., & Jayewardene, C. H. (1978). Philosophical consistency in public attitudes on crime and justice. *Australian and New Zealand Journal of Criminology, 11,* 182–184.

Skogan, W., & Maxfield, M. G. (1981). *Coping with crime: Individual and neighborhood differences.* Beverly Hills, CA: SAGE.

Smith, D. A., Visher, C., & Davidson, L. A. (1984). Equity and discretionary justice: The influence of race on police arrest decisions. *Journal of Criminal Law and Criminology, 75,* 234–249.

Sprott, J. B. (1999). Are members of the public tough on crime? The dimensions of public punitiveness. *Journal of Criminal Justice, 27,* 467–474.

Stinchcombe, A. L., Adams, R. G., Heimer, C. A., Schepple, K. L., Smith, T. W., & Taylor, D. G. (1980). *Crime and punishment: Changing attitudes in America.* San Francisco: Jossey Bass.

Tartaro, C., & Krimmel, J. T. (2003). The effect of race on criminal justice students' career choices. *American Journal of Criminal Justice, 28,* 109–124.

Taylor, D. L. (2000). Cultural mistrust and racial divides. *Social Pathology: A Journal of Reviews, 6,* 199–212.

Tsoudis, O. (2000). Does majoring in criminal justice affect perceptions of criminal justice? *Journal of Criminal Justice Education, 11,* 225–236.

Tuch, S. A., & Weitzer, R. (1997). Racial differences in attitudes toward the police. *Public Opinion Quarterly, 61*, 642–663.
Turk, A. (1976). Law as a weapon in social conflict. *Social Problems, 23*, 276–291.
Turner, M. G., Cullen, F. T., Sundt, J. L., & Applegate, B. K. (1997). Public tolerance for community-based sanctions. *The Prison Journal, 77*, 6–26.
Tyler, T. R., & Boeckmann, R. J. (1997). Three strikes and you are out, but why? The psychology of public support for punishing rule breakers. *Law and Society, 31*, 237–265.
Tyler, T. R., & Weber, R. (1982). Support for the death penalty: Instrumental response to crime or symbolic attitude? *Law and Society Review, 17*, 21–44.
US Bureau of Census. (2000). *Projected state populations, by sex, race, and Hispanic origin: 1995–2025.* Retrieved February 18, 2003 from http://www.census.gov/population/projections/state/ stpjrace.txt.
Vandiver, M., & Giacopassi, D. (1997). One million and counting: Students' estimates of the annual number of homicides in the US. *Journal of Criminal Justice Education, 8*, 135–143.
Waldner, L., Sikka, A., & Baig, S. (1999). Ethnicity and sex differences in university students' knowledge of AIDS, fear of AIDS, and homophobia. *Journal of Homosexuality, 37*, 117–133.
Walker, S., Spohn, C., & DeLone, M. (2000). *The color of justice: Race, ethnicity, and crime in America* (2nd ed.). Belmont, CA: Wadsworth.
Webb, V. J., & Marshall, C. E. (1995). The relative importance of race and ethnicity on citizen attitudes toward the police. *American Journal of Police, 14*(2), 45–66.
Weinrath, M., & Gartell, J. (1996). Victimization and fear of crime. *Violence and Victims, 11*, 187–197.
Weitzer, R. (1996). Racial discrimination in the criminal justice system: Findings and problems in the literature. *Journal of Criminal Justice, 24*, 309–322.
Weitzer, R. (2000). Racialized policing: Residents' perceptions in three neighborhoods. *Law and Society, 34*, 129–155.
Weitzer, R., & Tuch, S. A. (1999). Race, class, and perceptions of discrimination by the police. *Crime and Delinquency, 45*, 494–507.
Young, R. L. (1991). Race, conceptions of crime and justice, and support for the death penalty. *Social Psychology Quarterly, 54*, 67–75.

Selected Reading

# Perceived Criminal Threat from Undocumented Immigrants

## Antecedents and Consequences for Policy Preferences

*Elizabeth K. Stupi, Ted Chiricos, and Marc Gertz*

Since 2008, several thousand pieces of legislation have been proposed at the state level to deal with immigration. In 2013, as detailed by the National Conference of State Legislatures (2014), the most frequently engaged issues involve "IDs and driver's licenses," "budget," and "law enforcement." With regard to the latter, one of the most notorious was Arizona Senate Bill 1070, a 2010 law that not only creates new categories of crime specific to undocumented immigrants (i.e. trespassing by "illegal aliens," unlawful stopping and solicitation of work), but also grants local and state law enforcement agents greater powers to verify the immigration status of any person they come into contact with. Since then, several other states, including Alabama, Georgia, Indiana, and Utah, have passed similar laws based on the Arizona provision. Overall, since 2011, state legislatures have successfully enacted 90 laws relating to immigration and matters involving "law enforcement" (National Conference of State Legislatures, 2014).

The debate surrounding these laws has emphasized claims relating to the putative criminal threats posed by undocumented[1] immigrants. In Arizona, a key rationale behind SB 1070, known as the "Support Our Law Enforcement and Safe Neighborhoods Act," was "an illegal immigrant crime wave" presumed to be sweeping the state because of "disproportionately high numbers of criminals who are illegal immigrants" (FoxNews.com, 2010). At the federal level, a US Congressman released a statement claiming that "murderous illegal aliens" are responsible for taking an average of 12 US citizens' lives every day (King, 2006). Undocumented immigrants are described as extensively involved in a wide variety of criminal activities, ranging from DUI (Immigration Counters.com, 2012) to murder (Immigrations Human Cost.org, 2012). And one "researcher" estimated that "93 sex offenders and 12 serial sexual offenders" enter the US each day as undocumented immigrants (Schurman-Kauflin, 2006).

The myriad claims about the criminal proclivity of immigrants, both legal and undocumented, persist despite a sizable research literature that contradicts those claims with aggregate data (Martinez, Stowell, & Lee, 2010; Ousey & Kubrin, 2009; Stowell, Messner, McGeever, & Raffalovich, 2009); with individual level data (Hickman & Suttorp, 2008; Sampson, 2008); and with multi-level analyses (Desmond & Kubrin, 2009; Sampson, 2006; Sampson, Morenoff, & Raudenbush, 2005). The weight of evidence from this research supports a conclusion at substantial variance with popular claims inasmuch as immigration is most often negatively related to crime (Wang, 2012).

While empirical evidence of a connection between immigrants and crime remains to be established, the presumed link endures strongly in the realm of popular opinion (Wang, 2012). The mobilization of punitive anti-immigrant policy more clearly reflects popular discourse and opinion than it does assembled empirical evidence. Prior research has linked punitive popular attitudes to the perception of criminal threat from other minority groups, including African-Americans (Chiricos, Welch, & Gertz, 2004; King & Wheelock, 2007) and Latinos (Johnson, Stewart, Pickett, & Gertz, 2011; Unnever & Cullen, 2012). It is not unreasonable to anticipate that a similar relationship could be found with regard to undocumented immigrants.

The present study uses survey data from a national random sample of non-Latino adults in the United States ($N$ = 1,364) to examine the extent to which undocumented immigrants are perceived as a criminal threat. In addition, we test how perceived criminal threat relates to support for punitive social controls dealing with both undocumented immigrants trying to enter the country and those already present. Also, we examine whether support for those controls may be influenced by contextual indicators of presumed threat (living in a border state, as well as static and change measures of percent Latino).

## MINORITY GROUP THREAT AND SOCIAL CONTROL

The group threat perspective (Blalock, 1967; Blumer, 1958; Bobo, 1983) is the theoretical grounding for our discussion of undocumented immigrant criminal threat. This approach argues that subordinate (minority) groups often appear threatening to superordinate, dominant interests. Threat may take several forms, including economic, political, or criminal; may be understood in either objective or perceptual terms; and may be experienced by an individual or as part of a group (Bobo, 1983). Regardless of the specifics of threat, the response is generally hypothesized to involve discriminatory and/or controlling behaviors by the majority in relation to the threatening minority. Although the original focus of group threat research was on relations between African-Americans and Anglos[2], a number of recent studies have used the theory to examine relationships between immigrants and native groups both in the United States and in Europe (e.g. Espenshade & Hempstead, 1996; Hawley, 2011; McLaren, 2003; Quillian, 1995; Semyonov, Raijman, & Gorodzeisky, 2006; Sides & Citrin, 2007).

As originally proposed by Blalock (1967), "power threat" focuses on the size of and changes in minority populations. Blalock hypothesized that as a minority group increased in size, the majority could be threatened and act in a more discriminatory manner. In research focused on immigrants, contextual measures of this threat have included percent foreign born (Fetzer, 2000; Hawley, 2011; Hjerm, 2007; McLaren, 2003) but also percent Latino (Berg, 2009; Hawley, 2011; Rocha & Espino, 2009) and percent Asian (Hawley, 2011; Hood & Morris, 1997), the latter serving as proxies for immigrants. Some have recently argued that in order to more effectively tap contextual threat it is useful to go beyond static measures of the minority population. Bowyer (2009) posits, threat that is most apparent comes from growth rather than size and thus "is best measured by change in the relative size of the ethnic minority population" (p. 569). Hopkins (2010) similarly argues that it is "changes in demographics [that] will lead to political hostility in affected places" (p. 43). The present research examines demographic context as potentially threatening in both static and dynamic terms.

It is important to note however, that objective contextual circumstances may only be consequential in mobilizing support for controls if human actors situated in those circumstances are actually threatened by them. For this reason, Bobo (1983) emphasized the "subjective perception that out-group members pose a threat to valued resources or preferred states-of-affairs" (p. 1200). And Blalock (1967) considered "perceived competition and power threats" to be essential "intervening variables" in the mobilization of social threat and social control (p. 29).[3]

Numerous studies have made use of perceived immigrant threat to predict popular support for punitive or restrictive immigration policies. However, almost all of that research has focused either on *cultural* threat presumably posed by immigrants (Citrin, Green, Muste, & Wong, 1997; Hood, Morris, & Shirkey, 1997; McLaren, 2003; Wilson, 2001) or economic threat perceived to arise from immigration (Citrin et al., 1997; Espenshade & Hempstead, 1996; Hood et al., 1997; Fetzer, 2000; Lu & Nicholson-Crotty, 2010; Wilson, 2001). Research engaging perceived *criminal* threat from immigration is, as we note shortly, extremely limited and in only one instance (Wang, 2012) specifically concerns undocumented immigration.

Taken together, previous work on minority group threat and social controls hypothesizes a theoretical process containing four key dimensions: threatening context, individual perceptions of threat, individual support for punitive controls, and the implementation of social controls at the macro-level. The perspective argues that context may influence both individual perceptions of threat and support for punitive controls, and that certain contexts may be more threatening than others. Additionally, individual level perceptions of threat are expected to increase support for punitive controls. The final step is the implementation of social controls at the macro-level. The present research will address the first three dimensions in the threat/control process, testing how context, perceptions of criminal threat, and support for both border and internal control measures may all be related.

## PRIOR RESEARCH: PERCEIVED CRIMINAL THREAT

Before outlining our methods and results, we first discuss the limited body of research on immigrant criminal threat that has accumulated to date. Two studies of the potential criminal threat posed by immigrants have examined it as a dependent variable. Using 2007 data from four Southwestern states, Wang (2012) found that a contextual measure of presumed threat—percent Latino—was unrelated to perceived criminal threat as measured by whether respondents believed that undocumented immigrants commit more, less, or the same amount of crime as legal residents. However, she also found that the perceived size of the undocumented immigrant population and unemployment rates in some models were positively related to respondents' perception of criminal threat. Research using European data from 2002 to 2003 asked respondents to rate on an 11-point scale the degree to which their country's "crime problems are made worse or better by people coming to live here from other countries" (Ceobanu, 2011). Respondents living in countries with higher non-European immigrant concentrations were more likely to state that their country's crime problems are made worse by immigrants.

Using European data, several studies have looked at the predictors of an index of perceived immigrant threat, which generally includes not only indicators of perceived criminal threat but also of economic and cultural threat (Hjerm, 2007; Hjerm & Nagayoshi, 2011; Quillian, 1995; Semyonov et al., 2006; Sides & Citrin, 2007). These studies have mostly found no relationship between the size of the foreign-born population (Hjerm, 2007; Hjerm & Nagayoshi, 2011; Quillian, 1995), the perceived size of the foreign-born population (Hjerm, 2007; Hjerm & Nagayoshi, 2011), or the discrepancy between the perceived size and actual size of the foreign-born population (Sides & Citrin, 2007) and their indices of perceived immigrant threat. One study (Semyonov et al., 2006) did find that the size of the non-European Union immigrant population was positively related to anti-immigrant attitudes in three of the four time periods examined.

To date, only one piece of research has used US data to test a multifaceted measure of perceived threat as the dependent variable (Alba, Rumbaut, & Marotz, 2005). This study found using 2000 GSS data that a measure of perceived ethnic composition—the ratio of white to Latino and Black residents in the US—was inversely related to a measure of perceived immigrant threat (Alba et al., 2005). However, the reference to immigrants in the GSS data did not distinguish undocumented immigrants from others and the measure of perceived immigrant threat was an additive index that combined criminal with economic and cultural indicators of threat. Both of these measurement conditions limit the applicability of this outcome to the present research question.

Efforts to link support for anti-immigrant policies to perceived criminal threat are also quite limited. Palmer (1996) found that Canadian respondents to a 1989 survey who thought that immigration increased crime were more likely to support decreasing the level of immigration to that country. Lu and Nicholson-Crotty (2010) reported that respondents to a 2000 GSS survey who believed that immigration is likely to result in "rising crime rates" were more supportive of not only lower levels of immigration in general, but also lower levels of immigration specifically from Latin American countries. In both of these inquiries, perceived threat and policy attitudes were addressed by single-item questions that referenced immigration generally. In a third study using 2009 Russian data, Wheelock, Semukhina, and Demidov (2011) reported that perceived threat to "public safety" posed by immigrants from Central Asia and North Caucasus was unrelated to a three-item index of punitive attitudes.

## PRIOR RESEARCH: CONTEXTUAL THREAT

The relevance of using contextual measures of presumed immigrant threat is complicated by the fact that aggregate indicators such as percent Latino or percent foreign born could be proxies for economic, cultural, political, or criminal threat. Since prior research on support for anti-immigration policy attitudes has made extensive use of aggregate indicators, and because our analyses will make use of three such contexts—residence in a border state, percent Latino, and change in percent Latino, we briefly summarize results from studies using data from the United States that involve our measures of interest.

Living in a border state which is commonly defined as being immediately proximate to Mexico—Arizona, New Mexico, Texas, and California—has been related to the belief that immigration is the most important problem facing the country (Dunaway, Branton, & Abrajano, 2010) and opposition to increasing levels of immigration (Burns & Gimpel, 2000). In a third study, Hood and Morris (1997) determined that residents living in California were more opposed to increasing levels of immigration than those in other states.

Hawley (2011) and Hood and Morris (1997) concluded there is no relationship between percent Latino and immigration policy preferences. Berg (2009) found that percent Latino had no effect in 1996, but was significantly related in 2004 to support for "stronger measures to exclude illegal immigrants." Rocha and Espino (2009) reported that neither a measure of Spanish-speaking nor English-speaking Latinos was related to immigration level preferences among Anglos. However, spatial dispersion mattered inasmuch as opposition to immigration was greatest in areas with more segregation and Spanish-speaking Latinos and in less segregated areas with fewer Spanish-speaking Latinos (Rocha & Espino, 2009).

## EXTENDING PRIOR RESEARCH

Overall, research concerning the criminal threat posed by immigrants and its relation to support for punitive social controls has been limited. We are aware of just a single study that has used US data to assess the predictors of perceived criminal threat posed by undocumented immigrants. Wang's (2012) important work in this regard is seminal. We hope to build on her contribution in several ways. First, we make use of a national random sample that may warrant somewhat more generalizable results than the regional sample engaged earlier. Next, we make use of a dynamic measure of demographic context (change in percent Latino) in addition to the static measure employed in the previous study. This comports with suggestions from immigrant threat scholars not focused on crime (Hawley, 2011; Hopkins, 2010) who note that change in demographic context may be more noticeable, and on that account, threatening than enduring demographic composition. Finally, and most importantly, we use perceived criminal threat not only as a dependent variable, but as a predictor of support for immigrant control policies focused on the border and directed at undocumented immigrants already present.

To date, only one other study has used US data to assess support for immigration-related policy in response to perceived criminal threat from immigrants (Lu & Nicholson-Crotty, 2010). Their examination of support for future levels of immigration makes use of GSS data from 2000 that are not specific to undocumented immigration. The time lag in the study of popular support for immigration policy is surprising because so much about immigration, including numbers involved, policy debates, and claims-making activity has changed since 2000. Just in terms of numbers, between 2000 and 2008 (the year represented in our data), estimates of the "unauthorized" immigrant population in the US suggest that it may have grown by more than 36% (Hoefer, Rytina, & Baker, 2009). In addition to closing the temporal gap in the assessment of support for immigrant control policies, the present work adds to what is known in this regard by (1) explicitly focusing on "undocumented immigration" both in terms of perceived threat and in terms of policy preferences and (2) by examining popular support for policies that go beyond the traditional issue of future immigration levels and engage very detailed activities to secure the border on the one hand and deal with undocumented immigrants who are already in the country on the other. It is reasonable to imagine that very different attitudes could arise in relation to immigrants who are imagined as "others" outside and those with whom people may interact on a regular basis.

## THE PRESENT RESEARCH

Based on our reading of group threat theory as well as prior research, our analysis is organized by three main research hypotheses.

H1: Respondents who live in presumably more threatening contexts (border state residents, higher percent Latino and greater change in percent Latino) will perceive undocumented immigrants to be more of a criminal threat than those in less threatening contexts.

H2: Respondents who live in presumably more threatening contexts as noted above will also express more support for border and internal controls targeting undocumented immigrants than those in less threatening contexts.

H3: Respondents who perceive undocumented immigrants to be more of a criminal threat will express more support for border and internal controls targeting undocumented immigrants than those who do not perceive a criminal threat.

## Data

To address these hypotheses, we use data from a national random telephone survey of adults in US households conducted between January and April of 2008.[4] We limit our analyses to non-Latino respondents, which results in a sample size of 1364, including 1150 Anglos and 131 African-Americans. The characteristics of the final sample (with corresponding 2008 national data from the American Communities Survey for non-Latinos age 18+ in parentheses) include: median age of 43 (47), 56% (52%) female, 45% (28%) college graduates, 9% (13%) Black, and 55% (61%) living in households with annual incomes of at least $50,000. An overrepresentation of female and better educated respondents and an underrepresentation of minority respondents are not uncommon in telephone surveys (Lavrakas, 1993).

## Research Measures

### *Perceived Immigrant Criminal Threat*

This key measure which will serve as both a dependent and independent variable in our analyses is an index based on six items that asks respondents their level of agreement (five options: strongly agree to strongly disagree) with statements about "illegal immigrants." These include:

Illegal immigrants are no more violent than American citizens.
Illegal immigrants are more likely to use drugs than American citizens.
Too many illegal immigrants are trafficking drugs across the border.
Too many illegal immigrants with criminal records are coming to the US.
Gangs of illegal immigrant youth are a serious problem for this country.
Illegal immigrants are just as law-abiding as American citizens.

Items that expressed a negative opinion about undocumented immigrants (e.g. "Too many illegal immigrants ...") are reverse-coded, so that a score of 5 reflects higher levels of perceived threat. The additive index scores range from 6 to 30 with higher scores indicating that the respondent perceives undocumented immigrants to be more of a criminal threat. The final index has an alpha of .81. We also submitted these items to a confirmatory factor analysis in Stata (TLI = .99; CFI = .94) and the resulting factor scores were correlated at .97 with the additive index scores. Because the two are so highly correlated, we use the more easily interpreted additive index in our analyses.

## *Support for Controls Targeting Undocumented Immigrants*

Two of the three prior studies linking immigrant criminal threat and policy preferences focused on the preferred level of immigration, using that single-item indicator as their policy measure (Lu & Nicholson-Crotty, 2010; Palmer, 1996). The present study makes use of two additive indices to measure preferences with regard to two separate areas of policy relating to undocumented immigration: controls at the border and controls directed at undocumented immigrants already in the country. This distinction appears warranted for several reasons. First, undocumented immigrants present in the country will likely be interacting with native-born Americans and some have argued that such "contact" could mitigate feelings of threat (Allport, 1954; McLaren, 2003; Pettigrew, 1988). In addition, there are a number of policies, both enacted and proposed, that encourage undocumented immigrants already in the United States to assimilate. For example, a recent executive order by President Obama allows young undocumented immigrants who meet certain requirements to apply for work permits and temporarily avoid deportation (Cohen, 2012). Thus, undocumented immigrants already in the country may be regarded differently than those who have yet to enter, so we may reasonably expect to see this reflected in different levels of support for the two types of policies. Finally, we conducted a confirmatory factor analysis in Stata of the various control-related items used in the survey. We found that a two-factor solution provided a better fit to the data (TLI = .99; CFI = .93) than a one-factor solution (TLI = .93; CFI = .66). Items indicating support for stronger internal immigration controls loaded strongly on one factor, and items measuring support for border controls loaded strongly on another. This confirms our expectation that these items tap into two unique latent constructs. The two resulting indices have a bivariate correlation of .52.

The *border control* measure includes six questions regarding respondents' level of support (five options: strongly support to strongly oppose) for "some ways that have been proposed to deal with illegal immigration." These policies include:

Increased manpower for border patrol.
The use of military personnel to patrol the border.
Digging ditches in high entry areas to discourage crossing the border in a vehicle.
Constructing fences in high entry areas to discourage crossing the border on foot.
Erecting a wall along the border.
Increased electronic surveillance for monitoring the border.

All items are reverse-coded, so that a score of 1 indicates the least punitive attitude while a score of 5 reflects the most punitive. Scores on the additive index range from 6 to 30, with higher scores indicating more punitive attitudes. The final index has an alpha coefficient of .84. We compared the additive index with the previously described factor scores and, with a correlation of .99 between the two, we use the more easily interpreted additive measure for our analyses.

*Internal control* is measured using seven items asking respondents about their level of support (five options: strongly support to strongly oppose) for policies toward "the illegal immigrants who currently live in the United States." These include:

Allow illegal immigrants who have been in the US for seven years to stay.
Allow illegal immigrants to send their children to public schools.
Permit illegal immigrants to receive welfare assistance.
Allow illegal immigrants to receive emergency health care benefits.
Grant US citizenship to children of illegal immigrants born in the US.
Permit illegal immigrants to obtain a valid driver's license.
Send anyone the police can identify as an illegal immigrant back to their native country.

The punitive item (e.g. "Send anyone ...") is reverse-coded, so that on all items, a score of 1 indicates the least punitive attitude and a score of 5 indicates the most punitive. Scores on the additive index range from 7 to 35, with higher scores indicating more punitive attitudes toward undocumented immigrants. The final index has an alpha coefficient of .82. Again, we compared the additive index to factor scores from the confirmatory factor analysis and found a correlation of .99. Since the factor score was almost identical to the additive score, we use the more easily interpreted additive measure.

## Contextual Threat Measures

Our first measure of contextual threat, percent Latino, has been extensively used in research concerned with immigrant threat (Berg, 2009; Hawley, 2011; Rocha & Espino, 2009; Wang, 2012). Alternative possible measures include percent foreign born and percent non-English speaking. The choice of percent Latino is made because it is reasonable to assume that residents of a community would have a clearer sense of Latino presence than the presence of those who are foreign born. Also in popular discourse and claims-making about immigrant threat, the focus is predominantly on immigration from Latino countries. Percent Latino is measured with county-level data from the 2005 to 2009 ACS.[5]

The second indicator of contextual threat used here follows the lead of some recent immigrant threat research (Hawley, 2011; Hopkins, 2010) that argues for dynamic measures of context. *Change in percent Latino* is the relative percentage change between the 2000[6] and 2005–2009 measures of percent Latino. Specifically, the 2000 level of percent Latino is subtracted from the 2005–2009 level and then divided by the 2000 level. This measure of relative change is preferred to absolute change because it is likely a more sensitive indicator. For example, in a community with an original Latino presence of 6%, a three-point increase would be more dramatic than an equivalent increase in a community that was originally 20% Latino.[7]

Our third indicator of presumed contextual threat is whether respondents reside in a border state. Living in a border state raises the possibility that respondents may be more likely to encounter undocumented immigrants and thus may perceive more threat in that regard. *Border state* is a dichotomous variable, coded 1 if the respondent lives in any state contiguous to Mexico (Arizona, California, New Mexico, and Texas).

## Control Variables

We also control for demographic characteristics that have been shown to be salient in previous research on immigrant threat and/or punitive attitudes toward immigrants. These include: sex (Berg, 2009; Lu & Nicholson-Crotty, 2010; Wang, 2012); age (Burns & Gimpel, 2000; Lu & Nicholson-Crotty, 2010; Wang, 2012); race/ethnicity (Hawley, 2011; Rocha et al., 2011; Wang, 2012); education (Lu & Nicholson-Crotty, 2010; Rocha & Espino, 2009; Wang, 2012); income (Lu & Nicholson-Crotty, 2010; Wang, 2012); and political ideology (Lu & Nicholson-Crotty, 2010; Rocha & Espino, 2009; Wang, 2012).

Respondent sex is coded dichotomously, where 1 indicates male. Age is a continuous measure, ranging from 18 to 94. Race/ethnicity is a set of dichotomous variables, indicating whether the respondent self-identified as *Black* (yes = 1) or *other race* (yes = 1), with Anglo as the reference group. *Education* is the self-reported number of years of education that the respondent has completed. Respondents also self-reported which of the six categories their 2007 household income fell into: less than \$15 k, \$15 k to less than \$35 k, \$35 k to less than \$50 k, \$50 k to less than \$75 k, \$75 k to less than \$100 k, or more than \$100 k. *Income* is coded as the midpoint of the self-reported category, ranging from \$7.5 k to \$150 k, our established upper limit. To capture political ideology, respondents were asked to classify themselves on a scale from very liberal to very conservative. *Conservative* is a dichotomous variable with "very conservative" or "conservative" coded as 1 and all others coded as 0. Age, education, income, and conservative all have some missing values due to non-response. These values were imputed, using chained equations (the "ice" command in Stata) to create five data-sets as the basis for the imputation.[8]

We also control for three county-level characteristics. The first two are unemployment and income inequality, both of which Wang (2012) included in her models of perceived criminal threat. Because our survey respondents are non-Latino, we use 2005–2009 ACS data to construct a *percent non-Latino unemployed* measure. Using the same data, we take a ratio of the median household income for Anglos to the median household income for Latinos as our measure of *income inequality*. Finally, we control for county-level homicide rates on the assumption that the level of crime in one's county may have an impact on the perception of criminal threat, independent of its relation to undocumented immigrants. A similar approach by Wang (2012) utilized total crime rate.[9] It has been argued that

**Table 4.5** Descriptive statistics

| | Mean | SD |
|---|---|---|
| *Threat variables* | | |
| Perceived criminal threat | 18.67 | 4.30 |
| % Latino | 10.47 | 12.20 |
| Change % Latino | 39.13 | 31.03 |
| Border state | .15 | .36 |
| *Punitiveness variables* | | |
| Border control | 20.73 | 5.10 |
| Internal control | 23.40 | 5.69 |
| *Control variables* | | |
| Male | .44 | .50 |
| Age | 54.31 | 15.57 |
| Black | .09 | .29 |
| Other | .08 | .26 |
| Education | 14.77 | 2.59 |
| Income | 72.71 | 48.16 |
| Conservative | .38 | .48 |
| % Non-Latino unemployed | 6.83 | 2.06 |
| Income Inequality | 1.51 | .49 |
| Homicide Rate | 5.04 | 5.50 |

homicide rate may be a more reliable indicator of crime since it is less likely than other index crimes to have problems related to under-reporting and under-recording (Gove, Hughes, & Geerken, 1985). Our *homicide rate* per 100,000 in each county is taken from the 2007 Uniform Crime Report. Descriptive statistics for all of the variables in these analyses are reported in Table 4.5.

## Analytic Strategy

Although our 1,364 respondents are clustered in 759 counties across the United States, multi-level modeling is not appropriate since some counties contain one or two respondents and two-thirds of counties have three or less. Thus, using Stata, we run Ordinary Least Squares regression with robust standard errors at the county level for all of our modeling in order to help correct for correlated errors. We begin by looking at perceived criminal threat as a dependent variable in Table 4.6. Then in Tables 4.7 and 4.8, the predictors of support for border and

**Table 4.6** OLS regression coefficients: perceived criminal threat from undocumented immigrants on contextual threat and other predictors†

| | Model 1 | Model 2 |
|---|---|---|
| Percent Latino | .007 | |
| | (.015) | |
| Change in percent Latino | | .007 |
| | | (.004) |
| Border state | .140 | .499 |
| | (.478) | (.350) |
| Male | –.070 | –.072 |
| | (.225) | (.224) |
| Age | .033*** | .033*** |
| | (.007) | (.007) |
| Conservative | 2.155*** | 2.136*** |
| | (.232) | (.233) |
| Education | –.354*** | –.352*** |
| | (.047) | (.047) |
| Income | –.009** | –.009** |
| | (.003) | (.003) |
| Black | –.776* | –.807* |
| | (.363) | (.362) |
| Other | .421 | .451 |
| | (.490) | (.489) |
| Percent non-Latino unemployed | .029 | .046 |
| | (.069) | (.068) |
| Income inequality | –.374 | –.302 |
| | (.211) | (.215) |
| Homicide rate | .009 | .010 |
| | (.022) | (.022) |
| Constant | 22.246*** | 21.744*** |
| | (.990) | (1.015) |
| Adjusted R-square | .165 | .166 |
| | ($n$ = 1320) | ($n$ = 1320) |

†Standard errors in parentheses.
*$p \leq .05$.
**$p \leq .01$.
***$p \leq .001$.

**Table 4.7** OLS regression coefficients: support for border control on measures of threat and other predictors†

| | Model 1 | Model 2 | Model 3 |
|---|---|---|---|
| Perceived criminal threat | | | .561*** |
| | | | (.034) |
| Percent Latino | .012 | | |
| | (.017) | | |
| Change in percent Latino | | .010* | .006 |
| | | (.005) | (.004) |
| Border state | .559 | .872* | .592 |
| | (.579) | (.415) | (.362) |
| Male | .159 | .156 | .197 |
| | (.266) | (.265) | (.233) |
| Age | –.003 | –.003 | –.021** |
| | (.009) | (.009) | (.008) |
| Conservative | 3.059*** | 3.038*** | 1.839*** |
| | (.285) | (.283) | (.263) |
| Education | –.236*** | –.235*** | –.037 |
| | (.060) | (.060) | (.053) |
| Income | –.002 | –.002 | .033 |
| | (.004) | (.004) | (.003) |
| Black | –.954 | –1.009 | –.556 |
| | (.523) | (.520) | (.483) |
| Other | –1.007 | –.968 | –1.221** |
| | (.540) | (.540) | (.475) |
| Percent non-Latino unemployed | –.118 | –.091 | –.117 |
| | (.075) | (.075) | (.065) |
| Income inequality | –.178 | –.082 | .087 |
| | (.222) | (.222) | (.196) |
| Homicide rate | .019 | .017 | .011 |
| | (.027) | (.027) | (.024) |
| Constant | 24.345*** | 23.566*** | 11.363*** |
| | (1.132) | (1.166) | (1.259) |
| Adjusted R-square | .110 | .113 | .299 |
| | ($n$ = 1320) | ($n$ = 1320) | ($n$ = 1320) |

†Standard errors in parentheses.
*$p \leq .05$.
**$p \leq .01$.
***$p \leq .001$.

**Table 4.8** OLS regression coefficients: support for internal control on measures of threat and other predictors†

| | Model 1 | Model 2 | Model 3 |
|---|---|---|---|
| Perceived criminal threat | | | .713*** |
| | | | (.034) |
| Percent Latino | –.008 | | |
| | (.018) | | |
| Change in percent Latino | | .008 | .003 |
| | | (.005) | (.005) |
| Border state | .180 | .181 | –.175 |
| | (.578) | (.453) | (.394) |
| Male | .230 | .229 | .281 |
| | (.298) | (.297) | (.257) |
| Age | .010 | .010 | –.014 |
| | (.010) | (.010) | (.009) |
| Conservative | 3.533*** | 3.525*** | 2.001*** |
| | (.288) | (.287) | (.254) |
| Education | –.277*** | –.278*** | –.027 |
| | (.068) | (.067) | (.057) |
| Income | –.002 | –.002 | .004 |
| | (.004) | (.004) | (.003) |
| Black | –2.533*** | –2.582*** | –2.007*** |
| | (.580) | (.581) | (.515) |
| Other | –.446 | –.423 | –.745 |
| | (.573) | (.572) | (.494) |
| Percent non-Latino unemployed | –.089 | –.068 | –.101 |
| | (.084) | (.085) | (.068) |
| Income inequality | –.617* | –.559* | –.344 |
| | (.265) | (.265) | (.242) |
| Homicide rate | .036 | .033 | .026 |
| | (.033) | (.032) | (.027) |
| Constant | 27.444*** | 26.842*** | 11.331*** |
| | (1.336) | (1.377) | (1.272) |
| Adjusted R-square | .136 | .137 | .379 |
| | ($n$ = 1320) | ($n$ = 1320) | ($n$ = 1320) |

†Standard errors in parentheses.
*$p \leq .05$.
**$p \leq .01$.
***$p \leq .001$.

**Table 4.9** OLS regression coefficients: support for punitive controls on measures of threat, by subsamples[†]

| | Border control | | Internal control | |
|---|---|---|---|---|
| PANEL A | Anglos ($n$ = 1101) | Blacks ($n$ = 124) | Anglos ($n$ = 1101) | Blacks ($n$ = 124) |
| Perceived criminal threat | .571*** | .399*** | .709*** | .669*** |
| | (.038) | (.096) | (.037) | (.119) |
| Change in percent Latino | .004 | .031* | –.005 | –.011 |
| | (.005) | (.014) | (.005) | (.014) |
| Border state | .611 | –.266 | –.066 | .374 |
| | (.424) | (1.316) | (.475) | (1.085) |
| PANEL B | Conservative ($n$ = 494) | Non-Cons ($n$ = 826) | Conservative ($n$ = 494) | Non-Cons ($n$ = 826) |
| Perceived criminal threat | .534*** | .570*** | .603*** | .754*** |
| | (.047) | (.046) | (.057) | (.042) |
| Change in percent Latino | .013 | .001 | .015* | –.005 |
| | (.007) | (.005) | (.007) | (.006) |
| Border state | .728 | .450 | .012 | –.394 |
| | (.544) | (.487) | (.656) | (.450) |
| | p-values for significant slope differences are as follows: | | | |
| | Border Anglo/Black | | | |
| Perceived criminal threat | .048 | | | |
| Change in percent Latino | .035 | | | |
| | Internal Cons/Non | | | |
| Perceived criminal threat | .017 | | | |
| Change in percent Latino | .015 | | | |

[†]Standard errors in parentheses.
*$p \leq .05$.
**$p \leq .01$.
***$p \leq .001$.

internal controls, including perceived criminal threat are examined. Table 4.9 repeats the latter analyses for subsamples distinguished by virtue of respondent attributes that are strongly related to support for punitive controls. The objective here is to assess whether there are demographic contexts in which support for immigrant controls is already so high that contextual and perceived threat are less consequential (ceiling effect). As specified, the models presented appear unaffected by issues of multicollinearity with VIF scores consistently below 1.35.

## Results

### *Predicting Perceived Criminal Threat*

Model 1 in Table 4.6 examines the effects of our control variables in addition to percent Latino and border state residence on perceptions of criminal threat from undocumented immigrants. Sex, county unemployment level, county income inequality, and county homicide rate are unrelated to the index of perceived criminal threat. However, higher levels of perceived criminal threat from undocumented immigrants are indicated for conservative and for older respondents. Respondents who are Black and those with higher reported education and income see significantly less crime threat associated with immigrants. Neither measure of contextual threat—percent Latino or border state residence—is related to the perception of criminal threat from undocumented immigrants. Our significant results for Black and non-significant results for percent Latino, unemployment, and income inequality are consistent with those reported by Wang (2012).[10] The directions of our significant relationships reported for conservatives, education, income, and age are also consistent with the direction of non-significant coefficients for those variables reported by Wang (2012). It can be noted that standardized coefficients show that the strongest predictors of perceived criminal threat from immigrants are conservative ideology and education.

Model 2 in Table 4.6 substitutes change in percent Latino in place of the static measure of ethnic composition. All other predictors from Model 1 are retained and their effects are unchanged from those reported above. In this model, the relative change of percent Latino is non-significant. This does not support the arguments raised by several researchers (Hawley, 2011; Hopkins, 2010; Semyonov et al., 2006) who call for the use of dynamic contextual measures of immigrant threat.

### *Predicting Support for Anti-Immigrant Controls*

Table 4.7 describes the results achieved from estimates of support for enhanced border controls targeting undocumented immigrants. As shown in Model 1, support for these controls is unrelated to respondent sex, age, income, race, county-level non-Latino unemployment, county-level income inequality, or county homicide rate. However, more highly educated respondents are less supportive of enhanced border controls while conservatives are more likely to want them strengthened. In Model 1 of Table 4.7, both contextual measures of immigrant threat—border state residence and percent Latino—are unrelated to support for enhanced border control.

Model 2 in Table 4.7 substitutes change in percent Latino for the static measure of that presumed contextual threat. Support for enhanced border controls remains strong among conservatives and opposition to harsher controls is again expressed by better educated respondents. In terms of contextual threat, border state residence significantly predicts support for stronger border controls when change in percent Latino is in the model. The latter dynamic indicator of ethnic composition is also a significant predictor of support for enhanced border measures, whereas percent Latino (Model 1) was not. This supports the suggestion that dynamic indicators of contextual threat may be more useful in modeling immigration policy attitudes than the traditionally employed static measures.

Since the dynamic measure of ethnic composition is significant while the static indicator is not, we continue to use change in percent Latino in Model 3, adding perceived criminal threat from undocumented immigrants to the specification of Model 2. Doing so reduces the coefficients for education to non-significance and reduces the effect size for conservative by more than one third. With perceived threat in the model, the effects of age and being "other" race are negative and significant. The effects of both contextual threat measures—border state residence and change in percent Latino—are also reduced to non-significance in Model 3. Most important perhaps is that perceived immigrant criminal threat is by far the strongest predictor of that policy preference outcome, with a standardized coefficient (.47) more than 2.5 times greater than the next largest for conservative (.17). Adding the perceptual threat measure increases the explained variance from .113 to .299. The changes in coefficient size and significance when perceived criminal threat is introduced in Model 3 suggest that the perceptual threat measure may partially mediate and, on that account, help explain the positive effects on support for border controls of conservative, border state residence, and change in percent Latino and may also help account for the diminished opposition to such controls among better educated respondents.

Table 4.8 applies the modeling strategy just described to support for control measures directed toward undocumented immigrants who are currently in the United States (internal controls). In Model 1, there are only four significant predictors. Conservatives are more likely to support enhanced internal controls while Blacks and more highly educated respondents express less support for such measures. Additionally, greater income inequality in the county is associated with a lower level of support for internal controls. Neither contextual threat measure—border state residence and percent Latino—has a significant effect.

Model 2 replaces static percent Latino with its change analog. The coefficients for Black, education, conservative, and county-level income inequality remain significant and almost identical in magnitude, and they are again the only predictors to achieve statistical significance. Our dynamic measure of threat, change in percent Latino, is non-significant in this model.

However, the results from Model 3 in Table 4.8 reinforce those from Table 4.7 and suggest that perceived threat from immigrants may be the most useful predictor of support for control policies. Model 3 introduces perceived criminal threat from undocumented immigrants to the specification in Model 2. The coefficients for education and county-level income inequality are reduced to non-significance, and those for conservative and Black are reduced in magnitude by 43 and 22%, respectively. The explained variance is increased by more than 2.5 times and the standardized coefficient for perceived criminal threat (.54) is more than three times greater than for conservative (.17). Similar to policy preferences relating to border controls, the effects on internal controls for conservatives, Blacks, and better educated respondents appear to be at least partially mediated by the effects of perceived criminal threat from undocumented immigrants.

## Subsample Analyses

Because race and political ideology are strong predictors of support for more punitive controls, we examine the possibility that our contextual and perceptual measures of threat may have variable consequence for Black and Anglo respondents and for those who are conservative or not. Some previous work on support for punitive attitudes in relation to race found that perceived threat was less consequential for those who were otherwise more punitive, suggesting a possible "ceiling effect" for the influence of threat (e.g. Pickett, Chiricos, Golden, & Gertz, 2012). In the present instance, since Anglo and conservative respondents were consistently more supportive of strong border and internal controls, we might anticipate that the effects of immigrant threat would be less apparent for them than for the generally less punitive Black and non-conservative respondents.

Table 4.9 addresses this question in relation to support for both border and internal controls. Panel A reports the coefficients for immigrant threat variables from models predicting that support separately for Black and Anglo respondents. All estimates include the full complement of predictors employed in Model 3 from Tables 4.7 (border) and 4.8 (internal).

The first two columns of Panel A (border controls) show that while the effects of perceived criminal threat are positive and significant for both Anglo and Black respondents, the influence of this perceptual threat indicator is significantly stronger for Anglos than it is for Blacks ($p = .048$).[11] This is not consistent with a ceiling effect because perceived criminal threat matters more for Anglos even though they are consistently more punitive in general. Panel A also shows that the relevance of change in percent Latino for border control support is only significant for Black respondents and the slope difference between Black and Anglo respondents in this regard is also significant ($p = .035$). This result appears to be consistent with a ceiling effect because change in percent Latino is inconsequential for Anglo respondents, perhaps because they are already more punitive than others. While the signs for border state residence are positive for Anglos and negative for Blacks there is no significant difference in their slopes relating to border control support.[12]

The second two columns of Panel A compare the effects of perceived and contextual threat on support for internal controls among Black and Anglo respondents.

Simply put, there are no significant differences by race in the magnitude of these effects, and thus there is no suggestion of ceiling effects either.

Panel B in Table 4.9 repeats the foregoing analytic strategy for a comparison of conservative and non-conservative respondents. In predicting support for border controls, the first two columns show that perceived criminal threat is significant for both ideological groups and change in percent Latino and border state residence are both inconsequential irrespective of political ideology. None of the slope differences are significant in relation to border controls.

The last two columns in Panel B of Table 4.9 address possible ideological differences in the effects of immigrant threat on support for internal controls. Perceived criminal threat is significant for both groups but is significantly stronger among non-conservatives ($p = .017$). That perceived criminal threat would matter less for conservatives is not inconsistent with a ceiling hypothesis. However, the robust consequence of this perceptual threat measure in both ideological contexts suggests that political ideology may only modestly moderate the consequences of perceived criminal threat. Change in percent Latino is significant in predicting support for internal controls for conservatives but it is not for non-conservatives. The differences between these effects are significant ($p = .015$). This pattern is not consistent with a ceiling effect which would expect weaker effects of contextual threat among respondents who were already highly punitive. Border state residence is inconsequential in relation to policy preferences relating to controls on immigrants already in the country, regardless of political ideology.

Overall, the pattern of results from these subsample analyses indicates some significant differences between Black and Anglo respondents with regard to the effects of immigrant threat on support for border controls and between conservatives and non-conservatives in relation to the effects of threat on internal controls. But only one of four significant slope differences is consistent with a ceiling effect, wherein the effect of change in percent Latino predicted border control support for Black but not Anglo respondents.

## DISCUSSION AND CONCLUSIONS

While empirical evidence consistently contradicts the claim that immigration increases crime, those claims persist in many quarters with a particular emphasis on the presumed criminal threat posed by undocumented immigrants. The present study is the first to examine whether public support for enhanced controls against undocumented immigrants is linked to the perception that such immigrants are indeed criminally threatening. Survey data show that perceived criminal threat from undocumented immigrants is a consistently strong predictor of policy preferences that would strengthen border controls and impose increased costs on undocumented immigrants who are presently in this country.

More specifically, the results of the foregoing analyses of 1,364 responses by non-Latinos to a 2008 national survey can be briefly summarized. (1) Perceived criminal threat is consistently higher for respondents who are conservative or who have lower levels of income or education. (2) Contextual level threat matters, often in dynamic rather than static terms, in predicting support for enhanced border controls but not for enhanced internal controls. (3) Perceived criminal threat from undocumented immigrants is clearly more important than contextual measures of threat as well as demographic traits of respondents for understanding popular support for punitive controls. (4) There is little evidence of "ceiling effects" suggesting that threat may not matter more for those who are less punitive generally.

Our results modeling perceived criminal threat among undocumented immigrants depart somewhat from those recently reported by Wang (2012). In the present analyses, positive effects of conservative and age as well as the negative effects of education, income, and Black are statistically significant. Among those predictors, only the effect for Black respondents was significant in Wang's (2012) study, though the reported signs for the other variables are most often the same. Wang also found that the unemployment rate was a significant predictor of perceived criminal threat for native-born respondents whereas we found that county-level unemployment had no effect. The two studies include disparate contextual measures of presumed threat—percent Latino, unemployment, and specific southwestern state residence in Wang's research; change in percent Latino and border state residence in ours. In addition, there are important disparities in the dependent measures used in the two studies (three-ordered categories in the former, continuous measures in the present) as well as differences in sample size and composition that limit comparisons between the two studies.[13]

In terms of estimating support for controls against undocumented immigrants, it is notable that the only significant consequence of presumed contextual threat is found for those controls to be mobilized at the border—and not for controls directed at immigrants already present—and then only before perceived criminal threat is introduced. This pattern in the findings raises several issues relative to the ongoing examination of immigrant threat and social control that merit discussion.

First, the disparity in results for border and internal controls underscores the importance of distinguishing between the two kinds of controls that differ substantially in both content and focus. Much of the immigrant threat research—including the limited work on perceived criminal threat—has operationalized support for controls in terms of desired levels of future immigration. There is likely much to be learned from making finer distinctions that distinguish between policy preferences in relation to immigrants who are already living in this (or another) country and others who are "outside" and can only be imagined. Just in terms of the "unknown," those outside could reasonably be seen as more threatening and a basis for supporting stronger border controls.

But from another point of view, it is possible that for immigrants already present, some of whom are undocumented, ongoing interaction with US residents may contribute to a different dynamic. It has been suggested that "contact" between disparate groups can under certain circumstances temper their threatening disposition and even lead to positive sentiments (Allport, 1954; McLaren, 2003; Pettigrew, 1988). In relation to immigration, such contact may not necessarily lead to positive attitudes but to an attenuation of perceived threat and distrust. This may be one reason why change in percent Latino and border state residence are significant in estimates of support for border controls and are not in estimates of support for internal controls.

The results involving change in percent Latino, especially when compared with those for a static measure of that demographic, lend partial support to a growing sentiment among students of threat and social control that warrants the further but modified engagement of contextual threat measures. Immigrant threat and policy preference research has made much use of static compositional measures such as percent Latino (Berg, 2009; Hawley, 2011; Hood & Morris, 1997) and percent foreign born (Hawley, 2011; McLaren, 2003; Sides & Citrin, 2007), and frequently those results have been less than supportive of the presumed threat hypothesis. The results reported here for change in percent Latino are consistent with several prior studies that have fruitfully engaged dynamic or change measures of foreign-born population to predict immigrant policy preferences (Hawley, 2011; Hopkins, 2010; Meuleman, Davidov & Billiet, 2009). The rationale for emphasizing contextual change is well expressed by Hopkins (2010) who noted that "while *levels* of ethnic heterogeneity might escape notice" because of the consistency of experience, "*changes* are less likely to do so" because of the sudden prospect of a challenge to the status quo (p. 42).

Finally, from the view of the group threat process, it should not be surprising that perceived criminal threat is more consequential in predicting support for controls than observed contextual threat measures. When Blalock (1967) introduced his social threat perspective he posed the question: "why should the size of a minority affect discrimination?" (p. 28). His response made reference to what were termed "intervening variables" that operate at "the micro level" and which included "perceived competition and power threats" (Blalock, 1967, p. 29). As previously outlined, for structural conditions like demographic composition, exposure, and change to be consequential for the mobilization of controls, individuals living in those contexts must perceive them to be threatening in ways that lead to support for controlling responses. As Giddens (1976) observed, social structures "only exist in the reproduced conduct of situated actors" (p. 127). So perceived criminal threat directly measures at the level of "situated actors" what is assumed and unmeasured but absolutely necessary for contextual threat to have its hypothesized outcomes.

Although perceptions could theoretically mediate the relationship between contextual threat and policy preferences, our analyses do not find consistent evidence of mediation. Specifically, the effects of change in percent Latino and border state residence on support for border controls are reduced to non-significance upon the introduction of perceived criminal threat. However, the effects of contextual threat never reach significance in predicting either perceptions of criminal threat or support for internal controls.

An alternative rationale for why context may have less salience than perceptions with specific regard to immigrant threat was proposed by Sides and Citrin (2007). They observed that attitudes about immigration issues are becoming substantially more politicized and as a result "have become increasingly divorced from social reality" (Sides & Citrin, 2007, p. 501) or what one might describe as the social contexts in which people live. As a result, perceptions about immigration more often "rely on vivid events ... and messages from politicians and media and less on the demographic and economic conditions" (Sides and Citrin, 2007, p. 501) in which individuals, who may or may not be threatened, are situated. However apposite such an observation may have been in 2007, it is obvious that the mechanisms described as driving perceptions about immigration and crime, independent of empirical circumstances, have surely intensified not only with new forms of media and correspondence but with the heightened popular and political salience of the issues.

## Notes

1 While scholarly reference frequently makes use of the term "undocumented," the survey providing data for this project used the term "illegal" for a few reasons. First, claims made to the general public most often use the latter term. Additionally, since our focus is on measuring public perception, we felt the term "illegal" would create less confusion among respondents than either "undocumented" or "unauthorized." Moreover, it has been shown that the term used does not significantly influence policy preferences of survey respondents (Merolla, Ramakrishan, & Haynes, 2013).

2 In this paper, we use "Anglos" to reference non-Latino whites.

3 Individual perceptions may mediate the relationship between context and support for punitive controls or may be completely independent for reasons we discuss in our conclusion.

4 The Research Network, Inc., a public opinion polling firm in Tallahassee, Florida, completed the surveys using list-assisted random digit dialing. Using recommended criteria from the American Association for Public Opinion Research (AAPOR, 2009), a response rate of 38.5% and cooperation rate of 73% were obtained. These are generally consistent with rates reported in other recent studies that are using RDD telephone surveys (e.g. Hirschfield & Piquero, 2010; King & Wheelock, 2007). Also, while response rates have decreased in recent years (Pew Research Center, 2004), several researchers have found that response rates are not significantly related to non-response bias (Curtin, Presser, & Singer, 2005; Keeter, Kennedy, Dimock, Best, & Craighill, 2006; Keeter, Miller, Kohut, Groves, & Presser, 2000).

5 We used the 5-year pooled estimates instead of single-year estimates for 2008 because of limitations to the single-year data. Single-year ACS estimates are only available for large counties (at least 65,000 population), resulting in a considerable amount of missing data. Further, the larger sample size afforded by multi-year data provides for more reliable estimates, even in the largest counties.

6 2000 Census data were used for this measure of percent Latino.

7 We also examined the possibility that the effects of percent Latino and change in percent Latino could be non-linear. This prospect was first raised by Blalock (1967) in relation to minority composition posing either economic or political threats. Quadratic terms for percent Latino and change in percent Latino were not significant in any of the models estimating either perceived criminal threat or support for immigration controls (results available on request).

8 There were 18 missing responses on age, 13 on education, 203 on income, and 57 on conservative. For purposes of imputation, OLS regression was used for age; ordered logistic regression was used for education and income; and logistic regression was used for conservative. We also included male, white, black, other race, and perceived criminal threat in the models even though they were not missing data.

9 Each of the subsequent analyses was also conducted using the total crime rate. It was not significant in any model, and results for other predictors were substantively unchanged.

10 Our comparisons to Wang (2012) make reference to her full sample results (Table 4.6). Her analysis found unemployment to be a significant predictor of perceived criminal threat for Natives as opposed to Immigrant respondents.

11 The significance of slope differences was estimated using the method established by Paternoster, Brame, Mazerolle, and Piquero (1998). These differences used one-tailed tests for significance.

12 Although border state residence was marginally significant in the full sample analyses for border control, it fails to reach statistical significance for either the Anglo or Black subsamples. This is likely because of the reduced sample sizes for the subgroups.

13 It would have been helpful if we could have specified our models predicting perceived criminal threat in ways that corresponded more closely with Wang's estimates, but our survey unfortunately was conducted too early for that.

## References

Alba, R., Rumbaut, R. G., & Marotz, K. (2005). A distorted nation: Perceptions of racial/ethnic group sizes and attitudes toward immigrants and other minorities. *Social Forces, 84*, 901–919.

Allport, G. W. (1954). *The nature of prejudice.* Reading, MA: Addison-Wesley.

American Association for Public Opinion Research. (2009). *Standard definitions: Final dispositions of case codes and outcome rates for surveys* (6th ed.). Deerfield, IL: AAPOR.

Berg, J. A. (2009). White public opinion toward undocumented immigrants: Threat and interpersonal environment. *Sociological Perspectives, 52*, 39–58.

Blalock, H. M. (1967). *Toward a theory of minority group relations*. New York: Wiley.

Blumer, H. (1958). Race prejudice as a sense of group position. *The Pacific Sociological Review, 1*, 3–7.

Bobo, L. (1983). Whites' opposition to busing: Symbolic racism or realistic group conflict? *Journal of Personality and Social Psychology, 45*, 1196–1210.

Bowyer, B. T. (2009). The contextual determinants of Whites' racial attitudes in England. *British Journal of Political Science, 39*, 559–586.

Burns, P., & Gimpel, J. G. (2000). Economic insecurity, prejudicial stereotypes, and public opinion on immigration policy. *Political Science Quarterly, 115*, 201–225.

Ceobanu, A. M. (2011). Usual suspects? Public views about immigrants' impact on crime in European countries. *International Journal of Comparative Sociology, 52,* 114–131.

Chiricos, T., Welch, K., & Gertz, M. (2004). Racial typification of crime and support for punitive measures. *Criminology, 42,* 359–389.

Citrin, J., Green, D. P., Muste, C., & Wong, C. (1997). Public opinion toward immigration reform: The role of economic motivations. *The Journal of Politics, 59,* 858–881.

Cohen, T. (2012, June 15). *Obama administration to stop deporting some young illegal immigrants*. Retrieved from http://www.cnn.com/2012/06/15/politics/immigration/index.html.

Curtin, R., Presser, S., & Singer, E. (2005). Changes in telephone survey nonresponse over the past quarter century. *Public Opinion Quarterly*, 69, 87–98.

Desmond, S. A., & Kubrin, C. E. (2009). The power of place: Immigrant communities and adolescent violence. *Sociological Quarterly, 50,* 581–607.

Dunaway, J., Branton, R. P., & Abrajano, M. A. (2010). Agenda setting, public opinion, and the issue of immigration reform. *Social Science Quarterly, 91,* 359–378.

Espenshade, T. J., & Hempstead, K. (1996). Contemporary American attitudes toward U.S. immigration. *International Migration Review, 30,* 535–570.

Fetzer, J. S. (2000). *Public attitudes toward immigration in the United States, France and Germany.* Cambridge: Cambridge University Press.

FoxNews.com. (2010, April 29). *Border states deal with more illegal immigrant crime than most, data suggest.* Retrieved from http://www.foxnews.com/politics/2010/04/29/border-states-dealing-illegal-immigrant-crime-data-suggests/.

Giddens, A. (1976). *The new rules of sociological method: A positive critique of interpretive sociologies*. New York: Basic Books.

Gove, W. R., Hughes, M., & Geerken, M. (1985). Are uniform crime reports a valid indicator of the index crimes? An affirmative answer with minor qualifications. *Criminology, 23,* 451–502.

Hawley, G. (2011). Political threat and immigration: Party identification, demographic context, and immigration policy preference. *Social Science Quarterly, 92,* 404–422.

Hickman, L. J., & Suttorp, M. J. (2008). Are deportable aliens a unique threat to public safety? Comparing the recidivism of deportable and nondeportable aliens. *Criminology & Public Policy, 7,* 58–82.

Hirschfield, P. J., & Piquero, A. R. (2010). Normalization and legitimation: Modeling stigmatizing attitudes toward ex-offenders. *Criminology, 48,* 27–55.

Hjerm, M. (2007). Do numbers really count? Group threat theory revisited. *Journal of Ethnic and Migration Studies, 33,* 1253–1275.

Hjerm, M., & Nagayoshi, K. (2011). The composition of the minority population as a threat: Can real economic and cultural threats explain xenophobia? *International Sociology, 26,* 815–843.

Hoefer, M., Rytina, N., & Baker, B. C. (2009). *Estimates of the unauthorized immigrant population residing in the United States: January 2008.* Office of Immigration Statistics, U.S. Department of Homeland Security. Retrieved from http://www.dhs.gov/xlibrary/assets/statistics/publications/ois_ill_pe_2008.pdf.

Hood, M. V., & Morris, I. L. (1997). Amigo o Enemigo: Context, attitudes and Anglo public opinion toward immigration. *Social Science Quarterly, 78*, 310–323.

Hood, M. V., Morris, I. L., & Shirkey, K. A. (1997). ¡Quedate o Vente!: Uncovering the determinants of Hispanic public opinion toward immigration. *Political Research Quarterly, 50*, 627–647.

Hopkins, D. J. (2010). Politicized places: Explaining where and when immigrants provoke local opposition. *American Political Science Review, 104*, 40–60.

Immigration Counters.com. (2012). Retrieved January 6, 2012, from http://www.immigrationcounters.com/.

Immigrations Human Cost.org. (2012). *America's least wanted*. Retrieved January 6, 2012, from http://www.immigrationshumancost.org/text/criminals_2.html.

Johnson, B. D., Stewart, E. A., Pickett, J., & Gertz, M. (2011). Ethnic threat and social control: Examining public support for judicial use of ethnicity in punishment. *Criminology, 49*, 401–441.

Keeter, S., Kennedy, C., Dimock, M., Best, J., & Craighill, P. (2006). Gauging the impact of growing nonresponse on estimates from a national RDD telephone survey. *Public Opinion Quarterly, 70*, 759–779.

Keeter, S., Miller, C., Kohut, A., Groves, R. M., & Presser, S. (2000). Consequences of reducing nonresponse in a national telephone survey. *Public Opinion Quarterly, 64*, 125–148.

King, S. (2006. May 5). *Biting the hand that feeds you*. Retrieved from http://www.house.gov/apps/list/hearing/ia05_king/col_20060505_bite.html.

King, R. D., & Wheelock, D. (2007). Group threat and social control: Race, perceptions of minorities and the desire to punish. *Social Forces, 85*, 1255–1280.

Lavrakas, P. (1993). *Telephone survey methods: Sampling, selection and supervision* (2nd ed.). Beverly Hills, CA: Sage.

Lu, L., & Nicholson-Crotty, S. (2010). Reassessing the impact of Hispanic stereotypes on White Americans' immigration preferences. *Social Science Quarterly, 91*, 1312–1328.

Martinez, R., Stowell, J. I., & Lee, M. T. (2010). Immigration and crime in an era of transformation: A longitudinal analysis of homicides in San Diego neighborhoods, 1980–2000. *Criminology, 48*, 797–829.

McLaren, L. M. (2003). Anti-immigrant prejudice in Europe: Contact, threat perception, and preferences for the exclusion of migrants. *Social Forces, 81*, 909–936.

Merolla, J., Ramakrishnan, K., & Haynes, C. (2013). "Illegal," "undocumented," or "unauthorized": Equivalency frames, issue frames and public opinion on immigration. *Perspectives on Politics, 11*, 789–807.

Meuleman, B., Davidov, E., & Billiet, J. (2009). Changing attitudes toward immigration in Europe, 2002–2007: A dynamic group conflict theory approach. *Social Science Quarterly, 38*, 352–365.

National Conference of State Legislatures. (2014). *2013 immigration report*. Retrieved from http://www.ncsl.org/research/immigration/2013-immigration-report.aspx.

Ousey, G. C., & Kubrin, C. E. (2009). Exploring the connection between Immigration and violent crime rates in U.S. cities, 1980–2000. *Social Problems, 56*, 447–473.

Palmer, D. L. (1996). Determinants of Canadian attitudes toward immigration: More than just racism? *Canadian Journal of Behavioural Science/Revue canadienne des sciences du comportement, 28*, 180–192.

Paternoster, R., Brame, R., Mazerolle, P., & Piquero, A. (1998). Using the correct statistical test for the equality of regression coefficients. *Criminology, 36,* 859–866.

Pettigrew, T. F. (1988). Intergroup contact theory. *Annual Review of Psychology, 49,* 65–85.

Pew Research Center. (2004). *Survey experiment shows polls face growing resistance, but still representative.* Washington, DC: Pew Research Center.

Pickett, J. T., Chiricos, T., Golden, K. M., & Gertz, M. (2012). Reconsidering the relationship between perceived neighborhood racial composition and Whites' perceptions of victimization risk: Do racial stereotypes matter? *Criminology, 50,* 145–186.

Quillian, L. (1995). Prejudice as a response to perceived group threat: Population composition and anti-immigrant and racial prejudice in Europe. *American Sociological Review, 60,* 586–611.

Rocha, R. R., & Espino, R. (2009). Racial threat, residential segregation, and the policy attitudes of Anglos. *Political Research Quarterly, 62,* 415–426.

Rocha, R. R., Longoria, T., Wrinkle, R. D., Knoll, B. R., Polinard, J. L., & Wenzel, J. (2011). Ethnic context and immigration policy preferences among Latinos and Anglos. *Social Science Quarterly, 92,* 1–19.

Sampson, R. J. (2006, March 11). Open doors don't invite criminals. *New York Times.* Retrieved from http://www.nytimes.com/2006/03/11/opinion/11sampson.html?_r=0.

Sampson, R. J. (2008). Rethinking crime and immigration. *Contexts, 7,* 28–33.

Sampson, R. J., Morenoff, J. D., & Raudenbush, S. (2005). Social anatomy of racial and ethnic disparities in violence. *American Journal of Public Health, 95,* 224–232.

Schurman-Kauflin, D. (2006). *The dark side of illegal immigration: Nearly one million sex crimes committed by illegal immigrants in the United States.* Retrieved August 20, 2012, from http://www.drdsk.com/articles.html#Illegals.

Semyonov, M., Raijman, R., & Gorodzeisky, A. (2006). The rise of anti-foreigner sentiment in European societies, 1988–2000. *American Sociological Review, 71,* 426–449.

Sides, J., & Citrin, J. (2007). European opinion about immigration: The role of identities, interests and information. *British Journal of Political Science, 37,* 477–504.

Stowell, J. I., Messner, S. F., McGeever, K. F., & Raffalovich, L. E. (2009). Immigration and the recent violent crime drop in the United States: A pooled, cross-sectional time-series analysis of metropolitan areas. *Criminology, 47,* 889–928.

Unnever, J. D., & Cullen, F. T. (2012). White perceptions of whether African Americans and Hispanics are prone to violence and support for the death penalty. *Journal of Research in Crime and Delinquency, 49,* 519–544.

Wang, X. (2012). Undocumented immigrants as perceived criminal threat: A test of the minority threat perspective. *Criminology, 50,* 743–776.

Wheelock, D., Semukhina, O., & Demidov, N. N. (2011). Perceived group threat and punitive attitudes in Russia and the United States. *British Journal of Criminology, 51,* 937–959.

Wilson, T. C. (2001). Americans' views on immigration policy: Testing the role of threatened group interests. *Sociological Perspectives, 44,* 485–501.

# Chapter 5

# Injustice in Criminal Justice

## INTRODUCTION

What does it mean to examine the CJS from a larger justice perspective? Much has been written about injustices that exist within CJSs; in this chapter, we examine some of the pressing injustices in our current CJS using the framework for a broad justice analysis laid out in this book. As Chapter 1 describes, CJSs can be examined in terms of the ways they intersect with various types of justice, including formal/procedural justice, substantive justice, and social justice. We can also examine whether and how CJSs exhibit the qualities of fairness, equality, merit/desert, and need to assess them in terms of justice. We know, for instance, that formal/procedural justice is foundational to the structure of our legal system, and consequently our CJS. At any point in the CJ process, we can assess whether the system makes good on its fairness guarantees in terms of the rights afforded to people as they are arrested, interrogated, detained, tried, punished, and released back into society.

It is important to keep in mind, however, that not all types of justice are built into the goals and functioning of the CJS. Examining the CJS from a larger justice perspective sometimes means assessing the system based on external criteria, rather than according to its own internal justice goals. For instance, you should recall from Chapter 1 that social justice is a particularly tricky concept for the CJS, because the system's focus on individual cases makes it difficult to achieve justice at the societal level. The individual case orientation of the CJS would not be an issue if it weren't for the context of broader inequalities that characterize our society. Individual-level justice can produce or promote justice at the societal level—but only when society is functioning in a just way outside of the CJS.

For this reason, the distinction drawn in Chapter 2 among three different ways that justice can interact with the CJS is a pivotal one. Recall that there is injustice in the form of crime (the purview of the CJS), injustice that characterizes the CJS response to crime, and injustice in the broader context surrounding the CJS. When access to resources and opportunities is distributed unequally in society, the likelihood of interaction with the CJS is also unevenly distributed. Poor people, particularly people of color, represent a disproportionate number of people involved in our CJS, as both victims and offenders, because of the intertwining of social problems such as poverty and racism. Once people are entangled in the system, the social exclusion and oppression that poverty and racism entail are only compounded, further exacerbating injustice for groups that are already marginalized. This is the case even when the requirements of formal justice are satisfied by the CJS. In other words, even when individuals are treated fairly and processed through the system in a way that recognizes all of their rights, their system involvement can still represent social injustice and/or exacerbate other types of injustice that they have experienced in their lives.

## THE INJUSTICE OF CRIME

Most crimes represent injustice in some way, and the majority of these injustices can be understood at the individual level. A few types of crime, however, represent broader injustices that reach beyond the individuals involved in the crime. When crimes can be linked to broader inequalities or injustices, they become a social justice issue. Let's consider hate crimes as an example. Hate crimes occur when victims are selected on the basis of their actual or perceived membership in a particular social group. Hate crimes are typically motivated by prejudice on the basis of race, ethnicity, nationality, religion, sexual orientation, gender or gender identity, disability, and other similar statuses. Because perpetrators choose victims who represent (to the perpetrator) an undesirable group, hate crimes are not just interactions between individuals; they are also powerful manifestations of ideology.

Interestingly, in recent years the CJS has begun to orient to hate crime as categorically distinct from other crimes, with laws passed at the state and federal level that pertain exclusively to hate crimes. Hate crime laws take many different forms, but typically have provisions enhancing penalties for bias- or hate-motivated crimes. In 2009, Congress passed the Matthew Shepard and James Byrd, Jr., Hate Crimes Prevention Act, ensuring that federal hate crime protections covered people in states without their own hate crime statutes, and providing federal assistance in the investigation and prosecution of hate crimes. The very existence of hate crime statutes is evidence of the application of social justice goals to the CJS. This departure from the individual-level focus of the CJS has even been articulated at the highest levels of our government. Because hate crimes are "more likely to provoke retaliatory crimes, inflict distinct emotional harms on their victims, and incite community unrest," Chief Justice William Rehnquist noted, they are "thought to inflict greater individual *and societal harm*" (*Wisconsin v. Mitchell*, 1993, emphasis added).

Despite the progress that has been made in the CJS with regard to social justice in the area of hate crimes, the system is still not designed to handle most social problems. Let's turn to another example, violence against women, to further examine the mismatch between the individual-level orientation of the CJS and the societal level at which social problems operate. Although it may seem like violence against women is a type of hate crime, this is not usually the case. Violence against women is a broad category that includes domestic violence, intimate partner violence, and sexual assault. Unlike hate crimes, which are driven by consciously articulated prejudices against a group as a whole, the intended target of violence against women is not usually women as a group. Instead, the ideology that drives violence against women is more subtle. This ideology goes by many names: sexism, gender inequality, patriarchy, misogyny. Here, we'll call it misogyny: the devaluation of women relative to men. Misogyny is systemic and widespread in our society; moreover, it has deep historical roots. This engenders and perpetuates a culture of gender inequality that positions women as less socially valuable than men and therefore vulnerable to men in many ways (e.g., financially, physically, emotionally). The societal power structures that create this vulnerability link individual acts of violence against women to the larger social problem of misogyny.

But how can the CJS combat misogyny? Unfortunately, it can't. The 1994 Violence Against Women Act allocated funding for the prosecution of violent crimes against women, enhanced protections and restitution for victims, and established the Office on Violence Against Women within the U.S. Department of Justice. Unlike hate crimes legislation, however, the Violence Against Women Act does not change the way the CJS processes violent crimes against women. Let's consider a hypothetical scenario in which a woman is repeatedly pushed, slapped, and punched by her boyfriend. This repeated intimate partner violence escalates over time, and culminates in a blow to the head that sends her to the emergency room. Police take a report, and the boyfriend is charged with domestic assault. Although the Violence Against Women Act may provide federal funding that will help bring the case to trial, and may aid the victim in claiming her restitution, there is little other impact. No additional charges will be filed, nor harsher penalties enacted. Thus, despite a commitment at the national level to address the social problem of violence against women, the CJS is only equipped to address the issue of violence against individual women, one at a time.

Let's switch gears to a very different kind of crime: white collar crime. It has been suggested that white collar and corporate crime are underrepresented in criminal justice journals, criminology and criminal justice textbooks, and doctoral program curricula (Lynch, McGurrin, & Fenwick, 2004). One of the challenges to discussing white collar crime is in understanding who the victims are. Although not a victimless crime by any means, white collar crimes such as embezzlement or fraud could have millions of victims, some known and some unknown. The larger public, too, can be victimized by white collar crime, for instance in the form of fraudulent practices by banks that have far-reaching effects on the economy. This element—lack of an easily identifiable and recognizable victim—renders white collar crime challenging for both the CJS (in terms of combating white collar crime) and CJC studies (in terms of the analysis of white collar crime). Interestingly, this same element becomes advantageous when considering white collar crime as a social problem, rather than a criminal justice issue. The individual-level orientation of the CJS makes it difficult to prosecute and punish much white collar crime, particularly high-level crime. The societal level at which social problems operate, however, is the perfect space to analyze and address white collar crime. Thus, it is precisely because white collar crime is difficult to consider in terms of criminal justice that it makes sense to orient to it as a social justice issue.

Let's examine a concrete example of the difficulty the CJS has in dealing with white collar crime. When the financial crisis of 2008 struck, Americans suffered millions of job losses and home foreclosures as a result of widespread risky and fraudulent practices in our country's largest and most prestigious banks. A 2011 U.S. Senate report attributed the financial collapse to "high risk, complex financial products; undisclosed conflicts of interest; the failure of regulators, the credit rating agencies, and the market itself to rein in the excesses of Wall Street" (United States, 2011). Following the financial collapse, there was a loud and concerted public outcry for justice. This took many forms, including the Occupy Wall Street movement described in Chapter 4. Widespread public dissatisfaction with wealth inequality in our country and anger at what many saw as a "rigged system" (look, an example of conflict perspective!) fueled the public's desire to see the bankers responsible for the frauds underpinning the crisis punished. Although criminal prosecution following an economic bust is not unprecedented, this particular time it did not materialize. Only one high-level banker was sentenced to prison for his role in the financial crisis; in fact, the government opted to use the civil legal system to levy large financial penalties against the banks themselves, rather than prosecuting individuals for their fraud. The scale and complexity of the frauds, combined with their far-reaching societal effects, make such crimes incredibly difficult for the CJS to tackle.

## INJUSTICE IN THE CRIMINAL JUSTICE SYSTEM

Now let's turn our attention to injustices that are created within and by the CJS, rather than injustices that are dealt with (to varying degrees) by the CJS. To many, our country's practice of mass incarceration has become one of the most pressing civil and human rights issues of the 21st century. The United States is the leader by far in rates of incarceration worldwide, with Rwanda and Russia falling a distant second and third. For most of the 20th century, imprisonment was rare and its rate was low and steady. At 100 people incarcerated per 100,000, just one-tenth of 1% of the population was behind bars. This began to change in the mid-1970s (remember the "tough on crime" ideology discussed in Chapter 4?). Since then, our country has witnessed unprecedented growth in incarceration, with rates peaking in 2009 with 1,615,487 prisoners incarcerated under state or federal jurisdiction (Carson, 2015). As of year-end 2014, the number had dropped to 1,561,500 total prisoners, with an incarceration rate of 612 people per 100,000. More than one-half of the prison population consists of drug offenders: one-half of all incarcerated females (who make up 7% of those incarcerated) and 59% of males are serving time for drug offenses (Carson, 2015).

Although mass incarceration implicates corrections most obviously, it also involves the practices of police and the courts. Much of our current correctional reality can be attributed to crackdowns on crime rather than on crime itself—notably the tough-on-crime policies enacted throughout the 1970s, 1980s, and 1990s. Stricter enforcement of laws and harsh mandatory sentences were implemented with the goal of reducing crime through incapacitation or deterrence. Another causal factor may be the decline of funding and services for those with mental health and drug abuse issues, leaving prison as the most readily available response. Although all classes of people commit crime, it is typically the poor who experience the highest rates of arrest, criminal charges, convictions, lengthy sentences, and the denial of parole.

Despite being institutions of "correction," prisons can exacerbate underlying issues and create new problems for prisoners. Research has documented the lack of programs in institutions, from effective drug treatment (despite the fact that the majority of inmates report substance use), to programs that focus on the development of new skills. Insufficient mental health and medical care also frequently characterize prisons. In California—a state with one of the largest prison populations in the country—the Supreme Court found that the California Department of Corrections and Rehabilitation had consistently violated prisoners' 8th amendment rights by failing to provide adequate medical treatment, mental health care, and disability accommodations. Although many of these injustices are inherent to prison systems, crowded conditions only exacerbate them.

There are many deprivations and losses created by the experience of incarceration as well (Sexton, 2015). The degrading and dehumanizing culture of prison life, along with the omnipresent threat of violence, are unavoidable in prison. Looking outside prison walls, a loss of family ties occurs due to the often remote location of prisons (far from major metropolitan/residential areas) and many other policies and practices that discourage contact, such as inconvenient visiting times for brief visits devoid of physical contact that take place in crowded visiting rooms or through Plexiglas. Restrictions on prisoner mail and phone time, combined with the exorbitant cost of phone calls from prison, further strain family bonds. Beyond the negative effects experienced directly by those who are incarcerated, are the negative effects on children of prisoners. It is estimated that some two and a half million children are affected by incarceration in this way; as a result, they are more likely to experience poverty, abuse and neglect, be put in foster care, be labeled as like their parents, and end up entangled in the CJS themselves.

The price tag for our mass incarceration endeavor is high, with state expenditures on corrections at $51.9 billion in 2013. The numbers only grow when the jail population and those under community supervision (on probation or parole) are added, pushing the number of those under some form of correctional control well over 4 million (The Sentencing Project, 2015). Compare and contrast this with spending on education, and a very grim picture of our country's priorities is revealed. As of 2016, 11 states in the United States spent more money on incarceration than they did on education. Per-person costs can be up to four times as high for prison as they are for education (Lobosco, 2015). Thus, the size and reach of our prison system influences not just the CJS, but also other social institutions such as family and education, demonstrating that mass incarceration has become a social problem. Numerous CJC scholars have questioned our use of incarceration, challenging the practice on humanitarian, moral, and financial grounds, and in turn calling for alternatives (Alexander, 2012; Pratt, 2008; Soering, 2004). Once again, the intertwined and complex nature of justice—in terms of fairness, desert, equality of opportunity, and social justice, among others—leaves the CJS in a sticky situation (that is, admittedly, partially of its own making).

Another major area of injustice within the CJS is juvenile justice. Until recently, the United States permitted the execution of juvenile offenders (those who were younger than age 18 at the time of their crime). In 2005, the U.S. Supreme Court banned the execution of juveniles, bringing the United States into line with international standards prohibiting such executions. The United States also allows for life sentences (including life sentences without the possibility of parole) to be given to juvenile offenders, although life-without-parole for nonviolent offenses was ruled unconstitutional in 2009, and *mandatory* juvenile life-without-parole sentences for any crime were banned in 2012. Life sentences for child offenders are prohibited under the United Nations Convention on the Rights of the Child, a document signed, but not ratified by the United States. Many groups and individuals in the United States have called for an end to this practice, including the American Civil Liberties Union, the Sentencing Project, and the Equal Justice Initiative.

The application of life sentences for juveniles increased dramatically in the late 1980s as perhaps the epitome of the tough on crime ideology that gripped the nation. A 2005 report found that 2,225 people had been sentenced to life without parole (also known as "natural life," because it generally means that prisoners will die behind bars) for crimes committed when they were children (Human Rights Watch/Amnesty International, 2005). Of the cases examined, 16% of those prisoners were between age 13 and 15 at the time of the crime and 59% received the sentence for their first conviction. Many were convicted of "felony murder" based on evidence of their participation in a crime during which a murder took place, but without direct evidence of their involvement in the actual killing. This report called upon the United States authorities to stop sentencing children to life without parole and to juveniles serving such sentences immediate access to parole procedures.

The experience of detention can also produce grave injustices for juveniles. Whether detained in facilities designated specifically for juveniles, or incarcerated in adult prisons, younger prisoners are at risk for many serious abuses and injustices. The use of restraint chairs and solitary confinement is one of the most extreme—although unfortunately not uncommon—examples of this. Juvenile solitary confinement in particular has come under increasing public and political scrutiny in the past few years, primarily for the severe and long-term psychological consequences that it can have. In 2016, President Obama announced a ban on solitary confinement for juveniles in federal prisons—a measure that affects relatively few youth directly (as most youth are detained at the county or state level), but sets a powerful precedent nonetheless.

One of the starkest examples of injustice within criminal justice comes from the examination of disproportionate minority contact (DMC) with all components of the CJS (police, courts, and corrections). Evidence of this phenomenon exists in both adult and juvenile populations. For example, although African American youth make up 17% of the population, they make up 31% of those arrested, and are similarly more likely to be referred to the juvenile court, to be processed, to be securely confined, and to be transferred to an adult facility compared to their White counterparts (Puzzanchera & Hockenberry, 2013). It may be tempting to make the assumption that they are simply committing more crimes or delinquent acts, but self-report data show few group differences between White youth and youth of color (Lauritsen, 2005).

Curfew violations are a good example of a minor offense where few differences exist in self-report data, yet significant racial differences emerge in arrest rates. In 2011, Black youth were 269% more likely than White youth to be arrested for curfew violations (The Sentencing Project, 2014). Most research suggests that existing policies and practices, rather than actual behavioral differences, are at the root of the problem. As early as preschool, there are disproportionate suspensions for Black children compared with White children. It is widely known that secure, out-of-home placements are linked to negative outcomes for children in terms of health, well-being, educational achievement, and future employment opportunities, yet non-Hispanic Black youth make up 40% of those placements, whereas their representation in the population is at 14% (The Sentencing Project, 2014).

## INJUSTICE IN THE CONTEXT SURROUNDING THE CJS

Before turning to another type of injustice, let's examine how disproportionate minority contact with the CJS can also be an issue of justice in the context surrounding the CJS. Although it is clear that some causes of DMC originate from within the CJS, many of the root causes of DMC are societal in nature. The concepts introduced in Chapter 3—social stratification, social exclusion and oppression, and racism—all have bearing on the disproportionate contact that people of color have with the CJS. Social stratification results in an excess of burdens for those situated toward the bottom of the SES ladder (particularly poor people of color) and an excess of rewards for those situated near the top (picture any of the Wall Street CEOs who weren't charged with fraud after the financial collapse).

Although some of the disproportionality in minority contact with the CJS can be attributed to discriminatory policing practices, bias in the courtroom, and even racialized patterns of community supervision, a large part of the problem rests outside the CJS. When people live in disadvantaged neighborhoods characterized by poverty and social disorganization, crime often follows. So too does law enforcement presence, leading to increased opportunity for contact with the police. Thus, the social and financial disadvantages that are disproportionately faced by people of color in this country (the effect of persistent racism, discussed in Chapter 3) lend themselves to involvement in the CJS. Life in high-crime neighborhoods is structured in such a way that it encourages participation in crime, whereas society erects barriers that make it extremely difficult for poor people of color to exit these neighborhoods or thrive within them. Because poverty and racism are social problems that are very closely linked to criminal justice problems, the CJS is forced to either operate in a way that attempts to address larger societal injustice (despite not being designed to do so), or proceed according to the status quo, which can exacerbate injustice.

These same factors (poverty, racism, concentrated disadvantage) do not just affect individuals' likelihood of entry into the CJS; they also have powerful impacts on the lives of those who are returning to society after serving time in prison. Upon release, individuals generally return to the same neighborhoods from which they came, often to levels of social and financial support that are even lower than before their incarceration (Clear, Rose & Ryder, 2001). Those reentering the community frequently experience difficulty finding and maintaining employment, housing, and transportation. The sources of these difficulties are many, and include the financial and time-related challenges of poverty, the stigma of a felony conviction, and the lingering effects of incarceration. Long incarceration terms can cause individuals to become accustomed to an institutional setting (referred to as "prisonization"), which diminishes the abilities and characteristics they once had, including skills related to decision-making, trust, and the ability to exercise control over their lives. Formal barriers to successful reintegration (often referred to as "collateral consequences" of the CJS) take the form of exclusion from government benefits such as food stamps and public housing, and the loss of civil rights such as the ability to vote and eligibility to serve on a jury—powerful civil rights that are deeply embedded in our participatory government.

In this way, incarcerated (or formerly incarcerated) individuals can experience both injustice at the hands of the CJS and injustice in the larger context in which the CJS is situated. This creates a vicious cycle that is incredibly difficult to escape. The root causes of crime and system involvement (e.g., social disorganization, poverty) are social problems that are only exacerbated by incarceration, at both the individual level and a societal level. Thus, even when the internal goals of the CJS (e.g., crime control) are being met, social problems can once again rear their ugly heads.

There are many other societal injustices that interact with the CJS; in fact, just about every injustice that we've discussed thus far in the book can be related to criminal justice in some way. We discussed race and ethnicity in detail previously, but they are not the only statuses with implications for injustice in the CJS. Problems of disproportionate contact with, and disproportionate impact of, the CJS can also be seen related to sexual orientation, gender identity, ability, and mental health status. For instance, it is estimated that LGBT youth comprise only 7% of the larger population, but represent 15% of the youth involved in the juvenile justice system—a figure that jumps to 40% when broadened to include girls who are questioning or gender-nonconforming (Irvine & Canfield, 2016). The reasons for this disproportionality are debatable, but could include the stresses and stereotypes associated with growing up LGBTQ, including rejection by family and others upon coming out. For instance, homelessness and poverty are major justice issues facing this population, with one study estimating that 40% of homeless youth identify as LGBT (Durso & Gates, 2012).

In addition to being overrepresented in the CJS, LGBTQ individuals often find themselves at greater risk while incarcerated. Rates of physical and sexual assault for nonheterosexual prisoners are significantly higher than for heterosexual prisoners (Jenness, Maxson, Matsuda, & Sumner, 2007). This vulnerability is heightened for transgender prisoners, 59% of whom have reported sexual assault while in prison—a figure 13 times higher than that of the general prison population (Jenness, Sexton, & Sumner, 2010). Prisoners with disabilities and mental health issues are similarly vulnerable in a prison context; they, too, face higher rates of physical and sexual victimization, along with prison conditions that can exacerbate underlying medical and psychological issues. These conditions include, but by no means are limited to, insufficient medical care, the experience of greater and more frequent use of force, and overreliance on solitary confinement to control behavior deemed problematic by prison staff.

## RECONCILING CRIMINAL JUSTICE AND SOCIAL JUSTICE

In the previous sections, we have tried to provide a diverse range of examples of injustice in and around the CJS. We highlighted big, pressing issues as well as topics that tend to get overlooked in the CJC literature. There are many categories of injustice that get less attention still than those discussed in this chapter. Unlawful wiretapping, murder by military contractors, and cyber crime are just a few examples that could be given. Teaching about crimes committed by the state, be it our government or other governments, is also underdeveloped in CJC studies, despite high interest among students and criminologists (Ross & Rothe, 2007). To achieve a more comprehensive and holistic picture of the concept of justice and in recognition of the societal costs and impacts of these types of crimes, a critical focus on these crimes committed by the powerful and an analysis of our system response to them must also receive a greater focus.

Regardless of which type of injustice we consider, examining the CJS through a broad justice lens presents some difficulty. The individual-level justice focus of our CJS seems to be on something of a collision course with the social injustices that abound in our society. For the CJS to operate in a way that is just, it must strike a balance between individual justice and social justice; fairness and merit/desert must be considered alongside larger issues of equality and need. Because injustice is unfortunately pervasive in our society, this is quite a tall order for a system that is not designed or structured to address issues of social injustice on a large scale. To move forward, we need CJ practitioners who are trained in the rigorous and creative application of a social justice lens to criminal justice issues—including the CJS itself. In the next chapter, we provide a roadmap for doing so, detailing the link between theory, research, and policy to draw connections between CJC studies and the CJS systems they focus on.

## References

Alexander, M. (2012). *The new Jim Crow: Mass incarceration in the age of colorblindness.* New York: The New Press.

Carson, E.A. (2015). *Prisoners in 2014.* Washington, D.C.: U.S. Department of Justice.

Clear, T., Rose, D. R., & Ryder, J. A. (2001), Incarceration and the community: The problem of removing and returning offenders. *Crime & Delinquency, 47*(3), 335–351.

Durso, L. E., & Gates, G. J. (2012). *Serving our youth: Findings from a national survey of service providers working with lesbian, gay, bisexual, and transgender youth who are homeless or at risk of becoming homeless.* Los Angeles: The Williams Institute with True Colors Fund and The Palette Fund.

Human Rights Watch/Amnesty International (2005). *The rest of their lives: Life without parole for child offenders in the United States.* New York: Human Rights Watch/Amnesty International.

Hurlbert, M.A. (Ed.). (2011). *Pursuing justice: An introduction to justice studies.* Nova Scotia, Canada: Fernwood Publishing.

Irvine, A., & Canfield, A. (2016). The overrepresentation of lesbian, gay, bisexual, questioning, gender nonconforming and transgender youth within the child welfare to juvenile justice crossover population. *Journal of Gender, Social Policy, and the Law, 24*(2): article 2.

Jenness, V., Maxson. C., Matsuda, K., & Sumner, J. (2007). *Violence in California correctional facilities: An empirical examination of sexual assault.* Report submitted to the California Department of Corrections and Rehabilitation.

Jenness, V., Sexton, L., & Sumner, J. (2010). Transgender inmates in California's prisons: An empirical study of a vulnerable population. Report submitted to the California Department of Corrections and Rehabilitation.

Lauritsen, J. L. (2005). Racial and ethnic difference in juvenile offending. In D.F. Hawkins, & K. Kempf-Leonard (Eds.), *Our children, their children: Confronting racial and ethnic differences in American juvenile justice* (pp. 83–104). Chicago: University of Chicago Press.

Lobosco, K. (2015). 11 states spend more on prisons than on higher education. CNN, Oct. 1, 2015. Retrieved from http://money.cnn.com/2015/10/01/pf/college/higher-education-prison-state-spending/.

Lynch, M.J., McGurrin, D., & Fenwick, M. (2004). Disappearing act: The representation of corporate crime research in criminological literature. *Journal of Criminal Justice, 32*(5), 389–398.

Pratt, T. (2008). *Addicted to incarceration: Corrections policy and the politics of misinformation in the United States.* New York: SAGE.

Puzzanchera, C., & Hockenberry, S. (2013). *National disproportionate minority contact databook.* Washington, D.C.: National Center for Juvenile Justice for the Office of Juvenile Justice and Delinquency Prevention. Retrieved from http://www.ojjdp.gov/ojstatbb/dmcdb/.

Ross, J., & Rothe, D. (2007). Swimming upstream: Teaching state crime to students at American universities. *Journal of Criminal Justice Education, 18*(3), 460–475.

Sexton, L. (2015). Penal subjectivities: Developing a theoretical framework for penal consciousness. *Punishment & Society, 17*(1), 114–136.

Soering, J. (2004). *An expensive way to make bad people worse: An essay on prison reform from an insider's perspective.* New York: Lantern Books.

The Sentencing Project (2014). *Disproportionate minority contact in the juvenile justice system.* Washington, D.C.: The Sentencing Project.

The Sentencing Project (2015). *Trends in U.S. corrections.* Washington, D.C.: The Sentencing Project.

United States. (2011). Wall Street and the financial crisis: Anatomy of a financial collapse. Washington, D.C.: Permanent Subcommittee on Investigations, United States Senate.

*Wisconsin v. Mitchell*, 508 U.S. 476 (1993).

## Selected Readings

Olusanya, O., & Gau, J. (2012). Race, neighborhood context, and risk prediction. *Criminal Justice Studies, 25*(2), 159–175.

Richie, B. E. (2007). Women and drug use. *Women & Criminal Justice, 17*(2-3), 137–143.

## Discussion Questions/Writing Assignments

1. There are many injustices in criminal justice that we weren't able to cover in this chapter. What other types of injustice in CJ have you become aware of through your CJC education? Which relationship between the CJS and injustice do they represent (e.g., crime as injustice, injustice within the CJS, or injustice within the larger societal context)?
2. For each type of injustice in the chapter, and those from the previous question, note the types of justice that this social problem relates to. Articulate what makes this problem a social problem.
3. Twitter allows users to express their thoughts with a maximum of 140 characters. Create a tweet that expresses your concern over a particular injustice related to criminal justice.
4. Check out the Federal Bureau of Investigation's latest hate crime statistics here: https://www.fbi.gov/news/stories/2015/november/latest-hate-crime-statistics-available. Choose one finding presented on that page (either in the figure or the text) and explain it in terms of injustice.
5. At the outset of this chapter, we proposed an assessment of whether our CJS makes good on its fairness guarantees in terms of the rights afforded to people as they are arrested, interrogated, detained, tried, punished, and released back into society. After reading the chapter, do you think it does make good on these promises?
6. How well does the CJS handle issues of social justice? Give one specific example and explain how this social justice issue is dealt with by the CJS.
7. Look at the CNN Money infographic depicting state expenditures on corrections and education found here: http://money.cnn.com/infographic/economy/

education-vs-prison-costs/. How does your state compare with others? As a student, explain the justice implications this has had for you.
8. The subtitle of Richie's article included in this chapter is "The Case for a Justice Analysis." What does the author mean by "justice analysis"? Is this compatible with the broad justice analysis we propose in this book?
9. How do Olusanya and Gau blend individual-level and macro-level factors in their analysis of race, neighborhood context, and risk prediction?

# ACTIVITIES/ASSIGNMENTS

## Injustice in Criminal Justice

Choose one of the news articles below, identify the justice issue and the type of injustice it creates, and discuss the implications for both the CJS and social justice.

http://www.usatoday.com/news/nation/story/2012-03-01/buying-prisons-require-high-occupancy/53402894/1#.T10oTHFZv_c.email
http://www.usatoday.com/story/opinion/2015/10/05/domestic-violence-911-eviction-women-police-ordinance-column/73082434/
http://www.npr.org/2014/05/19/312158516/increasing-court-fees-punish-the-poor?important
http://www.nytimes.com/2014/09/08/opinion/charles-blow-crime-bias-and-statistics.html?_r=1
http://www.washingtonpost.com/world/national-security/fbi-director-acknowledges-hard-truths-about-racial-bias-in-policing/2015/02/12/023c6c6e-b2c6-11e4-854b-a38d13486ba1_story.html
http://www.philly.com/philly/news/politics/20150715_NAACP_to_hear_Obama_urge_criminal_justice_reforms.html
http://news.stlpublicradio.org/post/i-cry-during-sentimental-movies-prisoners-use-personal-stories-reflect-mass-incarceration
http://onpoint.wbur.org/2015/06/11/prison-reform-sentencing-reform-new-york-jail-break

## "Book Club" Activity: Interviews with Legal Scholars about Their Books

Interview with Michelle Alexander, author of *The new Jim Crow: Mass incarceration in the age of colorblindness*: http://www.npr.org/2012/01/16/145175694/legal-scholar-jim-crow-still-exists-in-america

What does Alexander add to the discussion of injustice in our CJS?
Interview with Adam Benforado, author of *Unfair: The new science of criminal justice*: http://www.npr.org/2015/07/06/418585084/the-new-science-behind-our-unfair-criminal-justice-system

What does Benforado add to the discussion of injustice in our CJS?
Interview with Bryan Stevenson, author of *Just mercy: A story of justice and redemption*: http://www.npr.org/2014/10/20/356964925/one-lawyers-fight-for-young-blacks-and-just-mercy

What does Stevenson add to the discussion of injustice in our CJS?
Based on these interviews, which book would you be most interested in reading? Why?

## *Pen Pal in Prison* (optional idea for interested students)

http://www.writeaprisoner.com/

## Reality versus Imagination

Pick several of the justice issues discussed in this chapter. Divide into small groups based on whether you'd rather be in the "reality" group or the "imagination" group. The reality group should develop a list of solutions that would be relatively easy and possible to implement. The imagination group is freed from the constraints of practicality and should develop the most creative solutions possible. Discuss your solutions; how well does each achieve justice? Was there value in approaching the problem in these two ways?

## SEMESTER-LONG JUSTICE PROJECT

Step Five: It is time to make a plan for creating justice. Once you've figured out your plan, write a two-page description of the concrete steps that you will be taking to achieve justice. Because we know it's difficult to find your initial footing, here are a few ideas to get you started—but try to think as creatively as possible, and don't feel constrained by these examples! You can volunteer with local agencies to find out what their needs are. Students in the past have done a variety of things for agencies, including working fund raising events, collecting donations, assisting with grant writing, conducting research, and providing translation work. You could create videos, blogs, start letter-writing campaigns, and/or write your elected representatives. You could create and distribute materials to raise awareness on your issue and/or speak to local community or campus groups. Other unique forms of activism include trips to the state capital to get involved in advocacy work, hosting a film screening on campus, attending community events for murder victims, and serving on student campus committees related to your topic.

Selected Reading

# WOMEN AND DRUG USE

## The Case for a Justice Analysis

*Beth E. Richie*

## INTRODUCTION

There is extensive data that links women's use of drugs and their subsequent involvement in illegal activity resulting in their growing presence in the population who are incarcerated or otherwise under the surveillance and control of the criminal legal system in this country. Scholars, policy makers, intervention specialists, criminal justice professionals, advocates and community members alike understand that this is one of the most serious problems facing society today, as evidenced by morbidity and mortality rates, incarceration statistics, data from child protective services and other bureaucratic institutions and court records. Moreover, anecdotal evidence from neighborhood level analyses attests to the pressing nature of the problem of women and substance abuse.

A review of the literature reveals several epistemological trends in the data that describe the problem. One body of research looks at individual level psychological analyses of causation. Other studies attempt to recognize the link between substance abuse and other social problems such as poverty and violence. There are important accounts of the ways that certain groups of women are disproportionately affected by the problem and significant evaluation research of program effectiveness and model intervention strategies.

Much of this is very good research that stands up to the most ambitious standards of scientific rigor; the research questions are good ones, the methodological approaches are sound, the samples are appropriate, and the analytic strategies are well thought out. In the aggregate, the conclusions from this body of work illuminate many of the factors that are important to the understanding about women and their drug abuse in contemporary society. These conclusions could be summarized in the following way.

Women use drugs for a number of reasons. While some of the causal factors have been established as similar to the reasons that men use drugs, there are particular risk factors that predispose women to substance abuse, including relational subordination and exposure to intimate partner violence. Another area of gender difference is the effect and consequences of drug abuse. Pharmacological research has established that certain drugs have a unique physiological effect on women and social analyses reveal that society's response to the problem of sub-stance abuse is, in many ways, more severe. In addition, it has been shown that the process of recovery for women is different and that programs need to take what is called a "gender-specific approach" to treatment. Finally, almost all studies have indicated that women of color from low-income communities are disproportionately represented in the population of women affected by illegal drug use in the United States.

This summative picture of the research findings could be stated another way. Consider the following assessment: Gender violence, with its root causes in male domination, predisposes women to substance abuse, as does economic marginalization and persistent poverty. These and other issues that affect women's sense of self worth–such as degrading interactions with social institutions, social stigma and punitive public policy–further increase their risk of substance abuse and the concomitant consequences. Institutional neglect is also indicated as a major risk factor, and given racial and class hierarchy, it follows that women of color from low-income communities are most likely to experience the negative consequences of substance abuse; their treatment needs are not addressed and they are sanctioned by the criminal legal system most harshly.

The two versions of the summary and the differential language used to describe the research findings represent more than semantic differences. On the one hand, the focus on individual pathology and the "empiricist" assessments can lead scholars, policy makers and intervention specialists to direct attention (and blame) and resources (including law enforcement apparatus) to individuals in a way that is harmful rather than helpful. In the second version of the problem, the larger concerns become paramount, bringing into focus issues such as poverty, racism, inequality, and gender oppression, which are typically outside the domain of study.

The second narrative also enables a justice perspective by reframing the research questions. It allows for the creation of a set of recommendations about how research on women and drugs could serve a broad social justice agenda goal as well as the goal of advancing the specific knowledge about women and crime. The reframing is built on the following four assertions. First, it is important to include the concept of justice as a theoretical area of inquiry when looking at the issue of women and substance abuse. Second, it is important to include questions about experiences of injustice among the variables considered when the causes and the consequences of substance abuse are measured in studies of women and substance abuse, particularly with regard to questions of desistance. Third, as research findings are translated into questions of intervention, it is essential that work addressing injustices appears in the array of services provided. Finally, researchers must ask how public policy can be refocused to include more than punishment so that it is reoriented towards the redistribution of power and resources to meet the goals of justice and equality.

Prior to elaboration on these issues, it is important to explain that in this paper, I am using the term "justice" to signify the range of conditions that would expand opportunity for those who have been constrained by their social position or lack of access to institutional privileges. The concept as I use it includes creating a set of circumstances where disadvantaged groups or individuals who experience injustice are compensated for their plight. Analytically, it means that our understanding of social problems includes the ways that disenfranchisement contributes to individual pathology and social deviance and the role of institutions and the state in creating opportunities for redress. Justice, in this sense, works to both validate the sense that macro variables play a role in the creation of individual pathology and treatment of injustice is corrective at the level of broader social forces. An analysis that points to the need for advancing justice as part of the solution to a social problem like drug abuse by women focuses attention on the role that the state and its institutions play in the creation of conditions that lead to individual dysfunction. Intervention is aimed at restoring rights, creating opportunity and strengthening the social position of those who suffer the most in contemporary society; as in the case of women who use drugs.

## JUSTICE AS A RESEARCH QUESTION

When we think of justice in this way, a new set of research questions emerges as significant. In addition to the very important work of exploring the link between women's substance abuse and conditions in their family of origin, the role of their peers in risk-taking behavior, women's individual reactions to stress or other individual factors that predispose them to the risk of substance abuse, asking questions about the role of injustice opens a broader area for researchers to explore. Such questions might include attention to the role that economic marginalization played in women's involvement in the illegal drug trade, the role that gender oppression played in women's use of drugs with their partners and the role that institutional policy played in their inability to comply with treatment protocols. Exploring these and related areas would allow researchers to expose the role that macro level forces play in women's substance abuse–not as a way to diminish or compete with the importance of individual characteristics–but as a way to look for additional causal factors.

## JUSTICE AS AN ANALYTIC VARIABLE

When justice is included in the research questions and hypotheses, it can then be treated as an analytic category. Here I am not only suggesting that an operationalized notion of justice be included on data collection instruments (survey instruments, questionnaires or interview schedules), but that researchers define and quantify the concept in such a way that participants' responses and/or field observations can be interpreted by researchers as issues of justice *even if* they are not defined in precisely those terms by the women substance abusers who make up the sample being studied. In the same way that depression is measured, for example, injustice could be operationalized in concrete terms that were generalizable and tested for validity. It must be recognized that there is some important literature that attempts to quantify related terms, such as "empowerment" or "self efficacy;" however, in the research on substance abuse, an analytic category that includes elements of justice is underdeveloped. To remedy this would be an ambitious scientific project, however I assert that without standardization, discussion of the role that injustice plays in women's substance abuse will remain at the level of rhetoric rather than "social science."

## JUSTICE AS A DESISTANCE FACTOR

The extent to which reallocating resources, changing institutional policies, restoring individual rights or other efforts towards decreasing social inequality will lead to reduction or desistance of substance abuse in women remains an empirical question. Moreover, the relationship between social arrangements that disadvantage certain groups of women and their concentration in the populations of substance abusers has not received much research attention except as a descriptive reality. I argue that this level of discussion is not only inadequate, it is dangerous. That is, to say that "most of the women in this study were women of color and/or poor" (as most reports of research findings on women and substance abuse do) leaves some readers feeling like that is neither an analytic problem nor a political one. It is stated as a fact rather than as a critical research question. Researchers interested in justice will want to understand (1) *why* that is the case and (2) what role the *social conditions that create injustice* had in the creation of the problem and society's response to it. Here a theoretical discussion the likes of which have been advanced by feminists of color and critical race theorists is warranted.

## JUSTICE AS AN INTERVENTION PROGRAM

In addition to challenging taken-for-granted over representation of women of color among illicit substance users and those more often sanctioned by the criminal justice system, and prompting new areas of inquiry, introducing justice as a research question allows for a new set of possibilities around intervention research. What would an intervention program that included social justice in its program goals look like? Who or what would be the "target" of the intervention? What activities would be included in the therapeutic menus offered to those who are suffering? What would the role of punishment or other state sanctions be in responding to the problem? How would program success be measured? These types of questions are being asked by a growing cohort of scholars/practitioners who are interested in advancing a different kind of feminist intervention on problems that marginalized groups of women face. These include programs that build community organizing skills, which engage so-called "clients" in action research that is aimed towards social transformation as opposed to only providing social services. The field of women's substance abuse treatment research could benefit from and build on this work were it to embrace the notion of justice research. Multi-method studies and analytical strategies that privilege those who are most affected as the people who validate knowledge are indicated. In addition, studies that look at resistance as well as protective factors would also serve the goal of advancing understanding of the relationship between women, drug abuse and justice.

## JUSTICE AS PUBLIC POLICY

The criminal legal system has, in a sense, hijacked the notion of justice to such an extent that feminist researchers and other scholars interested in exploring questions of substance abuse and women have avoided mentioning (let alone engaging in serious scientific debates about) the concept. I am arguing here that it is time to re-position the notion of justice as a key aspect of women's health and healing from drug abuse and other manifestations of social injustice. I am suggesting that we seriously consider questions of injustice as causal factors and that we develop scientific instruments and theoretical paradigms that help to explain what justice is and how injustice works as a causal mechanism. Such an endeavor would enable scientific research that results in findings that could not only be integrated into treatment programs, but would point to other avenues of desistance work. Lastly, public policy could emerge that is more effective and humane and that has longer-term results than the current agenda of sanctions and disenfranchisement, which the current research invokes.

We know a lot about the micro, individual causes and consequences of substance abuse among women. What we have yet to understand, is the link between these micro level issues and women's experience in the broader social sphere related to their disadvantaged social position, their limited access to resources and the ways that institutions fail them. Public policy that is aimed at changing that situation (as opposed to changing or sanctioning women themselves) is likely to be more effective in resolving the problem of substance abuse. At the very least, I am arguing that equal attention needs to be given to this assertion in our research agenda.

## Selected Reading

# RACE, NEIGHBORHOOD CONTEXT, AND RISK PREDICTION

***Olaoluwa Olusanya and Jacinta M. Gau***

## INTRODUCTION

Human obsession with predicting the future dates back to ancient Babylon (3200 BC) (Guehlstorf, 2004, p. 45). During that period haruspices examined animal entrails to divine future events (Collins, 2008, p. 320). In addition, be they reading tea leaves, tarot cards, palms, or a more sophisticated system such as the use of statistical prediction to estimate risk empirically, all divination systems are themselves diagnostic of the society that employs them. The anthropologist Victor Turner often expressed the opinion that after studying a people's social structure, he could predict the key themes of their divination system (Gordon, 2004).

Perceptions of future dangerousness and predictions of potential risk are staples of the modern Anglo-American criminal justice system (Garland, 2001; Lianos & Douglas, 2000). A combination of pre-emptive targeting and actuarialism is embedded in a risk discourse permeating contemporary society. Both processes typically operate in tandem to exclude risky population subgroups (Rose, 2002); i.e. 'groups with a statistical likelihood of criminality and/or disruptive incivilities' (Fitzgibbon, 2007, pp. 131–132) – which often become operationally defined as members of poor and/or minority communities (Quillian & Pager, 2001, note 5).

In this paper, we argue that the risk prediction tools that have been developed and introduced in the criminal justice system reflect social structures which are racially differentiated. Hacker (1992) for example observed that:

> America is inherently a 'White' country: in character, in structure, in culture. Needless to say, [B]lack Americans create lives of their own. Yet as a people, they face boundaries and constrictions set by the White majority. America's version of *apartheid*, while lacking overt legal sanction, comes closest to the system even now ... reformed in the land of its invention. (p. 4)

Due in part to economic shifts that disproportionately disadvantage black citizens (Wilson, 1987) and in part to racist laws and policies (Massey & Denton, 1993), US society has emerged as profoundly stratified along racial and socioeconomic lines. Blacks are substantially overrepresented among the poor and destitute and have thus borne a large share of the burden of public attitudes and social policies that blame impoverished persons for their own misfortunes and use low socioeconomic status as a sign of bad character (Hurwitz & Peffley, 1997; Peffley, Hurwitz, & Sniderman, 1997). As stated by Gilens (1999, p. 173), 'the stereotype of [B]lacks as lazy has a long history in American culture and is implicated in both media portrayals and public attitudes toward poverty and government anti-poverty policy'.

Given that risk prediction tools are a product of the society that created them and thus reflect the assumptions, biases, and stereotypes of the collective, criminal justice agents who make predictions of dangerousness bear a responsibility to prove that their predictions are free of such biases. No such attempts have been made on a national scale – indeed, the courts repeatedly turn a wilfully blind eye toward even clear evidence of racial discrimination (e.g. *McCleskey v. Kemp*, 1987; see Zeisel (1981) for a summary) – and the absence of racial bias within these predictions is therefore an untested, unproven assumption that seems at odds with social reality.

There is, in fact, evidence to suggest that bias and prejudice do pervade criminal justice actors' decision-making. According to Robinson (2010, p. 94), 'the poor and people of colour are disproportionately likely to be exposed to arrest, probation, jail, prison, and executions' (see also Barak, Leighton, & Flavin, 2006). For instance, arrest and police contact data show that blacks are treated more harshly than whites in the criminal justice system (Sampson & Lauritsen, 1997; Sorensen & Wallace, 1999). In general, blacks are much more likely to be imprisoned, and they serve longer prison terms than other racial groups (Bridges & Crutchfield, 1998; Rocque, 2011). Mauer and King (2007, p. 1) maintain that '[i]f current trends continue, one in three Black males born today can expect to spend time in prison during his life-time'.

In this paper, we propose a sociocognitive model that combines cognitive mechanisms of implicit racial bias (e.g. attitudes) and structural level (e.g. concentrated disadvantage) factors. In this regard, it should be pointed out that the role of neighborhood influence and context is largely absent from the literature on risk and prediction (Parker, MacDonald, Alpert, Smith, & Piquero, 2004, p. 944; Webster, MacDonald, & Simpson, 2006, p. 12). We contend that this is a serious oversight that warrants redress.

In our view, differential treatment of black and white suspects, defendants, and offenders may result from the social and spatial mismatch, or separation, between both groups (see Black, 1976). This mismatch, in turn, has implications for attitudes towards members of both racial groups in the criminal justice system. Black neighborhoods are locked in a cycle of disadvantage in which certain structural characteristics – concentrated disadvantage, residential instability, high crime rates, racial/ethnic heterogeneity, and implicit racial biases – reciprocally influence each other (Massey, 1995). It is well known that police use neighborhood crime rates and socioeconomic status as a proxy for the character, intentions, and criminal activity of individuals whom they encounter within those areas (Klinger, 1997; see also a line of US Supreme Court cases such as *Illinois v. Wardlow*, 1999). Racial stereotyping, in turn, assigns to blacks a distinct or homogeneous character, allowing criminal justice actors to make assumptions about individuals on the basis of their race, socioeconomic status, and neighborhood of residence. It is our contention here that more attention should be paid to the subtle, insidious ways in which the racial stereotypes and prejudices that are a prominent feature of US society may infiltrate the so-called 'neutral' decision-making of criminal justice system actors. The sociocognitive approach to risk prediction stresses the impact that personal beliefs and attitudes have on these actors' decisions about whom to arrest, prosecute, and imprison and thereby provides a framework for explaining why racial discrimination persists within an atmosphere that prides itself on being neutral and yet is often anything but.

## A SOCIOCOGNITIVE EXPLANATION OF RACIAL DIFFERENCES IN PREDICTION OUTCOMES

From a sociocognitive perspective, the labeling of Black communities as 'underclass', 'dangerous', or 'criminal' (Rose, 2002, p. 182) feeds back into the very problems of marginalization, isolation, and unemployment which lie at the heart of much of the criminality within these communities (Butler, 1999; Kubrin & Weitzer, 2003). That is, structural factors, such as residential and social segregation of blacks, are refracted socially in ways that reinforce negative images of persons who are members of these groups, which in turn fuels repressive law enforcement practices directed at these individuals (e.g. Fagan & Davies, 2000). These processes serve to further entrench the unemployability, alienation, and social outsider status of black Americans.

The following sections further explicate the social (i.e. concentrated disadvantage and the nexus between minority race and low economic status) and cognitive (i.e. racial biases) aspects of the sociocognitive perspective. It will be shown that due to the nature of the criminal justice system as a mechanism for controlling the 'worst of the worst', cognitive biases are reinforced on a daily basis and are rarely, if ever, challenged. The practice of using neighborhood crime rates and socioeconomic statuses to draw inferences about the deviance of individuals within those areas – and the fact that the widely invoked 'high crime neighbourhood' is itself a product of informal labeling rather than of data-driven analyses and conclusions – provides a backdrop against which implicit biases can unfold.

### Concentrated Disadvantage

Over the years, inner-city urban neighborhoods have become economically and racially/ethnically homogeneous as middle-class whites and blacks alike have systematically abandoned them in favor of suburbs. To capture such homogeneity, researchers have considered concentrated disadvantage as a structural, class-based measure that reflects the poverty embedded in racially segregated neighborhoods (Sampson & Raudenbush, 1999; Sampson, Raudenbush, & Earls, 1997; Wilson, 1987). The benefit of concentrated disadvantage is that it captures key risk factors leading to classification of a neighborhood as underclass (Land, McCall, & Cohen, 1990; Wilson, 1987) and which may be more appropriately associated with criminal threat than simple racial or ethnic composition would be. In this regard, the multiple race-specific measures of structural disadvantage that can be used to reflect the racial differences in urban disadvantage include poverty, income inequality, joblessness, female-headed homes with children, receipt of government benefits, and racial residential segregation. Sampson and Laub (1993, p. 293) have argued that 'counties characterized by ... a large concentration of the "underclass" (that is, minorities, poverty, female-headed families, welfare) are more likely than other counties to be perceived as containing offensive and threatening populations'. Werthman and Piliavin (1967) referred to the process as 'ecological contamination', whereby everyone encountered in neighborhoods designated as 'bad' assume moral liability. In a recent analysis, Sampson and Loeffler (2010) reiterated the previous opinion that 'concentrated inequality exacerbates existing patterns of criminal justice punishment' and in particular that:

> The attributions and perceptions of dangerousness attached to stigmatized and spatially concentrated minority groups ... increase the intensity of both unofficial beliefs about social disorder and official decisions to punish through incarceration ... offenders from communities of concentrated disadvantage are themselves stigmatized and are more likely to be incarcerated when compared to those in less disadvantaged communities with similar crime rates. (p. 4)

Ecological contamination is also evident in the tendency for police officers working urban, disadvantaged beats to begin seeing victims within these areas as having either actively precipitated their own victimization or as having passively brought it upon themselves by their failure to move to a better place (Klinger, 1997). People living in these areas may experience both overzealous and lackluster exercises of formal controls, as these individuals face heightened scrutiny in relation to suspected offenses, while crime victims who turn to the criminal justice system for help routinely feel ignored (Brunson, 2007; Brunson & Miller, 2006; Sampson and Bartusch, 1998). The belief that the law has failed can spur retaliatory violence (Kubrin & Weitzer, 2003), thus perpetuating not only violent crime but also the image of the neighborhood as being out of control and full of lawless, amoral people. Since the job of the police is to deal with the people whose actions are in question, they are repeatedly faced with examples of misbehaving black individuals and are not as often exposed to the members of this racial group who do abide by the law and act in accordance with prevailing norms of conduct. Implicit biases are thus consistently strengthened by reaffirmation and are never weakened by the challenge of counterexamples.

This problem is exacerbated by the US Supreme Court's express permission of the use of so-called 'high-crime areas' and 'areas known for drug trafficking' in police officers' establishment of reasonable suspicion to make *Terry*-type pedestrian and vehicle stops. Courts generally defer to officers' claims about the quantity of crime and drug activity in certain areas and do not require statistical data to corroborate these claims (Ferguson & Bernache, 2008). This has opened the door for profiling not just of people but of places (Harris, 1994).

## Implicit Racial Bias

Implicit racial prejudice includes sociocognitive mechanisms that underlie different aspects of race bias. Empirical research in implicit social cognition demonstrates that people automatically and unintentionally make distinctions between certain groups of people (e.g. black and white people; e.g. Bower & Karlin, 1974; McArthur & Baron, 1983) and particular attributes (e.g. 'good' and 'bad'; Dovidio, Kawakami, Johnson, Johnson, & Howard, 1997; Fazio, Jackson, Dunton, & Williams, 1995; Nosek, Banaji, & Greenwald, 2002). According to Quillian and Pager (2001, p. 722) 'the stereotype of Blacks as criminals is widely known and is deeply embedded in the collective consciousness of Americans, irrespective of the level of prejudice or personal beliefs' (Drummond, 1990; Russell, 2002).

In addition, the activation of automatic stereotypes within a semantic network serves as a possible psychological mechanism underlying this phenomenon. For instance, social learning theory and sociocognitive models (e.g. Anderson et al., 2003; Bandura, 1973; Huesmann, 1998) posit that from exposure to media coverage of crime stories on news broadcasts that are more likely to depict blacks as perpetrators than as victims (Dixon & Linz, 2000; Oliver, 1994), people develop mental primes and scripts which can then guide their later behavior in ambiguous situations (Sagar & Schofield, 1980).

Furthermore, objective demographic data constitute a primary source of stereotype (Blumstein, 1982; Harer & Steffensmeier, 1993; Peffly & Hurwitz, 2002; Percival, 2009; Tonry, 1995; Wilson, 1987). Quillian and Pager (2001, note 5) observe that 'studies find that Black neighborhoods do on average have higher rates of crime than White neighbourhoods' and that 'the bivariate correlation between neighbourhood racial makeup and crime rates is no doubt one reason that stereotypes associating race and crime remain widespread'.

Nevertheless, it should be pointed out that in terms of volume 'most crime is actually committed by Whites' (Gilens, 1996; Welch, 2007).

Moreover, with very little public discourse taking place that would emphasize that crime is actually not the disease itself but, rather, is a symptom of deeper structural problems (Sampson, 2011), black criminality becomes among the general public – just as among police officers – a stereotype that receives reaffirmation and minimal challenge – '[T]he image of violent criminals as young [B]lack males is routinely reinforced' (Young, 1985, p. 475). Amodio and Mendoza (2010) have identified a number of currently held stereotypes about blacks. These include, but are not limited to the following (see also Figure 5.1):

- Blacks are dishonest.
- Blacks are violent and prone to petty crime
- Blacks are lazy and will not work or keep a steady job.
- Blacks are unintelligent.
- Blacks are poor.

Moreover, an experimental study by Correll et al. (2007) vividly illustrates the power of implicit racial bias. They examined how racial bias plays into an officer's decision to shoot a suspect. They found that participants made the correct decision to shoot an armed target faster if the target was black than if he was white, but decided not to shoot an unarmed target more quickly if he was white, than if he was black (see also Eberhardt, Goff, Purdie, & Davies, 2004;

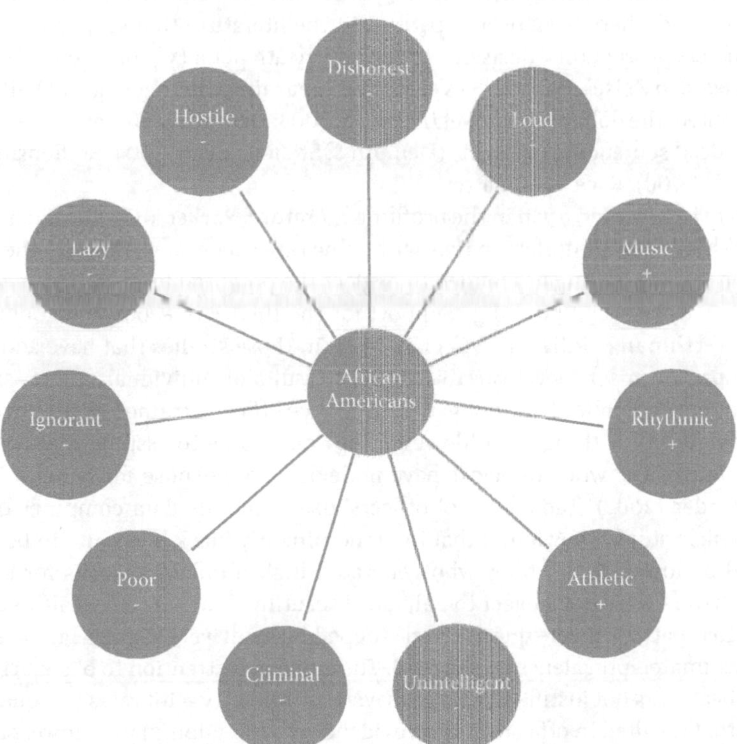


**Figure 5.1** Associational network of attributes related to the concept of 'African Americans'

Source: Amodio and Mendoza (2010).

Glaser & Knowles, 2008). Finally, implicit racism has been implicated in biased decision-making by criminal justice actors. The liberation hypothesis predicts that racial disparities in decisions such as arrest, prosecution, and sentencing will be greatest when the evidence against a suspect/defendant is ambiguous and decision-makers resort to their own personal beliefs and attitudes (including prejudices) to reach a conclusion about the best course of action (Kalven & Zeisel, 1966).

## THE SOCIOCOGNITIVE MODEL IN ACTION: WHEN 'BLACK' MEANS 'RISKY'

### Racial Profiling

Racial profiling in the USA has been described as a 'crude risk assessment tool' (Willis & Mastrofski, 2011, p. 12). Race, being highly visible, serves as an indicator of less visible characteristics such as a person's values, ethics, and proclivities. While individual studies differ with respect to the type and magnitude of the race effects found, there is an overall pattern in the literature that suspect/defendant race affects prosecutors' decisions to seek the death penalty (Sorensen & Wallace, 1999; see also Zeisel, 1981), judges' decisions regarding whether to grant bail and, if it is granted, the dollar amount set (Demuth, 2003; Demuth & Steffensmeier, 2004), and judicial sentencing decisions (Demuth & Steffensmeier, 2004; Steffensmeier & Demuth, 2000). Race does matter.

There is, however, a gap in the profiling literature. Parker and colleagues (2004, p. 944) have noted, '[u]nfortunately with a few rare exceptions, much of the literature on racial profiling has tended to neglect the potential importance of context in the study of racial profiling'. Support for the theory of ecological contamination (Werthman & Piliavin, 1967) is evident in those studies that have addressed the impact of macro-level variables on the results of individual officer–suspect encounters and police behavior generally. Police officers, trained as they are to be hyper-vigilant for things that 'don't add up', may come to assume that there are particular places wherein blacks have no legitimate purpose for being. Meehan and Ponder (2002) studied patrol officers' use of mobile data computer queries and vehicle stops. They found that in predominantly black beats and in beats occupied by lower-class whites who generated high numbers of calls for service, black drivers were not subject to enhanced scrutiny. It was in the wealthier white beats that patrol officers queried and stopped black drivers at rates far exceeding their estimated prevalence on the road. The enhanced attention to black drivers in these beats was not justified by these drivers' criminality – hit rates (i.e. queries or stops that resulted in officers finding evidence of wrongdoing) were lowest among this group.

Fagan and Davies (2000) found similar results with respect to *Terry*-type pedestrian stops and frisks in New York City: Stops of suspects of all races were driven in part by neighborhood-level poverty and social disorganization, an effect that was particularly pronounced for black and Latino suspects. Stewart, Baumer,

Brunson and Simons (2009), moreover, found that black youths' perceptions of biased treatment were greatest when those youths were in predominantly white neighborhoods at the time of the encounter. Finally, Terrill and Reisig (2003) discovered that the statistical significance of minority status on police officers' use of higher levels of force disappeared once neighborhood-level concentrated disadvantage and crime rate was controlled for. The neglect of macro-level contextual factors has been to the detriment of the body of knowledge regarding the racialization of formal social control.

## Courts

Concentrated disadvantage has been used in relation to the sentencing of adults and juveniles. For instance, Sampson and Laub (1993) employed it in analyses of juvenile court processing in 200 US counties guided by a group conflict perspective and found that among a variety of structural factors, concentrated disadvantage (underclass, as they termed it) significantly increased the likelihood of pre-trial confinement in secure facilities. In relation to disposition, they found a disproportionate use of out-of-home placement – the most serious form of control exercised by the juvenile court – especially for black youth adjudicated for property or drug crimes (1993, pp. 302–306). Sampson and Laub (1993) described this pattern of results as 'consistent with the idea that underclass Black males are viewed as a threatening group' and on that account subject to increased formal social control (1993, p. 306). Freiburger (2009) found that being unemployed did not impact white defendants' likelihood of being incarcerated, but increased black defendants' odds of incarceration. D'Alessio and Stolzenberg (2002) introduced controls for city-level unemployment rates and concluded that there was an interaction between city-level unemployment, defendants' race, and defendants' unemployment such that unemployed black defendants were more likely to be incarcerated pending trial when city-level unemployment was high, but not when city-level unemployment was more moderate.

In addition, Chiricos, Barrick, Bales, and Bontrager (2007) have studied the effect of adult felony conviction, and community-level characteristics, such as rates of crime and concentrated disadvantage, on the relationship between the felony conviction and recidivism. They found that as county levels of both concentrated disadvantage and percentage black increase, the odds of black defendants having adjudication withheld is found only for violent crimes. They also found that the cross-level effect of concentrated disadvantage on the race/adjudication withheld relationship is found for both violent and drug crimes but for percentage black is limited to violent crimes.

Furthermore, some researchers have sought to establish a relationship between racial stereotypes and disparity in judicial sentencing, claiming that both blacks and Latinos are more likely to receive harsher sentences than whites (Curry & Corral, 2008). The 'focal concerns' model has been put forward as an explanation for sentencing disparities for offenders according to racial, ethnic, and sociodemographic differences (Steffensmeier & Demuth, 2000; Steffensmeier, Ulmer, & Kramer, 1998). The focal concerns model holds that judges use three general considerations when making decisions about individual defendants: the defendant's culpability/ blameworthiness for the (alleged) crime; the defendant's dangerousness and the need to protect the community; and practical constraints, such as the defendant's perceived ability to handle being incarcerated (Freiburger, 2009).

All three aspects of the focal concerns model are vulnerable to the impact of implicit biases or prejudices possessed by judges. Assumptions about what 'real' offenders look like can lead to a tendency to assign greater guilt and malice to black defendants relative to white ones, and even within black defendants as a group, to see those with more stereotypically black features (e.g. darker skin) as especially dangerous (Eberhardt Davies, Purdie-Vaughns, & Johnson, 2006). With respect to practical constraints, judges may perceive black offenders as tougher than white ones, and better able to navigate the treacherous prison environment and protect themselves from harm (Steffensmeier, Ulmer, & Kramer, 1998).

Finally, as the above discussion attests, racial and ethnic disparities and/or discrimination in judicial sentencing may reflect the tendency for judges to place reliance on extralegal variables such as race, class, and gender as indicators of character, moral culpability, blameworthiness, or future dangerousness (Freiburger, Marcum, & Pierce, 2010; Steffensmeier & Demuth, 2000, 2001; see also Kalven & Zeisel, 1966), especially when confronted with a dearth of adequate information and data about cases or defendants.

## Corrections

Contemporary correctional practice requires an assessment of the likelihood of re-offending on at least two levels. First, risk assessments are necessary to decide which offenders should be targeted for rehabilitation (Allan, & Dawson, 2004; Andrews et al., 1990), as treatment programs have greater pay-off when they focus on offenders who have a high probability of recidivating. Second, risk assessment is necessary to deal with the increasing demand by the public and politicians that dangerous felons are not released from prison prematurely (Bonta, 1996). According to Benda, Corwyn, and Toombs (2001, p. 589) 'from the inception of correctional intervention, risk assessment has played a pivotal role in deciding the degree of sanction and/or treatment' (see also Campbell, French, & Gendreau, 2009).

In this section, we illustrate our argument by drawing on three generations of risk assessment that have evolved in corrections. First-generation assessment is non-actuarial. It involves the assessment of risk based solely on professional judgment or wisdom. The role of the practitioner here is to identify and prescribe preventative measures. The exercise of discretion by professionals has implications for black offenders. In addition, it is possible that focal concerns theory exerts influence over decisions regarding the release of offenders by correctional officials. In this respect, Benda and colleagues (2001, p. 589) point out that:

> although these assessments can be useful in allowing for individual differences and extenuating circumstances, they are fraught with potential idiosyncratic preferences and biases in the assembling and interpretation of information. Moreover, evidence is clear that the accuracy of these professional judgments is legally, ethically, and pragmatically unacceptable.
>
> (Alexander, 1986; Andrews & Bonta, 2006; Bonta & Motiuk, 1990)

Furthermore, second-generation assessment tools such as the Violence Risk Appraisal Guide developed by Quinsey et al. (1998) have been plagued by conceptual problems which have implications for black offenders. For example, Monahan and Steadman (1994) criticized second-generation assessment tools for employing a 'very narrow range of ... predictor variables ... chosen without conscious regard for any theory of violent behaviour' (p. 7). The main implications of the above statement for black ex-offenders is that by focusing on static variables that emphasize personality, demographic characteristics, and criminal history rather than situational factors, second-generation risk assessments lend the impression that certain people cannot and will not change, and are therefore not a good investment with respect to the expenditure of correctional resources. It is well established in the research literature on mainstream criminality that criminal history is the best predictor of re-offending (Andrews & Bonta, 2006); however, as pointed out by Webster, MacDonald, and Simpson (2006), the literature on risk and prediction has largely ignored 'the role of neighbourhood influence and context in the emergence of risk factors associated with criminal careers' (Sampson et al., 1997, p. 12). We maintain that static risk factors allow society to ignore the fact that black ex-offenders are more likely than white ex-offenders to return to communities with intense poverty, crime, and unemployment and that the former are therefore at a greater risk of returning to crime not because they suffer from immutable personal defects but because they are enmeshed in criminogenic environments. In this respect, Webster and his colleagues contend that:

> Numerous neighbourhood based studies have consistently shown that regardless of whether children and young people have accrued individual risk factors associated with chronic offending, serious offending is significantly more likely in the most disadvantaged neighbourhoods. Conversely, predictions of offending based on risk fail to materialize in the case of individuals living in more affluent neighbourhoods.
>
> (p. 12; Lizotte et al., 1994; Thornberry, 1994)

Also outside of consideration is racial discrimination in the criminal justice system as reflected in significantly higher arrest, charge, and conviction rates for blacks. To an extent as yet unquantified, these elevated rates are not attributable to more prevalent or more extreme crime commission among this group (e.g. Kochel et al., 2011), and instead reflect factors such as police deployment and surveillance patterns that result in intense scrutiny of these areas and the people in them. Second-generation risk assessment tools' reliance on static risk factors is woefully inadequate in light of what is known about the criminogenic impact of macro-level disadvantage.

Finally, unlike second-generation assessment tools, third-generation assessment tools such as the level of supervision inventory revised (LSI-R; Andrews & Bonta, 2001), historical, clinical, and risk management violence risk assessment scheme (HCR-20; Webster, Douglas, Eaves, & Hart, 1997); and Self-Appraisal Questionnaire (Loza, 2005) measure both static and dynamic risk factors (criminogenic needs). One advantage of third-generation risk assessment tools over the previous generations is their sensitivity to changes in risk over time and the fact that they can be used to measure whether an offender's risk is increasing or decreasing over time (Andrews & Bonta, 2006; Heilbrun, 1997). However, it should be pointed out that many dynamic risk or criminogenic need variables are related to race. For instance, the socioeconomic nature of some classifications such as education and employment may result in class and race bias (Smykla, 1986; Whiteacre, 2006, p. 331). In addition, the fact that many established risk assessment instruments have been developed and validated for white, male inmates has led some to question the utility of these tools for minorities (Bloom, Owen, & Covington, 2003; Smykla, 1986). Martel, Brassard, and Jaccoud (2011) have recently criticized the definitional criteria used to circumscribe risk markers that have been developed on the basis of dominant sociocultural worldviews. In their view:

> Structural markers such as poverty and social markers such as residential instability, family/marital problems, school/employment difficulties, absence of positive leisure or recreational activities as well as substance abuse that are melded actuarially with higher risks of (re)offending are ill-adapted to the historical, socio-economical and cultural specificities of Indigenous peoples. (p. 240)

The same argument can also be extended to African-Americans. In other words, since African-American communities face structural problems including high levels of poverty, unemployment, and family disruption such structural hardships expose these communities to being described as intrinsically criminogenic.

## Mixed Mechanisms

The concentrated disadvantage and implicit racial bias connection, along with the existing scholarship, brings us to a rather interesting crossroads, in that if we want to reduce racial prejudice and stereotypes and minimize their effects on judgments involving risk, then an increase in the number of blacks employed in the criminal justice system is paramount. Kim and Mengistu (1994) argue that blacks and women are still underrepresented in law enforcement (Angelique, Nolasco, & Vaughn, 2011; The President's Initiative on Race Advisory Board, 1998). Also in relation to black representation in the judiciary, Brest (1985, p. 669) maintains that:

> judges ... are far from a representative cross section of American society. They are overwhelmingly Anglo, male, well educated, and upper or upper middle class ... Women, [B]lacks, and [H]ispanics are only the groups most notoriously under-represented on the judiciary.

It follows that diversification of police, courts, and corrections serves several important functions. First, it will lead people to have more positive associations for blacks. In this respect, a number of scholars have suggested that affirming positive associations, such as counter-stereotypical contact with racial and other out-group members can lead to reduced automatic stereotypical activation (Blair, Ma & Lenton, 2001; Graham & Lowery, 2004, pp. 500–501; Sinclair, Lowery, Hardin, & Colangelo, 2005; Ward, Farrell, & Rousseau, 2009; Wittenbrink et al., 2001). Second, others have argued that diversity is indispensable for ensuring impartiality in decision-making by criminal justice agents (Ifill, 2000). In relation to judicial decision-making, Ifill (2000) advanced the following rationales:

> First, the creation of a racially diverse bench can introduce traditionally excluded perspectives and values into judicial decision-making. The interplay of diverse views and perspectives can enrich judicial decision-making ... Second, racial diversity on the bench also encourages judicial impartiality, by ensuring that a single set of values or views do not dominate judicial decision-making. (pp. 410–411)

Third, there is some empirical support for the position that police and court workforce diversity can encourage a culture of racially differential sanctioning of black defendants. For instance, Farrell, Ward, and Rousseau (2009) concluded in their recent study of racial diversity of federal courts that:

> Black defendants are more likely to be sentenced to prison than their White counterparts, even after controlling for legally relevant variables, but when Black defendants are sentenced in districts with increased representation of Black prosecutors, they have a decreased likelihood of being imprisoned, which results in more racially equitable sentences. (p. 131)

However, they found the opposite effect of black representation among probation officers and no effect of black representation among judges and defense attorneys, on disparities in being sentenced to prison (ibid., p. 131).

The results obtained by Farrell et al. (2009) illustrate that diversification is a good first step to greater equality, but is not a panacea allowing society to collectively wash its hands of the issue of racial bias and discrimination. Empirical evidence suggests that black citizens experience much of the same mistreatment at the hands of black police officers that they have encountered when dealing with white officers (Brunson and Gau, forthcoming; Weitzer, 2000) and that injustice perpetrated by black officers may be especially damaging to the recipients because of the expectations black citizens may have that black officers will treat them respectfully and with empathy (Brunson, 2007; Brunson and Miller, 2006). Similar results have been found for black judges. Analyses by Schanzenbach (2005) indicated that the proportions of judges in federal districts that were black did not affect sentencing practices in those districts; in fact, the counterintuitive result arose that larger Hispanic judge representation was possibly associated with harsher sentencing. Spohn (1990) found that black judges were slightly less likely than white judges to sentence black defendants to prison, but did not differ from white judges in the lengths of sentences handed down to those who were imprisoned. Even black judges were more likely to sentence black defendants to prison than they were to sentence white defendants, controlling for relevant legal variables.

Finally, all of this suggests that genuine change in the criminal justice system is about more than the demographics of the people who work within it. Diversification is a laudable goal for many reasons, but it should not be expected to magically transform the way in which black suspects, defendants, and offenders are treated. True change starts at the societal level.

## CONCLUSION

The sociocognitive perspective emphasizes the role that implicit racial bias and bias spurred by macro-level crime and disadvantage can play in criminal justice actors' decision-making. It is the contention of this paper that there needs to be greater recognition of the existence and society-wide impact of subtle forms of racial discrimination, as these can be more insidious and destructive than overt forms of racism, as the latter is considered by most people to be unacceptable and yet the former continues to be seen by the white majority as tolerable or even beneficial. An example of this is the difference between blacks and whites with respect to perceptions of racial profiling – while people of both races believe that police engage in this practice, whites who think profiling is widespread actually tend to think that this is a good thing, while blacks generally see it as purely discriminatory (Tyler & Wakslak, 2004). The stereotypes and prejudices that drive biased policing, prosecution, and sentencing are the same as those that drive the white public's support for these discriminatory policies and will hinder or possibly prevent progress towards genuinely race-neutral practices unless they are brought to the open, discussed, falsified, and abandoned. The first step to solving a problem is to admit that there actually is a problem; once the admission has been made, progress can proceed.

## NOTES ON CONTRIBUTORS

Olaoluwa Olusanya is currently Lecturer (Assistant Professor) in the Department of Law & Criminology at the University of Wales Aberystwyth. In general, he is interested in the intersection of social cognitive science and crime and deviance-related issues across multiple contexts: race, genocide, and military veterans. His most recent work has appeared or is forthcoming in journals such as the *New Criminal Law Review, Psychiatry, Psychology and Law, Critical Criminology, The Journal of Human Behavior in the Social Environment,* and in a chapter entitled 'The psychology of criminal behaviour and sentencing' in *Criminal Psychology.*

Jacinta M. Gau is an Assistant Professor in the Department of Criminal Justice at the University of Central Florida. Her work has appeared in journals such as *Justice Quarterly, Criminology & Public Policy, Journal of Criminal Justice,* and *Police Quarterly.*

## References


Advisory Board to the President's Initiative on Race. (1998). *One America in the 21st century: Forging a new future.* Washington, DC: The Board.

Alexander, J. (1986). Classification objectives and practices. *Crime & Delinquency, 32,* 323–338.

Allan, A., & Dawson, D. (2004). Assessment of the risk of reoffending by Indigenous male violent and sexual offenders, Trends & Issues in Crime and Criminal Justice No. 280, Australian Institute of Criminology, Canberra. Retrieved June 19, 2012, from http://www. aic.gov.au/documents/9/B/3/%7B9B3A99FC-C538-40B2-B921-2F1B77F1616F%7Dtandi280. pdf.

Amodio, D.M., & Mendoza, S.A. (2010). Implicit intergroup bias: Cognitive, affective, and motivational underpinnings. In B. Gawronski & B.K. Payne (Eds.), *Handbook of implicit social cognition: Measurement, theory, and applications* (pp. 353–375). New York, NY: Guilford Press.

Anderson, C.A., Berkowitz, L., Donnerstein, E., Huesmann, L.R., Johnson, J.D., Linz, D., … Wartella, E. (2003). The influence of media violence on youth. *Psychological Science in the Public Interest, 4,* 81–110.

Andrews, D.A., & Bonta, J. (2006). *The psychology of criminal conduct* (4th ed.). Cincinnati, OH: Anderson.

Andrews, D.A., Zinger, I., Hoge, R.D., Bonta, J., Gendreau, P., & Cullen, F.T. (1990). Does correctional treatment work? A clinically relevant and psychologically informed meta-analysis. *Criminology, 28*(3), 369–404.

Angelique, C., Nolasco, R., & Vaughn, M.S. (2011). Judicial scrutiny of gender-based employment practices in the criminal justice system. *Journal of Criminal Justice, 39*(2), 106–119.

Bandura, A. (1973). *A social learning analysis.* Englewood Cliffs, NJ: Prentice-Hall.

Barak, G., Leighton, P., & Flavin, J. (2006). *Class, race, gender, and crime: The social realities of justice in America* (2nd ed.). Lanham, MD: Rowman and Littlefield.

Benda, B.B., Corwyn, R.F., & Toombs, N.J. (2001). Recidivism among adolescent serious offenders – prediction of entry into the correctional system for adults. *Criminal Justice and Behavior, 28*, 588–613.

Black, D. (1976). *The behavior of law*. New York: Academic Press.

Blair, I.V., Ma, J.E., & Lenton, A.P. (2001). Imagining stereotypes away: The moderation of implicit stereotypes through mental imagery. *Journal of Personality and Social Psychology, 81*(5), 828–841.

Bloom, B., Owen, B., & Covington, S. (2003). *Gender-responsive strategies: Research, practice, and guiding principles for women offenders*. Washington, DC: US Department of Justice, National Institute of Justice.

Blumstein, A. (1982). On the disproportionality of United States' prison populations. *Journal of Criminal Law and Criminology, 73*, 1259–1281.

Bonta, J. (1996). Risk-needs assessment and treatment. In A. Harland (Ed.), *Choosing correctional options that work: Defining the demand and evaluating the supply* (pp. 18–68). Thousand Oaks, CA: Sage.

Bonta, J., & Motiuk, L.L. (1990). 'Classification to halfway houses: Aquasi-experimental evaluation'. *Criminology, 28*, 497–506.

Bower, G.H., & Karlin, M.B. (1974). Depth of processing pictures of faces and recognition memory. *Journal of Experimental Psychology, 4*, 751–757.

Brest, P. (1985). Who decides? *Southern California Law Review*, 58, 661–671.

Bridges, G., & Crutchfield, R. (1998). Law, social standing and racial disparities in imprisonment. *Social Forces, 66*, 699–724.

Brunson, R.K. (2007). 'Police don't like black people': African-American young men's accumulated police experiences. *Criminology & Public Policy, 6*(1), 71–102.

Brunson R.K. & Gau J.M. (forthcoming). Officer race versus macro-level context: A test of competing hypotheses about black citizens' experiences with and perceptions of black police officers. *Crime & Delinquency* (OnlineFirst).

Brunson, R.K., & Miller, J. (2006). Young black men and urban policing in the United States. *British Journal of Criminology, 46*, 613–640.

Butler, P. (1999). Racially based jury nullification: Black power in the criminal justice system. *The Yale Law Journal, 105*(3), 677–725.

Campbell, M.A., French, S., & Gendreau, P. (2009). The prediction of violence in adult offenders: A meta-analytic comparison of instruments and methods of assessment. *Criminal Justice and Behavior, 36*(6), 567–590.

Chiricos, T., Barrick, K., Bales, W., & Bontrager, S. (2007). The labeling of convicted felons and its consequences for recidivism. *Criminology, 45*(3), 547–581.

Collins, D. (2008). Mapping the entrails: The practice of Greek hepatoscopy. *American Journal of Philology, 129*, 319–345.

Correll, J., Park, B., Judd, C., Wittenbrink, B., Sadler, M.S., & Keesee, T. (2007). Across the thin blue line: Police officers and racial bias in the decision to shoot. *Journal of Personality and Social Psychology, 92*, 1006–1023.

Curry, T.R., & Corral, G.C. (2008). Sentencing young minority males for drug offenses. *Punishment & Society, 10*(3), 253–276.

D'Alessio, S.J., & Stolzenberg, L. (2002). A multilevel analysis of the relationship between labor surplus and pretrial incarceration. *Social Problems, 49*(2), 178–193.

Demuth, S. (2003). Racial and ethnic disparities in pretrial release decisions and outcomes: A comparison of hispanic, black, and white felony arrestees. *Criminology, 41*(3), 873–908.

Demuth, S., & Steffensmeier, D. (2004). Ethnicity effects on sentence outcomes in large urban courts: Comparisons among White, Black, and Hispanic defendants. *Social Science Quarterly, 85*(4), 994–1011.

Dixon, T.L., & Linz, D. (2000). Overrepresentation and underrepresentation of African Americans and Latinos as lawbreakers on television news. *Journal of Communication, 50*(2), 131–154.

Dovidio, J.F., Kawakami, K., Johnson, C., Johnson, B., & Howard, A. (1997). On the nature of prejudice: Automatic and controlled processes. *Journal of Experimental Social Psychology, 33*, 510–540.

Drummond, W.J. (1990). About face: Blacks and the news media. *American Enterprise, 1*, 23–29.

Eberhardt, J.L., Goff, P.A., Purdie, V.J., & Davies, P.G. (2004). Seeing black: Race, representation, and visual perception. *Journal of Personality and Social Psychology, 87*, 876–893.

Eberhardt, J.L., Davies, P.G., Purdie-Vaughns, V.J., & Johnson, S.L. (2006). Looking death-worthy: Perceived stereotypicality of black defendants predicts capital-sentencing outcomes. *Psychological Science, 17*(5), 383–386.

Fagan, J., & Davies, G. (2000). Street cops and broken windows: Terry, race, and disorder in New York City. *Fordham Urban Law Journal, 28*, 457–504.

Farrell, A., Ward, G., & Rousseau, D. (2009). Race effects of representation among federal court workers: Does black workforce representation reduce sentencing disparities? *The Annals of the American Academy of Political and Social Science, 623*, 121–132.

Fazio, R.H., Jackson, J.R., Dunton, B.C., & Williams, C.J. (1995). Variability in automatic activation as an unobtrusive measure of racial attitudes: A bona fide pipeline? *Journal of Personality and Social Psychology, 69*, 1013–1027.

Ferguson, A.G., & Bernache, D. (2008). The high-crime area question: Requiring verifiable and quantifiable evidence for fourth amendment reasonable suspicion analysis. *American University Law Review, 57*, 1587–1644.

Fitzgibbon, D.W. (2007). Institutional racism, pre-emptive criminalisation and risk analysis. *Howard Journal of Criminal Justice, 46*(2), 128–144.

Freiburger, T.L. (2009). Race and the sentencing of drug offenders: An examination of the focal concerns perspective. *Southwest Journal of Criminal Justice, 6*(2), 163–177.

Freiburger, T.L., Marcum, C.D., & Pierce, M. (2010). The impact of race on the pretrial decision. *American Journal of Criminal Justice, 35*, 76–86.

Garland, D. (2001). *The culture of control: Crime and social order in contemporary society*. Oxford: Oxford University Press.

Gilens, M. (1999). *Why Americans hate welfare: Race, media, and the politics of anti-poverty policy*. Chicago: University of Chicago Press.

Gilens, M. (1996). 'Race coding' and white opposition to welfare. *American Political Science Review, 90*, 593–604.

Glaser, J., & Knowles, E.D. (2008). Implicit motivation to control prejudice. *Journal of Experimental Social Psychology*, 44, 164–172.

Gordon, R.L. (2004). Divination and prophecy: Rome. In S. Johnston (Ed.), *Religions of the ancient world: A guide* (pp. 387–389). Cambridge, MA: Harvard University Press Reference Library.

Graham, S., & Lowery, B.S. (2004). Priming unconscious racial stereotypes about adolescent offenders. *Law and Human Behavior, 28*, 483–504.

Guehlstorf, N. (2004). *Political theories of risk analysis*. Dordrecht: Springer.

Hacker, A. (1992). *Two nations: Black and white, separate, hostile, unequal*. New York: Maxwell MacMillan.

Harer, M.D., & Steffensmeier, D. (1993). The differing effects of economic inequality on black and white rates of violence. *Social Forces, 70*, 1035–1054.

Harris, D.A. (1994). Factors for reasonable suspicion: When black and poor means stopped and frisked. *Indiana Law Journal, 69*, 659–687.

Heilbrun, K. (1997). Prediction versus management models relevant to risk assessment: The importance of legal decision making context. *Law and Human Behavior, 21*, 347–359.

Huesmann, L.R. (1998). The role of social information processing and cognitive schema in the acquisition and maintenance of habitual aggressive behavior. In R.G. Geen & E. Donnerstein (Eds.), *Human aggression: Theories, research, and implications for social policy* (pp. 73–109). San Diego, CA: Academic Press.

Hurwitz, J., & Peffley, M. (1997). Public perceptions of race and crime: The role of racial stereotypes. *American Journal of Political Science, 41*(April), 375–401.

Ifill, S.A. (2000). Racial diversity on the bench: Beyond role models and public confidence. *Washington & Lee Law Review, 57*, 405–495.

Kalven, H.,Jr., & Zeisel, H. (1966). *The American jury*. Boston: Little, Brown, and Company.

Kim, P., & Mengistu, B. (1994). Women and minorities in the work force of law enforcement agencies. *American Review of Public Administration, 24*(2), 161–180.

Klinger, D.A. (1997). Negotiating order in patrol work: An ecological theory of police response to deviance. *Criminology, 35*, 277–306.

Kubrin, C.E., & Weitzer, R. (2003). Retaliatory homicide: Concentrated disadvantage and neighborhood culture. *Social Problems, 50*, 157–180.

Land, K.C., McCall, P.L., & Cohen, L.E. (1990). Structural covariates of homicide rates: Are there any invariances across time and social space? *American Journal of Sociology, 95*, 922–963.

Lianos, M., & Douglas, M. (2000). Dangerization and the end of deviance: The institutional environment. *British Journal of Criminology, 40*, 261–278.

Lizotte, A.J., Thornbury, T.P., Krohn, M.D., Chard-Wierschem, D.J., & McDowall, D. (1994). Neighborhood context and delinquency. In E. Weitkamp & H. Kerner (Eds.), *Cross-national longitudinal research on human development and human behaviour* (pp. 217–227). Dordrecht: Kluwer.

Loza, W. (2005). *The self-appraisal questionnaire (SAQ): A tool for assessing violent and non-violent recidivism.* Toronto: Mental Health Systems.

Martel, J., Brassard, R., & Jaccoud, M. (2011). When two worlds collide: Aboriginal risk management in corrections. *The British Journal of Criminology, 51*(2), 235–255.

Massey, D.S. (1995). Getting away with murder: Segregation and violent crime in urban America. *University of Pennsylvania Law Review, 143*(5), 1203–1232.

Massey, D.S., & Denton, N.A. (1993). *American apartheid.* Cambridge, MA: Harvard University Press.

Mauer, M., & King, R. (2007). *Uneven justice: State rates of incarceration by race and ethnicity* (pp. 1–23). Washington, DC: The Sentencing Project.

McArthur, L.Z., & Baron, R. (1983). Toward and ecological theory of social perception. *Psychological Review, 90,* 215–238.

Meehan, A.J., & Ponder, M.C. (2002). Race and place. The ecology of racial profiling African American motorists. *Justice Quarterly, 19*(3), 399–430.

Monahan, J., & Steadman, H.J. (1994). Toward a rejuvenation of risk assessment research. In J. Monahan & H.J. Steadman (Eds.), *Violence and mental disorder: Developments in risk assessment* (pp. 1–17). Chicago: University of Chicago Press.

Nosek, B.A., Banaji, M., & Greenwald, A.G. (2002). Harvesting implicit group attitudes and beliefs from a demonstration web site. *Group Dynamics, 6,* 101–115.

Oliver, M.B. (1994). Portrayals of crime, race, and aggression in reality-based police shows: A content-analysis. *Journal of Broadcasting & Electronic Media, 38,* 179–192.

Parker, K.F., MacDonald, J., Alpert, G.P., Smith, M.R., & Piquero, A. (2004). A contextual study of racial profiling: Assessing the theoretical rationale for the study of racial profiling at the local level. *American Behavioral Scientist, 47*(7), 1–20.

Peffley, M., & Hurwitz, J. (2002). The racial components of 'race-neutral' crime policy attitudes. *Political Psychology, 23,* 59–75.

Peffley, M., Hurwitz, J., & Sniderman, P. (1997). Racial stereotypes and whites' political views of blacks in the context of welfare and crime. *American Journal of Political Science, 41*(January), 30–60.

Percival, G.L. (2009). Testing the impact of racial attitudes and racial diversity on prisoner reentry policies in the US states. *State Politics & Policy Quarterly, 9*(2), 176–203.

Quillian, L., & Pager, D. (2001). Black neighbors, higher crime? The role of racial stereotypes in evaluations of neighborhood crime. *American Journal of Sociology, 107*(3), 717–767.

Quinsey, V., Harris, G., Rice, M., & Cormier, C. (1998). *Violent offenders: Appraising and managing risk.* Washington, DC: American Psychological Association.

Robinson, M. (2010). Assessing criminal justice practice using social justice theory. *Social Justice Research, 23*, 77–97.

Rocque, M. (2011). Racial disparities in the criminal justice system and perceptions of legitimacy: A theoretical linkage. *Race and Justice, 1*, 292–315.

Rose, W. (2002). Crimes of colour: Risk, profiling and the contemporary racialization of social control. *International Journal of Politics, Culture and Society, 16*(2), 179–205.

Russell, K.K. (2002). The racial hoax as crime: The law as affirmation. In S.L. Gabbidon, H.T. Greene, & V.D. Young (Eds.), *African American classics in criminology and criminal justice* (pp. 349–376). Thousand Oaks, CA: Sage.

Sagar, H.A., & Schofield, J.W. (1980). Racial and behavioral cues in black and white children's perceptions of ambiguously aggressive acts. *Journal of Personality and Social Psychology, 19*, 590–598.

Sampson, R.J. (2011). The community. In J.Q. Wilson & J. Petersilia (Eds.), *Crime and public policy* (pp. 210–236). New York: Oxford University Press.

Sampson, R.J., & Bartusch, D.J. (1998). Legal cynicism and (subcultural?) tolerance of deviance. The neighborhood context of racial differences. *Law and Society Review, 32*, 777–804.

Sampson, R.J., & Laub, J.H. (1993). Structural variations in juvenile court processing: Inequality, the underclass, and social control. *Law & Society Review, 27*(2), 285–312.

Sampson, R., & Lauritsen, J. (1997). Racial and ethnic disparities in crime and criminal justice in the United States. *Crime and Justice, 21*, 311–374.

Sampson, R.J., & Loeffler, C. (2010). Punishment's place: The local concentration of mass incarceration. *Daedalus, 139*(3), 20–31.

Sampson, R.J., & Raudenbush, S.W. (1999). Systemic social observation of public spaces: A new look as disorder in urban neighborhoods. *American Journal of Sociology, 105*(3), 603–651.

Sampson, R.J., Raudenbush, S.W., & Earls, F. (1997). Neighborhood and violent crime: A multilevel study of collective efficacy. *Science, 277*(2), 918–924.

Schanzenback, M. (2005). Racial and sex disparities in prison sentences: The effect of district-level judicial demographics. *Journal of Legal Studies, 34*(1), 57–92.

Sinclair, S., Lowery, B.S., Hardin, C.D., & Colangelo, A. (2005). Social tuning of automatic racial attitudes: The role of affiliative motivation. *Journal of Personality and Social Psychology, 89*(4), 583–592.

Smykla, J.O. (1986). Critique concerning prediction in probation and parole: Some alternative suggestions. *International Journal of Offender Therapy and Comparative Criminology, 30*(31), 125–139.

Sorensen, J., & Wallace, D.H. (1999). Prosecutorial discretion in seeking death: An analysis of racial disparity in the pretrial states of case processing in a Midwestern county. *Justice Quarterly, 16*(3), 559–578.

Spohn, C. (1990). The sentencing decisions of black and white judges: Expected and unexpected similarities. *Law & Society Review, 24*(5), 1197–1216.

Steffensmeier, D., & Demuth, S. (2000). Ethnicity and sentencing outcomes in US federal courts: Who is punished more harshly? *American Sociological Review, 65*(5), 705–729.

Steffensmeier, D., & Demuth, S. (2001). Ethnicity and judges' sentencing decisions: His-panic–black–white comparisons. *Criminology, 39*(1), 145–178.

Steffensmeier, D., Ulmer, J., & Kramer, J. (1998). The interaction of race, gender, and age in criminal sentencing: The punishment cost of being young, black, and male. *Criminology, 36*, 763–797.

Stewart, E.A., Baumer, E.P., Brunson, R.K., & Simons, R.L. (2009). Neighborhood racial context and perceptions of police-based racial discrimination among black youth. *Criminology, 47*(3), 847–887.

Terrill, W., & Reisig, M.D. (2003). Neighborhood context and police use of force. *Journal of Research in Crime and Delinquency, 40*(3), 291–321.

Thornberry, T. (1994). *Violent families and youth violence*. Fact Sheet No. 21. Washington, DC: Office of Juvenile Justice and Delinquency Prevention.

Tonry, M. (1995). *Malign neglect*. New York: Oxford University Press.

Tyler, T.R., & Wakslak, C.J. (2004). Profiling and police legitimacy: Procedural justice, attributions of motive, and acceptance of police authority. *Criminology, 42*(2), 253–281.

Ward, G., Farrell, A., & Rousseau, D. (2009). 'Does racial balance in workforce representation yield equal justice? Race relations of sentencing in Federal Court organizations'. *Law & Society Review, 43*(4), 757–806.

Webster, C.D., Douglas, K., Eaves, D., & Hart, D. (1997). HCR-20: *Assessing risk for violence* (Ver. 2). Vancouver: Mental Health, Law, & Policy Institute, Simon Fraser University.

Webster, C., MacDonald, R., & Simpson, M. (2006). Predicting criminality? Risk factors, neighbourhood influence and desistance. *Youth Justice, 6*(1), 7–22.

Weitzer, R. (2000). White, black, or blue cops? Race and citizen assessment of police. *Journal of Criminal Justice, 28*(4), 313–324.

Welch, K. (2007). Black criminal stereotypes and racial profiling. *Journal of Contemporary Criminal Justice, 23*, 276–288.

Werthman, C., & Piliavin, I. (1967). Gang members and the police. In D.J. Bordua (Ed.), *The police: Six sociological essays* (pp. 56–98). New York: John Wiley & Sons.

Whiteacre, K.W. (2006). Testing the level of service inventory – revised (LSI-R) for racial/ethnic bias. *Criminal Justice Policy Review, 17*, 330–342.

Willis, J.J., & Mastrofski, S.D. (2011). Compstat and the new penology: A paradigm shift in policing? *British Journal of Criminology*. doi: 10.1093/bjc/azr063.

Wilson, W.J. (1987). *The truly disadvantaged*. Chicago: University of Chicago Press.

Wittenbrink, B., Judd, C.M., & Park, B. (2001). Spontaneous prejudice in context: Variability in automatically activated attitudes. *Journal of Personality and Social Psychology, 2001*(81), 815–827.

Young, R.L. (1985). Perceptions of crime, racial attitudes, and firearms ownership. *Social Forces, 64*, 473–486.

Zeisel, H. (1981). Race bias in the administration of the death penalty: The Florida experience. *Harvard Law Review, 95*, 456–468.

## Cases cited

*Illinois v. Wardlow*, No. 98-1036. Argued November 2, 1999-Decided January 12, 2000.

*McCleskey v. Kemp*, 481 U.S. 279 (1987).

# Chapter 6

# Linking Theory, Research, and Policy

## INTRODUCTION

Because criminologists study real-world issues with real-world impact, the theories we construct and the research we conduct often have policy relevance. In an ideal world, criminal justice policies would always be guided by theory or empirical evidence. Policies that are guided by theory are sometimes referred to as "theoretically grounded" or "theory-driven" policies, whereas those that are based on the findings of empirical research are referred to as "evidence-based." One of the most important skills for success as a criminal justice professional or academic is having an understanding of the important links that exist between theory, research, and policy. In this chapter, we discuss each of these three elements in detail, beginning with what each one is and how it is relevant to the CJS, and then examining the ways that these three elements are connected.

## THEORY

*Theories* are how we make sense of the world and explain things that occur. Theories provide abstract, conceptual propositions about why things happen. Because the social world is complex and phenomena often have vague or multifaceted antecedents, it is human nature to try to make sense of things in ways that are general and patterned. Take crime, for instance. When you tell people—your family, friends, or someone you just met—that you study CJC, do they respond by giving you their own personal theories on why people commit crime? They probably don't come right out and say "Well, my theory on crime is... ." Instead, they likely make a statement about crime that is based on an implicit or unstated theory about criminal behavior. Perhaps they talk about declining morality and "kids these days," point to certain sections of town that are known for high crime rates, or immediately begin talking about policing and corrections (often, we find, in the context of the TV show *Law & Order*). Each of these statements—although not theoretical propositions on their face—hint at underlying theories that people hold about what causes crime. Comments about "kids these days" often implicate the breakdown of social institutions such as family and religion—key concepts in theories of social disorganization and social control. Mentions of "bad" neighborhoods may also invoke ideas of social disorganization, or implicate social learning or subcultural theories (they may also indicate biased ideologies such as racism or classism). Responses that immediately orient to crime as a matter of detection and punishment through policing and corrections may hint at rational choice theory—the cornerstone of deterrence models.

Thus, theory is implicit everywhere. The social world is complex, and humans attempt to impose order on it by making conceptual generalizations about why things happen around us the way that they do. As societies attempt to understand events—especially pressing social problems such as crime—systematic explanations develop that help to organize existing knowledge and guide future knowledge production. When this happens, the move has been made from personal theoretical explanations (what we could refer to as proto-theory) to actual theory. Theories about the social world must not only advance conceptual ideas about the causes of a certain phenomenon, they must also make propositions that can be tested empirically through research. For instance, theories of crime propose explanations for why some people commit crimes and others do not; these propositions can then be tested through research, producing findings that either support or challenge the theory.

Because theory is created by people and because people are informed by their context (remember our discussion of reflexivity in Chapter 1?), it is important to keep in mind that theory is not objective. Social experiences and historical and cultural contexts shape the way people think about crime and what theories they come up with to explain crime. This is true for everyone, including CJC scholars, CJS practitioners, and even CJS policymakers such as government officials. One way to see this effect is to think about the ways prevailing theoretical explanations have shifted over time. For example, let's consider how explanations of deviant behavior have changed over the past few centuries. In the highly religious society of the U.S. colonists, the origins of crime were thought to be spiritual demons and sinfulness. In the late 1800s when ideas about natural selection and Darwinism were in vogue, crime was attributed to defective biological constitution. In the more recent past, the blame has been placed on social ills or a permissive society. Consider that there may be current theories about crime and criminals that will make little sense 20 years from now, as our thinking about the causes of crime will surely have evolved by then.

In criminology, all of the variables hypothesized to cause crime are studied, and there are several ways to categorize those causes. One easy distinction to make is the difference between individual theories of crime and sociological theories of crime. If the cause of crime originates inside the individual, for example, by being related to a person's biological or psychological makeup, it is likely an individual theory of crime. Examples of these types of independent variables are intelligence, heredity, and physical attributes such as hormones, temperament, or personality traits such as impulsivity, cognition or thought processes, moral development, or individual choices. If the cause of crime originates outside of the individual, for example, by being related to a person's experience with outside forces or the effects of sociodemographic variables, it is likely a sociological theory of crime. These explanations focus on ways in which individuals are the product of their environment.

In CJC studies, much attention is given to the study of crime as a behavior to understand, or the propensity to commit crime. But CJC is much broader than that. There are also theories that examine the operation or process of criminal justice systems in an effort to explain why these systems behave as they do, and what effects they have on the people caught up in them. This type of theorizing has focused on theories of social control, theories of trends in crime control, theories of oppression coming out of critical criminology, and theories of organizations.

Whether focusing on crime or system response, there are a number of criteria that can be used to evaluate CJC theories (Akers, 1994). Although it may seem obvious, theories should be logical, consistent, and as concise as possible. The goal of a theory is to distill a large amount of information to simple statements. Similarly, theories must be precise about what they explain. Does the theory explain all crime or just certain types of crime for certain subgroups of people? This is referred to as the scope of the theory. Theories can also be evaluated for how testable they are; the development of empirical research questions that help ascertain whether a particular theory is supported is where research begins.

## RESEARCH (AND MORE THEORY)

Although the term "research" can be used informally as a verb meaning to look into something, in the social sciences we orient to research as a noun—as something that is done deliberately and according to specific rules. Here, we define *research* as the systematic investigation of a social phenomenon. Research is *empirical*, meaning verifiable by observation or experience, rather than theory or logic. In other words, research allows us to draw conclusions based on *data*, or systematically collected information about the social world. These data can be explained in terms of theory. There are two primary ways that theory can be related to data, each associated with its own type of theory. *Deductive theory* begins with ideas about how the social world works. Deductive theorists use logic and prior knowledge to hone their ideas, generating testable propositions about the social world. Once a theory has been fully formulated, it can then be tested through quantitative or qualitative empirical research. *Inductive* or *grounded theory* turns this process on its head, beginning with data rather than ideas. First, information about the social world is collected systematically through qualitative research. The resulting data are carefully analyzed to detect patterns. Once these patterns have been discerned, theoretical propositions are developed based on the relationships seen in the data. As with deductive theory, these theories can later be tested empirically (quantitatively or qualitatively), creating a cyclical process between theory and data.

Social theories are comprised of statements linking various abstract concepts, for instance "crime" and "concentrated disadvantage." For relationships between concepts to be tested by researchers, they must be transformed into something that is observable and measurable. This process is referred to as operationalization. For example, the concept of "school performance" could be made measurable or observable by looking at a student's cumulative grade point average. What are some other ways to measure school performance? Should such factors as enthusiasm and participation be taken into account, perhaps measured by number of extracurricular activities? In social research, there are usually many possible ways to measure a concept; it is up to the researchers to choose the best, most parsimonious (simple, yet complete) measures of the concepts that they are investigating.

One way to assess the rigor of research is to examine whether the key concepts are being measured in a way that is both valid and reliable. *Validity* refers to how accurately and fully a given measure captures the concept it is supposed to represent. A valid measure of crime, for instance, would include all types of crime and exclude anything that isn't technically criminal. *Reliability* refers to the consistency of the measurement tool—how consistently it yields the same measurements of an unchanging phenomenon. Measures are like the bathroom scales of the social sciences. A valid scale displays the weight of the person standing on it; a valid social science measure accurately captures the concept that it represents. A reliable scale will display the same weight each time the person steps on and off it a few minutes apart, for instance; a reliable measure will yield the same values time and time again. A reliable measure is not necessarily a valid measure. Just as a bathroom scale that is consistently 3.5 pounds high is a reliable, but not valid, measure of weight, it follows that a measure of victimization that consistently underrepresents unreported incidents among youth of color is an invalid, and therefore poor, measure.

In deductive, quantitative research, measures take the form of variables. Variables can be *independent* or *dependent.* The *dependent variable* represents the concept that the researcher wants to explain. In CJC studies, the dependent variable is generally some type of crime, delinquency, victimization, or system response. *Independent variables* are the predictor variables; they represent the concepts that will help to explain variation in the dependent variable. Variables must be measured carefully using the correct *unit of analysis*: the thing that is being examined for variation. Because CJC researchers study many different things, there are many possible units of analysis: individuals (e.g., victims, incarcerated people, children), groups (e.g., gangs, juries, parole boards), organizations/systems (e.g., police, corrections, court systems), social artifacts (e.g., newspaper representations, tweets, student papers), or social interactions (e.g., divorces, fist fights, sexual assaults).

The relationship between the independent variable and the dependent variable is expressed as a *hypothesis*, or what the researcher expects to find based on the theory guiding the study. Let's revisit the school performance example from earlier in this chapter. Say you want to conduct research that examines the effect of school performance on juvenile delinquency at the individual level (i.e., with student as the unit of analysis). "School performance" would be the independent variable and "truancy" (a specific type of juvenile delinquency) would be the dependent variable. Your hypothesis could be that poor school performance increases the likelihood of truancy. It is also conceivable that truancy could cause poor school performance, as it is difficult to succeed in school without being there. If you wanted to examine this causal relationship, you would switch the independent and dependent variables. In deductive research, the placement of the independent variable and dependent variables is guided by theory.

In inductive, qualitative research, on the other hand, "measurement" doesn't occur at a numerical level. Qualitative research is designed to capture a phenomenon as fully as possible, delving deep into the context to collect data that reflect nuance and fine-grained detail; this type of data is difficult to capture with numbers. Qualitative research also strives to examine patterns in the data holistically. Rather than attempting to isolate or tease apart relationships between concepts, qualitative research acknowledges the intertwined nature of our messy social world, bringing order to the chaos rather than zeroing in on its individual elements. This emphasis on the holistic understanding of a complex phenomenon lends itself to inductive theory building, which begins with a large amount of data and uses analysis to discern patterns and relationships in the data to generate theory. This type of theory is often called "grounded" theory because it is firmly grounded in empirical data.

Across these types of research, there are many different study designs that can be used to examine CJC issues. The specific research design is informed by the goal of the research (e.g., developing theory, testing theory, determining causal relationships, exploring a new phenomenon, evaluating the effectiveness of a program). Unfortunately, we can't address all of the types of social research here; fortunately, you've probably already learned about many of them: ethnography, experiments, interviews, surveys, systematic social observation, archival research, content analysis, and the list goes on.

Let's imagine that you are going to conduct a CJC research study. No matter which study design you choose, the starting point is to determine the research question that you want to answer. Initially, you may think of shallow questions that have simple answers. That's okay—most researchers start here! Once there are answers to these questions, deeper questions, often with more complex answers, can be asked. For example, it is easy to determine the answer to the question, "What country in the world has the highest incarceration rate, and what is that rate?" This particular question would not qualify as a research question at this point because we already know the prevalence of incarceration across the globe. No research needs to be conducted to answer this question—a simple Internet search can yield the answer (the United States) in seconds.

The deeper question, and one of many appropriate social research questions, is "*Why* does the United States have the highest incarceration rate?" This is an example of a fairly broad research question. The answer could lie squarely in the field of CJC studies, or it could reside in the larger context in which the CJS operates, implicating schools, communities, family, or social values, for instance. When researchers already have ideas about the relationships that they want to explore (guided by theory, of course), they can pose more specific research questions. Many tests of criminological theories do just that. For example, a test of Currie's theory of market society discussed in Chapter 2 might ask a research question that implicates both the dependent and independent variables—for instance, "What effect does the intrusion of market principles into society have on crime rates?"

Developing good research questions requires first gathering extensive information to understand more about the problem, learn about the theoretical explanations that exist for the problem, and discover what prior research has demonstrated about the problem. Much of this information comes from peer-reviewed, academic journal articles. Journals are academic periodicals that publish empirical research articles (among other things). In the peer-review process, articles are carefully vetted and guided by experts in the field before publication to ensure high levels of rigor. You've probably read many journal articles over the course of your CJC education; if you pursue graduate study in CJC, you will probably even write some of your own. Despite this, many students are never taught what goes into a research article, or how to read one. Thus, we briefly touch upon the structure of a research article in the next paragraph.

Research articles typically follow a predictable pattern, beginning with an introduction that lays out the nature of the study, the research question(s), and the hypotheses (if applicable). This section is followed by a literature review in which previous research on the topic is presented. Next, the methods sections tells the reader everything about the research conducted, including the type of data used, who the study participants were, and how data were collected and analyzed. The next section presents the findings or results of the research, informs the reader of whether the hypotheses were supported or rejected, and presents the authors' explanation of the findings. Finally, the last section contains a discussion and set of conclusions that put the research into context by relating the findings to the larger field, noting the limitations of the study, and providing policy implications or recommendations.

## POLICY (AND RESEARCH AND THEORY)

Not all academic fields conclude journal articles with policy implications or recommendations. In fact, even within CJC studies, not all articles include explicit discussions of policy. But as we noted in the opening of this chapter, CJC studies is a field that examines real-world issues with real-world impact. If we as researchers don't see the policy relevance in the theories we construct and research we conduct, we are simply conducting an intellectual exercise. The perspective we advance in this book is one in which theory, research, and policy are considered in tandem to bridge the gap between academic CJC studies and CJS policy/practice. This notion of a responsibility for CJC studies to attend to policy concerns is supported by Aker's (1994) last criterion for evaluating theory—bringing us right back to where we began. This criterion entails assessing the policy implications of a theory to determine whether the theory is useful in providing guidelines for effective social and criminal justice policy and practice.

*Public policy* is any law, rule, or regulation around which our criminal justice system (and other related systems) operate. From a justice perspective, policy can be thought of as the actions that governments take based on the social contract that exists between society and the government. It is often just as relevant to examine what governments choose not to do, or their inaction. One major driver of policy change is the emergence of new problems or changing perceptions of problems, for example, health epidemics, inflation/recession, natural disasters, terrorism, drunk driving-related deaths, drugs, and gangs. Sometimes problems are identified and studied, and a response is developed in the form of policy. Many times, however, change is far less planned. Policy change can come about in response to a crisis, a dramatic event that is highly publicized, a political opportunity, or a lawsuit. Because of their quick-response, reactive nature, these types of interventions are often poorly planned and more likely to be ineffective and waste resources.

Most social problems have numerous root causes, which means there will likely be many components to an effective solution. Within the CJS, solutions often take the form of programs. Programs are developed to provide a set of services aimed at achieving specific goals for certain individuals, groups, organizations, or communities (e.g., the development of gender-responsive programs for female prisoners). There are many examples of these types of CJ interventions. Prisoner reentry policies and programs, such as the Second Chance Act, have included drug treatment, community aftercare, vocational and basic education, postrelease employment, and reintegration services. Many specialized problem-solving courts have been developed to provide a specialized arena that addresses issues such as drug use, domestic violence, mental health, and crimes committed by veterans. This innovative approach is one of the ways that the individually oriented CJS is making strides at addressing social problems. Problem-solving courts recognize that substance abuse or issues facing veterans, for instance, are complex social problems that must be dealt with by the CJS.

Thoughtful, theory-driven and evidence-based policies are the gold standard of public policy. Systematic approaches to policy development have been established that emphasize the need to rigorously analyze the problem, develop theoretically driven objectives, and then choose and implement an intervention that will address the factors theorized to create the problem. However, it is equally important to develop a plan for evaluating the effects and effectiveness of the intervention, beginning with determining the data that will need to be collected to allow for systematic investigation. For a policy to be truly evidence-based, there is a need to understand what the policy does, why it behaves the way it does, and whether it works—issues that require the combined strengths of theoretical and empirical explanations.

Every policy or action in the CJS is *in some way* based on an explanation of why crime occurs. Some of these explanations are formal theories, and some are what we called proto-theories earlier in this chapter. Different theories will have different policy implications; as we discussed in Chapter 1, the individual-level orientation of the CJS lends itself to individually-oriented explanations (i.e., individual-level theories) and policies that treat crime and justice as personal issues rather than social problems. One of the limitations of many current CJC policies and practices, however, is that they are not based on clearly articulated, sound criminological theories. Our system is fueled by deterrence theory, with a particular emphasis on the severity of the sanction. Unfortunately, research has consistently found that the deterrent value of sanctions is limited, and that severe sanctions can even have counterproductive effects. Other policies may be informed by implicit explanations of the way crime and offenders operate—explanations that are often only revealed when the assumptions underlying a policy are examined. In the absence of a tight link between theory, research, and policy, there is ample opportunity for ideologies (such as those discussed in Chapter 4) to fill the void and drive public policy.

Whether examining criminality using criminological theory or policy using criminal justice theory, Cooper and Worrall (2012) argue for the importance of theory and bridging the gap between criminology and CJ theory with theory-based evaluations. Unfortunately, few modern-day policies rely on contemporary research (Williams & Robison, 2004). Although the discipline of CJC has a substantial body of theory and research about criminality, crime control and criminal justice systems, it has not driven criminal justice policy as significantly as it should have (Cooper & Worrall, 2012). We have a long way to go to solve our complex social problems.

## References

Akers, R.L. (1994). *Criminological theories: Introduction and evaluation.* Los Angeles: Roxbury.

Cooper, J.A., & Worrall, J.L. (2012). Theorizing criminal justice evaluation and research. *Criminal Justice Review, 37*(3), 384–397.

Williams, E.J., & Robison, M.B. (2004). Ideology and criminal justice: Suggestions for a pedagogical model. *Journal of Criminal Justice Education, 15*(2), 373–392.

## Selected Readings

Chappell, A.T., Monk-Turner, E., & Payne, B.K. (2011). Broken windows or window breakers: The influence of physical and social disorder on quality of life. *Justice Quarterly, 28*(3), 522–540.

Rudes, D.S., Viglione, J., Lerch, J., Porter, C., & Taxman, F.S. (2014). Build to sustain: Collaborative partnerships between university researchers and criminal justice practitioners. *Criminal Justice Studies, 27*(3), 249–263.

## Discussion Questions/Writing Assignments

1. Describe the relationship between theory, research, and policy in two sentences.
2. Pick a CJC-related theory and create a research question to test that theory. What would your hypothesis be if you were going to conduct this study?
3. What is the theory of crime that you find most persuasive? State its general propositions. Has this theory been empirically supported? What are the policy implications of these research findings?

4. How does our current context inform the dominant CJC theories of the moment?
5. Operationalize the following concepts: punishment, juvenile, crime severity, and rehabilitation.
6. What is grounded theory?
7. Are you more interested in learning about issues of crime, or issues of the CJS response to crime? Why?
8. What is one possible challenge that policymakers face when trying to create theoretically driven, evidence-based policy? What is a challenge that academics face in getting their research to affect policy?
9. Explain the link between theory, research, and policy in *Broken Windows or Window Breakers?*
10. What are some of the obstacles to productive, lasting research-practitioner collaborations described in *Build to Sustain*? What suggestions do the authors offer to overcome these obstacles?

# ACTIVITIES/ASSIGNMENTS

## Drawing the Connections

Draw the relationship among research, theory, and policy. Make sure you include the various types of theory (inductive and deductive) and portray all of the ways that theory, research, and policy are related.

## Finding Journal Information

Find the websites for three academic journals in CJC. If you are having a hard time thinking of the names of journals, you can use your library's online resource search or Google Scholar to find some. Locate the following information on the journal websites: whether the journals are peer-reviewed, who the editors are, and some indication of the journal strength or quality (usually presented in terms of "impact factor" or ranking).

## Theory, Research, Policy Activity

This group activity is designed to get you thinking about the connection between theory, research, and policy in innovative ways. Specify a type of crime you want to focus on.

Part I: Designing Theory: Brainstorm with your group to come up with a new criminological theory that explains your specific crime type. You may incorporate elements of existing criminological theories, but be sure that your group's theory is original; your theory should present a new way of thinking about the factors that cause crime. Describe your new theory in the space below, providing a thorough rationale for its applicability to your chosen crime type.

Part II: Designing A Study to Test Your Theory: As a group, design a research study that would test the validity of your new criminological theory. Describe the basic study design. Be sure to include your chosen research method, research questions, hypotheses, proposed measurement of independent and dependent variables, and anticipated findings.

Part III: Examining Policy Implications: Imagine that you actually executed the research study that you designed in Part II. Describe the policy implications of your expected findings. Be sure to consider how the results of your study inform criminal justice practice, and offer specific, evidence-based policy recommendations based on these results.

## SEMESTER-LONG JUSTICE PROJECT

Step Six:

Choose one of the assignments below:

Locate and summarize a second academic article that relates to your injustice topic. How are theory, research, and policy connected in this article?

OR

What theories explain your issue? What empirical evidence exists supporting or challenging those theories? Given this evidence, start to think about how you could use your justice project to address this issue. Instead of theory-research-policy, figure out the theory-research-justice project progression for your semester-long project.

## ACTIVITIES FOR INSTRUCTOR

Share with your students examples of how you or others have used theory, research, and policy in your own work.

## Selected Reading

# Broken Windows or Window Breakers

## The Influence of Physical and Social Disorder on Quality of Life

*Allison T. Chappell, Elizabeth Monk-Turner, and Brian K. Payne*

## INTRODUCTION

The relationship between neighborhood disorder and fear of crime is well established (Hinkle & Weisburd, 2008). In fact, some research indicates that neighborhood disorder, or incivilities, is a better predictor of fear than serious crime (Kelling, 1981; Skogan & Maxfield, 1981). According to broken windows theory, neighborhood physical and social disorder cause residents to be fearful and retreat from their neighborhoods (Moore & Trojanowicz, 1988; Wilson & Kelling, 1982, p. 36). This breaks down informal social control mechanisms and suggests to residents and outsiders alike that the neighborhood is "uncontrolled and uncontrollable" (Wilson & Kelling, 1982, p. 33), which ultimately may lead to more serious crime. The idea is that disorder causes fear, and fear leads to activities that cause serious crime.

Broken windows theory has influenced policy, most notably in the policing arena. Policing strategies based on this approach, often termed "quality of life policing," focus on the elimination of problems, such as panhandling and public drunkenness, vandalism, prostitution, noise, loitering and unruly youths, graffiti and littering, and dilapidated buildings (Kelling, 1987; Kelling & Coles, 1996). It is a variation of community policing that takes a zero tolerance approach to misdemeanor crimes based on the premise that unattended disorder leads to more serious crime. In New York City, "quality of life" policing has been credited with contributing to the unprecedented 1990s crime drop (Bratton & Knobler, 1998; Kelling & Sousa, 2001).

While research in criminology has largely focused on the relationship between disorder, fear, and crime, our goal is to discern whether disorder is inextricably related to quality of life. Indeed, broken windows theory implies that disorder negatively impacts quality of life (Taylor, 2001). According to Kelling (1987) "disorderly behavior powerfully shapes the quality of urban life," (p. 95) and Moore and Trojanowicz (1988) argued that fear "produces a loss in personal well-being" (p. 3). Other researchers have touched on the fear-quality of life nexus, contending that fear of crime is only one component of a larger construct of quality of life (Garafolo & Laub, 1978; see also Hale, 1988). Furthermore, according to Xu, Fiedler, and Flaming (2005) "Citizen's fear is a significant predictor of the perceived quality of life, and both are in turn significantly influenced by disorder" (p. 174). Certainly, fear, which causes people to retreat into their homes, impacts subjective quality of life. However, this proposition— that disorder affects quality of life—has not yet been empirically examined in the USA.

While past research has found a relationship between disorder and fear, anger, hopelessness, and demoralization (Skogan, 1990), no studies to date have specifically examined the relationship between disorder and subjective quality of life. In fact, few studies have examined the link between perception of crime or victimization and quality of life and happiness (Michalos & Zumbo, 2000). Today, researchers generally understand quality of life (or happiness) as a sense of subjective well-being (SWB) and life satisfaction (Diener, 1984; Diener, Suh, Lucas, & Smith, 1999; Doland & White, 2006; Lu, 1995; Yang, 2008). In the current study, we aim to investigate the relationship between broken windows or neighborhood disorder, and subjective quality of life. In so doing, we will extend broken windows theory and examine whether one key assumption of the theory is empirically supported.

This research is important for policy, research, and theory. Broken windows theory suggests that quality of life can be improved by addressing disorder. But, is disorder actually related to quality of life? Our research has practical and theoretical importance in that this core assumption of broken windows theory—that disorder is predictive of quality of life—remains an empirical question.

## LITERATURE REVIEW

### Broken Windows Theory

According to Wilson and Kelling's broken windows theory, disorder (or incivilities) in a neighborhood causes citizens to be fearful and withdraw from neighborhood activities. Disorder is a "signal that no one cares" (Wilson & Kelling, 1982, p. 31), and symbolizes an increased likelihood of serious criminal activity. This, in turn, causes residents to limit their activities (Costa, 1984), decreasing informal social control, and eventually leading to more serious crime. According to Wilson and Kelling (1982), "serious crime flourishes in areas in which disorderly behavior goes unchecked" (p. 34). One of the implications of the theory is that policing efforts that focus on decreasing disorder will lead to increases in informal social control and therefore prevent more serious crime from occurring.

Broken windows theory has led to a number of policing initiatives (Bratton & Knobler, 1998; Kelling & Sousa, 2001; Weisburd & Braga, 2006) that advocate aggressive police tactics aimed to control minor crimes and disorder. These policing practices have been referred to with a variety of terms, such as "zero tolerance policing," "order maintenance policing," and "quality of life policing" (Cordner, 1998). The basic premise of such policing strategies, based on broken windows theory, is that the aggressive enforcement of minor offenses (i.e., disorder) will prevent more serious crime from occurring (Kelling & Sousa, 2001; Skogan, 1990). Examples of such aggressive enforcement include increasing arrests for disorderly behavior and loitering, increasing code enforcement, and eliminating graffiti (Kelling & Sousa, 2001; Skogan, 1990). Many of these policing efforts explicitly aim to decrease fear and crime as well as improve quality of life (Bennett, 1991). Broken windows theory has notably been credited for contributing to the crime drop in New York City in the 1990s (Bratton & Knobler, 1998; Kelling & Sousa, 2001).

While considerable research has established a relationship between disorder and fear (Covington & Taylor, 1991; Markowitz, Bellair, Liska, & Liu, 2001; Skogan, 1990), other studies have focused on the relationship between disorder and crime. For example, Kelling and Sousa (2001) found that the aggressive enforcement of disorder was associated with decreased violent crime, and Messner et al. (2007) concluded that order maintenance policing reduced gun-related homicides. Other scholars, however, have found that increased enforcement of disorder has had no effect on serious crime (Katz, Webb, & Schaefer, 2001; Novak, Hartman, Holsinger, & Turner, 1999; Sherman, 1990).

While some critics contend that broken windows theory lacks merit and has not been adequately tested (Harcourt, 1998; Sampson & Raudenbush, 1999), others suggest that addressing disorder is a worthwhile pursuit even if it has no direct effect on crime rates. Thacher (2004) argues that order maintenance policing is best judged by its direct impact on public order; that what should be considered is whether attacking public disorder is "intrinsically valuable" (p. 381). He attributes the skepticism by some commentators as a result of "strong causal reasoning" (p. 383) and a reliance on research methods that are unable to adequately capture the reality of order maintenance policing. He suggests that ethnographic techniques may be more appropriate for such an endeavor. Sousa and Kelling (2006) elaborate on this, arguing that "broken windows may have merit beyond the link between disorder and crime" (p. 87). Indeed, policing strategies based on broken windows theory may aim to improve public order with no intent to reduce serious crime. Certainly, research has shown that disorder may cause more fear and concern among the public than serious crime (Kelling, 1981; Skogan & Maxfield, 1981). Thus, even if quality of life policing does not have a direct impact on crime rates, it is possible that it is worthwhile in its own right.

No researchers to date have directly examined the relationship between broken windows theory and quality of life. Outside of criminology, however, a few key studies have looked at the impact of neighborhood disorder on a number of issues that relate to quality of life, such as health and mortality (Chaix, 2009; Cohen et al., 2003; Hill, Ross, & Angel, 2005; Yen, Yelin, Katz, Eisner, & Blanc, 2006), risky behavior (Latkin, Curry, Hua, & Davey, 2007), substance use (Cleveland, Feinberg, & Greenberg, 2010; Wilson, Syme, Boyce, Battistich, & Selvin, 2005), children's activity levels (Miles, 2008; Molnar, Gortmaker, Bull, & Buka, 2004), depression (Latkin & Curry, 2003; Ross, 2000), drinking (Hill & Angel, 2005), smoking (Miles, 2006), and perceived powerlessness (Geis & Ross, 1998).

Some research has found that the social and physical environment in neighborhoods plays an important role in health and mortality. Research in the health and medical fields suggests that those who live in neighborhoods plagued with physical and social disorder are less likely to be physically active, which is a risk factor for a number of diseases, including heart disease, diabetes, and cancer (Cohen et al., 2003; Kahn et al., 2002; King et al., 2000; Sallis & Owen, 1996). Research has found that people who perceive high levels of neighborhood disorder are more likely to restrict physical activity (e.g., walking in the neighborhood) and are more likely to have health problems (Wei, Hipwell, Pardini, Beyers, & Loeber, 2005). Furthermore, dilapidated neighborhood conditions likely affect social relationships with those in the neighborhood, and a lack of social relationships has a negative impact on health and quality of life (Cohen et al., 2003; Helliwell & Putnam, 2004; Putnam, 2000). In other words, researchers are recognizing the importance of neighborhood conditions in health and longevity, as people are more likely to spend time outdoors when the neighborhood is pleasant (Cohen et al., 2003).

Christmann and Rogerson (2004) conducted a study in the UK on crime, fear of crime, and quality of life. Interestingly, they found no association between the level of property and violent crime rates and quality of life. However, they did find that neighborhood disorder was a good predictor of quality of life. In fact, it was the third best predictor of quality of life after difficulty with financial debt and poor health. They concluded, "the most direct approach to improving quality of life ... is to address ... physical disorder" (p. i).

## Quality of Life

Stemming primarily from the disciplines of psychology and economics, quality of life research has focused on a number of indicators such as work, income and education, health and social relationships, and personal characteristics. For example, a number of studies have examined the impact of income on quality of life and found that income is positively associated with quality of life (Easterlin, 2001; Frey & Stutzer, 2000). However, other researchers challenge this assertion, citing data that the per capita income gap between wealthy and poor countries does not match the gap in quality of life (Layard, 2005; Nettle, 2005). At the individual level, income increases lead to variable outcomes. For the poor, an increase in income has a stronger impact than for the rich. In other words, there seems to be a "baseline;" income affects quality of life to the extent that it helps people meet their basic needs, but after that, the effect is negligible (see Diener, 2009; Diener et al., 1999). Furthermore, it appears that relative, rather than absolute, income is a better determinant of happiness (Ball & Chernova, 2008; Dorn, Fischer, Kirchgassner, & Sousa-Poza, 2007). Similarly, a few studies have examined the role of work in quality of life. This research tends to focus on how hours worked is related to quality of life (Bardasi & Francesconi, 2004; Benz & Frey, 2004;

Blanchflower, 2000; Blanchflower & Oswald, 1998, 2005). Little research has examined how employment status, specifically whether or not one works outside of the home, shapes SWB. Education has been found to have a positive influence on quality of life; notably, this effect is independent of income (Blanchflower & Oswald, 2004; Easterlin, 2001; Fahey & Smyth, 2004).

Extant research has examined the impact of demographic variables, such as age, race, and gender, on quality of life. The findings regarding the relationship between age and quality of life are mixed. Some research has found that quality of life increases as people get older (Charles, Reynolds, & Gatz, 2001; Yang, 2008), while others have found that it decreases (Rodgers, 1982) or stays the same (Costa et al., 1987). Ferrer-i-Carbonell and Gowdy (2007) found that those in their 30s and 40s reported lower life satisfaction than those who were younger or older. Women have been found to have higher quality of life than men (Easterlin, 2001), although one recent study found that while women are happier earlier in life, men are happier later in life (Plagnol & Easterlin, 2008). African Americans have been found to have lower quality of life than whites (Davis, 1984; Hughes & Thomas, 1998).

Health and relationships may also affect quality of life. Many researchers have found a positive relationship between health and quality of life (Bowling, 1996; Seligman, 2002; Shields & Wheatley Price, 2005), although this relationship is complicated by the fact that "the promotion of good health might be indistinguishable from the promotion of a good life" (Michalos, Zumbo, & Hubley, 2000, p. 247; also see Blane, Netuveli, & Montgomery, 2008; Michalos, 2004). Similarly, studies have found a positive relationship between having close family relationships, strong community ties, and friendships and quality of life (Argyle, 2001; Blanchflower & Oswald, 2004; Lelkes, 2006; Lucas & Dyrenforth, 2006; Myers, 2000; Pichler, 2006). Indeed, "social connectedness" and social capital have been linked to higher levels of reported quality of life (Helliwell & Putnam, 2004; Putnam, 2000).

While a few studies have examined the impact of crime on quality of life (Michalos & Zumbo, 2000), limited research has analyzed the role of neighborhood disorder, or broken windows, on quality of life. Commentators have repeatedly implied that a relationship between disorder and quality of life exists, but this relationship has never been directly tested in the USA (for a study in the UK, see Christmann & Rogerson, 2004). In this study, we aim to examine the relationship between disorder and quality of life while controlling for a number of factors that have been found to impact quality of life in prior research.

Our research is important for empirical reasons as well as policy and theory. Empirically, researchers need to be sure that they are accurately framing, understanding, and assessing the consequences of neighborhood disorder. At this point, the idea that disorder impacts quality of life is an empirical assumption. Furthermore, many policies advocate the aggressive enforcement of laws against disorder and low-level criminality in the spirit of improving quality of life. Such efforts may be misplaced if research fails to find a relationship between disorder and quality of life. Finally, our research is theoretically important because it examines broken windows theory in a new context. Some researchers have argued that the theory has never been adequately tested (Harcourt, 1998) and the present research tests a core assumption of the theory that has lacked empirical examination in the past.

## METHODS

To assess the impact of disorder on quality of life, a telephone survey of residents living in two large southeastern cities was conducted. The survey was part of a broader quality of life survey focusing on interdisciplinary issues related to quality of life. The survey included several sections including demographic questions and questions about (1) quality of life issues, (2) social networks, (3) neighborhood disorder, (4) health, and (5) interpersonal relationships. The survey took between 15 and 20 minutes to complete.

The telephone surveys were conducted by a research center based at the university where each of the authors worked when the study was conducted. The research center has conducted several different telephone surveys on an annual basis since its inception more than a decade ago. For this survey, the telephone interviewers included students, many of whom had extensive experience conducting telephone interviews. All of the interviewers participated in training that focused specifically on this study.

We purchased a list of 4,795 random telephone numbers from Marketing Systems Group (http://www.m-s-g.com/home.aspx). This total number was selected on the basis of a formula the research center had used in its previous telephone surveys. The goal was to develop a sample of 750 respondents. To estimate the amount of telephone numbers needed, research center staff divided the total number of desired completions by three figures: (1) the estimated working number rate, which was assumed to be 0.75, (2) the estimated cooperation rate, which was assumed to be 0.25, and (3) the eligibility rate, which was assumed to be 0.84. These assumptions were determined by previous telephone surveys conducted by the research center.

Of those 4,795 phone numbers, 1,765 were deemed to be unusable after 10 attempts were made to call the number. This resulted in 3,030 possible phone calls where someone answered the phone. Of the total list of numbers (e.g., 4,795), 746 respondents completed the survey for a response rate of 15.6%. While this rate is arguably low, it is probably more reasonable to calculate the response rate based on the number of phone calls where someone actually answered the phone. Of the 3,030 phone calls, 746 surveys were completed for a cooperation rate[1] of 24.6%. Others have calculated response rate based on answered calls—rather than the total number of telephone numbers—as well (see Payne, Tewksbury, & Mustaine, 2010). Response rates in this range are common in telephone surveys (see McCarty, House, Harman, & Richards, 2006).

A majority (69%) of our respondents were females and white (69%). The mean age of our sample was 49. Approximately a third (34%) of the sample reported incomes of $75,000 or higher. Half of respondents worked full time (49%) and 36% had acquired the bachelor's degree or better.[2] Many (37%) strongly agreed that they socialized with family and friends every week. Half (51%) of respondents said that their health was very good or excellent. Almost a third (31%) reported that 20% fall in income would make them feel very restricted or they would feel it would be difficult to survive (see Table 6.1).

**Table 6.1** Descriptive statistics ($N$ = 746)

| | M | SD | Range |
|---|---|---|---|
| *Dependent variable* | | | |
| Quality of life | 18.95 | 2.76 | 6–24 |
| *Independent variables* | | | |
| Race (1 = white) | 0.69 | 0.45 | 0–1 |
| Gender (1 = male) | 0.31 | 0.46 | 0–1 |
| Age | 48.89 | 16.59 | 19–94 |
| Income | 8.57 | 2.81 | 1–12 |
| Education (1 = bachelor's degree) | 0.36 | 0.48 | 0–1 |
| Employment (1 = full time) | 0.49 | 0.5 | 0–1 |
| Sees family regularly | 0.37 | 0.48 | 0–1 |
| Income drop | 0.31 | 0.46 | 0–1 |
| Health (1 = very good) | 0.51 | 0.5 | 0–1 |
| Resources | 14.82 | 2.43 | 5–20 |
| Health (scale) | 11.44 | 4.61 | 6–30 |
| Disorganization | 8.94 | 2.69 | 5–20 |
| Physical disorganization | 5.2 | 1.64 | 3–12 |
| Social disorganization | 3.76 | 1.27 | 2–8 |

## Dependent Variable

We created a quality of life index, which is a composite variable of six questions. Respondents were asked about whether or not they were as happy as anyone they knew, accepted things the way they were in their life, felt connected to other people, found much fulfillment in life, led a rich, spiritual life, and enjoyed their daily activities (alpha 0.79). Response options ranged from strongly disagree to strongly agree. The possible range on this variable was 6–24 with lower scores indicating less SWB compared to others (mean 18.95). Our measure is similar to those used in other quality of life studies (see Diener, 1984; Michalos et al., 2000; Yang, 2008). According to Yang,

> previous research defines subjective well-being as a state of stable, global judgment of life quality and the degree to which people evaluate the overall quality of their present lives positively ... general happiness is the measure of subjective well-being examined most frequently (2008, p. 204; see also, Diener, 1984).

## Independent Variables

Race was dichotomized between whites (1) and all others (0). Gender was dichotomized between males (1) and females (0). Age was in years (continuous). Respondents were asked their total household income. Response options included 12 categories and ranged from less than $10,000 to $110,000 and over (continuous). Educational attainment was dichotomized between those with at least a bachelor's degree (1) and others (0). Employment status was captured as employed full time (1) compared to others (0). Seeing family and friends was a dichotomized variable and coded 1 if the respondent strongly agreed with the statement that they socialized with family and friends every week (1) and (0) otherwise. Respondents who felt they would be very restricted or would find it difficult to survive if their disposable income fell by 20% were coded as (1) compared to those who felt such a drop in income would mean doing without the basics or not being able to do nice things (0). Respondents who rated their health as very good or better (1) were compared to others (0).

Three composite measures were constructed: resources, health, and disorder. Respondents were asked how they felt about their economic resources. Five questions were included in this composite measure with response options ranging from strongly disagree (1) to strongly agree (4); therefore, a low score on this measure would indicate that the respondent felt they did not have sufficient resources for their perceived needs. Respondents were asked if they had sufficient resources for housing, for their transportation, for their medical care, for their future needs, and if they were confident about the future of social security (alpha 0.75).

Questions from the *SF-8 Health Survey* were used to measure items related to health. This survey is designed to quickly assess different indicators of health and well-being (SF-8™ Health Survey, 2008). Respondents were asked six questions to capture health concerns with response options ranging from 1 to 5 (with 1 being no problems); therefore, the possible range on this variable was between 6 and 30 (mean 11.44). A low score would indicate that the respondent reported better health. Respondents were asked if, within the past four weeks, physical health limited activities, they had difficulty with daily work, how much pain they were in, how much energy they had (reverse coded), how much their health limited their social activities, and how much they were bothered by emotional problems (alpha 0.82).

Disorder was captured by five questions that were posed to respondents with response options ranging from strongly disagree (1) to strongly agree (4). The possible range on this variable was 5–20 with a low score indicating neighborhood disorder was not a problem (mean 8.94). Respondents were asked if litter was a major problem in the neighborhood, if there were major signs of vandalism, if a lot of houses around their house had burglar bars on the windows, if unsupervised youth were always in their neighborhood, and if public drinking was a problem in the neighborhood (alpha 0.82).[3] In order to capture possible differences between physical and social disorder, the disorder variable was dichotomized between physical disorder (litter, vandalism, and burglar bars) and social disorder (unsupervised youth and public drinking).

## Analytic Plan

Utilizing ordinary least-squares (OLS) regression, we explored differences in reported quality of life for a basic model that included demographic variables, an expanded model with composite predictor measures included, and a series of full models with disorder variables added. In this way, we capture how well disorder shapes reported differences in quality of life while controlling for variables that have been shown to impact quality of life in the extant literature.

## RESULTS

In our basic model, which included demographic variables of race, gender, and age, none of these variables significantly shaped differences in quality of life (see Table 6.2). Next, in our expanded model, we added composite measures of resources and health to the model while controlling for income,[1] education, employment status, how regularly one saw family and friends, health, and how one felt about a fall in income. Income, education, how often one saw family and friends, as well as our composite health and resource variables significantly shaped differences in reported quality of life. Completing at least the bachelor's degree as well as strongly agreeing to the statement that they regularly saw family and friends

**Table 6.2** OLS regression models predicting quality of life

| | Basic model ($n$ = 721)<br>$B$ (SE) | Expanded model ($n$ = 547)<br>$B$ (SE) |
|---|---|---|
| Race (1 = white) | 0.27 (0.23) | −0.11 (0.24) |
| Gender (1 = male) | −0.34 (0.22) | −0.41 (0.23) |
| Age | 0.00 (0.01) | 0.01 (.01) |
| Income | — | −0.10 (0.04)* |
| Education (1 = bachelor's degree) | — | 0.58 (0.22)** |
| Employment (1 = full time) | — | −0.05 (0.23) |
| Sees family regularly | — | 1.37 (0.22)** |
| Income drop | — | −0.01 (0.24) |
| Health (1 = very good) | — | 0.32 (0.24) |
| Resources | — | 0.33 (0.05)** |
| Health (scale) | — | −0.14 (0.03)** |
| Constant | 18.84 (0.34)** | 15.32 (0.92)** |
| $R$-square | 0.001 | 0.28 |

*$p < 0.05$; **$p < 0.01$; $p$ values computed for two-tailed significance tests.

was positively associated with quality of life. However, as income went up, respondents reported a decrease in their quality of life. Both of our composite predictor variables, health and resources, were significant in shaping perception of quality of life. Quality of life was positively associated with reporting fewer health problems and the feeling that one had sufficient economic resources for their needs.

## Deconstructing an Understanding of Disorder

In our full models, neighborhood disorder variables were included along with other control variables (see Table 6.3). Again, the initial measure of disorder was a composite variable which included questions that captured both social and physical aspects of neighborhood disorder. Next, this variable was disaggregated and two measures that captured possible differences between social disorder and physical disorder were included in the model. Physical disorder included three of the composite measures (litter, vandalism, houses with burglar bars) while social disorder was measured by how respondents felt about unsupervised youth always being in the neighborhood and public drinking in the neighborhood.

In the full models (see Table 6.3), results from the expanded model held. Looking at Model 1, we see that those who perceived less (total) disorder in their neighborhoods were significantly more likely than others to report greater quality of life. Looking at a possible difference between physical and social disorder in shaping quality of life, we found that both perceived physical disorder and perceived social disorder were significantly related to quality of life when included in the models separately (see Table 6.3, Models 2 and 3). Specifically, those who perceived less social and physical disorder in their neighborhoods reported greater quality of life compared to others.

Overall, quality of life differences are shaped by perceived social and physical disorders in neighborhoods; however, does this result hold when these variables are included in both the models? Our composite disorder variable, which included both social and physical disorders, was significant in shaping quality of life differences. Likewise, both social and physical disorder variables significantly shaped differences in quality of life. When respondents perceived less disorder, whether that be overall disorder, physical disorder, or social disorder, their perceived quality of life increased. However, when both social and physical disorder variables are included in our model only physical disorder remained significant in shaping differences in quality of life (Table 6.3, Model 4). It appears that physical disorder in neighborhoods is a key in shaping differences in quality of life. Social disorder (i.e., unsupervised youth and public drinking) is only significant in shaping quality of life when physical aspects of this measure are not included separately in the model.[5] It is worth noting that other researchers have found that measures of social disorder are "narrower in range and quite rare" compared to signs of physical disorder (Gault & Silver, 2008; see also, Sampson & Raudenbush, 1999). This may explain why they are less significant predictors of quality of life than physical disorder.

**Table 6.3** OLS regression models predicting quality of life

| | Model 1 ($n$ = 536) | Model 2 ($n$ = 540) | Model 3 ($n$ = 540) | Model 4 ($n$ = 536) |
|---|---|---|---|---|
| | $B$ (SE) | $B$ (SE) | $B$ (SE) | $B$ (SE) |
| Race (1 = white) | −0.05 (0.24) | −0.06 (0.24) | −0.08 (0.24) | 0.07 (0.24) |
| Gender (1 = male) | −0.45 (0.23) | −0.44 (0.23) | −0.41 (0.23) | −0.45 (0.23) |
| Age | 0.01 (0.01) | .01 (0.01) | 0.01 (0.01) | 0.01 (0.01) |
| Income | −0.11 (0.04)* | −0.11 (0.04)* | −0.11 (0.04)* | −0.11 (0.04)* |
| Education (1 = bachelor's degree) | 0.56 (0.23)* | 0.57 (0.22)* | 0.58 (0.23)* | 0.56 (0.23)* |
| Employment (1 = full time) | −0.04 (0.23) | −0.07 (0.23) | −0.04 (0.24) | −0.05 (0.23) |
| Sees family regularly | 1.21 (0.22)** | 1.20 (0.22)** | 1.27 (0.22)** | 1.20 (0.22)** |
| Income drop | 0.00 (0.24) | 0.00 (0.24) | 0.01 (0.25) | −0.01 (0.24) |
| Health (1 = very good) | 0.27 (0.24) | 0.27 (0.24) | 0.31 (0.24) | 0.26 (0.24) |
| Resources | 0.30 (0.05)** | 0.31 (0.05)** | 0.31 (0.05)** | 0.30 (0.05)** |
| Health (scale) | −0.13 (0.03)** | −0.13 (0.03)** | −0.13 (0.03)** | −0.13 (0.03)** |
| Disorganization | −0.14 (0.04)** | — | — | — |
| Physical disorganization | — | −0.22 (0.07)** | — | −0.20 (0.09)* |
| Social disorganization | — | — | −0.22 (0.09)* | −0.05 (0.11) |
| Constant | 17.03 (1.09)** | 16.91 (1.06)** | 16.58 (1.06)** | 17.02 (1.09)** |
| $R$-square | 0.29 | 0.29 | 0.28 | 0.29 |

*$p < 0.05$; **$p < 0.01$; $p$ values computed for two-tailed significance tests.

## DISCUSSION

These results provide intriguing insight into the relationship between disorder and quality of life. Analyses of the basic model found that none of our variables were significant in shaping quality of life. In the expanded model, regularly seeing family and friends, having acquired at least a bachelor's degree, feeling positively about one's economic resources and reporting fewer health problems were positively related to quality of life. As well, an increase in income was associated with a decrease in perceived quality of life. This variable was significant in both the expanded and full models and the sign and direction of the coefficient were consistent in both models. Extant research indicates that the relationship between income and quality of life is not linear; that is, income seems to affect quality of life to the extent that it helps people meet their basic needs, but after that, the effect is negligible (see generally Diener, 2009; Diener et al., 1999). Thus, the fact that our results indicate that income has a negative impact on quality of life is not that surprising, given the characteristics of our sample (which is wealthier than the general population). Finally, perceiving fewer problems with neighborhood disorder was positively related to quality of life; however, it appears that physical disorder in neighborhoods is what is key (rather than social disorder) in shaping differences in quality of life, all else equal.

This suggests that there is a link between neighborhood disorder (particularly physical disorder), our measure to capture variables tied to broken windows theory, and quality of life. In fact, it seems that—with regard to disorder—physical disorder plays a more significant role than social disorder in producing quality of life. Collectively, these findings point to a number of potential implications for policing, theory, and future research.

One clear implication from these findings is that policy makers and law enforcement executives should not assume that policing practices, such as broken windows policing, can positively influence quality of life by themselves. Certainly, quality of life is produced by a number of variables. When "quality of life" policing occurs, it is possible that addressing social disorder, absent the focus on other types of disorder, will not have a significant influence on quality of life.

Second, and somewhat related, these findings suggest that current policing practices designed to address social disorder may be shortsighted. The inability of policing strategies, such as broken windows policing, to address various issues has been noted elsewhere. In fact, according to Sampson and Raudenbush (1999), "the current fascination in policy circles on cleaning up disorder through law enforcement techniques appears simplistic and largely misplaced." The fact that social disorder is not significant while controlling for physical disorder suggests that law enforcement efforts to address social disorder independent of efforts to address physical disorder are quite possibly "simplistic and largely misplaced."

Third, law enforcement practices cannot be expected to solve issues of disorder by themselves; instead, law enforcement officials must work with other agencies and units better able to address issues related to disorder. In Oakland, California, the Specialized Multi-Agency Response Team (SMART) program, for example, involved police officers working with place managers to address crime, while other community officials were given the task of addressing physical disorder (Green, 1995, 1996; Green, Price, & Roehl, 2000; Mazerolle, Kadleck, & Roehl, 1998). Landlords and homeowners were fined if their residence showed continued signs of disorder. As place managers expanded their efforts to work together, drug activity decreased (Mazerolle et al., 1998). Indeed, the police themselves were not able to address physical disorder.

Fourth, in terms of policing implications, quality of life policing (Kelling, 1987) is possibly the inappropriate label given to these law enforcement techniques. This is important because members of the public might have expectations that the policing practices will change their quality of life. From these findings, however, it appears that the dynamics and contextual factors surrounding quality of life cannot be adequately addressed by quality of life policing efforts. In the end, if citizens expect policing practices to improve quality of life (because of the label given to the policing practices), then citizens will likely be disappointed in the results of the policing practices. In effect, the very label of "quality of life" policing may perpetuate negative attitudes about the police, and thereby potentially reduce, rather than improve, quality of life.

These findings have implications for criminological theory. At the broadest level, it seems safe to suggest that the lack of a link between quality of life and social disorder has implications for broken windows theory. In general, broken windows theorists suggest a link between disorder and quality of life. The results reported here support this assumption to a degree. Our results particularly point to the role of physical disorder in producing quality of life. Conversely, the minimal influence of social disorder suggests that the dynamics surrounding the disorder matter in terms of quality of life.

Another theoretical implication has to do with the need to better link broken windows theory and broken windows policing through criminological theory and empirical research. Many of the criticisms of broken windows policing (e.g., that the practice is shortsighted and narrowly defined) seem to stem from the fact that the practices are driven void of empirical theory and research. The current research provides but one set of findings that can be used to help drive broken windows policing. Additional criminological research and theory development is needed to better situate broken windows policing in various communities where it occurs.

A number of limitations warrant that these implications be approached with a degree of caution. Consistent with other studies on disordered communities, our sample was underrepresented in terms of minorities and lower-income residents—groups that have historically been distrustful of social science research (Button, 2008). As well, because we had to limit the number of questions on our survey due to budget constraints, our social disorder measure was somewhat narrow and excluded other possible indicators of disorder that may have led to different results. For example, drug dealing, prostitution, aggressive panhandling, and public drunkenness might be perceived differently by respondents than our indicators of social disorder were perceived.

Future researchers should consider how quality of life policing strategies are specifically tied to quality of life in communities where these strategies occur. Researchers should also focus on how quality of life and broken windows policing strategies are defined by law enforcement officers, policy makers, and citizens. Determining whether the conceptual focus of the practices is consistent with the perceived outcomes of the strategies will help to better understand how these law enforcement practices are received in the community.

In addition, researchers should focus more clearly on the actual goals of these practices, how those goals are defined, and whether the goals are actually met. Finally, researchers should expand their efforts to identify the links between quality of life, various types of disorder, police practices, and the presence of crime in a community. All too often, these relationships are over simplified or assumed. Empirically verifying the relationships will help to determine which response strategies should be most effective.

## NOTES ON CONTRIBUTORS

Allison T. Chappell is an Assistant Professor in the Department of Sociology and Criminal Justice at Old Dominion University in Norfolk, Virginia. She earned her PhD in Sociology from the University of Florida in 2005. Her primary research interests are policing and juvenile justice/delinquency. Her work has appeared in journals such as *Crime and Delinquency, Policing: An International Journal of Police Strategies and Management*, and the *Journal of Contemporary Ethnography.*

Elizabeth Monk-Turner is Professor of Sociology and Criminal Justice at Old Dominion University. Her most recent work focuses on subjective well being and how this varies by age, in unique samples (yoga practitioners), and between those who exchange money for sex in Thailand and Yunnan, China. How perceptions of personal and community safety shape subjective well-being will be a focus of future research. Other research examines work issues (including gender differences in promotional opportunities among correctional officers, how stakeholders perceive key issues in the selection of police chiefs, factors shaping police retention, meditation effects in correctional settings, and how bouncers do their job), factors shaping the decision of male assault survivors to seek counseling, hand washing behavior, and images in readily available internet pornography.

Dr. Brian K. Payne is Professor and Chair of the Department of Criminal Justice at Georgia State University. He received his PhD in 1993 in Criminology from Indiana University of Pennsylvania. His research focuses on elder abuse, crime policies, family violence, and community-based sanctions. He is the author of five books including *Crime and Elder Abuse: An Integrated Perspective*, *Crime in the Home Health Care Field*, and *Family Violence and Criminal Justice* and he has published more than 120 scholarly journal articles. His works have been reviewed in outlets such as the *New England Journal of Medicine*, *AgeVenture News*, and *The Gerontologist.* He is a recipient of numerous awards including the Southern Criminal Justice Association's Outstanding Educator Award and the Indiana University of Pennsylvania's Department of Criminology Distinguished Scholar Award.
Correspondence to: Allison T. Chappell, Department of Sociology and Criminal Justice, Old Dominion University, Norfolk, VA 23529, USA. E-mail: achappel@odu.edu

## Notes

1 "A cooperation rate is the proportion of all cases interviewed of all eligible units ever contacted" (American Association for Public Opinion Research, 2009, p. 37).
2 According to the 2000 US Census, the demographic characteristics of the region were 49.2% male, 62.1% white, 56.8% employed, and 27% with college degree. The median household income was $42,472 (20% make over 75,000), and the median age was 33.5 years (US Bureau of the Census, 2000).
3 Note that these items were included in sequential order on the survey, suggesting the respondents would recognize that "unsupervised youth" referred to "problematic" youth rather than kids simply hanging out on the streets.
4 One hundred and forty-two respondents did not respond to this question.
5 The correlation between physical and social disorder was 0.69 and collinearity diagnostics indicate that multicollinearity is not a problem (i.e., tolerances > 0.40 and variance inflation factors < 2.5 which is well within the acceptable range) (see Allison, 1999).

## References


Allison, P. (1999). *Multiple regression: A primer.* Thousand Oaks, CA: Pine Forge Press.

American Association for Public Opinion Research. (2009). *Standard definitions: Final dispositions of case codes and outcome rates for surveys* (6th ed.). Deerfield, IL: AAPOR.

Argyle, M. (2001). *The psychology of happiness.* London: Routledge.

Ball, R., & Chernova, K. (2008). Absolute income, relative income, and happiness. *Social Indicators Research, 88*(3), 497–529.

Bardasi, E., & Francesconi, M. (2004). The impact of atypical employment on individual wellbeing: Evidence from a panel of British workers. *Social Science and Medicine, 58*(9), 1671–1688.

Bennett, T. (1991). The effectiveness of a police-initiated fear-reducing strategy. *British Journal of Criminology, 31*(1), 1–14.

Benz, M., & Frey, B. S. (2004). Being independent raises happiness at work. *Swedish Economic Policy Review, 11,* 95–134.

Blanchflower, D. G. (2000). Self-employment in OECD countries. *Labour Economics, 7*(5), 471–505.

Blanchflower, D. G., & Oswald, A. J. (1998). What makes an entrepreneur? *Journal of Labor Economics, 16*(1), 26–60.

Blanchflower, D. G., & Oswald, A. J. (2004). Well-being over time in Britain and the USA. *Journal of Public Economics, 88,* 1359–1386.

Blanchflower, D. G., & Oswald, A. J. (2005). Regional wages and the need for a better area cost adjustment. *Public Money & Management, 25*(2), 86–88.

Blane, D., Netuveli, G., & Montgomery, S. M. (2008). Quality of life, health and physiological status and change at older ages. *Social Science & Medicine, 66*(7), 1579–1587.

Bowling, A. (1996). The effects of illness on quality of life: Findings from a survey of households in Great Britain. *Journal of Epidemiological and Community Health, 50*, 149–155.

Bratton, W., & Knobler, P. (1998). *The turnaround: How America's top cop reversed the crime epidemic.* New York: Random House.

Button, D. B. (2008). Social disadvantage and family violence. *American Journal of Criminal Justice, 33*(1), 130–147.

Chaix, B. (2009). Geographic life environments and coronary heart disease: A literature review, theoretical contributions, methodological updates, and a research agenda. *Annual Review of Public Health, 30*, 81–105.

Charles, S. T., Reynolds, C. A., & Gatz, M. (2001). Age-related differences and change in positive and negative affect over 23 years. *Journal of Personality and Social Psychology, 80*(1), 136–151.

Christmann, K., & Rogerson, M. (2004). *Crime, fear of crime and quality of life: Identifying and responding to problems. New deal for communities* (Research Report 35). Sheffield: The National Evaluation Centre for Regional Economic and Social Research at Sheffield Hallam University.

Cleveland, M. J., Feinberg, M. E., & Greenberg, M. T. (2010). Protective families in high-and low-risk environments: Implications for adolescent substance use. *Journal of Youth and Adolescence, 39*(2), 114–126.

Cohen, D. A., Mason, K., Bedimo, A., Scribner, R., Basolo, V., & Farley, T. A. (2003). Neighborhood physical conditions and health. *American Journal of Public Health, 93*(3), 467–471.

Cordner, G. (1998). Problem-oriented policing vs. zero tolerance. In T. Shelley & A. Grant (Eds.), *Problem oriented policing* (pp. 303–329). Washington, DC: PERF.

Costa, J. J. (1984). *Abuse of the elderly.* Boston, MA: Lexington Books.

Costa, P. T., Zonderman, A. B., McCrae, R. R., Huntley, J. C., Locke, B. Z., & Barbano, H. E. (1987). Longitudinal analysis of psychological well-being in a national sample: Stability of mean levels. *Journal of Gerontology, 42*(1), 50–55.

Covington, J., & Taylor, R. B. (1991). Fear of crime in urban residential neighborhoods: Implications of between-and within-neighborhood sources for current models. *Sociological Quarterly, 32*(2), 231–249.

Davis, J. A. (1984). New money, an old man/lady and "two's company": Subjective welfare in the NORC General Social Surveys, 1972–1982. *Social Indicators Research, 15*, 319–350.

Diener, E. (1984). Subjective well-being. *Psychological Bulletin, 95*, 542–575.

Diener, E. (2009). *The science of well-being: The collected works of Ed Diener* (Social Indicators Research Series, Vol. 37). New York: Springer.

Diener, E., Suh, E. M., Lucas, R. E., & Smith, H. L. (1999). Subjective well-being: Three decades of progress. *Psychological Bulletin, 125*, 276–302.

Doland, P., & White, M. P. (2006). Dynamic well-being: Connecting indicators of what people anticipate with indicators of what they experience. *Social Indicators Research, 75*, 303–333.

Dorn, D., Fischer, J. A., Kirchgassner, G., & Sousa-Poza, A. (2007). Is it culture of democracy? The impact of democracy, and culture on happiness. *Social Indicators Research, 82*, 505–526.

Easterlin, R. A. (2001). Income and happiness: Towards a unified theory. *Economic Journal, 111*, 465–484.

Fahey, T., & Smyth, E. (2004). Do subjective indicators measure welfare? Evidence from 33 European societies. *European Societies, 6*, 5–27.

Ferrer-i-Carbonell, A., & Gowdy, J. M. (2007). Environmental degradation and happiness. *Ecological Economics, 6*, 509–516.

Frey, B. S., & Stutzer, A. (2000). Happiness, economy and institutions. *Economic Journal, 110*, 918–938.

Garafolo, J., & Laub, J. (1978). Fear of crime: Broadening our perspective. *Victimology, 3*(3/4), 242–253.

Gault, M., & Silver, E. (2008). Spuriousness or mediation? Broken windows according to Sampson and Raudenbush (1999). *Journal of Criminal Justice, 36*, 240–243.

Geis, K. J., & Ross, C. E. (1998). A new look at urban alienation: The effect of neighborhood disorder on perceived powerlessness. *Social Psychology Quarterly, 61*(3), 232–246.

Green, L. (1995). Cleaning up drug hot spots in Oakland, California: The displacement and diffusion effects. *Justice Quarterly, 12*, 737–754.

Green, L. (1996). *Policing places with drug problems* (Drugs, Health, and Social Policy Series, Vol. 2). Thousand Oaks, CA: Sage.

Green, L. M., Price, J. F., & Roehl, J. (2000). Civil remedies and drug control: A randomized field trial in Oakland, CA. *Evaluation Review*, 24, 212–241.

Hale, D. C. (1988). Fear of crime and quality of life: A test of Garofolo and Laub's model. *Criminal Justice Review, 13*(1), 13–19.

Harcourt, B. E. (1998). Reflecting on the subject: A critique of the social influence conception of deterrence, the broken windows theory, and order-maintenance policing New York style. *Michigan Law Review, 97*(2), 292–389.

Helliwell, J. F., & Putnam, R. (2004). The social context of well-being. *Philosophical Transactions of the Royal Society London, 359*, 1435–1446.

Hill, T. D., & Angel, R. J. (2005). Neighborhood disorder, psychological distress, and heavy drinking. *Social Science and Medicine, 61*(5), 965–975.

Hill, T. D., Ross, C. E., & Angel, R. J. (2005). Neighborhood disorder, psychophysiological distress, and health. *Journal of Health and Social Behavior, 46*, 170–186.

Hinkle, J. C., & Weisburd, D. (2008). The irony of broken windows policing: A micro-place study of the relationship between disorder, focused police crackdowns and fear of crime. *Journal of Criminal Justice, 36*(6), 503–512.

Hughes, M., & Thomas, M. E. (1998). The continuing significance of race revisited: A study of race, class, and quality of life in America, 1972 to 1996. *American Sociological Review, 63*, 785–795.

Kahn, E. B., Ramsev, L. T., Brownson, R. C., Heath, G. W., Howze, E. H., Powell, K. E., …, Task Force on Community Preventive Services (2002). The effectiveness of interventions to increase physical activity: A systematic review. *American Journal of Preventive Medicine, 4*(S1), 73–107.

Katz, C. M., Webb, V. J., & Schaefer, D. R. (2001). An assessment of the impact of quality-of-life policing on crime and disorder. *Justice Quarterly, 18*(4), 825–876.

Kelling, G. L. (1981). *The Newark foot patrol experiment.* Washington, DC: Police Foundation.

Kelling, G. (1987). Acquiring a taste for order: The community and police. *Crime & Delinquency, 33*(1), 90–102.

Kelling, G. L., & Coles, C. M. (1996). *Fixing broken windows: Restoring order and reducing crime in our communities.* New York: Free Press.

Kelling, G. L., & Sousa, W. H. (2001). *Do police matter? An analysis of New York city's police reforms.* New York: Manhattan Institute for Policy Research.

King, A. C., Castro, C., Wilcox, S., Eyler, A. A., Sallis, J. F., & Brownson, R. C. (2000). Personal and environmental factors associated with physical inactivity among different racial-ethnic groups of US middle-aged and older-aged women. *Health Psychology, 19,* 354–364.

Latkin, C. A., & Curry, A. D. (2003). Stressful neighborhoods and depression: A prospective study of the impact of neighborhood disorder. *Journal of Health and Social Behavior, 44,* 34–44.

Latkin, C. A., Curry, A. D., Hua, W., & Davey, M. A. (2007). Direct and indirect associations of neighborhood disorder with drug use and high-risk sexual partners. *American Journal of Preventive Medicine, 32*(6S), S234–S241.

Layard, R. (2005). *Happiness: Lessons from a new science.* New York: Penguin Books.

Lelkes, O. (2006). Knowing what is good for you: Empirical analysis of personal preferences and the "objective good." *Journal of Socio-Economics, 35*(2), 285–307.

Lu, L. (1995). The relationship between subjective well-being and psychosocial variables in Taiwan. *Journal of Social Psychology, 135,* 351–357.

Lucas, R. E., & Dyrenforth, P. S. (2006). Does the existence of social relationships matter for subjective well-being? In K. Vohs & E. Finkel (Eds.), *Self and relationships: Connecting intrapersonal and interpersonal processes* (pp. 254–273). New York: Guilford Press.

Markowitz, F. E., Bellair, P. E., Liska, A. E., & Liu, J. (2001). Extending social disorganization theory: Modeling the relationships between cohesion, disorder, and fear. *Criminology, 39*(2), 293–319.

Mazerolle, L., Kadleck, C., & Roehl, J. (1998). Controlling drug and disorder problems: The role of place managers. *Criminology, 36,* 371–403.

McCarty, C., House, M., Harman, J., & Richards, S. (2006). Effort in phone survey response rates. *Field Methods, 18,* 172–188.

Messner, S. F., Galea, S., Tardiff, K. J., Tracy, M., Bucciarelli, A., Piper, T. M., …, Vlahov, D. (2007). Policing, drugs, and the homicide decline in New York City in the 1990s. *Criminology, 45*(2), 385–414.

Michalos, A. C. (2004). Social indicators research and health-related quality of life research. *Social Indicators Research, 65*(1), 27–72.

Michalos, A. C., & Zumbo, B. D. (2000). Criminal victimization and the quality of life. *Social Indicators Research, 50*(3), 245–295.

Michalos, A. C., Zumbo, B. D., & Hubley, A. (2000). Health and the quality of life. *Social Indicators Research, 51*(3), 245–286.

Miles, R. (2006). Neighborhood disorder and smoking: Findings of a European urban survey. *Social Science and Medicine, 63*(9), 2464–2475.

Miles, R. (2008). Neighborhood disorder, perceived safety, and readiness to encourage use of local playgrounds. *American Journal of Preventive Medicine, 34*(3), 275–281.

Molnar, B. E., Gortmaker, S. L., Bull, F. C., & Buka, S. L. (2004). Unsafe to play? Neighborhood disorder and lack of safety predict reduced physical activity among young urban children and adolescents. *American Journal of Health Promotion, 18*(5), 378–386.

Moore, M. H., & Trojanwicz, R. C. (1988). *Policing and the fear of crime.* Washington, DC: National Institute of Justice.

Myers, D. G. (2000). The funds, friends, and faith of happy people. *American Psychologist, 55*(1), 56–67.

Nettle, D. (2005). *Happiness: The science behind your smile.* Oxford: Oxford University Press.

Novak, K. J., Hartman, J. L., Holsinger, A. M., & Turner, M. G. (1999). The effects of aggressive policing of disorder on serious crime. *Policing: An International Journal of Police Strategies & Management, 22* (2), 171–194.

Oramas, M. N. (1994). *Drug enforcement in minority communities: The Minneapolis Police Department 1985–1990* (Case Studies Series #2). Washington, DC: Police Executive Research Forum.

Payne, B. K., Tewksbury, R., & Mustaine, E. E. (2010). Attitudes about rehabilitating sex offenders: Demographic, victimization, and community-level influences. *Journal of Criminal Justice, 38*(4), 580–588.

Pichler, F. (2006). Subjective quality of life of young Europeans. Feeling happy but who knows why? *Social Indicators Research, 75*(3), 419–444.

Plagnol, A. C., & Easterlin, R. A. (2008). Aspirations, attainments, and satisfaction: Life cycle differences between American women and men. *Journal of Happiness Studies, 9*(4), 601–619.

Putnam, R. D. (2000). *Bowling alone: The collapse and revival of American community.* New York: Simon & Schuster.

Rodgers, W. (1982). Trends in reported happiness within demographically defined subgroups, 1957–78. *Social Forces, 60*, 826–842.

Ross, C. E. (2000). Neighborhood disadvantage and adult depression. *Journal of Health and Social Behavior, 41*, 177–187.

Sallis, J. F., & Owen, N. (1996). *Ecological models.* San Francisco: Jossey-Bass.

Sampson, R. J., & Raudenbush, S. W. (1999). Systematic social observation of public spaces: A new look at disorder in urban neighborhoods. *American Journal of Sociology, 105*(3), 603–651.

Seligman, M. E. P. (2002). *Authentic happiness.* New York: The Free Press.

SF-8™ Health Survey (2008). Retrieved from http://www.sf-36.org/tools/sf8.shtml.

Sherman, L. W. (1990). Police crackdowns: Initial and residual deterrence. *Crime and Justice, 12*, 1–48.

Shields, M. A., & Wheatley Price, S. (2005). Exploring the economic and social determinants of psychological well-being and perceived social support in England. *Journal of the Royal Statistical Society, 168*(3), 513–537.

Skogan, W. G. (1990). *Disorder and decline: Crime and the spiral of decay in American neighborhoods.* Berkeley, CA: University of California Press.

Skogan, W. G., & Maxfield, M. G. (1981). *Coping with crime: Individual and neighborhood reactions.* Beverly Hills, CA: Sage.

Sousa, W. H., & Kelling, G. L. (2006). Of "broken windows," criminology, and criminal justice. In D. Weisburd & A. Braga (Eds.), *Police innovation: Contrasting perspectives* (pp. 77–97). Cambridge: Cambridge University Press.

Taylor, R. B. (2001). *Breaking away from broken windows—Baltimore neighborhoods and the nationwide fight against crime, grime, fear, and decline*. Boulder, CO: Westview Press.

Thacher, D. (2004). Order maintenance reconsidered: Moving beyond strong causal reasoning. *Journal of Criminal Law and Criminology, 94*(2), 381–414.

US Bureau of the Census (2000). *Census 2000*. Washington, DC: US Bureau of the Census.

Wei, E., Hipwell, A., Pardini, D., Beyers, J. M., & Loeber, R. (2005). Block observations of neighbourhood physical disorder are associated with neighbourhood crime, firearm injuries and deaths, and teen births. *Journal of Epidemiology and Community Health, 59*, 904–908.

Weisburd, D., & Braga, A. A. (Eds.). (2006). *Police innovation: Contrasting perspectives*. Cambridge: Cambridge University Press.

Wilson, J. Q., & Kelling, G. L. (1982). Broken windows. *Atlantic Monthly, 249* (3), 29–38.

Wilson, N., Syme, S. L., Boyce, T., Battistich, V. A., & Selvin, S. (2005). Adolescent alcohol, tobacco, and marijuana use: The influence of neighborhood disorder and hope. *American Journal of Health Promotion, 20*(1), 11–19.

Xu, Y., Fiedler, M. L., & Flaming, K. H. (2005). Discovering the impact of community policing: The broken window's thesis, collective efficacy, and citizens' judgment. *Journal of Research in Crime and Delinquency, 42*(2), 147–186.

Yang, Y. (2008). Social inequalities in happiness in the United States, 1972–2004: An age-period-cohort analysis. *American Sociological Review, 73*(2), 204–226.

Yen, I. H., Yelin, E. H., Katz, P., Eisner, M. D., & Blanc, P. D. (2006). Perceived neighborhood problems and quality of life, physical functioning, and depressive symptoms among adults with asthma. *American Journal of Public Health, 96*(5), 873–879.

Selected Reading

# BUILD TO SUSTAIN

## Collaborative Partnerships Between University Researchers and Criminal Justice Practitioners

*Danielle S. Rudes[1], Jill Viglione, Jennifer Lerch, Courtney Porter, and Faye S. Taxman*

## INTRODUCTION

It is paradoxical that two systems that greatly benefit from sustainable, collaborative partnerships often encounter obstacles finding and maintaining a working relationship. While criminal justice and criminology research faculty working within universities seek answers to questions about social and/or organizational phenomena, criminal justice practitioners often seek answers about which programs or practices to alter, implement or terminate to get the best results at the lowest cost. Yet, a legacy built upon distrust, ineffective communication, and the slow speed of science and ineffective communication (Bolton & Stolcis, 2003; Lane, Turner, & Flores, 2004) often leaves both researchers and practitioners feeling alone in their respective corners. Bridging the gap between these two disparate groups requires solid partnerships built on access, agreement, goal setting, feedback, and relationship maintenance. When these components coalesce, each group benefits from a durable partnership and can achieve better outcomes. A researcher–practitioner partnership is a challenging and complex process requiring careful attention to detail and an endless supply of energy and determination.

Considering what researchers and practitioners want and/or need is only part of the equation. Partnerships are often part of the broader sociopolitical spectrum as well. When President Barack Obama calls for greater attention to evidence-based practices, transparency, and accountability, he is signaling the need for researcher– practitioner relationships to achieve these goals. Likewise, and perhaps in turn, the National Institutes of Justice and Health look favorably upon researcher–practitioner partnerships – as implied in their continued funding of researcher–practitioner grants – indicating the inherent value in these relationships and the legitimacy the external environment gives these collaborations.

In this paper, we highlight some of the many successful researcher–practitioner partnerships our research team at the Center for Advancing Correctional Excellence (ACE!) has with criminal justice agencies. We detail four specific partnerships with federal, state, and county criminal justice organizations spanning from probation and parole to problem-solving courts. While some follow a grant cycle, one of our partnerships spans over two decades, offering key insight into the development and nurture of these mutually beneficial – if at times perplexing – collaborations. To open this world to readers, we first review prior literature on researcher–practitioner partnerships. Then, we provide a five-pronged framework defining research– practitioner partnerships complete with project-specific examples. Finally, we offer some conclusions about the collaborative benefits of a researcher–practitioner team approach.

## RESEARCH–PRACTITIONER PARTNERSHIPS IN THE LITERATURE

A current theme in the literature suggests that universities should 'engage' in research 'of consequence.' That is, universities should invest in improving the quality of life and address some social or natural problems that can make a difference and improve outcomes. The emergent interest is in how collaborations and partnerships between community service agencies, universities, and governmental agencies can address social and other problems in thoughtful ways. Collaboration is a decision-making process between two or more organizations (Davey & Ivery, 2009) usually uniting separate groups to achieve a mutual goal (Reilly, 2001). These relationships occur for various reasons including shared vision (Wolff, 2001), opportunity (e.g. attending conferences or meetings, agencies seeking volunteers), adversity or crises (e.g. a natural disaster or mandate) (Bringle & Hatcher, 2002; Reilly, 2001), and shared desire to address a social problem (Taxman, Henderson, Young, & Farrell, 2012; Young, Farrell, & Taxman, 2012). Many funding opportunities from both federal and private organizations require interdisciplinary research (e.g. criminal justice and psychology) combined with collaborative partnerships (Allen-Meares, 2008; Mizrahi & Rosenthal, 2001) such as those between universities and governmental agencies. Collaborative relationships between practitioners and researchers mobilize agencies; expand networks (Davey & Ivery, 2009); enhance capacity building; respond to community problems; create more community-driven initiatives (Reilly, 2001); and produce research that is practical for the field (Bell et al., 2004).

Differences between universities and community/government organizations make these types of partnerships complex (Bringle & Hatcher, 2002). Many practitioners harbor an 'Ivory Tower' mentality toward research universities believing that researchers are too theoretical and cannot comprehend what work is like 'on the ground.' Likewise, researchers have difficulty believing organizations grasp the beneficial impact of involvement in research and many times move forward in research studies without complete participation from community/government organizations. This cycle of mistrust can hinder communication between partners and impact the shared vision strived for through these partnerships. However, these types of partnerships are critical for successfully translating research to practice (Elder et al., 2013). Incorporating agency or organizational input from the beginning of a research project ensures that outcomes are realistic for and useable to both researchers and practitioners in ways that may not be available without collaboration. Successful collaborations between universities and organizational partners help create research grounded in best practice where both partners invest in quality outcomes (Bell et al., 2004). Collaborations and partnerships also yield insight into issues and challenges facing those in the field (Jaffe, Berman, & MacQuarrie, 2011) leading to opportunities for study (Fawcett et al., 1995) and new questions for research and the field.

## Strategies to Create Successful Collaborations and Partnerships

Prior research identifies many strategies and components necessary for creating and sustaining successful collaborations. A few strategies leading to successful collaborations include open, frequent, on-going communication (Elder et al., 2013; Johnson, Zorn, Yung Tam, Lamontagne, & Johnson, 2003), partner-ready leadership (Austin et al., 1999; Johnson et al., 2003; Minkler, Vasquez, Tajik, & Peterson, 2008), and a clear research purpose or agenda (Davey & Ivery, 2009). During a collaborative partnership with the local community, the San Diego Prevention Research Center found that open communication lines lead to quality input and feedback from all partners (Elder et al., 2013). Citing a shared purpose or vision as a necessity, Minkler and colleagues (2008) found a sense of solidarity and shared values led to an enhanced commitment among the partners studied. Along with a shared vision, researchers identified respect and equal representation among partners (Davey & Ivery, 2009; Kent, 2005) as adding to the success of collaborations. Looking at four case studies, researchers found that a high level of mutual respect characterized each partnership (Minkler et al., 2008).

A number of prior research studies express the importance of strong leadership in creating collaborative partnerships. Each of the four partnerships studied by Minkler and colleagues (2008) included a community partner recognized as a leader in their field. Participants of the study credited the executive directors of the organizations as playing a substantial role in furthering the partnerships. Their ability to mobilize and develop support in the community enabled the creation of sustainable partnerships. Additionally, Kent (2005) cites a need for evaluation to ensure continued improvement within the collaboration and research. To that end, Reilly (2001) also argues that a successful collaboration requires buy-in from those in power. Supportive university leadership and commitment to respond to the emerging needs in the field facilitate ongoing community/research partnerships (Jaffe et al., 2011).

The creation of collaborative partnerships is only the first step, as successful collaborations require durable or sustainable relationships (Reilly, 2001). This includes a strong initial foundation that can adjust to changing conditions within communities such as social, political, or economic pressures. For example, collaborations created on a framework that includes frequent communication and shared visions are more likely to withstand challenges such as economic hardships found in decreased funding streams. Partnerships that can weather challenges and external pressures are more likely to accomplish shared goals (Reilly, 2001).

## Strategies to Sustain Collaborations and Partnerships

The process of creating collaborations and partnerships should focus on how to sustain the partnerships. In forming partnerships and collaborations, memorandums of understanding (MOUs) help maintain and solidify long-term relationships among partners (Elder et al., 2013). MOUs include critical components that allow partnerships to grow and flourish. Such components include developing projects that meet both researcher and partner agency needs, responding to requests of technical assistance, providing capacity-building opportunities, sharing funding opportunities, collaborating on dissemination activities including conference presentation and other publications, advocating on behalf of community partners and participating in regular community events and meetings (Elder et al., 2013).

Collaborative efforts employ several strategies to perpetuate the partnerships. Monthly meetings, monthly newsletters, annual reports celebrating successes, task forces to address specific issues, and evaluations promote longevity (Wolff, 2001). Monthly organizational meetings and newsletters focusing on innovative interventions by affiliates, emerging research, and disseminating information help preserve collaborative partnerships (Busch-Armendariz, Johnson, Buel, & Lungwitz, 2001).

## Benefits of Collaborations and Partnerships

Participants face many benefits after establishing collaborations/partnerships. Collaborations between different organizations provide a unique combination of perspectives (Busch-Armendariz et al., 2001) that stem from different disciplines (e.g. education, law, and criminal justice) to guide research and policy implementation. Having different perspectives at the table enables the collaborative group to look at research questions from different angles and potentially leads to additional research questions.

Working with community partners lessens the isolation sometimes felt among researchers (Bell et al., 2004) by connecting the research to larger goals and policy. Many researchers work on projects alone or with select colleagues with similar interests. Researchers focusing solely on the academic aspects of research make it difficult for practitioners to use the findings in meaningful ways. Collaborating with community partners helps connect academic research to larger, real-world issues. Other benefits include increasing the ability to gain input from a broad range of people with diverse economic, experiential and employment backgrounds (Bell et al., 2004; Fawcett et al., 1995), and utilizing diverse expertise and resources (Bickel & Hattrup, 1995; Israel, Schulz, Parker, & Becker, 2001). Diversity among individuals involved in collaboration allows members to play to their strengths and provide knowledge that others may lack. In academic and community partner collaborations, academics often have knowledge of research methods and the subject matter. Likewise, community partners possess intrinsic knowledge of the community context and recognize nuances within their organization that may impact the research partnership if not addressed.

From the organizational partners' perspective, collaborating with university researchers increases an agency's ability to identify additional resources and funding (Bell et al., 2004; Rollison et al., 2013), obtain technical assistance, and increase staff knowledge (Bickel & Hattrup, 1995; Reed & Collins, 1994). Each of these can improve partners' position and likelihood for obtaining future funding. Organizations trying something new as part of a research collaborative also benefit from receiving technical assistance from their research partners that they would not otherwise receive. Finally, participating in new research on innovative programming sets organizations apart creating exemplars or leaders in their respective fields.

From the university perspective, collaborating with community partners enhances the research design (Harper & Salina, 2000), process (Reed & Collins, 1994) and relevance and use of research data (Israel et al., 2001). Incorporating local knowledge into the research design and process improves the quality and validity of the research (Allen-Meares, 2008; Israel et al., 2001). Additionally, universities and community partnerships assist students with translating knowledge into real-world practice (Allen-Meares, 2008). Partnering with organizations brings a relevance to the field that might not otherwise exist. When thinking about research design, process and data, working closely with organizations provides an understanding of the data as well as the context of where that data comes from. Additionally, researchers gain background knowledge of data processes that are unique to each organization.

Universities can also offer support to agencies willing to conduct research themselves as well as fund efforts of new and seasoned investigators by providing opportunities for graduate students to learn about research in practice. Research and activities developed in partnership with community and government organizations increases researchers' ability to overcome distrust from communities that historically have been the subjects of research (Israel et al., 2001).

## Challenges of Collaborations and Partnerships

Despite the benefits discussed above, participants in organizational partnerships report several challenges such as preventing misuse of research findings, using appropriate and non-offensive language, and influencing funders' perceptions of important research questions (Bell et al., 2004). Additional barriers that challenge partnerships include funding issues (Kent, 2005), the tendency to lose steam when the original vision is limited or gets lost along the way (Kent, 2005), lack of time (Bell et al., 2004; Ouellette, Briscoe, & Tyson, 2004), lack of support from upper management, lack of commitment to the collaboration, and lack of trust (Johnson et al., 2003).

Bell and colleagues (2004) found that in domestic violence (DV) collaborations challenges lie in preventing the misuse of research and using appropriate and non-offensive language. Specific to DV research, collaborators frequently struggle with framing questions to avoid victim blaming. Another issue is how to use language that does not offend other collaboration participants. Bell and colleagues (2004) found that crafting a message with the right context was difficult when developing collaborations as specific words have different meanings to academics and practitioners. Alternatively, Kent (2005) found funding issues as the largest challenge to successful collaborations. Many collaborative efforts require outside funding to jumpstart the initiative. This is an issue if there is no way to sustain the partnership once the original funding is gone. To combat this, many collaborations look for multiple sources of funding to lessen or eliminate relying on only one funding source.

Power imbalances within the research process create another challenge for collaborative partnerships (Bell et al., 2004; Harper & Salina, 2000; Israel et al., 2001). Power imbalances occur when researchers make decisions about what research questions to ask, how to ask those questions and how to interpret findings with little or no input from practitioners (Busch-Armendariz et al., 2001). It is difficult to create or sustain collaborations when these imbalances exist. However, identifying and overcoming this power imbalance is possible. Giving partners a voice in the research process and ensuring all benefit from findings is one way to lessen a power imbalance (Hamberger & Ambuel, 2000). Participants can share power by openly discussing individual research agendas throughout the collaborative process (Bell et al., 2004). Collaborative research agendas should be thoughtful, comprehensive, and include strong, active university-community, and practitioner alliances resulting in 'real dialogue, discourse and useable outcomes' (Busch-Armendariz et al., 2001, p. 1204). 'Successful campus-community partnerships must find ways to preserve the integrity of each partner and at the same time honor the purpose of the relationship and growth of each party' (Bringle & Hatcher, 2002, p. 513).

## Examples of Collaborative Efforts and Partnerships

To consider some of these findings in action, we discuss four collaborative projects from over two decades of these relationships between the authors at their affiliated research center, The Center for ACE! at George Mason University and local correctional agency partners in many US states and the federal government. These projects include: the Maryland Department of Public Safety and Correctional

Services (MDPSCS; previously the Maryland Division of Parole and Probation), the Motivational Assessment Program to Initiate Treatment (MAPIT), the VA-DOC, and Juvenile Justice.

Originating over 25 years ago, the MDPSCS collaboration focuses on improving outcomes in custody and community corrections using evidence-based practices (EBPs). ACE!'s work with this organization varies dependent on the nature of individual projects. For instance, the current, agency-funded work operates under an MOU. However, we have also conducted research funded through grants in partnership with the agency. The Virginia Department of Corrections (VA-DOC) and Juvenile Justice projects also aim to improve outcomes and processes throughout the agencies through the use of EBP's. MAPIT is a National Institute on Drug Abuse (NIDA) funded grant in which both Maryland and Texas partnered with ACE! and the University of North Texas Health Science Center to conduct study probationers. This study tests innovative tools aiming to improve probation processes through motivational interviewing. This project builds on the sustained and beneficial relationships that the researchers have with both Maryland and Texas to allow access to their targeted probation process. Juvenile Justice operates as a collaboration between ACE! and a local probation agency supervising juvenile and adult (family/ domestic violence) probationers.

Each of these four projects offers various challenges to sustaining these collaborations. A few of the most challenging obstacles these organizations face when developing sustained relationships include: (1) coping with staff attrition; (2) determining the appropriate stakeholders; and (3) locating and securing funding. Staff attrition, particularly of upper level decision-makers, makes sustaining a collaboration challenging for both the researcher and agency partner. With ACE!'s partnerships, we find that maintaining collaboration and support among most of the staff (if not all) at all levels is imperative since many of the criminal justice agencies recruit upper management directly from front line staff ranks. When front line staff experience firsthand a positive, working collaboration between their agency and researchers, this relationship can be sustained for years to come. Reaching out to all staff ensures that the collaborative relationship sustains with anyone within the organization so that staff attrition does not damage continuing working relationships too severely.

ACE! and their collaborating organizations often struggle with determining which appropriate stakeholders to include at various stages of a project. At times individuals or stakeholders enter into project discussions too early or too late or with antithetical goals. This can derail the project and potentially the partnership overall. Additionally, the lack of funding or resources often places a strain on ACE! partnerships. At different points in ACE!'s extensive years of work with MDPSCS, VA-DOC, and Juvenile Justice, limited funds caused work stoppage or inability to deliver products that put the collaborations in jeopardy. One way we try to overcome this obstacle is by regularly applying for grant funds jointly with partners to ensure project continuation even if the agency cannot provide the funds/ resources. This demonstrates both the commitment to continued work from both ACE! and these organizations as well as an understanding of the realities of the contextual environment within which these studies occur.

The previous examples of successful research/organizational collaborations illustrate elements of strategies required for successful collaborations including open, frequent, and on-going communication, leadership, and a clear research purpose or agenda. Research consistently demonstrates that collaborations succeed by following these strategies and working to overcome challenges such as power imbalances, lack of commitment, funding, and time.

# COMPONENTS OF GOOD PARTNERSHIPS

Given the consistent array of relational and temporal components of partnerships noted by prior research, we use the remainder of this article to provide case specific examples on five key facets of practitioner-researcher partnerships. These include: (1) access; (2) agreements; (3) goal setting; (4) feedback; and (5) relationship maintenance (see Figure 6.1).

## Access

For researchers housed within universities, gaining access to the target study population is the first step in developing and sustaining a collaborative relationship (Elder et al., 2013). This is often a slow process, focused on developing and maintaining relationships with specific individuals within the organization who possess

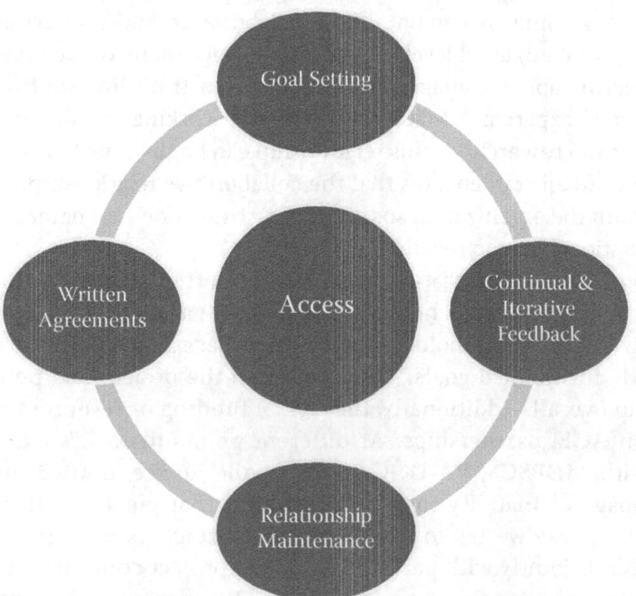


**Figure 6.1** Five main components of researcher–practitioner partnerships.

rich knowledge and understanding of the target research population (Elder et al., 2013). Gaining initial access generally occurs in one of two ways: (1) researchers seek out access to conduct research within an organization or (2) organizations seek out researchers to conduct research of interest. An established relationship often makes both methods of access more likely to occur and succeed. For many ACE! projects, including MDPSCS, VA-DOC, and Juvenile Justice, we begin by building on previously cultivated relationships with individuals within the organizations.

Part of access is not just having relationships that grant researchers access to populations or organizations of interest, but it is also about creating open entree for criminal justice staff to access researchers (Rudes, Lerch, & Taxman, 2012). A reoccurring theme throughout this manuscript is the importance of a mutually beneficial relationship. In the early stages of developing a relationship and gaining access to criminal justice agencies, it is critical that both parties participate in clearly defining the goals of the research project and see the value in forming the collaborative partnership (Reilly, 2001; Wolff, 2001). It is often useful for research and criminal justice staff to write down their goals for the research project. Working together to set expectations incorporates research project buy-in and ensures that both researchers and agency staff have similar expectations moving forward. Within ACE!'s collaborations, we accomplish access and building relationships through holding regular meetings with organizations to brainstorm research questions and topics of interest so our work will mean the most to their everyday operations. Such meetings lead to population access via addressing these questions/ topics, but also help build strong, sustainable relationships through relevant research.

Additionally, gaining access to one criminal justice agency may open other doors. Networking and developing a record of conducting strong research within criminal justice agencies lays a foundation to support the development of new relationships and often provides access to new organizational partners and settings (Minkler et al., 2008). If relationships do not currently exist, research staff can seek out 'gatekeepers' or those 'who patrol the boundaries of formal and private settings' and wield power in granting access to the organization (Morrill, Buller, Buller, & Larkey, 1999; 52). Gatekeepers vary depending on the organization, and may be a single individual or a group of individuals operating at any one (or multiple) level(s) within the organization. Identifying and building relationships with gatekeepers can assist in gaining access in otherwise inaccessible organizations. After gaining initial agency access, there are several areas researchers must address in order to develop and sustain relationships within the agency. This involves a variety of important components such as negotiation and agreement development, collaborative goal setting and planning, provision of continued feedback, and maintaining relationships.

## Negotiating Research Agreements

An essential part of any good partnership is a formal, written agreement in the form of a memorandum of understanding (MOU) (e.g. research agreement) between the agency and researcher (Elder et al., 2013; Fowler, 1982).

Whether the project is part of a federal research grant or directly funded by the agency, a MOU lays the groundwork for the collaboration. The MOU plays an essential role in outlining both parties' expectations regarding project implementation and project outputs. Research in various fields suggests several essential components of research agreements that are worthy of consideration when starting any project. A few of these include: (1) clearly outlined project scope; (2) extent of funding and resource commitment; (3) roles regarding implementation of the project; (4) expectations for products reported; and (5) expectations for publishing and use/sharing of information/data (Elder et al., 2013; Fowler, 1982). While not all of these components exist in every MOU, varying combinations of these should be included depending on the nature of the partnership.

Even within long-term partnerships or existing MOUs, each new project should begin with the development of a research agreement specific to the needs of that particular project (Fowler, 1982). Developing new research agreements begins with planning meetings where collaboration on the goals and needs of the research project occurs. These planning meetings provide an opportunity to work through ideas and expectations for the project before creating a formal MOU. Final research agreements always outline the scope of the project, reporting expectations from the researcher to the department, and resource requirements on both sides of the partnership, such as the space used or data provided. Outlining essential components allows for clear, tangible expectations from both sides of the partnership, while providing some clarity to the purpose of the research (Elder et al., 2013). An imperative part of these agreements is clearly defining expectations for both parties so that both receive benefits from the arrangement and will not have unmet expectations later.

For instance, our research agreements with MDPSCS clearly outline expectations and delivery of results as well as the expected data requirements. Similarly, in the Juvenile Justice project, a research agreement outlines the expectations and deliverables for both partners. However, as projects grow, so do opportunities and needs. In both cases, the collaborative teams added new research tasks and goals, but never revisited the research agreement to make formal changes in expectations. This creates challenges, as the agency partner expected deliverables not budgeted for by the research team. This approach also adds strain given possible misunderstandings or lack of clarity about new expectations set between the research partners. Revising the original research agreement to reflect updated expectations and deliverables is one way to avoid confusion and misunderstandings. Formally revising the agreement provides an opportunity for both partners to communicate regarding changes to the project scope.

## Collaborative Goal Setting and Planning

One method of developing and fostering mutually beneficial partnerships with criminal justice agencies is collaboration. Engaging criminal justice staff in the goal setting and planning phase of research projects is critical to foster buy-in and support for the study, as well as for learning from organizational experts about how implementation can best occur in their agency (Johnson et al., 2003; Reilly, 2001; Rogers, 2003). For example, when researchers first began MAPIT at ACE!, the goal was to be as minimally intrusive to normal probation processes as possible. Prior to the start of the project, researchers from both universities (George Mason University and University of North Texas Health Science Center) met with participating probation organizations to elicit feedback from probation staff on how best to implement the study. Even though the probation agencies were not able to give input into the actual design of the intervention, engaging in an open discussion prior to the start of a project increased support from staff. Additionally, information gained from these meetings informed research staff about important considerations when planning the implementation of MAPIT, such as when to recruit potential study participants during their existing probation intake process.

Another way researchers collaborate with criminal justice agencies is through providing knowledge and resources to practitioners regarding the current research evidence (Reilly, 2001). This helps researchers better meet agency needs and goals. For example, as part of the VA-DOC project, ACE! actively collaborated with correctional executives and probation leadership during their strategic planning process. Researchers attended all working group meetings over the course of a year to provide guidance on research evidence, sometimes leading meetings, and other times acting as a participant. Researchers were critical to this process, providing guidance and direction on issues important to the VA-DOC such as building organizational support for change and better implementing a standardized risk and needs assessment tool throughout the state. Additionally, researchers assisted the VA-DOC team members with thinking critically about the issues that concerned them such as creating overall culture shifts in the organization and ensuring support for that shift throughout the state. In collaboration with VA-DOC personnel, researchers also participated in developing one part of the actual strategic plan by serving on a committee devoted to the organizational development component. VA-DOC personnel valued the inclusion of researchers in the strategic planning process.

## Continued and Iterative Feedback

One of the most important ways researchers build relationships with non-academic organizations is through active participation in discussions and the provision of continuous and iterative feedback (Busch-Armendariz et al., 2001). The strategic planning process held by the VA-DOC is an excellent example as practitioners identified areas of concern and researchers provided ideas based on previous research to jumpstart the brainstorming process – all of which fed into the development of the strategic plan. This feedback and active participation of researchers in the planning process helped strengthen the partnership between VA-DOC and ACE! and led to the development of trust and mutual understanding regarding key concepts.

When implementing a research study within a criminal justice agency, it is critical to provide feedback regarding study progress (Busch-Armendariz et al., 2001). Researchers must determine the appropriate level of feedback depending on their specific study and needs of the criminal justice agency and staff. For all four ACE! studies discussed, researchers provide regular status updates. This feedback varies in terms of frequency and depth. For MDPSCS, researchers provide in-depth, written monthly reports documenting the study's progress. On the MAPIT project, funded by NIDA, researchers provide regular updates about study progress to agency leaders who have been crucial to implementing the study (e.g. providing space to conduct the study and recruiting participants). In addition, on MAPIT, researchers requested key agency staff members to act as members of the Data Safety Management Board (DSMB) so that an agency staff member receives regular updates on study flow semi-annually. The DSMB consists of individuals external to the research study who review the study's progress on aspects such as participant risks and recruitment progress. These individuals raise concerns and/or make suggestions of improvement to the research team regarding the study. A DSMB is only one example out of many (e.g. proposal writing, reviewing papers, co-presenting study experiences and findings) of how researchers can provide feedback to the organization (Elder et al., 2013; Israel et al., 2001). Feedback within the Juvenile Justice project occurs at bi-monthly meetings of the research and agency executive teams and periodic findings rollouts and trainings with select agency staff. The ACE! team also contributes a monthly column to the agency's internal newsletter that reports new information from academe and study finding highlights.

In the MDPSCS, VA-DOC, and Juvenile Justice projects ACE! collects staff data (e.g. organizational surveys, interviews). A key component of these surveys is to provide clear and concise summary reports of findings. These summaries allow staff to understand important issues in their organization and see how surveys can provide meaningful information for them and their organization. These reports are integral for obtaining staff support to conduct further research and building upon working relationships with organizational partners (Wolff, 2001). Whenever possible, all levels of staff should have access to the survey results so they can see the usefulness of research. For example, as part of the Juvenile Justice project, researchers provided a full survey report to agency staff who used the results in staff trainings and in development of their own strategic plan. The report provides important data for the agency to build future initiatives on and demonstrates the value of research. Recent survey results found a discrepancy between the perception of available services for clients and the number of referrals actually made to those services. Staff reported believing services for clients less available than the number of referrals made to those services. This finding interests agency partners, who – as a result – plan further examination of this discrepancy within their agency.

## Relationship Maintenance

Through continuous, active participation and provision of feedback, often researchers' ultimate goal is to maintain an ongoing relationship with partner organizations. Ideally, this should be a mutual relationship, where researchers approach new ideas with criminal justice partners and criminal justice partners come to researchers with ideas or questions. Beyond initiating new projects, continuing partnerships are sustainable through addressing such questions as: *What should we do next? How has this research benefited us as a partnership so far?* or *What does the agency need?* A give-and-take relationship is critical for maintaining a research–organization relationship as it allows both parties to see and experience mutual collaboration benefits (Allen-Meares, 2008; Minkler et al., 2008). This type of maintenance can take many forms from answering a quick question over the telephone to presenting research to partners or vice versa. For example, many of ACE!'s organizational partners inquire about research to support ideas or practices in which they are interested. Several of our organizational partners are interested in writing and submitting grants and want our expertise on current research or in preparing grant applications. This process affords researchers active engagement with organizational partners in areas of research interesting to them. This also provides opportunities for graduate students to gain important skills and experience in grant writing, while helping partners.

A critical component of maintaining relationships with organizations is to continue to provide assistance, even after funding ends. ACE! participates in a number of projects and initiatives that are not funded. Agreeing to these projects displays a willingness to be of assistance to and a commitment to the field directly and provides the added benefit of providing opportunities for graduate students to become directly involved with criminal justice agencies. Additionally, participation in non-funded initiatives highlights the research capabilities and strengths of the research center and staff. Another way of maintaining relationships is simply to remain in touch with contacts at collaborating agencies (Minkler et al., 2008). This may involve occasional emails with research updates or articles that might interest the organization or phone calls to discuss any new or upcoming research initiatives. Although it might not seem like much, continuing this type of contact with past or current partners keeps the window of opportunity open for future research collaborations. While potentially challenging at times, continued involvement in discussing research and showing an interest maintains relationships and provides access to organizations that might not otherwise exist.

# DISCUSSION AND CONCLUSION

Forming a mutually beneficial relationship is ideal and essential for building long-lasting partnerships. Organizations and staff members should never feel like researchers are using them to conduct research only with no benefit to the agency.

Emphasis on building and maintaining solid and positive relationships can provide collateral benefits that make extra hours spent grant writing, presenting, or researching previous studies for organizational partners well worth the effort. For example, participation in the VA-DOC strategic planning process led to many additional activities and research projects. VA-DOC management personnel asked researchers to help write and develop a grant, which included several graduate students' participation. By combining resources and interests, at least two funded research projects within the VA-DOC and one graduate student dissertation project resulted from this partnership. In a time when resources are scarce, it is critical for organizations and researchers to look for opportunities to work together and combine resources and building new research projects out of existing projects is a an excellent example of how to do so. For instance, as a direct result of relationships formed with various criminal justice agencies, four additional graduate students' dissertations are currently in progress. With this, agencies and students receive the benefits of developed partnerships. The formation and maintenance of relationships over time also help to build trust between researchers and organizations. This trust is critical in testing out new and innovative projects like MAPIT, and developing interesting ideas for future research that works to improve policy and practice outcomes to benefit criminal justice organizations, their clients, and communities.

## NOTES ON CONTRIBUTORS

Danielle S. Rudes is an associate professor of Criminology, Law, and Society and the deputy director of the Center for Advancing Correctional Excellence at George Mason University. Her research focuses on how middle managers and street-level workers within social control organizations understand, negotiate, and at times, resist change. Dr. Rudes' publications include work in the journals Law & Policy, Journal of Crime & Justice, and Justice Quarterly.

Jill Viglione is a PhD candidate in the Criminology, Law, and Society program and a research assistant at the Center for Advancing Correctional Excellence at George Mason University. Her areas of research include evidence-based practice implementation, organizational change, and decision-making within correctional settings. Publications include articles in Criminal Justice & Behavior and Victims & Offenders.

Jennifer Lerch is a doctoral student in the Criminology, Law, and Society program and a research assistant at the Center for Advancing Correctional Excellence at George Mason University. Her published work includes articles in the Journal of Offender Rehabilitation.

Courtney Porter is a doctoral student in the Criminology, Law, and Society program at George Mason University and research analyst at the Fairfax County Juvenile & Domestic Relations District Court. Her published work includes work in the journal Federal Probation.

Faye S. Taxman is a university professor in the Criminology, Law, and Society department and director of the Advancing Correctional Excellence Center at George Mason University. She is recognized for her work in the development of the seamless systems of care models that link the criminal justice with other service delivery systems as well as re-engineering probation and parole supervision services. Her publications include a book with Dr. Steven Belenko titled Implementing evidence-based practices in community corrections and addiction treatment (2011), many research articles and editorship at the journal Health & Justice.

## Note

1 Corresponding author. Email: drudes@gmu.edu.

## References

Allen-Meares, P. (2008). Schools of social work contribution to community partnerships: The renewal of the social compact in higher education. *Journal of Human Behavior in the Social Environment, 18*, 79–100.

Austin, M. J., Martin, M., Carnochan, S., Goldberg, S., Berrick, J. D., Weiss, B., & Kelly, J. (1999). Building a comprehensive agency-university partnership. *Journal of Community Practice, 6*, 89–106.

Bell, H., Busch, N. B., Heffron, L. C., White, B., Angelelli, M. J., & Rivaux, S. (2004). Balancing power through community building: Setting the research agenda on violence against women. *Affilia, 19*, 404–417.

Bickel, W. E., & Hattrup, R. A. (1995). Teachers and researchers in collaboration: Reflections on the process. *American Educational Research Journal, 32*, 35–62.

Bolton, M. J., & Stolcis, G. B. (2003). Ties that do not bind: Mustings on the specious relevance of academic research. *Public Administration Review, 63*, 626–630.

Bringle, R. G., & Hatcher, J. A. (2002). Campus-community partnerships: The terms of engagement. *Journal of Social Issues, 58*, 503–516.

Busch-Armendariz, N. B., Johnson, R. J., Buel, S., & Lungwitz, J. (2001). Building community partnerships to end interpersonal violence: A collaboration of the schools of social work, law and nursing. *Violence Against Women, 17*, 1194–1206.

Davey, T. L., & Ivery, J. M. (2009). Using organizational collaboration and community partnerships to transition families from homelessness to home ownership: The homebuy5 program. *Journal of Prevention and Intervention in the Community, 37*, 155–165.

Elder, J. P., Ayala, G. X., Arredondo, E. M., Talavera, G. A., McKenzie, T. L., Hoffman, L., ... Patrick, K. (2013). Community health partnerships for chronic disease prevention among Latinos: The San Diego prevention research center. *Journal of Primary Prevention, 34*, 17–19.

Fawcett, S. B., Paine-Andrews, A., Francisco, V. T., Schultz, J. A., Richter, K. P., Lewis, R. K., … Lopez, C. M. (1995). Using empowerment theory in collaborative partnerships for community health and development. *American Journal of Community Psychology, 23,* 677–697.

Fowler, D. R. (1982). University-industry research relationships: The research agreement. *Journal of College and University Law, 9,* 515–532.

Hamberger, L. K., & Ambuel, B. (2000). Community collaboration to develop research programs in partner violence. *Journal of Aggression, Maltreatment & Trauma, 4,* 239–272.

Harper, G. W., & Salina, D. D. (2000). Building collaborative partnerships to improve community-based HIV prevention research. *Journal of Prevention & Intervention in the Community, 19*(1), 1–20.

Israel, B. A., Schulz, A. J., Parker, E. A., & Becker, A. B. (2001). Community-based participatory research: Policy recommendations for promoting a partnership approach in health research. *Education for Health, 14,* 182–197.

Jaffe, P. G., Berman, H., & MacQuarrie, B. (2011). A Canadian model for building university and community partnerships: Centre for research and education on violence against women and children. *Violence Against Women, 17,* 1159–1175.

Johnson, L. J., Zorn, D., Yung Tam, B. K., Lamontagne, M., & Johnson, S. A. (2003). Stakeholders' views of factors that impact successful interagency collaboration. *Exceptional Children, 69,* 195–209.

Kent, J. C. (2005). Getting the best of both worlds: Making partnerships between court and community ADR programs exemplary. *Conflict Resolution Quarterly, 23,* 71–85.

Lane, J., Turner, S., & Flores, C. (2004). Researcher-practitioner collaborations in community corrections: overcoming hurdles for successful partnerships. *Criminal Justice Review, 29,* 97–114.

Minkler, M., Vasquez, V. B., Tajik, M., & Peterson, D. (2008). Promoting environmental justice through community-based participatory research: The role of community and partnership capacity. *Health Education Behavior, 35,* 119–137.

Mizrahi, T., & Rosenthal, B. B. (2001). Complexities of coalition building: Leaders' successes, strategies, struggles, and solutions. *Social Work, 46,* 63–78.

Morrill, C., Buller, D. B., Buller, M. K., & Larkey, L. L. (1999). Toward an organizational perspective on identifying and managing formal gatekeepers. *Qualitative Sociology, 22,* 51–72.

Ouellette, P. M., Briscoe, R., & Tyson, C. (2004). Parent–school and community partnerships in children's mental health: Networking challenges, dilemmas and solutions. *Journal of Child and Family Studies, 13,* 295–308.

Reed, G. M., & Collins, B. E. (1994). Mental health research and service delivery: A three communities model. *Psychosocial Rehabilitation Journal, 17,* 69–81.

Reilly, T. (2001). Collaboration in action. *Administration in Social Work, 25,* 53–74.

Rogers, E. (2003). *Diffusion of Innovations* (5th ed.). New York: Free Press.

Rollison, J., Banks, D., Martin, A. J., Owens, C., Thomas, N., Dressler, K. J., & Wells, M. (2013). Improving school-justice partnerships: Lessons learned from the safe school/safe health students initiative. *Family Court Review, 51,* 445–451.

Rudes, D. S., Lerch, J., & Taxman, F. S. (2012). Implementing a reentry framework at a correctional facility: Challenges to the culture. *Journal of Offender Rehabilitation, 50*, 467–491.

Taxman, F. S., Henderson, C., Young, D., & Farrell, J. (2012). The impact of training interventions on organizational readiness to support innovations in juvenile justice offices. *Administrative Policy of Mental Health*, 177–188.

Wolff, T. (2001). A practitioner's guide to successful coalitions. *American Journal of Community Psychology, 29*, 173–191.

Young, D. W., Farrell, J. L., & Taxman, F. S. (2012). Impacts of juvenile probation training modules on youth recidivism. *Justice Quarterly, 30*(6), 1–22.

# Part III

# Creating Justice

As we've discussed throughout the book, social justice demands that equal opportunities be afforded to all people. In reality, this demand is seldom met. From our perspective, this makes "second" chances an absolute necessity for the achievement of justice. (We put the word "second" in quotation marks because a society that falls short of social justice—like ours—may find itself providing *first* chances later in life for some than others.) A just system must provide people with opportunities to get what they need to survive and thrive; some individuals may have had chances for this before becoming involved in the CJS, while others may never have had these opportunities. The lives of system-involved individuals are often characterized by an interconnected series of disadvantages and a dearth of opportunities. Thus, the question that many graduating CJC students ask themselves is "How can we break that cycle and allow for second chances?" The answer is a simple one that belies a deceptively complicated task: by transforming social institutions so that they function in ways that combat and eliminate inequality rather than perpetuating it.

This stance on second chances can be applied well beyond the CJS. Take, for instance, our discussion of basic writing skills in Chapter 7. For some, this may be a refresher; for others, it could be their first exposure to the nuts and bolts of using proper grammar, constructing an argument, or writing in a formal academic style. We decided to cover writing in this book not just because communication skills are crucial for CJC students (and all students, really), but also because we believe so strongly in second chances. When students from underfunded schools move on to college, they arrive having missed out on opportunities to learn how to write well. The college environment, unfortunately, is not designed to impart this knowledge, and often presumes that entering students have these skills in hand upon arrival. Professors make this same mistake, too. Chapter 7, then, represents a chance for students to make up for missed opportunities.

The concrete, practical nature of the communication skills presented in Chapter 7 extends throughout the remainder of Part III of this book. To revisit the metaphor from the very beginning of the book, if Parts I and II helped to fill in your roadmap to justice, Part III can teach you to drive. Part I of this book is broad and abstract, and hopefully prompted you to think about justice in a big way—both in terms of depth and breadth. Part II related the concepts introduced in Part I to the CJS without losing this broader perspective. In this sense, Part I of this book can be seen as an introduction to the broader context of justice, whereas Part II situates the CJS within this larger social context. We bring the book to a close with Part III, which emphasizes the practical skills necessary to create justice in the realm of criminal justice: communication skills, employment within the CJS and related careers, and navigating the opportunities and constraints of the CJS to create social change.

# Chapter 7

# WRITING AND SPEAKING FOR JUSTICE

## INTRODUCTION

Strong communication skills are critical for succeeding in all justice-related professions. Communication skills may be particularly relevant for obtaining promotions and opening up new job opportunities. Bad writing, for example, is likely to be judged harshly and can limit advancement. Employers, colleagues, and clients all benefit from oral and written communication that is thoughtful, clear, and concise. Strengthening communication skills is a life-long endeavor. Even professors and professional writers/public speakers put a great deal of effort into these forms of communication. It is hard work!

Unfortunately, not everyone who enters college is adequately prepared for college-level writing, and this diversity in ability is often directly linked to the quality of high school preparation. When students have unequal access to opportunities to develop their communication skills and uneven guidance in doing so, writing can become a justice issue. For students who struggle with the nuts and bolts of writing, college can present a second chance to learn the foundational aspects of good communication and make up for previous deficits. Given the range in writing levels that we see in our college classes, we begin this chapter with the very basics of strong writing—content that may serve as a refresher for some, and for others may simply be a starting point for further study. There is an exercise at the end of this chapter that should serve as a test of your writing ability and can help you determine how much time you will need to devote to mastering the basics. This activity will help you assess your skill at spotting bad writing as well as your ability to correct it.

After basic college-level writing expectations have been covered, we move on to more advanced and specialized communication topics. First up is formal, academic writing, including instruction on writing style, citations and references, and the writing process. Then we shift gears to more applied types of communication (public speaking and job application materials) in anticipation of Chapter 8's focus on jobs in criminal justice.

## WRITING BASICS

The most basic element of writing that we'll address here is grammar. Rather than providing an introductory primer on grammar (which can be found in better form in the "recommended readings" at the end of this chapter), instead we have decided to focus our attention on the most common mistakes that we see in student papers. These mistakes can result from a lack of knowledge about grammar (either because students never learned grammar in school or because they have since forgotten it), rushed or careless writing, or a lack of editing. No matter the cause, however, the end result is writing that is sloppy and poorly representative of the thoughts that it is meant to convey. The good news is that these errors are fairly easy to fix. In the rest of this section, we provide examples of good and bad writing for the common errors that we see, and the activities and assignments at the end of the chapter give you a chance to practice and assess your mastery of grammar.

The most basic grammatical errors pertain to punctuation and sentence construction. Each sentence that you write should express a grammatically complete thought. This means that it must contain, at the very least, a noun and a verb. If your (alleged) sentence is missing either of these components, it is not actually a sentence; it is a *fragment*. Although fragments contain too little information, too much information is also a problem. If your sentence has more information than it needs, you may have a run-on. One way to spot run-on sentences is to look for two whole sentences that are linked with a comma. Consider, for instance, the sentence: "The young man was nervous in court, he wanted to know as soon as possible whether he could go home to his family." We can tell this is a run-on sentence because the chunks of text before the comma ("The young man was nervous in court") and after the comma ("he wanted to know as soon as possible whether he could go home to his family") both qualify as complete sentences. When strung together like this, they provide either too much or not enough information. If we simply want to convey that the man was nervous and that he wanted to know whether he could go home, then two sentences would do this best. If we want to link these two thoughts, we could use a *conjunction* ("and," "or," "but," "for," "nor," "so," "yet"). Conjunctions allow for the two thoughts (or *clauses*) to be meaningfully linked. For instance, we could write: "The young man was nervous in court, because he wanted to know as soon as possible whether he could go home to his family." The addition of a single word ("because") helps us to understand a causal relationship that would not be conveyed by two separate sentences, or by the run-on sentence. It is best to use conjunctions in the middle of sentences to link two clauses. Starting sentences with conjunctions is not advisable. Instead, use words that act as a transition for the reader, such as "additionally," "nevertheless," or "alternatively."

Punctuation is critical to sentence structure. All sentences should end with a period, exclamation point, or question mark. Many other punctuation marks can be used mid-sentence: colons, semicolons, commas, and parentheses. Colons are most commonly used to introduce a list, but only after a complete sentence. Take, for instance, the third sentence of this paragraph. The clause before the colon ("Many other punctuation marks can be used mid-sentence") could actually stand on its own as a complete sentence. The addition of the colon followed by a list of examples is a clear and easy way to provide additional information.

Semicolons are a bit more complicated, and require some judgment calls. Semicolons are used to join two closely related independent clauses, each of which could be a complete, stand-alone sentence. Let's revisit the example of the young man's court experience as an illustration. We know that the original sentence, "The young man was nervous in court, he wanted to know as soon as possible whether he could go home to his family." is a run-on. We solved this problem previously by adding a conjunction. Another way to address this problem is to use a semicolon: "The young man was nervous in court; he wanted to know as soon as possible whether he could go home to his family." Without additional context from the surrounding sentences, it's difficult to know whether this is a strong use of a semicolon. It is certainly appropriate, as it links two clauses that could each be stand-alone sentences. Whether it is *necessary* is another matter. Generally, it is advisable to avoid using semicolons unless there is a strong reason to indicate to the reader that two discrete thoughts—and only those two—are particularly closely related, in the context of the larger point the author is trying to make.

Another form of punctuation that requires some discretion is the comma. It is difficult to present formalized rules for the use of commas. In general, writing that uses too few or too many commas can confuse the reader. When writing is especially confusing, sometimes a sentence will need to be read multiple times to ascertain its meaning and relationship to the rest of the paragraph. There are many uses for commas, including setting apart nonessential material from the rest of a sentence, separating items in a list (like this), or showing relationships between ideas. The most important function of commas is to prevent confusion on the part of the reader. Think of a comma as an indicator to pause while reading or take a breath while speaking. If you follow this rule, reading a sentence out loud can reveal whether there is an excess of commas making sentences cumbersome to read.

A more simple form of punctuation that can nonetheless cause confusion when used incorrectly is the apostrophe. Apostrophe errors are often related to possession or contractions. Apostrophes can be used to indicate possession or ownership of a noun, as in the case of the following phrases: the officer's report, several years' work, women's substance abuse rates. When a noun is singular, the apostrophe is positioned before the "s," as is the case with "officer's report." When the noun is plural and ends in "s" (such as "several years' work") the apostrophe is positioned after the "s." When the noun is plural and does not end in "s," as is the case with irregular words such as "women," the apostrophe is put before the "s" like it is for singular nouns (e.g., "women's substance abuse rates"). Apostrophes can also be used to indicate an omitted letter or letters, as is the case with contractions such as "isn't" or "you're." Apostrophes will seldom be used for contraction in formal, academic writing, but you'll see them all over other kinds of writing (like this book).

Another common grammatical error is a lack of *agreement* between subjects and verbs or between nouns and the pronouns that represent them. Agreement involves whether a word is singular or plural. For example, the sentences "The manual is helpful for beginning police officers" and "The manuals are helpful for beginning police officers" use the correct conjugation of the verb for the subject of the sentence. Follow-up sentences could require agreement between nouns and pronouns. For instance, "The manual is helpful for beginning police officers. They find it particularly useful in their first six months." and "The manuals are helpful for beginning police officers. They find them particularly useful in their first six months." These sentences are fairly straightforward, so it is easy to see the agreement. The more complicated your sentence structure, and the more complex the ideas you are trying to convey, the easier it is to lose track of the subject and accidentally use a verb or pronoun that doesn't agree.

Another common error involving pronouns is unclear pronoun references. Pronouns are generic words such as "it," "they," "this," "that," "these," "those," and "which." As a writer, it is easy to have a clear idea of what a pronoun refers to—but it isn't always obvious to your reader. Pronouns should clearly refer to a specific noun in the same sentence, or the sentence immediately preceding it. Consider, for example, the sentence: "If students do poorly on the quizzes, they must not be very good." In this case, we do not know if it is the students or the quizzes that are not good. To clarify, the sentence should be reworded to say, "If students do poorly on the quizzes, the quizzes must not be very good." To avoid confusion, it is always helpful to use more specific information. When talking about a new crime prevention strategy, for instance, it is better to say "In her speech, the mayor proposed a new focus on violent crime in the city. <u>This strategy</u> will reduce crime overall." instead of "In her speech, the mayor proposed a new focus on violent crime in the city. <u>This</u> will reduce crime overall." Even though the correct meaning can probably be gleaned from context, it is still possible to interpret the latter example as proposing that the mayor's speech (rather than the mayor's new strategy) will reduce crime.

One error that is easy to make while writing is to use the wrong word. This is a particularly easy mistake to make when the words sound similar, or even exactly the same, when spoken aloud. A classic example in the social sciences is the use of "effect" versus "affect." "Effect" is most often a noun that means a result (e.g., "The effect of the intervention was clear."). "Affect" is almost always a verb that means to influence (e.g., "The intervention affected juveniles' involvement in gangs."). If you affect something, you can cause an effect. Other common words that are easily and frequently confused include: their/there/they're, lead/led, then/than, and accept/except to name a few. Relatedly, it is very easy to mistake the contraction "should've" (a shortened form of "should have") for "should of" (a grammatically incorrect phrasing).

The best writing is not just grammatically correct, but strong, clear, and concise. Ways to strengthen your writing include the use of active voice, consistent verb tense, proper placement of modifiers, parallel sentence structure, and appropriate introduction of acronyms. Strong writing uses an active, rather than a passive, voice as much as possible. For example, "the probation officer contacts her clients" is an example of an active verb form, whereas "the clients are contacted by the probation officer" uses a passive verb form. The passive voice uses verbs of being (in this case, "the clients <u>are</u> contacted"), which removes the actor from the sentence and focuses our attention on the object being acted upon. The active voice, by contrast, emphasizes the person doing the acting by making her the subject of the sentence and using a more active verb (e.g., "the probation officer contacts"). Use of the active voice makes your writing stronger, clearer, and more concise.

For clarity, you should avoid switching verb tenses as you write. It is good practice to choose a tense (e.g., past, present, or future) before starting to write. Sometimes switching tense in the context of a writing assignment makes sense to show a change in time, but arbitrarily switching between tenses can easily confuse your reader. For an example of tense switching, consider the following sentence: "During his testimony, the disgruntled witness stood up and then walks out of the courtroom." Because this sentence is describing a scenario that has already happened, the past tense is appropriate. "Stood" is already in the past tense, but "walks" is in the present tense. To accurately describe the complete scene as having occurred in the past, the word "walks" should be changed to "walked."

For strong and clear writing, be sure to place *modifiers*—words or phrases that describe a noun (e.g., "disgruntled witness")—near the things they describe. Misplaced modifiers can change the meaning of a sentence. For example, in the sentence, "My dog was hit by a truck running across the road" it is unclear whether the dog or the truck was running across the road. A clearer telling of this unfortunate incident would be "While running across the road, my dog was hit by a truck." Another practice is to avoid *faulty parallelism*, or the lack of similar structure in the various parts of a sentence. Be sure to use grammatically equivalent sentence elements to express two or more matching ideas or items in a series. For example, the sentence "The police are trained to conduct searches, make arrests, and in questioning witnesses" displays faulty parallelism. It should be rewritten to say, "The police are trained to conduct searches, make arrests, and question witnesses."

Before we move on to formal academic writing, one more specific writing mistake bears mentioning: the use of unspecified acronyms. It is easy to think that acronyms such as FBI, for instance, speak for themselves. The best writing, however, takes little for granted—including knowledge of what acronyms stand for. Therefore, it is important to only use acronyms after they have been properly introduced. After using the acronym the first time in conjunction with the complete phrase, you can simply use the acronym to refer to the entity. For example, we could include the following sentence in this book, "One can learn about scholarly research in the field of CJC by attending meetings of the American Society of Criminology (ASC)." The acronym "CJC" here can remain unspecified because we already introduced that acronym in Chapter 1 of this book. The acronym "ASC," however, has not appeared thus far in the text, and therefore requires clarification. On a related note, when referring to our country, be sure to either write "United States" or use the acronym "U.S." Because "America" includes more than just the U.S., it is inaccurate at best (and offensive at worst) to use this word to refer only to the United States.

# FORMAL ACADEMIC WRITING

## Style

In formal academic writing, there are additional guidelines that produce stronger, more professional writing that is easy to read and digest. Formal writing requires extra effort beyond simply being attentive to sentences and paragraphs. It requires the development of thesis statements and meaningful arguments, and the appropriate attribution of words, thoughts, and ideas (also known as citation). In this section, we describe the elements of the formal academic writing style, address issues of citation, reference, and plagiarism, and offer suggestions for finding your ideal academic writing process.

As with all forms of writing, formal academic writing should be extremely clear. The goal of good writing is to make the reader do as little work as possible. Consequently, what you are seeking to accomplish in your writing should be obvious and clearly stated. This is usually made clear in the very first paragraph of a piece of writing (the *introduction*), particularly in the *thesis statement* that sums up the main point that you, the author, are trying to make. Most introductions begin with an engaging opening sentence that draws the reader in and provides an idea of the topic that you are addressing. Early in the introductory paragraph is your thesis statement (often called a "topic sentence" in high school English classes). The *thesis statement* is a clear, concise presentation of the main argument that you are making in your writing. All academic writing should advance an *argument*—a point that you are trying to convey to the reader or convince her of. After your thesis statement is presented, the rest of your text will be dedicated to explaining and supporting that argument, and convincing the reader of its importance. For strong writing, it is crucial to stay on topic, and avoid redundancy or repetition. In the words of Strunk and White (1979, p. 23), "Vigorous writing is concise. A sentence should contain no unnecessary words, a paragraph no unnecessary sentences, for the same reason that a drawing should have no unnecessary lines and a machine no unnecessary parts." Overall decisions about organization and transitions between sentences should provide a flow from beginning to end that keeps the paper from being an unorganized jumble of ideas.

Formal writing sounds professional. This means avoiding writing that is overly dramatic, emotional, or biased. This doesn't mean that you need to avoid sensitive, emotional issues in academic writing. You can address these issues in a compelling way without overdoing it; the key is moderation. Especially when talking about sensitive topics, avoid using terms that are pejorative or insulting toward others. This should also be kept in mind when referencing or citing the work of other authors in a less than positive light (e.g., "the author attempts to," "a waste of time").

There are certain words, phrases, sentences, and practices to avoid in formal academic writing that would be perfectly acceptable in spoken conversation or informal writing. We present a few of these below, along with definitions and examples for clarity.

1. *Idioms* are phrases that do not have a literal meaning. Imagine how difficult it would be to translate these phrases into another language (e.g., "on pins and needles," "follow suit," "flat broke," "going the extra mile," "at the end of the day," "on the wagon").
2. *Slang* is an informal type of speech used by specific social groups that could be defined by age, time period, or culture (e.g., "dude," "dough," "cop," "my bad," "dis").

3. *Clichés* are phrases that are common to the point of being overused. Using clichés (e.g., "strong as an ox," "at all costs," "fall on deaf ears") can make your writing sound unoriginal, unprofessional, or unpersuasive.
4. *Jargon* is a type of word or phrase that is familiar only to a specific group, field, or industry. Jargon should be avoided whenever possible in formal writing. For example, CJS professionals use "SHU" (i.e., security housing unit) or "ad-seg" (i.e., administrative segregation) to refer to short-term solitary confinement and "beat" to refer to a specified area designated to officers for patrol. CJC scholars also have specialized vocabulary that includes terms not commonly used outside of the discipline. For examples of these, just look for the italicized concepts in all of the chapters. *Social justice, intersectionality,* and *concentrated disadvantage* are examples of CJC jargon. In formal academic writing, jargon should only be used when it would be unclear or confusing to use an alternative word or phrasing. For instance, the concept of intersectionality is a fairly complex one that cannot easily be summed up by a more common word or phrase. Consequently, "intersectionality" is an appropriate piece of jargon to use in formal, academic writing—but only after it has been properly introduced and explained.
5. *Stage directions* are when you explicitly tell your reader what to expect from your writing. For example, "This paper will explain..." Although we use these types of directives often in this book (because it isn't formal writing), this type of direction is unnecessary in formal, academic writing. A clearly organized and well-written academic paper will convey everything on its own without being overly didactic.
6. *Contractions*, defined earlier as phrases that use apostrophes to shorten single words or collapse multiple words together, are not used in formal writing. Even though it may sound stiff, this is commonly accepted practice.
7. *Shortened or abbreviated words* (e.g., "TV," "combo," "info") should not be used. In formal academic writing, make sure you write out the entire word.
8. *First- and second-person point of view (POV)* entails the use of personal pronouns that refer to the author (first person) or the reader (second person). There are many examples of first- and second-person POV in this book. To make the information in this chapter less dry and more accessible, we (the authors) try to use conversational language and draw the reader in by referring to you directly. In the previous sentence, "we" is the first person pronoun and "you" is the second person pronoun. If this book were written in a formal academic style, it is likely that neither of those pronouns would appear. First- and second-person perspectives are appropriate in some circumstances and for some assignments, however. This is often the case when the author is drawing upon her own perspective to shape or advance her argument. When in doubt about a class assignment, ask whether the use of personal pronouns is allowable to indicate first- and second-person POV.
9. *Rhetorical questions* are questions posed by an author that are not intended to be answered. Do not ask (or answer) rhetorical questions in your writing (e.g., "Why do indigenous populations continue to experience so much injustice?"). This is partially because it brings first- and second-person POV into

the writing, and partially because it implies a dialogue or conversation that is not generally part of formal academic writing.

10. The *imperative voice* is another construction that implies first-person POV by directly addressing the reader. Examples of the imperative voice are "recall that..." or "you must"). Instead, you can refer the reader to an author and the year of publication in the text for more details.

At this point, you may be wondering why we, the authors of this book, are violating so many of these rules for formal, academic writing. The answer is simple: this book is not intended to be formal. Even though this is technically an academic book, we chose to write it in an informal style to make the book more enjoyable, rather than a formal style that demonstrates mastery. It is our hope that the content of this book will be more easily and enjoyably absorbed by students because the writing sounds like teaching.

## Citations and References

Because academic writing builds on knowledge gathered from other sources (e.g., books, journal articles, class lectures), it is crucial to differentiate between your own work and the work of others. The way we do this in formal academic writing is through the use of citations and references. This practice helps prevent *plagiarism*, or passing off another person's words, thoughts, ideas, or findings as your own. Plagiarism can happen intentionally or can be the unintentional result of writing about someone else's work without proper attribution. To avoid plagiarism, make sure that you give appropriate credit whenever you present someone else's work, even when you aren't using their exact words. In general, anything that isn't considered common knowledge (things known widely and likely to be found in multiple sources) should be clearly attributed to the appropriate source.

There are two ways to incorporate another author's work into your own writing: *paraphrasing* and *quoting*. *Paraphrasing* involves accurately presenting someone else's work in your own words. "In your own words" means more than just swapping out a few words from the author's original text or moving around the pieces of a sentence or thought. To ensure that you are paraphrasing, rather than plagiarizing, we recommend looking away from the text that you want to summarize and trying to represent its content from memory without peeking at the original. Then, check your paraphrased summary against the original text to ensure accuracy. This is an excellent way to make sure that you fully understand what you are incorporating into your writing. A common cause of student plagiarism is an incomplete or superficial understanding of the original source material; when we don't understand something fully, it is difficult to express it in our own words. *Quoting* text involves using the original author's text to capture her ideas. When this is done, the text that is borrowed from the original source must be put inside quotation marks and clearly presented as someone else's thoughts *and* words. It can be tempting to use quotations liberally, but the best writing uses them only minimally. When deciding whether to paraphrase or quote, ask yourself whether the original author has stated the point in a way that is so eloquent, concise or compelling that it couldn't possibly be represented as well another way. If this is the case, you have good reason to quote. If not, then you'd better get to paraphrasing.

Regardless of whether you paraphrase or use a direct quotation, all ideas and information that you pull from another author must be clearly attributed to that author. In this book, we recommend the use of APA citation style guidelines for in-text parenthetical citations and end-of-text references. There are many resources available online, including the excellent Purdue University Online Writing Lab (https://owl.english.purdue.edu/owl/resource/560/01/). We also cover a few very basic elements here. When referencing authors in text, include their last names and the year of publication in parentheses at the end of your sentence; this is your in-text *citation*. Page numbers are not required unless a direct quotation is presented; in this case, the page number is included in the parenthetical citation. In-text citations direct the reader to a more comprehensive list of sources with complete bibliographic information at the end of the document (called the *references*). It is important to never misspell an author's last name in either the citations or the references, as these are tools for the reader to find further information.

One tricky issue with citations, for both paraphrased and quoted material, is punctuation. When using APA citation style, as we do in this book, parenthetical citations should be placed at the end of a sentence, before the period. If a direct quotation is used, the citation comes after the quotation marks, but still before the period. Most punctuation belongs inside the quotation marks, except when the last item in the quotation marks is a letter or a number (e.g., The highest ranking on the Level of Service Inventory is a "40".), or when the punctuation is a colon, semicolon, or question mark that is not part of the quoted material. For more instruction along these lines, the APA style blog has a handy reference guide (http://blog.apastyle.org/apastyle/2011/08/punctuating-around-quotation-marks.html). Always use double quotation marks to indicated quoted material. For quotations embedded within another quotation, use single quotation marks. Many examples of the proper placement of quotation marks can be seen in this chapter.

## The Writing Process

Now that we've covered the mechanical aspects of academic writing, let's take a holistic look at the process of writing. In this section, we'll trace the writing process across the following stages: understanding the assignment, brainstorming, locating sources, organizing your thoughts, putting text on the page, and finalizing your draft. Because most of the academic writing that you do as a CJC student is for class assignments, we focus on this particular type of writing.

The first part of the writing process actually doesn't involve writing at all. It begins with understanding your assignment. Make sure you read the assignment fully and carefully, making note of the different components while keeping the overall task in mind. The *task* is important; it is the thing you are being asked to do. Schmidt and Hooper (2003) developed a useful typology of tasks that students are asked to perform: analyze, critique, develop, evaluate, explain, identify, illustrate, interpret, and review. Each task is associated with a specific thinking pattern. An analysis task calls for you to break the topic into parts and understand each part. To critique, you express and substantiate opinions about something. To develop, you elaborate or expand upon an idea. An evaluation is an appraisal or judgment. To explain, you give reasons for or clarify something. To identify, you choose or select and explain why. To interpret, you explain the meaning or significance. A review is a reexamination or overview.

Once you have identified the main task in your assignment, the next step is to break it down into parts. Some assignments are simple, whereas others are complex. Most assignments of substantial length can be broken down into parts. If an assignment has multiple tasks, for instance, each task could be a part. If the assignment asks you to consider numerous concepts or dimensions (e.g., "make sure you cover theory, research and policy in your paper"), each of these would be a part. The only hard-and-fast rule to breaking an assignment down into parts is to make the parts meaningful to you. Once you've broken the assignment down, create a checklist that you can revisit at the end of your writing process to ensure that you've fulfilled all of the requirements of the assignment.

Now that you've imposed order on the assignment, the next step is to cultivate some chaos. Brainstorm a few ideas in response to the assignment. Consider topics to choose, positions to take, arguments to advance, questions to explore. Make your brainstorming visual. It doesn't matter what form it takes; just make sure you are typing, writing, sketching, or even finger painting to get the thoughts out of your head and into the world. Be as messy as you'd like. This is the time for wild, undisciplined thinking and "free writing" (jotting down all the ideas that come to your mind without editing). See where your thoughts take you. If this part of the process makes you nervous or seems a little silly, set a timer for three minutes and see what you can come up with—just make sure that your hands are constantly typing, writing, drawing, sculpting, or anything else that helps your creativity flow.

At the end of your brainstorming session, you should have some documentation of your ideas. Some of them will be good, and others not as much. Choose the strongest ideas and begin to find information about them. The scope and depth of your search for information will vary from assignment to assignment, but the best place to start is with the materials for your class. Read through your notes, assigned and suggested readings on the syllabus, and any other course materials that you have. Then, move on to academic books and peer-reviewed journal articles (remember these from Chapter 6?). A thorough search of these works will give you a comprehensive overview of the existing literature on a topic. If you are having a hard time finding sources, reference librarians can be helpful, and there are a number of criminal justice databases that can be used (e.g., ncjrs.org) or generic search engines such as Google Scholar. As you conduct your search, review the sources that you find, and file away the ones that are helpful (if it's an article, either save the PDF or print it out). Take notes on your sources as you go, if that is helpful. Expand or narrow your search as necessary, depending on the amount of information that you find. It's always better to find and file away more information than you think you'll need, so err on the side of overinclusion.

Once you've found and reviewed your sources, it's time to start organizing your thoughts. Remember all that chaos from a few steps earlier? It's time to impose some order on it. Start by thinking about how your paper could be best organized on a broad level. Some common organizational plans include moving from general to specific, moving from specific to general, chronological ordering, spatial organization, and cause-and-effect organization (Schmidt & Hooper, 2003). Make sure that you choose an appropriate scope for your assignment, so you aren't trying to tackle too much or finding yourself with too little to write.

Next, begin to outline your paper. Even if you're "just not an outline person," try to become one. Outlines make it easier to break complex ideas down into parts, help you arrange your thoughts in a logical order, and can even make it easier to spot organizational or logical inconsistencies in the flow of your paper. There are many different ways to create an outline; in the following paragraphs, we present a very simple option that can be tweaked and tailored to fit your style and can be subdivided for longer, more complex assignments.

In terms of general structure, each first-level heading in your outline will be the thesis statement for a new paragraph. The second-level text will be the content of the paragraph in support of the thesis. All outlines should begin with an *introduction* and end with a *conclusion*. The substance in between the introduction and conclusion should be broken up into *body paragraphs* by main point or topic.

Your *introduction* paragraph should include an engaging opening sentence, followed shortly after by a thesis statement that presents your main argument clearly and concisely. Remember that all papers should advance an argument of some type; the argument is what you, as the writer, are trying to convince the reader of. The remainder of the introduction paragraph will consist of basic information about your topic—anything that the reader will need as background on the big picture before getting into the nitty-gritty.

*Body paragraphs* (not including the introduction or conclusion) are where you provide support for your argument. The number of body paragraphs will depend on the length of the paper and the complexity of your argument. Organize each first-level heading in your outline (i.e., each paragraph) around a single point that you want to make. Each body paragraph should have its own topic sentence and then supporting points. All paragraphs must be at least three sentences long and shouldn't be much longer than half a page. Make sure the body of your paper follows a logical order. Each piece should build incrementally on what came before. Outlines make it easy to determine whether your paper has a logical flow. You should be able to read only the first-level headings (disregarding all of the second-level text below) and still get a complete, if thin, version of the argument.

Once you've outlined the entire body of the paper, it's time to move on to the *conclusion* paragraph. Conclusions should start by restating your argument. (Note that you should *restate* rather than *reiterate* your argument; say it in different words!) Next, very briefly summarize the evidence that you've provided to support your argument. End your paper with the "so what?" factor—explain the impact, importance, or implications of your argument.

With your outline now complete, you've actually already done most of the work! Transfer all of your ideas from your outline into paper format. Some people even prefer to write directly into their outline, deleting Roman numerals and letters as they go. No matter how you choose to transform your outline into a paper, there are a few things to keep in mind. We address these briefly next.

Be sure to give some thought to who your reader or audience is. Language choices, including the use of jargon and acronyms, will need to be adjusted accordingly. Help yourself avoid typographical errors (typos) and misspellings. Make sure that your software's spellcheck tool is activated—but keep in mind that spellcheck is not infallible. Many spellcheck tools have limited dictionaries that erroneously mark some specialized CJC vocabulary as misspelling. Conversely, spellcheck will fail to catch errors that are words… but aren't the *right* words. For instance, despite being incorrect, the phrase "aren't the write words" would not get flagged by spellcheck. The best way to catch these errors (and others) is a thorough, out-loud reading of your paper before you turn it in. Ask yourself whether each sentence makes sense and is written as clearly as possible. Note any spots where you stumble, and check for errors or awkward phrasing.

Be mindful of formatting and other specific directions from your instructor. Avoid extra spaces between words and paragraphs, and incorrect paragraph indentation. It is now standard to use just one space between sentences. Some instructors are very specific about formatting, and others are less so. Unless otherwise instructed, use Times New Roman, 12-point font with one-inch margins and double spacing between lines. Keep in mind that these are not the default settings in some word processing software, so you might have to change your formatting settings when you open a new document. Refrain from altering the formatting and font style or size to make a paper appear longer. These paper-lengthening strategies are very easy for professors to spot and give the impression of laziness or dishonesty. Similarly, padding a paper with "fluff" to add length is a bad idea. Wade (2014) notes that phrases such as "Since the beginning of time…" add little, but can easily pad a paper. Take the time to come up with smart and meaningful introductions and conclusions without simply repeating what has been said, or stating what is so obvious it does not need to be said.

Also be sure to accurately distinguish between facts and opinions. Wade (2014) provides the following quotation as evidence of the confusion between fact and opinion: "Considering that Clinton's departure will leave only 16 women in the Senate out of 100 senators, many feminists believe women are underrepresented on Capitol Hill." The problem with this sentence is that it misrepresents fact as opinion. This is a common mistake found in student papers, along with its closely related cousin: stating unfounded or inaccurate facts as opinion (and thus avoiding citations). For instance, many students "believe" that the crime rate is increasing (or at least say so in their papers). Had they taken the time to look into this belief, though, they would have found that crime rates have steadily fallen since the 1990s.

Once you've finished a draft of your paper, the best thing you could possibly do is set it aside for a bit and return to it with fresh eyes, so to speak. Of course, this is only possible if you start the paper well before the deadline. When you do sit down to review your draft, you should first check your paper against the assignment. Remember that checklist you made in the very first step? This is the time to use it. Cross-check your paper against the assignment, ensuring that you've thoroughly addressed all of the parts of the task. Next comes proofreading. Read through your paper silently, considering whether your argument is as tight as it can be, whether you're missing any important pieces of the argument, and whether your ordering of topics is logical as written. Then, read through your paper *out loud* from start to finish, proofreading for writing style, grammar, and typos as you go. This might feel awkward, but it is a great way to catch errors that might not be as apparent to you in text.

## PUBLIC SPEAKING

Written communication is not the only way to convey your knowledge. It is also important to be able speak accurately, concisely, and persuasively in public arenas. Without a doubt, most people find public speaking nerve wracking. When people are asked to list their greatest fears, public speaking or giving a speech comes up for the majority of those asked. Given exposure to public speakers, all of us have ideas about what makes someone a good (or bad) public speaker. Public speaking requires a different method of delivery compared with writing, yet is not the same as regular conversational speech. To be clearly heard and understood, it is important to speak more slowly than you usually do and increase your volume and enunciation. It is always worth taking the time beforehand to organize your thoughts and develop an outline, similar to the type described previously for papers. It is a mistake to think a good presentation can be given without preparing in advance or by "winging it." Even if you are charismatic and good on your feet, a lack of preparation will show in your presentation. Tailor your message to your audience, which may require altering your natural word choices. Consider approaching your talk as a story that could be told. This technique tends to draw the listener in. No matter your approach, make sure you practice giving the talk out loud both to yourself and to a test audience. There's a good chance this will feel awkward and strange, but that might not be such a bad thing! It will make the actual public speaking event seem like a breeze in comparison.

## RESUMES AND PERSONAL STATEMENTS

One of the most important forms of communication for you, as a soon-to-be CJC graduate, is the communication of your capabilities and qualifications for jobs or further academic study. Resumes, cover letters, and personal statements are just a few ways that you can demonstrate your qualifications, expertise, and ambitions to prospective employers before even meeting them. Resumes are brief, well-organized lists of your education and work experience. There are many different formats and guidelines for resumes; you can find templates or examples online or base yours off a friend's or classmate's resume. No matter the style that you choose, be sure to keep the formatting clear and consistent. The information on your resume should speak for itself; jobs with specialized titles should be accompanied by a list of job responsibilities, and career interests should be relevant and easily recognizable to the position you are seeking.

For many jobs, and for applications for graduate study, your resume will be accompanied by a cover letter or personal statement. These documents are professional in nature and should follow most of the rules for formal academic writing. (It is often acceptable to use first person pronouns in these documents, but use your judgment or ask a professor to be completely sure.) The form/style of these documents matters almost as much as the content, as they are often used to assess your writing abilities. Cover letters and personal statements should highlight the most important elements of your resume, not by restating the information that is already available, but by demonstrating *why* they make you a strong candidate for the position you are seeking. These documents should describe your career goals, reveal your motivation for pursuing this career path, and persuade the employer that you are the right candidate for the position (both by highlighting your strengths and demonstrating knowledge of the position itself). Keep these items in mind as you turn to Chapter 8, where we cover career paths in criminal justice.

## References

Schmidt, J.H., & Hooper, M.K. (2003). *6 steps to effective writing in criminal justice.* Belmont, CA: Wadsworth.

Strunk, W., & White, E.B. (1979). *The elements of style* (3rd ed.). Boston: Allyn and Bacon.

Wade, L. (2014). 10 things every college professor hates. *Business Insider.* Retrieved from http://www.businessinsider.com/10-things-every-college-professor-hates-2014-11.

## Recommended Readings

Frye, K., & Kirton, R. (2012). *Grammar for grown-ups: A straightforward guide to good English.* London: Square Peg.

Thurman, S. (2003). *The only grammar book you'll ever need: A one-stop source for every writing assignment.* Avon, MA: Adams Media.

Truss, L. (2006). *Eats, shoots, & leaves: The zero tolerance approach to punctuation.* New York: Avery.

Yagoda, B. (2013). *How to not write bad: The most common writing problems and the best ways to avoid them.* New York: Riverhead Books.

# ACTIVITIES/ASSIGNMENTS

## Writing and Speaking for Justice

What does it mean to write for justice? What does it mean to speak for justice? What are the all the ways someone could write or speak for justice?

## Bad Writing

Rewrite the following sentences to make them correct. What is wrong with each sentence?

1. Crime has no generally accepted definition. For many people, behavior that is harmful to individuals or groups.
2. Visher observed that police chivalry exists only for White women, Black women were far more likely to be arrested.
3. The hearing was planned for Monday, December 2, but not all of the witnesses could be available, so it was rescheduled for the following Friday, and then all the witnesses could attend.
4. Many tourists visit Arlington National Cemetery, where veterans and military personnel are buried every day from 9:00 a.m. until 5:00 p.m.
5. The candidate's goals include winning the election, a national health program, and the educational system.
6. Some critics are not so much opposed to capital punishment as postponing it for so long.
7. Einstein was a brilliant mathematician. This is how he was able to explain the universe.
8. Because Senator Martin is less interested in the environment than in economic development, he sometimes neglects it.
9. The professor asked the students to quickly take the quiz.
10. When it comes to eating people differ in their tastes.
11. The "child-savers" who were largely women from the middle-class exhibited a concern for the welfare of children.
12. Internships are required, in several departments, such as, criminal justice and political science.
13. In the current conflict its uncertain who's borders their contesting.
14. One of my professors always spill coffee on my papers.
15. Feminism as an approach to studying crime and delinquency focuses on womens and girls experiences, typically in the areas of victimization, gender difference's in crime, and differential treatment of women and girl's by the justice system.
16. The recession had a negative affect on sales.
17. In my opinion, a continued emphasis and focus on training of juvenile court personnel is essential and critical. So, I always take advantage of training when it is offered! You should too:)

## 10 Steps Toward Better Writing

Read the following article. What advice did you find most helpful?
http://www.lifehack.org/articles/communication/advice-for-students-10-steps-toward-better-writing.html

## Understanding the Assignment: Assignment Analysis

Using the document link that follows, what additional factors might you now consider prior to beginning a writing assignment?
http://sbcc.edu/clrc/writing_center/wc_files/handout_masters/Understanding%20the%20Assignment.pdf

## Task, Thinking Pattern, Reader, Organizational Activity

For each fictional assignment, identify your task and the related thinking patterns, audience, and organizational plan.

1. The probation agency you work for is trying to understand why most violations are occurring around failure to secure employment. Because you are soon to be a CJC graduate, they have asked you to explore this topic in a paper to be presented at the next monthly staff meeting. Hopefully, your research will help interpret why this is happening and identify the steps that can be taken to address this problem.
2. In graduate school, you are assigned the following paper: Explain and illustrate how our current practices in juvenile justice can be traced back to how juveniles were treated at different times in the history of the United States.
3. You work in an alternative school for children who have been suspended from other schools. You are concerned about the quality of the food the children receive. Because everyone "knows" that nutrition is related to learning and behavior, you have decided to write up a proposal to fund a more nutritious school lunch program.
4. You work in law enforcement in Kansas City. Recently, a high-crime area of a well-defined geographical region has been identified. You have been asked to analyze this area in an attempt to explain the possible reasons for the concentration of crime and develop preventative efforts that may prove useful.
5. As a law student, you have closely followed a case in which a woman has been accused of cutting a baby from the womb of another person. The pregnant woman died as a result, but the baby survived. You have strong beliefs on whether the baby should be considered a legal person in a court of law. You intend to review this case to explain your position.

## Walking and Talking About Justice

This activity could be done outdoors on a nice day or done within a building. Engage in active listening by taking turns answering and asking follow-up questions about the following three questions: What injustice(s) do you feel passionate about eradicating? Why is it a justice issue? What do you do/could you do when confronted with social injustice? After about 10 minutes, switch walking partners and have each person share what you have learned this semester and what you hope to learn in the remaining weeks.

## Journaling in Class

As a follow-up to the activity discussed previously, write two journal entries to share with your instructor that reflect your thoughts on justice and your own learning.

## Plagiarism Tutorial

Go to the following web site and go through the eight steps given, including the pretest, two quizzes, and posttest.

http://www.lib.usm.edu/legacy/plag/plagiarismtutorial.php

## Improving Student Writing

After reading the article by Doyle and Meadows, which of the proposed strategies do you think would be most effective in improving student writing?

## SEMESTER-LONG JUSTICE PROJECT

Step Seven: In preparation for your final paper, write a one-page paper that explains why you chose the justice topic that you did. How does this topic relate to the types of justice that we've covered in this book? How does it relate to other relevant concepts from the book?

## Selected Reading

# A Writing-Intensive Approach to Criminal Justice Education

## The California Lutheran University Model

*Michael Doyle and Robert J. Meadows*

## INTRODUCTION

Writing as a central academic process has been widely touted in American higher education over the past decade. Labeled either as "writing-to-learn" or "writing-across-the curriculum," the emphasis on writing began in the early 1980's and had spread to over one-third of the colleges and universities in the United States by the academic year 1987–88 (Watkins, 1990). Regardless of the name, the goals of these writing initiatives have been to encourage greater use of writing as a means to promote active learning (Bonwell and Eison, 1991), improve the teaching of critical thinking (Clark and Biddle, 1993; Henry, 1993) and more effectively teach content (Murray, 1984).

Criminal justice educators have also praised the pedagogical value of writing as a means for personally connecting students with subject matter (e.g. Gladis, 1991) while others implicitly acknowledge the importance of writing to the learning process by requiring a traditional term paper to supplement a favored pedagogical approach (e.g. Cederblom and Spohn, 1991). Furthermore, the use of writing and critical thinking exercises for criminal justice educators has proven successful at many institutions (Blankenship, Janikowski, & Sparger, 1990). Regardless of pedagogy, writing is, and arguably should be, an essential ingredient in developing the intellectual capacity of students. Thus, the challenge facing each of us as educators is to devise appropriate strategies which are likely to improve the thinking-writing skills for our students. This article will describe the curricular efforts toward making writing a central feature of the academic program at a small, liberal arts institution and the strategies adopted by the criminal justice faculty to accommodate the heightened emphasis on writing within the general education and major requirements. First, we will describe the university-wide, cross-disciplinary, integrative initiative which pairs or "clusters" core courses while emphasizing writing across the curriculum. In Criminal Justice, this has been a cluster with a single section of Freshman English. Second, we will describe how other writing in nearly all criminal justice courses has been strengthened to meet the university's General Education Requirements for proficiency in written communication.

## THE CLUSTER PROGRAM

Begun in 1984, the goals of the cluster program are to...

...integrate knowledge across departmental lines and to give students practice and support in making discriminating judgments. The key instructional method, however, has been writing because it stimulates thinking and provides the best demonstration of a student's ability to integrate ideas from various sources, infer relationships among them, and arrive at independent judgments (Bowman, 1991).

Thus, the pairing of separate core courses is aimed at accomplishing discrete course objectives while offering opportunities for regularly scheduled interaction between clustered courses during the semester. The purpose of the interaction is "...integrating concepts, ideas and content while emphasizing writing, understanding of texts, analysis of ideas, and ability to synthesize" (Bowman, 1991). Efforts by Criminal Justice and English faculty toward achieving cluster goals have resulted in a significantly revised approach to teaching Introduction to Criminal Justice.

## THE MECHANICS OF CLUSTERING

In the fall of 1993, Freshman English and Introduction to Criminal Justice courses were paired. The English course was required of all freshmen, and Introduction to Criminal Justice was required of all criminal justice majors. However, there were a number of students enrolled who were not majors in criminal justice. The clustering students registered for both discrete courses which were offered at different times. Each instructor provided a syllabus detailing his/her specific course requirements as well as requirements which were unique to the cluster. In other words, while there were specific content requirements for each course, the major thrust of the cluster was to collaboratively analyze texts and explore various perspectives on justice.

The process of coordinating the cluster began when both instructors met prior to the start of the semester in order to select texts and develop five writing topics or convergence papers which were relevant to each course. Additional coordination occurred during the semester when both instructors met with the clustering students at the time the assignments were made in class. This afforded an opportunity to clarify the assignments, which constituted a significant proportion of the grade in each course. Once a student paper was submitted, each instructor evaluated the *paper* for purposes of grading within his/her discrete course. The same student evaluation procedure was employed regardless of the focus or content of the assignments.

The convergence papers were either reflective, documentary, or a combination of both. A reflective paper required students to assess or analyze a theory of crime or significant issue regarding justice. The first convergence paper required students to reflect on the meaning of law and justice. In other words, can law exist without justice, or are there some situations where the law may not apply?

The second assignment was documentary writing which required each student to gather information on community policing or some other aspect of policing in a contemporary society. Students were required to use both primary research techniques (interviews or other methods for gathering new information) and secondary techniques (Journal articles or prior studies of policing).

Assignment three was again reflective and focused on the courts, the rights of the accused, or a topic related to sentencing. A number of students wrote on sentencing disparity and community corrections.

The fourth paper returned to documentation but in combination with reflection. For this assignment, the topic was youth violence and gangs. To assist in this process, several gang members currently on probation visited the class (along with their probation officer). Students directed a variety of questions to the gang members. Based on this discussion, a reflective paper was generated which also included relevant secondary research sources.

The final paper was reflective and addressed the issue of incarceration. In order to provide the students with a variety of perspectives, assigned readings included fairly traditional material about prisons and punishment and the novel Treblinka. Not surprisingly, some students found the novel to be depressing. However, the account of confinement, oppression, torture and murder of Jews in a Nazi death camp afforded a view of imprisonment which is quite different from contemporary corrections. While the novel did provide students with a more graphic sense of the Holocaust, it also raised the issues of formal and informal controls within institutions dedicated to confinement. The final reflective papers produced by the students addressed the effects of confinement on inmates, custodial staff and prison administrators.

Regardless of the type of convergence assignment, the papers were graded on the basis of writing style and content. Each paper, for example, had to begin with a clearly defined thesis statement, followed by a logical expression of ideas supported by documentation when necessary. A number of the weaker students were given an opportunity to rewrite an unsatisfactory paper. When rewriting produced a marked improvement over the first effort, the higher grade was recorded. This was quite consistent with the instructors' philosophy that writing with a purpose is a continuous process leading to improvement.

In-class, informal writing assignments also contributed to the continuity of the writing process. Impromptu assignments based on the assigned readings or topics were techniques to engage the students with a topic in order to promote discussion, apply a concept or solve a problem. Students were encouraged to draw upon these expressive pieces of writing when composing their convergence papers. Additional in-class attention to writing was also encouraged by structuring opportunities for students to serve as peer reviewers for their classmates. This involved reading, discussing and critiquing the work done by others and offered each peer reviewer a chance to compare writing styles and other topical perspectives with his/her own.

Overall, the emphasis on writing in a discrete course operating within a cluster is a unique strategy to help students integrate knowledge across disciplinary lines. Furthermore, as an interdisciplinary enterprise, clustering and writing offer new opportunities for students to develop and practice critical thinking skills. While the clusters are aimed at Freshmen and Sophomores, other writing proficiency strategies are focused on lower- and upper-division students.

## IMPROVING WRITING PROFICIENCY IN CRIMINAL JUSTICE

As part of a complete revision of the general education requirements, the university established four sets of core requirements: Proficiencies, Perspectives, Cultures and Civilizations, and Integrated Studies. Regardless of academic major, all students must complete each core requirement. Within the Proficiency requirement, written communication is particularly emphasized. In order to satisfy the writing proficiency, each student is required to complete two "writing intensive" courses beyond Freshman English and excluding cluster courses. Furthermore, one of the two courses must be at the Junior-Senior level.

Each academic department was encouraged to develop writing intensive courses which met the following criteria established by the University General Education Committee.

The course must require students to engage in critical thinking through writing and should include:

a. A minimum of 4000 words of writing (about 16 double-spaced pages) which can include required drafts, essay test writing and formal, graded journal writing.
b. At least two assignments which require drafts. Drafts should be responded to by other editors, including some combination of instructor, peer writing groups, departmental assistants, or writing center editors.
c. Evaluation or tests which include essay components; they may not be exclusively multiple choice or T/F.
d. Some methodology for discussing the kinds and styles of writing that are specific to this course.

The criteria are fairly clear regarding the quantity of writing which is necessary to qualify a course as writing intensive but say nothing about how to create written assignments which emphasize critical thinking or integrate more writing into existing courses. Furthermore, as criminal justice faculty, we had not been trained to teach writing and the kind of written work which we assigned was typically modeled after our own experiences as students. Needless to say, we were also concerned about reading and grading a significantly greater volume of written work within an already filled course schedule. The answers to these and other faculty questions and concerns were provided via a series of writing workshops sponsored by the Committee.

## OLD AND NEW ASSIGNMENTS

To appreciate the changes in devising writing assignments within the department as a result of the writing intensive workshops, consider the following example of a former assignment for Introduction to Criminal Justice.

> Prepare a 3–5 page paper on some aspect of the criminal justice system. The paper should demonstrate knowledge of the complexity of the system and the relationships between agencies and components. It may be helpful to provide examples of how the CJS attempts to control crime and why it is often unsuccessful.

The assignment sheet also exhorted the students to comply with standard expectations for college level written work and specified a due date.

From the perspective of the faculty, the only steps in the writing process were assigning, collecting, reading, grading, and returning the papers to the students. Not surprisingly, and always the source of much grumbling among the faculty, the quality of the papers was often below what had been expected. In fact, the quality of any paper was highly dependent on the prior writing proficiency of that student. Note that the example offered little direction to the student about how to complete the assignment and no opportunity for learning from any mistakes. In this respect, the example is also fairly typical by prescribing a deadline for submission of the paper and offering the student a single chance at succeeding on the assignment. More importantly, the assignment does not make clear what the students were supposed to learn nor does it require any particular kind of thinking.

In terms of Bloom's Taxonomy of Educational Objectives (1956), there is a significant difference between knowledge (what the student recalls or remembers) and application (applying knowledge to a new situation). Assignments which develop critical thinking skills should help hone the ability to analyze and synthesize (to see relationships and put parts together in new ways) and make informed evaluations (judge the worth or value of material). To elicit critical thinking skills, however, the assignment has to be sufficiently focused to lead the students from simple inquiry to more sophisticated application, analysis and synthesis.

## A REVISED ASSIGNMENT

With only a modest amount of creativity, our introductory writing assignment can be revised as follows:

> As an educated person who has begun the study of criminal justice, you have been asked to address a group of senior citizens on the topic of criminal justice in the United States. The questions which most concern the group are listed below. You are well aware that there is usually a gap between public perception and the reality of how the system works. Your position is that the criminal justice system is a complex network of agencies, officials, rules and law and it is that complexity which has practical consequences for how the CJS responds to crime. You will illustrate what that means by responding to two of the questions posed for you by the senior citizen group.

1. It seems like the police do a better job of clearing murder than burglary. Will increasing the number of police officers lead to an increase in the burglary conviction rate?
2. A friend told me that the reason so few criminals go to prison is that there are too many technical legal rules like the Miranda warning and search and seizure laws. Is this true? If not, why don't more criminals go to prison?
3. I think that the reason we have so much crime in the U. S. is because we don't punish criminals severely. Could we reduce burglary, for example, by increasing the possible sentence for someone convicted of burglary?
4. One of my friends said that X and Y counties have very different responses to persons convicted of drunk driving. If the state law regarding drunk driving is applicable to both counties, why is county X so much tougher on drunk drivers than county Y?
5. Our District Attorney has a special program for prosecuting career criminals. Will the crime rate go down if he convicts these people?

The revised assignment clearly requires that the student demonstrate factually correct knowledge of how the criminal justice system works. It also offers an opportunity to apply that knowledge to a new situation and helps to "cue" the students to the progression from simple to more complex thinking.

## STRUCTURE AND PROCESS

Redesigning assignments to elicit good work is also enhanced by providing the students with sufficient information about the process of writing. Our former assumption, usually false, was that college students knew how to produce a good paper.

Consequently, we now include information (below) about how to approach the assignment.

a. Re-read the assigned readings, underlining and making notes to yourself to identify the main points.
b. Choose the two questions you will respond to as examples which support your thesis.
c. Make notes and an outline to help you plan your essay. (Your final paper should be about four typed, double spaced pages.)
d. Write a first draft.
e. Set the draft aside for a few hours/days; then revise and rewrite it.
f. Have a friend or tutor in the writing center read your essay and comment on it. Take notes on what the reader says.
g. Revise and rewrite your essay.
h. Repeat steps f and g as often as you like.
i. Type your final paper which must be double-spaced with one-inch margins and should not exceed four pages. Edit for correctness. Staple in the upper left-hand comer.

## GRADING CRITERIA

In addition to these suggestions for completing the assignment, we also now include the grading criteria in the assignment sheet. For our revised assignment, the criteria consist of the following:

1. How accurately does the content of the essay reflect understanding of the assigned reading?
2. Is the essay logical, coherent and well-organized?
3. Is the essay appropriate to its audience and occasion? Are the explanations and examples clear and to the point?
4. Is the essay carefully proofread and edited so that errors of grammar, spelling and punctuation are avoided?

Overall, the redesigned assignments are now much shorter in length. However, written assignments, particularly in writing intensive courses, are now more frequent. Furthermore, in order to maximize the learning-writing potential, many assignments are first submitted as a "clean draft". This allows each student to receive formal feedback on the quality of the paper and affords them an opportunity to incorporate that information into a revision.

To facilitate the increased faculty workload arising from the greater number of writing assignments, much of the initial "official" feedback comes in the form of structured peer editing. Each paper is read by at least one other student in the class. Using a Peer Editing Sheet (see Appendix 1), the peer editor makes detailed comments about the content and structure of the paper. Interestingly, the peer editors, with minimal instruction, are able to do a very thorough job of critiquing papers. The professor then provides a cursory review of each paper in light of the editor's comments. Most often, comments by the faculty affirm the findings of the peer editor. Additionally, some faculty also note what the grade for the paper would be if it were graded "as is."

Each student is then offered an opportunity to revise the paper before it is officially graded. Students may elect not to revise; in which case the "as is" grade is recorded. For students who choose to rewrite, the only requirement is that any revision must take into account all of the deficiencies noted by the peer editor and professor. Generally, about 2/3 of the class will elect to rewrite, and the revisions are usually markedly better than the initial effort.

## CONCLUSION

At this point, the writing intensive emphasis has helped faculty do a much better job of creating the kinds of assignments which develop critical thinking and good writing skills.

Furthermore, the "draft and rewrite" process affords students an opportunity to improve their writing skills in a structured way. The faculty have also acquired a new sense of responsibility for improving the written communication and thinking skills of our students. The English Department is no longer seen as the sole source of writing instruction and the primary repository for complaints about under-prepared students. While the faculty will always grouse about problems of student preparation and writing ability, the writing intensive requirements have forced each of us to be a part of the solution.

### References

Blankenship, Michael B., W. Richard Janikowski, and Jerry R. Sparger (1990). The impact of general education on criminal justice pedagogy. Journal of Criminal Justice Education, I, 87–98.

Bloom, B.S., et.al. (1956). Taxonomy of Educational Objectives: Cognitive Domain. New York: David Mckay Co.

Bonwell, Charles C., and James Eison (1991). Active Learning: Creating Excitement in the Classroom. ASHE-ERIC Higher Education Report No. I.

Bowman, Janice (1991). California Lutheran University Cluster Program. Instructor's Handbook. California Lutheran University.

Cederblom, Jerry, and Cassia Spohn (1991). A model for teaching criminal justice ethics. Journal of Criminal Justice Education, 2, 201–17.

Clark, John H., and Arthur W. Biddle (1993). Teaching Critical Thinking: Reports from Across the Curriculum. Englewood Cliffs, NJ: Prentice Hall.

Gladis, Stephen (1991). Writing to learn strategies for criminal justice educators. Journal of Criminal Justice Education, 2, 237–243.

Henry, Louis H. (1993). Clustering, writing and discussing economic issues. In J. Clark and A. Biddle (Eds.), Teaching Critical Thinking: Reports from Across the Curriculum. Englewood Cliffs, NJ: Prentice Hall.

Murray, Donald (1984). Write to Learn. New York: Holt, Rinehart and Winston.
Watkins, Beverly T. (18 July 1990). More and more professors in many academic disciplines routinely require students to do extensive writing. Chronicle of Higher Education, 36, Al3+.

# APPENDIX 1

## Paper Editing Sheet*

Your Name ________________ Author's Name ________________

Talk with your partner about any concerns s/he may have about the paper. Read through the paper fairly quickly to get a sense of the whole thing. *Underline passages of sentences that aren't clear to you.* Put a check mark or exclamation point next to things you like.

Now reread the paper carefully, paying attention to the following questions.

## Form Issues

1. Introduction. Does the opening paragraph clearly set the context for what the paper is about? Does it establish a thesis? Make suggestions for change as necessary.
2. Transitions. Check all first sentences of paragraphs. Do they make logical transitions from the ideas in the previous paragraphs? Are there abrupt shifts? Mark good and weak transitions. Do you have suggestions for change?
3. Organization. Are the paragraphs arranged logically? Would you rearrange anything? What? Does each paragraph advance the thesis?
4. Development. Should the author add any more discussion of ideas? Where? Which is the weakest paragraph? Why?
5. Conclusion. Does the writer tell you what is significant? Do they suggest the implications of their discussion or do they simply repeat their main points? How would you improve the conclusion?

## Content Questions

1. Does the paper provide evidence that the author understands the assigned readings? Note one or two examples which support your judgment.
2. Are the questions answered by the author used to illustrate the complexity of the CJS? Note one or two examples which support your judgment.

3. Has the author provided adequate support (logical argument and/or reference to an authoritative source) for any assertions regarding the complexity of the CJS?
4. Do you think the sources used by the author (if any) are authoritative and credible? Why or why not? Are the sources properly documented in the body of the paper and in a bibliography or list of references at the end of the paper?

* This form is adapted from one developed by Dr. Susan Hahn. MD-c:\wp51\data\class\edit

**Chapter 8**

# Working in Criminal Justice

## INTRODUCTION

An undergraduate degree in CJC studies will present you with many career options to consider, from working in the CJS or surrounding fields to continuing your education via graduate school. In this chapter, we will examine the realities and misconceptions of jobs in criminal justice and help you think about which of the many available career paths is the best fit for you. A wide variety of careers will be explored, with the goal of expanding the array of opportunities you have to consider. Many careers in criminal justice are dynamic and interesting, and provide you opportunities to work with diverse populations. This chapter will address the skills that can help you work effectively and meaningfully with the populations that interact with the CJS. Hopefully the many activities at the end of this chapter will be helpful in charting your career trajectory.

## CAREER PATHS IN CRIMINAL JUSTICE

Depictions of criminal justice jobs on television and in film are not generally accurate reflections of the reality of this work. Unfortunately, the glamour, pay scale (as implied by the characters' apparent SES), excitement, and distinct lack of paperwork are simply not normative aspects of this line of work. Most criminal justice careers start with entry-level positions and modest pay—although a Master's degree in CJC studies can facilitate a higher starting rank or salary. It is unrealistic to expect to immediately begin a career as a detective, special agent, crime scene investigator, or prison administrator right after you earn your degree, however. Oftentimes, students envision working for the federal government, for instance in the Federal Bureau of Investigating (FBI) or the Central Intelligence Agency (CIA). This is certainly possible—but these are the most competitive jobs in the CJS and individuals generally spend a few years working their way up to positions in these agencies by way of municipal-, county-, or state-level employment.

In fact, the majority of CJS professionals working in the field are employed by local-, county-, or state-level agencies.

Continuing your education is also an important option to consider. Although a CJC degree will provide a great starting point for a career in the CJS, some jobs require advanced degrees or specialization in other areas as well. Whether you pursue graduate study right away or after obtaining some experience in the field, a graduate degree can benefit your career immensely. This can be done in CJC, or in public administration, law, psychology, social work, or business. For example, to work in forensics or arson investigation, a degree in chemistry or another science-related degree would be expected alongside a CJC credential. Similarly, the FBI often seeks out accountants, lawyers, psychologists, computer specialists, and individuals fluent in languages other than English. None of this information should deter or dishearten you, though. There are many jobs for those with undergraduate degrees in CJC studies!

There are also jobs in agencies outside of the criminal justice realm that CJC graduates are well-suited for, including jobs in human and social services, corporate operations, domestic and foreign policy, and the nonprofit sector. There are several questions to contemplate as you choose your path. See the self-assessment activity at the end of this chapter for a great place to start your exploration. There are likely more job opportunities open to CJC graduates than you may have initially thought. We group them here into five main categories: law enforcement/security, judiciary/law/courts, corrections/counseling/juvenile justice, social services/victim advocacy, and teaching/research. The more you know about your ideal job, the better prepared you will be to determine your individual career path.

## Law Enforcement/Security

For many CJC majors, the law enforcement careers that come to mind most readily are police officer, detective, and crime scene investigator. There are a variety of other types of law enforcement jobs that might be less prominent, such as working as a fish and game warden, park ranger, airport security worker, deputy marshal, military officer, school public safety officer, border patrol or immigration officer, or witness protection program worker. If you are interested in law enforcement, you may want to expand your job search to include a wide variety of agencies, such as the Transportation Security Administration (TSA), the United States Post Office (USPS), the Internal Revenue Service (IRS), the Bureau of Alcohol, Tobacco, Firearms and Explosives (ATF), the Drug Enforcement Administration (DEA), the FBI, the CIA, and the many local- and state-level agencies in your area. You might also consider employment in loss or fraud prevention for a company, insurance or private investigator, service as a bodyguard, and providing either industrial or private security.

Applying for a position in law enforcement can be a complex and time-consuming process. Begin by researching jobs that you are interested in, making sure to develop a working knowledge of the department in which the position is located; as with everything we've discussed in this book, context matters! Apply for jobs through the appropriate agency websites. Be prepared to demonstrate the knowledge of criminological theory and Evidence Based Practices (EBPs) that you acquired while obtaining your degree. Make sure your application materials are strongly written. Police work requires an ability to write clearly and concisely in reports and other short formats, and agencies look for this skill when hiring. And remember that in this line of work, honesty is critical. The application process is likely to include a written test, a physical test, a background check, psychological testing, medical clearance, drug tests, polygraph testing, and multiple interviews. Once hired to work for a police department, training both at the Academy and in the field is extensive, including qualifying on the use of firearms, and continues on posthire. Expect to begin working shifts that no one else wants (e.g., weekends, midnights, evenings), with minimal control over your schedule for the first few years.

## Judiciary/Law/Courts

When most people think of the court system, they envision snappily dressed attorneys and somber judges. Both of these careers require law degrees, but an undergraduate degree in CJC lays a great foundation for law school. There are many other jobs within the court system that do not require a law degree, such as court coordinator, court reporter, clerk, jury coordinator, court services officer, bailiff, paralegal, community liaison officer, presentence investigator, victim advocate, pretrial supervision officer, and diversion service personnel. This diverse array of jobs requires varying degrees of education and special certifications, and the exact qualifications necessary will vary by agency and jurisdiction. The application process for many of these court positions would involve an online or written application, at least one interview, and potentially a drug test. Jobs are likely to be posted through county or state websites and private organizations.

## Corrections/Counseling/Juvenile Justice

In the field of corrections, the most commonly thought-of careers involve the supervision of correctional populations: correctional officer, parole officer, and probation officer. These positions are widely available at both the adult and juvenile levels across jurisdictions. There are also many other positions that focus less (or not at all) on supervision, with an emphasis instead on treatment provision, skill development, and diversionary programs. Individuals may also serve as residence supervisors, counselors, community liaison officers, and, with experience and further education, warden or program director. Many positions in corrections blend these two elements (captured roughly by the categories of supervision and service provision). This is particularly the case in juvenile justice, which has a stronger treatment orientation than adult corrections, and in community corrections. In a prison setting, some employees start out as correctional officers (working "custody") and later transition to a noncustody role (e.g., correctional counselor) with more of a focus on service provision.

Because there is a wide range of corrections positions, the application process varies greatly. Again, it is important to research the field and the organization and be ready to demonstrate your knowledge about CJC studies, including theoretical perspectives and EBPs. The process for applying to correctional officer positions will likely be similar to the law enforcement application process, whereas applications for other jobs in corrections generally resemble the court application process. Make sure your application materials are strongly written and that you are honest in your application. Many of these jobs will also require a background check and/or drug test, so make sure you are prepared.

## Social Services/Victim Advocacy

Many organizations—both government agencies and nongovernmental organizations—partner with criminal justice agencies to provide services and counseling to people involved in or affected by the CJS. Government agencies that interface with the CJS include social services, children's and family services, and housing and urban development. Many nonprofit organizations hire advocates to safeguard the rights and integrity of victims, particularly abused and neglected children and battered women. Nonprofit organizations also do important community work in the areas of awareness raising, prevention, and service provision. Community organizing is a great way to address existing social problems that, as we know, are intricately intertwined with CJS issues. For those who find the individual-level focus of the CJS constraining in the face of a desire to remedy broader social problems, nonprofit organizations have great potential.

These agencies operate at national and local levels, and there are many job opportunities if you know where to look. For instance, the National Coalition of Anti-Violence Programs (NCAVP) is an organization that "works to prevent, respond to, and end all forms of violence against and within LGBTQ communities" (http://www.avp.org/about avp/coalitions-a-collaborations/82-national-coalition-of-anti-violence-programs). Although NCAVP is based in New York, member organizations and local affiliates are located across the United States. Positions at NCAVP include victim advocacy, community training and outreach, data analysis, and policy development. Job opportunities with NCAVP and many other nonprofit organizations can be found on websites such as idealist.org, nonprofitjobs.org, and npconnect.org. Because the range of positions is so wide, application procedures and qualifications are too diverse to cover here. As with all jobs, make sure to research your options diligently, learning everything you can about the position and the organization (including the mission and goals of the organization, which may not be as obvious with nonprofits as they are with certain government jobs).

## Teaching/Research/Analysis

If you just can't get enough CJC studies, there is always the option of more. In fact, there are two options: a Master's degree and a Ph.D. Continuing your studies in a

Master's program can serve many purposes. As discussed earlier, it can prepare you for employment as a CJS practitioner, often starting you off at a higher wage or rank than if you began working straight out of college. A Master's degree will also qualify you for an additional category of jobs that can roughly be understood as "analyst" positions: crime analyst, research analyst, data analyst. These positions exist within many agencies, and generally require proficiency in basic quantitative analysis. Although a Master's degree can qualify you to teach at the college level on an adjunct (course-by-course) basis, it is difficult to sustain a career this way. If you are interested in college-level teaching, a Ph.D. is necessary to obtain full-time, tenure-track employment. A Master's degree can be used as a stepping stone to a Ph.D., although many Ph.D. programs do not require a Master's degree for admission. Continuing your education to obtain a Ph.D. in CJC studies would provide the expertise and credentials to be a tenure-track professor, work as a researcher or senior data analyst, and do consulting work for CJ agencies.

## LOOKING FOR AND GETTING A JOB

You may think that the factors that will most strongly affect your job prospects right out of college are grade point average, the reputation of your school, or the relevance of your coursework. A recent study revealed, however, that none of these even make it into the top five attributes used in evaluating new graduates on the job market. The most important factors were, in this order: whether students completed an internship, whether they were employed during college, their major (the only academic factor in the top five), whether they had volunteer experience, and whether they participated in extracurricular activities (Thompson, 2014).

Looking to secure employment is a full-time job in itself, and preparing for an interview requires doing research on the organization. The more you know, the better. Although there is a plethora of information available on how to be a strong interview candidate, here are a few tips. Be on time or even early to the interview, making sure you are dressed appropriately. Remember to turn your cell phone off. You will make a great first impression by preparing answers before the interview, and asking questions that build on what you have already learned doing research on the organization. Be positive, confident, and enthusiastic. Greet the interviewer with a firm handshake. When the interview is over, thank the interviewer in person, but also send a note afterwards. Do not leave without knowing what their next steps and timetable are, as this communicates interest and can help assuage your nerves as you await a response.

Before an interview, you should review commonly asked questions and practice answering them. Here are a few questions to start considering:

- Why do you want to be a [insert position applying for]?
- Why do you want to work for our department/agency?
- Where do you see your career in five years?
- What would your current supervisor tell us about you as an employee?
- What are your strengths and weaknesses?

- Why are you qualified for this position?
- What are some evidence-based practices you could use in this position?
- How do you feel about working with different populations (e.g., those who face domestic violence, sex, drug, or DUI [driving under the influence] cases)?
- Explain a time where you had to interact with someone who was not happy. How did you respond?
- Give an example of a team experience that you found disappointing. What would you go back and do differently?

In addition to these general questions, it would not be uncommon to be asked scenario questions, asking what you might do in a very specific situation. If you have a friend or colleague who works in the field that you are applying for, ask her for advice on what might come up during the interview, and how she has handled various situations on the job.

## SKILLS NEEDED TO WORK TOWARD JUSTICE

Take a minute to consider the skills that you think are needed to work effectively and justly with the individuals involved in the CJS. Jot down your ideas. Were your lists mostly technical, including things such as writing skills and statistics? Or did they involve qualities necessary to interact with people? What other kinds of skills appeared on your list? Now consider which of these skills you already possess and which you need to develop. For instance, do any of your skills demonstrate a willingness to connect with system-involved individuals in a professional capacity? If not, you might want to add this. The literature on corrections has demonstrated that the attitude a CJS professional holds toward offenders and the quality of the relationship between them are key factors predicting offender success (Bonta et al., 2011; Lowenkamp, Holsinger, Robinson, & Cullen, 2012).

A willingness to engage with the diverse populations that are entangled in the CJS requires an understanding of many of the topics we've covered in this book. For instance, your sociological imagination will allow you to see the broader justice implications of the individual cases you encounter in your daily work. An understanding of social stratification and privilege based on race, gender, and class will help provide context for your interactions with people who are different from you; reflexivity will help you overcome the natural tendency toward ethnocentrism that may obscure some of the relevant factors and impede your ability to relate to a client. Last, a working understanding of the structural and cultural impacts of poverty will help you meet your clients where they are at by providing insight into their circumstances.

Working with people in poverty requires a closer examination of the multiple causes of poverty. In the absence of a thorough understanding of the causes and effects of poverty, it is easy to make assumptions based on erroneous or incomplete information. Typical assumptions about poverty focus on the behaviors of individuals, their choices, characteristics, and habits. However, this narrow focus obscures other important factors, such as the resources available in poor communities, historical legacies of exploitation that create and reinforce poverty, and the larger political and economic structures that result in poverty (Payne, 2005). If you have not personally dealt with poverty, it will help you in your job to spend time considering the barriers created by poverty (many of which were discussed in Chapter 2) and the role that these barriers play in the lives of system-involved individuals.

Working with individuals whose lives intersect with the CJS involves an understanding of their resources as much as their constraints. An overemphasis on challenges and barriers may leave important strengths and skills unacknowledged. Resources can be financial (not just money, but also knowledge), emotional (e.g., healthy emotional responses, motivation and persistence), cognitive (e.g., reading skills, aptitude for numbers, compassion), spiritual (e.g., beliefs, cultural support), physical (e.g., health and mobility), or social (e.g., social support, positive relationships and role models) (Payne, 2005). Ultimately, it is important to recognize the humanity and individuality of everyone you work with and recognize your ability to be in a supportive role to individuals who may need to make major life changes, including breaking addiction and/or dealing with mental health issues or problems as seemingly intractable as poverty. Approaching others without judgment, displaying an understanding of their circumstances, and communicating a belief in their humanity is critical. By knowing yourself—in terms of your strengths, limitations, positionality, etc.—you can figure out how to best work with others who may be significantly different from you to achieve justice in an imperfect system.

## References

Bonta, J., Bourgon, G., Rugge, T., Scott, T., Yessine, A.K., Gutierrez, L., & Li, J. (2011). An experimental demonstration of training probation officers in evidence based community supervision. *Criminal Justice & Behavior, 38*(1), 1127–1148.

Lowenkamp, C.T., Holsinger, A.M., Robinson, C.R., & Cullen, F.T. (2012). When a person isn't a data point: Making evidence-based practice work. *Federal Probation, 76*(3), 11–21.

Payne, R.K. (2005). *A framework for understanding poverty.* Highlands, TX: aha! Process Inc.

Thompson, D. (2014). The thing employers look for when hiring recent graduates. *The Atlantic,* August 19, 2014. Retrieved from http://www.theatlantic.com/business/archive/2014/08/the-thing-employers-look-for-when-hiring-recent-graduates/378693/.

# ACTIVITIES/ASSIGNMENTS

## Empathy Versus Sympathy

Watch this three-minute video clip. What does that add to your ideas about empathy versus sympathy?

https://www.youtube.com/watch?v=1Evwgu369Jw

## Recognizing Resources

Using the typology of resources presented in this chapter, provide an assessment of your own resources in each category. Where are your deficits and strengths in terms of resources?

## Chapter Review

What does this chapter provide in terms of best practices for working with people living in poverty? What characteristics must you possess to work effectively with CJS-involved individuals?

## Discovering Your Core Values

Read this article and complete the activity.
http://www.taproot.com/archives/37771

## Self-Assessment for CJ and CJ-related Jobs

1. How comfortable would you be working with offenders? Careers in policing, corrections (probation, parole, and work within institutions) and counseling/psychology in the CJS will require daily interaction with offenders, many of whom have committed serious offenses. This is different from the work of police who typically have little interaction with offenders and usually only for brief encounters.
2. How comfortable would you be carrying a firearm? This is an important question. If you are not comfortable around firearms and do not believe you could use one against another person, even if the circumstances required it, then you should avoid jobs that will require this. This includes policing (patrol and detectives), parole in some states, and several federal law enforcement agencies.
3. How important is salary? This is a tough question to answer and will likely require balancing other considerations (e.g., how much you enjoy what you do, benefits, hours). Careers in criminal justice tend to pay reasonably well. However, you will not become wealthy working in the CJS. Salaries for police officers are becoming increasingly competitive and many larger police departments begin officer salaries in the upper $30K (and many higher than $40K) plus the potential for overtime. The median salary for police officers is around $57K. Probation and parole officers tend to start at the mid to upper $30K per year, and have a median salary around $48K. Careers working with juveniles are usually some of the lower paying jobs, though they clearly have the potential to be rewarding in a number of other ways.
4. Consider your personal values and identities. This refers to a number of issues and questions that all students should think about when making major decisions that will affect their lives and the lives of others. Remember that most people change jobs and/or careers during their lifetime. There is no reason why your

first job out of college must be the one you stay with until retirement. There are, however, some basic questions you can think about to decide whether you would be happy with a particular job. People tend to be happiest in their work when it is consistent with and reinforces their own beliefs, values, goals, and principles.

## Answer these questions

1. What is important to you?
2. What type of person are you?
3. Would you feel more comfortable in a supervision role, a service provision role, or a combination of the two?
4. Do you like to work collaboratively with others or would you rather rely on your own skills and abilities?
5. What kind of life do you want?
6. What type of job would you find rewarding—protecting people, helping others, being in a position of authority and responsibility, being intellectually or physically challenged?

## Looking for Jobs

To begin the research, look at www.bls.gov for recent information about career outlooks, average salaries, and potential jobs for your specific degree. Another interesting site is http://www.degreescout.com/criminal-justice-degrees/criminal-justice-careers-on-the-rise

Look at the websites in your area for police departments, department of corrections, and county services.

For federal jobs look at: http://federalgovernmentjobs.us/

For a large nonprofit jobs database, see: http://www.npconnect.org/page/jobs/

Also look at ATF, DEA, FBI, and CIA websites for career descriptions and opportunities.

This last website is a resource for nonprofit job opportunities in nonprofit work. https://www.myphilanthropedia.org/all-nonprofit-reviews/national/criminal-justice/2011

## Interviewing Practice

In pairs of two, practice answering the interview questions posed in this chapter. Create one scenario question based on your partner's job interest.

## Social Class Quiz

Take the social class quiz found here: http://www.asanet.org/introtosociology/Documents/Hidden%20Rules%20of%20Social%20Class.htm. Where do you have the most check marks? Where do you have the least? Were you surprised by the outcome? How did you feel when doing the exercise? Analyze the type of taken-for-granted information found in the questionnaire. What is the knowledge about? How and where do you learn it? How do you gain access to the people and places where it can be learned?

## The Place of Ethics in Criminal Justice Education

After reading the article by Rhineberger-Dunn and Mullins, what is your position on the place of teaching ethics in academic CJPs? What types of ethical issues do you expect to encounter working in the CJS? Which ones would you like to discuss in class?

## Changing Police Organizational Culture

After reading the article by Kingshott, what are the barriers that exist to changing existing police culture and broadening ideas about leadership? How might police departments look different if they incorporated feminist perspectives on leadership?

Selected Reading

# Women in Policing

## Changing the Organizational Culture by Adopting a Feminist Perspective on Leadership

***Brian F. Kingshott***

## INTRODUCTION

This paper will not attempt to seek new definitions of leadership but to discuss concepts found within the literature review relating to classical leadership in general and discuss their relevance to leadership within the police organization. The majority of existing research 'in leadership studies is centered on the individual leader rather than the process of leadership' (Komives, Lucas, & McMahon, 1998, p. 11). Within the hierarchical structure of the police service it may be argued that 'leadership is not something a leader possesses so much as a process involving followership' (Hollander, 1993, p. 29). Alternatively, it may be argued that much of the leadership comes from the lower ranks due to a developing situation and that at that moment in time the resolution does not call for 'a process involving followership.' It is because little emphasis is placed upon the ethical parameters of policing that the roles of leadership and management are important. The role of leadership in the police service will be discussed with reference to the classical models of leadership identified in the literature review. In that literature review it was identified that early approaches explored leadership via the notions of traits and behaviors contained within contingency theory, although later authors explored 'transformational' theories and some issues of practice. It is acknowledged that the discussion relating to classical leadership within this paper owes its format to the discussions of Doyle and Smith (1999).

Many of the images and perceptions associated with leadership within the police service have their roots in conflict, and within military models associated with British colonialism. From a military perspective we consider leaders of major conflicts from Joan of Arc, Napoleon, and the Duke of Wellington, to actions during the Zulu Wars, the Boer War, and later conflicts. Regardless of one's affiliations military leadership was demonstrated by all sides to a greater or lesser degree. Other perspectives identify politicians whose oratory and passion mobilize individuals and groups to action and people from all walks of life are destined to take control of a crisis. We are directed to special individuals like Winston Churchill, Mohandas Karamchand (Mahatma) Gandhi, Nelson Mandela, or Martin Luther King. The biographies of these individuals identify that there are moments of crisis or decision where their actions were pivotal. They each had a vision of what can, and should be, achieved and were able to communicate this to others to initiate irrevocable change and are an inspiration to future leaders. From their examples it may be argued that the quality of leadership is pivotal to the survival and success of groups and organizations regardless of ethnicity, religion, or political orientation. *The Art of War*, the oldest known military text (*c.*400 BC), describes the role of leader as, 'the leader of armies is the arbiter of the people's fate, the man on whom it depends whether the nation shall be in peace or in peril' (Phillips, 1985, p. 26).

The question is raised, what is leadership? It seems to be one of those ethereal qualities that you know when you see it, but is difficult to articulate. It may simply be described as an action where one person leads. If that is so there are four issues identified within the literature that are referred to as 'divisions.' The first is the ability to lead in such a manner as to influence followers. Secondly, it is accepted that where there are leaders there are followers. Thirdly, leaders are identified when individuals, who may or may not be part of a group, are faced with a crisis or special problem to which there has to be a response solution and the leader is the one who initiates a response. Fourth, leaders are individuals who have a vision of what they want to achieve to resolve the crisis and a strategy that initiates that change. Then leaders are individuals, of either gender, who are able to identify the problem and initiate a response solution. That solution will influence the actions of others but the leader will also be aware of individual and group social norms, beliefs, and emotions of those stakeholders impacted by the response solution. That being said, then being a 'leader' is personal and many leaders are identifiable by a charismatic personality (the question of charisma will be addressed later in this paper). However, a charismatic personality does not make a leader as that role requires additional management skills and here the roles become confused because not all managers are leaders; and not all leaders are managers.

In the recent literature relating to 'classical' leadership there have been four main 'generations' of theory identified as Trait, Behavioral, Contingency, and Transformational Theories. However, it is important to acknowledge that none of the four 'generations' is mutually exclusive and they should not be considered in isolation (Van Maurik, 2001). The literature review tends to suggest that each generation identifies or redefines aspects of leadership that adds to the continuing debate on leadership qualities and those qualities are not mutually exclusive to one school or another. This is perhaps the most important aspect of leadership as it relates to the police service as hierarchical organizations are often too rigid in rules, regulations, and procedures to allow the development of effective leaders. The police service may be viewed as a specialist group therefore framing that group into a community will identify that relational leadership is often effective because '*When force is used, conflict and argument follow. The group field degenerates. The climate is hostile, neither open nor nourishing*' (Heider, 1985, p. 59).

The fourfold division, identified earlier in this paper, of 'modern' leadership/management can be identified under different descriptions (e.g., charismatic may be described as transformational leadership), and there are other possible candidates, for example, skill-based approaches and self-management or shared leadership (discussed elsewhere on these pages). However, regardless of the syntax of descriptions identified within these four formations there are identifiable qualities that are held in common and from this perspective they can be approached as variations of the 'classical' model of leadership.

> Leaders are people who are able to express themselves fully ... they also know what they want, why they want it, and how to communicate what they want to others, in order to gain their cooperation and support ... they know how to achieve their goals.
>
> (Bennis, 1998, p. 3)

Then the question is raised, what is it that makes someone an exceptional leader? Whoever is identified as an effective leader, personal qualities, influenced by but not limited to, gender, ethnicity, education, and personal traits are all influential qualities. However, those qualities are all very different; comparison of political figures such as Mahatma Gandhi, Nelson Mandela, Golda Meir, or Thabo Mbeki will confirm this.

## Traits

The literature attempts to identify the general qualities or *traits* that are believed should be present in effective leaders. Early trait research by Stogdill (1948) and Mann (1959) reported that many of the studies identified personality characteristics that appear to differentiate leaders from followers. This was later contradicted by Wright (1996, p. 34) who commented, '*others found no differences between leaders and followers with respect to these characteristics, or even found people who possessed them were less likely to become leaders.*' The early researchers assumed that there was a definite set of characteristics that made a leader and if those traits could be identified then, whatever the situation that confronted them, whether it was on a battlefield or a factory production line, the identified traits provided leadership skills. Such flawed thinking minimized the impact of the situation (Sadler, 1997). In the literature review the search for an identifiable list of traits that were thought to be central to effective leadership was a continuing theme on the assumption that if a person possesses this he/she will be able to take the lead in very different situations.

The problem is that in the literature some authors identified and mixed qualities that may be better categorized elsewhere within a personality profile because the identifying of qualities was a subjective decision of individual authors. Qualities may be identified as aspects of a person's behavior, skills, or as temperament and intellectual ability (Gardner, 1989), but the conclusion was that there were some qualities or attributes that did appear to mean that a leader in one situation could lead in another. Personality dimensions were addressed by Eysenck (1977, 1989) and Eysenck and Gudjonnson (1990) with the theory that there are three major personality dimensions, namely, *psychoticism*, *extraversion*, and *neuroticism*. Although in the above theory the emphasis was on criminal behavior the point is that personality dimensions are much more complex than simply providing a typology of required qualities of attributes desirable in a leader. It is acknowledged that the literature review broadly addressed *business* organizations and even where that business was seen to be a service provider (e.g., hotel or restaurant), that service provider's output was limited, constant, and with a limited number of variables that would allow for improvement to the service. This is important because the police as a service provider do not have a constant output as policing has a much broader base of service. There are many more variables associated with each individual problem and resolution decisions are often autocratic and made within microseconds as opposed to committee decisions as in other service provider environments.

The identified qualities or attributes were not exclusive to leaders as many were also applicable to management which raises the question, what is leadership as opposed to management? (This question will not be addressed within this paper.) Those qualities or attributes included, but were not limited to, Intelligence and action-oriented judgment; Eagerness to accept responsibility; Task competence; Understanding of followers and their needs; Assertiveness; Physical vitality and stamina; Skill in dealing with people; Courage and resolution; Trustworthiness; Capacity to motivate people; Decisiveness; Self-confidence; as well as Adaptability/flexibility.

Regardless of the author the typologies produced vary in length and are not exhaustive and often ignore other 'leadership qualities' identified by other authors which raises the question, what happens when someone has some but not all of the qualities? What combinations of traits are required by a leader and who decides? Stogdill (1948) argues that it may be possible to link clusters of desirable personality traits to succeed in identified situations but it is based upon personal opinion not science and therefore must be flawed according to Wright (1996), who continued to explore modern trait theories in relation to leadership qualities.

One problem associated with such trait typologies relates to gender as many typologies are gender specific (Rosener, 1997). It is apparent that when men and women are asked to define each other's characteristics and leadership qualities, significant patterns emerge (Lipman-Blumen, 1984). The difficulties in seeing women as leaders were identified by all respondents. The attributes associated with leadership typologies are often viewed as male which identifies the problems of identifying typologies of gender-specific leadership traits. The issues relating to gender and qualities of leaders from a feminine perspective will be discussed later in this paper.

## Behaviors

The early literature identified that there were flaws in the methodology of leadership traits because the methodology moved focus from trait typologies to what leaders did in relationships linked to their behavior. The move, from leaders to leadership, was to become the dominant way of approaching leadership within organizations in the 1950s and early 1960s. This was to be achieved by grouping different patterns of behavior together and labeled as styles. This is exemplified by Blake and Mouton's Managerial Grid (1964, 1978), and here the author argues that the inextricable link between leadership and management was made. The model can be categorized as having four styles categorized as: Concern for Task; (2) Concern for People; (3) Directive Leadership; and (4) Participative Leadership.

### *Concern for Task*

In this style leaders emphasize the achievement of defined objectives. They look for high levels of productivity, and ways to organize people and activities in order to meet those organizational objectives. In the police service this style may be effective from an administrator's perspective but limited for the patrol officer.

### *Concern for People*

In this style leaders look upon their employees (followers) as individuals who have needs, as identified in Weber's model of management. The employees are not simply units of production or means to an end. Concern for task is set against concern for people. In the police service the culture and anecdotal evidence would suggest that this does not occur.

### *Directive Leadership*

This style is characterized by leaders, who are often autocratic in management styles, taking decisions for others and expecting followers or subordinates to follow instructions. It is because of the hierarchical structure of the police service that this style of leadership is often the most commonly applied. Directive leadership is contrasted with participative leadership (for example, McGregor's 1960 portrayal of managers as 'Theory X' or 'Theory Y').

Theory X Assumptions:
- People inherently dislike work
- People must be coerced or controlled to do work to achieve objectives
- People prefer to be directed

Theory Y Assumptions:

- People view work as being as natural as play and rest
- People will exercise self-direction and -control towards achieving objectives they are committed to
- People learn to accept and seek responsibility

## *Participative Leadership*

This style is characterized by leaders who demonstrate a democratic approach to leadership as they attempt to share decision-making with others (Wright, 1996).

The literature review identified that many of the early authors that analyzed participative and people-centered leadership, argued that it brought about greater satisfaction amongst followers (subordinates). Sadler (1997) argued that this was not true because of the differences and inconsistencies between studies. Those inconsistencies made it difficult to support the statement that style of leadership was significant in enabling one group to work better than another. Wright (1996, p. 47) argued that, as with the authors who argued for traits, researchers did not identify the context or setting in which the style was used. This was an important omission by those researchers because the styles that leaders adopt are affected by those they are working with, and the environmental constraints they are operating within. From the literature it is apparent that because of the complexity and diversity of the policing task there is no one model of leadership that suits the police service but that all models have aspects that may, in certain situations, be of value. Therefore, police leaders need to be educated in all aspects of organizational leadership in order that they may choose the most appropriate model, or combination of models, to suit the situation they face because the situations will dictate the strategies for a successful resolution to the problem being addressed.

## Situations

The literature review relating to classical leadership models identified that later researchers began to turn to the contexts in which leadership is exercised and accepted that each situation requires different attributes and skills of leadership and management. Within any given policing scenario identifying the contexts assists in identifying the style required for a given situation. That is important because each policing problem is unique therefore particular contexts would demand particular forms of leadership dependent upon the variable associated with the policing problem.

The acceptance that each situation requires different attributes and skills of leadership and management led to the development of a *contingency* approach, an approach that identifies that effective leadership is dependent on many factors. For an effective leader effectiveness depends upon leadership style and the degree to which the situation gives the leader control and influence. The three factors influence the outcome and they are: (1) the relationship between leaders and followers; (2) the structure of the task; and (3) the position of power. A summary of the argument is as follows:

- *The relationship between the leaders and followers.* If leaders are popular and respected they are more likely to have the support of followers.
- *The structure of the task.* If the task is clearly identified through a management structure relating to goals, methods, and standards of performance then it is the leader's ability to exert influence that will be enhanced.
- *Position of power.* If an organization or group confers powers on the leader for the purpose of enforcement of organizational or group goals then the influence of the leader is enhanced (Fiedler, 1997; Fiedler & Garcia, 1987).

The literature identified that Reddin (1970, 1987) examined the interaction of the characteristics of the leader, the characteristics of the followers, and the situation from the perspective of Blake and Mouton's Managerial Grid. In addition, Hersey and Blanchard (1977) argued that it was necessary to identify the appropriate leadership style for the particular situation because one style will not suit all situations. To support their argument they identified four different leadership styles that could be drawn upon to deal with contrasting situations which they listed as: (1) Telling (high task/low relationship behavior); (2) Selling (high task/high relationship behavior); (3) Participating (high relationship/low task behavior); and (4) Delegating (low relationship/low task behavior). However, caution is advised when appraising these leadership styles because they relate to general organizations and not specifically police service delivery organizations, although aspects of the model may be incorporated into an effective police leadership style if the *situation* warrants it.

## Telling (High Task/Low Relationship Behavior)

This approach is characterized by involvement of providing specific direction to subordinates and by directing attention to defining roles and goals. The negative concepts associated with this style were that it was recommended for dealing with new employees, or where the work defined is menial or repetitive, or where time factors are important. In this model the assumption was that subordinates are viewed as being unable and unwilling to 'do a good job.'

## Selling (High Task/High Relationship Behavior)

This approach relies upon direction given by the leader, but there is an attempt at encouraging individuals to agree and support the designated task. The 'coaching' approach was found to be effective when the tasked individuals are willing and motivated but are identified as lacking the required 'maturity' or 'ability' to achieve the designated task.

## *Participating (High Relationship/Low Task Behavior)*

This democratic approach allows for a partnership where decision-making is shared between leaders and followers. In this model the main role of the leader is to facilitate and communicate the designated task. This model entails high support and low direction and is effective when individuals are able, but are perhaps unwilling or insecure. This was identified by Hersey (1984) in that such individuals are of moderate to high maturity.

## *Delegating (Low Relationship/Low Task Behavior)*

This approach allows for the leader to identify and articulate the problem or issue, but the responsibility for carrying out the response is given (delegated) to followers although the leader will retain overall responsibility for the outcome. It entails having a high degree of competence and maturity (people know what to do, and are motivated to do it).

There is no consensus of agreement among authors as Bolman and Deal (1997) comment that authors Blake and Mouton (1964, 1978) and Hersey and Blanchard (1977) '*focus mainly on the relationship between managers and immediate subordinates, and say little about issues of structure, politics or symbols*' (Bolman & Deal, 1997, p. 302). It is acknowledged that the observation of Bolman and Deal (1997) identifies the limitations of the model for police purposes although knowledge of such a model can only enhance a leader's arsenal of options.

The question raised is what leadership qualities are ideal for the police service? Robert McMurray (1992) argued that the realities of organization life make participative management virtually impossible and suggests that a benevolent autocrat is needed. Renis Likert (1992) at the Institute of Social Research at the University of Michigan did not support this. His conclusion was that those studied for their leadership qualities were classified as either 'job centered' or 'employer centered.' Based on that research Likert recommends that supportive employee-centered leadership models be developed where possible, and such models would be of value in the police service.

To improve the management and leadership qualities of the individual within any organization knowledge of the psychological principle underlying motivation will allow for lateral development. The most influential theory of motivation is the needs hierarchy formulated by Maslow (1954). Maslow identified five distinct need categories which were (a) physiological needs, (b) safety and security needs, (c) belongingness and love needs, (d) self-esteem needs, and finally (e) the need to self-actualize. Furthermore, he proposed that these needs are organized into a hierarchy because the needs higher up in the hierarchy emerge to play a prominent role in the control of behavior only when needs lower down the hierarchy are satisfied. Self-actualization, the highest level in the hierarchy, concerns the need for self-fulfillment and the complete achievement of the individual's full potential. In the police service many individuals do not seek promotion simply because they are allowed to achieve their full potential in a specialist role and are valued for their contribution.

In this model Maslow attempts to emphasize the positive side of human nature. This is achieved by stressing that despite the requirement for the satisfaction of lower level needs individuals strive to achieve their full potential thereby attaining satisfaction that they are using their abilities and skills to maximum effect. Maslow's theoretical model identifies possible implications of the need hierarchy for organizations and would appear popular in police management circles. However, despite its obvious appeal and relevance to the police service as an organization, the theory has not been well supported by empirical studies of its validity. As a result of those studies Alderfer (1972) produced a revision of Maslow's theory using three categories of needs with less emphasis on the hierarchical ordering and this reformulation has been validated to a certain degree by empirical studies.

If, in its broadest terms, leadership is concerned with personnel and management is concerned with other resources then both roles have a correlation and important to both is the need to motivate. The motivational process is based on human behavior patterns, which are directed towards a need or desire. Some needs are common, others arise from environmental factors, the people we work with, the community we serve and some are purely related to one's ego. It is worth remembering that all the management and leadership concepts discussed so far were conceived for their industrial application where there was an identifiable product and a quantifiable production run. There must be caution applied with any one, or combination of models, that are used in the police organization scenario because in both the law enforcement role and the service role, there is no identifiable product and no quantifiable production run.

## Authority

On occasions there is confusion between leadership and authority. Heifetz (1994) argues that authority is often viewed as the possession of powers based on a formal role. In organizations the focus is often on the manager or supervisor or officer, being individuals who have the right to direct others. Such individuals are obeyed when their exercise of power is legitimate although it is acknowledged that they may be obeyed if those ordered to complete a task fear the consequences of not following their orders. In addition, it is the possibility of sanctions (sacking, demoting, or disadvantaging the individual) that may lead to compliance to the given direction. In comparison direction may be followed because the individual giving the direction may show leadership. That leadership direction is generally informal – the ability to make sense of, and act in, situations that are out of the ordinary. Leaders may have formal authority, but they will also rely in large part on informal authority that is underpinned by their charismatic personal qualities and actions. They may be respected for their expertise, followed because of their ability to persuade or because they command respect from the group. The leader also relies on individual and group feedback and contributions because without these the leader will not have the information and resources to achieve the goal. Then it follows that leaders and individual 'followers' are interdependent.

In the police organization having formal authority has duality and may be viewed as both a resource and a constraint. This is because formal authority provides access to resources and organizational systems thereby engendering feelings of security within the group, but formal authority will also carry personal and organizational expectations. Heifetz (1994, p. 180) articulates that it, *'raise hard questions and one risk's getting cut down, even if the questions are important for moving forward on the problem.'* Then it may be argued that there is an advantage of being outside the formal power structure, but remaining within an organization. In such a situation the leader has the advantage of focusing on the issue rather than the organization's goal allowing for empathetic focus on those individuals tasked with implementing the action.

## Transactional and Transforming Leaders

In discussing the perceived qualities and attributes of transactional and transforming leaders the literature identifies that Bass (1985) disagreed with Burns (1978), who argued that transactional and transformational leaders should be seen as polar opposites. Burns (1978, p. 4) argues that there is a distinction between transactional and transforming leaders. The former, *'approach their followers with an eye for trading one thing for another,'* whilst the latter are visionary leaders who seek to appeal to their followers' *'better nature and move them towards a higher and more universal needs and purposes'* (Bolman & Deal, 1997, p. 314). Then accepting those observations it is argued that the leader is not only an instigator but an agent of change.

*Transactional leaders* will tend to have the following attributes:

- Recognize what it is they want to obtain from work
- Ensure that there is a reward if the effort merits it
- Exchange rewards and promise for effort
- Responsive to immediate self-interests if they can be met by completing the assigned task (Bass, 1985; Wright, 1996).

*Transformational leaders* will tend to have the following attributes:

- Raise the followers' level of awareness concerning the significance and value of designated outcomes
- Identify strategies to achieve designated outcomes
- Inspire followers to place the team/organization above self-interest
- Alter the followers' level of 'need'
- Expand the followers' range of 'wants and needs' (Bass, 1985; Wright, 1996, p. 213).

It is accepted that the qualities between transactional and transformational leaders are not mutually exclusive as any or all of these qualities may be adapted and adopted into other leadership models for a police leader because that leadership style has been identified within the literature as to be dependent upon the *situational* variable associated with the policing problem.

## CHARISMA – A NECESSARY CHARACTERISTIC FOR EFFECTIVE LEADERSHIP?

However, regardless of how a leader is categorized the literature identifies that analysts of leaders often refer to a charismatic character; then the question is raised, what is this elusive ethereal quality of charisma? It is an aspect of character whereby supporters feel empathy and trust in the actions and decisions that individuals make having faith in the projected outcome (Howell & Avolio, 1988). Wright (1996, p. 194) argues that this quality is, literally, a gift of grace or of God although it was Max Weber who brought this characteristic into consideration when discussing leadership. Weber used the term 'charisma' to describe the attributes of self-appointed leaders whose followers are individuals who are in some form of psychological distress and seeking a direction in their lives. The argument was that such leaders both gain and sustain influence because followers have identified an empathetic understanding that can provide relief from the psychological pain that they are in (Gerth & Mills, 1991, pp. 51–55).

In exploring the concept of the charisma of individual leaders, researchers may examine the qualities of the leaders, in particular paying attention to their skills, personality, and presence. However, there is a requirement to evaluate the situations in which charisma arises. In those situations when emotions and psychological distress are prevalent individuals will turn to those who can alleviate that distress and who appear to have the answers. Then it may be argued that individual followers in some form of psychological distress place the burden of identifying the problem and providing a solution to the leader thereby providing a role that a charismatic leader may step into.

The charismatic leader, who accepts the proffered role, will seek to articulate their individual skills to ensure the followers that they have made the correct choice, thus ensuring continued support. The leader will identify and articulate a vision of resolution and develop appropriate strategies, however, there are consequences to abrogating personal responsibilities because charisma involves dependency. Individuals may find it easier to offer control to another rather than face up to situations and providing solutions; it is often easier to abrogate responsibility and control to someone else and remain a follower, and are encouraged by the leader to remain a follower. If an individual does seek to face the problem and seek the solution it is possible to turn against a charismatic leader. However, history will often identify that when one charismatic leader falls he or she is replaced by another who assumes an identical mantle.

It is accepted that within the literature review there are flaws associated with many of the models discussed, the most obvious being that the literature review has a North American bias. There is evidence that identifies that cultural factors influence the way that people carry out, and respond to, different leadership styles. Many cultures are more individualistic, or value family as against bureaucratic models, or have very different expectations about social intercourse and all this impacts on the choice of style and approach.

Earlier in this paper, when discussing traits, the issue of gender was raised as an important factor because gender has influence upon leadership style and there may be different patterns of leadership linked with men and women (Helgesen, 1990). The feminist literature (Funk, 2004; Gilligan, 1982; Held, 1983; Jaggar, 1992; Ruddick, 1983; Tong, 2003) has argued that women may have leadership styles that are more nurturing, caring, and sensitive. They look more to relationships. Kohlberg's analysis (1971) argues that men are said to look to task which raises the question as to whether Kohlberg's six stages of moral developments are indeed: (1) universal, (2) invariant, and (3) hierarchical.

The literature review identified that there was a correlation between management and leadership, and that the modern police service will require an input of both management and leadership to develop and evolve. By reasoned argument and definition it may be possible to state the ideal combination of constituent management and leadership skills necessary to provide, if not the ideal, then a progressive model that will allow the police service to move towards an effective, efficient, and accountable police service and, in the UK, that was the objective of the Home Office (Circular 114/1983) and, by legislation, (Police Act 1964) Parliament.

All actions have consequences and to be effective is to bring about an intended result; to be efficient is to perform an action and bring about a desired result. To achieve either or both the question raised is what is the relationship/correlation between the management and leadership roles within the police service? To answer that what is perceived as management and what is perceived as leadership within the police service must be identified. However, this paper will not attempt to identify the relationship of leadership and management roles within the police service.

In discussing leadership in general terms it is apparent that the term leadership has entered the common vocabulary and been encapsulated into the technical vocabulary of a science discipline without being precisely redefined (Yukl, 2002). That failure to redefine has consequences, namely, it creates ambiguity of meanings because it carries extraneous connotations (Janda, 1960). Then what is leadership? A comprehensive review of the literature concluded that 'there are almost as many definitions of leadership as there are persons who have attempted to define the concept' (Stoghill, 1974, p. 259). Some of the definitions to be found include the following.

Leadership is

> the behavior of the individual ... directing the activities of a group towards a shared goal.
>
> (Hemphill & Coons, 1957, p. 6)

> a process of giving purpose (meaningful direction) to collective effort, and causing willing effort to be expended to achieve purpose.
>
> (Jacobs & Jacques, 1990, p. 281)

> the ability to step outside the culture ... to start evolutionary change processes that are more adaptive.
>
> (Schein, 1992, p. 2)

> the process of making sense of what people are doing together so that people will understand and be committed.
>
> (Drath & Palus, 1994, p. 4)

> about articulating visions, embodying values, and creating the environment within which things can be accomplished.
>
> (Richards & Engle, 1986, p. 199)

> the ability of an individual to influence, motivate, and enable others to contribute towards the effectiveness and success of an organization.
>
> (House et al., 1999, p. 184)

The literature review generally did not identify leadership as having gender associations although when reviewing the literature relating to leadership and ethics there was an obvious difference in language associated with gender. For that reason issues of ethics and leadership from a feminist perspective, as opposed to a classical leadership perspective, will be further explored.

It is accepted that many police forces and law enforcement agencies subscribe to a code of ethics and assume that both the organization, and the individuals within that organization, subscribe to the published ethical rules. If that were true then why do we have police misconduct reported on such a regular basis? Is this a leadership or a management problem or simply an individual problem, that is, just a few rotten apples in the barrel? Funk (2004, p. 1) identifies leadership characteristics to include: '*being brave, caring, creative, courageous, committed, confident, energetic, healthy, honest, industrious, introspective, intuitive, knowledgeable, open-minded, passionate, pragmatic, reflective, responsible, risk-taking, trustworthy, and well-informed.*' In addition she identifies '*Essential leadership roles that these women school executives described were: analyzer, change agent, communicator, delegator, dreamer, hirer, nurturer, reader, risk-taker, and team-builder.*' It is of interest that Funk (2004, p. 4) then identifies qualities of leadership to include '*character, integrity, vision, courage, and passion,*' whilst critical skills identified are those of '*visioning, determining the real needs for their districts, communicating, hiring the right people, delegating, developing team support, working effectively with people, and producing meaningful and lasting change.*'

Ethicist Alison Jaggar faults traditional Western ethics for failing women in five related ways. First, it shows little concern for women's as opposed to men's interests and rights. Second, in the private world where women cook, clean, and care for the young, the old, and the sick, issues that arise in that arena are dismissed as morally uninteresting. Thirdly, the inference is that women are not as morally developed as men. Fourth, there is an overvaluation of perceived culturally masculine traits such as independence, autonomy, separation, mind, reason, culture, transcendence, war, and death. Whereas, culturally feminine traits such as interdependence, community, connection, body, emotion, nature, peace, and life are grossly undervalued. Jaggar's fifth point is that Western ethics favors culturally masculine ways of moral reasoning that emphasize rules, universality, and impartiality over culturally feminine ways of moral reasoning where that emphasis is on relationships and partiality (Jaggar, 1992, pp. 363–364).

Feminist Ethics may be viewed as an attempt to revise, reformulate, or rethink those aspects of traditional Western ethics that depreciate or devalue women's moral experience (http://plato.stanford.edu/entries/feminism-ethics/, accessed 29 September 2004). From the review of the literature it may be argued that the various adjectives used would support Gilligan's perspective (1982) on feminist ethics where with a more caring, nurturing role being suggested in the leadership and management roles. In discussing leadership and management the question is raised, why should this be a gender issue? Surely ethical conduct is not bound by gender?

Although it may be inappropriate to divide leadership and management ethics into gender-related issues it is appropriate that the perceived gender issues are revisited. In Kohlberg's analysis (1971) moral development is a six stage process. Stage one is the punishment and obedience orientation. To avoid the 'stick' of punishment and/or to receive the 'carrot' of a reward, children do as they are told. Stage two is 'the instrumental relativist orientation.' Based on a limited principle of reciprocity – you scratch my back and I'll scratch yours – children meet others' needs only if others meet their needs. Stage three is the 'good boy–nice girl' orientation. Kohlberg argues that adolescents conform to prevailing norms to secure others' approval and love. Stage four is the law and order orientation. In this process of development adolescents begin to do their duty, show respect for authority, and maintain the given social order to secure others' admiration and respect for them as honorable, law abiding citizens. Stage five relates to the social contract legalistic orientation. In this stage it is suggested that adults adopt an essentially utilitarian moral point of view according to which individuals are permitted to do as they please, with the proviso that they refrain from harming other people in the process. Stage six, the final stage of moral development, is the universal ethical principle orientation. Here Kohlberg argues that adults adopt an essentially Kantian moral perspective that seeks to transcend and judge all conventional moralities. That being so then adults are no longer ruled by self-interest, the opinion of others, or the fear of legal punishment, but by self-legislated and self-imposed universal principles such as those of justice, reciprocity, and respect for the dignity of human persons (Kohlberg, 1971, pp. 164–165).

Tong (2003) argues that although Gilligan concedes that Kohlberg's six-stage scale appeals to many people schooled in traditional Western ethics, she insists that the popularity of a theory of moral development is not an index of its truth. The questions raised include whether Kohlberg's six stages of moral development are indeed: (1) universal, (2) invariant, and (3) hierarchical. Gilligan also identifies in the Kohlbergian work with which she is most familiar, that women rarely climb past stage three, whereas men routinely ascend to stages four and even five? The question raised by Tong's analysis (2003) asks whether this gender difference means that women are less morally developed than men. Or, were there flaws in Kohlberg's methodology – some bias that permits men to achieve higher moral development scores than women? Tong (2003, p. 4) further argues that Gilligan's analysis *'seem(s) no more an account of human moral development than Kohlberg's Stages, with Kohlberg focusing on men's moral experience, and Gilligan on women's.'*

Then as Tong (2003, p. 6) observes:

> even if women are better carers than men, it may still be epistemically, ethically, and politically imprudent to associate women with the value of care. To link women with caring is to promote the view that because women can care; they should care no matter the cost to themselves.

Other feminine approaches to ethics include the maternal approaches to ethics. Supporters of maternal ethics include, but are not limited to, Sara Ruddick (1983), Virginia Held (1983, 1987, 1993, 1995), and Rosemarie Tong (1984, 1993, 2003) who continue to affirm the feminine psychological traits and moral virtues that society in general associates with women. They argue that gender-equal ethics do not favor paradigms, such as the contract model, that addresses male experience in the public arena and female and children's experience in the private arena.

Tong (2003, p. 6) observes that:

> Although feminine, maternal, feminist, and lesbian approaches to ethics are all women centered, they do not impose a single normative standard on women. Rather they offer to women multiple standards that validate women's different moral experiences in ways that points to the weaknesses as well as the strengths of the values and virtues culture has traditionally labeled 'feminine.' In addition, they suggest to women several paths, all of which lead toward the one goal that is essential to the project of any women-centered ethics; namely, the elimination of gender inequality.

In the USA according to the National Center for Women and Policing (NCWP, 2002) their data analysis for 2001 indicated that women accounted for only 12.7% of all sworn law enforcement positions in large agencies (with 100 or more sworn personnel).[1] In small agencies (with less than 100 sworn personnel), women accounted for only 8.1% of the total personnel. With the figures combined in a weighted estimate, they indicate that women represent only 11.2% of all sworn law enforcement personnel in the USA. Without further research the assumption is made that in Western democracies the percentage of women represented in sworn law enforcement will be about the same.

## POLICE ORGANIZATIONAL CULTURE

One important aspect relating to both management and leadership is that of the 'canteen culture,' and its influence upon both police and the public they serve. There have been a number of academic enquiries into police culture that have produced concepts such as Skolnick's symbolic assailant (1994), Manning's impossible mandate (1989), Niederhoffer's cynicism (1967), Wilson's craftsmen (1968),

Reuss-Ianni's two cultures (1983), and Van Maanen's kinsmen and asshole (1978). However, Crank (1998) argues that far too much emphasis has focused upon the use of force, coercion, danger, and corruption (Bittner, 1970; Kappeler, Sluder, & Alpert, 1994; Klockars, 1991), and that these themes are too unwieldy to mete out the subtlety of police culture. *'Culture is a diffusion of the work-a-day world in which ways of doing work become habitual and habits become meaningful'* (Crank, 1998, p. 14).

Diverse aspects of organizational activity merge into a whole united by commonly held values and shared ways of thinking. Then culture carries important values that are shared by members of that group and the organizations themselves are carriers of important institutional values. It is that very organizational culture that has an impact upon female officers to their detriment but the author posits that female officers can change the organizational culture.

## WHAT/HOW DOES BEHAVIOR IMPACT UPON ORGANIZATIONAL CULTURE?

In discussing culture the literature in the field often quotes Kroeber and Kluckhohn's identification (1952) of 164 definitions of culture, or Ajiferuke and Boddewyn's observation (1970) that *'culture is one of those items that defy a single all purpose definition and meanings of culture as people using the term,'* quoted in Greenberg (2003, p. 378). Tayeb (1994, p. 431) argues that *'culture is too fundamental to be solved through a tighter definition.'* Whilst Hofstede (1983, p. 77) argues that *'there is no commonly accepted language to describe a complex thing such as a culture.'* It is acknowledged that the term culture is used in a wide range of social sciences (e.g., anthropology, sociology, and psychology), and it has different meaning in different disciplines and it may be argued that many recently developed definitions of culture are mainly based on value orientations (Kluckhohn & Strodtbeck, 1961) and predictions of common human problems (Schneider, 1997).

It is public expectation that sets the police culture apart from other organizational cultures (Kingshott, 1999). Cultures and sub-cultures are part of the normal evolution of an organization and will contain both positive and negative influences that will impact upon the efficiency and effectiveness of the organization (Rigakos, 2002). The questions raised and discussed within this paper include, what constitutes an organizational culture, the component parts of the culture, why it occurs, what influences it exerts and how it can be changed. *'The ethical decisions confronting the police in a democracy are so extraordinary that there is no other occupation in which its members are and should be held to a high standard of professional and personal conduct'* (Jetmore, 1997). Harrison (1998, pp. 1–2) observed:

> Many police leaders have been thwarted in their attempts to engender change in the organization due to existing cultural barriers inside their own departments. Much of the research regarding police culture appears in

> the literature relating to police deviant behaviour, ethics, and the misuse of force and discretion ... the discussion of culture tend to be cast in the light of its potential negative effects. Little has been written about the possible beneficial effects of these same cultural characteristics on the organisation.

Geertz (1983) argues that we create meaning daily and meaning emerges in the form of common sense. These meanings tend to provide a sensibility out of which future action is conditional. Accepting that statement as common sense is part of a communal cultural expectation, then it is no surprise that observers of culture have described the interactive process as shared typifications (Berger & Luckmann, 1966); as common-sense knowledge (Geertz, 1983); as figurative action (Shearing & Ericson, 1991); as documentary interpretation (Garfinkle, 1967); as a toolkit (Swidler, 1986); and as a humanistic coefficient (Znaniecki, 1936). The common theme that emerges from the literature review is *'that culture is a body of knowledge that emerges through the shared application of practical skills to concrete problems encountered in daily routines and the normal course of activities'* (Crank, 1998, p. 17).

Selznick (1949) argued that in the police service thinking and actions become institutionalized and valued in themselves. This view is called an *institutional perspective* and is used to seek to identify meanings that underlie ways of thinking and acting that are often taken for granted within an organizational environment (DiMaggio, 1991). It was argued that institutions constrain rational decision-making vis-à-vis hidden assumptions and accepted practices (Douglas, 1986). That being so then it is argued that values and meanings are inclusive and are part and parcel of what it means to act human, and are intrinsic elements of all cultures. Institutional perspectives have failed to identify how values can spontaneously emerge from what police officers do on a daily basis and that the police organization exists in an institutional environment (Crank & Langworthy, 1992; Mastrofski & Worden, 1991).

Cultural themes stem from everyday interactions of the police with their various environments, and the people they meet within those environments. Those environments will include other agencies, accident and crime scenes, the organizations' managers, and the general public. In addition, there are the media influences, radio, television, newspapers, and training films that carry stereotypes and common notions of police values and behaviors. Then it is in the context of these influential environments, and the particular patterns by which the culture is articulated with the environments, that cultural themes become meaningful, and that the public may gain an understanding of the various bonds that exist between officers (Crank, 1998). Ortiz and Peterson (1994, p. 24) caution: *'The irony of culture is that, like the air people breathe, its powerful effects normally escape the attention of those it most affects.'*

The police culture has been extensively written about. It has been described as isolationist, elitist, misogynist, racist, and authoritarian. Such a culture may be at odds with effective policing and public relations. In addition, managers must be aware of the culture of their group as well as the organization in order to utilize cultural diversity. One of the most consistent complaints from leaders of minority communities is that police officers are not sensitive to differing cultures. Gould (1997) argues that research suggests that police officers are somewhat divided in their views of the necessity for cultural diversity training. New recruits tend to be more accepting of the training while experienced officers tend more often to see the training as a waste of time. However, it may be argued that experienced officers are always cynical of any type of training. In examining any organizational culture the first step would be to identify the norms (attitudes and beliefs held by members of a group) that are operating.

From the literature review it may be argued that organizational norms found within a police organization can be identified and may include, but not limited to:

- Conformity
- Discipline elitism
- Formal inter-office memos
- Inflexible organization
- Interest in technology
- Lateral transfers
- Maintenance of distance from citizens
- Militarism
- Negative perception of innovation
- Numerous meetings
- Organizational loyalty to employees
- Physical fitness
- Reluctance to share credit for results
- Selective recruitment
- Specialized police language
- Coarse language
- Loutish behavior
- Territorialism.

The above list should not be considered definitive and will change. Gould (1997, p. 340) defined police culture as *'the sum of the beliefs and values held in common by those within the organisation, serving to formally and informally communicate what is expected.'* The norms are, in effect, what is 'normal' and as most officers do not want to be considered 'abnormal' they do and say what others expect from them. They are influenced by the organizational culture and to be accepted as part of the organization they accept the organizational norms.

Organizational workplace norms were identified by Buchholz (1985) and the following are examples of workplace norms:

- Do the job the way you're told, even if it's not the best way.
- It is okay to come in late every morning.
- Always eat your breakfast on the company's time.
- Always look busy, even if you haven't any work to do.
- Padding out expenses is okay.
- First one to arrive in the morning makes coffee.

Accountability, and especially individual level accountability, has profound implications for the development and sustenance of police culture. Firstly, it misdirects problems away from organizational sources towards the individual. The various reviews of the Knapp Commission (the inquiry into police corruption in New York) indicate that about every 20 years New York citizens are confronted with a headline exposé of police corruption. Crank (1998) argues that the intense focus on individual responsibility prohibits organizational assessments of problems that might create conditions for their resolution.

Secondly, it is argued that to protect themselves officers will develop strategies that obstruct external enquiry into their personal affairs. Then efforts aimed at the external imposition of accountability will always engender the paradox of personal accountability. Crank (1998, p. 236) argued that the more officers are held responsible for the outcome of police–public interactions, the more difficult it will be to hold them administratively accountable. '*The corollary paradox is that administrative and citizen-based efforts to control accountability of individual officers will result in increased strengthening of the police culture and diminish the ability of administrators to hold individual officers accountable for their behaviour.*'

## HOW CAN THE POLICE CULTURE BE CHANGED?

The workplace culture is considered to be the sum of the beliefs and values held in common by those within the organization, serving to formally and informally communicate what is expected. It is acknowledged that the issue of police culture is complex and that there is a requirement for change for the benefit of the individual, the organization, and the public. Then how can change be achieved? The need for change can only be accomplished by examining the existing workplace culture, and sub-cultures. The transformation of police organizations, and the police culture, has proven extremely difficult given the conservative nature and the general resilience to change.

Wallace, Hunt, and Richards (1999) argue that with all aspects relating to change the managers of the organization should be aware of the relationship between the organizational culture and their managerial values in order to effectively manage that change. Then to institute change there must be a reshaping of the workplace culture. Buchholz (1985) identified that to shape workplace culture you must evaluate the existing culture and:

- *Identify existing norms*
- *Evaluate the norms*
- *Change the counterproductive norms.*

The keys to changing workplace culture, according to Dumaine (1990) include:

- *Understanding your old culture*
- *Encourage employees for ideas*

- *Find the best sub-culture and hold it up as an example*
- *Do not attack the culture head on*
- *Change will take time*
- *Live the culture you want.*

Dumaine (1990, pp. 129–130) further argues that it is within the police culture that the individual and the group can grow and develop personally and professionally the culture must expect, encourage, and reward growth. *'A company trying to improve its culture is like a person trying to improve his or her character. The process is long, difficult, often agonizing. The only reason people put themselves through it is that it's correspondingly satisfying and valuable.'*

The organizational culture, the 'canteen culture,' can be changed and that change must be underpinned by ethical behavior and the concept of accountability, which can be characterized as a demand that is made or a condition that exists. Wagner (1990, p. 8) argues for a normative understanding of accountability, *'in saying that a particular agent is accountable we could imply that he is obligated to give a report, relation, description, explanation, justifying analysis or some form of exposition.'* Although Kleinig (1996, p. 317) agrees that Wagner is right to see that there is a difference between requiring a report or an explanation or justification, he states:

> my own belief, however, is that accountability for the authority one is accorded is almost always implicitly justificatory. A public trust is involved, and giving account is not merely a matter of reporting or explaining but of showing that the trust has been justified.

Theories that attempt to explain this dynamic between an organizational culture that has a hyper-masculine social structure and the adverse experiences of the female police officers were discussed by Franklin (2006). Those women who do enter policing are not only faced with a male-dominated organizational culture that emphasizes male homophobia, gender bias, and racism (Kingshott, 2006; Kingshott & Prinsloo, 2004), it is also argued that policing strategies may be gender biased. The argument for gender-biased strategies was articulated by Eterno (2006) who used the Compstat model, developed by New York Police Department, and adopted by numerous police agencies across the country (Walker & Katz, 2008, pp. 104–105), to argue that inappropriate and illegal behavior that may include, but is not limited to, unlawful searches and seizures.

The literature identifies that although retention and promotion are linked, there are additional barriers facing women in policing (Burlingame & Baro, 2005). These include, but are not limited to, discrimination against African American women (Martin, 1991), race and gender issues (Martin, 1994), discrimination against minorities (Felkenes & Schroeder, 1993), and the law enforcement recruit training that emphasizes 'tearing down individuals and rebuilding them to the military model' (National Center for Women and Policing, 2002, p. 83). In such a situation recruits are

> often yelled at, humiliated before their peers, called names, and punished for any evidence of weakness. Their success and graduation may depend

> upon not only their skills, but also their ability to tolerate such humiliation and to relinquish any appearance of personal identity.
>
> (Kingshott, Bailey, & Wolfe, 2004, p. 195)

The author argues that there are two identified factors that would allow for leadership potential to be identified and leadership skills learnt from the literature. First, there is a need to develop police training programs that do not use a militaristic foundation as that model is flawed (Sykes, 1989), and second, there has to be a change in the police culture. The last recommendation is an immense undertaking and acknowledged by Reiner (1992) and the proposed change will not be easy (Dumaine, 1990). The change is necessary because in the USA an influential text on effective police leadership (Baker, 2002) has its roots embedded in the military model, which the author argues is flawed when used as a police model (Cowper, 2000). The model proposed is the BE, KNOW, DO leadership approach based on a military model (HQ TRADOC, 1983, p. 50) which ignores the complexity of the policing task and the fact that there can be no one inclusive police model but a model that includes aspects of many leadership models driven by the *situation* that is faced by the leader. Police leadership cannot be reduced to a simple typology as given by Baker (2002, p. 35), '*Leaders must role model for loyalty, integrity, courage, and competence.*'

The future will see the appointment of more senior police women to leadership and management positions within the policing role, this raises the question of whether accepted masculine 'norms' associated with leadership, such as cronyism, nepotism, and autocratic decision-making, may be confined to history. The classical role of leadership must be seen as a constantly evolving model that accepts environmental and cultural changes that embrace diversity to achieve a goal. This is especially relevant to policing as the policing role is not a constant therefore leadership and management must also evolve. The future will see the appointment of more senior police women to leadership and management positions within the policing role. This raises the question as to whether accepted masculine 'norms' associated with leadership, such as cronyism, nepotism, and autocratic decision-making, may be confined to history. The classical role of leadership must be seen as a constantly evolving model that accepts environmental and cultural changes that embrace diversity to achieve a goal. This is especially relevant to policing as the policing role is not a constant therefore leadership and management must also evolve.

With the continued move towards policing philosophy that embraces both Community Policing (CP) and Problem Oriented Policing (POP) the lower ranks will be empowered and decision-making will be delegated to them. The increase in police women within policing may be the first steps in dismantling the code of silence so prevalent within policing. It was not the purpose of this paper to redefine leadership models but to underscore some of the key elements found within each typology of defined leadership.

# IN CONCLUSION

A literature review has identified that there has been a historical underrepresentation of women in policing. In addition, the same literature review has also identified that the police culture has allowed for the oppression of women in terms of opportunities and in social encounters with male peers. The fact that, in general terms, the police culture is dominated by macho organizational norms (Kingshott, 2006), it is no surprise to find that there is not only resistance but opposition to women in policing (Franklin, 2006) because in many instances the police culture is misogynist (Kingshott & Prinsloo, 2004).

The research into the reluctance of male police officers to accept female officers was primarily focused on whether women can be effective in a male-dominated profession. With the advent and adoption of community policing the necessity for officers to have strong interpersonal people-oriented skills has had an effect upon the role perceptions of female officers. No longer is research focused upon whether women can do the job of policing but how women do the job differently. This aspect of women in law enforcement and their nurturing role was discussed by DeJong (2005) whose focus was on how male and female officers respond to citizens differently in terms of providing comfort following police – citizen interactions. DeJong's analysis (2005) identified other variables to explain attitude and behavior and that environmental and situational factors are important in determining officer behavior. Although in the past three decades women have entered the field of law enforcement in increasing numbers and have played a pivotal role in the development of modern policing, often achieving the highest ranks, the number of women entering the profession has remained relatively low. This observation was supported by Lonsway (2006) whose research findings suggest that although considerable progress has been achieved for women within policing barriers still exist.

Many integration barriers stem from traditional, but often anecdotal, assumptions about police work, and one such barrier relates to the perceived male cultural mandate to use coercive authority over citizens, who are categorized as per Van Maanen's typology (1978). Female police officers are often perceived as unwilling to accept the Van Maanen's typology as well as being unwilling or unable to effectively use coercion in interactions. Paoline and Terrill (2005) identified that contrary to traditional assumptions, female police officers, compared to their male counterparts, were reluctant to use coercive force. The implication being that if this perceived integration barrier was based upon a false premise then the question raised is how many other false premises exist in relation to the full integration of women into the policing role?

In this paper the author has attempted to identify some of the elements of a 'classical' view of leadership that may be acceptable within the policing environment and included in leadership decisions that will be an amalgamation of many models driven by the *situation*. The literature review has identified how many authors have searched for special traits and behaviors that may be defined in typologies as well as briefly identify the different situations in which leaders work and emerge. From the limited and selected literature review it is acknowledged that bias may have been inadvertently introduced. However, from the literature it is possible to identify some of the common elements from which a classical view of leadership may be broadly extrapolated.

- Leaders are perceived to have special qualities
- Leaders tend to be part an hierarchical structure
- Leaders tend to be identified by position rather than personality
- Leaders' strengths are often enhanced by the weakness of the followers
- Leaders tend to become the focus for answers and solutions
- Leaders have a vision that they can communicate to followers
- Leaders give direction.

The view of leadership identified within this paper may be found within organizational structures that are common in business, the armed forces, government, and the police service. In the police service some 'classical' leaders may have a more participative style, it remains simply a style. It is important to acknowledge that in the police service much of the power remains with the lower rank therefore everyone in the organization, to a greater or lesser degree, are leaders and managers within the organization.

It is argued by the author that it is difficult to accept a definitive typology of leadership traits or acceptable personality traits that would be found within the character of charismatic and effective leaders. At this time the effects of cultural, ethnic, religious, family, educational, geographic, and environmental factors that will impact an individual in his or her lifetime will all affect that individual's ability to become an effective leader. To support that individual in leadership decisions education in all models of leadership should be part of the training curriculum. Often the role of leadership is thrust upon an individual due to circumstances which are beyond human control and the effects of that individual's upbringing and personal resolve are used to impact the situation thrust upon them. This is particularly so in the police service when a developing situation is often thrust upon the lowest rank. The resolution of that situation is often one of autocratic decisions that 'were the right thing to do at that moment in time.'

To be an effective leader requires human personality traits and attributes that may not be apparent or even known to the individual or the bystander until the situation demands an action that provides an intended solution. However, one fact emerges in relation to police leaders from the literature review: there is no single model of leadership. For that reason it may be argued that police leadership remains indefinable; it seems to be one of those ethereal qualities that you know when you see it, but it remains difficult to articulate.

## NOTE ON CONTRIBUTOR

Brian F. Kingshott, PhD., FRSA, obtained his BA degree at Open/Keele University (England) and his MA and PhD at the University of Exeter (England) in Police Studies. Areas of specialty: terrorism and counter terrorism, law enforcement, community policing, criminal investigation, Human Rights Auditor and Ethicist. MODACE Officer (Management of Disaster and Civil Emergency), police media advisor and trainer. Former member of the United Kingdom Cadre of International Hostage Negotiators. Kingshott retired from the Devon & Cornwall Constabulary after 32 years service in 2001 with an exemplary service record that included a number of commendations as well as a Commendation with Star for Bravery & Leadership. For his work on personal and organizational ethics he was elected Fellow of the Royal Society of Arts (London). At present he is Associate Professor in the School of Criminal Justice at Grand Valley State University, Grand Rapids, MI.

## Note

1 The National Center for Women and Policing is the only organization that annually tracks the number of women in policing, including the numbers of sworn, correctional, and civilian women broken down by rank (http://www.womenandpolicing.org/statusreports.html, accessed 18 November 2005).

## References

Ajiferuke, M., & Boddewyn, J. (1970). Socio-economic indicators in comparative management. *Administrative Sciences Quarterly, 15*(4), 453–458.

Alderfer, C. (1972). *Existence, relatedness & growth.* New York: Free Press.

Baker, T.E. (2002). *Effective police leadership.* New York: Looseleaf Law Publications.

Bass, B.M. (1985). *Leadership and performance beyond expectation.* New York: Free Press.

Bass, B.M. (1990). *Bass and Stogdill's handbook of leadership: Theory, research and managerial applications.* New York: Free Press.

Bennis, W. (1998). *On becoming a leader* (p. 3). London: Arrow.

Berger, P., & Luckmann, T. (1966). *The social construction of reality.* Garden City, NY: Doubleday.

Bittner, E. (1970). *The functions of police in modern society.* Washington, DC: National Institute of Mental Health.

Blake, R.R., & Mouton, J.S. (1964). *The Managerial Grid.* Houston, TX: Gulf.

Blake, R.R., & Mouton, J.S. (1978). *The New Managerial Grid.* Houston, TX: Gulf.

Bolman, L.G., & Deal, T.E. (1997). *Reframing organizations. Artistry, choice and leadership* (2nd ed.). San Francisco: Jossey-Bass.

Buchholz, S. (1985). *The positive manager.* New York: John Wiley.

Burlingame, D., & Baro, A.L. (2005). Women's representation and status in law enforcement: Does CALEA involvement make a difference? *Criminal Justice Policy Review, 16*(4), 391–411.

Burns, J.M. (1978). *Leadership.* New York: HarperCollins.

Cowper, T.J. (2000). The myth of the 'military model' of leadership in law enforcement. *Police Quarterly, 3*(3), 228–246.

Crank, J.P. (1998). *Understanding police culture.* Cincinnati, OH: Anderson.

Crank, J.P., & Langworthy, R. (1992). An institutional perspective of policing. *The Journal of Criminal Law and Criminology, 83,* 338–363.

DeJong, C. (2005). Gender differences in officer attitude and behavior: Providing comfort to citizens. *Women & Criminal Justice, 15*(3/4), 1–32.

DiMaggio, P. (1991). Interest and agency in institutional theory. In W. Powell & P. DiMaggio (Eds.), *The new institutionalism in organisational analysis* (pp. 3–19). Chicago: University of Chicago Press.

Douglas, M. (1986). *How institutions think.* Syracuse, NY: Syracuse University Press.

Doyle, M.E., & Smith, M.K. (1999). *Born and bred? Leadership, heart and informal education.* London: YMCA George Williams College/The Rank Foundation.

Drath, W.H., & Palus, C.J. (1994). *Making common sense: Leadership as meaning-making in a community practice* (p. 4). Greensboro, NC: Center for Creative Leadership.

Dumaine, B. (1990, January 15). Creating a new company culture. *Fortune,* 127–131.

Eterno, J.A. (2006). Gender and policing: Do women accept legal restrictions more than their male counterparts? *Women & Criminal Justice, 18*(1/2), 49–78.

Eysenck, H.J. (1977). *Crime and personality.* London: Routledge and Kegan Paul.

Eysenck, H.J. (1989). Personality and criminality: A dispositional analysis. In W.S. Laufer & F. Adler (Eds.), *Advances in criminological theory* (*Vol. 1,* pp. 89–110). New Brunswick, NJ: Transaction.

Eysenck, H.J., & Gudjonnson, G.H. (1990). *The causes and cures of crime.* New York: Plenum.

Felkenes, G.T., & Schroeder, J.R. (1993). A case study of minority women in policing. *Women & Criminal Justice, 4,* 65–89.

Fiedler, F.E. (1997). Situational control and a dynamic theory of leadership. In K. Grint (Ed.), *Leadership. Classical, contemporary and critical approaches.* Oxford: Oxford University Press.

Fiedler, F.E., & Garcia, J.E. (1987). *New approaches to effective leadership* (pp. 51–67). New York: John Wiley.

Franklin, C.A. (2006). Male peer support and the police culture: Understanding the resistance and opposition to women in policing. *Women & Criminal Justice, 16*(3), 1–25.

Funk, C. (2004, Spring). *Outstanding female superintendents: Profiles in leadership.* Retrieved September 28, 2004, from http://www.advancingwomen.com/awl/spring2004/FUNK.html.

Gardner, J. (1989). *On leadership.* New York: Free Press.

Garfinkle, H. (1967). *Studies in sociology.* Englewood Cliffs, NJ: Prentice Hall.

Geertz, C. (1983). *Local knowledge.* New York: Basic Books.

Gerth, H.H., & Mills, C.W. (Eds.). (1991). *From Max Weber. Essays in sociology* (pp. 51–55). London: Routledge.

Gilligan, C. (1982). *In a different voice: Psychological theory and women's development.* Cambridge, MA: Harvard University Press.

Gould, L.A. (1997, July 25). Can an old dog be taught new tricks? Teaching cultural diversity to police officers. *Policing, 20*(2), 339–356.

Greenberg, J. (2003). *Organizational behavior: The state of science.* New York: Lawrence Erlbaum Associates.

Harrison, S.J. (1998). *Police organizational culture: Using ingrained values to build positive organisational improvement.* Penn State University. Retrieved from www.jxrll@psu.edu.

Heider, J. (1985). *The tao of leadership: Lao Tzu's tao te ching adapted for a new age.* New York: Bantam.

Heifetz, R.A. (1994). *Leadership without easy answers*. Cambridge, MA: Belknap Press.
Held, V. (1983). The obligations of mothers and fathers. In J. Trebilcot (Ed.), *Mothering: Essays in feminist theory* (p. 7). Totowa, NJ: Rowman and Allanheld.
Held, V. (1987). Feminism and moral theory. In E. Kittay & D. Meyers (Eds.), *Women and moral theory*. Savage, MD: Rowman and Littlefield.
Held, V. (1993). *Feminist morality: Transforming culture, society, and politics*. Chicago: University of Chicago Press.
Held, V. (Ed.). (1995). *Justice and care: Essential readings in feminist ethics*. Boulder, CO: Westview Press.
Helgesen, S. (1990). *The female advantage; Women's ways of leadership*. New York: Doubleday.
Hemphill, J.K., & Coons, A.E. (1957). Development of the leader behavior description questionnaire. In R.M. Stogdill & A.E. Coons (Eds.), *Leader behavior: Its description and measurement* (pp. 6–38). Columbus: Bureau of Business Research, Ohio State University.
Hersey, P. (1984). *The situational leader*. New York: Warner.
Hersey, P., & Blanchard, K.H. (1977). *The management of organizational behaviour* (3rd ed.). Upper Saddle River, NJ: Prentice Hall.
Hofstede, G. (1983, Fall). The cultural relativity of organisational practices and theories. *Journal of International Business Studies, 75–92*.
Hollander, E.P. (1993). Legitimacy, power, and influence: A perspective on relational features of leadership. In M.M. Chemers & R. Ayman (Eds.), *Leadership theory and research: Perspectives and directions* (pp. 29–47). San Diego: Academic Press.
Home Office. (1983). *Manpower, effectiveness and efficiency* (Circular 114/1983). London: Home Office.
House, R.J., Hanges, P.J., Ruiz-Quintanilla, S.A., Dorfman, P.W., Javidan, M., Dickson, M., et al. (1999). Cultural influences on leadership and organizations: Project GLOBE. In W.H. Mobley, M.J. Gessner, & V. Arnold (Eds.), *Advances in global leadership* (pp. 171–233). Stamford, CT: JAI Press.
Howell, J.M., & Avolio, B.J. (1988). Two faces of charisma: Socialized and personalized leadership in organizations. In J.A. Conger, R.N. Kanungo, & Associates (Eds.), *Charismatic leadership: The elusive factor in organizational effectiveness* (pp. 213–236). San Francisco: Jossey-Bass.
HQ TRADOC. (1983). *Military leadership* (Fm 22–100, p. 50). Washington, DC: Department of the Army.
Jacobs, T.O., & Jacques, E. (1990). Military executive leadership. In K.E. Clark & M.B. Clark (Eds.), *Measures of leadership* (pp. 281–295). West Orange, NJ: Leadership Library of America.
Jaggar, A.M. (1992). Feminist ethics. In L. Becker & C. Becker (Eds.), *Encyclopaedia of ethics* (pp. 363–364). New York: Garland Press.
Janda, K.F. (1960). Towards the expectation of the concept of leadership in terms of the concept of power. *Human Relations, 13*, 345–363.
Jetmore, L.F. (1997). *The path of the warrior*. New York: Looseleaf.
Kappeler, V.E., Sluder, R.D., & Alpert, G.P. (1994). *Forces of deviance: The dark side of policing*. Prospect Heights, IL: Waveland Press.
Kingshott, B.F. (1999). To a higher standard. *Ethics Roll Call, 6*(1), 2–4.

Kingshott, B.F. (2006). The role of management and leadership within the context of police service delivery. *A Critical Journal of Crime, Law and Society, 19*(2), 121–137.

Kingshott, B.F., Bailey, K., & Wolfe, S.E. (2004). Police culture, ethics & entitlement theory. *Criminal Justice Studies, 17*(2), 187–202.

Kingshott, B.F., & Prinsloo, J. (2004). The universality of the police culture. *Acta Criminologica – The South African Journal of Criminology, 17*(1), 1–16.

Kleinig, J. (1996). *The ethics of policing.* Cambridge: Cambridge University Press.

Klockars, C.B. (1991). The rhetoric of community policing. In C. Klockars & S. Mastrofski (Eds.), *Thinking about policing* (2nd ed., pp. 530–542). New York: McGraw-Hill.

Kluckhohn, F., & Strodtbeck, F. (1961). *Variations in value orientations.* Evanston, IL: Row, Peterson & Company.

Kohlberg, L. (1971). From is to ought: How to commit the naturalistic fallacy and get away with it in the study of moral development. In T. Mischel (Ed.), *Cognitive development and epistemology* (pp. 164–165). New York: Academic Press.

Komives, S.R., Lucas, N., & McMahon, T.R. (1998). *Exploring leadership* (p. 11). San Francisco: Jossey-Bass.

Kroeber, A., & Kluckhohn, F. (1952). *Culture: A critical review of concepts and definitions.* Cambridge, MA: Harvard Business Review.

Likert, R. (1992). *Advanced supervision skills* (p. 2). Alexandra, VA: International Association of Chiefs of Police.

Lipman-Blumen, J. (1984). *Gender roles and power.* Englewood Cliffs, NJ: Prentice Hall.

Lonsway, K.A. (2006). Are we there yet? The progress of women in one large law enforcement agency. *Women & Criminal Justice, 18*(1/2), 1–48.

Mann, R.D. (1959). A review of the relationship between personality and performance in small groups. *Psychological Bulletin, 66*(4), 241–270.

Manning, P.K. (1989). The police occupational culture in Anglo-American societies. In L. Hoover & J. Dowling (Eds.), *Encyclopaedia of police sciences.* New York: Garland.

Martin, S.E. (1991). The effectiveness of affirmative action; The case of women in policing. *Justice Quarterly, 8*(4), 489–504.

Martin, S.E. (1994). Outsiders within the station house: The impact of race and gender on Black women police. *Social Problems, 41*(3), 383–400.

Maslow, A. (1954). *Motivation & personality.* New York: Harper.

Mastrofski, S., & Worden, R. (1991). Community policing as reform: A cautionary tale. In C. Klockars & S. Mastrofski (Eds.), *Thinking about police: Contemporary readings* (2nd ed., pp. 515–529). New York: McGraw-Hill.

McGregor, D. (1960). *The human side of enterprise.* New York: McGraw-Hill.

McMurray, R. (1992). *Advanced supervision skills* (p. 2). Alexandra, VA: International Association of Chiefs of Police.

National Center for Women and Policing (NCWP). (2002). *Equality denied: The status of women in policing 2001* (p. 83). Washington, DC: US Department of Justice.

Niederhoffer, A. (1967). *Behind the shield.* Garden City, NY: Doubleday.

Ortiz, R.L., & Peterson, M.B. (1994, August). Police culture: A roadblock to change in law enforcement? *The Police Chief, 61*(8), 68–71.

Paoline, E.A., & Terrill, W. (2005). Women police officers and the use of coercion. *Women & Criminal Justice, 15*(3/4), 97–119.

Phillips, T.R. (Ed.). (1985). *The art of war.* Harrisburg, PA: Stackpole Books.

Police Act 1964 from recommendations of the Royal Commission 1962. London: Home Office.

Reddin, W.J. (1970). *Managerial effectiveness.* New York: McGraw-Hill.

Reddin, W.J. (1987). *How to make management style more effective.* Maidenhead: McGraw-Hill.

Reiner, R. (1992). *The politics of the police* (pp. 36–37). London: Harvester Wheatsheaf.

Reuss-Ianni, E. (1983). *Two cultures of policing: Street cops and management cops.* New Brunswick, NJ: Transaction.

Richards, D., & Engle, S. (1986). After the vision: Suggestions to corporate visionaries and vision champions. In J.D. Adams (Ed.), *Transforming leadership* (pp. 199–214). Alexandria, VA: Miles River Press.

Rigakos, G.S. (2002). Solidarity, fear and subculture. *The new parapolice* (pp. 119–146). Toronto: University of Toronto Press.

Rosener, J.B. (1997). Sexual static. In K. Grint (Ed.), *Leadership. Classical, contemporary and critical approaches.* Oxford: Oxford University Press.

Ruddick, S. (1983). Maternal thinking. In J. Trebilcot (Ed.), *Mothering: Essays in feminist theory* (pp. 213–230). Totowa, NJ: Rowman and Allanheld.

Sadler, P. (1997). *Leadership.* London: Kogan Page.

Schein, E.H. (1992). *Organizational culture and leadership* (2nd ed., p. 2). San Francisco: Jossey-Bass.

Schneider, S. (1997). *Managing across cultures.* Hemel Hempstead: Prentice Hall Europe.

Selznick, P. (1949). *TVA and the grass roots.* Berkeley, CA: University of California Press.

Shearing, C., & Ericson, R.V. (1991). Culture as figurative action. *British Journal of Sociology, 42,* 481–506.

Skolnick, J. (1994). A sketch of a policeman's working personality. *Justice without trial: Law enforcement in a democratic society* (3rd ed., pp. 41–68). New York: Wiley.

Stogdill, R.M. (1948). Personal factors associated with leadership. A survey of the literature. *Journal of Psychology, 25,* 35–71.

Stogdill, R.M. (1974). *Handbook of leadership. A survey of theory and research.* New York: Free Press.

Swidler, A. (1986). Culture in action: Symbols and strategies. *American Sociological Review, 51,* 273–286.

Sykes, G.W. (1989). The functional nature of police reform: The myth of controlling the police. In R. Dunham & G. Alpert (Eds.), *Critical issues in policing: Contemporary readings* (pp. 450–482). Prospect Heights, IL: Waveland Press.

Tayeb, M. (1994). Organisations and national culture: Methodology considered. *Organisational Studies, 15*(3), 429–446.

Tong, R. (1984). The maternal instinct. In J. Trebilcott (Ed.), *Mothering: Essays in feminist theory* (pp. 185–198). Totowa, NJ: Rowman and Allanheld.

Tong, R. (1993). *Feminine and feminist ethics.* Belmont, CA: Wadsworth.

Tong, R. (2003). *Feminist ethics.* Retrieved September 29, 2004, from http://plato.stanford.edu/ entries/feminism-ethics/.

Van Maanen, J. (1978). The asshole. In P.K. Manning & J. Van Maanen (Eds.), *Policing: A view from the streets* (pp. 221–238). Santa Monica, CA: Goodyear.

Van Maurik, J. (2001). *Writers on leadership* (pp. 2–3). London: Penguin.

Wagner, R.B. (1990). *Accountability in education: A philosophical inquiry.* New York: Routledge.

Walker, S., & Katz, C.M. (2008). *The police in America* (6th ed., pp. 104–105). Boston: McGraw-Hill.

Wallace, J., Hunt, J., & Richards, C. (1999). The relationship between organisational culture, organisational climate and managerial values. *The International Journal of Public Sector Management, 12*(7), 54–56.

Wilson, J.Q. (1968). *Varieties of police behavior: The management of law and order in eight communities.* Cambridge, MA: Harvard University Press.

Wright, P. (1996). *Managerial leadership.* London: Routledge.

Yukl, G. (2002). *Leadership in organizations* (p. 2). Upper Saddle River, NJ: Prentice Hall.

Znaniecki, F. (1936). *The method of sociology.* New York: Farrar & Rinehart.

## Further Reading

Bennis, W., & Nanus, B. (1997). *Leaders: Strategies for taking charge.* New York: Harper Business.

Bethel, S.M. (1990). *Making a difference.* New York: Berkley Books.

Covey, S.R. (1989). *The seven habits of highly effective people.* New York: Simon & Schuster.

Funk, C. (2004, Spring). Outstanding female superintendents: Profiles in leadership. *Advancing Women in Leadership.* Retrieved September 28, 2004, from http://www.advancingwomen.com/awl/spring2004/FUNK.html.

Griffith, S.B. (1963). *Sun Tzu: The art of war.* Oxford: Oxford University.

Kingshott, B.F. (1992). Do we need a graded response to violent situations? *Police Journal, LXV*(4), 297–306.

Kingshott, B.F. (1993). Police behaviour in crowd situations: A recipe for violence. *Police Journal, LXVI*(4), 366–375.

Kouzes, J.M., & Posner, B.Z. (1995). *The leadership challenge.* San Francisco: Jossey-Bass.

Nanus, B. (1992). *Visionary leadership. Creating a compelling sense of direction for your organization.* San Francisco: Jossey-Bass.

Ruddick, S. (1989). *Maternal thinking: Toward a politics of peace.* New York: Ballantine Books.

Senge, P.M. (1990). *The fifth discipline. The art and practice of the learning organization.* London: Random House.

Taylor, R.L., & Rosenbach, W.E. (Eds.). (1996). *Military leadership: In pursuit of excellence* (3rd ed.). Boulder, CO: Westview Press.

Tong, R. (1998). *Feminist thought: A more comprehensive introduction* (2nd ed.). Boulder, CO: Westview Press.

Trojanowicz, R., & Bucqueroux, B. (1990). *Community policing.* Cincinnati, OH: Anderson.

Selected Reading

# EXPLORING ACADEMIC DISCOURSE ON CRIMINAL JUSTICE ETHICS

## Where Are We?*

***Gayle M. Rhineberger-Dunn and Megan C. Mullins***

## INTRODUCTION

Regardless of the discipline in which it is specifically applied, ethics generally refers to the study of what is right and wrong behavior, policies, or practices. Applied to the criminal justice discipline, ethics can be defined as ethical issues related to both broad social and legal policies as well as ethical dilemmas specific to particular criminal justice professions (Pollock, 2004). For example, the field of criminal justice ethics encompasses such discipline-specific questions as: Is the death penalty wrong? Is the Patriot Act a just piece of legislation? Are Sex Offender Registries fair? Is it wrong for police officers to accept gratuities?[1]

Although the subject of ethics is not new to the fields of criminal justice and criminology, its history is tenuous. It has only been in the past twenty-five years that ethics has emerged as a visible subfield in these disciplines. Prior to the 1980s, only a handful of programs offered criminal justice ethics courses, and very few required them as part of their curriculum. Similarly, very few academic publications focused on criminal justice ethics.

While criminal justice ethics has experienced an increased presence in both program curricula and academic journals over the past twenty-five years, no literature currently exists that assesses faculty and student participation in various forms of discourse on ethics or their perceptions about its place in the academic curriculum.

Understanding whether or not faculty and students are engaged in discourse on criminal justice ethics and the extent to which they are engaged in such discussion is an important issue for both criminal justice professionals and academics as a result of the increased call for accountability in social service professions, particularly in the area of professional conduct, and the rise in criminal justice programs in colleges and universities. Recent cases publicized in the mass media bring to light serious problems endemic to the criminal justice profession, such as police racial profiling and use of force, overzealous investigators and prosecutors manipulating evidence to obtain convictions, wrongful convictions, and race and class-biased sentencing. It is important for students of criminal justice to be exposed to such topics before they enter their chosen profession, whether it is in criminal justice or elsewhere. Exposure to profession-specific ethical dilemmas (e.g., police accepting gratuities) can provide students with an understanding of the types of dilemmas they will face if they choose to work in that profession. Similarly, exposure to social policy-based ethical issues is important for the production of educated citizens who will inevitably impact such policies through their behavior (e.g., voting) or be impacted by them as a community citizen.

The purpose of this exploratory research is to understand the current state of discourse on ethics in the disciplines of criminal justice and criminology, in terms of pedagogy, verbal dialogue, and scholarly activities. Using both quantitative and qualitative data obtained from an email survey of American Society of Criminology members, we attempt to ascertain the extent to which criminal justice and criminology faculty and students talk about ethics, with whom they have these discussions, (e.g., students, fellow academics, criminal justice professionals), where they have them (in or outside of the classroom), and if they are presenting conference papers or publishing peer-reviewed articles on criminal justice ethics. This paper begins with a brief history of the state of ethics in criminal justice and criminology. Next, we provide a description of the methods used to conduct this study, followed by a detailed description and analysis of the research findings as they relate to the nature of the discourse on ethics in the disciplines of criminal justice and criminology. Lastly, we discuss the implications these findings have on the state of ethics within these two disciplines.

## HISTORICAL BACKGROUND

Prior to the early 1980s, there appears to have been a general lack of discourse on ethics in two primary areas: program curriculum and written publication. In the early 1980s, Sherman (1982) suggested that ethics had been virtually ignored in the fields of criminal justice and criminology, even at a time when it was increasing in other disciplines (e.g., medical schools, nursing, law, and journalism). This perception is substantiated by the virtual absence of academic ethics courses in the 1970s. Sherman (1982:13) speculated the following:

> It may be safe to say that even where ethics is taught, it is only marginal to the curriculum (as at Albany, where there is almost no link between ethics per se and any of the comprehensive doctoral examinations, the central focus of the curriculum). In most institutions, separate courses on criminal justice ethics are probably unknown, and the teaching of ethics in other courses is unlikely to be explicit in its use of formal philosophical tools.

Although a 1978 report by the Police Foundation's National Advisory Commission on Higher Education for Police Officers recommended academic education in ethics for officers in training, few criminal justice programs at that point in time required an ethics class as part of their curriculum (Sherman, 1982; Southerland, 2002). While there was a relative absence of stand-alone ethics courses, the issue of ethics and ethical practice in criminal justice was not necessarily ignored in academe. In fact, as Sherman (1982) suggested, ethical issues were likely being discussed within various classes throughout the criminal justice curriculum. Therefore, some discussion of ethics was likely taking place within classes and among colleagues, just not in the form of stand-alone ethics courses. However, there is no data on how much or in what form (e.g., informal or formal conversations outside of class, classroom lecture) this dialogue was taking place.

In addition to the lack of stand-alone ethics courses in criminal justice curricula, there was minimal publication discourse on criminal justice ethics. The absence of academic research speaks volumes about the perceived importance of ethics in university or college curricula for criminal justice and criminology programs, whether this absence was due to a lack of faculty expertise or interest in publishing in this area, the quality or lack thereof of those submissions, or its marginalization by journal editors and reviewers in the form of manuscript rejections. Publications in academic journals represent principle current topics in the discipline and provide academics with an overview of what the core disciplinary issues are not only for research, but for teaching as well. Presumably, research findings are to be used in the classroom to teach students about the reality of crime, criminal justice, victims, offenders, and policy. Academic research reinforces for academics and for students what they should be concentrating on within their research and classroom discussions.

The lack of ethics-related publication discourse in academic journals reinforces the perception that ethics was not considered a vital core topic in the discipline. If its absence was due to reviewer and editorial decisions, this marginalization reflects at least to some degree a lack of willingness by some members of the discipline to engage in professional written discourse on ethics. This in itself does not indicate a lack of interest in teaching on, talking about, or publishing in the area of criminal justice ethics. However, there are no data available to assess the extent to which ethics was being discussed in non-ethics specific classes, outside the classroom, or the degree to which academics were interested in engaging in ethics-related research.

It was not until the early 1980s that substantial academic literature on ethics appeared in criminal justice-related journals. Criminal justice and criminology are ever-changing fields; as the dominant culture changes, so does the teaching and research focus within the discipline. Several developments contributed to changing the presence of ethics in academic courses and written publications. The first development was the discovery of various governmental scandals, namely Watergate, ABSCAM, and the Iran-Contra investigations (Hyatt, 1991). The tumultuous political and social landscape of the 1970s and 1980s was beginning to push professional ethics to the forefront of the academic and public arenas. Citizens increasingly demanded accountability and proof of ethical behavior by government and other leaders, including criminal justice system professionals (Hyatt,

1991). The 1990s Rodney King incident further influenced the call for ethical conduct for criminal justice actors. This case raised a multitude of ethical issues, including but certainly not limited to police conduct generally, the use of force, racial profiling, response to and control of the subsequent riot, police department procedures for investigating and disciplining complaints against officers, criminal prosecution and sentencing of police officers involved in the incident, media coverage of crime, criminals, and trials, and the dissection of the incident in academic and media forums.

The second development occurred in the policing profession. The creation of the Law Enforcement Assistance Administration and the Law Enforcement Education Program provided funding for post-secondary criminal justice programs, thereby directly contributing to a rise in the number of these programs nationwide (Durham, 1992 and Weirman and Archambeault 1983 as cited by Durham, 1992). From 1960 to the late 1970s, the number of institutions offering a degree of any type, from associate to doctoral, in criminal justice rose to 600 (Durham, 1992). With this increase in criminal justice students, particularly future police officers, police organizations took an increased interest in the curriculum of this academic training. In 1978 the Police Foundation's National Advisory Commission on Higher Education for Police Officers recommended academic training in ethics (Sherman, 1982). This recommendation may have facilitated increased attention to the development of ethics courses, both for potential police officers, and for criminal justice students generally.

The last development focused on the need for ethics in academic curricula. In 1981 and 1982, Sherman (1982:6) called for the need to increase the teaching of and research on ethics in criminal justice:

> No matter what personnel arrangements are made for research and teaching, the subject matter of criminology will be incompletely taught unless ethics is brought into the curriculum. A student of crime who has not thought about whether and when violence is right or wrong can hardly be said to have a thorough understanding of the subject. Moreover, the nature of the subject matter makes it almost impossible for ethics to be ignored in teaching.

Simultaneously, a general academic debate arose over the meaning of an "educated person," which translated into the need to train university students to be good citizens by teaching them to analyze moral and ethical questions, as the "inability to examine difficult issues in a careful and unemotional way will leave students lacking in one of the most essential tools for making them good citizens" (Hyatt, 1991:79). While this debate centered on the general university student, Hyatt (1991:79) postulated that ethics courses were particularly needed more broadly across the criminal justice field and included in a range of institutions, since it "vests a higher measure of coercion and discretion at its lowest ranks than any other occupation or profession that comes to mind. Criminal justice as a discipline is, after all, a field of moral (or non-moral) behavior." Similarly, criminal justice programs across type of institution have historically been viewed as non-rigorous, less-than-legitimate academic programs (Durham, 1992). Durham (1992:42) outlined several recommendations for obtaining legitimacy, such as "integrating academic with field-based education" and "increasing the role of research." What is interesting, however, is that he recommended teaching ethics not as an attempt to increase legitimacy in the discipline itself, but rather as a strategy for making criminal justice fit within university objectives in order to give it more academic legitimacy. To do this, he suggested the following:

> Again, criminal justice education is a splendid vehicle for accomplishing objectives that serve the general goals of the liberal arts education. The recurrent dilemmas of crime and justice offer innumerable case studies and examples that can be used to consider the classic problems in ethics. Issues such as defining good and evil, the nature of human responsibility, and the right of the state to enforce behavioral conformity are not only important in criminal justice, but also are matters of significant general concern.
>
> (Durham, 1992:48)

For him, offering ethics courses would not only benefit professionally-oriented criminal justice students (i.e., police or correctional officers), but also aid in the production of soundly "educated persons" who will be better equipped to act as good citizens.

Together, these three developments combined to aid the emergence of a discourse on ethics in academia. Since then, both pedagogical and scholarly discourse has increased dramatically. Compared to the late 1980s, more schools currently require an ethics course as part of their undergraduate curriculum. Southerland (2002) found that in a sample of criminal justice programs stratified by U.S. region (northeast, south, midwest, southwest, and west) in 1999 to 2000, the southwest reported 30 percent of the sample programs in that region required a course on ethics. Comparatively, 15 percent of the sample programs in the midwest required ethics, while 8 percent of sample programs in the each of the northeast, south, and west regions reportedly required ethics courses in their criminal justice curriculums. However, this picture differs significantly from the 1988 to 1989 sample, when no region reported 30 percent or more of the sample programs requiring ethics courses.

Publication data also clearly show an increase in criminal justice ethics-related books and articles since the mid-1980s. A handful of edited volumes and other published works appeared that provided insight on how to teach criminal justice ethics courses (see, for example, Sherman, 1981, 1982; Heffernan, 1982; Pollock-Byrne, 1988, 1990, 1993; Pring, 1988, 1990; Schmalleger, 1990; Cedarblom and Spohn, 1991; Hyatt, 1991; and Kleinig and Smith, 1997). When searching for ethics in the Criminal Justice Abstracts database, one can see there are a fairly substantial number of articles written since the 1980s on various aspects of ethics in criminal justice. These articles span such topical areas as ethics in law enforcement (e.g., Kania, 1988; Kingshott, Bailey, and Wolfe, 2004; Peak, Stitt and Glensor, 1998; Westerland, 2005), courts and the legal profession (e.g., Cohen, 2001; Cunningham, 1999; O'Grady, 2002), corrections (e.g., Schwartz and Nurge, 2004; Haag, 2006), and criminal justice research (Esbensen, 1991; DuVal and Salmon, 2004), as well as such topics as offender profiling (Wilson, Lincoln, and Kocsis, 1997) and mass media coverage of crime (Cramer, 1995). Additionally, two journals are currently devoted to ethical issues in criminal justice, namely, *Criminal Justice Ethics* (originating in 1982) and *Online Quarterly Review of Crime, Ethics, and Social Philosophy* (originating in 2004).

While not extensive, these results show that the place and importance of ethics in criminal justice has changed. The topic of ethics has now emerged as a critical issue worth formally incorporating in the discipline through publications as well as through criminal justice program curricula. As college and university faculty are in the position to shape the discipline for students, it is vital to understand if academics are teaching, discussing, and researching ethics in criminal justice.

The primary purpose of this research is to explore the degree to which the call for integrating ethics in academic curriculum has been answered. A secondary purpose is to provide a baseline understanding of the extent to which faculty, students and criminal justice professionals are engaged in discourse on criminal justice ethics, and the importance faculty and students place on having discussions revolving around criminal justice ethics.

# METHODS

To explore the extent to which academic faculty are engaged in discourse on ethics in criminal justice, we distributed an Internet-based survey questionnaire[2] to members of the America Society of Criminology (ASC).[3] The ASC is "an international organization concerned with criminology, embracing scholarly, scientific, and professional knowledge concerning the etiology, prevention, control, and treatment of crime and delinquency," and membership "includes professionals, academicians, and students in the many fields of criminal justice and criminology" (www.asc4l.com). Its membership directory is on-line and available to the public.[4] The ASC list of current and past members was chosen for the population base of this survey, as it most likely contains a great diversity of members representing all types of colleges and universities nation-wide. All current and past members listed in the online directory as of March 7, 2006, were eligible for participation in the study. The membership directory was formatted into an Excel file. Duplicate member entries were deleted, as were members who did not have an email address listed in the directory. All additional contact information except email addresses was also deleted from the file. This process resulted in 5,939 ASC members available for participation in the survey.

Utilizing a service provider for on-line surveys (www.questionpro.com), we uploaded the email addresses and sent all members an email invitation to participate that included a link to the survey. A follow-up email was sent to all participants who did not respond to the initial survey. The software allowed for all emails to be sent blindly, so that no individual participant was able to identify any other participant's email address. Additionally, this software allowed us to track emails that were rejected by the recipient's email server. Emails are generally rejected if they contain a bad or no longer usable email address or if they are captured by some of the more progressive SPAM filters. This process resulted in the loss of 786 potential participants, reducing the number of available subjects to 5,153. Further, as we wanted to focus our study on questions related to academic work (teaching and scholarship), we added a screener question in the questionnaire asking participants if they were currently affiliated with an academic department in which they were teaching or taking classes. This resulted in 119 participants being removed from the database, and reduced the population of subjects to 5,034. A total of 721 surveys were returned between March 28 and May 17, 2006, yielding a response rate of 14 percent.

# RESEARCH VARIABLES

## Dependent Variables

This study examines two outcome measures for use with binary logistic regression. In order to understand the extent to which academic faculty discuss criminal justice ethics and with whom they have these discussions, respondents were asked if they had discussed criminal justice ethics in the past year with any criminal justice professional (0 = no, 1 = yes) and if they had discussed ethical issues involving criminal justice actors with any of their colleagues or students within the past 12 months (0 = no, I = yes).

## Extent of Ethical Dialogue

A further purpose of this paper is to assess the extent to which academic criminologists engage in discussions of ethics with criminal justice professionals and with their colleagues and students. Respondents who indicated they had spoken with any criminal justice professional in the past year were asked to further identify which criminal justice professionals they had these discussions with (check all that apply): police, courts/legal professionals, correctional personnel, policy makers, or other (all yes/no responses). Respondents were further asked how often they discussed criminal justice ethics with each type of professional (regularly, sometimes, rarely, or never).

Similarly, respondents were asked to indicate where these conversations primarily take place (in class, out of class, or both in and out of class). They were also asked which faculty members they tend to discuss criminal justice ethics with more (members within their department, members outside their department, or both included equally in these discussions), and which students they tend to discuss ethics with more (undergraduates, graduate, or both included equally in these discussions). Respondents were further asked how often (regularly, sometimes, rarely/never)[5] they discuss criminal justice ethics with 1) other faculty members and 2) students.

If respondents answered rarely/never to either the faculty or student question, they were asked to explain why they rarely or never discuss criminal justice ethics with other faculty members. Qualitative responses were reviewed and a coding structure for data analysis was created in three phases. First, responses were reviewed and initial codes were assigned based on the content of participant responses. Second, the responses were reviewed again and categories were created that clustered together coded responses with similar themes (such as personal interest in the topic, lack of interaction with students, etc.). Third, a final review of the data was performed to confirm categories and themes and thus increase the reliability and validity of the coding process and results. In this way, the researchers were able to systematically develop categories, explore relationships between categories, and then refine the final themes and categories for discussion. All potentially identifying information in these responses was omitted from the presentation of results.

## Independent Variables

Five categories of independent variables were included in the analysis (see Table 8.1 for frequency distributions of the independent variables). Gender was coded as a dichotomous variable, with 1 for female and male as the reference category. Academic rank reflects the respondent's current status as a student, a non-tenure track faculty member, assistant professor, associate professor, or full/emeritus professor.[6] For degree field, respondents were asked to indicate one of five fields in which they obtained their highest degree: sociology, criminal justice, criminology, criminal justice and criminology, or other (and to specify the "other" field).[7] These were recoded to dummy variables, with criminal justice as the reference category. The variable, institution, represents the type of institution in which respondents indicated they were currently teaching or taking classes (community or junior college, 4 year Baccalaureate/liberal arts college, Master's university, and Doctoral university, or other). Four dummy variables were created, representing undergraduate institution, Master's university, and Doctoral university.[8]

Lastly, we included a series of professional teaching and scholarly experience variables. Respondents were asked if, in the past 12 months, they had taught an entire course on criminal justice ethics, participated in team-teaching a course on criminal justice ethics, or included material on criminal justice ethics in another course, published a peer-reviewed article on criminal justice ethics (including pedagogical pieces), presented a paper on criminal justice ethics at a professional conference, or attended a session on criminal justice ethics at a professional conference. Dummy variables were created for each of the following variables: having ever taught or team-taught a criminal justice ethics course, having ever included criminal justice ethics material in other courses, ever published a peer-reviewed article on criminal justice ethics, and ever presented a paper or attended a session on criminal justice ethics at a professional conference.[9]

# FINDINGS

## Academic Exposure

Very few respondents have pedagogical or scholarly experience with criminal justice ethics (see Table 8.1). Only 10.4 percent[10] had ever taught or team-taught a criminal justice ethics course. However, just over half (51.7 percent) of respondents indicated they have included material on criminal justice ethical issues in their other (non-ethics) courses. A mere 6.2 percent had ever published a peer-reviewed

**Table 8.1** Descriptive Statistics*

| Dependent Variables | | n | % |
|---|---|---|---|
| Any CJ Professional | (*N* = 683) | 388 | 56.8 |
| Policy Maker | (*N* = 721) | 134 | 18.6 |
| Police | (*N* = 721) | 272 | 37.7 |
| Courts/Legal Professionals | (*N* = 721) | 188 | 26.1 |
| Correctional Personnel | (*N* = 721) | 181 | 25.1 |
| Colleagues or Students | (*N* = 721) | 614 | 85.5 |
| **Independent Variables** | | **n** | **%** |
| **Gender** | (*N* = 623) | | |
| Male | | 309 | 49.6 |
| Female | | 314 | 50.4 |
| **Academic Rank** | (*N* = 593) | | |
| Student | | 204 | 34.4 |
| Non-Tenure Track Faculty | | 60 | 10.1 |
| Assistant Professor | | 148 | 25.0 |
| Associate Professor | | 72 | 12.1 |
| Full/Emeritus | | 109 | 18.4 |
| **Degree Field** | (*N* = 633) | | |
| Criminal Justice | | 149 | 23.5 |
| Sociology | | 222 | 35.1 |
| Criminology | | 70 | 11.1 |
| CJ and Criminology | | 68 | 10.7 |
| Other | | 124 | 19.6 |
| **Institution** | (*N* = 615) | | |
| Undergraduate Institution | | 121 | 19.7 |
| Master's Institution | | 103 | 16.7 |
| Doctoral Institution | | 391 | 63.6 |
| **Academic CJ Ethic Exposure** | | | |
| Ever Taught/Team-Taught | (*N* = 704) | 73 | 10.4 |
| Ever Included Material | (*N* = 706) | 365 | 51.7 |
| Ever Published | (*N* = 705) | 44 | 6.2 |
| Ever Presented at Conference or Attended Session | (*N* = 701) | 153 | 21.8 |

*Valid Percents

article on criminal justice ethics. A total of 21.8 percent of respondents have ever presented a paper or attended a conference session on ethics.

## Dependent Variables

As shown in Table 8.1, it is clear that academic faculty and students are engaged in some dialogue with both criminal justice professionals and other faculty and students. Just over half (56.8 percent) of respondents indicated they had discussed criminal justice ethics with any criminal justice professional in the past year. Respondents have the most contact with police (37.7 percent), and the least contact with policy makers (18.6 percent). Nearly 86 percent of respondents had discussed ethical issues involving criminal justice professionals with their colleagues or students in the past year.

## Extent of Dialogue Variables

Table 8.2 displays the extent to which respondents have discussions with criminal justice professionals and with their colleagues and students. A full 66.6 percent of respondents who say they have had a discussion with a criminal justice

**Table 8.2** Extent of Ethical Discussions*

| | Regularly n(%) | Sometimes n(%) | Rarely n(%) | Never n(%) |
|---|---|---|---|---|
| **Professional Discussions** | | | | |
| Police | 81 | 164 | 77 | 46 |
| | (22.0) | (44.6) | (20.9) | (12.5) |
| Courts/Legal Personnel | 52 | 131 | 99 | 74 |
| | (14.6) | (36.8) | (27.8) | (20.8) |
| Correctional Personnel | 54 | 125 | 83 | 86 |
| | (15.5) | (35.9) | (23.9) | (24.7) |
| Policy Makers | 42 | 101 | 79 | 116 |
| | (12.4) | (29.9) | (23.4) | (34.3) |
| Other CJ Professionals | 25 | 64 | 65 | 115 |
| | (9.3) | (23.8) | (24.2) | (42.8) |
| **Academic Discussions** | | | **Rarely/Never n(%)** | |
| Colleagues | 98 | 348 | 243 | |
| | (14.2) | (50.5) | (35.3) | |
| Students | 216 | 341 | 127 | |
| | (31.6) | (49.9) | (18.6) | |

*Valid Percents

professional in the past year indicate they either regularly or sometimes have these discussions with police, while only 12.5 percent indicate they have never had a discussion about ethics with a police officer. Of interest is the fact that nearly half (42.3 percent) of the respondents answering this set of questions indicate they have spoken either regularly or sometimes with a policy maker about ethics.

When asked how often they discuss criminal justice ethics with other faculty members, the majority of respondents indicated sometimes (50.5 percent). However, a full 35.3 percent indicated they rarely or never discuss criminal justice ethics with other faculty. Respondents indicating they regularly or sometimes discuss criminal justice ethics with faculty members ($n$ = 446) are having these discussions with other faculty members in their own departments (60.1 percent, $n$ = 268) or both members of their department and members outside their department (26.0 percent, $n$ = 116). A small portion (11.7 percent, $n$ = 52) said they discuss criminal justice ethics more with faculty members outside their department. Additionally, the majority of the 614 respondents who indicated they had discussed ethical issues involving criminal justice actors in the past year with their colleagues or students indicated they had these discussions both in and out of the classroom (53.9 percent, $n$ = 331), followed by discussions only in the classroom (29.2 percent, $n$ = 179), and only outside the classroom (16.9 percent, $n$ = 104).

Table 8.3 shows the most common open-ended responses for why respondents rarely or never discuss ethics with other faculty members. One hundred forty-six respondents provided an explanation for this lack of discussion. The most common response for rarely or never discussing this type of ethics with faculty members was that the subject is rarely or never raised (39 percent). Of these 57 respondents, 21 percent added that ethics as a distinct subject matter gets discussed after an unethical situation has occurred or when students ask a specific question about it in class. For example, one participant noted, "The program is geared towards Criminology not Criminal Justice. However, it does come up during class among us, the students with a criminal justice background." Graduate students also reported that it is sometimes difficult to have discussions with faculty outside of the classroom in general, and if they get the chance, they prefer to discuss their formal progress through the program.

The second most prevalent reason for not discussing ethics with faculty members is that it is not in an individual's area of expertise and/or they are not required to teach it as a course in their teaching schedule (14 percent). Others noted that criminal justice itself is not a department emphasis (10 percent) and that there is a general lack of university and department interest in criminal justice ethics (4 percent). For example, one respondent noted that, "Faculty and even my dean seem uninterested in the topic. I had to fight to teach an ethics course at my university. Everyone hated the idea and thought it was a waste of time." A final viewpoint on institutional nonsupport of ethics is reflected by one respondent's comment that "I think many of them are not interested in or concerned about ethics. I observe many engaging in unethical behavior."

Other explanations focused on faculty time constraints on interactions (7 percent). Some faculty members indicated that faculty interaction is limited overall and wrote that interaction is thus focused more on departmental governing issues, or that when ethics are discussed, the topics revolve around the subject

**Table 8.3** Explanations for Why Rarely or Never Discuss Ethics with Faculty*

| Participant Response | N | Percentage | Cumulative Percentage |
|---|---|---|---|
| Does not come up | 57 | 39% | 39% |
| Not in individuals' area of expertise/ teaching assignment | 20 | 14% | 53% |
| Lack of regular contact and Communication with faculty members | 15 | 10% | 63% |
| Criminal Justice not departmental emphasis | 14 | 10% | 73% |
| Time constraints limit faculty discussions | 10 | 7% | 80% |
| Lack of university/department Interest in topic | 6 | 4% | 84% |
| Don't know | 5 | 3% | 87% |
| To avoid conflict | 3 | 2% | 89% |
| Other | 16 | 11% | 100% |
| Total | 146 | 100% | 100% |

*Valid Percents

of research ethics or academia in general. One respondent indicated this by stating, "We don't discuss ethics with regard to criminal justice; we do so more often in regards to academia in general. I'm not sure why." Some also mentioned that discussions are more likely to arise after an incident has occurred, as indicated by a respondent who stated that "It seems like ethics only really come[s] up after someone does something unethical." Finally, a few in this group explained their lack of discussion of criminal justice ethics with other faculty because interaction with full-time professors is difficult or even discouraged in the work climate due to other time and resource commitments as well as being a product of their non-tenure track status. For example, one participant stated that, "I very rarely interact with the CJ faculty because 90% are adjunct faculty" while another noted that, "I'm adjunct and most of the other faculty in the department would not demean themselves by talking to me."

Respondents appear much more willing or able to discuss criminal justice ethics with students than with faculty. Of the 684 respondents who answered the question, how often do you discuss criminal justice ethics with students, the majority (49.9 percent) indicate sometimes having these discussions (see Table 8.2). When they discuss ethics with students,[11] they do so more with undergraduate students (46.6 percent, $n$ = 255), than with graduate students (27.8 percent, $n$ = 152). One quarter of respondents (25.6 percent, $n$ = 140) indicate they discuss criminal justice ethics equally with undergraduate and graduate students.

**Table 8.4** Explanations for Why Rarely or Never Discuss Ethics with Students*

| Participant Response | N | Percentage | Cumulative Percentage |
|---|---|---|---|
| Does not come up | 15 | 20% | 20% |
| Courses taught are not CJ related/ Criminal Justice not departmental emphasis | 14 | 19% | 39% |
| Not currently teaching | 11 | 15% | 54% |
| Lack of personal interest in subject | 5 | 6% | 60% |
| Lack of interaction with students | 4 | 5% | 65% |
| Students don't bring up subject/ up are not interested | 4 | 5% | 70% |
| Teach/discuss ethics more generally | 4 | 5% | 75% |
| Don't know | 3 | 4% | 79% |
| Students are not CJ students | 2 | 3% | 82% |
| Too busy/too much other Material to cover in class | 2 | 3% | 85% |
| Other | 11 | 15% | 100% |
| Total | 75 | 100% | 100% |

*Valid Percents

Table 8.4 displays the most common responses for why respondents rarely or never discuss criminal justice ethics with students. Seventy-five participants provided a reason for why they rarely or never discuss criminal justice ethics with students. Similar to the reasons for a lack of discussion with faculty members, the most reported reason why ethics involving criminal justice professionals is rarely or never discussed with students is because the topic rarely comes up (20 percent), they are not teaching in the field of criminal justice (19 percent), or that they were not teaching at the time the survey was taken, either because they were a student or for other reasons related to their positions as faculty members (15 percent). Finally, 6 percent reported that they were not interested in ethics, while 5 percent indicated their students are not interested in the topic, as illustrated by one respondent's comment that, "They (students) are both uninformed and uninterested in the issues." Still others responded that ethics is more likely an issue that arises in a general sense, such that "It just comes up as part of a conversation about another general theme. It's not a subject taught in the department; thus we are sort of not encouraged (or discouraged) to discuss ethics." Other comments described reasons such as limited interaction with students, too much material to cover, students not being CJ students, that the issue is inherent to many other courses, not knowing why these dialogues do not take place, and the lack of resources on the subject. For example, one respondent noted that, "Few if any resources exist on the topic and large lecture classes make open discussion difficult without preparatory readings." Another respondent noted that, "They have a moral component already due to the subject matter (i.e. crime, victimization, white collar crime, theory and explanation, poverty)."

## Binary Logistic Regression

We used binary logistic regression to explore the influence various personal and institutional factors have on whether or not ASC members have discussed ethics with specific criminal justice professionals and with colleagues and students in the past year. Tables 8.5 through 8.7 show the binary logistic regression results.[12] Table 8.5 displays the models for discussing criminal justice ethics with any criminal justice professional and with policy makers. Four variables increase the probability of discussing criminal justice ethics with any criminal justice professional in the past year: being a non-tenure track faculty (25.55 percent); currently working in a Master's level institution (16.56 percent), having taught or team-taught an ethics course (21.67 percent), and having ever included ethics material in other (non-ethics specific) courses (19.70 percent). Having a sociology degree decreases the probability of discussing ethics with a criminal justice professional by 12.81 percent. Four variables have a statistically significant relationship with having discussed criminal justice ethics with policy makers in the past year. Being a non-tenure track faculty member (20.93 percent), having ever taught or team-taught criminal justice ethics (18.94 percent), and having ever presented a paper or attended a session on ethics at a professional conference (16.67 percent) increase the probability of having spoken to a policy maker in the past year. However, being female (-12.50 percent) decreases the probability that respondents had spoken with a policy maker in the past year.

Table 8.6 displays the models for discussing ethics with specific criminal justice professionals. Six variables have a statistically significant relationship with discussing ethics with police. Being a non-tenure track faculty (27.12 percent), having taught or team-taught (24.29 percent), and having ever included ethics material in a non-ethics class (20.06 percent) increase the probability of having discussed ethics with police in the past year. Being female (–17.57 percent), having a degree in sociology (–22.46 percent), and having a degree in criminal justice and criminology (–21.17 percent) decrease the probability of having discussed ethics with a police officer in the past year.

Three variables increase the probability of discussing ethics with courts/legal professionals: being a non-tenure track faculty (17.43 percent), working in a Master's level institution (13.50 percent), and having ever included ethics material in a non-ethics course (18.94 percent).

Three variables are statistically related to respondent dialogue with correctional personnel. Working in a Master's level institution (17.00 percent), having taught or team taught ethics (22.40 percent), and having ever included ethics material in a non-ethics course (14.83 percent) increase the probability of having discussed ethics with correctional personnel in the past year.

**Table 8.5** Past Year Discussed CJ Ethics with a CJ Professional or Policy Makers

| | Model A: Any CJ Professional | | | Model B: Policy Makers | | |
|---|---|---|---|---|---|---|
| Variables | Odds Ratio | Logit | Prob. Diff. % | Odds Ratio | Logit | Prof. Diff. % |
| Constant | --- | −0.12 | --- | --- | −2.02 | --- |
| **Gender (male = 0)** | | | | | | |
| Female | 0.77 | −0.27 | −6.50 | 0.60 | −0.51 | −12.50* |
| **Academic Rank (student = 0)** | | | | | | |
| Non-Tenure Track Faculty | 3.09 | 1.13 | 25.55** | 2.44 | 0.89 | 20.93* |
| Assistant Professor | 0.59 | −0.53 | −12.89 | 0.78 | −0.24 | −6.18 |
| Associate Professor | 1.28 | 0.24 | 6.14 | 1.80 | 0.59 | 14.29 |
| Full/Emeritus Professor | 0.80 | −0.23 | −5.56 | 1.59 | 0.46 | 11.39 |
| **Degree Field (Criminal Justice = 0)** | | | | | | |
| Sociology | 0.59 | −0.53 | −12.81* | 1.00 | 0.00 | 0.00 |
| Criminology | 1.06 | 0.06 | 1.46 | 0.68 | −0.38 | −9.52 |
| CJ and Criminology | 0.81 | −0.22 | −5.25 | 1.70 | 0.53 | 12.96 |
| Other | 1.01 | 0.01 | 0.25 | 1.34 | 0.29 | 7.26 |
| **Institution (doctoral = 0)** | | | | | | |
| Undergraduate Institution | 1.39 | 0.33 | 8.16 | 0.98 | −0.02 | −0.51 |
| Master's Institution | 1.99 | 0.69 | 16.56* | 1.09 | 0.08 | 2.15 |
| **Academic CJ Ethics Exposure (never = 0)** | | | | | | |
| Ever Taught/Team Taught | 2.53 | 0.93 | 21.67* | 2.22 | 0.80 | 18.94* |
| Ever Included Material | 2.30 | 0.83 | 19.70*** | 1.22 | 0.20 | 4.95 |
| Ever Published | 1.25 | 0.22 | 5.56 | 1.61 | 0.48 | 11.69 |
| Ever Presented at a Conference or Attended a Session | 1.57 | 0.45 | 11.09 | 2.00 | 0.69 | 16.67* |
| Model $\chi^2$ | | 90.72*** | | | 68.27*** | |

***$p \leq 0.001$, **$p \leq .010$, *$p \leq .050$ (two-tailed tests)

**Table 8.6** Past Year Discussed CJ Ethics with a CJ Professional or Policy Makers

| Variables | Model C: Police | | | Model D: Courts/Legal Professional | | | Model E: Correctional Personnel | | |
|---|---|---|---|---|---|---|---|---|---|
| | Odds Ratio | Logit | Prob. Diff. % | Odds Ratio | Logit | Prob. Diff. % | Odds Ratio | Logit | Prob. Diff. % |
| Constant | --- | −0.60 | --- | --- | −1.89 | --- | --- | −1.55 | --- |
| **Gender (male = 0)** | | | | | | | | | |
| Female | 0.48 | −0.74 | −17.57*** | 0.91 | −0.10 | −2.36 | 0.90 | −0.11 | −2.74 |
| **Academic Rank (student = 0)** | | | | | | | | | |
| Non-Tenure Track Faculty | 3.37 | 1.21 | 27.12** | 2.07 | 0.73 | 17.43* | 1.18 | 0.17 | 4.11 |
| Assistant Professor | 0.90 | −0.10 | −2.58 | 0.84 | −0.18 | −4.35 | 0.63 | −0.47 | −11.50 |
| Associate Professor | 1.89 | 0.64 | 15.40 | 1.02 | 0.02 | 0.50 | 1.22 | 0.20 | 4.91 |
| Full/Emeritus Professor | 10.50 | 0.05 | 41.30 | 0.94 | −0.06 | −1.55 | 0.56 | −0.58 | −14.18 |
| **Degree Field (Criminal Justice = 0)** | | | | | | | | | |
| Sociology | 0.38 | −0.97 | −22.46*** | 1.05 | 0.05 | 1.22 | 0.79 | −0.24 | −6.02 |
| Criminology | 0.97 | −0.04 | −0.76 | 1.37 | 0.31 | 7.81 | 0.81 | −0.21 | −5.34 |
| CJ and Criminology | 0.41 | −0.90 | −21.17* | 1.32 | 0.27 | 6.90 | 1.41 | 0.34 | 8.47 |
| Other | 0.87 | −0.14 | −3.48 | 1.05 | 0.05 | 1.22 | 1.25 | 0.22 | 5.52 |
| **Institution (doctoral = 0)** | | | | | | | | | |
| Undergraduate Institution | 1.35 | 0.30 | 7.45 | 1.58 | 0.46 | 11.24 | 1.36 | 0.31 | 7.66 |
| Master's Institution | 1.66 | 0.51 | 12.41 | 1.74 | 0.55 | 13.50* | 2.03 | 0.71 | 17.00** |
| **Academic CJ Ethics Exposure (never = 0)** | | | | | | | | | |
| Ever Taught/Team Taught | 2.89 | 1.06 | 24.29** | 1.64 | 0.50 | 12.12 | 2.62 | 0.96 | 22.40** |
| Ever Included Material | 2.34 | 0.85 | 20.06*** | 2.22 | 0.80 | 18.94** | 1.84 | 0.61 | 14.83* |
| Ever Published | 1.63 | 0.49 | 11.98 | 0.79 | −0.24 | −5.87 | 1.11 | 0.11 | 2.70 |
| Ever Presented at a Conference or Attended a Session | 1.23 | 0.21 | 5.16 | 1.67 | 0.51 | 12.55 | 1.31 | 0.27 | 6.62 |
| Model $\chi^2$ | | 128.38*** | | | 52.75*** | | | 55.30*** | |

***$p \le 0.001$, **$p \le .010$, *$p \le .050$ (two-tailed tests)

Table 8.7 shows the results of the logistic regression for having discussed ethical issues involving criminal justice professionals with colleagues or students in the past year. Three variables increase the probability of having such discussions: working in an undergraduate institution (37.62 percent), having ever included ethics material in a non-ethics class (25.82 percent), and having ever presented a paper or attended a session on ethics at a professional conference (37.34 percent). However, having a degree in sociology (-24.85 percent) decreases the probability of having discussed ethics with colleagues or students in the past year.

**Table 8.7** Past Year Discussed Ethical Issues Involving CJ Actors with Colleagues or Students

| | Model F: Colleagues or Students | | |
|---|---|---|---|
| Variables | Odds Ratio | Logit | Prob. Diff. % |
| Constant | — | 1.67 | — |
| **Gender (male = 0)** | | | |
| Female | 0.85 | −0.17 | −4.20 |
| **Academic Rank (student = 0)** | | | |
| Non-Tenure Track Faculty | 0.60 | −0.52 | −12.62 |
| Assistant Professor | 1.35 | 0.30 | 7.48 |
| Associate Professor | 1.31 | 0.27 | 6.69 |
| Full/Emeritus Professor | 0.51 | −0.53 | −16.27 |
| **Degree Field (Criminal Justice = 0)** | | | |
| Sociology | 0.34 | −1.09 | −24.85** |
| Criminology | 0.54 | −0.62 | −15.06 |
| CJ and Criminology | 0.40 | −0.92 | −21.58 |
| Other | 0.58 | −0.54 | −13.25 |
| **Institution (doctoral = 0)** | | | |
| Undergraduate Institution | 7.08 | 1.96 | 37.62** |
| Master's Institution | 1.30 | 0.26 | 6.50 |
| **Academic CJ Ethics Exposure (never = 0)** | | | |
| Ever Taught/Team Taught | 1.69 | 0.53 | 12.83 |
| Ever Included Material | 3.14 | 1.14 | 25.82*** |
| Ever Published | 1.20 | 0.18 | 4.50 |
| Ever Presented at a Conference or Attended a Session | 6.90 | 1.93 | 37.34* |
| Model $\chi^2$ | | 84.77*** | |

***$p \leq 0.001$, **$p \leq .010$, *$p \leq .050$ (two-tailed tests)

## Constructing Dialogue from Respondent Comments

At the end of the survey, participants were asked to include any additional thoughts they had concerning ethics in criminal justice/criminology. Ninety-four respondents (13 percent) took the opportunity to reflect on the subject of criminal justice ethics, criminal justice practices in general, and the teaching of criminal justice ethics. The authors view these comments as a form of dialogue, whereby respondents were given the chance to "talk" about criminal justice ethics. We find them particularly telling, in an exploratory manner, of the divergent opinions on the relative importance of criminal justice ethics and discourse for academics belonging to this association.

Several respondents took this opportunity to critique the field of criminal justice and criminology generally, while some more specifically questioned whether criminal justice courses did anything more than support the status quo conditions of current policies and programs. For example, one respondent noted that, "Ethics in criminal justice is often a throw-away course used to justify the criminal justice system. CJ departments usually want to maintain relations with law enforcement and other parts of the criminal justice system- thus, a lack of critical thinking or approaches to this topic." Another respondent indicated that criminal justice/criminology courses were not the place to teach ethics, when he/she stated that, "I have never had an intelligent discussion with an academic in CJ about general principles of ethics. This group seems singularly unqualified to teach or study the issue." Still another respondent simply stated that, "I observe little use of ethics in the field."

Others reported that developing a discourse on the subject was critical for criminal justice/criminology, particularly as the subject relates to students. One respondent indicated that, "[Ethics) is a critical subject in CJ/Criminology. Police, guards, probation officers, etc. face ethical decisions all the time. So I think it is critical that CJ students read and think about ethical issues while they are in school before they go out and work in the real world." Another respondent indicated that, "Ethics is a subject matter overlooked by an increasingly quantitatively-driven research enterprise. We discount it to our peril."

While respondents indicated criminal justice ethics is an important topic worth teaching (and thereby having our students take), there appears to be controversy over how ethics should be taught. For example, one respondent noted that ethics is "an extremely important area of concern, but the central focus of educational efforts should be more on personal growth and self-awareness than on field-specific issues. Not that they should not be addressed, but the ethical line of development in the individual is the more salient issue or focus," while another respondent noted that, "It is very controversial. What is ethical to me might not be ethical to someone else. Guidelines must be clearly established." Another participant noted that experience in the field was necessary. "For ethics, it is not as much about knowledge as it is about experience in that particular area. It is difficult to teach police ethics if your decision is not based on first-hand knowledge since reaction to the situation often causes textbook ethics to be quickly abandoned. If you have never experienced it, it is difficult to relate." An additional respondent noted that, "In the international setting, I find most police officers dedicated to working for what is best in their society but with little education and guidance on making the decisions that achieve these goals. To a lesser degree, I find the same in the US." Another respondent noted that, "Politicians and national administration agencies have eroded, if not destroyed, any person's concerns about ethics."

# DISCUSSION

The purpose of this research was to explore the extent of academic discourse on ethics. Specifically, we explored whether or not academic faculty are teaching about criminal justice ethics, conducting scholarly activities related to ethics, and talking about ethics (and with whom they are having these discussions). Our results show that while American Society of Criminology (ASC) members are engaged in some dialogue with colleagues and students about criminal justice ethics, they are much less involved in directly teaching and conducting scholarly activities focused on ethics. Very few respondents have experience teaching an ethics-specific criminal justice course. The most frequent format for criminal justice ethics discourse is through teaching by inclusion of ethics material within other courses. Respondents have more experience attending conference presentations or presenting papers than they do publishing articles on ethics.

While faculty members discuss criminal justice ethics less with criminal justice professionals than they do with faculty or students, there is clear evidence that these conversations are occurring at some level. When they talk with professionals about ethics, they are least likely to have these conversations with policy makers and other non-specified criminal justice professionals. Faculty and students are much more likely to talk with police professionals than with courts/legal professionals or correctional personnel. This seems to limit the majority of the discourse on criminal justice ethics to just one component of the criminal justice system.

## Implications

There are several important implications of this exploratory study. First, the results indicate that there is controversy over the place of ethics in criminal justice and criminology courses and curricula in general. Both quantitative and qualitative responses indicate that some respondents find ethics to be crucial to the academic experience, while others believe it is not useful or are not interested in engaging in any form of discourse related to criminal justice ethics. This suggests that much more research is needed in this area in order to understand how ethics fits within the current academic curriculum. While there is literature discussing what topics individual researchers believe should be included in criminal justice ethics courses, as well as literature outlining how one should teach a criminal justice ethics course, there is no empirical evidence investigating how faculty or criminal justice professionals, with whom our students will be eventually employed, feel about the place of ethics in criminal justice and criminology program curricula. Currently, no literature exists discussing whether or not criminal justice faculty or criminal justice professionals are in favor of requiring ethics courses, nor is there research investigating the topics that faculty and criminal justice professionals believe should be addressed in such courses, on a more general scale than can currently be found in individual teaching-related journal articles. Before we start advocating the necessity of teaching ethics, we need to ask both criminal justice faculty and professionals if they believe it should be required, and if so, what topics they believe are the most pertinent to student needs, both practically and intellectually.

Second, our research suggests that non-tenure track faculty, particularly those at Master's level institutions, are more actively engaged in ethics-related conversations with criminal justice professionals. It is likely that many non-tenure track faculty are also working or have worked in the criminal justice system, and therefore have regular access to and conversations with these professionals. Interacting with criminal justice professionals may make these faculty members more informed of the ethical issues facing professionals in the field and how they must deal with these issues in the course of doing their everyday jobs. This may allow faculty to bring real-life examples into the classroom, albeit these examples seem to come primarily from police officers, thereby limiting the practical knowledge of professional conduct to one type of professional. Our results suggest that undergraduate students at doctoral institutions may not be receiving the same kind of practical knowledge in the classroom. We are not arguing that this practical knowledge is in any way better or worse than the knowledge brought to the classroom by faculty who do not have experience working in the criminal justice field or who do not have access to dialogue with such professionals. We are simply suggesting it is something to take note of and reflect on how this may influence perceptions of ethical responsibilities in professional conduct.

Third, our research suggests that academic exposure influences dialogue with professionals and students. Having taught or team-taught increases the probability of having ethics discussions with various professionals (any criminal justice professional, police, correctional personnel, and policy makers). Having ever included criminal justice ethics materials in non-ethics courses increases the probability of having discussions with all types of professionals (except policy makers) and with colleagues and students. These results seem to support the call of Sherman and others to incorporate ethics into the academic curricula. Additionally, we would expect individuals who have taught ethics or incorporated such material into their courses to have more discussions with colleagues and students about these issues as their previous inclusion of this material reflects the value they place on the subject.

## Limitations

The primary limitation of this study is generalizability. The results of this survey cannot be generalized, neither to all criminal justice and criminology faculty, nor to all members of the ASC. We did not have access to a manageable and cost-efficient national database of all academics teaching criminal justice and criminology classes. While we would have preferred to survey both the Academy of Criminal Justice Sciences (ACJS) members and the ASC members, we were unable to obtain the ACJS membership list for survey research purposes. Therefore, we were limited to the ASC membership. While this association has a substantial number of members representing all types of colleges and universities, it is not representative of all faculty who teach criminal justice and criminology-related courses (e.g., sociologists, psychologists, political scientists). Additionally, the membership itself is diverse, representing academics (faculty and students), professionals, administrators, and policy-makers. However, participants who did not have an academic affiliation, either through teaching or taking classes, were excluded from the survey.

Another issue related to generalizability is the method used to distribute the survey. Using an email survey, while economically advantageous, is not without peril. Although the survey provider we chose allowed us to assess how many surveys were distributed and how many surveys were undeliverable or "bounced" due to bad email addresses, it did not allow us to track how many surveys were automatically filtered into a "junk" email box and therefore never opened by respondents who do not manually check these components of their email system service. Therefore, we have no way of determining how many ASC members were aware of the opportunity to participate in this survey.

A third issue related to generalizability is the low response rate of 14 percent. While this rate was lower than expected for a survey directed at a specific professional population, it is a conservative estimate, as the online survey provider was unable to track the number of emails that were prevented from reaching the intended participant due to Internet firewall protections and SPAM filtering software.

A related concern is the possibility of inflated findings, particularly concerning the extent to which respondents discuss ethics. It is quite possible that the relatively high percentages of individuals indicating they regularly or sometimes discuss ethics with various criminal justice professionals, colleagues, and students, is in part a reflection of who completed the survey. Individuals who are interested in the topic of criminal justice ethics were probably far more likely to fill out the survey than those with little interest in the topic.

A final limitation of this study is variable measurement. Most critical is the measurement of how often respondents discuss ethics with faculty and students. Respondents could indicate regularly, sometimes, or rarely/never. The primary issue here is the lack of distinction between the rarely and never categories; these two categories were not separated in the questionnaire. This is problematic in that it potentially confounds the two issues this paper seeks to address: first, whether ethics is being discussed or not (the "never" element of the item) and secondly, to what extent it is being discussed (the "rarely" element of the item).

## Future Research

It is clear that criminal justice ethics has risen to the forefront of pertinent topics for the discipline, both pedagogically and scholarly in nature. While ethics has experienced an increased presence in both program curricula and academic journals over the past twenty-five years, there is still relatively little empirical evidence on how criminal justice and criminology faculty perceive the role of ethics in program curricula. It does not appear as if the academic faculty who plan program curricula, teach ethics courses, talk about various ethical issues with students and professionals, and conduct research on ethics topics, were consulted on the need for such courses for their students. Before we begin advocating it as a necessity in academic curricula, we need to better understand whether or not criminal justice faculty believe it should be required, as well as the topics they perceive as essential for student learning about criminal justice ethics.

Additionally, future research points us in the direction of understanding the types of ethical issues and dilemmas necessary for criminal justice or criminology students that criminal justice professionals feel students or new graduates should have been taught at an institute of higher education before they enter the career field. It is essential to investigate the differing roles that criminal justice professionals play as teachers to students or new graduates upon entering a criminal justice profession. Obtaining this information will allow criminal justice professionals to respond to the viewpoints expressed by academics and others affiliated with colleges and universities and inform academics of how this positioning works on the teaching and dialogue on criminal justice ethics from another vantage point, thus strengthening the key points that each group brings to the discourse.

## Notes

1 While we believe strongly that criminal justice ethics also refers to conduct associated with being an academic or student in the field of criminal justice (e.g., cheating, plagiarism, student-faculty relationships, or creating and enforcing academic policies), this paper focuses specifically on discussing ethics related to criminal justice policy and law and the practices of criminal justice professionals.
2 The survey instrument is available upon request from the first author.
3 While we surveyed American Society of Criminology members, this is not an ASC sponsored or sanctioned research effort.
4 As the directory is available to the general internet community, explicit permission from the American Society of Criminology was not needed to conduct this research.
5 Unlike the similar item asking respondent how often they discuss ethics with criminal justice professionals, this item did not contain separate categories for rarely and never.
6 Respondents were initially asked to indicate one of the following categories: graduate student without teaching appointment, graduate student with teaching appointment, adjunct faculty, assistant professor, associate professor, full professor, professor emeritus, dual position lecturer/criminal justice practitioner, or other (with specification). However, there were so few responses in some categories that the data were recoded to reflect the five most common ranks. Additionally, several respondents indicating a rank of "other" fit into one of these 5 final categories. Twenty-nine of them (e.g., Dean, "just graduated with [a degree], etc.), however, did not fit and were coded as missing for the statistical analyses.

7 The "other" category was analyzed for similarities among responses. However, the responses were diverse, with few responses in each category. For example, 10 respondents indicated a law or jurisprudence degree, 10 a public administration/public policy-related degree, 16 a political science or government degree, 17 a psychology degree, 15 indicated multiple degrees, and 56 responses did not fit together or into any of these other categories. Therefore, we determined that it was best to leave the "other" category as is without further delineation of the responses.
8 Only 17 individuals indicated they worked/were taking courses at a community or junior college. In order to maintain the integrity of the data, these responses were merged with responses for four-year Baccalaureate/liberal colleges to create a new variable of Undergraduate Institution. Additionally, only 12 individuals indicated "other" as the type of institution they were currently at; these responses were recoded as missing.
9 Due to the relatively small number of cases, and in the interest of preserving the integrity of the binary regression analysis, categories of ever taught and ever team-taught were combined to create one variable of ever taught or team-taught a course on criminal justice ethics. Similarly, categories of ever presented at a conference and ever attended a conference session were combined to create one variable of ever presented at a conference or attended a session on criminal justice ethics.
10 All percents are valid percents unless otherwise noted.
11 547 respondents answered the question of which type of student they have these discussions with more.
12 To compute the probability difference, we used Hanushek and Jackson's (1977) formula: [(odds ratio)/(odds ratio + 1)]-.5). The probability differences were multiplied by 100 to obtain percentage values.

# References

Cedarblom, J. and C. Spohn (1991). "A Model for Teaching Criminal Justice Ethics." *Journal of Criminal Justice Education* 2(2):201–217.

Cohen, N.J. (2001). "Nonlawyer Judges and the Professionalization of Justice: Should an Endangered Species Be Preserved?" *Journal of Contemporary Criminal Justice* 17(1):19–36.

Cramer, C.E. (1995). "Ethical Problems of Mass Murder Coverage in the Mass Media." *Journal on Firearms and Public Policy* 7:113–133.

Cunningham, L. (1999). "Taking on Testifying: The Prosecutor's Response to In-Court Police Deception." *Criminal Justice Ethics* 18(1):26–40.

Durham III, A.M. (1992). "Observations on the Future of Criminal Justice Education: Legitimating the Discipline and Serving the General University Population." *Journal of Criminal Justice Education* 3(1):35–52.

DuVal, G. and C. Salmon (2004). "Ethics of Drug Treatment Research with Court-Supervised Subjects." *Journal of Drug Issues* 34(4):91–1006.

Esbensen, F.A. (1991). "Ethical Considerations in Criminal Justice Research." *American Journal of Police* 10(2):87–104.

Haag, A. M. (2006). "Ethical Dilemmas Faced by Correctional Psychologists in Canada." *Criminal Justice & Behavior* 33(1):93–109.

Hanushek, E. A. and J.E. Jackson (1977). *Statistical Methods for Social Scientists.* New York: Academic Press.

Heffernan, W. (1982). "Two Approaches to Police Ethics." *Criminal Justice Review* 7(2):28–35.

Hyatt, W.O. (1991). "Teaching Ethics in a Criminal Justice Program." *American Journal of Police* 10(2):77–86.

Kania, R. (1988). "Should We Tell the Police to Say 'Yes' to Gratuities?" *Criminal Justice Ethics* 7(2):37–49.

Kingshott, B.F., K. Bailey, and S.E. Wolfe (2004). "Police Culture, Ethics and Entitlement Theory". *Criminal Justice Studies* 17(2):87–202.

Kleinig, J. and M.L. Smith (eds.). (1997). *Teaching Criminal Justice Ethics: Strategic Issues.* Cincinnati, OH: Anderson.

O'Grady, J.C. (2002). "Psychiatric Evidence and Sentencing: Ethical Dilemmas." *Criminal Behavior and Mental Health* 12(3):179–184.

Peak, K.J., B.G. Stitt, and R.W. Glensor (1998). "Ethical Considerations in Community Policing and Problem Solving." *Police Quarterly* 1(3):19–34.

Pollock, J.M. (2004). *Ethics in Crime and Justice: Dilemmas and Decisions,* Fourth Edition. Belmont, CA: Wadsworth.

Pollock-Byrne, J. (1988). "Teaching Criminal Justice Ethics." *The Justice Professional* 3(2):283–297.

Pollock-Byrne, J. (1990). "Teaching Criminal Justice Ethics." In F. Schmalleger (ed.), *Ethics in Criminal Justice: A Justice Professional Reader.* Bristol, IN: Wyndham Hall.

Pollock-Byrne, J. (1993). "Ethics and the Criminal Justice Curriculum." *Journal of Criminal Justice Education* 4(2):372–390.

Pring, R. (1988). "Logic and Values: A Description of a New Course in Criminal Justice and Ethics." *The Justice Professional* 3(1):94–106.

Pring, R. (1990). "Logic and Values: A Description of a New Course in Criminal Justice and Ethics." In *Ethics in Criminal Justice: A Justice Professional Reader.,* F. Schmalleger (ed.). Bristol, IN: Wyndham Hall.

Schmalleger, F. (ed.). (1990). *Ethics in Criminal Justice: A Justice Professional Reader.* Bristol, IN: Wyndam Hall.

Schwartz, M.D. and D.M. Nurge (2004). "Capitalist Punishment: Ethics and Private Prisons." *Critical Criminology* 12(2):133–156.

Sherman, L.W. (1981). *The Study of Ethics in Criminology and Criminal Justice Curricula.* Washington, D.C.: U.S. Department of Justice.

Sherman, L.W. (1982). *Ethics in Criminal Justice Education.* Hastings-on-Hudson, NY: The Hastings Center.

Southerland, M.D. (2002). "Criminal Justice Curricula in the United States: A Decade of Change." *Justice Quarterly* 19(4):589–601.

Westmarland, L. (2005). "Police Ethics and Integrity: Breaking the Blue Code of Silence." *Policing & Society* 15(2):145–165.

Wilson, P., R. Lincoln, and R. Kocsis (1997). "Validity, Utility and Ethics of Profiling for Serial Violent and Sexual Offenders." *Psychiatry, Psychology and Law* 4:1–11.

Chapter 9

# Translating Justice into Practice

## INTRODUCTION

Many injustices related to the CJS will require social change to remedy. When learning about the complexity and far-reaching implications of different forms of injustice, a logical response is to speculate as to how they can be combatted or fixed—or, as one of our students aptly put it, to determine the "justice maneuvers" that are needed. Studying the structure and functioning of the CJS, its relation to other institutions, and how it interacts with the larger social context, leaves many CJC students eager to create justice in a broad sense. One way that this can be achieved is through *social change*—the structural transformation of systems to create a more equal and just society. Working toward social change requires that we determine the underlying causes of problems and address them in a meaningful way that will promote social justice moving forward.

This proactive, societal-level approach sets social change apart from the sorts of individual- or institutional-level responses that characterize work within the CJS, and even volunteer or charity work outside the CJS. When society or individuals respond to the needs created by social problems without attempting to eliminate the social problems at their root, they are not engaging in social change. For instance, soup kitchens and donation drives are important means of ensuring that people experiencing homelessness receive some form of sustenance. This type of intervention is immediate, often local, and can produce marked improvement in individuals' daily lives. In contrast, social change is slow, often only yielding results in the long term, though it can have far-reaching and lasting impact. To achieve social change in the area of food insecurity for the homeless population, for instance, we would need to do more than just continually provide food to those in need; we would need to eliminate homelessness and food insecurity altogether. Most of our existing avenues for addressing injustice are reactive in nature. While reactive strategies can alleviate some of the harms of injustice, they often fail to combat the problem on a societal level and they are unable to ensure justice in the future. Effective and sustained social change renders piecemeal but proactive strategies moot by eliminating the problem at its roots, rather than trimming its branches every so often.

If this all seems deceptively simple (just identify the roots of a problem, and uproot it)... it is. Social change challenges and dismantles the status quo, which is often uncomfortable. Further, discussions of social change quickly become wrapped up in political ideology, making them even more fraught and fractious. In the current political climate, the progressive approach that social change requires is more aligned with the Democratic Party than the Republican Party. This is not to say that all Democrats are progressive advocates for social change, or that Republicans are opposed to social change. And as we know, the core platforms of U.S. political parties, and even the issues that tend to distinguish Republicans from Democrats, have changed over time. For instance, consider a remark made by Republican President Dwight D. Eisenhower (1953): "Every gun that is made, every warship launched, every rocket fired signifies, in the final sense, a theft from those who hunger and are not fed, those who are cold and not clothed." It is difficult to imagine such a statement being made by the past few Republican presidents in office. In fact, it's a bit of a stretch to imagine any sitting president, Democrat or Republican, juxtaposing security with poverty in such a stark, zero-sum way.

We have to consider that quote in the proper historical context, though. Recall from Chapter 4 that crime and crime control were not highly politicized until the 1970s. Since that era, political responses to crime control have been fairly homogenous across the political spectrum. Where variations on the tough-on-crime approach do emerge between political parties, they are largely differences of degree rather than kind. This may seem contradictory when considering the divergent views that Republicans and Democrats tend to have regarding other pressing social issues, also discussed in Chapter 4. One way to make sense of this apparent contradiction is by considering the incongruent ways that crime and social problems are framed. Although crime has been seen as a pressing social *issue* in the United States since the 1960s, it is seldom oriented to as a *social problem*. Thus, the political response to crime—the response carried out by the CJS that has been created through our political system—is not one of social change that eradicates the conditions that cause crime. Instead, it is a reactive system designed to combat crime by processing individual cases and meting out individual justice.

This does not mean that it is impossible to work toward social justice, or to effect social change, from within the CJS, as a CJC scholar, or even as a CJC student. In the remainder of this chapter, we will discuss the prospect of bringing about social change from each of these three positions. Let's start by discussing what it means to work toward social change from within the CJS, and what needs to be accomplished before this can begin.

## CREATING JUSTICE WITHIN THE CRIMINAL JUSTICE SYSTEM

Despite the CJS itself not being an agent of social change, there are many possible avenues to pursue social change within the CJS. CJS professionals at all levels have insight, expertise, and access that afford them a measure of power not available to those who work outside the CJS. This is a double-edged sword right now for many CJC students reading this book who may find themselves frustrated by lack of access to the very agencies and institutions that they are seeking to improve. Even entry-level CJS practitioners have gained insider access to government agencies that are fairly closed off from the public. Prisons represent the obvious extreme; they are physically closed institutions that grant access to few outsiders (e.g., visitors, journalists, researchers), and only after meticulous screening. While law enforcement agencies and court systems have far more permeable boundaries, they are still fairly difficult for average people to really know, let alone have the ability to influence. Thus, working within the CJS affords practitioners a unique opportunity in terms of access and knowledge.

This opportunity is not without constraints, however. Access is the first step, but it certainly isn't everything. Working *within* the CJS means working *for* the CJS—operating according to policy and customary practice designed and executed to handle individual cases, not social problems (as discussed in Chapter 5). While many CJS professionals have discretion in how they do their jobs, they are not at liberty to simply shift the focus of their concern from an individual level to a societal one. In a sense, then, working toward social change while working as a CJS professional means doing two jobs instead of one: dealing with individual cases and considering how these cases are linked to larger social problems. By carrying out their jobs in a way that attends to the broader social context and affords priority to the social justice impact of their actions, CJS professionals can begin to work toward social change. To use the language of Chapter 1, CJ practitioners can use their sociological imaginations to lay the groundwork for social change. We also know from Chapter 1 that different justice goals often exist in tension with one another, which means that there may be times when individual-level justice simply cannot be reconciled with social justice. The more CJ practitioners can work toward these two goals in tandem, however, the easier it will become to create social change. Institutional cultures within the CJS have formed slowly and ossified over time, leaving them resistant to change.

Let's turn to a more concrete example to illustrate this. Working toward social change as a practitioner within the correctional system, for instance, might involve working with prisoners in ways that acknowledge the structural factors that played a role in their incarceration (for instance, poverty, systemic racism, and other factors discussed in Chapter 2) and incorporate this understanding into practices of correctional rehabilitation and treatment, or even prisoner supervision. This can sometimes be an uneasy fit with correctional treatment paradigms that emphasize individual-level factors related to risk and need (e.g., Bonta, Rugge, Scott, Bourgon, & Yessine, 2008) to the exclusion of structural factors, or prison regimes that use techniques of responsibilization that demand that prisoners internalize blame for their actions without an acknowledgment of the contributing context (Myers & Schept, 2015). Luckily, there are many correctional treatment programs that are compatible with a holistic approach to social change. In fact, the most recent wave of evidence-based practices (Chapter 6) that have shown promise are those that combine an emphasis on individual change and recognition of social and cultural context (Andrews, Bonta, & Wormith, 2006). In terms of prisoner supervision, the challenge to acknowledging structural factors that affect prisoners is that the prison *is* such a structure, in both an institutional and physical sense. Even as a correctional officer tasked with supervising a housing unit full of prisoners, an orientation that acknowledges the humanity of prisoners and treats them accordingly would go a long way toward diminishing some of the harm that prison can produce.

While a commitment to social change on an individual level is all that is possible within U.S. prison systems in the current era, we can look to other countries for new perspectives that might facilitate social change even within our most rigid institutions. Denmark is one such example. There are many stark empirical differences between U.S. prisons and Danish prisons. Danish prisoners wear their own clothes, often purchase and cook their own food, and many live in facilities without perimeter fences. Danish prisoners and prison staff (even the wardens!) address each other using first names. On the face of things, Danish prisons may barely seem related to the fortified and harsh prisons that we have in the United States—but they serve as institutions that incapacitate, rehabilitate, and punish. Beyond the prison system, there are just as many differences evident between the United States and Denmark on a national level. Denmark has extremely low income inequality, a strong social welfare state that ensures citizens a high standard of living, and a far more ethnically homogenous society than the United States. Strongly held cultural values in Denmark—emphasizing family, community, and humanity—provide a powerful context that informs the structure, functioning and purpose of Denmark's CJS, the Ministry of Justice.

Despite the nation's low crime rates and a small incarcerated population, however, Denmark is far from perfect. What makes it noteworthy is the way in which its CJS acknowledges this imperfection and functions in a way that accounts for it by leaving room for error (Reiter, Sexton & Sumner, forthcoming). As Reiter, Sexton, and Sumner (2016, p. 1) found in their research,

> ... Danish prison officials assume some prisoners will get in fights, smuggle in drugs, commit suicide or escape. They expect and accept imperfections in their system. Their response to these unpleasant, unsanctioned events is rarely a crackdown, a drastic change in policy or even a public apology. For instance, even though prison officials know that drugs are smuggled into prisons through various body cavities, they do not conduct searches of prisoners or prison visitors. Prison officials prioritize dignity over implementing more stringent drug enforcement policies.

Operating a prison system in an imperfect world requires engaging with that imperfection fully. In the United States, our prison systems have no problem orienting to prisoners as flawed individuals; indeed, the systems are organized around responding to these flaws. There is even a growing recognition of challenges that prisoners may face in society upon release from prison, as evidenced by an orientation toward "prisoner reentry"—a phrase that is commonplace now, but surprisingly wasn't even coined (let alone discussed broadly) until the 1990s. Before social change can truly be pursued from within corrections, however, correctional practitioners and policymakers need to more fully understand the role that structural factors play in crime and incarceration (Chapter 2). These include many of the same factors that will affect prisoners once they are released, but it is important to also recognize their effects on the lives of incarcerated people *before* they were prisoners. Given what we know about the nature and remedies for social problems, a necessary precursor to social change is a full understanding of the problem. While it may be disheartening that there is still so much work to be done before social change can even be pursued within the CJS, the silver lining is that there is great potential for you as a CJC student to bring your knowledge to bear within the system.

## CREATING JUSTICE AS CRIMINAL JUSTICE AND CRIMINOLOGY SCHOLAR

The example of Denmark's prison system presented here can function not just as a model of creating a CJS that can facilitate social change; it also sheds light on how CJC scholars can work toward social change. CJC research and teaching have enormous potential to create social change through knowledge. Some scholars have suggested that our capacity to apply our knowledge base to real-world problems is underdeveloped (Arrigo, 2008; Rhineberger, 2006). This is all the more reason to focus on translational and applied research. As CJC scholars, we are in the business of knowledge creation and transmission, and if we're doing our jobs well (and responsibly), that means using our work to make the world better. As we've discussed throughout this book, CJC is a problem-centered discipline. We study real social problems with real-world impact—which makes it our responsibility to have a real-world impact of our own. Check out the box in this chapter for an example of how one of us worked toward social change as a CJC scholar!

**Dr. Holsinger reflects on justice in her career:** At the beginning of my academic career, the focus of my research agenda was on girls and young women who were involved in the juvenile justice system. This effort included trying to understand more about the pathways that brought them into contact with the system, how they were processed and treated once in the system, and what types of rehabilitative and skill development services they received. Given the greater focus on theory development and research for system-involved boys, much of this work examined how girls' circumstances and experiences were different. This type of research received national attention in the 1990s, thanks in part to federal funds to study the problem, and led to research that suggested the need for gender-specific and gender-responsive services for girls. It soon became clear that, although this new girl-centered focus made sense, there simply were not the resources to implement gender-specific services on a wide scale, much less conduct good research on the effectiveness of these approaches.

This dilemma caused me to think deeply about how to be more responsive to the unique needs of system-involved girls, particularly in light of the lack of innovation and change on the part of systems. By this point, I had learned so much about who they were, the challenges they faced, and how ill-equipped the juvenile justice system was in terms of responding to their unique needs. After making a contact within the local Family Court, we devised a mentoring class where college students would undergo background checks and training and then mentor incarcerated girls. This class eventually evolved into the students developing eight weeks of programs for the girls, which included career and skill development, educational sessions, guest speakers, and fun activities, including a hip-hop dance class. In another class I teach, *Women, Crime and Criminal Justice,* I incorporated service learning projects, one of which was the development of programming and donation drives for needed items (Holsinger, 2008; Holsinger & Ayers, 2004).

Another unique experience involved applying for an internal grant to diversify the curriculum in the college where I teach. I developed a Restorative Justice class to offer a unique educational experience to incarcerated youth and traditional college students. I knew that many court-involved youth, while having the intelligence and desire to succeed in college and, in many cases, concrete career aspirations, did not have the social support or financial support to attend college.

Restorative justice was a purposeful choice for the content of this class. This perspective sees crime as an opportunity to address social problems and as a potential catalyst for social change. Through short lectures, class activities, assignments, films, guest speakers, a tour of the facility where the youth lived, and a community service project, the class explored restorative justice concepts on both the interpersonal and societal level. Obstacles to restorative justice were discussed, such as how to get past feelings of revenge, how to reintegrate victims and offenders when the community is dysfunctional, and the difficulties of delivering "needs-based justice."

Several culminating events brought the class to an end: a luncheon ceremony was held at a nearby restaurant where course grades and framed certificates were given to the court-involved students. The certificates commended each student, acknowledging their "great attitude, thoughtful contribution, and demonstrated academic potential." The certificates contained contact information (business card of the professor) on the back so that the student would always know of one source of support should they decide to attend college in the future.

The results of the class for the court-involved youth were positive. The youth reported that they enjoyed the class and the break from their time at the residential facility, and being in a college setting with older adults. They gained exposure to and knowledge about college life, and some began to envision college as a possibility. They were surprised to learn about the many theories and research pertaining to juvenile delinquency, and were surprised to learn of all the efforts that went into addressing the problem of youth crime. Many had concrete ideas for how to improve schools and juvenile justice facilities. They also advocated for greater family involvement and more caring adults to talk to. One unanticipated outcome for the youth was the new perspective they developed on the effects of their delinquent actions. One individual stated, "When you do something it affects your family and the community, I realized what I did was wrong." Another wrote, "I respect victims more and understand how they feel. Should be what the JJS [juvenile justice system] does!"

The college students also enjoyed the course, largely due to the different style of the class and the interaction with the youth. This interaction gave the students an opportunity to learn about the lives of the youth and resulted in changes in attitudes toward "juvenile delinquents," which included a deeper understanding of their potential. They felt that the class had a positive impact on the younger, court-involved students. The college students emerged from the experience with strong critiques of the current system, and generated many ideas on changes needed in the juvenile justice system, again including the need for caring and passionate staff to work with the youth. Finally, the class provided them with direction in their career interests.

Positive media coverage provided an upbeat ending to the restorative justice class. An article ran in the local paper titled, "Students Seek New Solutions to Crime." The article represents yet another unanticipated outcome of the class. The story served to educate the public of the incredible potential of youth currently involved in the juvenile justice system and presented new, nonpunitive ways of responding to juvenile crime (Holsinger & Crowther, 2005).

## CREATING JUSTICE AS A CRIMINAL JUSTICE AND CRIMINOLOGY STUDENT

The semester-long projects are an opportunity for you to engage in your own justice work as a CJC student: to identify social problems or issues of injustice, understand your topic from both a theoretical and an empirical perspective (including the social context and related institutions), and creatively take action to combat injustice. Past justice projects undertaken by students have been impressive and inspiring. The problem-based learning approach used by CJC studies can be particularly helpful for students who want to effect change, because it often emphasizes working with local communities in meaningful partnerships to address the causes and responses to crime (Klofas, 2010). Next, we provide two examples of students' justice projects to put many of the concepts that we've discussed thus far into the context of the semester-long project.

One student chose to focus on domestic violence in his local Spanish-speaking community. While serving as an intern for the police department the previous summer, he noticed that the police officers often referred to the Latinx population as one that never caused any trouble because there were seldom calls for service from Latinx residents. As part of the Mexican American community, this student drew on his own knowledge to interpret the lack of police calls from the Latinx areas a bit differently. (Remember positionality from Chapter 2? Here it is in action.) He surmised that language barriers, combined with fear and distrust of the police and concerns about immigration status, might be stopping Latinx residents from calling upon the police in general. After learning about patriarchy and social stratification in class, and incorporating this newfound knowledge with his preexisting cultural knowledge of *machismo,* he thought this might be particularly problematic with regard to domestic violence.

He notes in his paper, "My personal strategy for achieving justice was to make the Hispanic population more aware of the steps that they can take to prevent domestic violence, or in instances when it has already occurred, to let them know what to do and how to report it." To do so, he capitalized on his contacts to translate printed and online materials from the Victims' Services Unit from English to Spanish, and disseminated the printed materials to local churches, businesses, and schools in Latinx areas of town. This project identified an existing injustice, sought to remedy this injustice using both the knowledge that he had learned from his CJC classes and his personal expertise, and achieved a great deal of success in providing access and understanding of police services to an underserved population.

Another student was troubled by the portrayal of female characters in law enforcement, particularly in policing-focused films. She deemed the portrayal by film and media as both minimal and negative, noting the influence of patriarchy, racism, and the inherent masculinity of the crime film genre. She effectively presented why this is a justice issue by drawing on the history of women in law enforcement, and the portrayal of female law enforcement officers in film and television. She then drew on the theory of cultivation (Wilson & Blackburn, 2014; Wimmer & Dominick, 2003), to explain how exposure to long-term, repetitive media messages produces "cumulative repercussions," including the acceptance of these depictions as reality. She explained why this is a justice issue in her paper by noting, "Positive representation is everyone's problem because society determines who has more social worth. That ideal is then reflected in the entertainment the public consumes, which affects and influences the minds of the next generation."

To change the status quo, she acknowledged that casting more women, particularly more women of color, in well-rounded and complex character roles is the obvious solution. However, given the profit-driven nature of the industry, she noted that such changes will require greater public awareness of the gendered, sexist, and racist nature of the film industry, and calls for more and better representation of women. Her creative and well-executed project sought to raise awareness about the importance of positive portrayals of female characters in law enforcement positions. She created a YouTube video, entitled, "Women in Cop Films" (https://www.youtube.com/watch?v=I5O7tpx5M-8), which was widely circulated on social media sites.

Many students' justice projects fall into the category of public education or awareness raising. Writing editorials, assembling resource packets, creating pamphlets, designing websites, and strategically using social media have been a handful of strategies that students have used to educate specific groups or simply raise awareness about a relatively unknown or misunderstood issue. Students have also created presentations to give to local community groups, including Girl Scout troops, high school students, sororities, mock trial teams, and CJ professionals. Other unique forms of awareness raising have included hosting documentary film screenings on campus, attending community prayer vigils for murder victims, serving on student campus committees, and targeted awareness raising through letters to government representatives, other organizations, and policy makers.

One common element of the most successful and inspiring justice projects is connections to the local (or larger) community. Although some students are fortunate to have had internships or employment with local agencies, or simply have established connections through their personal networks, many students find themselves feeling disconnected from others tackling similar issues and unsure of where to begin. A great place to start is by finding local agencies, nonprofit organizations, or grassroots movements that share your justice concerns, and contacting them to set up an informational meeting. Discussing the justice needs of the community with experts who are already working on the same issues (or even related issues) will not only help you understand the scope and nature of the problem, but will also shed light on what is currently being done to address it. Your justice strategy should complement and build on existing justice work in the community, rather than duplicating it. If current efforts are lacking completely in your community, you might need to look more broadly, at state or national-level agencies and organizations. If you aren't sure how to find these like-minded organizations, remember that your CJC professors might have some insight and be able to help you make valuable connections.

Another important—and often overlooked—aspect of working toward justice is creativity. It is a tall order to ask someone to dream up unique approaches to combat complex social problems—but that is precisely what you were tasked with doing in the semester-long project assignments for previous chapters. Some of the best justice projects we have seen have come from ideas that seemed off-the-wall, impossible, or just plain strange at first. Of course, not all bizarre ideas end up being fruitful. In fact, most successful justice projects started out looking very different from the finished product. Try to use the creative process detailed in Chapter 7 to help spark ideas. The more ideas you have, the better, because some avenues will be dead ends. Eventually, though, you will create a justice strategy that reflects a nuanced understanding of an existing injustice; use theory and research to design a response to that injustice; and then begin to take concrete steps toward creating justice.

The last thing to keep in mind as you work toward justice—in your semester-long projects, your studies, your career, or just life in general—is one of the first topics that we addressed in the book: reflexivity. Remember that the ways that you understand justice and identify injustices are necessarily going to be different from the ways that other people do. While your unique positionality in the world is an asset in approaching justice, it can also be a limitation if not understood fully and attended to responsibly. The antidote to this is, of course, more knowledge. The more you can learn about theory, research, practice, and policy pertaining to your justice issue, and its surrounding context, the better. The skills that you've learned (or honed) throughout this book will hopefully guide you on your path toward justice. Our hope is that you keep developing your sociological imagination, interrogating justice conceptually so you can achieve it empirically, critically analyzing social problems as you see them in the world around you, and thinking about interconnections—between social institutions, individuals and their context, or theory, research and policy. Keep writing and speaking for justice as much as you are able, and you will make social change a little more possible every day.

## References

Andrews, D. A., Bonta, J., & Wormith, S. J. (2006). The recent past and near future of risk and/or need assessment. *Crime and Delinquency, 52*(1), 7–27.

Arrigo, B.A. (2008). Crime, justice, and the under-laborer: On the criminology of the shadow and the search for disciplinary identity and legitimacy. *Justice Quarterly, 25*(3), 439–468.

Bonta, J., Rugge, T., Scott, T., Bourgon, G., & Yessine, A.K. (2008). Exploring the black box of community supervision. *Journal of Offender Rehabilitation, 47*(3), 248–270.

Eisenhower, D.D. (1953), from a speech before the American Society of Newspaper Editors, April 16. Retrieved from https://www.eisenhower.archives.gov/all_about_ike/speeches/chance_for_peace.pdf.

Holsinger, K. (2008). Teaching to make a difference: Activism and teaching, *Feminist Criminology, 3*(4): 319–335.

Holsinger, K., & Ayers, P. (2004). Mentoring girls in juvenile facilities: Connecting college students with incarcerated girls. *Journal of Criminal Justice Education, 15*(2): 351–372.

Holsinger, K., & Crowther, A. (2005). College course participation for incarcerated youth: Bringing restorative justice to life. *Journal of Criminal Justice Education, 16*(2): 328–339.

Klofas, J.M. (2010). Postscript: Teaching the new criminal justice. In J. Klofas, N. Kroovand Hipple, & E. McGarrell (Eds.), *The new criminal justice: American communities and the changing world of crime control* (pp. 147–155). New York: Routledge.

Myers, R. R., & Schept, J. (2015). Youth under control: Punishment and "reform" in the neoliberal state. *Social Justice, 41*(1), 1–7.

Reiter, K., Sexton, L., & Sumner, J. (2016). *Denmark doesn't treat its prisoners like prisoners—and it's good for everyone*. Washington Post, Feb. 2, 2016.

Reiter, K., Sexton, L., & Sumner, J. (Forthcoming). Negotiating Imperfect Humanity in the Danish Penal System. In T. Ugelvik and P. S. Smith (Eds.) *Embraced by the welfare state? Punishment, welfare, and the Nordic model*. London: Palgrave.

Rhineberger, G.M. (2006). Research methods and research ethics coverage in criminal justice and criminology textbooks. *Journal of Criminal Justice Education, 17*(2), 279–296.

Wilson, F.T., & Blackburn, A.G. (2014). The depiction of female municipal police officers in the first four decades of the core cop film genre: "It's a man's world." *Women & Criminal Justice, 24*(2), 83–105.

Wimmer, R.D., & Dominick, J.R. (2003). *Mass media research: An introduction*. Belmont, CA: Wadsworth.

## Discussion Questions

1. In this chapter, we discussed how social change could be facilitated from within the corrections system. Come up with an example from policing or the court system that demonstrates how CJS practitioners could pave the way for social change while on the job.
2. Why is social change so difficult to accomplish through work in the criminal justice system? Is this particular to the CJS, or do you think it applies to other government systems or institutions as well (e.g., education, health, social services)?
3. According to Nooe and Patterson (2010), how does the "ecology of homelessness" incorporate both individual- and societal-level factors into an understanding of homelessness as a social problem?
4. How are homelessness and the CJS related? What other social institutions are implicated in an understanding of homelessness? How can these institutions function to help assuage homelessness, rather than exacerbate it?
5. Welsh, Braga, and Sullivan (2014) discuss the utility of a public health model for understanding and preventing youth violence. What other lessons might CJC scholars and CJC practitioners be able to learn from public health?

# ACTIVITIES/ASSIGNMENTS

## Strategies to Achieve Justice

Evaluate these efforts and ideas on ways to achieve justice. Classify these examples according to the type of justice being breached (e.g., social justice, formal justice), and the kind of strategy being used (proactive/reactive, individual-/societal-level). Would you expect this approach to be helpful in achieving justice? Why or why not?

Hospitals Preventing Violence:
http://health.usnews.com/health-news/hospital-of-tomorrow/articles/2015/08/24/some-hospitals-boost-health-by-preventing-violence-attacking-social-determinants
Ideas for a Cop Free World:
http://www.rollingstone.com/politics/news/policing-is-a-dirty-job-but-nobodys-gotta-do-it-6-ideas-for-a-cop-free-world-20141216
Reducing Mass Incarceration:
http://webapp.urban.org/reducing-federal-mass-incarceration/

Prosecutorial Behavior:
http://www.urban.org/urban-wire/reduce-federal-prison-population-prosecutor-behavior-needs-change?utm_source=iContact&utm_medium=email&utm_campaign=Justice%20Policy%20Update&utm_content=Justice+Policy+Update+-11%2F04%2F2015
Using Data:
https://www.ted.com/talks/anne_milgram_why_smart_statistics_are_the_key_to_fighting_crime?language=en

## Three Ways to Fight Mass Criminalization

This video series presents three ways to decrease our reliance on incarceration by addressing the problems of mental illnesses, drug addiction, and homelessness in different ways. Do these strategies increase justice or not? How so?

http://www.huffingtonpost.com/jordan-melograna/three-ways-to-fight-mass-_b_5953978.html

## Fixing the Criminal Justice System

Read the following article. Which ideas are most worthwhile and why?

http://www.ru.org/index.php/society/79-seven-ways-to-fix-the-criminal-justice-system

## Criminal Justice Reforms at the State Level

What trends may emerge from these state-level reforms?

http://nationswell.com/7-states-progressive-criminal-justice-prison-reform/

## Social Change

What important lessons can be learned from this video clip on one person's response to the problem of homelessness.

http://www.thisblewmymind.com/she-gets-yelled-at-for-giving-coats-to-the-homeless-her-response-brilliant/#_

## Crime Control

In the article found below, Dolovich presents a variety of ideas about the causes of crime and how current (and past) crime control strategies, particularly incarceration, are falling short, and even supporting criminality in society. Based on this reading and your own ideas as a criminal justice major, what three recommendations do you have for making the biggest impact on reducing crime and/or incarceration in the United States?

http://scholarship.law.georgetown.edu/facpub/19

## Supporting Equality by Voting with your Wallet

Evaluate the helpfulness, strengths, and weaknesses of this type of information.
http://mic.com/articles/102220/vote-with-your-wallet-companies-to-avoid-if-you-support-equality-in-america?utm_source=huffingtonpost.com&utm_medium=referral&utm_campaign=pubexchange_facebook

## SEMESTER-LONG JUSTICE PROJECT

Write a 10-page final paper that examines and addresses your chosen injustice issue. Include why you chose this issue, why it is a justice issue and what type of justice it concerns, what you learned about it, and what concrete steps you took to achieve justice in this area, and how your positionality affected your understanding of the issue and strategy for achieving justice. Papers should demonstrate an understanding of course material and ability to engage with the material in a thoughtful and analytic way. Prepare a persuasive presentation for the class that conveys the content of your paper.

## Selected Reading

# THE ECOLOGY OF HOMELESSNESS

***Roger M. Nooe and David A. Patterson***

From an ecological perspective, homelessness can be understood as the result of interactions among risk factors ranging from individual conditions to socio-economic structures and environmental circumstances (Toro, Trickett, Wall, & Salem, 1991; Baron, 2004; National Coalition for the Homeless, 2007). Homelessness manifests itself on a temporal continuum as situational, episodic, or chronic. Over time, homeless individuals may experience changes in housing status that include being on the street, shared dwelling, emergency shelter, transitional housing, and permanent housing and hospitalization and incarceration in correctional facilities. Episodes of home-lessness result in individual and social consequences, which are commonly detrimental to individual well-being and negatively affect social interactions within the community (Phelan, Link, Moore, & Stueve, 1997; Saelinger, 2006; National Coalition for the Homeless [NCH], 2004; National Law Center on Homelessness and Poverty [NLCHP], 1997.)

The intention of this article is to propose a broad conceptual model of homelessness that examines biopsychosocial risk factors associated with homelessness in relation to the constructs of temporal course, housing status, and individual and social outcomes. We employ an ecological perspective to situate and describe known biopsychosocial risk factors in a hierarchy of systems/domains. The goal is to transcend the classic debate that posited homelessness as the result of either individual or structural factors (Burt, Aron, Lee, & Valente, 2001; Fisher & Breakey, 1991; Calsyn & Roades, 2006; United States Conference of Mayors, 2007). Though framing the debate of the origins of homelessness within this artificial causal dichotomy may have served political and policy objectives, this reductionism does not advance an etiological understanding of homelessness reflective of the phenomenon's actual complexity nor does it foster robust, multi-systemic response options from communities, agencies, organizations, and practitioners. More-over, homelessness cannot be understood or addressed by focusing solely on causal factors and ignoring its varying temporal dimensions, the spectrum of consequential individual and social outcomes, and the resulting limited housing options associated with homelessness. To view homelessness only from the perspective of why and how individuals and families became homeless is to see only half the picture. The conceptual model presented here is intended to articulate a gestalt of homelessness not only recognizing the constituent parts of the phenomenon but offering a map of the dynamic interactions of the elements of the model.

The proposed model is consistent with recognition of the complexity of homelessness. There are increasing attempts to analyze the transactional nature of factors contributing to homelessness (Burt et al., 2001; NCH, 2007; Coolen, 2006; Martijn & Sharpe, 2006; Toro et al., 1991). In our model, the four primary components are biopsychosocial risk factors, individual and social outcomes, the temporal dimension, and housing outcomes. Figure 9.1 illustrates this model of the ecology of homelessness. It is intended to depict the dynamic relationship between the domains and elements of the model.

## BIOPSYCHOSOCIAL RISK FACTORS

Biopsychosocial risk factors encompass a range of factors including individual biology and development and circumstances such as poverty and its many facets to housing availability and stability (NCH, 2007). The concept of biopsychosocial implies an ecological perspective. It recognizes the interaction of multiple factors on different levels, including individual factors (e.g., personality, developmental experiences, health-mental health, race, and ethnicity) and social factors, such as resource availability, policies, culture, discrimination, and social situations. It moves away from dichotomies such as micro vs macro or individual versus structural to appreciate the continuous transactions between person and environment. The concept underscores the complexity of interactions on different systems levels and encourages analysis of homeless as resulting from individual and family risks or vulnerability within a social context.

### Structural

#### *Poverty*

Poverty is overriding and intertwined in homelessness. People without financial resources are unable to meet basic needs such as housing and food, nor can they obtain other needed services. Poverty is a risk factor that makes people vulnerable for homelessness:

> ... poverty represents a vulnerability, a lower likelihood of being able to cope when the pressure gets too great. It thus resembles serious mental illness, physical handicap, chemical dependency, or any other vulnerability that reduces one's resilience and the resilience of one's family and friends.
>
> (Burt, 1992)

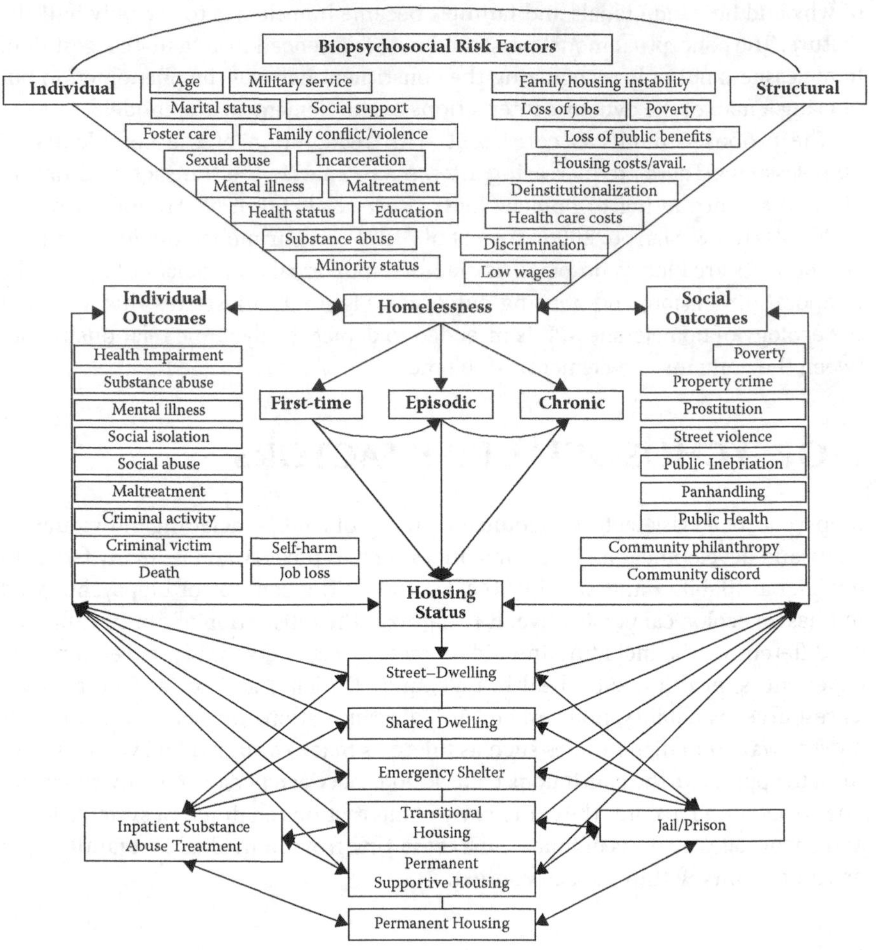


**Figure 9.1** Ecological model of homelessness.

A number of factors contribute to poverty including unemployment, the declining value of the minimum wage, housing costs, and health care and other services (NCH, 2007; US Conference of Mayors, 2005).

## Employment and the Minimum Wage

Lack of employment is often identified as a major cause of homelessness; however, many homeless persons report being employed or having occasional work (Economic Policy Institute, 2005; US Conference of Mayors, 2005). The difficulty is that many of these jobs do not provide adequate wages and benefits for self-sufficiency, a trend spanning a number of years. Mishel, Bernstein, & Schmitt

(1999) recognized that the value of the minimum wage had not kept up with economic growth. The United States Interagency Council on Homelessness (USICH) found that the median monthly income for persons who were homeless was about 44% of the federal poverty level (1999). Though the value of the minimum wage has not kept up with inflation, there has also been a decline in manufacturing jobs, a corresponding increase in low-paying service employment, globalization, decline in union bargaining power, and increase in temporary work, all factors in wage decline (USICH, 1999).

Many of the temporary jobs held by homeless persons do not provide sufficient wages and benefits such as health insurance to ensure self-sufficiency. The Interagency Council on the Homeless (ICH, 1999) recognized that employment prospects are dim for those who lack appropriate skills or adequate schooling. The labor market has changed, as evidenced by "plant relocations and closures, persistent racial discrimination, changes in industry that have increased the demand for highly educated people, the decline in the real value of the minimum wage, and the globalization of the economy" (ICH, p. 27). Employment instability has been identified in several studies as a risk factor for homelessness (Wagner & Perrine, 1994). Women and minorities seem to experience fewer employment opportunities (Anti-Discrimination Center of Metro New York, 2005; American Civil Liberties Union [ACLU], 2004; Butler, 1997). Furthermore, the duration of homelessness may decrease the prospects of employment. It is not surprising that homelessness itself may further diminish one's chances of employment, as prolonged idleness may cause loss in work habits, responsibility, and commitment to employment.

## Loss of Public Benefits

The decline in availability of public assistance and its declining value is a risk factor for homelessness. The welfare reform legislation in the late 1990s resulted in a number of individuals and families losing benefits. The Institute for Children and Poverty found that more than one-third of homeless families had benefits reduced (2001). The loss of health insurance also increases vulnerability (Families USA, 2001).

Welfare reform, including the shift from aid to families with dependent children (AFDC) to the block grant program temporary assistance to needy families (TANF) and the reduction in eligibility for SSI based on chronic substance abuse, has had an especially devastating impact. A study of TANF benefits, for example, found that assistance to a single mother of two children provided an income at approximately 29% of the federal poverty level (Nickelson, 2004). In essence, as homeless families experience reduced benefits, additional barriers to escaping homelessness result (Institute for Children and Poverty, 2001).

## Housing Costs and Availability

The shortage of affordable, particularly rental, housing is a major risk factor for homelessness. Approximately 2.2 million low-rent units were lost between 1973 and 1993 owing to abandonment, conversion to condominiums, or becoming unaffordable because of competition and costs (Daskal, 1998). The Institute for Children and Poverty (2001) estimated a gap of more than 4 million units between affordable units and low-income renters. Quigley and Raphael (2001) indicate that individuals on the lowest end of the economic scale are extremely vulnerable to homelessness secondary to shifts in the housing market.

Nationally, urban change and policy initiatives in the United States and global changes have contributed to a decline in affordable housing (National Low Income Housing Coalition, 2005). The loss of single room occupancy (SRO) housing has been particularly devastating (NCH, 2007). Dolbeare (1996) estimates that more than one million units were lost in the 1970s and 80s. For example, in 1960, 640,000 people in New York lived in SROs and rooming houses, but by 1990, this number was reduced to 137,000 (Stegman, 1993). Most cities have witnessed private-sector hotels and rooming houses that provided cheap lodging being razed or converted to condominiums in the apparent gentrification of the inner city (Wright & Rubin, 1997). In smaller urban areas, it may be that the "new SROs" are the increasing number of suburban motels, formally tourist-focused but now offering low rates and catering to a transient population (Nooe, 2006).

As affordable housing units and especially SROs were lost, the competition for (and rent levels of) remaining units increased. Those with mental illness and addiction disorders were significantly impacted in terms of not being able to locate and afford housing. As the NCH (2007) points out, in the last two decades, competition for increasingly scarce low-income housing grew so intensely that those with disabilities such as addictive and mental disorders were more likely to lose out and find themselves on the streets.

## Family Housing Instability

Families with children are the most rapidly growing group of the homeless population (US Conference of Majors, 2007). The lack of affordable housing, exacerbated by low incomes of families often with a history of housing instability, is a major factor in family homelessness (Burt, 2001; Shin et al., 1998). Housing instability involves a number of factors such as the lack of income, unavailability of supportive housing, and discrimination. It often manifests in doubling up with other families and living in shelters and cars (United States Department of Housing and Urban Development [USDHUD], 2009).

Homeless families are most frequently headed by single mothers (Rog & Buckner, 2007). A number of studies have found that female-headed households have greater risks for poverty (United States Department of Commerce, 1999) and subsequently have greater risks of homelessness (Caton et al., 1995; DiBlasio & Belcher, 1995). Similarly, women who have experienced violence may encounter discrimination from landlords who are reluctant to rent to them (ACLU, 2004).

## Deinstitutionalization

According to a survey by the US Conference of Majors (2005), approximately 16% of the single adult homeless population has a severe and persistent mental illness. However, a number of studies suggest a higher incidence, perhaps one-third of the homeless suffering severe mental illness (ICH, 1994; Nooe, 2006; Task Force on Homelessness and Severe Mental Illness, 1992). The estimated rates are wide ranging depending on methodology, definitions, sample selection, and diagnostic criteria; for example, shelter users seem to have higher rates of mental illness than do non-sheltered homeless persons. The Annual Homeless Assessment Report to Congress (USDHUD, 2009) indicted that 25% of all sheltered persons have a disability condition. Though the report does not specify the specific type of disability, severe mental illness and chronic substance abuse are frequently reported.

The relationship of homelessness to mental illness was initially highlighted when Bassuk asked the question, "Is homelessness a mental health problem?" (Bassuk, Ruben, & Lauriat, 1984). Underlying this deceptively simple question are a number of issues about individual causes versus structural causes, including the role of deinstitutionalization. Discussion of the influence of mental illness on homelessness has continued in the literature (Bassuk et al., 1984; Baum & Burnes, 1993; North, Pollio, Smith, & Spitznagel, 1998; HCH Clinicians' Network, 2000).

The role of deinstitutionalization in homelessness is a complex one that is compounded by the lack of national data on the outcomes of persons discharged from mental institutions. While deinstitutionalization increased through the 1980s, federal policies reduced funding for social programs with transfer of fiscal responsibility to state and local governments. Concurrently, conservative public housing policies reduced the availability of low-income housing, increasing competition, and the mentally ill became at greater risk for homelessness (Jansson & Smith, 1996; NCH, 2008). The importance of housing availability is also underscored by the decline in persons discharged from institutions returning to live with families (Talbott, 1980).

In summary, the history of the deinstitutionalization movement is fairly clear; however, there continues to be debate about its causal relationship to homelessness. Torrey (1989) argued:

> The homeless mentally ill are a product of the best intentions followed by the worst of operations. They are the result of deinstitutionalization, the policy that evolved in the 1950s and 60s to shift care of the seriously mentally ill from state mental hospitals to community facilities.

The NCH (Mental Illness and Homelessness, 1997) initially asserted that deinstitutionalization was not a major factor but more recently identified it as a contributing factor (2008).

The foregoing illustrates the different viewpoints. Most likely deinstitutionalization is a contributing factor but not the sole cause. Failure to provide support to those deinstitutionalized and the reduced availability and accessibility of resources for both treated and untreated persons are factors. For those persons with a mental illness, homelessness has a detrimental effect and, like any other crisis or trauma, may "catalyze and/or exacerbate mental illness, producing disorder where previously it did not exist" (Koegel & Burnam, 1992, p. 96).

## Health Care Costs

The unavailability of health care is a critical factor for homelessness. Faced with the challenge to pay rent and secure food and other basic necessities, persons with serious illness or disability can find themselves in a crisis that ends in homelessness. Between 2005 and 2006, the number of people without health insurance coverage increased from 44.8 million (15.3%) to 47 million (15.8%; US Bureau of the Census, 2007). More than a third of persons living in poverty have no health insurance. In recognizing this risk factor, the National Health Care for the Homeless Council calls for the establishment of a national health plan that guarantees access to affordable, high-quality and comprehensive health care, which is essential in the fight to end homelessness (NHCHC, 2008). In essence, health care costs may increase the risk for homelessness while lack of access to health care may be heightened by homelessness.

## Low Wages

The study, *Homelessness: Programs and the People They Serve* (US Interagency Council on Homelessness, 1999) found that median monthly income for persons who were homeless was about 44% of the federal poverty level. The value of the minimum wage, as noted previously, has not kept up with inflation. Decline in the value of minimum wage with the parallel decreased availability, but increased competition for affordable housing has heightened the risk for homelessness.

Employment prospects are especially dim for those who lack appropriate skills or adequate schooling. The labor market has changed, as evidenced by "plant relocations and closures, persistent racial discrimination, changes in industry that have increased the demand for highly educated people, the decline in the real value of the minimum wage, and the globalization of the economy" (US Interagency Council on Homelessness, 1999). Women and minorities are especially vulnerable and seem to experience fewer employment opportunities and lower wages (Anti Discrimination Center of Metro New York, 2005; ACLU, 2004; Butler, 1997). Employment instability is a risk factor for homelessness (Wagner & Perrine, 1994) and may create a cyclical phenomenon. Thus, homelessness itself may decrease the prospects of employment (NCH, 2008).

## Discrimination

The foregoing discussion recognizes that women and minorities often experience discrimination that manifests in lower wages or discriminatory practices and increases the risk of homelessness. People experiencing homelessness experience further stigmatization and discrimination in a range of contexts including access to health/mental health care, education, employment, and shelter (NCH, 2004; Phelan et al., 1997). Laws can operate in a manner that disadvantages homeless persons. The report "Illegal to Be Homeless: The Criminalization of Homelessness in the United States" describes violations to the basic human rights to homeless persons through passage of possibly unconstitutional laws, selective enforcement, and incorporation of discriminatory regulations (NCH, 2004). Ordinances prohibiting large group feedings, for example, have been found to be discriminatory against the homeless (ACLU, 2008). These discriminatory practices may involve criteria for Social Security, banning activities in public spaces, or more subtle denial of housing or employment without a fixed address or owing to past history (e.g., domestic violence, history of incarceration; ACLU, 2004; Anti-Discrimination Center of Metro New York, 2005; Human Rights and Equal Opportunity Commission, 2008; Tolman, Danziger, & Rosen, 2001).

The foregoing discussion has focused on risk factors that are structural or represent the social context within which the individual or family functions. Interacting with these factors are risk factors that can be viewed as individual.

## Individual

Individual risk factors include personal characteristics or conditions such as age, marital status, race, mental illness, substance abuse, and educational level and personal experiences such as childhood trauma and foster care that increase vulnerability for homelessness. These factors tend to imply personal responsibility. These risk factors are integrated and interacting as reflected in Figure 9.1, rather than representing linear causation. The point for emphasis is that they often increase vulnerability for homelessness.

## Age

Age can be considered a factor in homelessness both in children, as discussed earlier in family homelessness, and also in older persons, generally those older than 50 years of age. The number of older persons living in poverty and becoming homeless has increased, and the demand for affordable housing for elderly persons exceeds the supply (US Census Bureau, 2007). Elderly persons falling below the poverty level face greater challenges in maintaining housing and food, and unavailability of health care often creates a crisis situation that ends in homelessness. Once on the street, the elderly homeless may experience exacerbated health problems (Cohen, 1999) and being more vulnerable to crime and exploitation (NCH, 2007). It is not surprising that the premature mortality rate is three to four times greater for the elderly homeless (O'Connell, 2005).

## Marital Status

The question of the relationships between marital status and homelessness has been addressed in a number of studies (AHAR, 2007; Burt et al., 1999; Rossi, 1989). Forty-eight percent of homeless individuals have never married. The Annual Homeless Assessment Report to Congress (2007) noted that the majority of shelter users were unaccompanied adults. Among those who have been married (52%), 39% have ended in divorce or separation. Earlier discussion noted research evidence that single female-headed households were more vulnerable to homelessness, in that homeless families are most frequently headed by single mothers (Rog & Buckner, 2007). Jencks observed that "married couples hardly ever become homeless as long as they stick together" (1994). Marriage may provide social support, sharing of responsibilities, and pooling of resources. Though marital status may not be causal, it is likely a risk factor that affects vulnerability to homelessness and influences the duration of homelessness (Calsyn & Roades, 2006).

## Social Support

The research literature indicates homeless persons typically have smaller social networks than the non-homeless (Calsyn & Winter, 2002; Shinn, Knickman, & Weitzman, 1991). Bassuk et al. (1997) report that 220 homeless mothers in family shelters in Worcester, MA had significantly fewer members in their social networks than a comparison group of housed women. Further, the homeless women reported more conflict in their relationships than the housed women. This finding is echoed in an Anderson and Rayens (2004) study of 255 women, of whom 98 were homeless, 88 had never been homeless but experienced childhood trauma (physical and/or sexual abuse), and 73 had never been homeless and did not experience childhood trauma. When compared to the two groups of non-homeless women, the homeless women had significantly lower levels of social support and significantly higher levels of relationship conflict.

Letiecq, Anderson, & Koblinsky (1998) found homeless mothers in emergency shelters and in transitional housing had significantly less social support, as evidenced by less help from families, fewer people to count on, and lower levels of weekly contact with friends and relatives, than a control group of housed mothers. Kingree, Stephens, Braithwaite & Griffin (1999) found that after completion of a substance abuse treatment program, low levels of support from friends were associated with homelessness. Similarly, adolescents running away from or being kicked out by families are at risk for homelessness (Maclean, Embry, & Cauce, 1999). The availability of ongoing support for those exiting foster care, mental health, and correctional facilities is especially critical for avoiding or escaping homelessness.

## Foster Care

Several studies of homelessness have found that a history of foster care may be a childhood precipitant to becoming homeless (Roman & Wolfe, 1997). In a study of 220 homeless mothers, Bassuk et al. (1997) found the two most important childhood predictors of family homelessness were foster care placement and drug use by primary female caretakers. Though there is an over-representation of persons who have been in foster care among the homeless, the casual relationship is not conclusive. Most likely foster care and other childhood disruptions represent risk factors. Roman and Wolfe (1997) suggest that foster care may also be associated with homelessness at an earlier age and a longer duration of homelessness. Among children "aging out" of foster care, estimates suggest as many as 22% become homeless within a year (Pecora et al., 2005). There is some evidence that remaining in foster care until 21, as compared to aging out at 18, reduces the risk.

## Family Conflict and Violence

In Congressional testimony, Burt points out that "Very high proportions of homeless youth report family conflict as a reason for being homeless" (2007, p. 5).

Family conflict and family breakdown are frequently identified by homeless youth as contributing to their homelessness (Mallett, Rosenthal, & Keys, 2005). The pathways leading to youth homelessness often involve strained family relationships, conflict, communication problems, and parental substance abuse or mental health problems (Rosenheck, Bassuk, & Salomon, 2008). In a qualitative study of homeless youth, Miller, Donahue, Este, and Hofer (2004) found that in descriptions of families of origin, violence was common, whereas nurturance and support were lacking or absent.

Though family conflict is often cited as a contributing factor to youth homelessness, it is also a factor in homelessness among households with children and among singles. A survey of cities conducted by the US Conference of Mayors (2007) found that family disputes were reported as a cause of homelessness by 17% for both households and singles. Though not all family conflict involves domestic violence, studies have indicated that as many as 50% of homeless women are victims of abuse (Zorza, 1991). Among households with children, domestic violence as a cause was reported by thirty-nine percent of cities responding (US Conference of Mayors, 2007).

## Sexual Abuse

Childhood sexual abuse appears to be a risk factor for adult homelessness (Cauce et al., 2000; McChesney, 1995; Nyamathi et al., 2001; Toro et al., 1995). The US Department of Health and Human Services (1997) found that 17% of runaway and homeless youth were victims of sex abuse. Research indicates that each year, thousands of children run away from home to escape sexual abuse (Johnson, Rew, & Sternglanz, 2006). Even children placed in foster care may be at risk for running away to homelessness in that the system often fails to provide therapy to deal with the effects of sexual abuse (Roman & Wolfe, 1997). The trauma of sex abuse may well impact school performance, mental health, and other functioning that results in increased vulnerability. Homeless women in particular report a high incidence of childhood sexual abuse. (Bassuk et al., 1997). These childhood experiences are risk factors contributing to impaired healthy development and subsequent difficulties in social and psychological functioning (Molnar, Buka, & Kessler, 2001). In essence, adverse childhood experiences and trauma are strong risk factors for adolescent and adult homelessness (Herman, Susser, Struening, & Link, 1997; Rew, Fouladi, & Yockey, 2002).

## Maltreatment

Maltreatment may include sexual abuse, as was discussed earlier. However, maltreatment may be viewed in a broader sense, including physical and emotional abuse, neglect, family conflict, and failure to deal with trauma experiences.

Maltreatment and victimization are risk factors, especially for adolescent homelessness (Cauce, Tyler, & Whitbeck, 2004). Childhood maltreatment is a risk factor for homelessness and housing instability in that it may lead to a cycle of adult victimization and maltreatment by spouses or other relationships (Stein, Leslie, & Nyamathi, 2002). In essence, maltreatment disrupts normal development creating vulnerability. There is evidence that maltreatment may be linked to post-traumatic stress disorder and later homelessness (Gwadz, Nish, Leonard, & Strauss, 2007). Interestingly, there may be gender differences with females more vulnerable. As noted earlier, family maltreatment has been linked to adolescent runaways and flight into homelessness (Gwadz et al., 2007; Kimball & Golding, 2004).

## Incarceration

Increasing attention is being given to the relationships between incarceration and homelessness. Homelessness and incarceration are interacting factors in that homelessness increases the risk for incarceration, and the individual being released faces a greater risk of becoming homelessness (Cho, 2008). Research has been consistent in finding that persons from lower socioeconomic levels or minority status are at greater risk for arrest and incarceration (Greenberg & Rosenheck, 2008). Incarceration of these individuals, who have limited resources and social support, tends to isolate them from their communities, thus reducing ability to reestablish or reintegrate into the community (Rosenheck et al., 1998). Six percent of the persons in the 2007 AHAR data had been incarcerated in prison, jail, or detention facilities the evening before entering a shelter. Incarceration as a risk factor is not limited to the United States. A study of more than 22,513 homeless individuals seeking medical services in Moscow found that 30.3% reported being former convicts (Gutov & Nikiforov, 2004). Incarceration increases risks as it interacts with various other factors, such as stigma, loss of skills, discrimination, and often ineligibility for housing or other services.

Being homeless and mentally ill heightens the risk for incarceration (Cho, 2008; Greenberg & Rosenheck, 2008; McNiel, Binder, & Robinson, 2005). The homeless mentally ill have become criminalized and, in a sense, jails have become today's asylums. Even if not initially homeless, the mentally ill person who goes to jail has a significantly increased future risk of housing loss and community disenfranchisement hampering reintegration (Hartwell, 2003; HCH Clinician's Network, 2004; Soloman & Draine, 1995).

## Mental Illness

The extent of mental illness among the homeless and its role in causation is a source of contention. Studies suggest a range of mental illness from approximately 16% to more than one-third of homeless persons suffering from a severe and persistent mental illness (Federal Task Force on Home-lessness and Severe Mental Illness, 1992; US Conference of Majors, 2005; National Resource and Training Center on Homelessness and Mental Illness, 2003). A study of patients discharged from a state hospital was conducted at 13 month and at 3 months after discharge (Belcher, 1988). At the end of 3 months, approximately 35% had become homeless, with more than one-half classified as "aimless wanderers" without any specific plans. Complicating the incidence of mental illness is the number dually diagnosed or with co-occurring disorders such as substance abuse. Being homeless and mentally ill and abusing substances increases the risk for incarceration in criminal justice facilities and subsequently increases the risk of stigmatization and loss of competitive skills for achieving housing and employment.

## Domestic Violence

Considerable evidence indicates that domestic violence is a primary cause of homelessness, especially for women (ACLU, 2004; US Conference of Mayors, 2007; Zorza, 1991; Homes for the Homeless, 2000). A study sponsored by the Conference of Mayors in 2005 found that 50% of cities surveyed identified domestic violence as a primary cause of homelessness (United States Conference of Mayors, 2005). Ninety-two percent of homeless women report having experienced physical or sexual abuse at some time in their lives (Browne, 1998). Those on welfare seem particularly vulnerable to abuse and subsequent homelessness (Institute for Women's Policy Research, 1997). Domestic violence also involves children (Homes for the Homeless Survey, 2000; Institute for Children and Poverty, 2001), and one study found that 61% of homeless girls and 19% of homeless boys had experienced sexual abuse (Benson & Fox, 2004).

Though leaving the home to escape abuse represents a solution to one problem, the lack of employment and the absence of affordable housing often results in vulnerability for homelessness. The victims of domestic violence are often further challenged by difficulty in finding apartments owing to poor credit and employment histories attributable to the domestic violence (Anti-Discrimination Center of Metro New York, 2005). Discrimination against victims may occur as landlords adopt policies to evict tenants when violence occurs (Tolman et al., 2001). Likewise, some landlords may be reluctant to rent to women who have experienced domestic violence (ACLU, 2004). In a sense, the abused woman is a primary victim of domestic violence but then experiences secondary victimization as she is denied housing and employment because of the history of abuse.

## Health Status

Health problems such as mental illness and substance abuse are well recognized as risk factors for homelessness. Additionally, other medical problems and infirmities often represent risk factors for homelessness (Rosenheck et al., 1998). Studies of health problems in the homeless population indicate that 46% have chronic health problems such as arthritis, high blood pressure, diabetes, and cancer; 26% report acute infections conditions such as bronchitis, pneumonia, and tuberculosis. Various other conditions including HIV/AIDS are present (Kushel, Vittinghoff, & Ha, 2001; Schanzer, Dominguez, Shrout, & Caton, 2007; Burt et al., 1999).

Health problems in themselves often create stress and anxiety and a sense of vulnerability, which affects one's psychological functioning, further heightening the risk for homelessness. (Rogers, 2008). Just as lack of health care can be identified as a risk factor, medical illness and disability may result in loss of employment and income and bankruptcy (Himmelstein, Warren, & Woolhandler, 2005). For individuals and families struggling to barely meet daily living expenses, a medical crisis can deplete financial resources and push them into homelessness (NHCHC, 2008).

## Education

Given the increased requirement for technical and education competence to be self-sufficient, it is logical to assume that poor education is a risk factor for homelessness. In the study "Homelessness: Programs and the People They Serve," 53% of the parent clients in homeless families had less than a high school education (Urban Institute, 1999). Similarly, in a separate study, fewer than half of young homeless individuals were high school graduates (Burt, Aron, Lee, & Valente, 2001). The percentage completing high school may be misleading as proficiency levels in basics, such as reading and math, may be lower than the actual grade completed (Nooe, 1994).

## Substance Abuse

Habitual heavy substance use is often cited as a major contribution to homelessness. Compared with the general population, adult homeless persons have a much higher rate of substance abuse (Barber, 1994; Lehman & Cordray, 1993; NCH, 2007; Federal Task Force on Homelessness and Severe Mental Illness, 1992; Tam, Zlotnick, & Robertson, 2003). The presumption that first episodes of homelessness are frequently the result of alcohol abuse was supported by a study of 303 homeless individuals and people at risk of homelessness in Cook County, IL, finding that substance abuse was highly associated with first episodes of homelessness (Johnson, Freels, Parsons, & Vangeest, 1997). Additionally, these findings suggested a multi-directional model in which substance abuse is both a precursor and consequence of homelessness. In a sample of homeless persons at a city soup kitchen, 75% had used drugs in the preceding month (Magura, Nwakeze, Rosenblum, & Joseph, 2000). Single homeless men are especially likely to have histories of substance abuse (Toro et al., 1995). However, care should be taken in interpreting the statistical relationship since studies may over represent shelter users and single men (NCH, 2005). The relationship between homelessness and substance abuse is complex and involves interaction of many of the factors identified in Figure 9.1. For example, those who are addicted may be impacted by the decrease in SROs. Likewise, the lack of health insurance becomes a barrier in dealing with addiction. Changes reducing eligibility for SSI and Social Security Disability Insurance (SSDI), based on chronic substance abuse, further increase the risk for homelessness. The SSI policy change in 1996 was especially devastating to persons with addictive disorders. These changes resulted in denying SSI and SSDI and disability benefits, including denial of Medicaid eligibility, to persons whose addictions were defined as contributing to their disability status. For many persons, the loss of disability benefits resulted in the subsequent loss of housing (National Health Care for the Homeless Council, 1997, 2005). Similarly, policy changes that result in persons convicted of drug abuse/sale being barred from public housing create additional dilemmas.

In addition to lack of available, appropriate housing, there is also the issue of treatment resources. Many homeless individuals are dually disordered, suffering from both a major mental illness and substance abuse (Barber, 1994; Task Force on Homelessness and Severe Mental Illness, 1992). These dually disordered individuals frequently fall between the cracks because neither mental health nor substance abuse treatment facilities provide comprehensive services. Though substance abuse contributes to the lack of funds and eligibility for housing, it may also increase family conflict leading to family unwillingness to allow individuals to reside in the home.

Although addiction frequently is cited as a contributing factor, it must be considered within the context of housing, employment, and treatment availability (Oakley & Dennis, 1996). Public attitudes around addiction and the earlier cited stereotypes regarding homelessness and substance use may well impact the lack of programs to address these problems and the elimination of disability benefits.

## Minority Status

Minority status as a risk factor is based on the fact that blacks and other minorities are more likely to be poor, thus at greater risk for homelessness. Perhaps the most telling factor is that in 2006, approximately 21% of Hispanics and 24% of blacks were in poverty (US Census Bureau News, 2007). Therefore, minority status may not only increase the risk for homelessness but increase the barriers to escaping homelessness (Task Force on Homelessness and Severe Mental Illness, 1992; Rosenheck et al., 1998). Homelessness disproportionately impacts minorities constituting about 59% of the sheltered population compared with representing 31% of the US population (USDHUD, 2007). The homeless population is disproportionately black, approximately 45%, compared to the general population wherein blacks are about 12% (US Census Bureau, 2003). The loss of jobs in the inner city, housing segregation, and other structural factors are obviously intertwined with poverty to increase the risk for minorities. There may be racial differences among the causes of homelessness in that whites report more internal causes, such as substance abuse and mental illness, compared to nonwhites reporting more external factors such as low income and unemployment (North & Smith, 1994).

Studies on homeless whose minority status is based on sexual orientation are scarce. However, studies examining the sexual orientation of homeless youth suggest rates ranging from 6% to 40% (Cochran, Stewart, Ginzler, & Cauce, 2002). The National Gay and Lesbian Task Force suggests that between 20% and 40% of all homeless youth identify as lesbian, gay, bisexual, or transgender. The report goes on to say that family conflict over a youth's sexual orientation often leads to exclusion from the home and subsequent homelessness (Ray, 2006). Shelters and other care facilities may also react to a youth's sexual orientation in a manner that results in leaving and becoming homeless (Hyde, 2005).

## Military Service

Approximately 41% of homeless men are veterans compared to 34% of male veterans in the general population (National Coalition for Homeless Veterans, 2008; National Coalition for the Homeless, 2008; Rosenheck, Frisman & Chung, 1994). Gamache, Rosenheck, & Tessler (2003) found that women veterans are 3.6 times more likely to be homeless than non-veteran women. However, Rosenheck asserts that homelessness among veterans is not clearly related to military experience, but the same factors—poverty, lack of housing, alcohol and drugs—that contribute to homelessness among non-veterans are significant risk factors for homelessness among veterans (Rosenheck, Leda, Frisman, Lam, & Chung, 1996). Military service may be associated with other risk factors such as substance abuse and criminal behavior in becoming homeless. In a study of 188 homeless veterans, Benda, Rodell, and Rodell (2003) found that among those who were substance abusers, 41% reported committing crimes in the past year. Drug and alcohol abuse, lower levels of education, unemployment, physical or sexual abuse before age 18, and habitation with a substance abuser elevated the likelihood of homeless veterans committing crimes. The odds of committing a crime were decreased by resilience, ego integrity, and self-efficacy, all of which are individual factors.

# Individual and Social Outcomes

As is evident from the preceding discussion, multiple biopsychosocial risk factors can interact to produce homelessness. Once homeless, individuals and families are vulnerable to a number of harmful individual and social outcomes. Figure 9.1 displays these individual and social outcomes in the context of our model of the ecology of homelessness. It is to these outcomes of homelessness that the discussion now turns.

## *Individual Outcomes*

*Health impairment.* Health and health care reflect the interrelationship between personal and structural factors contributing to homelessness and may represent both a risk factor for homelessness and a result of homelessness. Chronic and acute health problems are frequent among the homeless (NHCHC, 2005). At the same time, homeless individuals are often uninsured and lack access to basic health care (O'Connell, Lozier, & Gingles, 1997) Illness or disability often results in lost employment and eviction followed by homelessness and overwhelming challenges to regaining stability.

Kushel, Perry, Bangsberg, Clark, and Moss (2002) surveyed 2,578 marginally housed and homeless persons in San Francisco regarding their use of hospital emergency department services in the prior year. Slightly more than 40% visited the emergency department at least once during the year. Strikingly, 7.9% respondents were responsible for 54.4% of all visits for the group. High use rates were associated with substance abuse, physical and mental illness, victimization, arrests, and less stable housing.

Homeless smokers ($n$ = 107) were compared to 491 non-homeless smokers in a study of the smoking habits of homeless smokers (Butler et al., 2002). Homeless smokers were found to smoke more cigarettes per day, to have begun smoking at a younger age, to have smoked for longer period of time, had a higher level of depression, and were more likely to use recreational drugs.

Homeless individuals are at greater risk of latent and active TB secondary to time spent in homeless shelters and other homeless services delivery facilities. In a study of 415 homeless persons in Los Angeles, Nyamathi et al. (2004) found a notable lack of knowledge regarding the risk factors associated with TB infection and modes of transmission. Injecting drug users and Latinos evidenced lower rates of TB knowledge.

Homeless children in particular suffer health problems, often resulting from hunger and poor nutrition. Development delays are frequent among children.

Psychological problems such as anxiety, depression and behavioral problems are elevated (Rafferty & Shinn, 1991). Various childhood diseases, delays in immunizations, and lack of health care are much greater among homeless children than the housed poor and national norms (Wright, 1991).

*Substance abuse.* The relationship between substance disorders and homelessness is complex. It is likely that for many individuals, the risk of homelessness is increased by substance abuse/dependence, but substance use may be accelerated by homelessness. Among cities surveyed by the United States Conference of Mayors (2008), 68% reported substance abuse as one of the leading cause of homelessness. Many persons become addicted while homeless (NCH, 2007). A critical factor is that homelessness may create additional barriers to treatment for substance disorders, including lack of insurance, lack of supportive resources, and general inaccessibility of programs (NASADAD, 2007).

*Mental illness.* Burt (1992) reports that mental illness and/or chemical dependency problems affect more than 50% of the US homeless population. As was noted in earlier discussion, for persons with mental illness and substance abuse, homelessness has a detrimental effect and, like any other crisis or trauma, may "catalyze and/or exacerbate mental illness producing disorder where previously if did not exist" (Koegel & Burnam, 1992). Banyard and Graham-Bermann (1998) found that homeless mothers had more depression and used avoidant coping strategies more than housed mothers. However, it may well be that depression and avoidance are a consequence rather than cause of homelessness.

*Social isolation.* Regardless of the factors involved, the availability of social support whether from friends, relatives, or agencies appears to influence both risks for and recovery from homelessness. Kingree et al. (1999), for example, found that low levels of support from friends were associated with homelessness after completion of a substance abuse treatment program. Similarly, personal crises such as divorce and widowhood remove support systems and may make individuals more vulnerable to homelessness.

*Impaired education.* Poverty and homeless have a devastating impact on educational achievement. In both the housed poor and the homeless; children in particular experience an increased risk of inability to succeed in school or community environments (Ziesemer, Marcoux, & Maxwell, 1994). Homeless children often experience difficulty accessing and staying in school. Even when enrolled, instability and shelter-living are not conducive to learning. Compared to their peers, homeless children are likely to experience educational underachievement and often are required to repeat grades (Rafferty & Shinn, 1991; Institute for Children and Poverty, 2003). Impaired education in childhood likely has long-term consequences, increasing the risk for adult poverty and homelessness.

*Sexual abuse.* There is increasing evidence that the incidence of childhood sexual abuse in the histories of chronically homeless women and clinical populations is much higher than the general population (Bassuk, Dawson, Perloff, & Weinreb, 2001; Kushel, Evans, Perry, Robertson, & Moss, 2003; Molnar et al., 2001). After becoming homeless, the risk of sexual assault may be heightened, with some, such as transgendered persons, being particularly vulnerable (Kushel et al., 2003). The limited studies available suggest that more than 10% of homeless women have been raped, many multiple times, during the past year (Wenzel, Leake, & Gelberg, 2000; Heslin, 2004). In addition to the trauma of sexual assault, many of these homeless individuals encounter barriers to services, including social stigma, lack of information or access, and lack of insurance and transportation (Pennsylvania Coalition Against Rape [PCAR], 2006).

*Maltreatment.* Earlier, maltreatment was recognized as a contributing or risk factor for homelessness. Once homeless, the incidence of maltreatment may be no less severe. Perhaps one of the most impacting outcomes is being stigmatized and blamed for being homeless. Thus, in addition to the hardships of homelessness, these individuals are often labeled and ostracized by their communities (Phelan et al., 1997).

Advocates identify a trend toward "criminalization of homelessness." In other words, using the criminal justice system to respond to homelessness rather than seeking more human solutions (NLCHP, 2006). The NCH and Saelinger (2006), for example, cite the trends of revitalization of downtowns and compassion fatigue toward the poor as underlying this shift.

In addition to stigma and criminalization, homeless persons face increased risk of physical maltreatment. Homelessness places women at higher risk of assault and rape (Heslin, 2004; PCAR, 2006). Homeless persons are victimized disproportionately as compared to the domiciles population (Lee & Schreck, 2005). According to the NCH, from 1999 through 2006, there were 774 acts of violence, resulting in 217 murders of homeless people and 557 victims of non-lethal violence in 200 cities from 44 states and Puerto Rico (2008). These attacks seem to be increasing, suggesting that these figures may be conservative in that studies often report as many as two thirds of homeless persons experience victimization (Mallory, 2002).

*Criminal activity.* Just as homeless persons tend to be victimized more than the general domiciled populations, they also have disproportionately higher incarcerations rates. Homeless jail inmates comprise more than 15% of jail inmates. Compared to other inmates, they are more likely to have committed a property crime, have a history of justice system involvement, suffer from mental illness and substance abuse, and be older, unemployed, and single (Greenberg & Rosenheck, 2008). Given these characteristics, it is logical to assume that they are more disadvantaged and face greater barriers to community reintegration.

Though the foregoing suggests that homeless persons are disproportionately incarcerated, care should be taken before concluding that homelessness has an outcome of increased criminal activity. The passage of anti-nuisance laws in recent years has expanded the definition of criminal activity and increases the risk of arrest and incarceration. Ordinances that prohibit pan-handling, camping, and eating and loitering in public spaces increases the risk of arrest for activities that may be part of survival for homeless persons (NCH & NLCH, 2006). Though the research is limited, it may well be that criminal activity by homeless persons may be higher for larceny offenses and ordinance violations but not significantly higher for violent, property and sexual offenses. (Polczynski, 2007). However, in an earlier study, Martell (1991) found the mentally ill homeless represented 50% of all admissions to a New York City maximum security hospital. This study suggested a higher base rate of violent criminal behavior in this population and the existence of a subgroup that might pose a threat to public safety secondary to violent behavior.

*Criminal victimization.* Homeless people are victimized disproportionately compared to the domiciled population entailing various forms of victimizations (Lee and Schreck, 2005). Sexual and physical assault are particularly common experiences among the homeless. A study found that 32% of women, 27% of men, and 38% of transgendered homeless persons reported physical or sexual assault in the previous year (Kushel et al., 2003). A California study found that 66% had been victimized in the previous year, with many reporting multiple victimization; assault and robbery were the most frequent reported by approximately three-fourths of the respondents (Mallory, 2002).

It has been pointed out that dimensions of marginality—disaffiliation, health problems, and traumatic events, for example—significantly increase the odds of being victimized (Lee & Schreck, 2005). Homeless persons with severe mental illness or other disabilities may be particularly vulnerable to violent criminal victimization, with some studies indicating a two-and-a-half times greater risk (Hiday et al., 1999). The NCH (2006) details the increasing rate of violent crimes in its report, "Hate, Violence and Death on Main Street USA: A Report on Hate Crimes and Violence Against People Experiencing Homelessness 2006." Perhaps most disturbing is that many of these crimes are committed by adolescents and young adults for no motive other than boredom. It is the NCH's position that these constitute hate crimes, even though not currently included in federal law.

*Job loss.* Job loss and unemployment were identified earlier as risk factors for homelessness. The loss of long-term jobs and involuntary job loss has increased in recent years (Mishel et al., 1999). It is not surprising that being homeless may further diminish one's chances of employment, both in terms of opportunities and as prolonged idleness may result in loss of skill and work habits, responsibility, and commitment to employment. Those with limited education, experience, or skills are especially at risk for prolonged homelessness. In addition to struggling with basic issues of survival such as food and shelter, the homeless worker often faces barriers such as lack of transportation, childcare and treatment for health problems. (Long, Rio, & Rosen, 2007; US Department of Labor, 1994). Even the lack of appropriate clothing for employment may pose a risk for maintaining or finding employment.

*Self-harm.* Service providers offer many anecdotal accounts of suicidal ideation and attempts by homeless persons, but the research is sparse. The frequent characteristics among the homeless—social isolation, mental illness, substance abuse, and poverty along with previous attempts of self-harm—represent high suicidal risk factors (Christensen & Garces, 2006). A study of homeless and runaway adolescents found that more than one-half had experiences suicidal ideation and more than one-fourth had made an attempt during the previous year (Yoder, Hoyt, & Whitbeck, 1998).

Suicidal ideation and attempts among mentally ill homeless persons are especially high. There is some evidence that young middle-aged persons are at greatest risk of suicidal behavior, a pattern quite different from the risk factors in non-homeless populations of older individuals (Prigerson, DeSai, Liu-Mares, &

Rosenheck, 2003). Regardless of the age group or health status, homeless often result in a sense of extreme hopelessness, which often underlies self-harm.

*Death.* One of the tragic outcomes of homelessness for some is death. Multiple studies have found elevated morality rates among homeless individuals ranging from 2 to 8.3 times higher than the general population, depending on gender, age group, and setting (Hibbs et al., 1994; Hwang, Orav, O'Connell, Lebow, & Brennan, 1997; Barrow, Herman, Cordova, & Struening, 1999; Hwang, 2000). In a study of 1981 women, Cheung and Hwang (2004) found morality rates for homeless women 10 times higher than for women in the general population. When they examined mortality data for homeless women in seven cities, they found women younger than 45 years had a mortality rate near or equal to men of a similar age. The most common cause of death was HIV/AIDS and drug overdose.

## Social Outcomes

*Poverty.* Poverty and homelessness are intertwined. In a sense, homelessness represents the "poorest of poor." In 2002, people below the official thresholds numbered 34.6 million, a figure 1.7 higher than the 32.9 million in poverty in 2001 (Proctor & Dalaker, 2003). An earlier study of single homeless individuals found an average income approximately 51% of the 1996 federal poverty level (US Interagency Council on the Homeless, 1999). The declining value of public assistance and shifts in welfare policy have resulted in fewer resources and stricter guidelines for subsidies and services (Berger & Tremblay, 1999; NCH, 2009; Dunlap & Fogel, 1998). These trends have increased the poverty level for homeless persons and make escape more difficult. Resources such as AFDC were important in preventing homelessness, but more exclusionary guidelines have negatively impacted preventing and escaping of homelessness.

*Public safety.* McNeil et al. (2005) found in a study of 12,934 individuals incarcerated in the San Francisco County Jail that 16% were homeless, with 30% of the homeless inmates having a severe psychiatric disorder. The homeless were significantly more likely to (1) receive a diagnosis of a co-occurring disorder, (2) be charged with a felony, but (3) not be charged with a violent crime. Inmates who were both homeless and diagnosed with a serve mental illness and substance abuse were more likely to have multiple incarcerations than inmates who were neither homeless nor dually diagnosed. As Greenberg and Rosenheck (2008) found, homeless inmates are more likely to have been charged with violent offenses, thus raising questions about public safety. The previously noted factors of untreated mental illness, substance abuse, disaffiliation, and lack of social support may increase issues of recidivism and subsequently public safety (Martell, 1991; Polczynski, 2007).

*Property crime.* There is often a public perception that homeless persons frequently commit property crimes (Tepper, 2006). As noted, in comparison with other jail inmates, the inmate who has been homeless is more likely to be incarcerated for a property crime. The homeless inmate is more likely to have a history of criminal justice involvement, have mental health and substance abuse problems, and be unemployed and less educated (Greenberg & Rosenheck, 2008). However, findings have been consistent that the majority of arrests, around 80%, are for substance abuse and offenses such as trespassing. However, there are mixed results. There is evidence that the homeless arrest rate for serious crime exceeds the arrest rates for those with permanent addresses. The rates for both property crimes and violent crimes have been significantly higher in some studies (Snow & Anderson, 1993). At the same time, other studies suggest that violent and property crimes are not correlated in areas close to homeless services (Polczynski, 2007).

*Prostitution.* Homeless women and runaway youth are especially vulnerable to falling into prostitution. Studies of homeless youth involved in prostitution range from ten to fifty percent. (Greenblatt & Robertson 1993). A Chicago study found that 50% of women involved in prostitution had been homeless (Mueller, 2005). Prostitution is frequently associated with drug addiction (McClanahan, McClelland, Abram, & Teplin, 1999; Silbert, Pines, & Lynch, 1982). However, survival sex—the exchange of sex for money to secure food, shelter, and other basic needs—is likely intertwined with other factors.

Earlier, childhood sex abuse was discussed as a risk factor for homelessness. Similarly, childhood sex abuse has been identified as an antecedent to prostitution (Simmons & Witbeck, 1991; Seng, 1989; McClanahan et al., 1999; Bagley & Young, 1987). Most likely the path is not linear but represents the interaction of abuse, runaway behavior, homelessness, substance abuse, and prostitution. Unfortunately, these factors create additional barriers to escaping homelessness and negative social consequences.

*Street violence.* Street violence is interlinked with homelessness. Earlier discussion recognized the rates of sexual abuse and other types of criminal victimization. It takes many forms ranging from assault by homeless persons on one another to thrill assaults and killings by teens and even to abuse by police and medical responders. Homeless persons experience physical and sexual violence much more frequently than housed persons (Street Health, 2007) The NCH publishes annual reports on hate crimes and violence, noting "In 2006 homeless individuals in America faced another year of brutality that ranged from assault to killings" (NCH, 2007). A study in Toronto, Canada, found a rate of physical assaults 35 times higher than the housed population (Street Health, 2007). Persons living outside, especially those with mental illness or substance abuse are particularly vulnerable to violence (NCH, 2007; Hiday et al., 1999). Street violence is pervasive and wide-ranging, with approximately 10% of homeless persons report being assaulted by police (Street Health, 2007; Hwang, 2004).

*Public inebriation.* Habitual heavy substance abuse is not uncommon among the homeless, increasing the risk for public inebriation and subsequent arrest (NCH, 2007; US Conference of Mayors, 2005, 2007; Toro et al., 1995). In some community studies, closer to 60% of homeless adults had been arrested for public inebriation within the past 3 years (Nooe, 2006). Public inebriation and incarceration may become cyclic, creating additional barriers to reintegration (Hartwell, 2003; NHCHC, 2005). The lack of health insurance, the limited number of resources for treating dually diagnosed individuals, and lack of support services are additional elements (Hartwell, 2003; HCH, 2007). Likewise, policy changes that result in persons convicted of drug abuse/sale being barred from public housing have created additional dilemmas. Another social outcome is the cost of public inebriation. Dunford found that 15 randomly selected chronic alcoholics amassed costs of $1.5 million for emergency department care during an 18-month period (Dunford et al., 2006).

*Panhandling.* The president of the Denver Metro Convention and Visitors Bureau is quoted as saying, "Panhandling and homelessness is still the number 1 negative comment from our tourists and conventioneers" (Steers, 2007). Whether accurate, there appears to be a widely held public view that homelessness and panhandling are closely related (Lee & Farrell, 2003; Rimer, 1989). However, studies offer different estimates of the number who panhandle, ranging from around 5% to more than a third of homeless people (Burt et al., 1999; Rossi, 1989; Snow, Anderson, Quist, & Cress, 1996). Likewise, results are mixed in addressing questions about panhandling being necessary for survival and the productivity of it (Lankenau, 1999; Snow et al., 1996; Stark, 1992). The literature is fairly consistent in suggesting that a person panhandling is more likely to be male and minority, and increases with duration of homelessness. (Lankenan, 1999; Stark, 1992). Lee and Farrell, 2003, reviewing the literature, indicate that panhandlers are generally "more isolated, troubled and disadvantaged," having more extensive histories of mental illness, substance abuse and criminal records than non-panhandling homeless persons.

Though information about homelessness and panhandling is limited, it is apparent that cities throughout the United States are enacting ordinances prohibiting or severely restricting panhandling (NCH & NLCHP, 2006). Thus, panhandling may be received as a social outcome of homelessness and stimulating social outcomes of ordinances and regulations.

*Strained health services.* The increased risk for health problems due to homelessness is well documented (Schanzer et al., 2007; Plumb, 1997). A Baltimore study found that homeless adults have an average eight to nine concurrent medical illnesses (Breakey et al., 1989). Rates of substance abuse and mental illness among the homeless are likely double those of other lowincome patients (Fisher & Breakey, 1991). The nature of homelessness—extreme poverty, social isolation, and lack of support networks—suggests greater risk for poor health status.

Homeless individuals use more impatient and emergency department services rather than outpatient or clinic services (Salit, Kuhn, Hartz, Vu, & Mosso, 1998; Folsom et al., 2005). The Centers for Disease Control National Health Survey found that approximately one-third of homeless individuals, as compared to 1% of the general population, used emergency facilities rather than clinics or private physicians for primary care.

The high incidence of substance abuse and mental illness among homeless persons frequently seen in emergency departments results in strained health services in terms of treatment and financial resources (Dunford, et al., 2006). When admitted, the homeless patient generally stays approximately 4 days longer than other comparable patients (Salit et al., 1998). Many of these individuals will be discharged back into homelessness, increasing the risk for continued illness or relapse. As noted earlier, most homeless persons are uninsured and, as need for treatment increases, the health system is further strained (O'Connell, Lozier, &

Gingles, 1997). An area of concern is the estimation that 6% to 27% of the homeless population in the United States are HIV positive (Kim, Kertesz, Horton, Tibbetts, & Samet, 2006).

*Community philanthropy.* Although they may experience "compassion fatigue," the public seems willing to support efforts to solve homelessness (Link et al., 1995). An earlier study by Toro and McDonnell (1992) found that more than 50% of respondents were willing to pay more taxes to help homeless persons. Though there is an expressed willingness to give, a number of factors my influence actual giving. Morgan, Goddard, and Givens (1997) examined the relationship between expressed willingness to assist the homeless and an individual's level of empathy, religion, household income or political orientation, gender, and race. In a study of 204 undergraduates, the authors found empathy and expressed religiosity strong predictors of willingness to assist the homeless.

Religious organizations play a major role in philanthropy. Cnaan and Handy (2000) examined the social services provided by religious congregations in Ontario and the United States. They found that 56.5% of Canadian congregations provided shelter for men compared to 28.7% of U.S. congregations; 54.3% of Canadian congregations provided shelter for women/children as compared to 28.3% of U.S. congregations.

Community philanthropy directed toward programs for the homeless also can be considered in terms of foundation giving and support from faith-based organizations. Historically, only about 1% of foundation giving has been for homeless giving; however, there are renewed efforts to involve foundations (National Center on Family Homelessness, 2008). Overall, churches and other faith-based organizations have played a more prominent role in addressing homelessness. The 1996 National Survey of Homeless Assistance Provides and clients found that the majority of all food programs and one-fourth of all shelters are operated by faith-based organizations (Aron & Sharkey, 2002).

*Community discord.* Community discord is often a social outcome of the increase in homelessness. Newspapers reflect these conflicts in stories such as "Atlanta Puts Heat on Panhandlers" (*USA Today*); "Pressed on the Homeless, Subways Impose Rules" (*New York Times*, 1989); and "Church Sued for Housing Homeless" (*Erie Times–News*, 2008). Saelinger (2006), summarizing a number of studies, notes that during the 1980s, homelessness was viewed as a critical social issue needing human solutions but, as cities revitalized and compassion fatigue increased, communities turned to anti-nuisance laws. Two major manifestations of community discord are the anti-nuisance ordinances regulating activity in public spaces, including prohibiting sleeping, feeding, and begging (NCH, 2005) and conflict and protest against location of shelters and homes for the homeless (NLCHP, 1997; Lyon-Callo, 2001).

The NCH report "Illegal to be Homeless: The Criminalization of Homelessness in the United States" (2004) documents the organization's view that "through the passage of possibility unconstitutional laws, the 'selective enforcement' of existing laws, arbitrary police practices and discriminatory public regulations, people experiencing homelessness face overwhelming hardships in addition to their daily struggle for survival." An indication of the level of discord is reflected in a

*New York Post* article suggesting that the American Civil Liberties Union is an instigator:

> What the homeless industry really wants is total exemption from the law for street vagrants so that they can remain publicly visible until the final thieves of alcoholism and schizophrenia drive them to the hospital or the grave. It is the enforcement of the laws—period—that infuriates these advocates, not their alleged "selective" enforcement. (MacDonald, 2002)

Community discord is often heated regarding the location of shelters and housing of homeless persons as reflected in "Not in My Backyard or NIMBY" (NLCHP, 1997). Though advocates often cite accessibility to resources, transportation, and centralization of services, those opposing cite decreased property values and increased crime rates (NLCHP, 1997).

The underlying reasons for community discord are complex, often involving an interplay between representations of homeless people and historical, class, and power dynamics within communities (Lyon-Callo, 2001). Takahashi (1998) points out that interconnections such as HIV/AIDS and homelessness add an additional dynamic that many be represented in NIMBY as a product of the changing social construct of stigma. As noted earlier, homelessness was a major issue for resolution in the 1980s, but Americans often grow impatient when solutions are slow in coming, perhaps reflecting "compassion fatigue" (Link et al., 1995).

## Temporal Dimension

Homelessness is a phenomenon of variable duration. Individuals and families may experience homelessness over the course of a single evening or extending multiple years. The categorization of temporal dimension of homelessness presents a significant definitional challenge. Commonly used terms describing the duration of homelessness include "first time," "short-term," "situational," "transitional," "episodic," and "chronic." Each of these terms has associated limitations, though "first time" conveys the most obvious specificity. The period of time denoting "short-term" homelessness is not well defined in the research literature. Perhaps more concretely, though researchers might legitimately view a 2-week period of homelessness as "short-term," to a family experiencing 2 weeks of living in an emergency shelter, "short-term" might seem interminable. "Transitional" was defined by Kuhn and Culhane (1998) as one stay in an emergency shelter for a "short-period" (p. 207). Alternatively, "transitional" housing programs typically provide residents shelter up to 24 months. Episodic homelessness is defined by frequent short periods of homelessness alternating with periods of time spent in temporary housing or institutions such as jails, detoxification centers, or psychiatric facilities (Farr, Koegel, & Burnam, 1986; Kuhn & Culhane).

The US federal government defines a "chronically homeless" person as "an unaccompanied homeless individual with a disabling condition who has either been continuously homeless for a year or more, or has had at least four episodes of homelessness in the past three years" (Notice of Funding Available for the Collaborative Initiative to Help End Chronic Homelessness, 2003). This definition conflates duration with condition. A person who has been "continuously homeless" for 1 year or experienced "homeless episodes during the last three years" could be considered chronically homeless and must also have a "disabling condition." Disabling conditions can include severe and persistent mental illness, severe and persistent alcohol and/or drug abuse problems, and HIV/AIDS.

It is noteworthy that the absence of a permanent residence or repeated periods of homelessness is insufficient to meet criteria for chronic homelessness. The US federal definition requires linkage to a plausible causal factor, a disabling condition. Strikingly, the allowable plausible causal factors center around individual disability, eschewing socioeconomic engendered causality such as unaffordable housing, low wages, and job loss. Further, the definition excludes children who are homeless with their parents, unaccompanied individuals without disabilities, and unaccompanied individuals who elect not to declare a disability.

Some researchers have posited a typology of homelessness that links duration or number of episodes of homelessness to groups or types of homeless individuals (Caton et al., 2005; Kuhn & Culhane, 1998). For instance, Kuhn and Culhane assert that transitionally homeless individuals are younger and typically have fewer problems associated with mental health, substance abuse, or medical conditions. Others have noted greater similarity than differences between the first-time homeless and those individuals with multiple episodes of homelessness (Goering, Tolomiczenko, Sheldon, Boydell, & Wasylenki, 2002).

The temporal dimension of homelessness is represented in our ecological model of homelessness (see Figure 9.1) with the categories First Time, Episodic, and Chronic, as these three terms are the most definitionally distinct. Biopsychosocial risk factors associated with homelessness can result in any one of these three temporal categories. It is important to recognize that every first-time homeless individual is at some risk of becoming episodically or chronically homeless. Individuals may move from being episodically homeless to chronically homeless by having a disabling condition and four or more episodes of homelessness in the previous 3 years. Conversely, it is possible that an individual previously categorized as chronically homeless could after a period of housing stability again become episodically homeless. This discussion now turns from the temporal dimension of homelessness to its locus and residential alternatives.

## Housing Status

The ecological model of homelessness in Figure 9.1 depicts a continuum of living arrangements experienced by homeless individuals and families. The arrows connecting these housing arrangements are intended to represent the real and potential pathways of transition between these housing categories. The arrows linking housing status categories to individuals and social outcomes represent the array of consequences associated with homelessness. This discussion begins with perhaps the most visible manifestation of homelessness: street dwelling.

## Street Dwelling

The term *street dwelling* is used here to denote a spectrum of impermanence or transitory sleeping options including on the streets, in vehicles, and in temporary camps. *Sleeping rough* is the British term for individuals who eschew staying in homeless emergency shelters for nights on the street (Urban Dictionary, 2008). In the 2007 Annual Homeless Assessment Report (AHAR) to Congress (Khadduri et al., 2007, p. i.), "unsheltered" is the term used for persons "who do not use shelters and are on the streets, in abandoned buildings, or in other places not meant for human habitation." For many residents of urban centers, street dwelling homeless may be the most familiar or commonly encountered among the wider homeless population. They sleep on the streets, under overpasses, in abandoned buildings, and in public spaces. Street-dwelling homeless traverse urban environments commonly carrying their few possessions, having limited or no access to sanitary facilities, and encountering an array of unsafe and unhealthy conditions (Cousineau, 1997)

O'Connell et al. (2004) conducted a 4-year prospective study of 30 street-dwelling individuals older than the age of 60. Over the course of the study, 30% (9) died, 27% (7) continued to live on the streets, 20% (6) moved into nursing homes, 17% (5) were housed, and 1 was lost to follow-up. The health and safety risks associated with street dwelling are not limited to elderly homeless. Ferguson (2007) lists high-risk survival behaviors of street-dwelling youth including prostitution, panhandling, pornography, drug dealing, and other criminal activities. Health problems of street-dwelling youth include HIV/AIDS and other sexually transmitted diseases, substance abuse and dependence, malnutrition, skin and respiratory infections, and a host of mental health problems.

The 2007 AHAR study (Khadduri et al., 2007) reports in a point-in-time study conducted in January 2005 that 45% of all homeless individuals were unsheltered. Of that group, 30% were chronically homeless, compared to the 17% rate of chronically homeless found among the sheltered homeless in the same point-in-time study. The authors point out that street counts of the unsheltered homeless may be inflated owing to methodological problems.

Some studies have attempted to differentiate unsheltered homeless persons from those found in emergency shelters and transitional housing. Larsen, Poortinga, and Hurdle (2004) used an unmatched, case control study to compare 85 homeless individuals who used the services of local shelters with 45 individuals who did not use shelters. The homeless individuals who elected to not use shelters were more frequently employed as day laborers, consumed large quantities of alcohol more frequently, and were more likely to be Native-American and to have received court-ordered psychiatric treatment. Lam and Rosenheck (1999) report that unsheltered homeless have a greater probability of being less interested in treatment and are more likely to have psychotic disorders, to be older, to be male, and to be more difficult to engage in case management.

## Shared Dwelling

The housing category "shared dwelling" refers to an option employed by individuals at risk of becoming homeless or transitioning out of homelessness for some period of time. Individuals using the shared dwelling option are sometimes referred to as *couch homeless, precariously housed, doubled up, couch surfers*, or the *hidden homeless* owing to the methodological challenges of finding and counting them. Nonetheless, Hoback & Anderson (2006) estimate that on any night in 2000 there were 4,700,000 couch homeless in the United States. This represents 1.65% of the population. Burt (1996) suggests that the "precariously housed" typically are unable to afford housing and that their shared dwelling arrangement usually lasts less than 60 days. According to the 2007 AHAR study (Khadduri et al., 2007), these individuals are commonly "doubled up" with relatives and friends and are at risk of homelessness.

## Emergency Shelter

The term *emergency shelter* refers to shared housing provided to homeless individuals and families. This shelter option is sometimes referred to as a homeless shelter or mission. They are typically found in urban settings and commonly have few restrictions on admission. The allowable length of stay in an emergency shelter depends on shelter policies and funding source restrictions. A Google search of the term *homeless shelter length of stay* produced documents reporting shelter policies on length of stay ranging from one night to up to 1 year. Wong, Park, and Nemon (2006) report that in a survey of 300 homeless residential programs, 43% of emergency shelters had either no length-of-stay restrictions or had no formal policy on length of stay.

Services provided by emergency shelters range from the basic bed and meals to more rehabilitative services including substance abuse treatment, domestic violence assistance, job placement skills, case management, and housing assistance. Many shelters discharge clients each morning and readmit them in the late afternoon, forcing clients to spend their days outside the shelter. Other shelters provide around-the-clock shelter, food, and services. Callicutt (2006, p. 169) suggests that homeless shelters, much like jails and prisons, are now part of a "de facto mental health system" that now provides housing to the severely persistently mentally ill who formerly would have received care in long-term psychiatric facilities.

Emergency homeless shelters are operated by city or county agencies, nonprofit groups, churches, and religious organizations supported by local and national church organizations. HUD provides funding for homeless shelters to its emergency shelter grants program. This funding is available to faith-based, secular organizations and local government agencies, though faith-based organizations are required to provide services in a manner free from religious influence (HUD, 2008).

## Jail and Prison

Jails and prisons across the United States regularly house the homeless and individuals destined for future homelessness. The relationship between homelessness and incarceration appears reciprocal; being homeless increases ones chance of arrest and once incarcerated, the risk of homelessness increases. Burt et al. (1999) found 54% of homeless individuals reported having been incarcerated for 5 days or more in a city or county jail, state or federal prison, or juvenile detention.

McNeil et al. (2005) examined their records of 12,934 individuals incarcerated in the San Francisco County Jail in the course of 6 months in 2000. They found that 16% of those incarcerated were homeless and that 30% of those individuals had a diagnosis of a mental disorder. Co-occurring substance abuse–related disorders were found in 78% of individuals with a severe mental disorder. Individuals with severe mental disorders and co-occurring substance abuse disorders were found to be held in jail longer than inmates charged with similar crimes.

Greenberg and Rosenheck (2008) studied data from a national survey of adults in state and federal prison. They found that the rate of homelessness among inmates was four to six times higher than the general population's estimated rate of homelessness. Strikingly, homeless inmates were more likely to be poor and have a history of trauma, substance abuse, mental health problems, and poor health. Additionally, homeless inmates also were more likely to have a record of prior property and violent offenses.

Metraux and Culhane (2006) matched data from New York City jails and New York State prisons to the homeless shelter records of 7,022 individuals who had spent time in a New York City public shelter over a 2-year study period. They found that 23.1% of the population had been incarcerated in the previous 2 years. Individuals released from jail, 17% of the study group, were more likely to have used shelters more frequently and evidenced a sequential pattern of alternating jail and shelter stays resulting in continuing residential instability. Individuals released from prison constituted 7.7% of the study group. This group was more likely to have a shelter stay within 30 days of release from prison and were less likely to have subsequent shelter stays when compared to individuals released from jail. The authors called for the development of differential approaches to preventing homelessness for individuals released from prison versus those released from jail.

## Hospitalization

Inpatient hospitalization of homeless individuals, whether for substance abuse, mental illness, or health reasons, accounts for an expensive but unknown proportion of the time the homeless are sheltered. Moore (2006) examined the 5-year cost of health care and incarceration of 35 duly diagnosed, chronically homeless individuals in Portland, OR. The average annual cost per individual was $42,075. Hospitalizations associated with health care, mental illness, and substance abuse accounted for 90% of the total 5-year expenditure of $7,363,214. The average annual cost per person found by Moore is similar to the findings of Culhane,

Metraux, and Hadley (2001). Their study of a similar population in New York City found the approximate annual cost of major services to be $40,500.

Salit et al. (1998) compared 18,864 homeless adults hospitalized in New York City in 1992 and 1993 to 383,986 low-income adults admitted for non-maternity reasons during the same time period. They found that homeless adults remained in the hospital 36% longer, which was partially attributed to the difficulty of finding appropriate discharge placements. In 80.6% of the admissions of homeless adults, substance abuse or mental illness was a primary or secondary diagnosis, double the rate for non-homeless, low-income adults in the study. The authors called for the development of supportive and low-cost housing options.

Culhane, Metraux, and Hadley (2002) found that placement in supportive housing (described further) reduced the number of days spent in inpatient psychiatric hospitals by 61% and public (non-psychiatric) hospitals by 21%. Similarly, Perlman and Parvensky (2006) found an 80% reduction of inpatient hospitalization nights associated with the placement of chronically homeless individuals in supportive housing.

## Transitional Housing

Transitional housing programs enable homeless individuals and families to move into a more stable housing situation for up to 24 months. During this time period, clients can address issues associated with their prior homelessness including substance abuse, mental health problems, poor credit/rental histories, employment, and other personal and situational impediments to permanent housing. Transitional housing programs are typically smaller and more focused on client rehabilitation, behavior change, and resource linkage than emergency shelters (Levinson, 2004). Crook (2001) found that residents reported more positive experiences in transitional housing programs that evidenced greater indigenous participatory leadership, decreased bureaucratic control, and higher levels of personalized interaction with residents.

HUD funds transitional housing programs through its Supportive Housing Program (HUD, 2008). These programs are designed to facilitate the movement of previously homeless clients to permanent housing by providing support services including home furnishings, childcare, and job training. Wong et al. (2006) found transitional housing programs had more selective admissions policies and consequently may serve clients evidencing higher levels of functioning. As a condition of continued stay, transitional housing residents are commonly required to participate in the program's services and training opportunities.

## Permanent Supportive Housing

HUD-funded permanent supportive housing (PSH) is intended to provide housing and appropriate support services for homeless individuals with disabilities including mental illness, physical disabilities, substance abuse problems, or AIDS and associated illnesses (HUD, 2002). Wong et al. (2006) point out that "support" is the critical distinguishing feature of PSH as it enables individuals with significant disabling conditions to acquire and retain housing. Martinez and Burt (2006) report that for a sample of 236 single adults, PSH residents had significantly fewer emergency room visits, lower per-person rates of emergency room visits, reduced rates of psychiatric hospitalization, and fewer psychiatric hospitalizations per person.

Wong et al. (2006) found that whereas up to 30% of emergency shelters and transitional housing programs serve families, 61% of permanent supportive housing programs serve only single adults. Further, these authors found that permanent supportive housing programs typically provide more privacy to clients, were more accepting of behavioral problems, and were more lenient in regards to length of stay and program requirements.

One emerging manifestation of permanent supportive housing is the Housing First model. Housing First is an evidence-based approach to providing permanent, independent housing to homeless individuals with mental illness, co-occurring substance abuse, or other health problems by removing barriers to housing entry. For instance, Housing First programs typically do not require sobriety and treatment compliance as prerequisites to housing placement (Stefancic & Tsemberis, 2007). Promotion of consumer choice, recovery, and community integration are goals of Housing First programs. Tsemberis, Gulcur, and Nakae (2004) conducted a study of 225 homeless individuals with a history of mental illness and substance abuse who were randomly assigned to either a control or experimental group. For the control group, the provision of housing was dependent on achieving sobriety and participating in treatment, whereas the experiment group was immediately provided housing without expectation of sobriety or treatment participation. The study participants were interviewed every 6 months over the course of 24 months. Participants in the experimental group had a significantly higher rate of rate of obtaining housing and remaining housed compared to the control group. There was no significant difference in alcohol and drug use between the two groups despite the fact that the control group had a significantly higher use of substance abuse treatment programs. Further, there was no significant difference in psychiatric symptoms between the two groups.

## Permanent Housing

*Permanent housing* refers to a house or apartment owned or rented by an individual or family or some other non-transitory living arrangement. For instance, an adult living in the home of his or her parents, without the expectation of finding another housing arrangement, might be said to have permanent housing. For our purposes, permanent housing is distinguished from permanent supportive housing by the absence of formal supportive services provided to the occupant to assist him or her in retaining permanent housing.

Not all homeless individuals need or require supportive services to leave homelessness and remain housed. This may be particularly true for individuals and families with longer histories of stable housing, who then lose their housing owing to economic conditions and transient disruptions such as domestic violence. For these individuals and families, especially those who are first-time homeless, remediation conditions and risk factors that produced the episode of homelessness can be sufficient to facilitate resumption of permanent housing (Shin et al., 1998; Wood, Valdez, Hayashi, & Shen, 1990).

## CONCLUSION

In the United States, the efforts to prevent, remediate, and end homelessness extend from local governmental and faith-based endeavors offering food, clothing, employment, and housing to state and federal initiatives to coordinate care and provide suitable housing. The present-day national economic crisis is constraining the financial and material resources available to respond to homelessness while simultaneously increasing the number of individuals at risk of becoming homeless. Efficacious responses to homelessness require an appreciation of the complexity of homelessness; its multiple, interacting causes; diverse manifestations; variable duration; and costly financial and social consequences.

The ecological model of homelessness presented here attempts to represent the domains and complexity of this tragically persistent social phenomenon. Our ecological model, represented in Figure 9.1, is a conceptual map depicting the relationships and interactions between the constituent elements of the model. Scientist and philosopher Alfred Korzybski famously said, "The map is not the territory." This insight is especially germane to the map presented in Figure 9.1. No set of lines can portray the territory of the experienced realities of homelessness, its precursors, and its consequences. Instead, this ecological model of homelessness and its explication in this article is our effort to distill a large body of social science literature into a coherent and cogent map to guide individuals, agencies, and communities in their efforts to prevent and redress homelessness.

## References


American Civil Liberties Union. (2004). *Domestic Violence and Homelessness*. Retrieved January 9, 2009, from http://www.aclu.org.

American Civil Liberties Union. (2008). Housing discrimination and domestic violence. Women's Rights Project. New York: ACLU. Retrieved January 9, 2009, from http://www.aclu.org/pdfs/womensrights/discrimination_housing_ 2008.pdf.

Anderson, D. G., & Rayens, M. K. (2004). Factors influencing homelessness in women. *Public Health Nursing, 21*(1), 12–23.

Anti Discrimination Center of Metro New York. (2005). *Adding insult to injury: Housing discrimination against survivors of domestic violence*. Retrieved December, 12, 2008, from http://www.antibiaslaw.com/dvreport.pdf.

Aron, L., and Sharkey, P. (2002). *The 1996 National Survey of Homeless Assistance Providers and Clients: Faith-based and secular non-profit programs*. Retrieved January 9, 2009, www.urban.org/url.cfm?IDD410496.

Bagley, C., & Young, L. (1987). Juvenile prostitution and child sexual abuse: A controlled study. *Canadian Journal of Community Mental Health, 16*, 5–26.

Banyard, V., & Graham-Bermann, S. (1998). Surviving poverty: Stress coping in the lives of housed and homeless mothers. *American Journal of Orthopsychiatry, 68*(3), 261–166.

Barber, J. G. (1994). Working with resistant drug abusers, *Social Work, 40*, 17–23.

Baron, J. (2004). The "No Property" problem: Understanding poverty by understanding wealth. *Michigan Law Review, 102*, 1000–1023.

Barrow, S. M., Herman, D. B., Cordova, P., & Struening, E. L. (1999). Mortality among homeless shelter residents in New York City. *American Journal of Public Health, 89*(4), 529–534.

Bassuk, E. L., Buckner, J. C., Perloff, J. N., & Bassuk, S. S. (1998). Prevalence of mental health and substance use disorders among homeless and low-income housed mothers. *American Journal of Psychiatry, 155*, 1561–1564.

Bassuk, E. L., Buckner, J. C., Weinreb, L. F., Browne, A., Bassuk, S. S., et al. (1997). Homelessness in female-headed families: Childhood and adult risk and protective factors. *American Journal of Public Health, 87*(2), 241–248.

Bassuk, E. L., Dawson R. Perloff, S., & Weinreb, L. (2001) Post-traumatic stress disorder in extremely poor women: Implications for health care clinicians. *Journal of American Medical Women's Association, 56*(2), 79–85.

Bassuk, E. L., Rubin L., & Lauriat, A. (1984). Is homelessness a mental health problem? *American Journal of Psychiatry, 141*, 1546–1550.

Baum, A. S., & Burnes, D. W. (1993). Facing the facts about homelessness. *Public Welfare, 51*(2), 20–27.

Bazelon Center for Mental Health Law. (2008). *Individuals with mental illness in jail and prison*. Retrieved November 22, 2008, from http://www.bazelon.org/issues/criminalization/factsheets/criminal3.html.

Belcher, J. R. (1988). Are jails replacing the mental health system for the homeless mentally ill? *Community Mental Health Journal, 24*, 185–195.

Belcher, J., & Toomey, B. (1988). Relationship between the deinstitutionalization model, psychiatric disability, and homelessness. *Health and Social Work, 13*, 145–153.

Benda, B., Rodell, D., & Rodell, L. (2003a). Crime among homeless military veterans who abuse substances. *Psychiatric Rehabilitation Journal, 26*(4), 32–345.

Benda, B., Rodell, D., & Rodell, L. (2003b). Homeless alcohol/other drug abusers: Discriminators of non-offenders, nuisance offenders and felony offenders. *Alcoholism Treatment Quarterly, 21*(3), 59–80.

Benson, M., & Fox, G. (2004). When violence hits home: How economics and neighborhood plays a role. *Research in Brief.* Washington, DC: National Institute of Justice.

Berger, P. S., & Tremblay, K. R. (1999). Welfare reform's impact on homelessness. *Journal of Social Distress and the Homeless, 8*, 1–20.

Breakey, W., Fischer, P., Kramer, M., Nestadt, G., Romanoski, J., et al. (1989). Health and mental health problems of homeless men and women in Baltimore. *Journal American Medical Association, 262*(10), 1352–1357.

Brown, J., Shepard, D., Martin, T. & Orwat, J. (2007). *The economic cost of domestic hunger: Estimated annual burden to the United States.* An Analysis Commissioned by the Sodexho Foundation in Partnership with the Public Welfare Foundation and Spunk Fund, Inc. Retrieved January 9, 2009, from http:www.sodexhofoundation.org/hunger.

Browne, A. (1998). Responding to the needs of low income and homeless women who are survivors of family violence. *Journal of American Medical Women's Association, 53*(2), 57–64.

Browne, A., & Bassuk, S. (1997). Intimate violence in the lives of homeless and poor housed women: Prevalence and patterns in an ethically diverse sample. *American Journal of Orthopsychiatry, 67*(2), 261–278.

Bufkin, J., & Bray, J. (1998). Domestic violence, criminal justice responses and homelessness: Finding the connection and addressing the problem. *Journal of Social Distress and the Homeless, 7*(4), 227–240.

Burt, M. (2001). *What will it take to end homelessness?* Washington, DC: Urban Institute. Retrieved January 9, 2009, from http://www.urban.org/publications/310305.htm.

Burt, M. (2007, June 19). *Understanding homeless youth: Numbers, characteristics, multi-system involvement, and intervention options. Testimony before the United States House Committee on Ways and Means: Sub-Committee on Income Security and Family Support*. Washington, DC: Urban Institute. Retrieved January 9, 2009, from http://www.urban.org/uploadedPDF/.901087_Burt_Homeless.PDF.

Burt, M. R. (1992). *Over the edge*. New York: Russell Sage.

Burt, M. R. (1996). Homelessness: Definitions and counts. In J. Baumohl (Ed.), *Homelessness in America: A statistical handbook and resource guide* (pp. 15–23). Phoenix, AZ: The Oryx Press.

Burt, M. R., Aron, L. Y., Douglas, T., Valente, J., Lee, E., et al. (1999). *Homelessness: Programs and the people they serve*. Washington, DC: Urban Institute.

Burt, M. R., Hedderson, J., Sweig, J., Oritz, M. J., Aron-Turnham, L., et al. (2004). *Strategies for reducing chronic street homelessness*. Washington, DC: United States Department of Housing and Urban Development.

Burt, M., & Cohen, B. E. (1993). *America's homeless*. Washington, D.C.: Urban Institute.

Burt, M., Aron, L., Lee, E., & Valente, J. (2001). *Helping America's homeless: Emergency shelter or affordable housing?* Washington, DC: Urban Institute Press.

Butler, J., Okuyemi, K. S., Jean, S., Nazir, N., Ahluwalia, J. S., et al. (2002). Smoking patterns of a homeless population. *Substance Abuse, 23*(4), 223–231.

Butler, S. S. (1997). Homelessness among AFDC families in a rural state: It is bound to get worse AFFILIA. *Journal of Women and Social Work, 12*(4), 427–451.

Callicutt, J. W. (2006). Homeless shelters: An uneasy component of the de facto mental health system. In J. Rosenberg and S. Rosenberg (Eds.), *community mental health: Challenges of the 21st century* (pp. 169–180). New York: Routledge.

Calsyn R., & Roades, L., (2006). Predictors of past and current homelessness. *Journal of Community Psychology, 22*(3), 272–278.

Calsyn, R. J., & Winter, J. P. (2002). Social support, psychiatric symptoms, and housing: A causal analysis. *Journal of Community Psychology, 30*(3), 247–259.

Caton, C. L. M., Shrout, P. E., Dominquez, B. D., Eagle, P. F., Opler, L. A., et al. (1995). Risk factors for homelessness among women with schizophrenia. *American Journal of Public Health, 85*(8), 1153–1156.

Caton, C. L., Dominguez, B., Schanzer, B., Hasin, D. S., Shrout, P. E., et al. (2004). Maltreatment and victimization in homeless adolescents: Out of the frying pan and into the fire. *The Prevention Researcher, 11*(1), 12–14.

Cauce, A., Paradise, M., Ginzler J., Embryl, L. Morgan C., et al. (2000). The characteristics and mental health of homeless adolescents. *Journal of Emotional and Behavioral Disorders, 8*(4), 230–239.

Cauce, A., Tyler, K., & Whitbeck, L. (2004). Maltreatment and victimization in homeless adolescents: Out of the frying pan and into the fire. *The Prevention Researcher, 11*(1), 12–14.

Centers for Disease Control and Prevention. (n.d.). *National Center for Health Statistics. National Health Interview Survey Data*. Retrieved October 16, 2008, from http://www.cdc.gov/nchs/data/nhsr/nhsr007.pdf.

Cheung, A., & Hwang, S. (2004). Risk of death among homeless women: A cohort study and review of the literature. *Canadian Medical Association Journal, 170*(8), 1243–1247.

Cho, R. (2008 March). *Overlap and interaction of homelessness and incarceration: A review of research and practice*. Baltimore: NAHC Research Summit.

Christensen, R. C., & Garces, L. K. (2006). Where is the research on homeless persons and suicide? *Psychiatric Services, 5*, 447.

Cnaan, R. A., & Handy, F. (2000). Comparing neighbors: Social service provision by religious congregations in Ontario and the United States. *The American Review of Canadian Studies, 30*(4), 521–543.

Cochran, B., Stewart, A., Ginzler, J., & Cauce, A. (2002). Challenges faced by homeless sexual minorities: Comparison of gay, lesbian, bisexual, and transgender homeless adolescents with their heterosexual counterparts. *American Journal of Public Health, 92*(5), 773–777.

Cohen, C. (1999). Aging and homelessness. *The Gerontologist, 39*(1), 5–14.

Coolen, H. (2006). The meaning of dwellings: An ecological perspective. *Housing, Theory and Society, 23*(4), 185–201.

Copeland, L., & Jones, C. (2005, August 15). Atlanta puts heat on panhandlers. *USA Today*, p. A3.

Cousineau, M. R. (1997). Health status of and access to health services by residents of urban encampments in Los Angeles. *Journal of Health Care for the Poor and Underserved, 8*, 70–82.

Crook, W. P. (2001). Trickle-down bureaucracy: Does the organization affect client responses to programs? *Administration in Social Work, 26*(1), 37–59.

Culhane, D. P. Metraux, S., & Hadley, T. (2000). Public service reductions associated with placement of homeless persons with severe mental illness in supportive housing. *Housing Policy Debates, 13*(1), 107–163.

Culhane, D., Metraux, S., & Hadley, T. (2001). *The New York/New York agreement cost study: The impact of supportive housing on services use for homeless mentally ill individuals*. New York: Corporation for Supportive Housing.

Daskal, J. (1998). *In search of shelter: The growing shortage of affordable rental housing*. Washington, DC: Center on Budget and Policy Priorities.

DiBlasio, F. A., & Belcher, J. R. (1995). Gender differences among homeless persons: Special services for women. *American Journal of Orthopsychiatry, 65*, 131–137.

Dolbeare, C. (1996). Housing policy: A general consideration in homelessness in America. In J. Baumohl (Ed.), *Homelessness in America* (pp. 34–45), Washington DC: Oryx Press.

Dunford, J. V., Castillo, E. M., Chan, T. C., Vike, G. M., Jenson, P., et al. (2006). Impact of the San Diego Serial Inebriate Program on use of emergency medical resources. *Annals of Emergency Medicine, 47*(4), 328–336.

Dunlap, K. M., & Fogel, S. J. (1998). A preliminary analysis of research of recovery from homelessness. *Journal of Social Distress and the Homeless, 7*(3), 175–188.

Economic Policy Institute. (2005). *Minimum wage: Facts at a glance*. Retrieved January 9, 2009, from www.epinet.org.

Erie Times. (2008, September 22). *Church sued for housing homeless*. Retrieved October 7, 2008, from http://www.goerie.com/apps/pbcs.d11/article?Date D20080922.

Families USA. (2001). *Losing health insurance: The unintended consequences of welfare reform*. Washington, DC: Author.

Farr, R., Koegel, P., & Burnam, A. (1986). *A survey of homelessness and mental illness and the skid row area of Los Angeles*. Los Angeles: Los Angeles County Department of Mental Health.

Federal Task Force on Homelessness and Severe Mental Illness. (1992). *Outcasts on mainstreet: A report on the task force on homeless and severe mental illness*. Washington, DC: Interagency Council on the Homeless.

Ferguson, K. M. (2007). Implementing a social enterprise intervention with homeless, street-dwelling youth in Los Angeles. *Social Work, 52*(1), 103–112.

Fisher, P., & Breakey, W. (1991). The epidemiology of alcohol, drug, and mental disorders among homeless persons. *American Psychologist, 46*(11), 1115–1128.

Folsom, D., Hawthorne, W., Lindamer, L., Gilmer, T., Bailey, A., et al. (2005). Prevalence and risk factors for homelessness and utilization of mental health services among 10,340 patients with serious mental illness in a large public mental health system. *The American Journal of Psychiatry, 162*, 370–376.

Gamache, G., Rosenheck, R., & Tessler, R. (2003). Overrepresentation of women veterans among homeless women. *Journal of Public Health, 93*, 1132–1137.

Goering, P., Tolomiczenko, G., Sheldon, T., Boydell, K., & Wasylenki, D. (2002). Characteristics of persons who are homeless for the first time. *Psychiatric Services, 53*, 1472–1474.

Greenberg, G. A., & Rosenheck, R. A. (2008). Homelessness in the state and federal prison population. *Criminal Behavior and Mental Health, 18*, 88–103.

Greenberg, G. A., & Rosenheck, R. A. (2008). Jail incarceration, homelessness, and mental health: A national study psychiatric services. *Criminal Behavior and Mental Health, 59*, 170–177.

Greenblatt, M., & Robertson, M. J. (1993). Life-styles, adaptive strategies, and sexual behavior of homeless adolescents. *Hospital and Community Psychiatry, 44*, 1177–1180.

Greene, J. M., Ennett, S., & Ringwalt, C. L. (1999). Prevalence and correlates of survival sex among runaway and homeless youth. *American Journal of Public Health, 89*(9), 1406–1409.

Gutov, R. N., & Nikiforov, A. (2004). Homelessness and trends in its development. *Sociological Research, 43*(3), 67–74.

Gwadz, M., Nish, D. Leonard, N., & Strauss, S. (2007). Gender differences in traumatic events and rates of post-traumatic stress disorder among homeless youth. *Journal of Adolescence, 30*, 117–129.

Hahn, J., Kushel, M., Bangsberg, D., Riley, E., & Moss, A. (2006). The aging of the homeless populations: Fourteen year trends in San Francisco. *Journal of General Internal Medicine, 21*(7), 775–778.

Hartwell, S. W. (2003, August). *Persons with mental illness and substance abuse problems in the criminal justice system*. Paper presented at the annual meeting of the American Sociological Association, Atlanta, GA. Retrieved August 1, 2008, from http://www.allacademic.com/meta/p107302_Index.html.

HCH Clinicians' Network. (2000). Mental illness & chronic homelessness: An American disgrace. *Healing Hands, 4*(5), 1–2. Retrieved February 5, 2009, from http://www.nhchc.org/Network/HealingHands/2000/October2000HealingHands.pdf.

HCH Clinician's Network. (2004). *Keeping homeless people out of the justice system*. Nashville, TN: Healing Hands. 8(6). Available: http://nhchc.org2004.

Herman, D., Susser, E., Struening, E., & Link, B. (1997). Adverse childhood experiences: Are they risk factors for adult homelessness? *American Journal of Public Health, 87*(2), 249–255.

Heslin, K. (2004). *Neighborhood characteristics and violence against homeless women: A multi-level analysis in Los Angeles County*. Paper presented at the annual meeting of the American Sociological Association. Retrieved January 9, 2009, from http://www.allacademic.com/meta/p mla apa research citation/1/1/0/2/9/p110293_index.html.

Hibbs, J., Benner, L., Klugman, L., Spencer, R., Macchia, I., et al. (1994). Mortality in a cohort of homeless adults in Philadelphia. *New England Journal of Medicine, 331*(5), 304–309.

Hiday, V., Swartz, M., Swanson, J., Borum, R., & Wagner, H. (1999). Criminal victimization of persons with severe mental illness. *Psychiatric Services, 50*, 62–68.

Himmelstein, D., Warren, E., & Woolhandler, S. (2005). Illness and injury as contributors to bankruptcy. *Health Affairs*: The Policy Journal of the Health Sphere. Retrieved January 19, 2009, from http://www.healthaffairs.org/or http://ssrn. com/abstractD664565.

Hoback, A., & Anderson, S. (2006). *proposed method for estimating local populations of precariously housed*. National Coalition for the Homeless. Retrieved January 9, 2009, from http://www.nationalhomeless.org/housing/Hobackreport.pdf.

Homes for the Homeless. (2000). The other America: Homeless families in the shadow of the new economy. *Homes for the Homeless & Institute for Children and Poverty*, 3. Retrieved November 5, 2008, from http:www.homeforthehome less.com.

Human Rights and Equal Opportunity Commission. (2008). *Homelessness is a human rights issue*. Retrieved January 9, 2009, from http://www.hreoc.gov.au/human_rights/housing/homeless_2008.html.

Hwang, S. (2000). Mortality among men using homeless shelters in Toronto, Ontario. *Journal of the American Medical Association, 283*(16), 2152–2157.

Hwang, S. (2001). Homelessness and health. *Canadian Medical Association Journal, 164*(2), 229–233.

Hwang, S. (2004). Homeless people's trust and interactions with police and paramedics. *Journal of Urban Health, 81*(4), 596–605.

Hwang, S., Orav, E., O'Connell, J., Lebow, J., & Brennan, T. (1997). Causes of death in homeless adults in Boston. *Annals of Internal Medicine, 126*(8), 625–628.

Hyde, J. (2005). From home to street: Understanding young people's transitions into homelessness. *Journal of Adolescence, 28*(2), 171–183.

Institute for Children and Poverty. (2001). A shelter is not a home: Or is it? Retrieved January 9, 2009, from www.homesforthehomeless.com.

Institute for Children and Poverty. (2003). Miles to go: The flip side of the McKinney–Vento Homeless Assistance Act. Retrieved January 9, 2009, from www.homesforthehomeless.com.

Institute for Women's Policy Research. (1997). Domestic violence and welfare receipt. *Welfare Reform Network News, 4*.

Interagency Council on the Homeless. (1992). *Implementation of actions for the federal plan to help end homelessness*. Washington, DC: Author.

Interagency Council on the Homeless. (1994). *Priority: Home! The federal plan to break the cycle of homelessness*. Washington, DC: Author.

Interagency Council on the Homeless. (1999). *Homelessness: Programs and the people they serve*. Washington, DC: Author.

Jansson, B., & Smith, S. (1996). Articulating a "new nationalism in American policy." *Social Work, 41*, 441–450.

Jencks, C. (1992). *Rethinking social policy*. Cambridge, MA: Harvard University Press.

Jencks, C. (1994). *The homeless*. Cambridge, MA: Harvard University Press.

Johnson, R., Rew, L., & Sternglanz, R. (2006). The relationship between childhood sexual abuse and sexual health practices of homeless adolescent. *Adolescence, 41*(162), 221–234.

Johnson, T., Freels, S., Parsons, S., & Vangeest, J. (1997). Substance abuse and homelessness: Social selection or social adaptation? *Addiction, 92*(4), 437–446.

Khadduri, J., Culhane, D. P., Holin, M., Buron, L., Cortes, A., et al. (2007). *The first annual homeless assessment report to congress*. Retrieved September 10, 2008, from http://www.huduser.org/Publications/pdf/ahar.pdf.

Kim, T. W., Kertesz, S., Horton, N., Tibbetts, N., & Samet, J. (2006). Episodic homelessness and health care utilization in a prospective cohort of HIV-infected persons with alcohol problems. *BioMed Central Health Services Research, 6*(19). Retrieved October 27, 2006, from http://www.biomedcentral.com/1472-6963/6/19.

Kimball, C., & Golding, J. (2004). Adolescent maltreatment: An overview of the research. *The Prevention Researcher, 11*(1), 3–6.

Kingree, J., Stephens, T., Braithwaite, R., & Griffin, J. (1999). Predictors of homelessness among participants in a substance abuse treatment program. *American Journal of Orthopsychiatry, 69*(2), 261–166.

Koegel, P., & Burnam, M. A. (1992). Issues in the assessment of mental disorders among the homeless: An empirical approach. In M. J. Robertson & M. Greenblatt (Eds.), *Homelessness: The national perspective*. New York: Plenum.

Koegel, P., Burnam, M., & Farr, R. (1988). The prevalence of specific psychiatric disorders among homeless individuals in the inner city of Los Angeles. *Archives of General Psychiatry, 45*(12), 1085–1092.

Koegel, P., Melamid, E., & Burnam, A. (1995). Childhood risk factors for homelessness among homeless adults. *American Journal of Public Health, 85*(12), 1642–1649.

Kuhn, R., & Culhane, D. (1998). Applying cluster analysis to test a typology of homelessness by pattern of shelter utilization: Results from the analysis of administrative data. *American Journal of Community Psychology, 26*, 207–232.

Kushel, M., Evans, J., Perry, S. Robertson, M., & Moss, A. (2003). No door to lock: Victimization among homeless and marginally housed persons. *Archives of Internal Medicine, 163*, 2492–2499.

Kushel, M., Perry, S., Bangsberg, D., Clark, R., & Moss, A. (2002). Emergency department use among the homeless and marginally housed: Results from a community-based study. *American Journal of Public Health, 92*(5), 778–784.

Kushel, M., Vittinghoff, E., & Haas, J. (2001). Factors associated with the health care utilization of homeless persons. *Journal of the American Medical Association, 285*(2), 200–206.

Lam, J., & Rosenheck, R. (1999). Street outreach for homeless persons with serious mental illness: Is it effective? *Medical Care, 37*(9), 894–907.

Lankenau, S. E. (1999). Stronger than dirt: Public humiliation and status enhancement among panhandlers. *Journal of Contemporary Ethnography, 28*(3), 288–318.

Larsen, L., Poortinga, E., & Hurdle, D. E. (2004). Sleeping rough: Exploring the differences between shelter-using in non-shelter-using homeless individuals. *Environment and Behavior, 36*(4), 578–591.

Lee, B., & Farrell, C. (2003). Buddy, can you spare a dime? Homeless, panhandling, and the public. *Urban Affairs Review, 39*(3), 299–324.

Lee, B., & Schreck, C. (2005). Danger on the streets. *American Behavioral Scientist, 48*(8), 1055–1081.

Lehman, A., & Cordray, D. (1993). Prevalence of alcohol, drug, and mental disorders among the homeless: One more time. *Contemporary Drug Problems, 20*(3) 355–383.

Letiecq, B., Anderson, E., & Koblinsky, S. (1998). Social support of the homeless and housed mothers: A comparison of temporary and permanent housing arrangements. *Family Relations, 47*(4), 415–421.

Levinson, D. (2004). *Encyclopedia of homelessness*. Thousand Oaks, CA: Sage Publications.

Levy, B., & O'Connell, J. (2004). Health care for homeless persons. *The New England Journal of Medicine, 350*(23), 2329–2332.

Lindhorst, T., Oxford, M., & Gillmore, M. (2007). Longitudinal effects of domestic violence on employment and welfare outcomes. *Journal of Interpersonal Violence, 22*(7), 812–828.

Link, B., Schwartz, S., Moore, R., Phelan, J., Struening, E., et al. (1995). Public knowledge, attitudes, and beliefs about homeless people: Evidence for compassion fatigue? *American Journal of Community Psychology, 23*(4), 533–555.

Long, D., Rio, J., & Rosen, J. (2007). Employment and income supports for homeless people. Available at http://www.huduser.org/publications/homeless/p11.html.

Lyon–Callo, V. (2001). Making sense of NIMBY: Poverty, power and community opposition to homeless. *City and Society, 13*(2), 183–209.

MacDonald, H. (2002, December 7). Homeless holiday hype. *New York Post*. Retrieved September 23, 2008, from http://www.manhattan_institute.org/html/_nypost_homeless.htm.

MacLean, M., Embry, L., & Cauce, A. (1999). Homeless adolescent's paths to separation from family: Comparison of family characteristics, psychological adjustments, and victimization. *Journal of Community Psychology, 27*(2), 179–187.

Magura, S., Nwakeze, P., Rosenblum, A., & Joseph, H. (2000). Substance misuses and related infectious diseases in a soup kitchen population. *Substance Use and Misuse, 35*(4), 551–583.

Main, T. (1998). How to think about homelessness: Balancing structural and individual causes. *Journal of Social Distress and the Homeless, 7*(1), 41–54.

Mallett, S., Rosenthal, D., & Keys, D. (2005). Young people, drug use and family conflict: Pathways into homelessness. *Journal of Adolescence, 28*(2), 185–199.

Mallory, P. R. (2002, October). *Special report to legislature on Senate resolution 18: Crimes committed against homeless persons*. Sacramento, CA: California Criminal Justice Statistics Center.

Markowitz, F. E. (2006). Psychiatric hospital capacity, homelessness and crime and arrest rates. *Criminology, 44*(1), 43–72.

Martell, D. (1991). The homeless mentally disordered offenders and violent crimes: Preliminary research findings. *Law and Human Behavior, 15*(4), 333–347.

Martijn, C., & Sharpe, L. (2006). Pathways to youth homelessness. *Social Science and Medicine, 62*(1), 1–12.

Martinez, T., & Burt, M. (2006). Impact of permanent supportive housing on the use of acute care health services by homeless adults. *Psychiatric Services, 57*(7), 992–999.

McChesney, K. (1995). A review of the empirical literature on contemporary urban homeless families. *Social Service Review, 69*(3), 429–460.

McClanahan, S. F., McClelland, G. M., Abram, K. M., & Teplin, L. A. (1999). Pathways into prostitution among female jail detainees and their implications for mental health services. *Psychiatric Services, 50*, 1606–1613.

McNiel, D. E., Binder, R. L., & Robinson, J. C. (2005). Incarceration associated with homelessness, mental disorders, and co-occuring substance abuse. *Psychiatric Services, 56*(7), 840–846.

McQuistion, F., Opler, L. A., & Hsu, E. (2005). Risk factors for long-term homelessness: Findings from a longitudinal study of first-time homeless single adults. *American Journal of Public Health, 95*, 1753–1759.

Metraux. S., & Culhane, P. (2006). Recent incarceration history among a sheltered homeless population. *Crime and Delinquency, 52*(3), 504–517.

Miller, P., Donahue, P., Este, D., & Hofer, M. (2004). Experiences of being homeless or risk of being homeless among Canadian youths. *Adolescence, 39*(156), 735–755.

Mishel, L., Bernstein, J., & Schmitt, J. (1999). *The state of working America*: 1998–99. Washington, DC: Economic Policy Institute.

Molnar, B., Buka, S., & Kessler, R. (2001). Child sexual abuse and subsequent psychopathology: Results from the national commodity survey. *American Journal of Public Health, 91*(5), 753–760.

Moore, T. L. (2006). *Estimated cost-saving swallowing enrollment in the Community Engagement Program: Findings from a pilot study of dually diagnosed adults.* Portland, OR: Central City Concern.

Morgan, M. M., Goddard, H. W., & Givens, S. N. (1997). Factors that influence willingness to help the homeless. *Journal of Social Distress and the Homeless, 6*(1), 45–56.

Mueller, D. (2005). *Curbing the demand for prostitution.* Chicago Coalition for the Homeless. Retrieved February 18, 2009, from http://www.chicagohomeless.org.

National Association of State Alcohol and Substance Abuse Directors. (2007). *Report on September 2007 Behavioral Health Information Technology Forum.* Retrieved February 18, 2009, from http://www.nasadad.org/resource.

National Center on Family Homelessness. (2008). *Ending homelessness: The philanthropic role.* Retrieved January 30, 2009, from http://www.nfg.org/publications/ending-homelessness.pdf.

National Center on Family Homelessness. (2008). *Re-engaging philanthropy in the fight to end homelessness.* Retrieved from http://www.familyhomelessness.org.

National Coalition for Homeless Veterans. (2008). *Background and statistics.* Retrieved January 23, 2009, from http://www.nchv.org/background.cfm.

National Coalition for the Homeless and the National Law Center on Homelessness and Poverty. (2006). *A dream denied: The criminalization of homelessness in United States cities.* Washington, DC: Author.

National Coalition for the Homeless. (2004). *Illegal to be homeless: The criminalization of homelessness in the United States.* Retrieved February 18, 2009, from http://www.nationalhomeless.org/publications.

National Coalition for the Homeless. (2005). *Addiction disorders and homelessness, Fact Sheet #6.* Washington, D.C.: National Coalition for the Homeless.

National Coalition for the Homeless. (2007). *Addiction disorders and homelessness.* Retrieved October 15, 2007, from http://www.nationalhomeless.org.

National Coalition for the Homeless. (2007). *Hate, violence, and death on Main Street USA.* Retrieved February 18, 2009, from http://www.nationalhomeless.org.

National Coalition for the Homeless. (2007, September). *Who is homeless?* Retrieved June 17, 2008, from http://www.nationalhomeless.org.

National Coalition for the Homeless. (2008). *How many people experience homelessness?* Retrieved February 18, 2009, from http://www.nationalhomelessness.org.

National Coalition for the Homeless. (2009). *Why are people homeless?* Retrieved August 1, 2009 from, http://www.nationalhomeless.org/publications.

National Health Care for the Homeless Council. (2005). *Addiction: mental health and homelessness.* Retrieved February 18, 2009, from http://www.nhchc.org.

National Health Care for the Homeless Council. (2008). *The basics of homelessness.* Nashville, TN: Author. Retrieved January 15, 2009, from http://www.nhchc.org/publications/basics-of-homelessness.html.

National Health Care for the Homeless Council [NHCHC]. (1997). SSI/SSDI study. *Healing Hands, 1*(6).

National Law Center on Homelessness and Poverty. (1996). *Mean sweeps: A report on anti-homeless laws, litigation, and alternatives in 50 United States cities.* Retrieved January 15, 2009, from http://www.nlchp.org/content/pubs/access delayedaccessdenied3.pdf.

National Law Center on Homelessness and Poverty. (1997). Access delayed, access denied. Washington, DC: Author. Retrieved January 15, 2009, from http://www.nlchp.org/content/pubs.

National Law Center on Homelessness and Poverty. (2004). Homeless in the United States and the human right to housing. Washington, DC: Author.

National Low Income Housing Coalition. (2005). The crisis in American's housing. Retrieved February 18, 2009, from www.nlihc.org.

National Resource and Training Center on Homelessness and Mental Illness. (2003). *Get the facts.* Retrieved February 18, 2009, from www.nrchmi.samhsa.gov.

Nickelson, I. (2004). *The district should use it's upcoming TANF bonus to increase cash benefits and remove barriers to work.* Washington, DC: Fiscal Policy Institute. Retrieved February 18, 2009, from www.dcfpi.org.

Nooe, R. M. (1994). *Homelessness in Knoxville/Knox County, 1994.* Knoxville, TN: Knoxville Coalition for the Homeless.

Nooe, R. M. (2006). *Homelessness in Knoxville-Knox County: A twenty-year perspective, 1986–2006.* Knoxville, TN: Knoxville, East Tennessee Coalition to End Homelessness.

North, C., & Smith, E. M. (1994). Comparison of white and nonwhite homeless men and women. *Social Work, 39,* 639–647.

North, C., Pollio, D., Smith, E., & Spitznagel, E. L. (1998). Correlates of early onset and chronicity of homelessness in a large urban homeless population. *Journal of Nervous and Mental Disorders, 186*(7), 393–400.

Notice of Funding Availability (NOFA) for the Collaborative Initiative to Help End Chronic Homelessness. (2003, January 27). *Federal Register,* 68(17), 4018–4022.

Nyamathi, A., Longshore, D., Keenan, C., Lesser, J., & Leake, B. D. (2001). Childhood predictors of daily substance abuse use in women of different ethnicities. *American Behavioral Scientist, 45*(1), 35–50.

Nyamathi, A., Sands, H., Pattatucci-Aragon, A., Berg, J., & Leake, B. (2004). Tuberculosis knowledge, perceived risk and risk behaviors among homeless adults: Effect of ethnicity and injection drug use. *Journal of Community Health, 29*(6), 483–497.

O'Connell, J. J., Roncarati, J. S., Reilly, E. C., Kane, C. A., Morrison, S. K., et al. (2004). Old and sleeping rough: Elderly homeless persons on the streets of Boston. *Case Management Journals, 5*(2), 101–106.

O'Connell, S. (2004). Dying in the shadows: The challenge of providing health care for homeless people. *The Canadian Medical Association Journal, 170*(8), 1251–1252.

O'Connell, S. (2005). *Premature mortality in homeless populations: A review of the literature.* Nashville, TN: National Health Care for the Homeless Council.

O'Connell, J., Lozier, J., & Gingles, K. (1997). *Increased demand and decreased capacity: Challenges to the McKinney Act's Health Care for the Homeless Program.* Nashville, TN: National Health Care for the Homeless Council.

Oakley, D., & Dennis, D. (1996). *Responding to the needs of homeless people with alcohol, drug, and/or mental disorders in homeless in America.* Washington, DC: Oryx Press.

Page, T., & Nooe, R. M. (2002). Life experiences and vulnerabilities of homeless women: A comparison of women unaccompanied versus accompanied by minor children, and correlates with children's emotional distress. *Journal of Social Distress and the Homeless, 11*(3), 215–231.

Pardeck, J. (2005). An explanation of child maltreatment among homeless families: Implications for family policy. *Early Child Development and Care, 175*(4), 335–342.

Pecora, P., Kessler, R., Williams, J., O'Brien, A., English, D., et al. (2005). *Improving family foster care: Findings from the Northwest Foster Care Alumni Study.* Seattle, WA: Casey Family Programs.

Pennsylvania Coalition Against Rape. (2006). Sexual violence and homelessness. *Technical Assistance Bulletin, 3*(1), 1–2. Retrieved January 30, 2009, from http://www.pcar.org/resources/bulletins/Winter%202006%20TAB.pdf.

Perlman, J., & Parvensky, J. (2006). *Denver housing first collaborative: Cost benefit analysis and program outcomes report.* Denver, CO: Colorado Coalition for the Homeless. Retrieved December 31, 2008, from http://www.shnny.org/documents/FinalDHFCCostStudy.pdf.

Phelan, J., Link, B. G., Moore, R. E., & Stueve, A. (1997). The stigma of homelessness: The impact of the label homeless on attitudes toward poor persons. *Social Psychology Quarterly, 60*(4), 323–337.

Plumb, J. (1997). Homelessness: Care, prevention and public policy. *Annals of Internal Medicine, 126*(12), 973–975.

Polczynski, C. G. (2007). *Homeless shelter hot spots: An analysis of crime around homeless shelters in Orlando.* Paper presented at the annual meeting of the American Society of Criminology, Atlanta, GA.

Preliminary research findings. *Law and Human Behavior, 15*(4), 333–347.

Prigerson, H. G., Desai, R. A., Liu-Mares, W., & Rosenheck, R. A. (2003). Suicidal ideation and suicide attempts in homeless mentally ill persons. *Social Psychiatry and Psychiatric Epidemiology, 38*(4), 213–219.

Proctor, B., & DaLaker, J. (2003). *United States Census Bureau, Current Population Report. Poverty in the United States: 2002* (pp. 60–222). Washington, DC: US Government Printing Office.

Quigley, J., & Raphael, L. (2001). The economics of homelessness: The evidence from North America. *European Journal of Housing Policy, 3*, 323–336.

Rafferty, Y., & Shinn, M. (1991). The impact of homelessness on children. *American Psychologist, 46*(11), 1170–1179.

Ray, N. (2006). *Lesbian, gay, bisexual and transgender youth: An epidemic of homelessness.* New York: National Gay and Lesbian Task Force Policy Institute and the National Coalition for the Homeless.

Rew, L., Fouladi, R., & Yockey, R. (2002). Sexual practices of homeless youth. *Journal of Nursing Scholarships, 34*(2), 139–145.

Rimer, S. (1989, October 25). Pressed on the homeless, subways impose rules. *New York Times*, p. B5.

Rog, D., & Buckner, J. (2007). *Homeless families and children.* Washington, DC: National Symposium on Homeless Research.

Rogers, A. C. (2008). Vulnerability, health and health care. *Journal of Advanced Nursing, 26*(1), 65–72.

Roman, N. P., & Wolfe, P. B. (1997). The relationship between foster care and homelessness. *Public Welfare, 55*(1), 4–9.

Roman, N., & Wolfe, P. (1995). *Web of failure: The relationship between foster care and homelessness*. Washington, DC: National Alliance to End Homelessness.

Rosenheck, R., & Fontana, A. (1994). A model of homelessness among male veterans of the Vietnam War generation. *American Journal of Psychiatry, 151*, 421–427.

Rosenheck, R., Bassuk, E., & Salomon, A. (1998). Special populations of homeless Americans. In L. B. Fosburg & D. L. Dennis (Eds.), *Practical lessons: The 1998 National Symposium on Homelessness*. Washington, DC: United States Department of Housing and Urban Development and United States Department of Health and Human Services. Retrieved August 1, 2008, from: http://aspe.hhs.gov/progsys/homeless/symposium/2-spclpop.htm).

Rosenheck, R., Frisman, L., & Chung, A. M. (1994). The proportion of veterans among homeless men. *American Journal of Public Health, 84*(3), 466–469.

Rosenheck, R., Kasprow, W., Frisman, L., & Liu-Mares, W. (2003). Cost effectiveness of supported housing for homeless persons with mental illness. *Archive of General Psychiatry, 60*(9), 940–951.

Rosenheck, R., Leda, C., Frisman, L., Lam, J., & Chung, A. (1996). Homeless Veterans. In J. Baumohl (Ed), *Homeless in America.* Westport, CT: Oryx Press.

Rossi, P. H. (1989). *Down and out in America.* Chicago: University of Chicago Press.

Saelinger, D. (2006). Nowhere to go: The impacts of city ordinances criminalizing homelessness. *Georgetown Journal on Poverty Law & Policy, 13*(3), 545–566.

Salit, S., Kuhn, E., Hartz, A., Vu, J., & Mosso, A. (1998). Hospitalization costs associated with homelessness in New York City. *The New England Journal of Medicine, 338*(24), 1734–1740.

Schanzer, B., Dominquez, B., Shrout, P., & Caton, C. (2007). Homelessness, health status and health care use. *American Journal of Public Health, 97*(3), 464–465.

Seng, M. (1989). Childhood sexual abuse and adolescent prostitution: A comparative analysis. *Adolescence, 24*, 664–675.

Shinn, M., Weitzman, B. C., Stojanovic, D., Knickman, J. R., Jiménez, L., et al. (1998). Predictors of homelessness among families in New York City: From shelter requests to housing stability. *American Journal of Public Health, 88*(11), 1561–1567.

Shinn, M., Knickman, J., & Weitzman, B. (1991). Social relationships and vulnerability to becoming homeless among poor families. *American Psychologist, 46*(11), 1180–1187.

Silbert, M. H., Pines, A. M., & Lynch, T. (1982). Substance abuse and prostitution. *Journal of Psychoactive Drugs, 14*, 193–197.

Simons, R., & Whitbeck, L. (1991). Sexual abuse as a precursor to prostitution and victimization among adolescent and homeless women. *Journal of Family Issues, 12*(3), 361–379.

Snow, D. A., & Anderson, L. (1993). *Down on their luck*: A study of homeless people. Berkley: University of California Press.

Snow, D. A., Anderson L., Quist, T., & Cress, D. (1996). Material survival strategies on the street: Homeless people or bricoleurs. In J. Baumohl (Ed.), *Homelessness in America* (pp. 86–96). Phoenix: ORYX.

Soloman, P., & Draine, J. (1995). Issues in serving the forensic client. *Social Work, 40*(2), 25–33.

Stark, L. R. (1992). From lemons to lemonade: An ethnographic sketch of late twentieth century panhandling. In P. O. Malley (Ed.), *Homelessness: New England and beyond* (pp. 341–352). Amherst: University of Massachusetts Press.

Steers, S. (2007, January 29). Signs point to decline in Denver panhandling: Business owners credit stricter laws for curbing beggars downtown. *Rocky Mountain News*. Retrieved October 7, 2008, from http://www.rockymountainnews.com.

Stefancic, A., & Tsemberis, S. (2007). Housing first for long-term shelter dwellers with psychiatric disabilities in a suburban county: A four-year study of housing access and retention. *Journal of Primary Prevention*, 283(3/4), 265–279, 1180–1187.

Stegman, M. (1993). *Housing and vacancy report: New York City*. New York: Department of Housing, Preservation and Development.

Stein, J., Leslie, M., & Nyamathi, A. (2002). Relative contributions of parent substance use and childhood maltreatment to chronic homelessness, depression and substance abuse problems among homeless women: Mediating roles of self esteem and abuse in adulthood. *Child Abuse and Neglect, 26*, 1011–1027.

Street Health. (2007). *Street Health Report 2007*. Toronto, Canada: Author. Available: www.streethealth.ca.

Takahashi, L. (1998). *Homelessness, AIDS, and stigmatization: The NIMBY syndrome In the United States at the end of the twentieth century*. Oxford: Clarendon Press.

Talbott, J. A. (1980). Toward a public policy on the chronic mentally ill patient. *American Journal of Orthopsychiatry, 50*(10), 43–53.

Tam, T. W., Zlotnick, C., & Robertson, M. J. (2003). Longitudinal perspective: Adverse childhood events, substance use, and labor force participation among homeless adults. *American Journal of Drug and Alcohol Abuse, 29*(4), 829–846.

Tepper, P. (2006, August 28). Busting the myths on downtown L. A.'s homeless problems. *Los Angeles Business Journal*. Retrieved September 26, 2008, from http://goliath.ecnext.com/coms2/gi_0199-5768042/Busting-the-myths-downtown.html.

Tolman, R., & Rosen, D. (2001). Domestic violence in the lives of women receiving welfare: Mental health, substance dependence, and economic well-being. *Violence Against Women, 7*(2), 141–158.

Tolman, R., Danziger, S., & Rosen, D. (2001). *Domestic violence and economic well-being of current and former welfare recipients.* Retrieved January 25, 2009, from http://www.northwestern.edu/pr/jcpr/workingpapers.

Toro, P. A., & McDonnell, D. M. (1992). Belief, attitudes and knowledge about homelessness: A survey of the general public. *American Journal of Community Psychology, 20*, 53–80.

Toro, P., Bellavia, C., Daeschier, C., Owens, B. J., Wall, D. D., et al. (1995) Distinguishing homelessness from poverty: A comparative study. *Journal of Consulting and Clinical Psychology, 63*, 280–289.

Toro, P., Trickett, E., Wall, D., & Salem, D. (1991) Homelessness in the United States: An ecological perspective. *American Psychologist, 46*(11), 1208–1218.

Torrey, E. F. (1989, August). *Why are there so many homeless mentally ill? The Harvard Medical School Mental Health Letter.* Cambridge: Harvard Medical School.

Tsemberis, S., Gulcur, L., & Nakae, M. (2004). Housing first, consumer choice, and harm reduction for homeless individuals with a dual diagnosis. *American Journal of Public Health, 94*(4), 651–656.

United States Bureau of the Census. (1990). *S-night counts 1990.* Retrieved February 25, 2009, from http://www.census.gov.

United States Bureau of the Census. (2003). *American Community Survey, 2003.* Available at www.census.gov.

United States Bureau of the Census. (2005). *Selected social characteristics in the United States.* Retrieved February 25, 2009, from http://www.census.gov.

United States Bureau of the Census. (2007). *Household income rises, poverty rate declines, number of uninsured up.* Available at http://www.census.gov/PressRelease/www/releases/archives/income_wealth/010583.html.

United States Conference of Mayors. (2004). *Hunger, homelessness still on the rise in major U.S. cities; 25-city survey finds unemployment, lack of affordable housing account for increased needs.* Retrieved March 16, 2004 from http:// www.usmayors.org/uscm/news/press_releases/documents/hunger_121803.

United States Conference of Mayors. (2005). *A status report on hunger and homelessness in American's cities: A 24-city survey (December).* Retrieved February 25, 2009, from http://www.usmayors.org/uscm/home.asp.

United States Conference of Mayors. (2007). *Hunger and homelessness survey.* Retrieved February 25, 2009, from http://usmayors.org/uscm/home.asp.

United States Department of Commerce. (1999). *Poverty in the United States: Current population reports: Consumer income.* Washington, DC: Author.

United States Department of Health and Human Services. (1997). *National evaluation of runaway and homeless youth.* Silver Springs, MD: National Clearing-house on Families and Youth.

United States Department of Housing and Urban Development. (2009). *The 2008 annual homeless assessment report to Congress.* Washington, DC: United States Department of Housing and Urban Development.

United States Department of Housing and Urban Development Office of Policy Development and Research. (2002). *Evaluation of continuums of care for homeless people.* Rockville, MD: United States Department of Housing and Urban Development.

United States Department of Housing and Urban Development. (2008). *ESG Deskguide Section 8: Other Federal Requirements.* Washington, DC: U. S. Department of Housing and Urban Development Homeless Resource Exchange. Retrieved November 4, 2008, from http://www.hudhre.info/index.cfm?doDviewEsgDeskguideSec8#8-7.

United States Department of Labor. (1994). *Employment and training for American's homeless: Report on the job training for the Homeless Demonstration Programs.* Washington, DC: Author.

United States Interagency Council on the Homeless. (1994). *Priority: Home! The federal plan to break the cycle of homelessness.* Washington, DC: Author.

United States Interagency Council on the Homeless. (1999). Homelessness: Programs and the people they serve. Washington, DC: Author.

Urban Dictionary. (2008). Retrieved September 10, 2008, from http://www.urbandictionary.com/.

Wagner, J. K., & Perrine, R. M. (1994). Women at risk for homelessness: Comparison between housed and homeless women. *Psychological Reports, 75*(3), 1671–1678.

Weber, A., Boivin, J., Blais, L., Haley, N., & Roy, E. (2004). Predictors of initiation into prostitution among female street youth. *Journal of Urban Health, 81*(4), 584–595.

Wenzel, S., Leake, B., & Gelberg, L. (2000). Health of homeless women with recent experience of rape. *Journal of General Internal Medicine, 15*(4), 265–268.

Widom, C. S. (1995). *Victims of childhood sexual abuse—later criminal consequences.* Washington, DC: National Institute of Justice, United States Department of Justice.

Wong, Y. I., Hadley, T. R., Culhane, D. P., Poulin, S. R., Davis, M. R., et al. (2006). *Predicting staying in or leaving permanent supportive housing that serves homeless people with serious mental illness.* Rockville, MD: United States Department of Housing and Urban Development Office of Policy Development and Research.

Wong, Y. I., Park, J. M., & Nemon, H. (2006). Homeless service delivery in the context of continuum of care. *Administration in Social Work, 30*(1), 67–94.

Wood, D., Valdez, R. B., Hayashi, T. & Shen, A. (1990). Homeless and housed families in Los Angeles: A study comparing demographic, economic, and family function characteristics. *American Journal of Public Health, 80*(9), 1049–1052.

Wright, J. (1991). Poverty, homelessness, nutrition, and children. In J. H. Kryder-Cole, L. M. Salamon, & J. M. Molnax (Eds.), *Homeless children and youth: A new American dilemma* (pp. 71–104). New Brunswick: Transaction.

Wright, J. D., & Rubin, B. A. (1997). Is homelessness a housing problem? In D. P. Culhane and S. P. Hornburg (eds), *Understanding homelessness: New policy and research perspectives* (pp. 205–224). Washington, DC: Fannie Mae Foundations.

Yates, G., Mackenzie, R., Pennbridge, J., & Cohen, E. (1988). A risk profile comparison of runaway and non-runaway youth. *American Journal of Public Health, 78*(7), 820–821.

Yoder, K., Hoyt, D., & Whitbeck, L. (1998). Suicidal behavior among homeless and runaway adolescents. *Journal of Youth and Adolescence, 27*(6), 753–771.

Ziesemer, C., Marcoux, L., & Maxwell, B. E. (1994). Homeless children: Are they different from other low-income children? *Social Work, 39*, 658–668.

Zlotnick, C., Kronstadt, D., & Klee, L. (1998). Foster care children and family homelessness. *American Journal of Public Health, 88*(9), 1368–1369.

Zorza, J. (1991). Woman battering: A major cause of homelessness. In *Clearinghouse Review 25*(4). Chicago: National Clearinghouse for Legal Services.

Selected Reading

# SERIOUS YOUTH VIOLENCE AND INNOVATIVE PREVENTION

## On the Emerging Link Between Public Health and Criminology

*Brandon C. Welsh, Anthony A. Braga, and Christopher J. Sullivan*

In the early to mid-1990s, "epidemic" became a common modifier attached to "youth violence" (Cook & Laub, 1998). Today, although it is not universally recognized and there are some exceptions, the word "declining" is used far more frequently to describe trends in youth violence (cf. Cook & Laub, 1998, 2002). With a number of plausible explanations for the changing facts on the ground (see, e.g. Blumstein & Wallman, 2006), it is unlikely that this problem could have been so significantly affected without knowledge and effort from multiple fields of science and practice (Dodge, 2001). The migration of public health perspectives to the understanding of crime and justice appears to be part of the process by which this change came about. Whether implicit or explicit, some core ideas and technology from public health have influenced criminologists and practitioners alike in a way that has had a discernable impact on the shared problem of youth violence. With serious youth violence as its focus, this paper surveys the evolving connection between public health and criminology. It is concerned with both research and practice and how these efforts are contributing to improved public health-criminology collaborations or public health-influenced programs that have a discernable impact on youth violence.

## BACKGROUND

In 2001, the first US Surgeon General's report on youth violence was published (US Department of Health & Human Services [USDHHS], 2001). It drew heavily on the work of developmental and criminological research on risk factors. Prior to that, researchers in this area had begun to take a similar approach to under-standing research and policy problems as those in the public health field. This work led to the identification of conditions in individuals, families, communities, and society-at-large that foster violent behavior (Dodge, 2001; Hawkins, Arthur, & Catalano, 1995). Although perhaps more provisional in that literature, this is similar to the notion that certain conditions or behaviors, such as high cholesterol or smoking, increase the chance that an individual will suffer from heart disease later in life. The notion that identified risk factors can point toward targets for intervention and possibly inform its course is now inherent in the response to youth violence problems.

In recent years, the fields of violence prevention and criminology more generally have begun to place a greater emphasis on evidence-based decision-making. In the area of violence prevention and intervention, some of this work has followed the example provided by medical studies that utilize rigorous scientific research (specifically, randomized controlled trials) to establish program efficacy and effectiveness, followed by systematic reviews and meta-analyses of the best available evidence from that original research (Welsh & Farrington, 2011). Although the terminology and contexts are often different, there are a host of implicit links between public health and criminology/criminal justice researchers in terms of their approach to gathering and analyzing information. This is especially true when one considers research focused on preventing youth violence, which rests in part on risk factor and concentrated epidemic frameworks and informs intervention and problem solving research (Shepherd & Farrington, 1993).

Even in locations and populations where there are relatively high rates of risk factors (exposure), there tends to be some concentration of problem outcomes in individuals or subgroups (incidence). Rose (2001) discusses this in terms of distinguishing between causes of cases (i.e. those groups or populations that tend to be at higher risk such as national differences in hypertension) and causes of incidence within that pool (i.e. individual susceptibilities to heart disease). These principles are evident in youth violence as well. Relatively few individuals have been identified as being responsible for the bulk of observed violent behavior (Blumstein, Cohen, Roth, & Visher, 1986; Wolfgang, Figlio, & Sellin, 1972) and they tend to come from populations that are disproportionately exposed to general risk factors. This signals a need to focus on both individual-and group-level risk factors in both violence and disease. Additionally, just as disease can be viewed in a multicausation model, where risk is seen to emanate from several sources (Rothman & Greenland, 2005), violent juveniles tend to have other co-occurring problems and generally face a cumulative package of risks (Farrington & Loeber, 2000). The need to unravel the etiology of the observed problem—in order to develop a sense of the process that gives rise to it—is an essential part of the public health approach (Mercy, Rosenberg, Powell, Broome, & Roper, 1993).

Although both public health and criminology have come to rely on rigorous designs in intervention research (Moore, 1995; Moore, Prothrow-Smith, Guyer, & Spivak, 1994), in some ways the fields have faced similar challenges in sorting out the etiology of problem outcomes and identifying effective responses. In particular, the need to rely on nonexperimental, observational studies in the initial stages of that evidentiary process is apparent. For example, the link between cigarette smoking and disease had to be established via observational, nonintervention studies (Cochran, 1983; Rosenbaum, 1995), and the establishment of risk factors for youth violence has proceeded in a similar fashion (Farrington & Loeber, 2000).

Dodge (2001) draws parallels between the consideration of risk factors in health outcomes and the field of developmental psychopathology, where risk factors for violent behavior are identified and studied. Ideally, this is followed by research on the processes that link intervening mechanisms to problem outcomes. Researchers and officials can then in turn develop a sense of how to effectively intervene with the population that is at risk, using knowledge that emerges from this process—along with evidence of best practices in the area. The Seattle Social Development Project (SSDP) demonstrates this progression in a violence/problem behavior prevention context (Hawkins, Catalano, Kosterman, Abbott, & Hill, 1999; Hawkins, Smith, Hill, Kosterman, & Catalano, 2007). Evidence was drawn from a growing pool of research on risk and protective factors and subsequently used to develop a theory about the developmental process underlying the problem. At the same time, the researchers were engaged in primary and secondary prevention programming in which reductions in violent behavior were an important outcome.

While many crime researchers have embraced the knowledge of risk factors as a starting point for understanding problem outcomes, the approach has also begun to permeate practice. So, just as health practitioners rely on screening practices to evaluate symptoms and identify appropriate courses of treatment, the practice of screening and assessment for risk and needs has become commonplace in the juvenile justice system and other community agencies that have contact with this population (LeBlanc, 1998; Schwalbe, 2008).

While public health research has clearly influenced the understanding of individual at-risk cases and provided a platform against which they could be identified and explained, violence also stems from situational and environmental factors (Farrington & Loeber, 2000), such as the use of alcohol or the availability of weapons. Beginning with the youth gun violence epidemic of the 1990s and continuing through today, collaborations between public health researchers and criminologists have yielded crucial insights on the various pathways through which convicted felons, juveniles, and other prohibited persons illegally acquire firearms. As summarized in recent reviews (e.g. Wintemute & Braga, 2011; Wintemute, Braga, & Kennedy, 2010), among the main findings of these collaborative studies are: (1) New guns are recovered disproportionately in crime. (2) Some licensed firearm retailers are disproportionately frequent sources of crime guns; these retailers are linked to more guns traced by law enforcement agencies than would be expected from their overall volume of gun sales. (3) Under test conditions, significant proportions of licensed retailers and private party gun sellers will knowingly participate in illegal gun sales. (4) On average, about one-third of guns used in crime in any community are acquired in that community, another third come from elsewhere in the same state, and a third are brought from other states. (5) There are longstanding interstate trafficking routes for crime guns, typically from states with weaker gun regulations to states with stronger ones. The best known of these is the "Iron Pipeline" from the Southeast to the mid-Atlantic and New England.

Public health perspectives also point to the importance of identifying and understanding problems as they aggregate across individuals or groups (Moore et al., 1994). Frequently this involves some type of geographic or network-based concentration of violence that is not unlike a localized transmission of disease. For example, Braga, Papachristos, and Hureau (2010) and Morenoff, Sampson, and Raudenbush (2001) studies looking at the geographic concentration of violence in local areas has some parallels with Kerani, Handcock, Handsfield, and Holmes (2005) study of the concentration of four different sexually transmitted diseases in a large county. Localized violence problems have been the subject of a great deal of inquiry and analysis by both academics and police agencies. For example, research on violence hot spots is among the more practically useful contributions of academic criminology to emerge in the last 25 years (Braga & Weisburd, 2010). More recently, sophisticated network analyses of street gangs and high-rate youth offenders suggest that most of the risk of gun violence concentrates in small networks of identifiable individuals and that the risk of homicide and nonfatal gunshot injury is associated not only with individual-level risk factors, but also the contours of one's social network (see, e.g. Papachristos, 2010). The identification and analysis of violence problems with respect to area concentration and underlying networks bears a close correspondence to the idea of the "social epidemiology" of HIV/AIDS, as described by Poundstone, Strathdee, and Celentano (2004).

The underlying etiology of hot spots and their analogs (e.g. repeat offenders and victims) generally points toward the need for a concerted, targeted prevention strategy. In recent decades, a great deal of research on crime has grown out of the practical desire to understand these problems, develop viable interventions, evaluate the results, and disseminate successful strategies (Clarke, 1997; Elliott & Mihalic, 2004). This action-oriented approach is similar to the public health posture towards understanding and intervening in youth violence problems (Mercy et al., 1993). Figure 9.2 presents a well-known public health model of the scientific approach to serious youth violence prevention. The initial stage of the process entails identifying and tracking the problem (e.g. elevated level of violent crime in a neighborhood) by means of some surveillance system. This is followed by an effort to understand the risk factors that contribute to the problem (e.g. actions between rival gangs), and develop an approach to ameliorate the problem and evaluate it. Finally, the prevention strategy may be introduced to other areas that face similar problems.

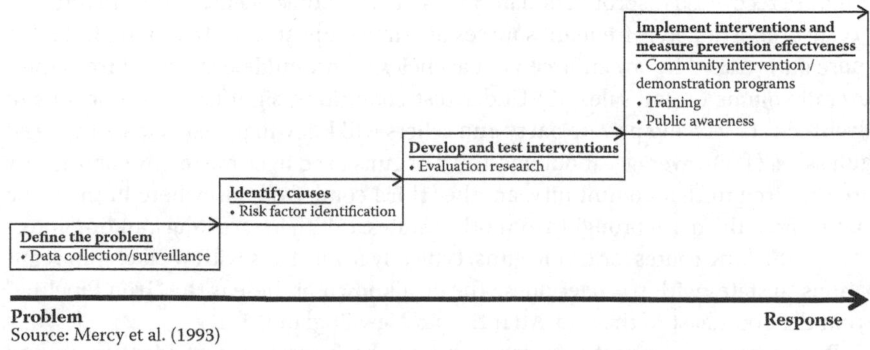


Source: Mercy et al. (1993)

**Figure 9.2** Public health model as a scientific approach to prevention.

Identifying something as a public health problem can mobilize more stakeholders, bringing the possibility of elevated buy-in to the possibility of intervention and potentially leveraging greater financial and human resources. Whereas the orientation of justice practitioners generally trends toward the reactive (Moore et al., 1994), framing the issue in this manner inherently calls for a proactive, multidisciplinary response (Dodge, 2001). Effective prevention strategy is frequently developed by, or in close association with, researchers and generally requires close adherence to an established model (Elliott & Mihalic, 2004; Welsh, Sullivan, & Olds, 2010). So, while the research/practice gap appears to have narrowed somewhat in the justice field, which bodes well for violence prevention, the gap between the ideas of practitioners in the two communities seems to have closed as well—particularly when compared to earlier analyses of the links between them (e.g. Moore et al., 1994). This is most evident in those communities where violence prevention strategies have been implemented and closely evaluated for targeted reductions in serious youth violence (see, e.g. McGarrell, Corsaro, Hipple, & Bynum, 2010).

In the sections that follow, we profile innovative primary, secondary, and tertiary prevention methods to reduce serious youth violence. We do so to illustrate the emerging and, in our view, highly promising link between public health and criminology.

## PRIMARY PREVENTION

A primary focus involves efforts to prevent youth violence well before it occurs; that is, before any signs of it become evident. It aims to positively influence early risk factors for violent offending, including childhood-behavior problems (e.g. aggressiveness and acting out in school), poor child-rearing practices (e.g. poor parental supervision, harsh or inconsistent discipline), and poor school performance or school failure (Farrington & Welsh, 2007). Pediatricians, family physicians, health nurses, and school teachers are among the many providers that are involved in primary prevention of youth violence.

One way that health nurses play a key role in primary prevention is through the provision of family support for new mothers and their children in the form of home visits. One of the main goals of home visits is the prevention of child abuse and neglect. This focus is particularly relevant to criminology, partly because children who are physically abused or neglected have an enhanced likelihood of becoming violent offenders later in life (Maxfield & Widom, 1996).

The best known home-visiting program and the only one with a direct measure of youth violence is the nurse-family partnership (NFP) developed by David Olds (see Olds, Sadler, & Kitzman, 2007). NFP was first tested in Elmira, New York, in the early 1980s. Four hundred first-time mothers were randomly assigned to receive home visits from nurses during pregnancy, or to receive visits both during pregnancy and during the first two years of life, or to a control group who received no visits. Each visit lasted just over 1 h and the mothers were visited on average every 2 weeks. The home visitors gave advice about prenatal and postnatal care of the child, about infant development, and about the importance of proper nutrition and avoiding smoking and drinking during pregnancy.

The results of this experiment showed that the postnatal home visits caused a significant decrease in recorded child physical abuse and neglect during the first two years of life, especially by poor, unmarried, teenage mothers; 4% of visited vs. 19% of nonvisited mothers of this type were guilty of child abuse or neglect (Olds, Henderson, Chamberlin, & Tatelbaum, 1986). In a 15-year follow-up (13 years after program completion), which included 330 mothers and 315 children, significantly fewer experimental compared to control group mothers were identified as perpetrators of child abuse and neglect (29 vs. 54%), and, for the higher risk sample only, significantly fewer treatment mothers, in contrast to the controls, had alcohol or substance abuse problems or were arrested. At the age of 15, children of the treatment mothers had committed significantly fewer violent and other major criminal acts than their control counterparts (a mean of 3.02 compared to 3.57; Olds et al., 1998). In the latest follow-up at age 19, compared to their control counterparts, girls of the full sample of mothers had incurred significantly fewer arrests and convictions and girls of the higher risk mothers had significantly fewer children of their own and less-Medicaid use; few program effects were observed for the boys (Eckenrode et al., 2010). Large-scale replications in Memphis and Denver have also shown a wide range of positive effects for children and mothers (Olds, Sadler, & Kitzman, 2007).

Today, NFP operates in 400 counties in 32 states, serving more than 21,000 families each year. It is also being implemented in many other countries, including Australia, Germany, Norway, and the UK. Crucial to each of these sites and the program's continued expansion is a commitment by local providers to insure fidelity to the model. As programs are implemented in new settings or scaled up for wider public use, there is the very real threat that the program will become diluted and its effectiveness greatly reduced. As a sign of the importance of this concern, a national office was established to work with local providers to make sure that NFP programs are implemented and operated as planned and to help address local needs. This marks a crucial advancement in the local delivery of evidence-based violence prevention programs.

Several recent systematic reviews and meta-analyses on the effects of youth violence prevention (see Derzon, 2006; Hahn et al., 2007; Limbos et al., 2007; Wilson & Lipsey, 2007) have also reported on the effectiveness of primary prevention in schools. Wilson and Lipsey's (2007) meta-analysis of school-based prevention programs included 249 studies, of which 77 were universal or primary prevention. Among the different intervention types (i.e. primary, secondary, special schools/classes, and comprehensive), primary prevention programs were found to be the most effective (along with secondary prevention programs) in reducing aggressive and disruptive behavior, with an overall weighted mean effect size of $d = 0.21$.

One effective school-based primary prevention program is the SSDP, which has drawn heavily on the connection between public health and criminology. As noted above, SSDP is founded upon criminological knowledge of risk and protective factors.

SSDP is a multicomponent program combining parent training, teacher training, and skills training for children. About 500 first grade children (aged 6) in 21 classes were randomly assigned to be in experimental or control classes in the original study. The parents and teachers of children in the experimental classes received instruction in methods of child management and instruction, which were designed to increase children's attachment to their parents and their bonding to school, based on the assumption that delinquency was inhibited by the strength of social bonds. The children also were trained in interpersonal cognitive problem solving. Their parents were trained to notice and reinforce socially desirable behavior in a program called "Catch Them Being Good." Their teachers were trained in classroom management, for example, to establish rules and routines at the beginning of the school year, to provide clear instructions and expectations to children, to reward children for participation in desired behavior, to use methods least disruptive to instruction to maintain order in the classroom, and to teach children prosocial methods of solving problems.

In an evaluation of this program 18 months later, when the children were in different classes, Hawkins, von Cleve, and Catalano (1991) found that the boys who received the program were significantly less aggressive than the control boys, according to teacher ratings. The experimental girls were not significantly less aggressive, but they were less self-destructive, anxious, and depressed. In a later follow-up, when the study participants were 18 years old, Hawkins et al. (1999) found that the full intervention group (those who received the intervention from grades 1–6) reported significantly less violence, less alcohol abuse, and fewer sexual partners than a late intervention group (grades 5–6 only) or the controls. In the latest follow-up, Hawkins, Kosterman, Catalano, Hill, and Abbott (2008) found that the full intervention group (compared to the comparison groups) reported significantly better educational and economic attainment, mental health, and sexual health by age 27 years. Interestingly, no effects were found for substance abuse and criminal activity at ages 24 or 27 years. This loss of effectiveness is unusual, and holds important implications for understanding the transition from adolescence to early adulthood.

Also noteworthy is the innovative and increasingly evidence-based "operating system" approach to violence prevention. This approach brings a dual focus on community mobilization and the use of scientific evidence. One of the best known and tested operating systems designed to prevent violence and other problem behaviors is communities that care (CTC; Hawkins, Catalano, & Arthur, 2002). CTC organizes knowledge of risk and protective factors into a strategy for strengthening protection in any social unit. It is modeled after large-scale community-wide public health programs designed to reduce illnesses such as coronary heart disease by tackling key risk factors in the community (e.g. Perry, Klepp, & Sillers, 1989). Consistent with health promotion approaches (e.g. Kaplan, 2000), there is great emphasis on enhancing protective factors and building strengths. The community could be a city, a small town, or even a neighborhood or public housing community. Violence and other problem behaviors can be prevented by aiding communities in assessing levels of risk and protection faced by their young people and then choosing and implementing prevention strategies that have demonstrated effectiveness. Primary prevention programs are important to this strategy as well as secondary and tertiary programs.

Results from the most recent CTC evaluation, known as the community youth development study (CYDS), point to the effectiveness of this operating system approach. The CYDS involved 24 matched communities across 7 states, which were randomly assigned to either implement the CTC system or to carry out prevention services as usual. In a panel of over 4,400 young people in CTC and control communities followed from grade 5 through grade 8, young people in CTC communities were 25% less likely to have initiated delinquent behavior than controls and 31% less likely to have engaged in a variety of delinquent acts (e.g. assault and theft). Significant reductions in alcohol and tobacco use were also observed in CTC communities compared with controls (Hawkins et al., 2009).

## SECONDARY PREVENTION

Whereas primary prevention is targeted broadly to the population, a secondary prevention focus entails implementation "on a selected scale, for children [or other relevant units] at enhanced risk of youth violence" (USDHHS, 2001, p. 111). These programs are also sometimes designated as "selective" prevention strategies (Farrell & Flannery, 2006). This is congruent with public health models that focus on identifying risk factors for disease in individuals and subsequently attempting to address those at-risk cases in order to forestall the emergence of later problematic outcomes. Early aggressive behavior, ineffective parenting, poor social skills, and exposure to delinquent peers are among the risk factors that might be used to identify possible candidates for secondary prevention efforts directed towards later violent behavior. If successful, these programs would reduce the chances that those youth—who appear to be the members of the population most likely to engage in violence at the point of intervention—actually become involved in violent behavior.

These initiatives tend to be implemented in schools and other community-based social service settings. Like the aforementioned primary prevention initiatives, secondary prevention can also be integrated into medical and public health settings (see Borowsky, Mozayeny, Stuenkel, & Ireland, 2004), but usually with enhancements to target specific risks of the youths and families involved (e.g. social skills training and parent training). Because this is a more selective group than the one targeted in primary prevention, there may be greater opportunity for delivery of intensive and varied services (Fields & McNamara, 2003). Secondary prevention programs still occur relatively early in a youth's development, so evaluators frequently have to consider intermediate outcomes, such as aggressive behavior, that may eventually lead to interpersonal violence. This is also the case in medical and public health interventions where there is a desire to impact "surrogate clinical endpoints," which are intermediary outcomes expected to mediate the effects between the intervention and its long-term target (Ludwig, 2012, p. 34).

Reviews of secondary prevention programs by Fields and McNamara (2003) and Molina, Dulmus, and Sowers (2005) indicated that the majority of interventions show positive effects on violence and related outcomes. In looking at randomized controlled trials, Limbos et al. (2007) identified three successful secondary-level interventions in their systematic review of an array of violence prevention programs. The three programs included the Baltimore Moving to Opportunity experiment, which involved residential relocation of families with children at-risk for violence (see Kling, Ludwig, and Katz (2005) for results from the multisite evaluation; Ludwig, Duncan, & Hirschfield, 2001); a community-based intervention that provided individual counseling and mentoring to youth and their families (Hanlon, Bateman, Simon, O'Grady, & Carswell, 2002); and therapeutic child care aimed at abused, neglected, and at-risk children (Moore, Armsden, & Gogerty, 1998).

The Chicago Child-Parent Center (CPC) program was targeted to black and Hispanic youth from low-income families and neighborhoods. The intervention, which can be characterized as "preschool-plus," comprised educational programming and family support services for children from 3 to 9 (Reynolds, Temple, Robertson, & Mann, 2001). The 25 centers were located in the most distressed areas of Chicago. Evaluations of the program compared CPC participants (Nrv900) to a group of youth matched on age, eligibility for government-funded programs, and family and neighborhood poverty (Nrv500) (Reynolds et al., 2001; Reynolds, Temple, Ou, Arteaga, & White, 2011). The 15-year follow-up study, which focused on educational and justice-related outcomes through age 20, showed that, on average, youth in the treatment group had a significantly lower prevalence of juvenile arrests (17%) relative to comparison cases (25%) (Reynolds et al., 2001). This significant effect was also observed for violent arrests specifically (9 vs. 15%). Positive results were found for official justice contact in a follow-up at age 28 as well (Reynolds et al., 2011).

The Incredible Years Parent, Teacher, and Child training series program is one of only 11 model programs identified by the Blueprints for Violence Prevention group at the University of Colorado (Center for the Study & Prevention of Violence, 2007). This program is selective in that it targets children who display behavior that suggests some level of conduct problems during early to late childhood. The program is delivered in a group training format and comprises elements of cognitive behavioral therapy and self-management principles. An evaluation of the parent training component of the Incredible Years found that youth in the treatment program had significantly lower levels of behavioral problems at the one-year follow-up point compared to baseline (Webster-Stratton, Hollinsworth, & Kolpacoff, 1989). Webster-Stratton and Hammond (1997) compared three Incredible Years treatment groups (Parent Training, Child Training, Parent and Child Training) against a waiting-list control and found that, in all cases, those groups had significantly lower levels of behavioral problems as measured by multiple validated instruments (e.g. Child behavior checklist [CBCL]). The positive intervention effects on behavioral problems, which can be considered an intermediate outcome that has a relationship with later violent offending, generally held at the one year follow-up. A similar pattern of treatment effects emerged when researchers observed children's interactions with their peers. In all three comparisons, the treatment group children exhibited significantly lower levels of negative conflict management with their best friend in a play situation where a potential quarrel was introduced.

The Montreal longitudinal-experimental study is mentioned in multiple reviews of effective secondary prevention initiatives. At-risk males were identified through teacher ratings of disruptive behavior in kindergarten (Tremblay, Pagani-Kurtz, Mâsse, Vitaro, & Pihl, 1995). Youth were also screened based on their ethnicity and parents' level of education. A total of 319 youth were then assigned to experimental and control conditions. The treatment involved multidisciplinary delivery (by trained child care and social workers and a psychologist) of (a) parental training in child rearing practices and (b) social skills development for children. The parental training program included behavioral monitoring and reinforcement practices, effective discipline, and family crisis management techniques. The children were exposed to social skills training in small groups with prosocial peers nominated by teachers; this included 10 sessions covering skills in problem solving and self-management in conflict situations. Specifically, coaching, peer modeling, role playing, and reinforcement on such topics as "how to help," "what to do when you are angry," and "how to react to teasing" were used in small group sessions in a school setting.

The effectiveness of the treatment was evaluated longitudinally (ages 10–15) across several dimensions, including self and teacher reports of problem behavior and juvenile court records. By age 12 (3 years post-treatment), boys in the experimental group were significantly less likely to be involved in fights than the controls (Tremblay et al., 1992). A study with a lengthier follow-up period revealed that youth in the treatment group had somewhat lower levels of teacher-reported disruptive behavior through age 15; the difference was not statistically significant, however. Trends in self-reported general delinquency increased over the follow-up period (consistent with general age trends in delinquent behavior), but the treatment group had significantly lower levels of delinquency than the control group during the 6 years following treatment. Juvenile record data did not show significant differences between the treatment and control groups. A later follow-up (to age 24) found that fewer treatment than control group youth had a criminal record (11%) and the effect was marginally significant (Boisjoli, Vitaro, Lacourse, Barker, & Tremblay, 2007).

A study by Borowsky et al. (2004) focuses on the degree to which medical professionals have increasingly become involved in the prevention of violence and associated injuries. They studied the effectiveness of a primary care-based violence prevention program for youth ages 7–15 that had an elevated score on a brief psychosocial risk screening instrument (Pediatric symptom checklist [PSC]). Eligible youth and their parents ($N$ = 224) were randomly assigned to intervention and control conditions. The intervention consisted of two parts. First, the clinician either saw the PSC screen results or they did not. If they saw the results, the clinician could then engage in appropriate follow-up and make referrals to indicated services (the vast majority of these cases were provided with referral services or additional follow-up). Second, a telephone-based, positive parenting curriculum was offered to the treatment group. The researchers found statistically significant differences between the two groups on parental-reported aggressive and delinquent behaviors (CBCL).

Secondary prevention may be targeted at areas identified on the basis of risk factors as well. For example, in Los Angeles, a business improvement district (BID) intervention was implemented in areas with identified community-ecological risk factors (e.g. physical disorder, concentrated poverty) (MacDonald et al., 2009). Using a nonequivalent matched comparison group ($n$ = 375), a BID intervention, which focused on public safety, area beautification, and promotional marketing, was shown to have a significant impact on some violent crimes (e.g. robbery) in areas in which it was implemented ($n$ = 362). It was also suggested that there was a "dose-response" relationship—as areas considered to have stronger BID interventions experienced greater reductions in violent crime.

As this review shows, in the last few decades, a number of secondary prevention programs, implemented in varied settings based on an array of risk factors, have been identified as effective for children and adolescents. This offers a clear sense that prevention programming can be successful with youth (and areas) already faced with risk factors for later violent behavior if it is properly targeted towards those at-risk and implemented with fidelity to the intervention model (Elliott & Mihalic, 2004). Further, because these cases are already at elevated risk, the potential cost-benefit yield of these interventions may be readily demonstrable in both the short and long term, serving as a useful midpoint between the global focus of primary prevention and the immediate corrective emphasis of tertiary prevention strategies. As Ludwig (2012) has pointed out, although earlier intervention may be recommended on several grounds, there are also reasons that developing and applying prevention (and even remediation) on the basis of observed risk levels may be beneficial. Specifically, looking at economies of scale, more intensive intervention may be provided to individuals or areas at greater risk for later violent behavior for the same cost as providing universal primary prevention.

## TERTIARY PREVENTION

Tertiary prevention involves attempts to minimize the course of a problem once it is already clearly evident and causing harm. In public health terms, tertiary prevention efforts intervene after an illness has been contracted or an injury inflicted, and seeks to minimize the long-term, devastating consequences of the disease or injury (Committee for the Study of the Future of Public Health, 1988). Criminologists and public health researchers have both contributed to a growing body of evaluation evidence that shows a wide range of effective tertiary treatments (e.g. cognitive behavioral therapy, functional family therapy (FFT); Lipsey, 2009). This development has been important and has helped to undergird the movement toward evidence-based violence prevention programs (Greenwood, 2006). Alongside it have developed some strategic innovations launched by criminal justice agencies, which have further established the emerging links between public health and criminology in youth violence prevention. This section begins with an overview of some of the leading evidence-based treatment programs for serious and violent youthful offenders. It then turns to a discussion of strategic innovations in criminal justice.

Greenwood (2006) identified three evidence-based treatment programs for adjudicated delinquents that operate outside of the juvenile justice system (but are often referred through the system): multisystemic therapy (MST), FFT, and multidimensional treatment foster care (MTFC). MST combines family and cognitive-behavioral therapies with a range of support services that are tailored to the needs of individual families. Treatment ingredients typically include parent management and communication skills training and work on establishing collaborative home-school links (Henggeler, Schoenwald, Borduin, Rowland, & Cunningham, 1998). MST has been evaluated under experimental conditions in more than 25 sites across the USA, Canada, and Western Europe. The weight of the evidence suggests that MST is highly effective in reducing aggression, violent offending, and other antisocial behaviors as well as time in custody compared with usual services (Curtis, Ronan, & Borduin, 2004).

FFT involves modifying patterns of family interaction—by modeling, prompting, and reinforcement—to encourage clear communication of requests and solutions between family members, and to minimize conflict (Alexander & Parsons, 1973). FFT's promise was first demonstrated almost 40 years ago in a randomized trial where adjudicated delinquents, whose families took part in a 10-week course, were significantly less likely to reoffend than their controls (Alexander & Parsons, 1973). Like MST, FFT has since been evaluated in multiple settings and is considered a highly effective treatment for serious and violent juvenile offenders (Greenwood, 2006).

MTFC involves individual-focused therapeutic care (e.g. skill building in problem solving) for the young person in an alternative, noncorrectional environment (foster care), and parent management training (Chamberlain, 2003). Evaluations by its originators at the Oregon Social Learning Center produced positive results in terms of lower rates of self-reported reoffending, including fewer serious and violent crimes, and lower institutional admission rates compared with controls placed in group homes (Chamberlain, 2003).

Tertiary prevention strategies represent a natural avenue for criminal justice agencies to respond to the problem of serious youth violence as well. Indeed, most everything the criminal justice system does—responding to calls for service, making arrests, prosecuting offenders, and incarcerating them—happens after rather than before a violent event. Unfortunately, criminal justice agencies have been traditionally oriented towards reactively resolving individual crime incidents or processing individual offenders rather than proactively seeking to halt recurring violence problems. Criminal justice agencies have also historically paid little attention to criminological research on violence problems and evaluations of violence prevention strategies. The criminology research community has long engaged in collection and analysis of data on serious youth violence in the same spirit as the epidemiological analyses carried out by public health researchers (Moore et al., 1994). Until recently, however, the close working relationships between practitioners and academics observed in the public health field have not been present in the criminal justice field (Moore, 1995). As an unfortunate result, much of this important criminological research languishes in scientific journals and is never brought to the attention of practitioners, who would benefit from the information.

The devastating harms generated by the 1990s youth violence epidemic helped to push criminal justice agencies, especially police departments, towards developing innovative violence prevention strategies (Weisburd & Braga, 2006). Some of the most important evidence-based practices emanating from this unprecedented period of police innovation parallel the basic public health approach to violence prevention. These violence prevention strategies are rooted in problem-oriented policing (Goldstein, 1990) and situational crime prevention (Clarke, 1997) perspectives that encourage officers to identify discrete problems, analyze the underlying conditions and dynamics that cause these problems to recur, implement strategies that are tailored to address these underlying causes, and to evaluate the impact of implemented strategies. These strategies are also characterized by close working partnerships between academics and practitioners.

Much of the devastating toll of urban gun violence can be linked to dynamics and situations generated by a small number of high-rate young offenders committing shootings at specific places. For instance, in 2006, roughly 1% of Boston youth between the ages of 15 and 24 participated in gangs, but violent gang dynamics generated more than half of all homicides and gang members were involved in roughly 70% of fatal and nonfatal shootings as either a perpetrator and/or a victim (Braga, Hureau, & Winship, 2008). Some 5% of Boston's street corners and block faces generated 74% of fatal and nonfatal shootings between 1980 and 2008, with the most active 65 locations experiencing more than 1,000 shootings during this time period (Braga, Papachristos, & Hureau, 2010). While concerning, these patterns represent important opportunities for more effective tertiary violence prevention. If police departments can organize themselves to control the small number of risky places and risky people that generate the bulk of their violent crime problems, they can more effectively manage citywide violent crime trends. Innovative focused deterrence and hot spots policing strategies take a problem-oriented approach to deal with these identifiable risks.

Pioneered in Boston during the 1990s, focused deterrence strategies are designed to prevent serious youth violence by reaching out directly to gangs, saying explicitly that violence would no longer be tolerated, and backing up that message by "pulling every lever" legally available when violence occurs (Kennedy, 2008; Kennedy, Piehl, & Braga, 1996). The chronic involvement of gang members in a wide variety of offenses make them, and the gangs they form, vulnerable to coordinated criminal justice responses. In concert with focused enforcement actions, youth workers, probation and parole officers, and churches and other community groups offer gang members services and other kinds of help. These partners also delivered an explicit message that violence was unacceptable to the community and that "street" justifications for violence were mistaken. The anti-violence message is delivered in formal meetings with gang members (known as "forums" or "call-ins"), through individual police and probation contacts with gang members, through meetings with inmates at secure juvenile facilities in the city, and through gang outreach workers. Quasi-experimental evaluations have found focused deterrence approaches to be effective in reducing serious youth violence in several US cities (e.g. Braga, Kennedy, Waring, & Piehl, 2001; McGarrell, Chermak, Wilson, & Corsaro, 2006).

The ultimate target of these gang interventions is the self-sustaining dynamic of retaliation that characterized many ongoing conflicts (Kennedy, 2008; Kennedy, Piehl, & Braga, 1996). Focused deterrence "crackdowns" are not designed to eliminate gangs or stop every aspect of gang activity, but to control and deter gang violence. The citywide communication of the anti-violence message, coupled with meaningful examples of the consequences that will be brought to bear on gangs that break the rules, sought to weaken or eliminate the "kill or be killed" norm as individuals recognize that their enemies will be operating under the new rules as well. The social service component of focused deterrence strategies serves as an independent good and also helps to remove excuses used by offenders to explain their offending. Social service providers present an alternative to illegal behavior by offering relevant jobs and social services. The availability of these services invalidates excuses that their violent behavior is the result of a lack of legitimate opportunities for employment, or other problems, in their neighborhood.

Youth violence is also linked to criminogenic dynamics and situations occurring at specific places within cities. In Chicago, street gang homicides have long been concentrated in a small number of gang turf and drug hot spots (Block & Block, 1993). In a longitudinal analysis of 14 years of juvenile arrest incident data in Seattle, Weisburd, Groff, and Morris (2009) found that one-third of all juvenile arrest incidents were concentrated on less than 1% of the city's street segments. The street segments with the highest juvenile arrest trajectories were characterized by facilities with high levels of juvenile activity such as schools, youth centers, and shopping malls.

A recent quasi-experimental evaluation of the Boston Police Department's Safe Street Team program found that problem-oriented policing interventions significantly reduced violent crime incidents in targeted hot spots (Braga, Hureau, & Papachristos, 2011). Many of the Safe Street Team problem-oriented interventions were designed to address violent crime problems caused by and perpetrated against local youth. For instance, in one violent hot spot, high school youth using public transportation were repeatedly robbed and often assaulted by other local youth when commuting between the train station and their high school. In addition to increasing their presence and making robbery arrests in the area, Safe Street Team officers made the place less attractive to youth robbers by collaborating with public works to fence a vacant lot and trim overgrown bushes and other vegetation that helped conceal robbers from their victims. The officers then collaborated with the local high school to raise awareness among the students that they should be aware of their surroundings and refrain from using smart phones and other items that were attractive to robbers when commuting in the risky area. The officers also sponsored a contest for students to design robbery awareness fliers and posters that used slogans and lingo that would appeal to youth. The fliers were distributed to all high school students and posters were displayed on school grounds, in the train station, and in the windows of stores on the route between the train station and the school.

These interventions are part of a growing body of rigorous scientific evidence that suggests police can reduce violence when they use an array of tactics and focus their efforts on identifiable risks (Weisburd & Eck, 2004). A recently completed Campbell Collaboration systematic review of 10 quasi-experimental evaluations and one randomized controlled trial of focused deterrence strategies found that these interventions were associated with significant violence reduction effects (Braga & Weisburd, 2011). A recently updated Campbell Collaboration systematic review of 9 quasi-experimental evaluations and 10 randomized controlled trials reported that hot spots policing interventions produced noteworthy violence reduction gains; it also found that problem-oriented policing strategies to control hot spots generated larger violence reduction effects relative to simply increasing levels of traditional policing activities, such as patrol and arrests, in hot spot areas (Braga, Papachristos, & Hureau, 2011).

## DISCUSSION AND CONCLUSIONS

Historically, public health researchers and practitioners have prevented many deaths and illnesses through the application of its fundamental problem solving capacity to develop actions such as water quality control, immunization programs, and food inspection regimes (Committee for the Study of the Future of Public Health, 1988). These successes exemplify the possibilities of dealing with very serious problems through an organized effort rooted in scientific knowledge. Public health research and practice does not separate scientific discussions on the nature of problems from discussions of solutions to those problems. As described by Mercy and Hammond (1999), a public health approach to violence prevention is action oriented and its main goal is the analysis of scientific evidence in order to improve injury prevention and violence reduction.

The public health approach starts with defining the problem, progresses towards identifying risk factors and causes, developing and implementing interventions, and measuring the effectiveness of these interventions. Public health researchers are careful to note that these steps sometimes do not follow this linear progression, because some may occur simultaneously or problems may need to be reanalyzed and ineffective interventions readjusted (Mercy & Hammond, 1999). They also note that information systems used to define and analyze youth violence problems can also be useful in evaluating the impacts of prevention programs.

Many criminologists will immediately recognize this public health model as a specific application of the basic action research model that has grounded applied social science inquiries for many decades (see, e.g. Lewin, 1947). As we show in this paper, the fields of criminology and public health often overlap and intersect in their examination of the nature of serious youth violence and the development of prevention responses to address it. In contrast to public health researchers, many criminologists have historically invested themselves in fundamental scientific inquiries that seek to test theories of criminality and crime causation rather than pursuing applied science research and development projects. In his well-known account of the role of criminologists in President Johnson's Commission on Crime and the Administration of Justice, James Q. Wilson (1975) observed that the research tradition in criminology, grounded in the sociological perspective, was focused on societal "root causes" of crime and had few implications for the potential effectiveness of available policy interventions.

The emerging link between criminology and public health in preventing serious youth violence is supported by a general rise in crime policy research in the criminology field. Indeed, one can argue that the emergence of the public health approach is somewhat connected to a more general movement toward evidence-based practice that emerged after the "nothing works" challenges began to recede. Moreover, the sociological perspective described by Wilson (1975) in the 1960s no longer dominates the field of criminology. Over the last 30 years, policy-oriented criminologists of many disciplinary backgrounds have made important scientific contributions to policy debates on crime and justice issues (Cook, 2003).

During this time period, the Academy of Criminal Justice Sciences and the American Society of Criminology have played significant roles in advancing applied research and developing connections with federal institutions to create a much stronger presence in the crime and justice policy world (Clear, 2010). The demand for on-the-ground action research partnerships has also increased as criminal justice practitioners have started to recognize the considerable value added by developing close working relationships with criminologists to address crime and justice problems (Petersilia, 2008).

Federal funding initiatives that support criminal justice practitioner-researcher partnerships could go far in improving our capacity to prevent serious youth violence. Academic researchers can help criminal justice agencies by conducting research on urban violence problems to focus limited prevention resources on high-risk offenders, victims, and places. Academic researchers also bring considerable skill to the evaluation of implemented programs. Success stories, such as the effective focused deterrence and hot spots policing strategies described here, have made academics an important part of new strategic violence prevention initiatives. For instance, the US Department of Justice-sponsored Project Safe Neighborhoods (PSN) initiative provided each of the 94 US Attorney's districts with funds to hire academic research partners to help understand and address serious gun violence problems in local jurisdictions. A recent national evaluation of PSN found that treatment cities with high levels of implementation, which includes in-depth problem analysis to tailor prevention strategies, were associated with declines in violent crime (McGarrell et al., 2010).

As we look to the future, youth violence prevention policy and practice would clearly benefit from a more sustained collaboration between criminologists and public health researchers on action research projects. One promising development is CDC's academic centers for excellence (ACE) for youth violence prevention. The centers are guided by four main goals: "(1) build the scientific infrastructure necessary to support the development and widespread application of effective youth violence interventions; (2) promote interdisciplinary research strategies to address the problem of youth violence; (3) foster collaboration between academic researchers and communities; and (4) empower communities to address the problem of youth violence" (Vivolo, Matjasko, & Massetti, 2011, p. 142). Notable collaborations between criminologists and public health researchers include the University of Chicago ACE site's study of the implementation of CeaseFire Chicago and Harvard University ACE site's evaluation of the StreetSafe initiative in Boston (Azrael & Hemenway, 2011; Vivolo, Matjasko, & Massetti, 2011).

Since 2000, a total of 20 ACE sites have been established across the country. In the most recent iteration of the ACE program (2010–2015), the Centers for Disease Control and Prevention (CDC) require researchers in each funded site to enhance the capacity and infrastructure of the local health department for youth violence prevention work, implement a coordinated set of youth violence prevention strategies in the local community, and evaluate the impact of the comprehensive youth violence prevention strategy on community rates of violence (http://www.cdc.gov/ViolencePrevention/ACE/index.html). Building on the capacities of these ACE collaborations (and others) and drawing upon the growing evidence base of primary, secondary, and tertiary prevention strategies signals a new era in the prevention of serious youth violence. We may be part way there, and criminology and public health are at center stage.

## References

Alexander, J. F., & Parsons, B. V. (1973). Short-term behavioral intervention with delinquent families: Impact on family process and recidivism. *Journal of Abnormal Psychology, 81*, 219–225.

Azrael, D., & Hemenway, D. (2011). Greater than the sum of their parts: The benefits of youth violence prevention centers. *American Journal of Community Psychology, 48*, 21–30.

Block, C. R., & Block, R. (1993). *Street gang crime in Chicago: Research in brief series.* Washington, DC: National Institute of Justice, US Department of Justice.

Blumstein, A., Cohen, J., Roth, J. A., & Visher, C. A. (Eds.). (1986). *Criminal careers and "career criminals".* Washington, DC: National Academy Press.

Blumstein, A., & Wallman, J. (Eds.). (2006). *The crime drop in America, rev. ed.* New York: Cambridge University Press.

Boisjoli, R., Vitaro, F., Lacourse, E., Barker, E. D., & Tremblay, R. E. (2007). Impact and clinical significance of a preventive intervention for disruptive boys: 15 year follow-up. *British Journal of Psychiatry, 191*, 415–419.

Borowsky, I. W., Mozayeny, S., Stuenkel, K., & Ireland, M. (2004). Effects of a primary care-based intervention on violent behavior and injury in children. *Pediatrics, 114*, 392–399.

Braga, A. A., Hureau, D. M., & Papachristos, A. V. (2011). An ex-post-facto evaluation framework for place-based police interventions. *Evaluation Review, 35*, 592–626.

Braga, A. A., Hureau, D. M., & Winship, C. (2008). Losing faith? Police, black churches, and the resurgence of youth violence in Boston. *Ohio State Journal of Criminal Law, 6*, 141–172.

Braga, A. A., Kennedy, D. M., Waring, E. J., & Piehl, A. M. (2001). Problem-oriented policing, deterrence, and youth violence: An evaluation of Boston's operation ceasefire. *Journal of Research in Crime and Delinquency, 38*, 195–225.

Braga, A. A., Papachristos, A. V., & Hureau, D. M. (2011). *The effects of hot spots policing on crime*. Report to the Campbell Collaboration Crime and Justice Group.

Braga, A. A., Papachristos, A. V., & Hureau, D. M. (2010). The concentration and stability of gun violence at micro places in Boston, 1980–2008. *Journal of Quantitative Criminology, 26*, 33–53.

Braga, A. A., & Weisburd, D. (2010). *Policing problem places: Crime hot spots and effective prevention*. New York: Oxford University Press.

Braga, A. A., & Weisburd, D. L. (2011). The effects of focused deterrence strategies on crime: A systematic review and meta-analysis of the empirical evidence. *Journal of Research in Crime and Delinquency*. Advance online publication. doi: 10.1177/0022427811419368.

Center for the Study and Prevention of Violence. (2007). *The incredible years: Parents, teachers, and children's training series*. Boulder, CO: Center for the Study and Prevention of Violence.

Chamberlain, P. (2003). *Treating chronic juvenile offenders: Advances made through the Oregon multidimensional treatment foster care model*. Washington, DC: American Psychological Association.

Clarke, R. V. (Ed.). (1997). *Situational crime prevention: Successful case studies* (2nd ed.). Albany, NY: Harrow and Heston.

Clear, T. R. (2010). Policy and evidence: The challenge to the American Society of criminology. *Criminology, 48*, 1–26.

Cochran, W. (1983). Planning and analysis of observational studies. New York, NY: Wiley.

Committee for the Study of the Future of Public Health. (1988). *The future of public health. Division of Health Care Services, Institute of Medicine*. Washington, DC: National Academy Press.

Cook, P. J. (2003). Meeting the demand for expert advice on drug policy. *Criminology & Public Policy, 2*, 565–570.

Cook, P. J., & Laub, J. H. (1998). The unprecedented epidemic in youth violence. In M. Tonry & M. H. Moore (Eds.), *Crime and justice: A review of research* (24, pp. 27–64). Chicago: University of Chicago Press.

Cook, P. J., & Laub, J. H. (2002). After the epidemic: Recent trends in youth violence in the United States. In M. Tonry (Ed.), *Crime and justice: A review of research* (29, pp. 1–37). Chicago: University of Chicago Press.

Curtis, N. M., Ronan, K. R., & Borduin, C. R. (2004). Multisystemic treatment: A meta-analysis of outcome studies. *Journal of Family Psychology, 18*, 411–419.

Derzon, J. H. (2006). How effective are school-based violence prevention programs in preventing and reducing violence and other antisocial behaviors? A meta-analysis. In S. R. Jimerson & M. J. Furlong (Eds.), *The handbook of school violence and school safety: From research to practice* (pp. 429–441). Mahwah, NJ: Erlbaum.

Dodge, K. A. (2001). The science of youth violence prevention: Progressing from developmental epidemiology to efficacy to effectiveness to public policy. *American Journal of Preventive Medicine, 20*(1S), 63–70.

Eckenrode, J., Campa, M., Luckey, D. W., Henderson, C. R., Cole, R., Kitzman, H., et al. (2010). Long-term effects of prenatal and infancy nurse home visitation on the life course of youths: 19-year follow-up of a randomized trial. *Archives of Pediatrics and Adolescent Medicine, 164*, 9–15.

Elliott, D. S., & Mihalic, S. F. (2004). Issues in disseminating and replicating effective prevention programs. *Prevention Science, 5*, 47–52.

Farrell, A. D., & Flannery, D. J. (2006). Youth violence prevention: Are we there yet? *Aggression and Violent Behavior, 11*, 138–150.

Farrington, D. P., & Loeber, R. (2000). Epidemiology of youth violence. *Child and Adolescent Psychiatry Clinics of North America, 9*, 733–748.

Farrington, D. P., & Welsh, B. C. (2007). *Saving children from a life of crime: Early risk factors and effective interventions*. New York: Oxford University Press.

Fields, S. A., & McNamara, J. R. (2003). The prevention of child and adolescent violence: A review. *Aggression and Violent Behavior, 8*, 61–91.

Goldstein, H. (1990). *Problem-oriented policing*. Philadelphia, PA: Temple University Press.

Greenwood, P. W. (2006). *Changing lives: Delinquency prevention as crime-control policy*. Chicago: University of Chicago Press.

Hahn, R., Fuqua-Whitley, D., Wethington, H., Lowy, J., Crosby, A., & Fullilove, M. (2007). Effectiveness of universal school-based programs to prevent violent and aggressive behavior: A systematic review. *American Journal of Preventive Medicine, 33*(2S), 114–129.

Hanlon, T. E., Bateman, R. W., Simon, B. D., O'Grady, K. E., & Carswell, S. B. (2002). An early community-based intervention for the prevention of substance abuse and other delinquent behavior. *Journal of Youth and Adolescence, 31*, 459–471.

Hawkins, J. D., Arthur, M. W., & Catalano, R. F. (1995). Preventing substance abuse. In M. Tonry & D. P. Farrington (Eds.), *Crime and justice: A review of research* (19, pp. 343–427). Chicago: University of Chicago Press.

Hawkins, J. D., Catalano, R. F., & Arthur, M. W. (2002). Promoting science-based prevention in communities. *Addictive Behaviors, 27*, 951–976.

Hawkins, J. D., Catalano, R. F., Kosterman, R., Abbott, R., & Hill, K. G. (1999). Preventing adolescent health-risk behaviors by strengthening protection during childhood. *Archives of Pediatrics and Adolescent Medicine, 153*, 226–234.

Hawkins, J. D., Kosterman, R., Catalano, R. F., Hill, K. G., & Abbott, R. D. (2008). Effects of social development intervention in childhood 15 years later. *Archives of Pediatrics and Adolescent Medicine, 162*, 1133–1141.

Hawkins, J. D., Oesterle, S., Brown, E. C., Arthur, M. W., Abbott, R. D., Fagan, A. A., et al. (2009). Results of a type 2 translational research trial to prevent adolescent drug use and delinquency: A test of communities that care. *Archives of Pediatrics and Adolescent Medicine, 163*, 789–798.

Hawkins, J. D., Smith, B. H., Hill, K. G., Kosterman, R., & Catalano, R. F. (2007). Promoting social development and preventing health and behavior problems during the elementary grades: Results from the Seattle social development project. *Victims and Offenders, 2*, 161–181.

Hawkins, J. D., von Cleve, E., & Catalano, R. F. (1991). Reducing early childhood aggression: Results of a primary prevention program. *Journal of the American Academy of Child and Adolescent Psychiatry, 30*, 208–217.

Henggeler, S. W., Schoenwald, S. K., Borduin, C. M., Rowland, M. D., & Cunningham, P. B. (1998). *Multisystemic treatment of antisocial behavior in children and adolescents*. New York: Guilford Press.

Kaplan, R. M. (2000). Two pathways to prevention. *American Psychologist, 55*, 382–396.

Kennedy, D. M. (2008). *Deterrence and crime prevention*. London: Routledge.

Kennedy, D. M., Piehl, A. M., & Braga, A. A. (1996). Youth violence in Boston: Gun markets, serious youth offenders, and a use-reduction strategy. *Law and Contemporary Problems, 59*, 147–196.

Kerani, R. P., Handcock, M. S., Handsfield, H. H., & Holmes, K. K. (2005). Comparative geographic concentrations of 4 sexually transmitted infections. *American Journal of Public Health, 95*, 324–330.

Kling, J. R., Ludwig, J., & Katz, L. F. (2005). Neighborhood effects on crime for female and male youth: Evidence from a randomized housing voucher experiment. *Quarterly Journal of Economics, 120*, 87–130.

LeBlanc, M. (1998). Screening of serious/violent juvenile offenders. In R. Loeber & D. P. Farrington (Eds.), *Serious and violent juvenile offenders: Risk factors and successful interventions* (pp. 167–196). Thousand Oaks, CA: Sage.

Lewin, K. (1947). Group decisions and social change. In T. Newcomb & E. Hartley (Eds.), *Readings in social psychology* (pp. 340–344). New York: Atherton Press.

Limbos, M. A., Chan, L. S., Warf, C., Schneir, A., Iverson, E., Shekelle, P., et al. (2007). Effectiveness of interventions to prevent youth violence: A systematic review. *American Journal of Preventive Medicine, 33*, 65–74.

Lipsey, M. W. (2009). The primary factors that characterize effective interventions with juvenile offenders: A meta-analytic overview. *Victims and Offenders, 4*, 124–147.

Ludwig, J. (2012). Cost-effective crime prevention. In R. Rosenfeld, K. Quinet, & C. Garcia (Eds.), *Contemporary issues in criminological theory and research: The role of social institutions* (pp. 29–39). Belmont, CA: Cengage.

Ludwig, J., Duncan, G., & Hirschfield, P. (2001). Urban poverty and juvenile crime: Evidence from a randomized housing-mobility experiment. *Quarterly Journal of Economics, 96*, 655–679.

MacDonald, J. M., Bluthenthal, R. N., Golinelli, D., Kofner, A., Stokes, R. J., Sehgal, A., et al. (2009). *Neighborhood effects on crime and youth violence: The role of business improvement districts in Los Angeles*. Santa Monica, CA: Rand.

Maxfield, M. G., & Widom, C. S. (1996). The cycle of violence revisited 6 years later. *Archives of Pediatrics and Adolescent Medicine, 150*, 390–395.

McGarrell, E., Chermak, S., Wilson, J., & Corsaro, N. (2006). Reducing homicide through a 'lever-pulling' strategy. *Justice Quarterly, 23*, 214–231.

McGarrell, E., Corsaro, N., Hipple, N., & Bynum, T. (2010). Project Safe Neighborhoods and violent crime trends in US cities: Assessing violent crime impact. *Journal of Quantitative Criminology, 26*, 165–190.

Mercy, J. A., & Hammond, W. R. (1999). Combining action and analysis to prevent homicide: A public health perspective. In M. D. Smith & M. A. Zahn (Eds.), *Homicide: A sourcebook of social research* (pp. 297–310). Thousand Oaks, CA: Sage.

Mercy, J. A., Rosenberg, M. L., Powell, K. E., Broome, C. V., & Roper, W. L. (1993). Public health policy for preventing violence. *Health Affairs, 12*, 7–29.

Molina, I. A., Dulmus, C. N., & Sowers, K. (2005). Secondary prevention for youth violence: A review of selected school-based programs. *Brief Treatment and Crisis Intervention, 5*, 95–127.

Moore, E., Armsden, G., & Gogerty, P. L. (1998). A twelve-year follow-up study of maltreated and at-risk children who received early therapeutic child care. *Child Maltreatment, 3*, 3–16.

Moore, M. H. (1995). Public health and criminal justice approaches to prevention. In M. Tonry & D. P. Farrington (Eds.), *Crime and justice: A review of research* (19, pp. 237–262). Chicago: University of Chicago Press.

Moore, M. H., Prothrow-Smith, D., Guyer, B., & Spivak, H. (1994). Violence and intentional injuries: Criminal justice and public health perspectives on an urgent national problem. In A. J. Reiss & J. A. Roth (Eds.), *Understanding and preventing violence* (4, pp. 167–216). Washington, DC: National Academy Press.

Morenoff, J., Sampson, R. J., & Raudenbush, S. (2001). Neighborhood inequality, collective efficacy, and the spatial dynamics of urban violence. *Criminology, 39*, 517–559.

Olds, D. L., Henderson, C. R., Chamberlin, R., & Tatelbaum, R. (1986). Preventing child abuse and neglect: A randomized trial of nurse home visitation. *Pediatrics, 78*, 65–78.

Olds, D. L. Henderson, C. R. Cole, R. Eckenrode, J. Kitzman, H. Luckey, D., et al. (1998). Long-term effects of nurse home visitation on children's criminal and antisocial behavior: 15-year follow-up of a randomized controlled trial. *Journal of the American Medical Association, 280*, 1238–1244.

Olds, D. L., Sadler, L., & Kitzman, H. (2007). Programs for parents of infants and toddlers: Recent evidence from randomized trials. *Journal of Child Psychology and Psychiatry, 48*, 355–391.

Papachristos, A. V. (2010). Murder by structure: Dominance relations and the social structure of gang homicide. *American Journal of Sociology, 115*, 74–128.

Perry, C. L., Klepp, K.-I., & Sillers, C. (1989). Community-wide strategies for cardiovascular health: The Minnesota health program youth program. *Health Education Research, 4*, 87–101.

Petersilia, J. (2008). Influencing public policy: An embedded criminologist reflects on California prison reform. *Journal of Experimental Criminology, 4*, 335–356.

Poundstone, K. E., Strathdee, S. A., & Celentano, D. D. (2004). The social epidemiology of human immunodeficiency virus/acquired immunodeficiency syndrome. *Epidemiologic Reviews, 26*, 22–35.

Reynolds, A. J., Temple, J. A., Ou, S. R., Arteaga, I. A., & White, B. (2011). School-based early childhood education and age-28 well-being: Effects by timing dosage and subgroups. *Science, 333*, 360–364.

Reynolds, A. J., Temple, J. A., Robertson, D. L., & Mann, E. A. (2001). Long-term effects of an early childhood intervention on educational achievement and juvenile arrest. *Journal of the American Medical Association, 285*, 2339–2346.

Rose, G. (2001). Sick individuals and sick populations. *International Journal of Epidemiology, 30*, 427–432.

Rosenbaum, P. (1995). *Observational studies*. New York: Springer.

Rothman, K. J., & Greenland, S. (2005). Causation and causal inference in epidemiology. *American Journal of Public Health, 95*, S144-S150.

Schwalbe, C. S. (2008). A meta-analysis of juvenile justice risk assessment instruments: Predictive validity by gender. *Criminal Justice & Behavior, 35*, 1367–1381.

Shepherd, J. P., & Farrington, D. P. (1993). Assault as a public health problem. *Journal of the Royal Society of Medicine, 86*, 89–94.

Tremblay, R. E., Pagani-Kurtz, L., Mâsse, L. C., Vitaro, F., & Pihl, R. O. (1995). A bimodal preventive intervention for disruptive kindergarten boys: Its impact through midadolescence. *Journal of Consulting and Clinical Psychology, 63*, 560–568.

Tremblay, R. E., Vitaro, F., Bertrand, L., LeBlanc, M., Beauchesne, H., Boileau, H., et al. (1992). Parent and child training to prevent early onset of delinquency: The Montréal longitudinal-experimental study. In J. McCord & R. E. Tremblay (Eds.), *Preventing antisocial behavior* (pp. 117–138). New York: Guilford.

US Department of Health and Human Services [USDHHS]. (2001). *Youth violence: A report of the surgeon general*. Rockville, MD: US Department of Health and Human Services.

Vivolo, A., Matjasko, J., & Massetti, G. (2011). Mobilizing communities and building capacity for youth violence prevention. *American Journal of Community Psychology, 48*, 141–145.

Webster-Stratton, C., & Hammond, M. (1997). Treating children with early-onset conduct problems: A comparison of child and parent training interventions. *Journal of Consulting and Clinical Psychology, 65*, 93–109.

Webster-Stratton, C., Hollinsworth, T., & Kolpacoff, M. (1989). The long-term effectiveness and clinical significance of three cost-effective training programs for families with conduct-problem children. *Journal of Consulting and Clinical Psychology, 57*, 550–553.

Weisburd, D., & Braga, A. A. (Eds.). (2006). *Police innovation: Contrasting perspectives*. New York: Cambridge University Press.

Weisburd, D. L., & Eck, J. E. (2004). What can the police do to reduce crime, disorder, and fear? *Annals of the American Academy of Political and Social Science, 593*, 42–65.

Weisburd, D. L., Groff, E., & Morris, N. (2009). Hot spots of juvenile crime: A longitudinal study of arrest incidents at street segments in Seattle, Washington. *Journal of Quantitative Criminology, 25*, 443–467.

Welsh, B. C., & Farrington, D. P. (2011). Evidence-based crime policy. In M. Tonry (Ed.), *The Oxford handbook of crime and criminal justice* (pp. 60–92). New York: Oxford University Press.

Welsh, B. C., Sullivan, C. J., & Olds, D. L. (2010). When early crime prevention goes to scale: A new look at the evidence. *Prevention Science, 11*, 115–125.

Wilson, J. Q. (1975). *Thinking about crime*. New York: Basic Books.

Wilson, S. J., & Lipsey, M. W. (2007). School-based interventions for aggressive and disruptive behavior: Update of a meta-analysis. *American Journal of Preventive Medicine, 33*(2S), 130–143.

Wintemute, G. J., & Braga, A. A. (2011). Opportunities for state-level action to reduce firearm violence: Proceeding from the evidence. *American Journal of Public Health, 101*, e1–e3.

Wintemute, G. J., Braga, A. A., & Kennedy, D. M. (2010). Private-party gun sales, regulation, and public safety. *The New England Journal of Medicine, 363*, 508–513.

Wolfgang, M., Figlio, R., & Sellin, T. (1972). *Delinquency in a birth cohort*. Chicago: University of Chicago.

# Index